THE POWER OF TWO LANGUAGES 2000

Effective Dual-Language Use Across the Curriculum

Josefina Villamil Tinajero
and Robert A. DeVillar, Editors

McGraw-Hill
School Division

New York   Farmington

This book complements the McGraw-Hill Spanish and English Programs.

ACKNOWLEDGMENTS

The publisher gratefully acknowledges permission to reprint the following copyrighted material:

"Alternative Assessment for Latino Students" by Ann Del Vecchio, Cyndee Gustke, and Judith Wilde from *Educating Latino Students: A Guide to Successful Practice,* edited by María Luísa González, Ana Huerta-Macías, and Josefina Villamil Tinajero. Copyright © 1998, Technomic Publishing Co., Inc.

"Effective Transitioning Strategies: Are We Asking the Right Questions?" by Lilia I. Bartolomé reprinted from *Cultural Diversity and Second Language Learning,* edited by B. MacLeod, by permission of the State University of New York Press. © SUNY Press.

"Making Inequality: Issues of Language and Meanings in Mathematics Teaching with Hispanic Students" by Lena Licón Khisty from *New Directions for Equity in Mathematics Education,* edited by Walter G. Secada, Elizabeth Fennema, and Lisa Byrd Adajian. Copyright © 1995, Cambridge University Press.

"Promoting Early Literacy Development Among Spanish-Speaking Children" by Claude Goldenberg from *Getting Reading Right from the Start: Effective Early Literacy Interventions* by Elfrieda H. Hiebert and Barbra M. Taylor. Copyright © 1994, Allyn and Bacon.

"Sociocultural Change Through Literacy: Toward the Empowerment of Families" by Concha Delgado-Gaitan from *Literacy Across Languages and Cultures,* edited by Bernardo M. Ferdman, Rose-Marie Weber, and Arnulfo G. Ramírez. Copyright © 1994, State University of New York Press.

"We Speak in Many Tongues: Language Diversity and Multicultural Education," an article by Sonia Nieto from the book *Multicultural Education in the Twenty-First Century,* edited by Carlos Diaz. Copyright © 1992, National Education Association. Reprinted by permission.

McGraw-Hill School Division
Two Penn Plaza
New York, New York 10121

Printed in the United States of America
ISBN 0-02-186934-0
1 2 3 4 5 6 7 8 9 079 04 03 02 01 00 99

Contents

Introduction 5
   Josefina Villamil Tinajero and Robert A. DeVillar

PART I: THEORETICAL PERSPECTIVES

Biliteracy, Empowerment, and Transformative Pedagogy 9
   Jim Cummins

The Two Goals of Bilingual Education: Development of Academic English and Heritage
Language Development 20
   Stephen Krashen

We Speak in Many Tongues: Language Diversity and Multicultural Education 30
   Sonia Nieto

Literacy Instruction Through Spanish: Linguistic, Cultural, and Pedagogical
Considerations 42
   Elly B. Pardo and Josefina Villamil Tinajero

Phonological Awareness in Spanish: A Summary of Research and Implications
for Practice 54
   Jan E. Hasbrouck and Carolyn A. Denton

Developing a Framework for Writing in Dual Language Settings 66
   Sarah Hudelson

Part II: PRACTICAL APPLICATIONS
Native Language Instruction

Promoting Early Literacy Development Among Spanish-Speaking Children:
Lessons from Two Studies 83
   Claude Goldenberg

Spanish Language, Literacy, and Cognition: Keys to Students' Success 102
   Juan R. Lira

Teaching Literacy in Spanish 126
   Kathy Escamilla

Second Language Instruction

Effective Transitioning Strategies: Are We Asking the Right Questions? 142
   Lilia I. Bartolomé

Official Versions: Encouraging Writing in Students' First Language in ESL Classrooms 155
   Paula Wolfe

Two-Way Bilingual Education: The Power of Two Languages in Promoting
Educational Success 163
   Kathryn J. Lindholm and Rosa Molina

Turning Transformative Principles into Practice: Strategies for English-Dominant Teachers in a Multilingual Context 175
    Joan Wink and LeAnn G. Putney

L1 Teachers and L2 Students: What Mainstream Classroom Teachers Know and Need to Know About English Language Learners 187
    Luisa Garro and Olga Romero

Sheltered Strategies: An Integrated Approach to Reading Instruction for Second Language English Speakers 209
    Julie Jacobson, Diane Lapp, and James Flood

Developing Biliteracy in a Two-Way Immersion Program 219
    Jennifer Martínez and Julie A. Moore-O'Brien

A Word Study on Word Study: Teacher-Researchers Use Computers to Accelerate Word Study in a Multicultural School with a Two-Way Bilingual Immersion Program 236
    Dennis Sayers

Part III: LANGUAGE AND LITERACY DEVELOPMENT ACROSS CONTENT AREAS

Content Area Instruction for Students Acquiring English: Focus on Social Studies 253
    Carrol Moran

Literacy and Science: Connections for English Language Learners 266
    Sally Blake, Sandra Rollins Hurley, and Josefina V. Tinajero

Making Inequality: Issues of Language and Meanings in Mathematics Teaching with Hispanic Students 283
    Lena Licón Khisty

Language and Literacy as a Bridge to Mathematics: Integrating Theory with Practice 295
    Eva Midobuche

Part IV: TECHNOLOGY

Global Learning Networks: Heartbeats on the Internet 309
    Kristin Brown

Literacy and the Role of Technology: Toward a Framework for Equitable Schooling 320
    Robert A. DeVillar

Part V: HOME AND COMMUNITY

Mother-Tongue Literacy as a Bridge Between Home and School Cultures 339
    Alma Flor Ada

Sociocultural Change Through Literacy: Toward the Empowerment of Families 346
    Concha Delgado-Gaitan

Part VI: ASSESSMENT

Alternative Assessment for Latino Students 365
    Ann del Vecchio, Cyndee Gustke, and Judith Wilde

Introduction

As our incipient global community prepares to cross the threshold of a new millennium, we are pleased to release the Millennium Edition of *The Power of Two Languages 2000*. In this volume, contributors explore the conditions within which students can effectively develop literacy in their native and second languages in distinct, but related, contexts. Home, community, and school settings are three general areas theoretically conducive to this dual language/biliteracy development. School settings, moreover, are comprised of curricular areas—such as math, science, and language arts—in which teachers can engage students in dual language/biliteracy development concomitantly with the learning of their subject matter. Dual language/biliteracy development also is enhanced by the use of technology within school and home settings. This volume addresses each area mentioned above. In doing so, we provide research-supported insights that both assist teachers to understand the nature of dual language/biliteracy development in distinct settings and describe effective classroom approaches they may use to foster this development among their students.

Our main goal in this edition of *The Power of Two Languages 2000* is to provide all teachers, particularly those within K–6 settings, theoretical and practical information about dual language instructional contexts to enhance their instructional performance. By enhancing instructional performance, we increase the possibility of students' academic, social, linguistic, cultural, and global success during, throughout, and beyond the K–6 cycle. To this end, this Millennium Edition covers three major sections organized under Theoretical Perspectives and Practical Applications: (1) Language and Literacy Development, (2) Language and Literacy Across the Curriculum, and (3) Language and Literacy Support in Informal Settings. Additional sections that complement the above include Technology and Assessment.

The theoretical base provides a meaningful and functional overarching framework within which to design instructional practices. The research cited provides substantive evidence for best and promising practices and sets the stage for the application section of the book. The application section brings together authors who provide state-of-the-art information, paradigms, and issues associated with effective teaching and learning within dual language contexts. This section addresses students' comprehensive learning needs within a dual language setting, that is, taking into account how social, linguistic, and cultural factors influence language/biliteracy development and academic outcomes. Our goal here is to enhance the confidence of teachers relative to the selection and use of best or most promising practices in dual language instructional contexts.

The Power of Two Languages 2000 presents paradigms, strategies, and techniques that best support the development of bilingualism and biliteracy. The authors featured in this Millennium Edition recognize that it is desirable and essential for each child to achieve competence in the language of the society at large—English in the case of the United States. At the same time, the contributors view as an inalienable right of children whose first language is not English that they retain and develop their mother tongue. Native language maintenance and development are indispensable to natural and effective communication within the home, family, and immediate community. Language also exerts a major influence on the formation of one's identity as a member of a group, a nation, and the world community. Thus, we view dual language and biliterate development for children within the United States as viable and necessary: viable in that contexts for second language acquisition and learning abound naturally throughout the nation; necessary in that integration and interaction among distinct groups in the U.S. must be actively fostered within school, community, and home environments for social and national understanding and cohesion to occur within our populace. A cohesive society, however complex in its demographic structure, can accommodate its schools and related institutions to promote and develop the language and academic potential of all of its populace. It will also reap rewards in terms of productivity, creativity, and harmony resulting from enlightened cohesion.

The Power of Two Languages 2000 provides teachers with the information to make powerful choices for themselves and for their students. It challenges them to use this information to create learning environments where learning is facilitated and stimulated by caring adults. Our hope in sharing this collection of articles is that best practices will be distributed across significantly more classrooms in the United States. Finally, we hope that the critical reading of this text will influence teachers to view students' dual language/biliterate abilities as an asset, as an intellectual accomplishment, and as a nationally treasured resource. The realization of the promise of dual language and biliterate development is the basis for building a solid academic future for individual students from all groups in our society, and for enhancing the general welfare of our nation.

The Power of Two Languages 2000 is empowering. It will empower you as a teacher to effectively reach and teach each and every one of your students.

Josefina Villamil Tinajero and Robert A. DeVillar
Co-Editors

Dedication: To second language learners, whose richness and diversity enhance our schools and our nation, and to you their teachers.

Josefina Villamil Tinajero and Robert A. DeVillar

Part I

THEORETICAL PERSPECTIVES

BILITERACY, EMPOWERMENT, AND TRANSFORMATIVE PEDAGOGY

Jim Cummins
University of Toronto

The continuing concern about preparing students for the technologically sophisticated workplace of the twenty-first century, with its requirement of higher literacy levels among workers, has given rise to concerted efforts at school reform in countries around the world. However, in most countries, despite the fact that linguistically and culturally diverse students tend to be strongly over-represented in school failure categories (e.g., dropout rates), few of the prescriptions for school reform specifically address the causes of educational failure among such students. Even fewer contemplate bilingualism and biliteracy as part of the solution rather than as part of the problem.

I argue in this article that biliteracy must become an essential component of educational reform efforts directed at underachieving Latino/Latina students. However, literacy and even biliteracy are insufficient as educational goals if they remain at the level of "functional literacy" and fail to promote "critical literacy." In other words, students must learn not only to "read the word," but also to "read the world" (Freire & Macedo, 1987). I argue that the public focus and apparent political commitment to improving the ability of students (and adults) to "read the word" represents a façade there that obscures an underlying societal structure that continues to discourage students from "reading the world." This reality implies that educators who strive to create educational contexts within which culturally diverse students develop a sense of empowerment, through acquisition of cultural and critical literacy, are of necessity challenging the societal power structure. By "power structure" I mean the division of status and resources in the society and also the ways in which discourse is mobilized through the media to legitimate and preserve the current division of status and resources.

A further distinction relating to the societal power structure is useful to make at this point. Throughout the article I distinguish between coercive and collaborative relations of power. *Coercive relations of power* refers to the exercise of power by a dominant group (or individual) to the detriment of a subordinated group (or individual). The assumption is that there is a fixed quantity of power that operates according to a balance effect; in other words, the more power one group has, the less, is there left for other groups.

Collaborative relations of power, in contrast, means that power is not a fixed, predetermined quantity, but rather can be generated in interpersonal and intergroup relations, thereby becoming "additive" rather than "subtractive." In other words, participants in the relationship are empowered through their collaboration, so that each is more affirmed in her or his identity and has a greater sense of efficacy to effect change in her or his life or social situation. Thus, power is created in the relationship and shared among participants. In educational contexts, cooperative learning activities and sister class networks constitute documented examples of the academic and personal benefits that accrue when coercive relations of power shift to collaborative relations of power (DeVillar & Faltis, 1990; Cummins & Sayers, 1995).

Within this context, *empowerment* refers to the collaborative creation of power. *Transformative pedagogy* refers to interactions between educators and students that foster the collaborative creation of power. These terms will be further elaborated throughout the article.

A fundamental argument of this article is that the root causes of academic failure among subordinate group students are to be found in the fact that the interactions between educators and students frequently reflect and reinforce the broader societal pattern of coercive relations of power between dominant and subordinate groups. Reversal of this pattern requires that educators resist and challenge the operation of coercive relations of power and actively seek to establish collaborative relations of power both in the school and in the broader society.

The next section focuses on the issue of biliteracy and examines the public debate on bilingual education in light of the research data. The goal is to demonstrate that biliteracy is a feasible educational outcome for all students, and what requires explanation is the public discourse that vehemently denies this reality. I then shift from a focus on "biliteracy" to the broader issue of literacy itself. I suggest that many educational policies not only are dedicated to reducing bilinguals to monolinguals, but also are structured to constrict the possibilities for students' identity formation and to limit the scope of their ability to think or, in Freire's terms, to read the world. Finally, drawing on

Ada's (1988a, 1988b) work, I suggest an alternative pedagogical orientation designed to promote critical biliteracy and student empowerment.

The Public Debate on Bilingual Education

In June 1998, California voters reversed almost 25 years of educational policy in that state by passing Proposition 227 by a margin of 61 to 39 percent. Proposition 227 was aimed at eliminating the use of bilingual children's first language (L1) for instructional purposes except in very exceptional circumstances. Despite the considerable impact of Proposition 227 on bilingual education, most dual-language or two-way bilingual immersion programs appear to have emerged relatively unscathed. These programs aim to develop bilingualism and biliteracy among both language-minority and language-majority students (e.g., Spanish L1 and English L1 speakers). Most of these programs use between 90 percent and 50 percent minority language instruction in the early grades, with instructional time equally split in the later elementary grades. These programs have been spreading rapidly in other states, such as Texas, and thus the potential for developing biliteracy among students is still very much a reality in spite of the strong rhetoric against bilingual education.

The debate leading up to the Proposition 227 referendum in California crystallized all the

arguments that had been advanced for and against bilingual education in the previous quarter century. Both sides claimed "equity" as their central guiding principle. Opponents of bilingual programs argued that limited-English-proficient students were being denied access to both English and academic advancement as a result of being instructed for part of the day through their L1. Exposure to English was being diluted, so it was not surprising that bilingual students continued to experience difficulty in academic aspects of English. Only maximum exposure to English (frequently termed "time on task") could remediate children's linguistic difficulties in that language on entry to school.

Proponents of bilingual education argued that L1 instruction in the early grades was necessary to ensure that students understood content instruction and experienced a successful start to their schooling. Reading and writing skills acquired initially through the L1 provided a foundation for strong English-language development. Transfer of academic skills and knowledge across languages was consistently evidenced by the research literature on bilingual development.

Thus, L1 proficiency could be promoted at no cost to children's academic development in English. Furthermore, the fact that teachers spoke the language of parents increased the likelihood of parental involvement and support for their children's learning. This, together with the reinforcement of children's sense of self as a result of the incorporation of their language and culture into the school program, contributed to long-term academic growth.

In the context of Proposition 227, advocates argued that bilingual education itself could not logically be regarded as a cause of continued high levels of academic failure among bilingual students, since only 30 percent of limited-English-proficient students in California were in any form of bilingual education. Fewer than 18 percent were in classes taught by a certified bilingual teacher, with the other 12 percent in classes most likely taught by a monolingual English teacher and a bilingual aide (Gandara, 1997). Thus, they argued, educational failure among bilingual (particularly Latino/Latina) students is more logically attributed to the absence of genuine bilingual programs than to bilingual education in some absolute sense.

The arguments on both sides of this debate can be articulated as theoretical propositions and examined in relation to the research data.

Theory Underlying Opposition to Bilingual Education

Three major propositions underlie many of the pedagogical arguments against bilingual education. These are:

1. The claim that "time on task" is the major variable underlying language learning, and hence immersion in English is the most effective means to ensure the learning of English

2. The claim that under these conditions of immersion, language-minority students will quickly (within one year) pick up sufficient English to survive academically without further special support

3. The claim that English immersion should start as early as possible in the student's school career, since younger children are better language learners than older children.

Rosalie Pedalino Porter (1990) clearly articulates the first and third principles in stating:

My personal experience and professional investigations together impel me to conclude that the two overriding conditions that promote the best learning of a second language are (1) starting at an early age, say at five, and (2) having as much exposure and carefully planned instruction in the language as possible. Effective time on task—the amount of time spent learning—is, as educators know, the single greatest predictor of educational achievement; this is at least as true, if not more so, for low-socioeconomic-level, limited-English students. Children learn what they are taught, and if they are taught mainly in Spanish for several years, their Spanish-

language skills will be far better than their English-language ones. (pp. 63–64)

Nathan Glazer (Glazer & Cummins, 1985) has articulated the second principle as follows:

. . . all our experience shows that the most extended and steady exposure to the spoken language is the best way of learning any language. . . How long? It depends. But one year of intensive immersion seems to be enough to permit most children to transfer to [regular] English-language classes. (p. 48)

Many other examples of these positions could be cited from both academic and media commentary (see Cummins, 1996). The opposition claims are in direct contrast to those made by academic advocates of bilingual education, as outlined below.

Theory Proposed by Bilingual Education Advocates

It is important first to highlight the fact that most bilingual education theorists have distanced themselves from the popular conception of the rationale for bilingual programs, namely the "linguistic mismatch" hypothesis. This position suggests that a home-school language switch (or linguistic mismatch) will inevitably lead to academic difficulties, since children cannot learn through a language they do not understand. While this claim has been persuasive to many policymakers and educators (and, in fact, underlies the quick-exit transitional focus of most U.S. bilingual education programs), it is seriously flawed. It fails to account either for the success of

English-background children in second language immersion or dual-language programs or for the fact that under certain conditions language-minority students can succeed academically in English-only programs (Cummins, 1979, 1996).

Academic advocates of bilingual education have consistently rejected compensatory (or transitional) bilingual programs and argued for programs that promote biliteracy. Cloud, Genesee, and Hamayan (in press) group these programs (second language immersion for majority students, developmental or late-exit programs for minority students, and dual-language programs for both groups) under the label of Enriched Education.

Three central psychoeducational principles, supported by empirical research, underlie this emphasis on enrichment or developmental bilingual education:

1. Continued development of both languages enhances children's educational and cognitive development.

2. Literacy-related abilities are interdependent across languages, such that knowledge and skills acquired in one language are potentially available in the other (Cummins, 1991; Verhoeven, 1991).

3. While conversational abilities may be acquired fairly rapidly in a second language, upwards of five years are usually required for second language learners to attain grade norms in academically related aspects of the second language (Collier, 1987; Cummins, 1981b).

Together, these principles suggest that reinforcing children's conceptual base in their first language throughout elementary school (and beyond) will provide a foundation for long-term growth in English academic skills. The theory also suggests that we should not expect bilingual children to approach grade norms in English academic skills before the later grades of elementary school.

Consistency of the Alternative Positions with the Research Data

There is virtually no disagreement among applied linguists regarding the consistency of bilingual program evaluation results with the theoretical principles advanced by advocates of bilingual education. The data clearly refute the validity of the "time on task" proposition, and they also refute the "linguistic mismatch" proposition. The distinction between conversational and academic language proficiency is supported, as is the significant relationship of academic proficiency across languages, even languages that are linguistically distant from each other (e.g., Basque and Spanish, Chinese and English) (see Genesee, 1979). The Ramirez report (Ramirez, 1992) shows very clearly, for example, that instruction through Spanish for part of the school day results in no loss in English academic skills. The data are completely inconsistent with the predictions of the time-on-task proposition. Even opponents of bilingual education, such as Christine Rossell (1992), acknowledge that the time-on-task hypothesis is refuted by the Ramirez data: "Large deficits in English language

instruction over several grades apparently make little or no difference in a student's achievement" (p. 183). Expressed more positively, instructional time devoted to promoting bilingual students' L1 literacy entails no adverse consequences for English language or literacy development.

The most clearcut evidence in relation to the alternative theoretical propositions comes from the outcomes of dual-language or two-way bilingual immersion programs. Evaluations of these programs have consistently shown strong academic performance over the course of elementary school for both language-minority and language-majority students (Cazabon, Nicoladis, & Lambert, 1998; Cloud et al., in press; Dolson & Lindholm, 1995). Let us just consider the outcomes of one program, at the Oyster Bilingual School in Washington, D.C., to illustrate the pattern.

The Oyster School's bilingual program was started in 1971 and involves instruction in both Spanish and English for about 50 percent of the time in each language from kindergarten through grade 6. Each class is taught by two teachers, one responsible for English-medium instruction and one for Spanish-medium instruction. This instructional organization is achieved primarily by means of creative management of resources rather than by additional external funds such as Title VII or Title I (personal communication, Elena Izquierdo, former principal of Oyster School), although the school fought successfully within the district to avoid cutbacks that were affecting other schools.

Students read in both languages each day, so there is simultaneous development of literacy in the two languages. The student body is composed of approximately 60 percent Spanish L1 (primarily Salvadorean) and 40 percent English L1 (about half African American, half European American).

The academic results of this program have been outstanding. For example, at the grade 3 level, Reading, Mathematics, Language, and Science scores were 1.6–1.8 median grade equivalents above norms (percentiles 74–81). The grade 6 grade equivalents were 4.4–6.2 above norms (percentiles 85–96) (1991 data reported in Freeman, 1998).

According to Freeman, the school has evolved a social identities project that positively evaluates linguistic and cultural diversity and communicates this strongly to students. In the words of one of the teachers, "It's much more than language." Freeman provides detailed discourse analyses that illustrate how the interactions between educators and students in Oyster Bilingual School "refuse" the discourse of subordination that characterizes the treatment of minorities in the wider society and in most conventional school contexts. She points out that the discourse practices in the school "reflect an ideological assumption that linguistic and cultural diversity is a resource to be developed by all students, and not a problem that minority students must overcome in order to participate and achieve at school" (p. 233). Specifically, educators have choices in the

way they organize discourse practices, and these choices entail significant consequences for both language-minority and language-majority students. The school requires all students to become bilingual and biliterate in Spanish and English and "to expect, tolerate, and respect diverse ways of interacting" (p. 27). In other words, the school "aims to promote social change on the local level by socializing children differently from the way children are socialized in mainstream U.S. educational discourse":

> Rather than pressuring language minority students to assimilate to the positively evaluated majority social identity (white middle-class native English-speaking) in order to participate and achieve at school, the Oyster educational discourse is organized to positively evaluate linguistic and cultural diversity. . . This socializing discourse makes possible the emergence of a wide range of positively evaluated social identities, and offers more choices to both language minority and language majority students than are traditionally available in mainstream U.S. schools and society. The Oyster educators argue that students' socialization through this educational discourse is the reason that [limited-English-proficient], language minority, and language majority students are all participating and achieving more or less equally. (p. 27)

The themes that Freeman emphasizes run through virtually all the programs for language-minority students that have proven successful in elevating academic achievement (Cummins, 1996). Respect for

students' language and culture is strongly communicated to students, and they are encouraged to see themselves as potentially fully bilingual and biliterate. Programs that are less successful (e.g., many quick-exit transitional programs) tend to see the students' L1 as simply a temporary bridge to English and do not aspire to bilingualism and biliteracy.

The Oyster School data clearly show that there is interdependence across languages within well-implemented bilingual programs. Students do not lose out in English despite spending only 50 percent of their instructional time learning through English. The time-on-task proposition would predict significant underachievement in English as a result of spending less time learning through that language. Clearly, the opposite is the case in this particular program.

The success of dual-language programs is not disputed by opponents of bilingual education. Porter (1990), for example, describes dual-language education as "particularly appealing because it not only enhances the prestige of the minority language but also offers a rich opportunity for expanding genuine bilingualism to the majority population" (p. 154). She notes that these programs "are also considered to be the best possible vehicles for integration of language minority students, since these students are grouped with English-speakers for natural and equal exchange of skills." (p. 154)

Charles Glenn, who has also expressed concerns about transitional bilingual education, is likewise an enthusiastic supporter of dual-language programs, as the following quotations illustrate:

> More than any other model of education for linguistic minority pupils, two-way bilingual programs meet the diverse expectations that we set for our schools. Properly designed and implemented, they offer a language-rich environment with high expectations for every child, in a climate of cross-cultural respect. Linguistic minority pupils are stimulated in their use of English, while being encouraged to value and employ their home language as well. (Glenn, 1990, p. 5)

> The best setting for educating linguistic minority pupils—and one of the best for educating any pupils—is a school in which two languages are used without apology and where becoming proficient in both is considered a significant intellectual and cultural achievement. (Glenn & LaLyre, 1991, p. 43)

What evidence do opponents of bilingual education advance to support their claims? The major evidence they refer to is a report written by Rossell and Baker (1996), which claims to show that 83 percent of the comparisons they reviewed between structured immersion (essentially English-only) and transitional bilingual education favored structured immersion, while there was no difference in 17 percent of comparisons. This literature review has been critiqued in detail elsewhere (e.g., Cummins, in press;

Greene, 1998; Krashen, 1999). It is sufficient to note here that nine out of the ten studies that Rossell and Baker claim show the superiority of monolingual structured immersion are in fact bilingual or trilingual programs whose success refutes the time-on-task theory and supports interdependence across languages.

In summary, the relevant distinction to make in understanding the research data on bilingual education is not between "English-only" and "bilingual education" in some absolute sense that ignores the huge variation in philosophy and implementation across programs. Rather, the appropriate distinction is between what Cloud et al. (in press) term Enriched Education, which aspires to biliteracy, and remedial programs that view students' bilingualism as a problem to be overcome and aspire only to monolingualism and monoliteracy. Enriched Education programs have overwhelming evidence of success in the research literature.

However, it is important to ask whether these programs could be even more successful than they currently are. There is considerable variation in the way literacy is taught in all programs, bilingual and monolingual. In the next part of this article, I suggest that optimal outcomes for students and society will accrue to programs that combine an Enriched Education focus on biliteracy with a transformative pedagogical orientation that actively challenges the operation of coercive relations of power in the wider society.

Transformative Pedagogy and Empowerment

The Persistence of "Banking Education"

One disturbing aspect of the findings of the Ramirez report is that the classroom environment in both bilingual and English-immersion programs reflects transmission models of pedagogy, or what Paulo Freire (1983) has called a "banking education." As expressed in the report:

> Of major concern is that in over half of the interactions that teachers have with students, students do not produce any language as they are only listening or responding with non-verbal gestures or actions. . . . Of equal concern is that when students do respond, typically they provide only simple information recall statements. Rather than being provided with the opportunity to generate original statements, students are asked to provide simple discrete close-ended or patterned (i.e., expected) responses. This pattern of teacher/student interaction not only limits a student's opportunity to create and manipulate language freely, but also limits the student's ability to engage in more complex learning (i.e., higher order thinking skills). In sum . . . teachers in all three programs offer a passive language learning environment, limiting student opportunities to produce language and develop more complex language and thinking skills. (Ramirez, Yuen, Ramey, & Pasta, 1991, p. 8)

The predominance of transmission models of pedagogy is not surprising in view of the fact that other large-scale studies of

American education have documented the same phenomenon (Goodlad, 1984; Sirotnik, 1983). However, there are additional unfortunate implications of transmission models for culturally diverse students, since the curriculum typically reflects the values and priorities of the dominant group and effectively suppresses the experiences and perspectives of subordinate groups. Thus, transmission models of pedagogy allow few opportunities to validate and amplify student identity. In other words, the late-exit programs documented in the Ramirez report appear to create conditions for student empowerment with respect to cultural and linguistic incorporation and parental involvement; however, their pedagogical orientation restricts the possibilities for genuine student empowerment.

This finding suggests that efforts to reverse the pattern of Latino/Latina academic underachievement must examine not only the language of instruction but also the hidden curriculum being communicated to students through that instruction. While improving literacy levels has been a major goal of educational reform reports, few policymakers have asked, "What kinds of literacy and for what purposes?" This question has been answered by Sirotnik (1983) in discussing the implications of Goodlad's major study of American classrooms. He points to the fact that the typical American classroom contains

a lot of teacher talk and a lot of student listening . . . almost invariably closed and factual questions . . . and predominantly total class instructional configurations around traditional activities—all in a virtually affectless environment. It is but a short inferential leap to suggest that we are implicitly teaching dependence upon authority, linear thinking, social apathy, passive involvement, and hands-off learning. (p. 29)

A Framework for Transformative Pedagogy

The remainder of this article focuses on the development of literacy for empowerment. I propose an academic language development framework that incorporates the orientation to critical literacy advocated by Alma Flor Ada (1988a, 1988b).

The framework outlined in Figure 1 is intended to provide a general guide to the implementation of pedagogy that will effectively promote second language learners' linguistic and cognitive development as well as encourage the growth of critical literacy skills. It assumes that for optimal progress to occur, cognitive challenge and intrinsic motivation must be infused into the interactions between teachers and students.

The starting point is to acknowledge that effective instruction in an L2 must focus initially on meaning or messages. Virtually all applied linguists agree that access to sufficient comprehensible input in the target language is a necessary condition for language acquisition. Most applied linguists, however, also assign a role to (1) a focus on formal features of the target language, (2) development of effective learning strategies, and (3) actual use of the target language. These components are incorporated in the Focus on Language and Focus on Use components of the framework.

The Focus on Message component argues that the interpretation of comprehensible input must go beyond just literal com-

INSTRUCTION FOR LANGUAGE LEARNING AND ACADEMIC ACHIEVEMENT

A. FOCUS ON MESSAGE
Making Input Comprehensible
Developing Critical Literacy

B. FOCUS ON LANGUAGE
Awareness of Language Forms and Uses
Critical Analysis of Language Forms and Uses

C. FOCUS ON USE
Using Language to:
Generate new knowledge
Create literature and art
Act on social realities

Figure 1

prehension and extend into critical literacy. This implies a process whereby students relate textual and instructional meanings to their own experience and prior knowledge (i.e., activate their cognitive schemata), critically analyze the information in the text (e.g., evaluate the validity of various arguments or propositions), and use the results of their discussions and analyses in some concrete, intrinsically motivating activity or project (e.g., making a video or writing a poem or essay on a particular topic). In short, for learning of academic content, the notion of comprehensible input must move beyond literal, surface-level comprehension to a deeper level of cognitive and linguistic processing. This perspective is elaborated below in considering Ada's work.

The Focus on Language component attempts to put such controversial issues as the appropriate time and ways to teach L2 grammar under the "umbrella" of Language Awareness. The development of language awareness includes not just a focus on formal aspects of the language but also the development of critical language awareness, which encompasses exploring the relationship between language and power. For example, students might carry out research on the status of different varieties of language (e.g., colloquial language versus formal, "standard" language) and explore why one form is considered by many educators and the general public to be "better" than the other. They might also research issues such as code switching and the role it plays in their own lives and their

bilingual communities. Or they might analyze letters to the editor on bilingual education and inquire why certain kinds of letters tend to get published while others do not.

In short, a focus on formal features of the target language should be integrated with critical inquiry into issues of language and power. Also, to be effective, a focus on language must be linked to extensive input in the target language (e.g., through reading) and to extensive opportunities for written and oral use of the language.

The Focus on Use component is based on the notion that L2 acquisition will remain abstract and classroom-bound unless students have the opportunity to express themselves—their identities and their intelligence—through that language. Ideally, there should be an authentic audience that motivates communication in both oral and written modes. The three examples of language use presented in Figure 1 (generate new knowledge, create literature and art, act on social realities) are intended to illustrate important components of critical literacy. Language must be used to amplify students' intellectual, esthetic, and social identities if it is to contribute to student empowerment, understood as the collaborative creation of power. Unless active and authentic language use for these purposes is promoted in the classroom, students' grasp of academic (and conversational) English and Spanish is likely to remain somewhat shallow and passive.

Ada's Critical Literacy Framework

One framework that elaborates a critical literacy approach to the education of culturally diverse students is presented by Ada (1988a, 1988b) on the basis of Paulo Freire's work. Ada's framework outlines how interpersonal spaces can be created between teachers and students that encourage students to share and amplify their experience within a collaborative process of critical inquiry. She distinguishes four phases in what she terms "the creative reading act." Each of the phases distinguished by Ada is characterized by an interactional process (either between the teacher and students or among peers) that progressively opens up possibilities for the articulation and amplification of student voice. The "texts" that are the focus of the interaction can derive from any curricular area or from newspapers or current events. The process is equally applicable to students at any grade level. Ada (1988a, p. 103) stresses that although the phases are discussed separately, "in a creative reading act they may happen concurrently and be interwoven."

Descriptive Phase In this phase the focus of interaction is on the information contained in the text. Typical questions at this level might be: Where, when, how did it happen? Who did it? Why? These are the types of questions for which answers can be found in the text itself. Ada points out that these are the usual reading comprehension questions and that "a discussion that stays at this level suggests that reading is a passive, receptive, and in a sense, domesticating process" (1988a, p. 104). When the process is arrested at this level, the focus remains on internalization of inert information and/or the practice of "reading skills" in an experiential and motivational vacuum. Instruction remains at a safe distance from any challenge to the societal power structure. This phase represents a focus on functional literacy isolated from both cultural and critical literacy.

Personal Interpretive Phase
After the basic information in the text has been discussed, students are encouraged to relate it to their own experiences and feelings. Questions that might be asked by the teacher at this phase are: Have you ever seen (felt, experienced) something like this? Have you ever wanted something similar? How did what you read make you feel? Did you like it? Did it make you happy? frighten you? What about your family? Ada (1988a) points out that this process helps develop children's self-esteem by showing that their experiences and feelings are valued by the teacher and classmates. It also helps children understand that "true learning occurs only when the information received is analyzed in the light of one's own experiences and emotions" (p. 104). An atmosphere of acceptance and trust in the classroom is a prerequisite for students (and teachers) to risk sharing their feelings, emotions, and experiences. It is clear how this process of sharing and critically reflecting on their own and other students' experiences opens up identity options for culturally diverse students. These identity options are typically suppressed within a transmission approach to pedagogy, where the interpretation of texts is non-negotiable and reflective of the dominant group's notions of cultural literacy. The personal interpretive phase deepens students' comprehension of the text or issues by grounding the knowledge in the personal and collective narratives that make up students' histories. It is also developing a genuine cultural literacy in that it is integrating students' own experience with "mainstream" curricular content.

Critical Analysis Phase
After children have compared and contrasted what is presented in the text with their personal experiences, they are ready to engage in a more abstract process of critically analyzing the issues or problems that are raised in the text. This process involves drawing inferences and exploring what generalizations can be made. Appropriate questions might be: Is it valid? Always? When? Does it benefit everyone alike? Are there any alternatives to this situation? Would people of different cultures (classes, genders) have acted differently? How? Why? Ada emphasizes that schoolchildren of all ages can engage in this type of critical process, although the analysis will always reflect children's experiences and level of maturity. This phase further extends students' comprehension of the text or issues by encouraging them to examine both the internal logical coherence of the information or propositions and their consistency with other knowledge or perspectives. When students pursue guided research and critical reflection, they are clearly engaged in a process of knowledge generation. However, they are equally engaged in a process of self-definition; as they gain the power to think through issues that affect their lives, they simultaneously gain the power to resist external definitions of who they are and to deconstruct the sociopolitical purposes of such external definitions.

Creative Action Phase
This is a stage of translating the results of the previous phases into concrete action. The dialogue is oriented toward discovering what changes individuals can make to improve their lives or resolve the problem that has been presented. Let us suppose that students have been researching (in the local newspaper, in periodicals such as National Geographic) problems relating to environmental pollution. After relating the issues to their own experience, critically analyzing causes and possible solutions, they might decide to write letters to congressional representatives, highlight the issue in their class/school newsletter in order to sensitize other students, write and circulate a petition in the neighborhood, write and perform a play that analyzes the issue, etc. Once again, this phase can be seen as extending the process of comprehension insofar as when we act to transform aspects of our social realities, we gain a deeper understanding of those realities.

Within Ada's framework, the process of making input comprehensible is an active, constructive process that can be facilitated or inhibited by those we are interacting with (or by characteristics of texts we are reading). The framework expresses the point that we cannot understand messages without acting on them either internally (through thinking about them) or externally (by acting on them in the "real" world). The personal interpretive and critical analysis phases represent internalized action on texts or messages. While this internalized action can be carried out by individuals, the process will usually be enhanced when the action is collaboratively constructed in the context of social interaction. The personal interpretive phase deepens the individual's comprehension by grounding the knowledge in the personal and collective narratives that make up our experience and history. The critical analysis phase further extends the comprehension process by examining both the internal logical coherence of the information or propositions and their consistency with other knowledge or perspectives. Finally, the creative action phase constitutes concrete action that aims to transform aspects of our social realities. This external action to transform reality also serves to deepen our comprehension of the issues.

With respect to expansion of possibilities for identity formation, culturally diverse students engaging in the critical literacy process outlined in Figure 1 have the possibility of actively voicing their own realities and their analyses of issues, rather than being constricted to the identity definitions and constructions of "truth" implicitly or explicitly transmitted in the prescribed curriculum. When classroom interaction progresses beyond the descriptive phase, students engage in a process of *self*-expression; in other words, by sharing and critically reflecting on their experience, they collaboratively construct an interpersonal space that expands their options for identity formation.

The operation of this process is evident in Freeman's account of the Oyster School bilingual program, where the instruction and interaction in the school actively encourage students to "refuse" the discourse of disempowerment that frequently characterizes dominant group/subordinated group interactions in the wider society. I would concur with Freeman in attributing the outstanding academic results obtained by students in this program primarily to the ways in which identities were being negotiated in the context of teacher-student interactions. For other Enriched Education programs to achieve similar results, their focus on promoting biliteracy must be integrated explicitly with a transformative pedagogy that affirms students' identities while simultaneously challenging coercive relations of power.

Conclusion

I have suggested that the debate on the merits or otherwise of bilingual education can be understood only by considering the power relations that are operating in the wider society. The history of the education of culturally diverse students in the United States and most other countries is a history of thinly disguised perpetuation of the coercive relations of power that operate in the wider society. The attempt to limit the framework of discourse so that promotion of biliteracy is not even considered as a policy response to the underachievement of Latino/Latina students illustrates the operation of coercive relations of power. Culturally diverse students are defined as deficient and confined to remedial programs that frequently act to produce the deficits they were ostensibly intended to reverse. Empirical evidence that points to biliteracy as a feasible (and readily attainable) educational goal for culturally diverse students has been either ignored or distorted by media and academic opponents of bilingual education. This is evidenced by the fact that most academic opponents of bilingual education are on record as supporting dual-language programs for majority and minority students, yet they persist in claiming that "bilingual education does not work." They also persist in defining bilingualism as part of the problem rather than as part of the solution.

Educators who aspire to challenge the operation of coercive relations of power in the school system must attempt to create conditions of collaborative empowerment. In other words, they must attempt to organize their interactions with students in such a way that power is generated and shared through those interactions. This involves becoming aware of, and actively working to change, the ways in which particular educational structures limit the opportunities that culturally diverse students might have for educational and social advancement. It also involves attempting to orchestrate their interactions with culturally diverse students in such a way that students' options for identity formation and critical inquiry are expanded rather than constricted. For Latino/Latina students, promotion of critical biliteracy is a necessary part of this empowerment process since, in the absence of critical biliteracy, students are unable to read either the word or the world in their two cultures.

REFERENCES

Ada, A. F. (1988a). Creative reading: A relevant methodology for language minority children. In L. M. Malave (Ed.), NABE '87. *Theory, research and application: Selected Papers.* Buffalo: State University of New York.

Ada, A. F. (1988b). The Pajaro Valleyexperience: Working with Spanish-speaking parents to develop children's reading and writing skills in the home through the use of children's literature. In T. Skutnabb-Kangas and J. Cummins (Eds.), *Minority education: From shame to struggle.* Clevedon, England: Multilingual Matters.

Cazabon, M. T., Nicoladis, E., & Lambert, W. E. (1998). *Becoming bilingual in the Amigos two-way immersion program.* Washington, DC: CREDE/CAL.

Cloud, N., Genesee, F., & Hamayan, E. (in press) *Dual language instruction: A handbook for enriched education.* Boston, MA: Heinle & Heinle.

Collier, V. P. (1987). Age and rate of acquisition of second language for academic purposes. *TESOL Quarterly, 21,* 617–641.

Cummins, J. (1981a). The role of primary language development in promoting educational success for language minority students. In California State Department of Education (Ed.), *Schooling and language minority students: A theoretical framework.* Los Angeles: Evaluation, Dissemination and Assessment Center, California State University.

Cummins, J. (1981b). Age on arrival and immigrant second language learning in Canada: A reassessment. *Applied Linguistics, 1,* 132–149.

Cummins, J. (1996). *Negotiating identities: Education for empowerment in a diverse society.* Los Angeles: California Association for Bilingual Education.

Cummins, J. (1999). Beyond adversarial discourse: Searching for common ground in the education of bilingual students. In I. A. Heath & C. J. Serrano (Eds.), *Annual editions: Teaching English as a second language* (pp. 204–224). Guildford, CT: Dushkin/McGraw-Hill.

Cummins, J. (in press). The ethics of doublethink: Language rights and the debate on bilingual education. *TESOL Journal.*

Cummins, J., & Sayers, D. (1995). *Brave new schools: Challenging cultural illiteracy through global learning networks.* New York: St. Martin's Press.

DeVillar, R. A., & Faltis, C. J. (1991). *Computers and cultural diversity: Restructuring for school success.* Albany: SUNY Press.

Freeman, R. D. (1998). *Bilingual education and social change.* Clevedon, England: Multilingual Matters.

Freire, P. (1983). Banking education. In H. Giroux & D. Purpel (Eds.), *The hidden curriculum and moral education: Deception or discovery?* Berkeley, CA: McCutcheon Publishing Corporation.

Freire, P., & Macedo, D. (1987). *Literacy: Reading the word and the world.* South Hadley, MA: Bergin & Garvey.

Genesee, F. (1979). Acquisition of reading skills in immersion programs. *Foreign Language Annals, 12,* 71–77.

Glazer, N., & Cummins, J. (1985). Viewpoints on bilingual education. *Equity and Choice, 2,* 47–52.

Glenn, C. L. (1990). Introduction, *Two-way integrated bilingual education.* Boston: Department of Education, Office of Educational Equity.

Glenn, C. L. (1991). Integrated bilingual education in the USA. In K. Jaspaert & S. Kroon (Eds.), *Ethnic minority languages and education* (pp. 37–55). Amsterdam: Swets & Zeitlinger.

Goodlad, J. I. (1984). *A place called school: Prospects for the future.* New York: McGraw-Hill.

Greene, J. (1998). *A meta-analysis of the effectiveness of bilingual education.* Claremont, CA: Tomas Rivera Policy Institute.

Krashen, S. D. (1999). *Condemned without a trial: Bogus arguments against bilingual education.* Portsmouth, NH: Heinemann.

Porter, R. P. (1990). *Forked tongue:The politics of bilingual education.* New York: Basic Books.

Ramírez, J. D. (1992). Executive summary. *Bilingual Research Journal, 16,* 1–62. Clevedon, England: Multilingual Matters.

Ramírez, J. D., Yuen, S. D., & Ramey, D. R. (1991). *Executive summary: Final report: Longitudinal study of structured English immersion strategy, early-exit and late-exit transitional bilingual education programs for language-minority children.* Contract No. 300-87-0156. Submitted to the U.S. Department of Education. San Mateo: Aguirre International.

Sirotnik, K. A. (1983). What you see is what you get—consistency, persistency, and mediocrity in classrooms. *Harvard Educational Review, 53,* 16–31.

Verhoeven, L. (1991). Acquisition of biliteracy. *AILA Review, 8,* 61–74.

The Two Goals of Bilingual Education: Development of Academic English and Heritage Language Development

Stephen Krashen

Introduction:
Two Goals, and Why We Need to Distinguish Them

We need to distinguish two aspects of, or goals for, bilingual education. The first is the development of academic English and academic success; the second is the development of the heritage, or primary, language. Both are worthwhile goals, and both are accomplished in quality bilingual education programs for the same price. It is, however, helpful to distinguish them when designing programs and also when dealing with the public.

As many professionals in the field know, for the public the bilingual education debate is portrayed as involving two camps: rational people who want children to learn English, and irrational extremists who, for mysterious reasons, want to keep children away from English and prevent them from acquiring it. Evidence that this is a common perception is the fact that when polls show parents want their children to learn English, anti-bilingual education forces interpret these findings as a strong argument against bilingual education.

Confusion about the goals of bilingual education was rampant during the Proposition 227 debate in California. This first became evident to me in the middle of the campaign. I remember the date, April 3, 1998, and I remember the place—Bed Bath & Beyond in West Los Angeles. It had been a frustrating day. I had been scheduled to debate Ron Unz at Cal State LA, my first chance to debate him face to face. To my disappointment, Unz did not show up, and he sent a substitute debater. Thanks to a very supportive, knowledgeable, and sophisticated audience, the substitute was overwhelmed, but little was accomplished. Unz wasn't there and therefore the press wasn't there. On the way home, I stopped at Bed Bath & Beyond to pick up some presents for a wedding shower. My disappointment and frustration at the morning's events must have shown on my face; while I was standing in line, waiting for my "professional shopper," the woman behind me asked me why I looked so depressed. I explained the situa-

tion briefly: I was supposed to debate someone, but he hadn't shown up. She asked what the debate was about, and I said that it was with Ron Unz and had to do with Proposition 227. Her response was immediate and animated: "Oh yes, English for the children! I've heard of that. I'm voting for it. I'm for English!"

I was stunned. I realized right then that my strategy of carefully presenting the research that contradicted the details of 227 had been all wrong. The woman had no idea what 227 was about: She was "voting for English," but *she clearly had no idea that a major goal of bilingual education was English language development.*

I think that when people understand what bilingual education is about, and why it helps English language development, many will support it. We need to communicate this to the media and to the public in general. When we appeal only to the second goal, when we discuss only the advantages of bilingualism, even when they come at no extra cost, we leap too far ahead.

The First Goal:
English Language Development

The idea that developing one language will help another seems to defy common sense. One would think that the more English children hear and read, the faster they will acquire it. It turns out that this is not so. When we give children a good education in their first language, they get two things: knowledge and literacy. Both the knowledge and the literacy they develop in their first language help English language development enormously. The effect is indirect, but powerful.

The knowledge you learn using your first language makes the input you hear and read in English much more comprehensible. This results in more language acquisition and more learning in general. The positive effects of background knowledge on language acquisition and learning have been thoroughly documented (Krashen, 1985), and the concept makes common sense. Consider the hypothetical case of a limited-English-proficient high school student enrolled in a U.S. history class, a student with clear limitations in English. But let us assume that she knows something about history. She has studied history extensively in her own language; she knows about World Wars I and II, knows where Istanbul, Addis Ababa, Copenhagen, and Dallas are, knows something about Louis XIV, Franklin Delano Roosevelt, and Fidel Castro, and knows how to read a complex academic text in her own language. Clearly, this student will

do well, possibly even better than many native English speakers. Thanks to the background knowledge she developed through her first language, U.S. history in English will be more comprehensible.

Developing literacy in the first language is a shortcut to English literacy. A simple three-step argument explains why:

1. As Smith (1994) and Goodman (1982) have argued, we learn to read by understanding what is on the page. (Of course, in light of the current debate, I need to point out that some consciously learned knowledge of phonics, of sound-spelling correspondences, can help make texts comprehensible, as noted by Smith, 1994; most phonics knowledge, however, Smith argues, is the result of reading, not the cause.)

2. If **(1)** is true, it is easier to learn to read if you understand the language.

3. Once you can read, you can read. When you are literate in one language, it is much easier to develop literacy in another, even if the alphabets are different (Krashen, 1996).

The Three Components of Bilingual Education

If the above principles are correct, we can conclude that effective bilingual programs have three components:

1. Subject matter teaching in the first language. This provides the background knowledge that makes the English that children read and hear more comprehensible. It is provided in the first language without translation.

2. Literacy development in the primary language, which transfers to the second. "Transfer" need not be delayed unduly. Students need not get a master's degree in Spanish literature before they are allowed to read in English; English reading can begin as soon as texts are comprehensible.

3. Comprehensible input in English, the second language. This is in the form of ESL at beginning levels and sheltered subject matter teaching as soon as the latter is comprehensible. In sheltered subject matter teaching (Krashen, 1991), intermediate second language acquirers are grouped for comprehensible instruction using the second language as a medium of instruction. Instruction can be made comprehensible for them, because they already have some knowledge of English and because they have some knowledge of the subject matter. In some program models, sheltered subject matter serves as a bridge between education in the primary language and in the mainstream.

There is good evidence that people understand and accept bilingual education when it is presented in terms of these underlying components and principles. In a series of studies, Shin (see Table 1) asked teachers, parents, and administrators not whether they supported bilingual education, but whether they agreed that learning subject matter through the first language helps make subject matter study in the first language more comprehensible, and whether they agreed that developing literacy in the first language facilitates literacy development in English. Shin found considerable support for these principles. Apparently, when described in terms of the underlying principles, bilingual education makes sense to a lot of people.

Table 1

OPINIONS ON THE UNDERLYING PRINCIPLES OF BILINGUAL EDUCATION

Developing literacy through the first language facilitates literacy development in English.

Percent agreement:

Hispanic parents = 53% (Shin & Gribbons, 1996)

Korean parents = 88% (Shin & Kim, 1996)

Hmong parents = 52% (Shin & Lee, 1996)

Administrators = 74% (Anton & Shin, forthcoming)

Teachers = 74% (Shin & Krashen, 1996)

Learning subject matter through the first language makes subject matter study in English more comprehensible.

Percent agreement:

Hispanic parents = 34% (33% were "not sure") (Shin & Gribbons, 1996)

Korean parents = 47% (Shin & Kim, 1996)

Hmong parents = 60% (Shin & Lee, 1996)

Administrators = 78% (Anton & Shin, forthcoming)

Teachers = 70% (Shin & Krashen, 1996)

Is Bilingual Education Effective?

In my reviews (Krashen and Biber, 1988; Krashen, 1996) I conclude that when bilingual programs are set up correctly—that is, when they contain the three components listed above—they work quite well. Children in these programs acquire academic English as well as or better than children in all-English programs. Studies done in other countries show similar results, with second language acquirers acquiring the language of the country as well as or better than comparison children (Krashen, 1999).

The Second Goal: Heritage Language Development

We turn now to the second goal of bilingual education, the continuing development of the child's primary, or heritage, language.

Advantages of Heritage Language Development

Continuing heritage language development has clear advantages for the individual and society. On the individual level, research clearly indicates that those who continue to develop their primary language have certain cognitive advantages over their English-only counterparts (Hakuta, 1986), which may be part of the reason why they do somewhat better in school and on the job market (studies reviewed in Krashen, 1998a).*

As for the social advantages, Wong Fillmore (1991) has pointed out that when the heritage language is weak, problems of intergenerational communication occur. Cho's work (Cho, Cho & Tse, 1997; Cho & Krashen, 1998) confirms Wong Fillmore's observations. Cho's subjects were adult Korean-Americans who were born in the United States or who arrived in the United States before age five. Many reported severe problems in communicating with their Korean-speaking parents. While ordinary communication was possible, discussion of complex and subtle issues was not. Here are comments from two of Cho's subjects:

> My parents and I do have a communication gap, a communication problem. . . . I can't even hold a normal conversation with my parents. I just say my thoughts once and I repeat it constantly until they understand.

> I can say the most subtle thing to my friends and they understand the whole color of it. But, with my parents, I have to literally say everything like, "I am sad! . . . This is why . . ." However, with my friends I just talk about all different aspects of how I am sad and how it reminds me of the time . . . and how I can get over it with what I have learned. But with my parents, I am just reporting to them. . . .

Cho's subjects' difficulties also extended to communication with members of the heritage language community:

> Whenever someone calls my home and they don't speak English, the only word I say is my parents went to "market" in Korean. That's all. After that, if they ask me anything else, I get so frustrated. I wish I could be very personable and ask about their kids . . . because many times I know who they are.

Wong Fillmore states the problem very well:

> What is lost is no less than the means by which parents socialize their children: When parents are unable to talk to their children, they cannot easily convey to them their values, beliefs, understanding, or wisdom about how to cope with their experiences. They cannot teach them about the meaning of work, or about personal responsibility, or what it means to be a moral or ethical person in a world with too many choices and too few guideposts to follow. What is lost are the bits of advice, the *consejos* [advice] parents should be able to offer children in the everyday interactions with them. Talk is a crucial link between parents and children. (p. 343)

The value to society of having bilingual citizens has been argued in many places. There are trade benefits (Fishman, Cooper, & Rosenbaum, 1977), and benefits to national security and diplomacy. In addition, there is no evidence that bilingualism and multiculturalism are the cause of economic or social problems (Fishman, 1990).

The Difficulty of Maintaining Heritage Languages

According to common knowledge, immigrants are reluctant to give up their heritage languages; they supposedly prefer to keep them rather than acquire English. I reviewed (Krashen, 1996, 1998a) a number of studies that showed that just the opposite is true: Heritage languages are typically not maintained and are rarely developed. This fact is one of the most solid and consistent results in language research, yet it appears to be nearly unknown to the general public.

In a recent example of this research, Rumbaut (1997) did two surveys of about 2,000 language-minority students in the San Diego area, one when they were in grades 8 and 9 and another three years later. About half of the students were foreign-born but came to the United States before age 12, and about half were born in the United States. In the first survey, 66 percent of the total sample said they preferred to speak English instead of their parents' language (56 percent of foreign-born, 78 percent of U.S.-born). Three years later, 82 percent of the total sample said they preferred English (72 percent of the foreign-born, 90 percent of the U.S.-born). There were differences among the various subgroups, but Rumbaut points out that "even among the most mother-tongue-retentive group, the Mexican-origin young living in a city adjacent to the Mexican border, the force of assimilation was incontrovertible; while at T1 (the first survey) only 32 percent of the Mexican-born preferred English, by T2 that preference had doubled to 61 percent; and while 53 percent of the U.S.-born had preferred English at T1, three years later that proportion had jumped to 79 percent" (p. 497).

Table 2

SELF-REPORTED COMPETENCE IN ENGLISH AND IN PARENTS' LANGUAGE

	KNOWS ENGLISH		KNOWS PARENTS' LANGUAGE		PREFERS ENGLISH
	Well	Very well	Well	Very well	
Total	93.6%	64.1%	44.3%	16.1%	72.3%
Mexican	86.1	43.7	69.1	34.9	44.8

Source: Portes & Hao (1998).

Portes and Hao (1998) compared English competence to heritage language competence with a larger sample of eighth and ninth graders of language-minority background (*n* = 5,266), which included the San Diego sample described above. All were native-born or had lived in the United States at least five years. Self-reported competence in the heritage language was much lower than self-reported competence in English, with only 16 percent claiming they spoke the heritage language "very well" (Table 2). Once again, even for the most English-resistant group, students of Mexican origin, the shift to English was obvious.

There are several reasons why heritage languages are hard to maintain, in addition to the obvious reason, lack of input.

Ethnic Evasion

Some language-minority-group members go through a stage in which the desire to integrate into the target culture is so strong that there is apathy toward or even rejection of the heritage culture. Tse (1998) refers to this stage as *ethnic ambivalence*, or *ethnic evasion*. Typically, this stage occurs during childhood and adolescence, but it may extend into adulthood. Those in this stage have little interest in the heritage language, and may even avoid using it.

> Maria Shao recounted how her knowledge of Chinese was a source of shame. She recalled that when she was in elementary school, "if I had friends over, I purposely spoke English to my parents. Normally, we only spoke Chinese at home. Because of the presence of a non-Chinese, I used to purposely speak English." (Tse, 1998, p. 21)

Those in this stage who did not know the heritage language had no interest in acquiring it:

> David Mura noted these feelings as a child: "I certainly didn't want to be thought of as Japanese-American. I was American, pure and simple. I was proud I didn't know Japanese, that English was my sole tongue." (p. 21)

For some, this stage gives way to another stage, *ethnic emergence*, in which minority-group members get interested in their ethnic heritage. Those in this stage, Tse points out, may be quite interested in heritage language development.

Language Shyness

This problem is faced by many heritage language (HL) speakers, but especially those who are "visible minorities" and who are among the younger siblings in a family. "Language shyness" occurs when an HL speaker knows the HL fairly well, but not perfectly. What is often lacking are late-acquired aspects of language, aspects that typically do not interfere with communication but that indicate politeness or mark social class differences.

Because HL speakers are members of the HL group, their imperfections are very salient to more proficient speakers, who may respond with correction or even with ridicule. Such responses can be devastating to less proficient HL speakers. Error correction and criticism do not help them, but have the opposite effect. Rather than risk error, they interact less in the HL. This sets up a vicious cycle: Less interaction means less input, and less input means less proficiency. Because language is such a clear marker of social group membership, it could also contribute to alienation from the HL group.

In Krashen (1998b) I present some case histories in which subjects confirm that correction and ridicule discouraged their use of the heritage language:

> I began to realize as I spoke Spanish to my relatives, they would constantly correct my grammar or pronunciation. Of course, since I was a fairly young child the mistakes I made were "cute" to them and they would giggle and correct me. This . . . would annoy me to no end. I wasn't trying to be "cute"; I was trying to be serious. My relatives would say, "You would never know that you are the daughter of an Argentine." Comments like these along with others are what I now believe shut me off to Spanish. . . .

> Growing up I was the butt of many jokes. . . . When I was nine years old . . . a man called, speaking Spanish very quickly. I stumbled through the conversation and got his name, Jorge. I left the message for my father that simply read "HORHEAD CALLED." They laughed about that for weeks and still bring it up to this day. . . . Every laugh and giggle chipped away at my self-esteem. . . . The innocent jokes and cracks took their toll on me and began the creation of a barrier between myself and my family. . . .

Some blamed themselves for not speaking the heritage language better:

> My self-esteem reached an all-time low in college. Several of my peers made well-meaning, but harsh comments upon hearing my Spanish. This was the final blow. It was then I made the decision that I wouldn't speak unless I could speak fluently, grammatically correct, and with a proper native accent. I couldn't even feel comfortable describing myself as bilingual on my résumé. I had to add "limited proficiency" in parentheses to ease my conscience. . . . I was ashamed of being Puerto Rican and living in a bilingual home and never learning Spanish. . . . The only conclusion I could come to was that it was somehow my fault. . . .

The high standards that heritage language speakers feel they must meet can be a disincentive to use the language. I was alerted to this by an insightful comment made by Fay Shin, who spoke Korean before she attended elementary school but feels she has serious gaps in her Korean today. We were having lunch in a Mexican restaurant in Stockton. Despite my modest (a.k.a. limited) command of Spanish, I enthusiastically ordered in Spanish. Shin commented that even though her Korean was much better than my Spanish, she would never order in Korean in a Korean restaurant; expectations for her Korean competence are far higher for her than for someone not of Korean heritage.

Language shyness often leads to less competence, and even more shyness. The consequences are serious: The speaker may eventually give up on the HL.

This means a loss of the economic and cognitive benefits of bilingualism, and can also result in estrangement from the HL community. Giving up on the HL can also prevent *ethnic emergence*, a stage that many minority members go through in which there is increased interest in one's ethnic heritage (see discussion above). It may be that ethnic emergence is an important step toward attaining a multicultural attitude and the acceptance of both cultures (Tse, 1998).

Heritage language speakers are in a no-win situation in foreign language classes. If they do well, it is expected. One of the subjects in Krashen (1998b) told me that her background with Spanish did not make high school Spanish a snap. The emphasis was on learning, not acquisition:

> Classmates' voices from high school keep ringing in my head: "What are you taking Spanish classes for? They must be easy for you. Oh, you're taking it for an easy A, aren't you?" Truthfully, the Spanish classes I took in high school were hard, and I had to work with my grammar and accent for long periods of time. (p. 45)

If HL speakers do not do well in foreign language classes, the experience is especially painful. Often, classes focus on conscious learning of grammatical rules that are late acquired and that some HL speakers may thus not have learned or acquired. It can happen that non-speakers of the HL who are good at grammar will outperform HL speakers on grammar tests and get higher grades in the language class, even though the non-speaker of the HL may be incapable of communicating the simplest idea in the language, while the HL speaker may be fairly competent in everyday conversation. This only adds to the HL speakers' problem, giving them even less confidence in their command of the HL.

Improving Bilingual Education

Bilingual education provides us with a double dividend. When done correctly, it helps children acquire academic English and also, for no extra cost, makes a strong contribution toward developing the child's heritage language—a benefit to the child and to society.

Of course, we must discuss improvement. It is important, however, to point out that when we do so, we are not necessarily saying that what we have now is bad (Rothstein, 1998). Computer companies are always coming out with (what they claim are) better products, but there is never the suggestion that what they had before was bad. Championship athletes are also always trying to improve, but when they break a world record, no one says the previous standard was inadequate. My suggestion is in this spirit. It is the same suggestion I made in Krashen (1996). I am repeating it here because I think it is very important and because there is even more reason to believe it will work. The suggestion is: The print environment in our bilingual programs should be vastly improved.

It is now firmly established that reading for meaning, especially free, voluntary reading, is the major source of our literacy competence. Those who report that they read more read better and write better (Krashen, 1993), and students who participate in free-reading activities in school (e.g. sustained silent reading) show superior literacy development when compared with students who do not (Krashen, 1993; Elley, 1998). Free reading appears to work for first language, for second language, for children, and for teenagers, and the research has confirmed these findings in many different countries.

A confirmation that is especially relevant to heritage language development is McQuillan (1996). Twenty HL speakers at the university level participated in a ten-week class that focused on free reading, literature circles (small-group discussion of what was read), and a survey of popular literature. There was no direct teaching of vocabulary or any other aspect of language. Sixteen of the 20 subjects increased their score on a vocabulary test, with only the highest-scoring pretest students not showing gains.

It is also firmly established that those with greater access to books read more. While access alone is not sufficient to guarantee reading, it is certainly necessary (Krashen, 1993; McQuillan, 1998b). It is also very clear that many limited-English-proficient children have little access to books in any language. I present here data on Spanish-speaking children.

The average Hispanic family with limited-English-proficient

children has about 22 books in their home (Ramirez, Yuen, Ramey, & Pasta, 1991). This refers to the *total* number of books in the home, including the Bible, cookbooks, and dictionaries. This is about one-sixth the U.S. average (Purves & Elley, 1992). School is not helping—in fact, school is making things worse. Pucci (1994) investigated libraries in schools in Southern California with strong bilingual programs and found that books in Spanish were scarce. Those that were available, while often of high quality, were usually very short and for younger children.

Enriching the print environment is not the only recommendation one can make for improving bilingual education, but it is a great place to begin. If it is true that learning to read in the primary language is in fact beneficial, children need something to read. My suggestion is a massive flood of books in the child's home language as well as in English. This suggestion is relatively inexpensive to implement. It would cost a fraction of what we are currently spending on new tests and computers, investments that have no demonstrated payoffs in increasing literacy. Providing a print-rich environment is also a strong investment in heritage language development. If HL speakers become readers in their primary language, they can continue to develop their primary language, whether or not other sources of input are available. Reading is also the perfect method for HL speakers who do not want to risk errors in interacting with others: It is the perfect method for the shy language acquirer.

NOTE

*Additional confirmation comes from Rumbaut (1995), who studied high school students from language-minority backgrounds in the San Diego area. Not surprisingly, those classified as English-only and fluent-English-proficient (bilingual) had higher grade-point averages than those classified as limited-English-proficient. But those classified as fluent-English-proficient had higher GPAs than English-onlys! While other factors may be at work here (English-onlys are typically U.S.-born, while FEPs tend to be foreign-born), the fact remains that bilingualism did not hurt academic achievement. Rumbaut (1995) reported similar results for a sample of 2,420 eighth and ninth graders with foreign-born parents: FEP students had a 2.86 GPA, while English-onlys were slightly behind them with 2.71, despite the fact that the English-onlys had socio-economic advantages and had lived in the United States longer. (See also Portes & Hao, 1998, for additional confirmation.)

Rumbaut also found that among Southeast Asian refugee families in the San Diego area, student GPAs were positively associated with parents' scores on a measure of "ethnic resilience and reaffirmation"; children's GPAs were higher when parents felt their ethnic group should stay together as a community "for social support and mutual assistance" (p. 51) and maintain their own identity, but at the same time should be committed to staying in the United States.

GRADE POINT AVERAGES
GRADES 9 TO 12

(for students from language-minority backgrounds)

Year	n	LEP	FEP	English-only
1986	12,288	2.00	2.21	2.03
1989	15,656	2.06	2.27	2.23

Source: Rumbaut (1995)

REFERENCES

CHO, G., K-S., & TSE, L. (1997). Why ethnic minorites want to develop their heritage language: The case of Korean Americans. *Language, Culture and Curriculum, 10* (2): 106–112.

Cho, G., &Krashen, S. (1998). The negative consequences of heritage language loss and why we should care. In S. Krashen, L. Tse, and J. McQuillan (Eds.), *Heritage language development.* (pp. 31–39) Culver City,CA: Language Education Associates.

Crawford, J. (1995). *Bilingual education: History, politics, theory and practice* (3rd ed.). Los Angeles: Bilingual Educational Services.

Cummins, J. (1989). *Empowering minority students.* Ontario, CA: California Association for Bilingual Education.

Elley, W. (1998). *Raising literacy levels in third world countries: A method that works.* Culver City, CA: Language Education Associates.

Fishman, J. (1990). Empirical explorations of two popular assumptions: Inter-polity perpective on the relationships between linguistic heterogeneity, civil strife, and per capita gross national product. In G. Imhoff (Ed.), *Learning in two languages.* (pp. 209–225) New Brunswick, NJ: Transaction Publishers.

Fishman, J., Cooper, R., & Rosenbaum, Y. (1977). English the world over: A factor in the creation of bilingualism today. In P. Hornby (Ed.), *Bilingualism: Psychological, social and educational implications.* (pp. 103–109) New York: Academic Press.

Goodman, K. (1982). *Language and literacy: The selected writings of Kenneth S. Goodman.* Boston: Routledge and Kegan Paul.

Hakuta, K. (1986). *Mirror of language: The debate on bilingualism.* New York: Basic Books.

Krashen, S. (1985). *The input hypothesis: Issues and implications.* Beverly Hills, CA: Laredo.

Krashen, S. (1991). Sheltered subjectsmatter teaching. *Cross Currents, 18*: 183–188.

Krashen, S. (1993). *The power of reading.* Englewood, CO: Libraries Unlimited.

Krashen, S. (1996). *Under attack: The case against bilingual education.* Culver City, CA: Language Education Associates.

Krashen, S. (1998a). Heritage language development: Some practical arguments. In S. Krashen, L. Tse, & J. McQuillan (Eds.), *Heritage language development* (pp. 3–13). Culver City, CA: Language Education Associates.

Krashen, S. (1998b). Language shyness. In S. Krashen, L. Tse, & J. McQuillan (Eds.), *Heritage language development* (pp. 41–49). Culver City, CA: Language Education Associates.

Krashen, S. (1999). *Condemned without a trial: Bogus arguments against bilingual education.* Portsmouth, NH: Heinemann.

Krashen, S., & Biber, D. (1988). *On course: Bilingual education's success in California.* Los Angeles: California Association for Bilingual Education.

McQuillan, J. (1996). How should heritage languages be taught? The effects of a free voluntary reading program. *Foreign Language Annals, 29*: 56–72.

McQuillan, J. (1998a). Is 99% failure a "success"?: Orange Unified's English immersion program. *Multilingual Educator, 21* (7): 11.

McQuillan, J. (1998b). *The literacy crisis: False claims and real solutions.* Portsmouth, NH: Heinemann.

Portes, A., & Hao, L. (1998). *E Pluribus Unum:* Bilingualism and loss of language in the second generation. *Sociology of Education, 71*: 269–294.

Pucci, S. (1994). Supporting Spanish language literacy: Latino children and free reading resources in schools. *Bilingual Research Journal, 18*: 67–82.

Purves, A., & Elley, W. (1994). The role of the home and student differences in reading performance. In W. Elley (Ed.), *The IEA study of reading achievement and instruction in thirty-two school systems* (pp. 89–121). Oxford: Pergamon.

Ramirez, D., Yuen, S., Ramey, D., & Pasta, D. (1991). *Final report: Longitudinal study of structured English immersion strategy, early-exit and late-exit bilingual education programs for language minority students* (Vol. 1). San Mateo, CA: Aguirre International.

Rothstein, R. (1998). *The way we were? Myths and realities in America's student achievement.* New York: Twentieth Century Foundation Press/Priority Press.

Rumbaut, R. (1995). The new Californians: Comparative research findings on the educational progress of immigrant children. In R. Rumbaut & W. Cornelius (Eds.), *California's immigrant children: Theory, research, and implications for educational policy* (pp. 17–69). San Diego: Center for U.S.-Mexican Studies, University of California, San Diego.

Rumbaut, R. (1997). Paradoxes (andorthodoxies) of assimilation. *Sociological Perspectives, 40* (3): 483–511.

Sahagun, L. (1999). L.A. students take to immersion. Los Angeles *Times*, Wednesday, January 13.

Shin, F., & Gribbons, B. (1996). Hispanic parent perceptions and attitudes of bilingual education. *The Journal of Mexican American Educators*, pp. 16–22.

Shin, F., & Kim, S. (1996). Korean parent perceptions and attitudes of bilingual education. In R. Endo, C. Park, J. Tsuchida, & A. Abbayani (Eds.), *Current issues in Asian and Pacific American education*. Covina, CA: Pacific Asian Press.

Shin, F., & Lee, B. (1996). Hmong parents: What do they think about bilingual education? *Pacific Educational Research Journal, 8*: 65–71.

Smith, C., Constantino, R., & Krashen, S. (1997). Differences in print environment for children in Beverly Hills, Compton, and Watts. *Emergency Librarian 24* (4): 8–9.

Smith, F. (1994). *Understanding Reading* (5th ed.). Hillsdale, NJ: Erlbaum.

Tse, L. (1998). Ethnic identity formation and its implications for heritage language development. In S. Krashen, L. Tse, & J. McQuillan (Eds.), *Heritage language development* (pp. 15–39). Culver City: Language Education Associates.

Wong Fillmore, L. (1991). When learning a second language means losing the first. Early *Childhood Research Quarterly, 6*: 323–346.

Wright, L. (1998). Report finds benefits in English immersion. Los Angeles *Times*, Orange County Edition, April 18.

We Speak in Many Tongues: Language Diversity and Multicultural Education

Sonia Nieto

University of Massachusetts at Amherst

Introduction

The United States is on the road to becoming a truly multilingual nation, if not in policy at least in practice. While the battle by the conservative right to make English the sole and official language of the country rages on, our classrooms, communities, and workplaces are becoming more linguistically diverse.[1] The increase in the number of students who speak a native language other than English has been dramatic and is expected to remain so. For instance, immigration to the United States during the 1970s and 1980s was among the largest in this nation's history. Legal immigration alone between 1980 and 1990 was almost 9 million, equaling that of the peak immigration decade of 1900–1910. About one-third of this immigration has been from Asia and another third from Latin America. In addition, it is estimated that the number of students who speak a language other than English will increase from just over 2 million in 1986 to over 5 million by 2020. Another indication of the enormous changes taking place in our society is the prediction that by the year 2050 the Latino population will have tripled in number and the Asian population will have increased tenfold.[2]

These statistics are cause for concern for the many teachers who must grapple with the dilemmas posed by the linguistic and educational differences that students bring to our schools. The purpose of this article is to explore the growing linguistic diversity in our society and schools in order to propose a different and more productive way of approaching the issue. Rather than continuing to view linguistic diversity as a problem to be corrected, we must change our thinking and consider it an asset for our classrooms and for society in general. Research focusing on the importance of native language development in school achievement will also be reviewed. Finally, I will propose several implications for school policies and practices based on the research reviewed and on a reconceptualization of language diversity within schools.

Language Diversity and Multicultural Education: Expanding the Framework

To understand language issues in a more comprehensive way, we need to expand the framework with which we view linguistic diversity. I will propose several ways in which to do this:

- understanding language diversity as a positive rather than as a negative condition;

- developing an awareness of the key role that language discrimination has played in U.S. educational history;

- removing the compensatory status of programs for linguistically diverse students;

- understanding the crucial role of bilingual education within a multicultural perspective; and

- redefining the benefits of linguistic diversity for all students.

Viewing Bilingualism as an Asset In the United States, we have generally been socialized to think of language diversity as a negative rather than as a positive condition. Yet in most other countries in the world, bilingualism and multilingualism are the order of the day. The prestige accorded to language diversity is a highly complex issue depending on the region of the country, the country itself, the language variety spoken, where and when one has learned to speak, and of course, the ethnicity and class of the speaker. Sometimes bilingualism is highly regarded. This is usually the case with those who are well educated and have high status within their society. At other times, bilingualism is seen as a sign of low status. This is usually the case with those who are poor and powerless within their society, even if they happen to speak a multitude of languages.[3] It is evident that issues of *status* and *power* must be taken into account in reconceptualizing language

diversity. This means developing an awareness that racism and ethnocentrism are at the core of policies and practices that limit the use of languages other than the officially recognized high-status language in schools and in society in general. That is, when particular languages are prohibited or denigrated, the voices of those who speak them are silenced and rejected as well.

Within the United States, the language of power is English. For those who speak it as a native language, monolingualism is an asset. In our society, bilingualism is usually considered an asset only for those who are dominant in English but have learned another language as a second language.

On the other hand, those who speak a language associated with low prestige and limited power as their native tongue are often regarded as deficient. Speaking with a Parisian French accent may be regarded as a mark of high status in some parts of the country, while speaking Canadian French or Haitian Creole usually is not. Likewise, speaking Castilian Spanish tends to be regarded more positively than speaking Latin American or Caribbean Spanish, which are often viewed within the general population as inferior varieties of the language.

For some groups, then, bilingualism is seen as a handicap. This is usually the case with our Latino, American Indian, Asian, and Caribbean students, those who represent the majority of the language minority students in our classrooms. Linguistically, there is nothing *wrong* with the languages they speak. That is, for purposes of communication, these languages are as valid as any others. However, socially and politically, they are accorded low status. Students who speak these languages are perceived as having a "problem," and the problem is defined as fluency in a language other than English. Because society in general and schools in particular define this as a problem, the purpose of education becomes to wipe out all signs of the native language. This is often done by well-meaning educators who perceive their students' fluency in another language as a handicap to their learning English and moving up the social ladder.[4]

Developing an Awareness of Linguicism
United States educational history is replete with examples of language discrimination or what Skutnabb-Kangas has called *linguicism*. Specifically, she defines linguicism as "ideologies and structures which are used to legitimate, effectuate and reproduce an unequal division of power and resources (both material and nonmaterial) between groups which are defined on the basis of language."[5] Entire communities, starting with Indian nations and enslaved Africans, have been prohibited the use of their native languages for either communication or education. This is evident in policies forbidding the use of other languages in schools, and in the lack of equal educational opportunity for youngsters who could not understand the language of instruction.[6] While this is particularly evident with racially and economically oppressed groups, linguicism has not been limited to these but has in fact been a widespread policy with *all* languages other than English in our society. The massive obliteration of the German language is a case in point. While German was almost on a par with English as a language of communication in the United States during the eighteenth and nineteenth centuries—and was in fact one of the most common languages used in bilingual programs during parts of our history—it was largely wiped out by xenophobic policies immediately prior to, during, and after World War I.[7]

Because of the tremendous pressures faced by those who spoke languages other than English, the fact that giving up one's language is a terrible and unnecessary sacrifice was often not questioned. Even today, it is still common to hear of children punished for speaking their native language, or of notes sent home to parents who barely speak English asking them not to speak their native language with their children. While nowadays there is more of an awareness of the extreme ethnocentrism of such practices, the fact that they continue to exist is an indication of our ingrained reluctance to perceive language diversity in positive terms. In developing a more positive framework for linguistic diversity, it is absolutely crucial that we learn how language discrimination has been used to discredit and disenfranchise those who speak languages other than English.

Removing the Compensatory Label from Linguistic Diversity Generally speaking, approaches geared toward students who speak a language other than English are compensatory in nature. That is, they respond to language diversity as if it were an illness to be cured. Thus, most approaches emphasize using the native language only as a bridge to English. When English is learned sufficiently well, the reasoning goes, the bridge can be burned and the student is well on her or his way to achieving academic success.

There are several problems with this reasoning. First, a compensatory approach assumes only that students are *lacking* in something, rather than that they also possess certain skills and talents. Instead of perceiving fluency in another language as an asset to be cherished, it is seen as something that needs fixing. Using the students' literacy in their native language as a basis for the development of literacy in their second language is not usually considered a viable option. Thus, students are expected to start all over again. Not only do they flounder in English, but they often forget their native language in the process.

In addition, even when language minority students are in bilingual programs, they are frequently removed too quickly and often end up in special education classes.[8] Most of the approaches used to help language minority students in school are based on this compensatory framework.[9] Yet, research in this area has suggested that in general students need between five and seven years to make a successful transition from their native language to English.[10] Ironically, when they fail to achieve, the blame is often placed on bilingual programs rather than on premature "exiting" from bilingual programs. Schools need to turn around preconceived notions of language diversity that may lead to policies and practices that jeopardize the very students we are trying to reach.

In order to expand our framework for linguistic diversity, then, we need to develop practices that build on students' language skills rather than tear them down. Programs such as *maintenance or developmental bilingual education*, in which students are encouraged to develop literacy and continued use of both English and their native language, represent a very different approach to language diversity. In programs such as these, students' native language is not considered a "crutch" to lean on until they master the "real" language of schooling. Rather, their native language is recognized as valid not only while they learn English but also in the acquisition of knowledge in general. *Two-way bilingual programs*, in which language minority students and monolingual speakers of English are integrated, afford another way of validating both languages of instruction. In addition, students in these programs learn to appreciate the language and culture of others and to empathize with their peers in the difficult process of developing fluency in a language not their own. Such programs have also been found to be successful in promoting academic achievement.[11]

Linguistic Diversity and Multicultural Education In expanding the framework for language diversity, we also need to redefine it within the field of multicultural education. One of the primary goals of multicultural education is to build on the strengths that students bring to school. Unfortunately, even within multicultural education, the strengths of language diversity are rarely considered. Even the most enlightened and inclusive frameworks for multicultural education fail to take into account the significance of language differences. Although race, class, and gender are often considered integral to multicultural education, language, which does not fit neatly into any of these categories, is not.[12] While it is true that most language minority students within U.S. schools are also from racially and economically oppressed communities, language differences cannot be relegated to either racial or class distinctions alone. Language diversity in and of itself needs to be considered as an important difference through which we can better understand both the talents and the needs students bring to school.

The failure of many proponents of multicultural education to seriously consider linguistic diversity or of supporters of bilingual education to understand the goals of multicultural education, leads to a curious schism: in one corner, we have multicultural education, while in the other we have bilingual education. This artificial separation often results in the perception that multicultural education is for African American students and other students of color who speak English, while bilingual education is only for Latino students and other students who speak a language other than English as their native language. This perception is reinforced by the fact that each of these fields has its own organizations, political and research agendas, and networks. Of course, this kind of specialization is both necessary and desirable because the questions we need to ask and the approaches we develop for each may be quite distinct. On the other hand, by positing the fields of bilingual and multicultural education as fundamentally different and unconnected ones, their common agendas are denied and each is left scrambling for limited resources. The unfortunate result is that proponents of bilingual and multicultural education sometimes become enemies with separate constituencies who know little about the other and may therefore respond with ignorance and hostility to one another.

Teachers need to understand that bilingual education is part and parcel of multicultural education. By allowing these two fields to be isolated from each other, the natural links between them are obscured. Language is one of the most salient aspects of culture. If the languages students speak, with all their attendant social meanings and affirmations, are either negated or relegated to a secondary position in their schooling, the possibility of school failure is increased. Because language and culture are so intimately connected, and because both bilingual and multicultural approaches seek to involve and empower the most vulnerable students in our schools, it is essential that we foster their natural links. This is not to imply that either bilingual or multicultural education is reserved for particular groups. On the contrary, both should be understood as necessary for *all* students. Nevertheless, given their roots and historical context, it is true that they began as responses to demands for improving the education of African American, Latino, Native American Indian, and Asian American students.

Redefining the Beneficiaries of Linguistic Diversity Generally speaking, programs that meet the needs of language minority students require the separation of these students from others. In fact, the dilemma posed by this kind of isolation has been seen as one of the knottiest questions facing the proponents of bilingual education. Landry has maintained that while the problems of race, class, gender, and disability discrimination are best resolved by integration, quite the opposite is true for language discrimination.[13] That is, bilingual education demands the opportunity to *separate* students, at least for part of their education. This makes it particularly troublesome in a democratic society that purports to afford all students an equal educational opportunity. While this claim of equal education is far from real, it is nevertheless an important ideal to strive for. Thus, we need to face the dilemma of segregation that bilingual education presupposes.

There are several ways that the needs of limited English proficiency and monolingual English speakers can be served at the same time. One is through two-way bilingual education, as previously mentioned. Other approaches include setting aside times for joint instruction and developing bilingual options within desegregation plans and magnet schools. Much remains to be done in expanding these options. Perhaps the most important shift in thinking that needs to take place is that *bilingual classrooms, teachers, and students are a rich resource for nonbilingual classrooms, teachers, and students*. When this shift happens, our schools will have taken the first step in committing society to making bilingualism and even multilingualism central educational goals for all students. This is hardly the case right now. For language minority students, for example, English language acquisition, often at the expense of their native language, is the primary goal rather than bilingualism. Even for our English monolingual students, the goal of bilingualism is an elusive one because foreign language courses are delayed until secondary school and are often ineffective. However, when language diversity becomes a benefit to all, we can be quite sure that the persistent underfunding of bilingual education will be eliminated and all students will benefit as a result.

We also need to mention, however, that bilingual education and other support services need to be understood as ensuring educational equity, particularly for language minority students. The issue is not simply one of language but goes much deeper than this. Bilingual education is a civil rights issue because it provides one of the few guarantees that children who do not speak English will be provided education in a language they understand. Given the increasing number of students who enter schools speaking a language other than English, it is clear that bilingual education will become even more important in the years ahead. Just as desegregation has been considered an important (and as yet unattained) civil right for those doomed to receive an inferior education because of inequality of resources, bilingual education is understood by language minority communities as an equally important civil right. Thus, in expanding the framework for linguistic diversity so that all students can benefit from it, we need to remind ourselves that for limited English proficient students, bilingual education is not a frill but *basic* education.

Native Language and School Achievement

Because language diversity has so often been viewed as a deficit, the positive influences of knowing a language other than English have frequently been overlooked.[14] Nevertheless, some recent research has examined the role of a native language other than English on the literacy development and academic achievement of students. Let me begin by stressing that the lack of English skills alone does little to explain the poor academic achievement of students classified as limited in their English proficiency. For example, Cuban students have the highest educational levels of all Latinos, yet they are also the most likely to speak Spanish at home.[15] Cubans are also the most highly educated and upwardly mobile of all Latino groups. It is clear then that speaking Spanish is not the problem. Rather, how language is viewed by the school and the larger society, how students themselves feel about their language, and most importantly, the economic class and professional background of parents seem to play key roles in the academic performance of students.

Given this caveat, research nonetheless suggests that native language maintenance seems to improve rather than jeopardize academic achievement. A study by Dolson, for instance, found that in measures of academic achievement, students who used Spanish at home generally outperformed their peers whose families had switched to only English. Clearly, the home language of these students gave them a distinct advantage in learning.[16] Another study found that recent Mexican immigrants were more successful in school in the United States than were longtime Mexican American residents. The same has been found with recent Puerto Rican arrivals as compared with those who have been here through all or most of their schooling.[17] Thus, the longer they are here, the worse their academic achievement. A major study of immigrant and nonimmigrant students in San Diego had similar findings. They concluded that Latino, Filipino, and Asian immigrants who were just becoming fluent in English were more academically successful than their U.S.–born counterparts.[18] Clearly, then, language differences are not the major problem.

Other recent research bolsters these findings. For example, studies by Moll and Díaz on successful reading and writing learning environments for Latino students found that the students' native language and culture did not handicap their learning. Instead, they concluded that the problems linguistic minority students face are generally due to instructional arrangements in schools that fail to capitalize on the strengths, including linguistic and cultural resources, that they bring to school.[19] In her research with four Mexican American students, Commins also found that the classroom setting for linguistic minority students can work as an intervening variable to support or to weaken students' perceptions of themselves and can thus contribute to their linguistic and academic development or lack of it. In fact, one of the major themes demonstrated by the student profiles was the ambivalence they experienced about their bilingualism.[20]

Thus, speaking a language other than English is not necessarily a handicap; on the contrary, it can be a great asset to learning. How such language use is interpreted is the real issue. For example, bilingual and other support services for students with a limited English proficiency frequently have a low status. Even their physical placement within schools is indicative of this. These programs are often found in large windowless closets, hallways, or classrooms next to the boiler room. Little surprise then that even the parents of children in these programs press for a quick exit for their children.

Yet, the fact is that bilingual education and other programs that support native language use, even if only as a transition to English, are generally more effective than programs such as ESL alone. This is true not only in terms of learning content in the native language, but in terms of learning *English* as well. This seemingly contradictory finding can be understood if one considers the fact that students in bilingual programs are provided with continued education in content areas *along with* structured instruction in English. In addition, they are building on their previous literacy, and thus it becomes what Lambert has called an *additive* form of bilingual education. *Subtractive* bilingual education, on the other hand, is when one language is substituted for another, and true literacy is not achieved in either.[21] This often happens in programs where the students' native language is eliminated and English grammar, phonics, and other language features are taught out of context with the way in which real day-to-day language is used.

Even in programs where English is not used or used minimally, results show dramatic gains in students' achievement. Campos and Keatinge, for instance, found that Latino children enrolled in a Spanish-only preschool program developed more skills that would prepare them for school than children in a bilingual preschool program where the main goal was to develop proficiency in English.[22] A comparative evaluation of bilingual and ESL-only programs also found that students in bilingual programs consistently outperformed those in ESL-only programs even in their English-language performance.[23] Ironically, the more native-language instruction students received, the better they performed in English! It is clear then that even if the primary purpose of education in our society is to learn English (a debatable position at best), bilingual programs seem to work more effectively than programs in which only English is used, because bilingual programs use students' acquired literacy as the basis for learning English. These findings have been consistently reported by researchers working in the field of bilingual education. Thus, when students' language is used as the basis for their education, when it is respected and valued, students tend to succeed in school.[24]

Although not explored as thoroughly with culture, a number of studies point to the same conclusions. For example, in a study of successful Punjabi students, Gibson found that parents consistently admonished their children to maintain their culture and made it clear that not doing so would dishonor their families and communities.[25] In addition, a major study of Southeast Asian students found an intriguing connection between grades and culture: higher grade-point averages were positively related to the maintenance of traditional values, ethnic pride, and close social and culture ties with members of the same ethnic group.[26]

In my own research with academically successful students, I found that maintaining language and culture were essential in supporting and sustaining their academic achievement. In a series of in-depth interviews with these linguistically, culturally, and economically diverse students, one of the salient features accounting for school success was a strong-willed determination to hold onto their culture and native language. Their pride in culture and language, however, was not without conflict. That is, most of these young people expressed both pride and shame in their culture. Given the assimilationist messages of our society, this is hardly surprising. What was surprising, however, was the steadfastness with which they maintained their culture and language in spite of such messages. Yet, for the most part, these were students who would not be expected to succeed in school given their disadvantaged economic position.[27]

What can we learn, then, from research

focusing on the importance of language and culture in the academic achievement of students? One intriguing conclusion is that the more students are involved in resisting assimilation while maintaining their culture and language, the more successful they will be in school. That is, cultural and linguistic maintenance seems to have a positive impact on academic success. This is obviously not true in all cases, as we can all think of examples of people who have felt they had to assimilate in order to succeed in school. The case of Richard Rodríguez, who felt compelled to choose between what he considered "public" and "private" worlds, comes to mind. That is, in order for him to succeed, he felt that he needed to reject his Mexican culture and the Spanish language.[28] We can legitimately ask whether his represents a healthy success, for in the bargain he lost part of himself. Thus, while it is important not to overstate that linguistic and cultural maintenance seems to have a positive impact on academic achievement, it is indeed a real possibility and one that severely challenges the "melting pot" ideology that has dominated U.S. schools and society throughout this century. The notion that assimilation is a necessary prerequisite for success in school and society is severely tested by current research.

Implications for Classroom Practice

The conclusion that maintaining native language and culture positively influences student achievement turns on its head not only conventional educational philosophy but also the policies and practices of schools that have done everything possible to effectively eradicate students' culture and language in order, they maintained, for all students to succeed in school. It would mean that rather than attempting to erase culture and language, schools should do everything in their power to use, affirm, and maintain them as a foundation for students' academic success. School policies and practices that stress cultural pride, build on students' native language ability, and use the experiences, culture, and history of the students' communities as a basis for instruction would be the result. We can even say that when their language and culture are reinforced not only at home but in school as well, students seem to develop less confusion and ambiguity about their ability to learn. Thus, regardless of the sometimes harsh attacks on their culture and language (as is the case in communities in which there are strident campaigns to pass "English-only" legislation), students whose language and culture are valued within the school setting pick up affirming messages about their worth.

If we move our thinking from *language diversity as deficit to language diversity as asset*, the implications for policy and practice become quite different from what they are at present. When linguistic diversity is seen as a handicap to be "fixed," policies and practices that focus on doing away with students' language differences are in operation. On the other hand, when linguistic diversity is seen as a valuable resource for students, schools, and communities, policies and practice reinforce the importance of and necessity for bilingualism and multilingualism. Three key implications of the reconceptualization of linguistic diversity in our schools become clear: strengthening bilingual programs, developing comprehensive multicultural education, and actively seeking ways to involve the parents of linguistic minority students in their children's education. Let us briefly review each of these.

1. Bilingual Programs Need to Be Valued and Strengthened

Bilingual education has always been a controversial program within U.S. schools, especially during the past 25 years when it has become such an important option for students with limited English proficiency. It is clear that a rethinking of the very goals of bilingual education needs to take place in order to reinforce the crucial role it has proven to have in supporting both English acquisition *and* native language maintenance. Thus, not only should these programs be promoted, but they should also be accorded more visibility and respect within schools. This implies at least the following:

- more funding for bilingual programs;
- availability of such programs for all students with limited English proficiency;
- changing the "quick-exit" mentality of bilingual programs; and
- more two-way programs in which bilingualism is promoted for all students.

2. Comprehensive Multicultural Programs Should Be Developed

Reconceptualizing language diversity as an essential component of multicultural education also means that the way in which schools view multicultural education needs to be changed. Multicultural education in many schools is reduced to a "Holidays and Heroes" approach where making exotic masks, eating ethnic foods, and commemorating safe heroes are the primary activities. Nevertheless, the research reviewed here has made it clear that if culture and language are to be respected and affirmed, a comprehensive approach to multicultural education needs to be developed. This means that linguistic differences of students not in bilingual programs need to be respected as well. In fact, most students who speak a language other than English are not in bilingual programs, at least not for most of their schooling. Strategies that would send these students the message that their language is important and worthy of respect might include:

- encouraging students to use their native language with language peers, both in academic and social situations;
- pairing students with a buddy more fluent in English and encouraging each to teach the other;
- motivating students to teach their peers about their language and culture;

- inviting guests who speak a variety of languages to the classroom; and
- using bilingual classrooms as a valuable resource for nonbilingual classrooms.

In addition, teachers who learn at least a working knowledge of one or more languages are telling their students that they appreciate the difficult work it takes to learn another language.

3. Parent Involvement of Linguistic Minority Students Should Be Promoted

The key role that parent involvement plays in the education of all students has been proven time and again.[29] In the case of linguistic minority students, this role can be even more central. That is, because the parents of these children are often directly involved in their native language literacy, their support of and participation in native language maintenance are crucial. Although parents are the first and most important teachers of their children, the secondary status accorded to parents of linguistic minority students has impacted on their involvement in school in negative ways. Schools and teachers need to develop strategies that welcome parents as important partners in the education of their children. This means seeking ways to involve them both in school and out, and to reaffirm the role they have in nurturing and maintaining children's literacy in their native language. One way of respecting the languages they speak as languages of knowledge and learning is to use these languages in activities that promote literacy both in school and at home. This reasoning was behind the literacy project developed by Ada in her research with Mexican American parents. Working with the parents of young elementary school children, she initiated a discussion-oriented project on children's literature. In the process of dialogue, reading, and writing, parents developed confidence and greater abilities in using the resources at their command, particularly their language and culture, to promote the literacy of their children.[30]

It is obvious from such research that parents can have a decisive effect on their children's literacy development and on their academic success in general. Schools need to acknowledge this important role and to seek innovative strategies to use the talents, hope, and motivation of parents in constructive ways. The view that poor parents and those who speak a language other than English are unable to provide appropriate environments for their children can lead to condescending practices that reject the skills and resources that parents do have.

Conclusion

Language is one of the fundamental signs of our humanity. It is "the palette from which people color their lives and culture. Intimately connected to the human experience, language oils the gears of social interactions and solidifies the ephemera of the mind into literature, history and collective knowledge."[31] While linguistic diversity is a fact of life in U.S. schools and society, many languages are not given the respect and visibility they deserve. Because English is the language of power in our society, monolingualism is perceived as an asset. Those who speak a language other than English are generally viewed as having a problem that must be solved. At the core of such perceptions are racist and ethnocentric ideas about the value of some languages and not others.

Given recent trends in immigration, the shrinking of our world, and the subsequent necessity to learn to communicate with larger numbers of people, it is clear that a reconceptualization of the role of languages other than English within our schools and society in general has to take place. Such a reconceptualization needs to have the following components:

■ a redefinition of linguistic diversity as an asset rather than a deficit;

■ building on students' strengths, including their language and culture, rather than tearing these resources down;

■ actively seeking out involvement by parents and other community people representing the linguistic diversity our students bring to school;

■ understanding bilingual education and other language approaches and services as important and necessary components of multicultural education; and

■ developing an awareness that all students can benefit from linguistic diversity, not only those with limited English proficiency.

Given this kind of reconceptualization, the policies and practices that schools have in place need to be reexamined. Those that build on students' diversity should be strengthened, while those that focus on differences as deficits should be eliminated. This means, at the very least, that bilingual and multicultural programs *for all students* have to be comprehensively defined, adequately funded, and strongly supported.

NOTES

* The title of this article refers to a statement made by Dr. Luis Reyes ("We speak in many tongues, but we are not confused") in response to *The New York Times Magazine* article entitled "A Confusion of Tongues." It was reported in *Speaking Out About Bilingual Education: A Report on the Testimony Presented at the Community Speak-Out on Bilingual Education* (Puerto Rican/Latino Education Roundtable, c/o Centro, Hunter College, New York City, June 15, 1983).

I would like to thank Jerri Willet for reading an earlier version of this article and providing helpful and critical suggestions for improving it.

1. The National Education Association, among many other organizations, has taken a strong stand against the "English Only" movement. See *Official English/English Only: More Than Meets the Eye* (Washington, DC: NEA, 1988). For in-depth reviews and analyses of the history and purposes of "English Only," see Harvey A. Daniels, ed., *Not Only English: Affirming America's Multilingual Heritage* (Urbana, IL: National Council of Teachers of English, 1990); and "English Plus: Issues

in Bilingual Education," *Annals of the American Academy of Political and Social Science* 508 (March 1990).

2. See, for example, John B. Kellogg, "Forces of Change," *Phi Delta Kappan* (November 1988): 199–204; Thomas Muller and Thomas Espenshade, *The Fourth Wave* (Washington, DC: Urban Institute Press, 1985); the National Coalition of Advocates for Students, *New Voices: Immigrant Students in U.S. Public Schools* (Boston, MA, 1988); Gary Natriello, Edward L. McDill, and Aaron M. Pallas, *Schooling Disadvantaged Children: Racing Against Catastrophe* (New York: Teachers' College Press, 1990); and E. Emily Feistritzer, *Teacher Crisis: Myth or Reality? A State-by-State Analysis, 1986* (Washington, DC: National Center for Education Information, 1986).

3. For a more comprehensive explanation of this, see Howard Giles, Klaus R. Scherer, and Donald M. Taylor, "Speech Markers in Social Interaction," in Klaus R. Scherer and Howard Giles, eds., *Social Markers in Speech* (Cambridge, England: Cambridge University Press, 1979); Einar Haugen, "The Language of Imperialism: Unity or Pluralism?" in N. Wolfson and J. Manes, eds., *Language of Inequality* (New York: Mouton Publishers, 1987); and Robert Phillipson, "Linguicism: Structure and Ideologies in Linguistic Imperialism," in Tove Skutnabb-Kangas and Jim Cummins, eds., *Minority Language: From Shame to Struggle* (Clevedon, England: Multilingual Matters Ltd., 1988).

4. See the research by Aida Hurtado and Raúl Rodriguez for a more comprehensive description of this phenomenon, "Language as a Social Problem: The Repression of Spanish in South Texas," *Journal of Multilingual and Multicultural Development* 10 (5): 401–419.

5. Tove Skutnabb-Kangas, "Multilingualism and the Education of Minority Children," in Tove Skutnabb-Kangas and Jim Cummins, eds., *Minority Language: From Shame to Struggle* (Clevedon, England: Multilingual Matters Ltd., 1988), p. 13.

6. For examples of language discrimination in our history, see Meyer Weinberg, *A Chance to learn: A History of Race and Education in the U.S.* (Cambridge, England: Cambridge University Press, 1977); and Jim Cummins, *Empowering Minority Students* (Sacramento, CA: California Association for Bilingual Education, 1989). Language discrimination was the basis for the unanimous Supreme Court decision in *Lau v. Nichols* (*Lau v. Nichols*, 414 U.S. 563, St. Paul, MN: West Publishing Co., 1974).

7. See, for example, Diego Castellanos, *The Best of Two Worlds* (Trenton, NJ: State Department of Education, 1983); and Gary S. Keller and Karen S. van Hooft, "A Chronology of Bilingualism and Bilingual Education in the United States," in Joshua Fishman and Gary Keller, eds., *Bilingual Education for Hispanic Students in the United States* (New York: Teachers College Press, 1982).

8. For an explanation of the relationship between premature removal from bilingual programs and special education, see Jim Cummins, *Bilingualism and Special Education* (Clevedon, England: Multilingual Matters Ltd., 1984).

9. For a review of program models in bilingual education, see Carlos J. Ovando and Virginia P. Collier, *Bilingual and ESL Classrooms: Teaching in Multicultural Contexts* (New York: McGraw-Hill Book Co., 1985).

10. See Jim Cummins, "The Role of Primary Language Development in Promoting Educational Success for Language Minority Students," in Office of Bilingual Bicultural Education, *Schooling and Language Minority Students: A Theoretical Framework* (Sacramento, CA: Evaluation, Dissemination, and Assessment Center, California State University, Los Angeles, 1981); and Virginia P. Collier, "How Long? A Synthesis of Research on Academic Achievement in a Second Language," *TESOL Quarterly* 23 (September 1989): 509–531.

11. Virginia P. Collier, "Academic Achievement, Attitudes, and Occupations Among Graduates of Two-Way Bilingual Classes." Paper presented at the annual meeting of the American Educational Research Association, San Francisco, CA, March 1989.

12. See, for example, Christine E. Sleeter and Carl A. Grant, "A Rationale for Integrating Race, Gender, and Social Class," in Lois Weis, ed., *Class, Race, and Gender in American Education* (New York: State University of New York Press, 1988).

13. Walter J. Landry, "Future *Lau* Regulations: Conflict Between Language Rights and Racial Nondiscrimination," in Raymond V. Padilla, ed., *Theory, Technology, and Public Policy on Bilingual Education* (Washington, DC: National Clearinghouse for Bilingual Education, 1983).

14. For extensive reviews of the research on bilingualism as a defect, see Cummins, *Empowering Minority Students*; and Kenji Hakuta, *Mirror of Language: The Debate on Bilingualism* (New York: Basic Books, Inc., 1986).

15. Ray Valdivieso and Cary David, *U.S. Hispanics: Challenging Issues for the 1990s* (Washington, DC: Population Trends and Public Policy, 1988).

16. David P. Dolson, "The Effects of Spanish Home Language Use on the Scholastic Performance of Hispanic Pupils," *Journal of Multilingual and Multicultural Development 6* (2): 135–156.

17. Maria E. Matute-Bianchi, "Ethnic Identities and Patterns of School Success and Failure Among Mexican-Descent and Japanese-American Students in a California High School: An Ethnographic Analysis," *American Journal of Education* 15 (1): 233–255; and Joseph O. Prewitt-Díaz, "A Study of Self-Esteem and School Sentiment in Two Groups of Puerto Rican Students," *Educational and Psychological Research* 3 (Summer 1983): 161–167.

18. Ruben G. Rumbaut and Kenji Ima, *The Adaptation of Southeast Asian Refugee Youth: A Comparative Study* (San Diego, CA: Office of Refugee Resettlement, 1987).

19. Luis C. Moll and Stephen Díaz, "Change as the Goal of Educational Research," *Anthropology and Education Quarterly* 18 (December 1987): 300–311.

20. Nancy L. Commins, "Language and Affect: Bilingual Students at Home and at School," *Language Arts* 66 (January 1989): 29–43.

21. W. E. Lambert, "Culture and Language as Factors in Learning and Education," in A. Wolfgang, ed., *Education of Immigrant Students* (Toronto: OISE, 1975).

22. S. Jim Campos and H. Robert Keatinge, "The Carpinteria Language Minority Student Experience: From Theory, to Practice, to Success," in Skutnabb-Kangas and Cummins, eds., *Minority Language.*

23. The study by Virginia P. Collier and Wayne P. Thomas was reported by James Crawford in "Study Challenges 'Model' E.S.L. Program's Effectiveness," *Education Week*, April 27, 1988.

24. See, for example, the research cited by Jim Cummins, *op. cit.*; see also Stephen Krashen and Douglas Biber, *On Course: Bilingual Education's Success in California* (Sacramento, CA: California Association for Bilingual Education, 1988); Shirley Brice Heath, "Sociocultural Contexts of Language Development," in *Beyond Language: Social and Cultural Factors in Schooling Language Minority Students* (Los Angeles, CA: Evaluation, Dissemination, and Assessment Center, Office of Bilingual Education, California State Department of Education, 1986); Carole Edelsky, "Bilingual Children's Writing: Fact and Fiction," in Donna M. Johnson and Duane H. Roen, eds., *Richness in Writing: Empowering ESL Students* (New York: Longman, 1989).

25. Margaret A. Gibson, "The School Performance of Immigrant Minorities: A Comparative View," *Anthropology and Education Quarterly* 18 (December 1987): 262–275.

26. Rumbaut and Ima, *The Adaptation of Southeast Asian Refugee Youth.*

27. Sonia Nieto, *Affirming Diversity: The Sociopolitical Context of Multicultural Education* (New York: Longman, 1991).

28. Richard Rodríguez, *Hunger of Memory: The Education of Richard Rodríguez* (Boston: David R. Godine, 1982).

29. Anne T. Henderson, *The Evidence Continues to Grow: Parent Involvement Improves Student Achievement* (Columbia, MD: National Coalition of Citizens in Education, 1987).

30. Alma Flor Ada, "The Pájaro Valley Experience," in Tove Skutnabb-Kangas and Jim Cummins, eds., *Minority Education: From Shame to Struggle* (Clevedon, England: Multilingual Matters Ltd., 1988).

31. William F. Allman, "The Mother Tongue," *U.S. News & World Report*, November 5, 1990.

Literacy Instruction Through Spanish: Linguistic, Cultural, and Pedagogical Considerations

Elly B. Pardo, *Educational Consultant*
and
Josefina Villamil Tinajero
University of Texas at El Paso

In the United States, the structure and content of bilingual education programs have been a topic of scrutiny and heated debate for some 25 years now. Of greatest concern to educational practitioners, researchers, policy makers, communities, and families has been the scholastic achievement of linguistic minority children, particularly the ways in which these youngsters successfully acquire and develop literacy skills in both their first and second languages (Cummins, 1989; Genesee, 1987; Goldenberg, 1994; Lambert, 1984; Macedo, 1991). It is widely accepted that literacy is the cornerstone of all academic competencies (Cummins, 1987, 1989; Heath, 1983, 1989; Snow, Burns, & Griffin, 1998). For this reason, in both bilingual and non-bilingual classrooms, a primary instructional goal is to teach students how to use oral and written language for meaningful communication.

Pedagogical problems arise, however, in the interpretation of what constitutes meaningful language and literacy instruction for students who are dominant in a mother tongue other than English. One school of thought considers bilingual education to be a kind of *internment program* in which limited English proficient students (LEPs) must spend several years before learning enough English to survive in regular education settings. Proponents of the *internment* model promote a structured English immersion approach to literacy development (Baker & de Kanter, 1981; Dunn, 1987; Gersten & Woodward, 1985). This approach is focused strictly on providing LEP youngsters with sufficient oral, reading, and writing skills in English so that they can eventually transition to a regular education program where their more analytical literacy learning will occur.

Another school of thought treats bilingual education as a *buffer program* that helps transition students from their home language and culture to the language and culture of the classroom. LEP children in this type of educational setting are initially provided with language and literacy instruction in their mother tongue (their L1) while simultaneously acquiring oral language skills in English (their L2). Nevertheless, as soon as they have sufficient conversational and oral comprehension ability in their L2 (perhaps after a year or two), they are gradually transitioned into an English literacy curriculum, even though they may still remain in a bilingual classroom. For this reason, the *buffer* model of bilingual education is not designed with the purpose of fully developing and preserving the speaking, reading, and writing skills of LEP students in their mother tongue (Medina & Escamilla, 1992; Troike, 1978).

And finally, a third school of thought advocates bilingual education as a way of cultivating and maintaining the literacy proficiency of LEP children in both their first and second languages. This method of bilingual instruction we shall call a *holistic* model of learning because it recognizes the societal value of developing literacy competence in a child's home language as well as in English. The rationale underlying the *holistic* model is that LEP children will have the best possible chance of becoming capable speakers, readers, and writers in both their L1 and L2 if they can transfer strong literacy skills from their native language to English (Cummins, 1981, 1987, 1989; Genesee, 1987; Goldenberg, 1994; Jimenez, Garcia, & Pearson, 1995; Krashen & Biber, 1988; Ramírez, Yuen, & Ramey, 1991; Snow, Burns, & Griffin, 1998; Thomas and Collier, 1997). For this reason, the model encourages long-term literacy instruction in both the L1 and the L2 as a means of sustaining literacy proficiency in two languages. It is the *holistic* method of bilingual education that will frame our discussion of the importance of native language instruction in promoting effective literacy skills in Spanish and English for Spanish-dominant elementary school children.

The Connection Between Language and Literacy Learning

Cognitive and Academic Considerations

Language is intimately linked both to conceptual development and to social experience (Brown 1973; Cummins, 1996; Hakuta, 1990; Skutnabb-Kangas, 1981; Snow, Burns, & Griffin, 1998). It is therefore an important tool for processing information about one's surroundings and for organizing personal perceptions of self in relation to these surroundings (Vygotsky, 1962). It reflects how humans view and interact with their world—why they say what they say and why they think in certain ways. In other words, language is the filter through which all sociocultural experiences and understandings must pass (Alexander, Schallert, & Hare, 1991).

Our discussion here will highlight the association between language background and literacy learning. In particular, it will underscore the importance of the mother tongue in teaching children to become competent readers, not only of words and phrases, but also of experience. Like others (Dechant, 1991; Smith, 1988), we argue that reading is an interactive process directed toward the sharing of meaning. To engage in this process effectively, readers must be able to comprehend a writer's text by drawing on their own literacy and sociocultural knowledge to reconstruct another's message. In other words, reading is intimately tied to comprehension, and comprehension is directly related to what the reader already knows (Smith, 1988). What this means is that children cannot become proficient readers of another's experiences if their own background has not equipped them with the cognitive, linguistic, and social tools that are relevant to the information communicated in print.

Heath (1989) explains that "for all children, academic success depends less on the specific language they know than on the ways of using language they know" (p. 144). In the arguments that follow, we propose that with Spanish-speaking elementary school students, literacy instruction in their native language is the most pedagogically sound way of teaching them about the relationships between meaning and print in both Spanish and English. This is because empirical evidence has shown that Spanish-dominant youngsters acquire English when they attain literacy proficiency in their mother tongue (Krashen, 1999; Krashen & Biber, 1988; Ramírez, 1994; Ramírez, Yuen, & Ramey, 1991; Thomas & Collier,

1997). In keeping with this finding, we contend that instruction in Spanish reading helps LEP children appreciate their linguistic heritage, develop positive literacy experiences, and attain competence in both academic Spanish and English. Therefore, to exclude the native language from a student's instructional program or to minimize its use in classroom pedagogy may seriously reduce the learning options for Spanish-dominant children as compared to those of their English-dominant peers.

Natural Language Learning and Literacy Competence

The Goodmans (1979) explain that for young children, literacy acquisition is an extension of natural language learning. Natural language learning occurs when youngsters draw upon the lexicon and grammar of their mother tongue to organize their thinking and to communicate their thoughts and needs to people who understand their cultural experience. We have already noted that culture and language are closely intertwined—language serving to re-create or interpret the accumulated experiences of a social group (González, 1989). For this reason, effective literacy practices must be tied to the cultural norms, values, belief systems, and behaviors of a community of speakers. When literacy learning is not linked to familiar information, it will be at odds with children's natural learning processes, "will neutralize or blunt the force of their language learning strength, and may (even) become counterproductive" (Goodman & Goodman, 1979, p. 138).

The position of "natural learning" is central to our argument concerning reading instruction for Spanish-speaking students in the elementary grades. We propose that for Hispanic youngsters with little or no proficiency in English, the native language is the most appropriate vehicle for teaching them about the complexities of the relationship between speech and print. This is because reading requires that people match their linguistic and sociocultural knowledge to a text (Goodman, 1967). It is a process of "building a representation of text by relating what is on the page to one's own fund of experience" (Dechant, 1991, p. 6). In fact, reading is often thought of as reasoning through print (Smith, 1988) because it relies on "higher order" thinking skills that involve message interpretation, the association of print with past experience, and the construction of new meanings and relationships. It follows then that children learning to read in a language they do not speak well will spend much of their time on deciphering graphic input instead of on message interpretation. Reading for them will thus become a rote activity focused on sound and vocabulary recognition instead of on the interplay between words and the images and ideas that these words evoke.

Literacy learning is most effective, then, when it is a natural outgrowth of the world knowledge that students bring with them from their home environment to school. Heath (1983) observes that each community has its own rules for socializing children through language and that "ways of taking" meaning from print differ across communities. Therefore, when the literacy instruction of LEP students helps them to "take meaning" from their own reservoir of sociolinguistic experiences, the school not only is establishing continuity between the home and school, but it is also validating the linguistic and cultural identity of these students. Moreover, in terms of achievement, scholars have argued strongly that positive self-identification affects educational success (Lambert, 1987; Matute-Bianchi, 1986; Padilla, 1990). For this reason, using the language of the home as a tool for linguistic empowerment is the most natural way of cultivating the self-worth and intellectual potential that LEP children often abandon when they enter the culture of the school.

Sociolinguistic Perspectives on Literacy Competence

When elementary school youth explore print in their mother tongue, they are learning about the lexical, grammatical, and semantic possibilities of a language that they already are able to use in purposeful speech. In other words, they have acquired a sociocultural perspective on how to explain, orient, prohibit, negate, mandate, and express emotions, etc., so that individuals in their speech community will think, feel, behave, or react in certain ways (Pardo, 1991). "Writing is not simply the language of speech written down (but) has its own set of characteristic grammatical structures," and children "generally do not master the constructions of the written language until they themselves become fluent readers" (Perera, 1987, p. 101). As a result, youngsters must be reading extensively to encounter some of these constructions.

Given the multifaceted nature of the reading process, we propose that when Spanish-dominant youngsters attain a level of reading proficiency in their L1 that enables them to do more than decode simple prose, they are learning a great deal about the science of linguistic communication. Specifically, they are gaining an analytical knowledge of the rhetorical potential of language: how to combine linguistic elements to develop cohesive arguments and how to create a mood and engage an audience through words. For this reason, providing young Spanish-dominant children with sufficient literacy instruction in their L1 furnishes them with an understanding of the expressive possibilities of language that they can later apply to literacy learning opportunities in their L2. (See the discussion on the *linguistic interdependence principle* in the following section for a consideration of psycholinguistic factors affecting the transfer of language knowledge.)

Commenting on the importance of literacy instruction in the native language, Snow (1990) observes:

> Practice in reading is possible only if children are willing to sit down and read, which is not likely if they are expected to read in a language they do not yet understand, or if they have to read material much below the level that interests them because of limitations on their language proficiency. (p. 69)

When LEP children must conduct their literacy activities in a language with which they have only little or moderate familiarity, they lose valuable opportunities to extract new ideas and forms of expression from texts that they can use in new language-based situations, in both their L1 and L2. We have already noted that printed material provides readers with numerous opportunities to discover how ideas are linked in ways that are not typical of everyday spontaneous speech. Pointing to the interplay between written and oral language, Perera (1987) explains that learning about the structural possibilities of written language enables readers to become more effective language users in general. She further notes that new structures "once mastered through writing . . . are available for use in speech . . . thereby increasing the power and flexibility of (an individual's) oral repertoire" (p. 115).

Nevertheless, as noted earlier, when native Spanish-speaking students develop literacy skills in English only, the potential for rapidly expanding their knowledge of how language works is considerably limited. This is because the students' familiarity with their L2 does not afford them opportunities to process the same amount of grammatical, semantic, and stylistic information in their L2 as they could process in their L1. Therefore, exposing Spanish-speaking students to an English-only curriculum does not guarantee that these students will have a greater awareness of English than LEP students who are instructed in both their L1 and L2. In fact, research has shown the opposite to be true.

A plausible explanation for the inability of Spanish-dominant students to process reading material in English as thoroughly as they are able to in Spanish stems from their limited exposure to the various contextual functions of English. The contextual functions of language refer to the culturally specific ways in which grammar and syntax are used in diverse social settings to convey meaning on a variety of topics to different audiences (Hymes, 1974). In order to be able to predict and identify with an author's message, a reader must therefore have strong *intuitions* about the structural and functional possibilities of the language he or she is attempting to comprehend. Nevertheless, when Spanish-speaking youngsters receive literacy instruction in their L2 before they acquire more than a superficial working knowledge of how to extract meaning from texts in their native language, they do not have well-developed intuitions about either English or Spanish. Consequently, as mentioned earlier, their involvement with print is often directed more to the mechanics of literacy, i.e., decoding of sounds and word meanings, than to anticipating the ways that language elements can co-occur to create relevant messages.

The Connection Between Literacy Instruction in the Native Language and Achievement

Conversational and Academic Language

Jim Cummins has written extensively on the importance of developing children's literacy skills in their mother tongue (1979, 1981, 1987, 1989, 1991, 1996). Both on psycholinguistic and sociolinguistic grounds, he argues strongly that overall, non-dominant speakers of English do better in school, in both their native language and English, if they are given ample opportunity to attain literacy proficiency through their L1.

Cummins (1989, 1996) has articulated an important linguistic distinction that highlights the relationship between language and achievement. This distinction, between *conversational* and *academic language*, describes a continuum of linguistic functions that children progressively acquire throughout their school years. At the lowest end of the continuum is conversational or everyday language, in which both paralinguistic cues (e.g., gestures and facial expressions) and situational props facilitate the transfer of meaning between speakers and listeners. Conversational language, therefore, is highly *context embedded* (Cummins, 1981, 1987, 1989); meaning is understood not only by what is said but also by what is surrounding a discourse (i.e., extralinguistic information). For this reason, the syntax of context-embedded speech is rather simple in comparison to that of other types of communicative events that do not rely on situational scaffolding.

As one moves towards the *academic* end of the continuum, however, the level of contextual support begins to decrease, and language exchanges eventually become *context reduced*. This means that as situational cues are gradually removed from a discourse, understanding must be achieved through more elaborate lexical, grammatical, and syntactic devices. Context-reduced communication thus requires language specificity for clear expression and accurate comprehension. It is far more characteristic of instruction in the upper elementary grades and beyond than of the early primary grades. Examples of the conversational/academic distinction as they might occur, from simple to most complex, along the proposed continuum are face-to-face talk with friends, a telephone conversation between a student and teacher about a homework assignment, reading one's own essay at a school assembly, and writing a critique of a Shakespearean play.

Of relevance to the discussion here is that LEP children are frequently exited from bilingual education programs or moved into a predominantly English curriculum within a bilingual classroom on the basis of their ability to use and comprehend only conversational English (Collier, 1987; Cummins, 1981; Krashen, 1999; Krashen & Biber, 1988; Medina & Escamilla, 1992). Their general knowledge of how to use their L1 in different settings for various purposes, however, is often quite limited and directed primarily to topics of a more concrete and descriptive nature. Ramírez (1992), however, highlights the importance of knowing several language varieties and specialized registers in order to attain *functional language proficiency* in academic subject matter:

> The acquisition of basic skills involves, in part, the learning of several language varieties that will allow the student to send (speak or write) or receive (listen or read) messages with different purposes (...write an essay to persuade, read an editorial for point-of-view). To acquire this competence, the individual may need to know and understand the specialized register (specific language structures and technical terminology) of the subject. (p. 269)

Given that mastery of subject matter content is the most important criterion for success in school, students with an insufficient knowledge of academic classroom language, in either their L1 or L2, will not have the functional linguistic proficiency to grasp material that is abstract, decontextualized, and problem-oriented. Consequently, their involvement with complex subject matter will be, at most, superficial, as they will not have the conceptual underpinnings or communication skills to analyze and discourse on a wide range of topics.

Transfer of Language Knowledge

A number of scholars (August & Hakuta, 1997; Cummins, 1987, 1996; Hakuta & Diaz, 1984; Lambert, 1984) have argued that the use of the native language to develop the academic skills of limited English proficient students is the best way of helping them avoid cognitive deficits and achievement lags in their school performance. In particular, Cummins (1989, 1996) explains that academic language learning requires two psycholinguistic prerequisites—concept formation and linguistic proficiency—and that these prerequisites constitute a global learning factor that he calls *common underlying proficiency* (CUP). CUP refers to the storage of cognitive and linguistic information that facilitates learning in general. In this way, the CUP model of bilingualism predicts that academic skills learned through one linguistic system will pave the way for the acquisition of skills in another. This is because, from an informational standpoint, the linguistic systems of bilinguals are interdependent (Cummins, 1989). Namely, when bilinguals use their language knowledge to construct and interpret meaning, they are drawing from a single storage space of information that funnels input into both their languages instead of from separate storage spaces for each language.

The *linguistic interdependence principle*, as Cummins describes the transfer of language knowledge from an individual's L1 to his or her L2, is useful in explaining why young native Spanish speakers perform well in English when they attain literacy proficiency in their mother tongue (González, 1989; Krashen & Biber, 1988; Ramírez, Yuen, & Ramey, 1991). Specifically, when these children learn about the intricacies of print relationships through materials that highlight their own language and social reality, the linguistic interdependence principle predicts that they will be able to extend their repertoire of literacy expertise to a range of language and social contexts in their L2. In fact, research shows that those students with high levels of literacy proficiency in their L1 perform better on tasks of academic English than do students with low levels of language and literacy proficiency in Spanish (Fischer & Cabello, 1978; Lindholm & Zierlein, 1991; Medina & Escamilla, 1992; Medina & de la Garza, 1989; Ovando & Collier, 1998; Snow, 1990; Snow, Burns, & Griffin, 1998;).

These findings, then, provide pedagogical evidence that academic literacy skills acquired in the mother tongue will transfer positively to English if they are sufficiently developed in the native language. Data from the studies cited above also suggest that primary language instruction in literacy may be the most educationally sound method for helping Spanish-speaking LEP children learn about the academic uses of school English. The rationale that underlies this thinking is that when LEP children develop reading and writing competencies first in their mother tongue, they are not forced to address issues of language and meaning separately. In other words, they do not have to learn *about* a language before they can construct meaning in that language. Therefore, teaching Spanish speakers about print relationships in their mother tongue enhances their opportunities to attend more to the semantic content of a writer's message and to the syntactic devices used to encode that message than to graphic input. Thus, acquisition of reading and writing skills and overall understanding of literacy as a tool for purposeful communication is not impeded by linguistic gaps.

The Connection Between Literacy Instruction in the Native Language and Pedagogy

Early in this paper we referred to a holistic model of bilingual education as one that cultivates and maintains the literacy skills of language minority children in both their L1 and L2. We explained that this model, which promotes literacy proficiency in both the home language and English, would frame our discussion on the importance of teaching Spanish-dominant elementary school children to speak, read, and write competently in their primary language. In keeping with our purpose, we have presented evidence in the previous two sections to show: (1) that language is a vehicle for expressing the sociocultural behaviors of a community of speakers, (2) that prior linguistic knowledge determines the extent to which students can interact with information in a text, and (3) that children cannot become proficient readers if their past linguistic and social experiences are not relevant to the literacy materials they are using.

In this final section, we will comment on the importance of designing an educational curriculum that fosters linguistic pluralism as a means of enhancing the literacy skills of Spanish-speaking children. We will also consider the effect of classroom instructional practices in the native language on student learning and self-esteem.

Linguistic and Curricular Concerns

Literacy can only be relevant and functional in the context of a relevant and functional curriculum. Such a curriculum allows for the natural acquisition of literacy and biliteracy by building on what learners know, their language, culture, interests, and common experiences. (Goodman, Goodman, & Flores, 1984, p. 35)

If the purpose of literacy is meaning and meaning is tied to what readers know, then it follows that a relevant curriculum for Spanish-speaking elementary school children will build on information from their home, community, and school life (August and Hakuta, 1997; Goldenberg, 1994; Handscombe, 1994; Wong Fillmore & Valadez, 1985). Krashen and Biber (1988) define literacy as "the ability to use language to discuss abstract ideas, to solve problems, (and) to clarify and stimulate thinking" (p. 22). A curriculum that fosters creative problem solving through Spanish will thus help bilingual youngsters achieve what English-only children achieve in an educationally stimulating environment. This is an awareness of how to use language to describe and reflect on one's own and others' actions, to organize thoughts through words, and to communicate ideas and intentions in a culturally appropriate way.

We have raised the issue of "creative" and "stimulating" literacy acquisition here because children develop a high degree of proficiency in speaking, reading, and writing only in educational settings where they are offered opportunities to become active participants in their learning experiences. Active literacy participation requires an identification with the topics and materials of the literacy event. Specifically, a literacy curriculum that promotes a high level of student involvement enables all youngsters to raise questions about learning activities and to critically examine the content of their literacy interactions. Discussing the classroom environment of Spanish-dominant bilinguals, Snow (1990) asserts that children will find literacy materials rich and challenging only in a language they speak well.

Of further importance to the literacy learning process is the way in which children are taught. The debate of the 1990s cannot be about the value of bilingual education for primary language students but instead about how to provide the most effective instructional environments for these students. For example, in a large-scale study of different program options available to Spanish-dominant bilinguals in the elementary grades, Ramírez, Yuen, and Ramey (1991) discovered that those students who did not receive the long-term benefits of native language instruction exhibited a decrease in their rate of growth in English language achievement and reading after the third grade. This outcome suggests that as learning material becomes progressively more complex (or *context reduced*) across grade levels, the native language may be the best resource for teaching bilinguals about academic literacy skills of an analytical nature. In other words, when children have a solid linguistic foundation in their primary language, they are prepared to acquire increasingly abstract concepts in that language. Once learned through the mother tongue, these concepts will then provide the backdrop for expressing similar ideas in their L2.

Another pertinent issue concerning literacy instruction in bilingual settings addresses the need to explore how students achieve academic language competence in both their L1 and L2. Little is still known about the process bilinguals use to transfer information from one linguistic system to another and about which pedagogical environments best facilitate this transfer (August and Hakuta, 1997; Hakuta, 1986; Ovando & Collier, 1998; Snow, Burns, & Griffin, 1998). To this end, Padilla (1990) suggests studying recent advances in the cognitive sciences and in educational technology to heighten our understanding of the way information is assimilated across languages and to articulate pedagogical practices with learning strategies.

To answer questions regarding information processing and the transference of skills between languages, Harvard University researchers initiated a two-year study in the fall of 1999. This study, conducted with Spanish-speaking students at the elementary school level, is exploring the psycholinguistic and educational factors that influence how youngsters use literacy skills in their first language to acquire literacy knowledge in their second language. The results of the Harvard research should shed considerable light on the nature and extent of the linguistic information learners must acquire before making a positive shift from one language to another.

Literary Practices and Student Self-Esteem

Certainly, no one would deny that professional accomplishment and socioeconomic mobility rest largely on an individual's skill at manipulating speech and print. Moreover, in a global society that relies heavily on international commerce and communication, there is a compelling need for individuals who are highly bilingual and biliterate. Nevertheless, when schools deny Spanish-speaking youngsters the tool that can be of greatest use to them in developing literacy proficiency—their native language—they are devaluing the self-worth of these youngsters and rejecting their most important personal asset for success in life. For this reason, Macedo (1991) asserts that "educators must develop radical pedagogical structures that provide students with the opportunity to use their own reality as a basis for literacy. This includes, obviously, the language they bring to the classroom" (p. 16).

All too often the success of bilingual education is judged by the number of LEP children who are reading in English or who are exited from bilingual programs into a regular education curriculum. The message these children receive from such instructional practices, both overtly and covertly, is that school achievement is measured primarily in terms of English competence. Bilinguals quickly learn that their native language and the cultural experiences it encodes have a low status in the classroom and in the society at large. Therefore, school personnel must seriously rethink how they transmit educational messages to students and whether the pedagogical practices they use in the classroom do, indeed, positively acknowledge the home background and cultural values of the students they serve.

A case in point comes from the Ramírez et al. study cited above. An examination of instructional personnel in different bilingual education program types shows that teachers in settings that promoted long-term study of literacy in Spanish generally had cultural backgrounds that were similar to those of their students. These teachers also had sufficient fluency in Spanish to be able to use the language as a medium of instruction. On the other hand, teachers in English immersion settings and in early-exit bilingual education programs tended not to be Hispanic or not to have the capability of teaching through Spanish. Their classroom behaviors thus reflected their pedagogical capabilities and the rationale underlying their respective program type.

To conclude, then, we recognize, as have others (Ferdman, 1991; Ramírez, 1994; Skutnabb-Kangas, 1981; Slavin, Karweit, Wasik, Madden, & Dolan, 1994; Thomas & Collier, 1997; Tinajero, Hurley, & Lozano, 1998), that the mother tongue is the primary vehicle for helping individuals establish their personal and social identity. It is the instrument that enables them to manage their thinking and the multitude of interactions, activities, and events in their surroundings. For this reason, if language minority children are to become competent readers, they must be able to share linguistic and cultural information with an author. Literacy instruction in their native language clearly helps them draw upon their own world knowledge to relate to texts in a meaningful way. When dominant speakers of Spanish learn to speak, read, and write proficiently in their primary language, they are building upon a firm foundation of linguistic, conceptual, and experiential information that paves the way for a high level of involvement with print. Snow (1990) underscores the need for schools to show sensitivity and appreciation for the language and cultural norms that young Spanish speakers bring with them to the classroom. Arguing this point on pedagogical grounds, she explains that by so doing, schools can maximize the self-esteem of students and that students with high self-esteem "work harder, learn better, and achieve more" (p. 64).

REFERENCES

Alexander, P. A., Schallert, D. L., & Hare, V. C. (1991). Coming to terms: How researchers in learning and literacy talk about knowledge. *Review of Educational Research, 61* (3), 315–343.

August, D., & Hakuta, K. (Eds.). (1997). *Improving schooling for language-minority children: A research agenda*. National Research Council. Washington, DC: National Academy Press.

Baker, K. A., & de Kanter, A. A. (1981). *Effectiveness of bilingual education: A review of the literature*. Washington, DC: Office of Planning and Budget, U.S. Department of Education.

Brown, R. (1973). *A first language: The early stages*. Cambridge, MA: Harvard University Press.

Collier, V. P. (1987). Age and rate of acquisition of second language for academic purposes. *TESOL Quarterly, 21*, 617–641.

Cummins, J. (1996). *Negotiating identities: Education for empowerment in a diverse society*. Sacramento: California Association for Bilingual Education.

Cummins, J. (1991). Language shift and language learning in the transition from home to school. *Journal of Education, 173* (2), 85–97.

Cummins, J. (1989). *Empowering minority students*. Sacramento: California Association for Bilingual Education.

Cummins, J. (1987). Bilingualism, language proficiency, and metalinguistic development. In Homel, P., Paliji, M., & Aaronson, D. (Eds.), *Childhood bilingualism: Aspects of linguistic, cognitive and social development* (pp. 57–73). Hillsdale, NJ: Lawrence Erlbaum Associates.

Cummins, J. (1981). *Schooling and language minority students*. Los Angeles: California State University; Evaluation, Dissemination and Assessment Center.

Cummins, J. (1979). Linguistic interdependence and the educational development of bilingual children. *Review of Educational Research, 49*, 222–251.

Dechant, E. (1991). Understanding and teaching reading: An interactive model. Hillsdale, NJ: Lawrence Erlbaum Associates.

Dunn, L. (1987). *Bilingual Hispanic children on the U.S. mainland: A review of research on their cognitive, linguistic, and scholastic development*. Circle Pines, MN: American Guidance Service.

Ferdman, B. (1991). Literacy and cultural identity. In *Language issues in literacy and bilingual/multicultural education* (pp. 347–371). Cambridge, MA: Newbury House Publishers.

Fischer, K., & Cabello, B. (1978). *Predicting student success following transition for bilingual programs*. Los Angeles: Center for the Study of Evaluation.

Freeman, D. E., & Freeman, Y. S. (1992). *Whole language for second language learners*. Portsmouth, NH: Heinemann.

Genesee, F. (1987). *Learning through two languages*. Cambridge, MA: Newbury House.

Gersten, R., & Woodward, J. (1985). A case for structured immersion. *Educational Leadership*, *43* (2), 75–79.

Goldenberg, C. (1994). Promoting early literacy development among Spanish-speaking children: Lessons from two studies. In Hiebert, E. H., & Baylor, B. M. (Eds.), *Getting reading right from the start: Effective early literacy interventions* (pp. 171–199). Boston: Allyn & Bacon.

Gonzalez, L. A. (1989). Native language education: The key to English literacy skills. In Bixler-Marquez, D. J., Green, G. K., & Ornstein-Galicia, J. L. (Eds.), *Mexican-American Spanish in its societal and cultural contexts*. Rio Grande Series in Language and Linguistics, no. 3, Pan American University at Brownsville.

Goodman, K. S. (1967). Reading: A psycholinguistic guessing game. *Journal of the Reading Specialist, 4,* 125–135.

Goodman, K. S., Goodman, Y., & Flores, B. (1984). *Reading in the bilingual classroom: Literacy and biliteracy*. Washington, DC: National Clearinghouse for Bilingual Education.

Goodman, Y., & Goodman, K. S. (1979). Learning to read is natural. In Resnick, L. B., & Weaver, P. A. (Eds.), *Theory and practice of early reading* (Vol. 1). Hillsdale, NJ: Lawrence Erlbaum.

Guerrero, M. D. (1997, Winter). Spanish academic language proficiency: The case of bilingual education teachers in the U.S. *The Bilingual Research Journal, 21* (1).

Hakuta, K. (1990). Language and cognition in bilingual children. In Padilla, A. M., Fairchild, H. H., & Valadez, C. M. (Eds.) *Bilingual education: Issues and strategies*. Newbury Park, CA: Sage Publications.

Hakuta, K. (1986). *Mirror of language*. New York: Basic Books.

Hakuta, K., & Diaz, R. M. (1984). The relationship between degree of bilingualism and cognitive ability: A critical discussion and some new longitudinal data. In Nelson, K. E. (Ed.), *Children's language* (Vol. 5, pp. 319–344). Hillsdale, NJ: Lawrence Erlbaum.

Handscombe, J. (1994). Putting it all together. In Genesee, F. (Ed.), *Educating second language children: The whole child, the whole curriculum, the whole community* (pp. 331–356). Cambridge: Cambridge University Press.

Heath, S. B. (1989). Sociocultural contexts of language development. In *Beyond language: Social and cultural factors in schooling language minority students*. Los Angeles: California State University; Evaluation, Dissemination and Assessment Center.

Heath, S. B. (1983). *Ways with words*. Cambridge: Cambridge University Press.

Hymes, D. (1974). *Foundations in sociolinguistics: An ethnographic approach*. Philadelphia: University of Pennsylvania Press.

Jimenez, R. T., Garcia, G. E., & Pearson, P. D. (1995, Spring). Three children, two languages, and strategic reading: Case studies in bilingual/monolingual reading. *American Educational Research Journal, 32* (1), 67–97.

Krashen, S. D. (1999). *Condemned without a trial: Bogus arguments against bilingual education*. Portsmouth, NH: Heinemann.

Krashen, S., & Biber, D. (1988) *On course: Bilingual education's success in California.* Sacramento: California Association for Bilingual Education.

Lambert, W. (1987). The effects of bilingual and bicultural experiences on children's attitudes and social perspectives. In Homel, P., Paliu, M., & Aaronson, D. (Eds.), *Childhood bilingualism: Aspects of linguistic, cognitive, and social development* (pp. 197–221). Hillsdale, NJ: Lawrence Erlbaum.

Lambert, W. (1984). An overview of issues in immersion education. In *Studies in immersion education: A collection for U.S. educators* (pp. 8–30). Sacramento: California State Department of Education.

Lindholm, K. J., & Zierlein, A. (1991). Bilingual proficiency as a bridge to academic achievement: Results from bilingual/immersion programs. *Journal of Education, 173* (2), 99–113.

Macedo, D. (1991). English only: The tongue-tying of America. *Journal of Education, 173* (2), 9–20.

Matute-Bianchi, M. E. (1986). Ethnic identities and patterns of school success and failure among Mexican-descent and Japanese-American students in a California high school: An ethnographic analysis. *American Journal of Education, 95,* 233–255.

Medina, J., Jr., & Escamilla, K. (1992). Evaluation of transitional and maintenance bilingual programs. *Urban Education, 27*, 263–290.

Medina, M., Jr., & de la Garza, J. V. (1989). Bilingual instruction and academic gains of Spanish-dominant Mexican American students. *NABE Journal, 13* (2), 113–123.

Ovando, C. J., & Collier, V. P. (1998). *Bilingual and ESL classrooms: Teaching in multicultural contexts*. New York: McGraw-Hill.

Padilla, A. M. (1990). Issues and perspectives. In Padilla, A. M., Fairchild, H. H., and Valadez, C. M. (Eds.), *Bilingual education: Issues and strategies* (pp. 1–26). Newbury Park, CA: Sage Publications.

Pardo, E. B. (1991, May) Cooperative education and technology: Preparing culturally diverse youth for today's challenges. An Interim Evaluation of Language-Minority Students in the Davidson Middle School's MacMagic Program, p. 10.

Pardo, E. B. (in press). Prerequisites for developing effective oral language skills. In Wheelock, A. (Ed.), *Crossing the tracks: How untracking can save America's schools* (pp. 147–150). New York: New Press.

Peregoy, S. F., & Boyle, O. F. (1997). *Reading, writing, and learning in ESL: A resource book for K–12 teachers* (2nd ed.). New York: Longman.

Perera, K. (1987). *Understanding language*. One of a series of occasional papers published by the National Association of Advisers in English.

Ramírez, A. G. (1994). Literacy acquisition among second-language learners. In Ferdman, B. M., Weber, R. M., & Ramírez, A. G. (Eds.), *Literacy across languages and cultures* (pp. 75–101). New York: State University of New York Press.

Ramírez, A. G. (1992). Language proficiency and bilingualism. In Padilla, R. V., & Benavides, A. (Eds.), *Critical perspectives on bilingual education research* (pp. 257–276). Tucson, AZ: Bilingual Review/Press.

Ramírez, J. D., Yuen, S. D., & Ramey, E. (1991). *Final report: Longitudinal study of structured English immersion strategy, early-exit and late-exit transitional bilingual education programs for language-minority children*. U.S. Department of Education, Contract No. 300-87-0156. San Mateo, CA: Aguirre International.

Skutnabb-Kangas, T. (1981). *Bilingualism or not: The education of minorities*. Bodmin, Cornwall: Robert Hartnoll Ltd.

Slavin, R. E., Karweit, N. L., Wasik, B. A., Madden, N. A., & Dolan, L. J. (1994). Success for all: Getting reading right the first time. In Hiebert, E. H., & Taylor, B. M. (Eds.), *Getting reading right from the start: Effective early literacy interventions* (pp. 125–147). Boston: Allyn & Bacon.

Smith, F. (1988). *Understanding reading: A psycholinguistic analysis of reading and learning to read*. New York: Holt, Rinehart and Winston; Hillsdale, NJ: Lawrence Erlbaum Associates.

Snow, C. E. (1990). Rationales for native language instruction. In Padilla, A. M., Fairchild, H. H., & Valadez, C. M. (Eds.), *Bilingual education: Issues and strategies* (pp. 60–74). Newbury Park, CA: Sage Publications.

Snow, C. E., Burns, M. S., & Griffin, P. (Eds.). (1998). *Preventing reading difficulties in young children*. National Research Council. Washington, DC: National Academy Press.

Thomas, W. P., & Collier, V. (1997). *School effectiveness for language minority students*. Resource Collection Series. Washington, DC: National Clearinghouse for Bilingual Education.

Tinajero, J., Hurley, S. R., & Lozano, E. V. (1998). Developing language and literacy in bilingual classrooms. In Gonzalez, M. L., Huerta-Macias, A., & Tinajero, J. V. (Eds.). *Educating Latino students: A guide to successful practice* (pp. 143–160). Lancaster, PA: Technomics.

Troike, R. C. (1978). Research evidence for the effectiveness of bilingual education. *NABE Journal 3*, 13–24.

Vygotsky, L. S. (1962). *Thought and language*. Cambridge, MA: MIT Press.

Wong Fillmore, L., & Valadez, C. (1985). Teaching bilingual learners. In Wittrock, M. C. (Ed.), *Handbook of research on teaching* (pp. 648–685). Washington, DC: American Educational Research Association.

PHONOLOGICAL AWARENESS IN SPANISH: A SUMMARY OF RESEARCH AND IMPLICATIONS FOR PRACTICE

Jan E. Hasbrouck and Carolyn A. Denton
Texas A&M University

Phonological awareness is the ability to discern units of sound in speech and to use those sound units in the cognitive processes involved in literacy activities. It entails the insight that words are made up of sounds that can be compared and manipulated as entities separate from the contextual meanings attached to them. It includes perception of separate, individual words, syllables within words, and smaller units of sound within a syllable. Children normally become aware of larger units, such as words and syllables, before they become aware of smaller units, such as individual phonemes (Adams, 1990). Phonological awareness can be operationally defined in terms of certain tasks that can be performed on words, such as segmenting a word into its component sounds, matching words that begin with the same sound, and identifying separate syllables within a word.

Levels of Phonological and Phonemic Awareness

Phonemic awareness is a subcategory of phonological awareness; it refers to the awareness of and the capacity to carry out mental operations on individual phonemes within language (as contrasted with the awareness of words, syllables, and other language segments). Yopp (1988) compared the relative difficulty of tasks in several measures of phonemic awareness and concluded that there are two levels of phonemic awareness: simple and compound. Both require the mental manipulation of sounds, but "simple" phonemic awareness tasks require a global or holistic analysis of sounds, while "compound" tasks require that a sound be held in memory while a series of operations are performed on it. Examples of simple phonemic awareness tasks include recognizing rhyme, blending phonemes to form a word, counting the number of phonemes in a word (often assessed by asking children to clap once for each sound they hear in a word), isolating sounds in words (such as saying only the first sound of a word), and segmenting phonemes (pronouncing the sounds in a word separately). According to Yopp's analysis, compound phonemic awareness tasks include phoneme deletion (removing one or more phonemes from a word and saying the remaining word or nonword), and word-to-word matching (matching initial, medial, or final sounds in two words; e.g., "I will say two words, and you tell me if they start with the same sound").

Adams (1990) described five levels of phonological and phonemic awareness. The simplest level involves a general awareness of sounds in spoken language, as measured by a child's knowledge of nursery rhymes. The second level involves the ability to compare and contrast similarities and differences in the sounds in syllables (such as telling which of three or four spoken words is different from the others or does not belong). The third level requires blending sounds into words and splitting syllables into component sounds. The fourth level consists of phonemic segmentation, or analysis of the words into a series of abstract phonemes. The fifth and highest level includes phoneme manipulation tasks: the addition, deletion, or moving of phonemes to make new words (or non-words). Chafouleas, Lewandowski, Smith, and Blachman (1997) identified a similar progression of difficulty in phonological awareness skills from rhyme to alliteration, blending, segmentation, and manipulation.

Research on Phonological Awareness

During the last decade, much attention has been given to the importance of phonological awareness and its relationship to reading development. Phonemic awareness has been shown to be a better predictor of reading achievement than IQ, general language proficiency, or traditional measures of reading readiness (Juel, Griffith, & Gough, 1986; Stanovich, Cunningham, & Cramer, 1984; Wagner, 1988). Early literacy interventions that foster the development of phonological and phonemic awareness skills may prevent the subsequent development of reading disabilities (Lyon, 1995; Snow, Burns, & Griffin, 1998; Stanovich, 1986), and may prevent the mislabeling of students as having learning disabilities (Vellutino et al., 1996).

Much of the theory and research on the topic of phonological awareness deals with its applications in the English language. However, phonological and phonemic awareness have been shown to be related to reading achievement in several non-English languages, including German (Näslund, 1990), Danish (Lundberg, Frost, & Petersen, 1988), Swedish (Lundberg, Olofsson, & Wall, 1980), Portuguese (Cardoso-Martins, 1991), Hebrew (Bentin, Hammer, & Cahan,

1991), French (Alegria, Pignot, & Morais, 1982), and Italian (Cossu, Shankweiler, Liberman, Katz, & Tola, 1988). In this article we review the current literature relating to phonological and phonemic awareness in Spanish and the implications for practice.

Questions Addressed in this Review

In this article we pose four sets of questions:

Question #1. What is phonological awareness (PA) in Spanish? How can PA be operationally defined in Spanish? What is the relative difficulty of different PA tasks in Spanish? Which linguistic properties of Spanish affect the relative difficulty of PA tasks?

Question #2. How can PA be assessed in Spanish? Are technically adequate instruments available for this purpose?

Question #3. What is the relationship between PA and reading progress in Spanish? Is Spanish PA a good predictor of reading achievement? Which aspects of Spanish phonological or phonemic awareness appear to develop before the onset of formal reading instruction, and which aspects appear to develop along with reading instruction? Does training in Spanish phonological or phonemic awareness have an impact on students' achievement in reading Spanish materials?

Question #4. Does cross-language transfer take place between Spanish and English PA? Do readers process text in fundamentally the same ways in Spanish and in English? Does increased phonological or phonemic awareness in one language have an impact on reading ability in the other language?

Question #1: What Is Phonological Awareness in Spanish?

In their study of Spanish illiterate adults, Adrián, Alegria, and Morais (1995) concluded that distinctions should be made among phonological sensitivity, phonological awareness, and phonemic awareness. They describe phonological sensitivity as the component of speech processing that allows a listener to distinguish between similar-sounding words or syllables. Phonological awareness requires phonological sensitivity, but it also entails "the capacity to represent consciously the phonological property on which some decision has to be taken" (p. 331). Phonemic awareness is distinguished as a subcategory of PA that deals specifically with the awareness of isolated sounds.

Cisero and Royer (1995) examined the question of whether PA skills develop in a specific order in English and in Spanish. Their subjects were monolingual English-speaking and bilingual Spanish-speaking (with limited English proficiency) kindergarten and first grade students. The researchers did not find statistical support for the theory that PA skills develop in a specific order in Spanish, but saw trends indicating that Spanish-speaking students may first develop sensitivity to onsets and rimes, and then to individual phonemes.

González and García (1995), in their investigation of the effects of different properties of words on Spanish-speaking children's performance on measures of PA, cite a study of Spanish PA conducted by Jiménez and Ortiz. These researchers found that even children who had not learned letter–sound correspondences could divide syllables into onsets and rimes, but that they did not demonstrate awareness of individual phonemes within these segments.

Spanish Linguistic Properties and PA

Some researchers have studied the effect of certain linguistic properties on the relative difficulty of PA tasks. Because Spanish has very regular phoneme–grapheme correspondences, the pronunciation of a sound unit can consistently be derived directly from print; thus, reading instruction in Spanish is often based on recognition and spelling of syllable units. Carreiras, Alvarez, and De Vega (1993) studied the question of whether Spanish readers use syllable information during word recognition and concluded that syllables are important processing units and that they have a strong effect on word recognition for Spanish language readers.

Researchers have theorized that the syllable may be a more important unit of PA in Spanish than it is in English. However, Adrián, Alegria, and Morais (1995) concluded that the manipulation of syllables is not a particularly accessible task in Spanish, because syllable deletion and reversal were difficult tasks for the subjects in their study, adult illiterates and adults with minimal literacy.

González and García (1995), in a Spanish replication of an English study by Treiman and Weatherston (1992), compared the influence of word linguistic properties on phonological awareness in the two languages. They found that initial "continuous" consonants (consonant sounds that can be pronounced for several seconds without distortion, e.g., /s/ and /m/) were much easier for children to isolate than initial "stop" consonants (consonant sounds that can be pronounced for only an instant without distortion, e.g., /t/ and /k/). They also compared initial phoneme deletion in two-syllable words in which the initial consonant belonged to stressed and unstressed syllables, but found no difference in children's ability to isolate initial sounds under those two conditions. González and García found that in Spanish as in English, children have greater difficulty isolating initial consonant sounds when they are a part of an initial consonant cluster, and that initial sound isolation is more difficult in longer words than in shorter words. In a related study, Manrique and Signorini (1994) also found that low-performing Spanish readers had difficulty spelling words containing clusters. Those students tended to spell the initial consonant in the cluster correctly and to omit the second one.

González and García (1995) also concluded that "the ability to segment syllables may be more important than the ability to segment phonemes in predicting students' response to instruction" (p. 199), a finding that coincides with the conclusion of Carrillo, Romero, & Sanchez, as cited in González and García (1995), that syllable awareness is a more important predictor of Spanish reading success than intrasyllable and phonemic awareness. However, González and García (1995) also cited Jiménez and Ortiz, who found that phonemic awareness is more important than syllabic awareness in predicting success in mastering the alphabetic code in Spanish.

Question #2: How Can Phonological Awareness Be Assessed in Spanish?

None of the studies located for this review described or implemented fully developed Spanish tests of phonological or phonemic awareness. Several of the reviewed studies implemented experimental procedures that were described in detail by the researchers.

Tasks Used to Assess PA Skills in Spanish

A variety of tasks were used to evaluate Spanish phonological or phonemic awareness in the studies reviewed for this article:

1. *Auditory discrimination:* Students hear pairs of similar words and identify the words as either the same or different (Adrián, Alegria, & Morais, 1995; Bravo-Valdivieso, 1995).

2. *Rhyme detection:* Students hear pairs of words and identify whether they rhyme (e.g., *ver/ser* = sí; *sed/van* = no) (Adrián, Alegria, & Morais, 1995; Cisero & Royer, 1995).

3. *Rhyme sensitivity:* Students hear a series of words and identify which one of the series does not rhyme with the others, or which one does not rhyme with a target word (Carrillo, 1994).

4. *Initial phoneme (onset) detection:* Students hear pairs of words and identify whether the words begin with the same sound (e.g., *ven/vid* = sí; *tal/sur* = no) (Cisero & Royer, 1995).

5. *Sensitivity to alliteration:* Students hear a set of words and identify the one that does not begin like a target word (Carrillo, 1994).

6. *Initial sound matching:* Students hear a target word and alternatives and choose the one alternative that starts with the same sound as the target word (Durgunoglu, Nagy, & Hancin-Bhatt, 1993).

7. *Final phoneme detection:* Students hear pairs of words and tell whether they end with the same sound (e.g., *con/ven* = sí; *luz/ver* = no) (Carrillo, 1994; Cisero & Royer, 1995).

8. *Syllable detection:* Students hear pairs of pseudowords and tell whether or not the pairs have an identical syllable (e.g., *mosa/moti* = sí; *lura/pebu* = no), or they hear a target syllable followed by a pseudoword and tell whether or not the target syllable is present in the pseudoword (Adrián, Alegria, & Morais, 1995).

9. *Phoneme detection:* Students hear two words or pseudowords and decide whether or not the words have an identical phoneme, or they tell whether or not a target phoneme is present in a word (e.g., */p/ -pal* = sí; */p/- bor* = no) (Adrián, Alegria, & Morais, 1995).

10. *Embedded phoneme detection:* Students hear a target word, then listen to three more words and identify which of these words contain the same phoneme as

the initial phoneme of the target word. The phoneme to be identified within the three choices may occur in any position within the word (Signorini, 1997).

11. *Onset-rime blending:* Students hear an onset and rime pronounced separately and blend them into a word (e.g., *d-on*) (Durgunoglu, Nagy, & Hancin-Bhatt, 1993).

12. *Syllable blending:* Students listen to two syllables pronounced separately and blend them into a word (e.g., *do-ce*) (Durgunoglu, Nagy, & Hancin-Bhatt, 1993).

13. *Phoneme blending:* Students listen to a sequence of phonemes pronounced separately and say the word formed by the phonemes as a single unit (Bravo-Valdivieso, 1995; Durgunoglu, Nagy, & Hancin-Bhatt, 1993).

14. *Phoneme isolation:* Students hear an intact word and pronounce either the initial or final phoneme of the target word separately (e.g., ¿Qué es la sonida primera en *mar*? ¿Qué es la sonida final en *sol*?) (Carrillo, 1994; González & Garcìa, 1995).

15. *Phoneme counting:* Students listen to a word, count the number of phonemes in the word, and put that number of chips on a board (Carrillo, 1994) or tap a pencil once for each phoneme they hear in the word (Manrique & Signorini, 1994).

16. *Phoneme segmentation:* Students segment two-, three-, and four-syllable words into their component phonemes, pronouncing the phonemes separately. (Bravo-Valdivieso, 1995; Durgunoglu, Nagy, & Hancin-Bhatt, 1993).

17. *Segmentation into syllables:* Students listen to pronounced words and separate them into separate syllables (Durgunoglu, Nagy, & Hancin-Bhatt, 1993).

18. *Position segment identification:* Students identify the position of a target sound within a word (beginning, middle, or end; e.g., ¿Donde está /a/ en *ola*, al principio, en el medio, o al fin? ¿Donde está /a/ en *ajo*?) (Carrillo, 1994).

19. *Phoneme deletion:* Students say a non-word by deleting a phoneme or group of phonemes from a target word or pseudoword (Adrián, Alegria, & Morais, 1995; Carrillo, 1994; Signorini, 1997).

20. *Syllable deletion:* Students delete a target syllable from a pseudoword and pronounce the remaining pseudoword (Adrián, Alegria, & Morais, 1995).

21. *Word reversal:* Students hear a pair of words and repeat them in reverse order (Adrián, Alegria, & Morais, 1995).

22. *Phoneme reversal:* Students hear syllables and then say the phonemes in them backward (e.g., *mil = lim; osa = aso*) (Adrián, Alegria, & Morais, 1995; Bravo-Valdivieso, 1995; Carrillo, 1994).

While studies of PA in Spanish have employed a wide variety of tasks, most did not present sufficient information regarding the reliability or validity of the measures used. There remains a need for fully developed and well-tested instruments for the assessment of PA in Spanish-speaking children for research as well as assessments in instructional settings. Riccio & Hasbrouck at Texas A&M University are completing work to establish the technical adequacy and utility of such a measure at this time (personal communication, April 1999).

Question #3: What Is the Relationship Between Phonological Awareness and Reading Progress in Spanish?

For four years, Bravo-Valdivieso (1995) followed the reading progress of Spanish-speaking urban Chilean children from low socioeconomic backgrounds. During the first year of the study, the students ranged in age from seven to nine years. Bravo-Valdivieso compared children within this group who learned to read normally with those who had severe reading difficulties. Eighty-seven percent of the reading difficulty group could read only a few letters and syllables and scored below the tenth percentile on a decoding test. Out of several measures administered to the students, the best predictor of reading achievement in the later years of the study was the initial score on the decoding measure. Students with weak decoding skills in the early grades never overcame this difficulty. Difficulties with phonological processing and verbal abilities were also strong predictors of reading underachievement.

Durgunoglu, Nagy, and Hancin-Bhatt (1993), in their study of Spanish-speaking first grade students in American schools, also found evidence of a relationship between Spanish PA and reading ability. In their study, PA was closely related to word-recognition ability. This conclusion is supported by Foorman et al. (1997), who found that the level of PA skills was a strong predictor of word reading performance in Hispanic children in the United States. It appears that Spanish phonological processing skills are closely tied to reading ability and are better predictors of reading achievement than IQ or other typical measures.

Carrillo (1994) found that performance on phoneme segmenting tasks differentiated good first grade Spanish readers from average and poor readers. Conflicting evidence was reported by Manrique and Signorini (1994), however, who found that even low-skilled Spanish first graders in Argentina performed well on a phoneme counting task (tapping a pencil for each phoneme heard in a word). Both skilled and less-skilled readers performed near ceiling on this task, with 95 percent of the children meeting the criterion for adequate performance. Manrique and Signorini found that the performance of the low-skilled Spanish readers on this task was significantly correlated with spelling ability, but not with word reading. The low-skilled readers could spell many words that they could not read. However, the authors point out that none of the students who per-

formed poorly on the phoneme segmentation task performed well in reading. They concluded that the regular orthography and open syllable structure of Spanish facilitates the early development of phonemic awareness and spelling. They suggest that these orthographic and phonological properties, along with exposure to print, have a strong effect on the development of phoneme segmentation ability.

In a later study Signorini (1997) found that a phoneme deletion task and an embedded phoneme identification task were only moderately related to first grade word reading once students had some reading instruction. She also found that these two tasks were not significantly correlated with each other, indicating that they may not have been measuring the same construct.

Order of Skill Development in PA and Reading

There is evidence from studies conducted in English (Bradley & Bryant, 1983; Foorman, Francis, Novy, & Liberman, 1991; Wagner, 1988) and in German (Näslund, 1990) that PA skills not only predict future reading ability but also have a causal relationship with reading development, especially in the early stages of reading acquisition. Some aspects of PA appear to develop independently of reading instruction and are necessary for successful reading acquisition. Other aspects of PA appear to have a reciprocally causal relationship with reading (Bentin, Hammer, & Cahan, 1991; Goswami & Bryant, 1990; Morais, Cary, Alegria, & Bertelson, 1979; Smith, Simmons, & Kameenui, 1995), meaning that PA facilitates reading, while engaging in reading causes fuller development of PA. Fully developed PA probably does not precede reading, but develops along with it, and is probably increased through exposure to print. Researchers have investigated the development of phonological and phonemic awareness to find out which forms of these skills are present before reading instruction has begun and which aspects may be developed after the onset of instruction in sound–letter correspondence.

Carrillo (1994) examined this question in a study conducted in Spain with K–1 students. She concluded that phonological and phonemic awareness develop prior to reading. As early readers in this study were exposed to the alphabetic code, they developed more advanced awareness of word segments. Tasks involving phoneme segmentation differentiated good first grade readers from average and poor readers in this study. Carillo concluded that the development of basic segmenting abilities is critical in the beginning stages of reading acquisition in Spanish, and that Spanish-speaking children who have not had reading instruction have difficulty in manipulating strings of phonemes. She also found that by the time children are in the first grade, more holistic PA tasks such as rhyme detection are no longer good predictors of reading ability. The more analytic phonemic awareness skills, such as phoneme manipulation, were associated with high decoding ability at this age.

Adrián, Alegria, and Morais (1995) confirmed that rhyme appreciation develops independently of literacy, since illiterate adults could perform these tasks well. However, tasks requiring conscious manipulation of syllables were difficult for these adult subjects, and they performed very poorly on tasks involving manipulation of individual phonemes. Adults who had achieved minimal literacy late in life outperformed the illiterate adults significantly on phonemic tasks. The authors supported Carrillo's (1994) conclusion that some forms of phoneme awareness develop after the onset of reading instruction.

Manrique and Signorini (1994) concluded from their study of first grade Spanish readers that exposure to print and to early reading instruction facilitate the development of PA in Spanish-speaking children. Some aspects of PA, such as phoneme counting ability, develop quite early, as a consequence of exposure to the regular orthography, accessible vowel sounds, and open syllabic structure of Spanish.

The Impact of Training in PA on Reading Ability

PA Studies in English

PA has been linked to the successful acquisition of reading, so it is important to examine the question of whether PA training provided to children in the early grades enhances reading achievement and prevents reading difficulty. Studies conducted with English-speaking children have provided evidence of the efficacy of this type of training (Ball & Blachman, 1991; Bradley & Bryant, 1983; Byrne & Fielding-Barnsley, 1991; Cunningham, 1990; Torgesen, Wagner, & Rashotte, 1997; Vellutino et al., 1996), although the methodological rigor of several of these studies has been questioned (Troia, 1999). Even considering such limitations, Troia found sufficient evidence to suggest that training can facilitate the development of early reading skills, although not all students appear to benefit from PA training. Troia also noted that there is no evidence in English language research of the effectiveness of this kind of training with older students or students with disabilities.

PA Studies in Spanish

Manrique and Signorini (1994) cite an earlier study they conducted, comparing the spelling performance of Spanish-speaking Argentine first grade students who had been trained in phonemic segmentation to that of students who had not received this training. Students who had received segmentation training were more likely than those who had not to spell unknown words conventionally or with invented spelling. Most students in the control group either wrote only the words they knew or were not able to write any word on the assessment.

Although few examples of PA training studies in Spanish were located for this review, there is some evidence of a link between instructional methods and the development of phonemic awareness. In

Carrillo's (1994) study of aspects of PA that precede and coincide with reading instruction, she compared performance on phonemic awareness tasks of kindergarten students taught by a phonics method, by a whole-word method which included letter-sound instruction, and by a whole-word method with no letter-sound instruction. Students from the phonics group outperformed students from the other groups in reading, and students who were better readers also had higher performance in phonemic awareness tasks. Phonics instruction in Spanish seems to promote early reading acquisition in kindergarten children, and high reading ability in this group had a strong correlation with high phonemic awareness.

Question #4: Is There Cross-Language Transfer of Phonological Awareness?

Students in American schools come from diverse linguistic backgrounds. A large number of these students speak Spanish as their primary language, but are enrolled in programs designed to facilitate the development of oral and written communication skills in English. It is believed that instruction in a student's native language supports literacy development in their second language (Cummins, 1979, 1981, 1984), although the transfer of some cognitive strategies from one language to the other may not be automatic, but may require instruction and support (Gersten, Brengelman, & Jiménez, 1994). Researchers have examined the question of whether training in PA in Spanish promotes reading achievement in English.

There are conflicting theories about whether the reading process is essentially the same in English and in Spanish. If the mental processes used by readers in the two languages are very similar, cross-language transfer of PA would appear more likely. In studies of the processes used by Spanish readers, Valle-Arroyo (1996) concluded that reading in Spanish requires essentially the same type of mental processing as reading in English. He found that young children read words principally through the application of letter—sound correspondences (phonological recoding), but by about sixth grade they read most words by directly recognizing the words and attaching meaning to them (direct lexical access). These development patterns mirror those in English beginning readers (Adams, 1990; Snow, Burns, & Griffin, 1998). Carreiras, Alvarez, and De Vega (1993) found conflicting evidence, concluding that even mature Spanish readers may access words by phonological recoding, that the activation of letter–sound relationships may be an automatic part of word identification in Spanish, and that the syllable unit is important for Spanish word recognition.

In a 1997 study of first and third grade skilled and less skilled readers in Argentina, Signorini concluded that these children rely on phonological recoding in the early stages of literacy acquisition. In the first grade, less skilled readers attempted to read all words presented to them but had difficulty with blending phonemes together to form words. By the third grade, even the low-skilled readers were fairly proficient at sounding out unfamiliar words, but they could not correctly pronounce words with irregular stress patterns. Skilled third grade readers identified words fluently and had no difficulty with the irregular stress patterns of some words.

Koda (1990) found evidence that cognitive word-recognition strategies developed in native language reading are retained in second language reading, even among advanced readers. Once habitual ways of processing print are developed in one language, these methods are applied in second language reading. Habits developed in processing of Spanish text may be applicable to English reading, particularly those habits and skills which relate to phonological processing.

In their study of English- and Spanish-speaking first grade students, Cisero and Royer (1995) administered measures of phonological and phonemic awareness in each student's native language (L1) and second language (L2) at two points during the school year. Many students had little or no familiarity with the L2. The researchers found that students' ability to isolate initial phonemes in their native and non-native language in December contributed significantly to the prediction of their L2 performance on this task on the May assessment, providing some evidence of cross-language transfer of this phonological skill. This pattern was not observed in other measures of PA, however.

Durgunoglu, Nagy, and Hancin-Bhatt (1993) also investigated the question of cross-language transfer of PA and its effect on word reading. They studied the impact of phonemic awareness developed in Spanish on English word recognition. Their subjects were Spanish-speaking first grade students in the United States, who were instructed in transitional bilingual programs, receiving their primary instruction in Spanish along with instruction designed to develop oral English fluency (but not English literacy). Spanish reading was taught using Spanish basal readers that emphasized syllables as an important unit of analysis. The researchers found that students who performed well on Spanish PA tests had significantly greater success in reading English words and English-like pseudowords than those students with low PA in their native language. This was especially true when the students read pseudowords that would be pronounced differently in Spanish and in English. They found that both Spanish PA and Spanish word-reading ability seem to transfer to English word recognition.

There is some evidence of cross-language transfer from a study of at-risk English-speaking adolescents who received direct instruction in Spanish phonology in their study of Spanish as a foreign language (Ganschow & Sparks, 1995). The researchers found that explicit instruction in Spanish phonology using a structured multisensory approach increased the English PA skills of these students, many of whom had learning disabilities. Students in the study made sig-

nificant gains in English spelling, PA, and word attack. Ganschow and Sparks concluded that the development of PA skills in the native and foreign languages is essentially the same, reflecting basic language functions, and that metacognitive skills, including the ability to reflect on language, can be applied across languages.

Summary and Implications

Phonological awareness (PA) in Spanish can be defined in terms of increasingly complex levels of awareness of sounds in language, summarized as (1) a functional ability to discern similarities and differences between sounds to comprehend speech, (2) an awareness of syllables, (3) a sensitivity to rhyme, (4) an awareness of onsets, particularly single initial consonants, and (5) an awareness of individual phonemes in words. The relative difficulty of PA tasks also seems to depend on certain linguistic properties of words, including word length, the presence of "continuous" and "stop" consonant sounds, and the presence of initial consonant clusters. Native Spanish-speaking students seem to have cognizance of the onset and rime within a syllable before they are aware of individual phonemes. Sensitivity to syllables appears to be a particularly important component of PA in Spanish language speakers, and this sensitivity may be an important predictor of later reading success.

In Spanish, as in English, PA develops in stages. Literate and preliterate Spanish speakers appear to be sensitive to likenesses and differences in sounds, including sensitivity to rhyme and alliteration. Spanish-speaking students probably first develop syllabic awareness followed by the ability to isolate onsets and rimes within spoken words or syllables. Eventually, as they begin to acquire reading and spelling skills, they achieve fully developed phonemic awareness.

Certain word linguistic properties appear to affect the relative difficulty of PA tasks in Spanish. These tasks are more difficult in long words than in short ones, in words beginning with "stop" consonants than in words with initial "continuous" consonants, and in words with initial consonant clusters rather than single initial consonants. Sensitivity to syllables in Spanish may be particularly important for later reading success, and the ability to segment words into their phonemes appears to play a critical role in reading acquisition.

There is evidence of a close relationship between PA and reading in Spanish, although the correlation between some phonemic awareness skills and word reading has been found to be weak in some studies of students who had already received at least one year of reading instruction. Phonological awareness in Spanish-speaking children has been shown to be a better predictor of reading success or failure than IQ or other traditional measures. Students with poor PA and poor decoding in the early years of school may be expected to have difficulty in overcoming these weaknesses. As Stanovich (1986) suggests, deficiencies in core phonological processes may cause slowed reading acquisition, a condition that produces a snowballing effect of increasing failure, as students have few opportunities to interact with print and poor educational opportunities. The result can be a generalized reading disability (Lyon, 1995; Snow, Burns, & Griffin, 1998).

Awareness of rhyme and of similarities and differences between words seems to precede the onset of reading instruction in normally developing Spanish-speaking children. Higher-level phonemic awareness abilities, such as phoneme segmentation and manipulation, appear to emerge, along with minimal acquisition and the alphabetic code. Some aspects of phonemic awareness may develop almost spontaneously as a result of exposure to the orthographic and phonemic regularity of the Spanish language. The development of phonemic awareness skills is probably supported by reading instruction, and likely contributes to development of skillful literacy as well.

We have not encountered empirical evidence that training in PA increases Spanish reading performance, although—given other similarities between English and Spanish phonemic awareness, along with evidence of the effectiveness of phonological training in English—it is reasonable to believe that this is true. There is an indication of a relationship between Spanish reading instruction and the development of phonemic awareness, because students taught by explicit phonics methods demonstrated higher levels of phonemic awareness.

High levels of PA in Spanish may facilitate the acquisition of these skills in English, and may predict success in English reading. The basic processes used in reading Spanish and English appear similar, and generic strategies and insights that students acquire in one language may be readily applied to the other.

There is a need for fully developed and empirically validated instruments for the assessment of PA in Spanish. Although many experimental procedures have been documented, there is insufficient information about the reliability or validity of these procedures. Stanovich, Cunningham, and Cramer (1984) found that in English, combinations of PA measures administered in sets were very strong predictors of reading progress. There is a need for examination of which types of measures, in which combinations, are the most reliable predictors of this progress in Spanish-speaking children.

Further study of PA in Spanish-speaking children is needed. In particular, there is a need for studies to evaluate training in PA and its impact on future reading achievement in both Spanish and English. A critical question is whether educators should spend valuable instructional time in activities designed to increase students' phonological and phonemic awareness, and what types of instructional activities produce the greatest gains. Results from studies in English indicate that, for students who are low-performing and at-risk, PA instruction can be an important investment that may prevent future reading difficulty, and even serious reading disability (Lyon, 1995; Snow, Burns, & Griffin, 1998; Stanovich,

1986, Velluntino et al., 1996). It is crucial that the efficacy of this type of training be evaluated directly in Spanish.

REFERENCES

Adams, M.J. (1990). *Beginning to read: Thinking and learning about print.* Cambridge, MA: MIT Press.

Adrián, J.A., Alegria, J., & Morais, J. (1995). Metaphonological abilities of Spanish illiterate adults. *International Journal of Psychology, 30* (3), 329–353.

Alegrìa, J., Pignot, E., & Morais, J. (1982). Phonetic analysis of speech and memory codes in beginning readers. *Memory & Cognition, 10* (5), 451–456.

Ball, E.W., & Blachman, B.A. (1991). Does phoneme awareness training in kindergarten make a difference in early word recognition and developmental spelling? *Reading Research Quarterly, 26,* 49–66.

Bentin, S., Hammer, R., & Cahan, S. (1991). The effects of aging and first-grade schooling on the development of phonological awareness. *Psychological Science, 2,* 271–274.

Bradley, L., & Bryant, P.E. (1983). Categorizing sounds and learning to read—a causal connection. *Nature, 301,* 419–421.

Bravo-Valdivieso, L. (1995). A four-year follow-up study of low socioeconomic status, Latin American children with reading difficulties. *International Journal of Disability, Development, & Education, 42* (3), 189–202. LC4661.S 564.

Byrne, B., & Fielding-Barnsley, R. (1991). Evaluation of a program to teach phonemic awareness to young children. *Journal of Educational Psychology, 83* (4), 451–455.

Cardoso-Martins, C. (1991). Awareness of phonemes and alphabetic literacy acquisition. *British Journal of Educational Psychology, 61,* 164–173.

Carreiras, M., Alvarez, C.J., & De Vega, M. (1993). Syllable frequency and visual word recognition in Spanish. *Journal of Memory and Language, 32,* 766–780.

Carillo, M. (1994). Development of phonological awareness and reading acquisition: A study in Spanish language. *Reading and Writing, 6* (3), 279–298.

Chafouleas, S.M., Lewandowski, L.J., Smith, C. R., & Blachman, B.A. (1997). Phonological awareness skills in children: Examining performance across tasks and ages. *Journal of Psychoeducational Assessment, 15,* 334–347.

Cisero, C.A., & Royer, J.M. (1995). The development and cross-language transfer of phonological awareness. *Contemporary Educational Psychology, 20,* 275–303.

Cossu, G., Shankweiler, D., Liberman, I.Y., Katz, L., & Tola, G. (1988). Awareness of phonological segments and reading ability in Italian children. *Applied Psycholinguistics, 9,* 1–16.

Cummins, J. (1979). Linguistic interdependence and the educational development of bilingual children. *Review of Educational Research, 49,* 222–251.

Cummins, J. (1981). Empirical and theoretical underpinning of bilingual education. *Journal of Education, 163,* 16–29.

Cummins, J. (1984). *Bilingualism and special education: Issues in assessment and pedagogy.* Austin, TX: Pro-ed.

Cunningham, A.E. (1990). Explicit versus implicit instruction in phonemic awareness. *Journal of Experimental Child Psychology, 50,* 429–444.

Durgunoglu, A.Y., Nagy, W.E., & Hancin-Bhatt, B.J. (1993). Cross-language transfer of phonological awareness. *Journal of Educational Psychology, 85* (3), 453–465.

Foorman, B.R., Francis, D.J., Novy, D.M., & Liberman, D. (1991). How letter-sound instruction mediates progress in first-grade reading and spelling. *Journal of Educational Psychology, 83,* 456–469.

Foorman, B.R., Francis, D.J., Winikates, D., Mehta, P., Schatschneider, C., & Fletcher, J.M. (1997). Early interventions for children with reading disabilities. *Scientific Studies of Reading, 1,* 255–276.

Ganschow, L., & Sparks, R. (1995). Effects of direct instruction in Spanish phonology on the native-language skills and foreign-language aptitude of at-risk foreign-language learners. *Journal of Learning Disabilities, 28* (2), 107–120.

Gersten, R., Brengelman, S., & Jiménez, R. (1994). Effective instruction for culturally and linguistically diverse students: A reconceptualization. *Focus on Exceptional Children, 27,* 1–16.

González, J.E.J., Garcìa, C.R.H. (1995). Effects of word linguistic properties on phonological awareness in Spanish children. *Journal of Educational Psychology, 87* (2), 193–201.

Goswami, U., & Bryant, P. (1990). *Phonological skills and learning to read.* Hillsdale, NJ: Erlbaum.

Juel, C., Griffith, P.L., & Gough, P.B. (1986). Acquisition of literacy: A longitudinal study of children in first and second grade. *Journal of Educational Psychology, 78*, 243–255.

Koda, K. (1990). The use of L1 reading strategies in L2 reading: Effects of L1 orthographic structures in L2 phonological recoding strategies. *Studies in Second Language Acquisition, 12* (4), 394–410.

Lewkowicz, N.K. (1980). Phonemic awareness training: What to teach and how to teach it. *Journal of Educational Psychology, 72*, 686–700.

Lundberg, I., Frost, J., & Petersen, O. (1988). Effects of an extensive program for stimulating phonological awareness in preschool children. *Reading Research Quarterly, 23*, 263–284.

Lundberg, I., Olofsson, A., & Wall, S. (1980). Reading and spelling skills in the first school years predicted from phonemic awareness skills in kindergarten. *Scandinavian Journal of Psychology, 21*, 159–173.

Lyon, G. R. (1995). Toward a definition of dyslexia. *Annals of Dyslexia, 45*, 3–27.

Manrique, A.M.B., & Signorini, A. (1994). Phonological awareness, spelling and reading abilities in Spanish-speaking children. *British Journal of Educational Psychology, 64*, 429–439.

Morais, J., Cary, L., Alegria, J., Bertelson, P. (1979). Does awareness of speech as a sequence of phonemes arise spontaneously? *Cognition, 7*, 323–331.

Näslund, J.C. (1990). The interrelationships among preschool predictors of reading acquisition for German children. *Reading and Writing: An Interdisciplinary Journal, 2*, 327–360.

Signorini, A. (1997). Word reading in Spanish: A comparison between skilled and less skilled beginning readers. *Applied Psycholinguistics, 18*, 319–344.

Smith, S.B., Simmons, D.C., & Kameenui, E.J. (1995). *Synthesis of research on phonological awareness: Principles and implications for reading acquisition* (Tech. Rep. No. 21). Eugene: University of Oregon, National Center to Improve the Tools of Educators.

Snow, C.E., Burns, M.S., & Griffin, P. (Eds.) (1988). *Preventing reading difficulties in young children.* Washington, DC: National Academy Press.

Stahl, S.A., & Murray, B.A. (1994). Defining phonological awareness and its relationship to early reading. *Journal of Educational Psychology, 86* (2), 221–234.

Stanovich, K. E. (1986). Matthew effects in reading: Some consequences of individual differences in the acquisition of literacy. *Reading Research Quarterly, 21*, 360–397.

Stanovich, K.E., Cunningham, A.E., & Cramer, B.B. (1984). Assessing phonological awareness in kindergarten children: Issues of task comparability. *Journal of Experimental Child Psychology, 38*, 175–190.

Torgesen, J.K., Wagner, R.K., & Rashotte, C.A. (1997). Prevention and remediation of severe reading disabilities: Keeping the end in mind. *Scientific Studies of Reading, I*, 217–234.

Treiman, R., & Weatherston, S. (1992). Effects of linguistic structure on children's ability to isolate initial consonants. *Journal of Educational Psychology, 84*, 174–181.

Troia, G.A. (1999). Phonological awareness intervention research: A critical review of the experimental methodology. *Reading Research Quarterly, 34*, 28–52.

Valle-Arroyo, F. (1996). Dual-route models in Spanish: Developmental and neuropsychological data. In M. Carreiras, J.E. García-Albea, & N. Sebastian-Galles (Eds.), *Language processing in Spanish* (pp. 89–118). Mahwah, NJ: Erlbaum.

Vellutino, F.R., Scanlon, D.M., Sipay, E.R., Small, S.G., Pratt, A., Chen, R., & Denckla, M.B. (1996). Cognitive profiles of difficult-to-remediate and readily remediated poor readers: Early intervention as a vehicle for distinguishing between cognitive and experiential deficits as basic causes of specific reading disability. *Journal of Educational Psychology, 88*, 601–638.

Wagner, R.K. (1988). Causal relations between the development of phonological processing abilities and the acquisition of reading skills: A meta-analysis. *Merrill-Palmer Quarterly, 34*, 261–279.

Yopp, H.K. (1988). The validity and reliability of phonemic awareness tests. *Reading Research Quarterly, 23*, 159–177.

DEVELOPING A FRAMEWORK FOR WRITING IN DUAL LANGUAGE SETTINGS

Sarah Hudelson
Arizona State University

Introduction

A few weeks ago I attended a meeting of a local school district governing board. Recent elections had changed the composition of the board, and some of the new members had been contemplating doing away with the bilingual education programs that had existed for quite a few years in this particular location. As a result, many of us had come to testify in support of these programs during the public comment portion of the board meeting. As I sat in the audience, six fifth grade children from one of the district schools stepped, one at a time, to the microphone, and read essays that they had created for a contest sponsored by the state bilingual education association. The topic for the essays was the advantages of being bilingual. (In fact, the children who won the contest were some of the essay readers.) The children had written their essays in both Spanish and English, and they read them to the assembled board members and audience.

Each essay told the story of how a child began school speaking only Spanish, became literate initially in Spanish and then gradually added on English literacy. The children wrote of their dreams of future careers where they might use their bilingualism and biliteracy; they wrote of the importance of being able to use two languages in both spoken and written forms; they thanked the teachers who had worked with them over the years.

These essays were particularly striking to me because of the current rhetoric surrounding bilingual education, including claims that learners enrolled in bilingual programs never learn to use English. Some of the children who read their work had been students in the bilingual program since Head Start or kindergarten. Others had been in this country and school only a year or two and came to the United States already literate in Spanish. Yet all of them articulated the importance of being able to use both English and Spanish effectively, and all were in schools

that worked hard to enable students to become bilingual and biliterate.

This district is typical of many in the state in that the school-age population of Spanish-speaking children has increased greatly over the last ten years. Immigrant families from Mexico and Guatemala have joined the Spanish-speaking families who have been in the community for one to several generations. In neighborhoods around some of the schools, changing demographics have resulted in community environments in which Spanish now has a visible public presence. Within several school settings, Spanish-speaking adults have become increasingly active in parent–teacher–community councils. A response to the increase in numbers by many schools has been to provide opportunities for children to learn in and through both their primary language (L1) and English. Some bilingual programs that began, about 20 years ago, with a strictly transitional focus have shifted to maintenance models. At several sites, Title VII funding has been used to plan and begin to implement two-way bilingual education programs, thus offering the possibility of bilingualism and biliteracy to non-Spanish-speaking children in the district. Parents at several schools have advocated for the strengthening of bilingual programs and for the inclusion of native English speakers in these efforts.

All these realities struck me simultaneously, and I have continued to think about them as I have worked on this article, particularly as I have struggled with how to present current knowledge with regard to children's writing development in dual language settings. Because my own work has focused on young children's development as writers in Spanish and English, my first thought had been to begin with children themselves—with what we know about how children construct their knowledge of written language and with how writing serves multiple purposes for children. Since most of the research on writing development has taken place within the context of schools, I thought that I would then consider the beliefs and understandings that teachers and schools hold with regard to writing, how those beliefs and understandings play themselves out in classrooms, and what this means for children's writing. From there I planned to consider briefly the influence of families and local communities on children's understandings of writing and their written products.

However, as my more recent reading has reminded me over

and over again, literacy is always culturally and socially situated, literacy is a socioculturally constructed activity, and it varies across social and cultural settings (Delgado-Gaitan, 1990; Perez, 1998; Street, 1995). Children do not become literate in a vacuum. Rather, they see demonstrations of literacy events, they often participate in these events, and they come to understand literacy practices within specific sociocultural contexts, both outside and within formal schooling. (In this discussion I am using Street's distinction between *literacy events* as specific occasions in which literacy is integral to the interactions of participants and *literacy practices* as not only the specific occasions but also the cultural meanings given to literacy, or the meanings that communities assign to particular events.) Given that stance, I decided to start this article with the idea of writing as socioculturally constructed activity and to examine writing events in children's homes and communities before addressing writing in school contexts and before considering children's individual construction of written language systems. So instead of moving from the individual to the classroom and then out to the community, this article moves from Spanish-speaking communities and families to dual language classrooms and then to child writers learning to manipulate the sytems of Spanish and English and using writing for multiple purposes in their lives.

Writing as social and cultural practice in neighborhoods and families

I have worked in bilingual and second language education for 30 years. Over the decades I have heard terms such as *culturally deprived, culturally and socially disadvantaged, poverty-stricken, economically and socially disadvantaged, illiterate, semilingual,* and *semiliterate* used to describe children of working-class families who are not speakers of what has been termed standard English and who don't share many of the cultural and social experiences and values of middle-class children (Flores, Cousin, & Diaz, 1991). Many assumptions and claims have been made about the literacy practices and abilities of these children's families, most of them suggesting that illiteracy is rampant and that literacy at home and in the local community does not exist. In her now classic work *Ways with Words* (1983), Shirley Brice Heath demonstrated that such claims have little basis in fact, as she delineated the multiple and varied ways that working-class African American and white families from the Carolina Piedmont used spoken and written language in their homes and neighborhoods. What she also made clear was that the ways with words in the communities of Trackton and Roadville differed significantly from the ways with words of the middle-class townspeople and that teachers often recognized the townspeople's literacy practices while failing to acknowledge the literacy practices of other communities. A few years later Denny Taylor and

Catherine Dorsey-Gaines (1986) documented the varied kinds of and purposes for reading and writing found in the homes of working-class African Americans in an urban setting in the Northeast, another disputation of the claim that literacy did not occur in certain homes and communities. Recently Taylor (1998) has compiled a collection of family literacy stories from around the United States and beyond; these stories provide many examples of the rich variety of literacy practices of families across racial, ethnic, social class, and gender lines.

For me personally and for many of us involved in Spanish–English bilingual education, these studies raised questions about literacy practices in Spanish-speaking homes and neighborhoods. Since the focus of this article is writing, I chose to review several studies that I knew had been carried out among Spanish speakers in varied communities around the United States. As I reread the studies, I kept in mind questions such as: How is writing used in Spanish-speaking homes, meaning what kinds of writing and for what purposes? What demonstrations of writing do children see in their homes? In what language or languages? Do children as well as adults engage in writing at home? For what purposes? What significance does writing have?

In an examination of 20 families in a working-class immigrant Mexican Spanish-speaking community called Portillo in Southern California, for example, Delgado-Gaitán (1990) discovered that a significant writing practice for adults in the 20 families she

studied was writing letters to relatives in Mexico. Writing was a way to keep in contact with loved ones, and many parents also made sure that their children wrote to cousins, aunts and uncles, and grandparents. Delgado-Gaitán also discovered that this purposeful, meaningful writing in Spanish that children both saw demonstrated and participated in contrasted significantly with the kinds of writing that children carried out in school and for homework, which basically involved completing worksheets and other workbook-like tasks.

In another California Mexican Spanish-speaking community, Sequoya, researchers discovered that parents used writing for accomplishing day-to-day business (for example, paying bills and purchasing groceries), as well as for staying in contact with distant family members (Delgado-Gaitán & Trueba, 1991). In still another *barrio*, Spanish-dominant adults shared that writing was part of what they had to do on their jobs (for example, answering the telephone and taking messages). In addition, writing was a part of the homework for ESL classes that many adults attended, as the ESL students were asked to write answers to questions from their ESL texts (Delgado-Gaitán, 1987).

In Chicago, Juan Guerra (1998) spent many years documenting the oral and written language practices of a group of Mexican immigrants in the neighborhood known as Pilsen/Little Village. For these Spanish-speaking adults, too, letter writing was a culturally significant writing practice, and

letters received from those far away were kept for years as a way of representing and connecting to those who were not physically present. Only when family members joined one another were years-old letters thrown away, no longer needed because families were now in close proximity. Over the course of his work, Guerra became friends with two generations of community members. He learned that, depending upon the audience for the writing, younger adults were expected to write in English as well as in Spanish. Thus letters to family in Mexico were composed in Spanish, but other documents such as school notes, application forms, and lists often were written in English. Predictably, Guerra also found that younger community members with more formal education in the United States were more comfortable speaking and writing English than those educated in Mexico. Some younger adults on occasion translated from Spanish and wrote in English for their Spanish-speaking elders.

In another study done in a Mexican immigrant neighborhood in Chicago, Marcia Farr (1994) examined writing and reading practices of 45 individuals within the contexts of: home and family, school, religion, commerce, and the state/law. She determined that writing took place in both Spanish and English in all these settings and that, for the most part, the purpose of writing was to accomplish specific tasks—for example, filling out forms from the IRS or INS, completing homework or *doctrina* (catechism) assignments, keeping track of Tupperware sales, and the like. Writing was an integral part of what people needed to do to accomplish many daily living tasks.

In addition to demonstrations of writing for varied purposes, the Spanish-speaking adults in all the studies described above placed a high value on education, both for themselves and for their children. Parents encouraged their children to study hard in school. They talked with them about the importance of learning and of being able to write and read in both English and Spanish. Torres Guzmán (1998) has noted a similar valuing of literacy and formal education among Puerto Rican families and communities.

In considering what this information might mean for writing instruction, many literacy scholars who share a sociocultural view of literacy suggest that educators and schools need to view working-class Spanish-speaking children's homes, families, and communities as sociocultural resources that may be used in creating more effective learning environments for children, including environments for writing (Torres Guzmán, 1998). One proponent of this perspective is Luis Moll, who, with his colleagues, has developed the concept of *funds of knowledge*. Funds of knowledge are bodies of knowledge and skills that families have accumulated over time, and that enable families to function and to provide for the needs of family and community members (Moll et al., 1992; also see González, 1995; Vélez-Ibañez & Greenberg, 1992). These funds of knowledge exist in all households, including those traditionally thought of as deprived of or lacking in resources. Working with this concept, bilingual teachers have identified funds of knowledge among selected families and then have utilized this knowledge within their own classrooms.

One primary grade teacher-researcher, for example, discovered that the family of one of her students sold candy from Mexico to enhance the family's income. Beginning with family and child knowledge about how the candy was purchased, marketed, and resold (including how writing and reading were used in these transactions), this teacher created a unit of study in which children used their Spanish and English writing and reading abilities to compare and contrast U.S. and Mexican candy and to determine classmates' favorite candies (González, 1995). In another bilingual intermediate grade classroom, children conducted research on their own families, using Spanish and English writing (in the forms of notes, logs, and journals) to record information as they interviewed family members to determine: family genealogy and history, family migration, family use of Spanish and English, family members' knowledge of stories, sayings, poems, games, and so on from the oral tradition, and special skills of family members (Craig, 1995).

Another bilingual educator who has advocated incorporating parental and family knowledge into the literacy curriculum is Alma Flor Ada (1988). Her work with migrant parents began by involving them in choosing Spanish-language picture books to share with their children. These interactions around literature, plus multiple opportunities to talk about their own lives and to tell their own stories, culminated in many parents' writing their own poetry and stories, which became a part of the material that was available for their children to read. In work inspired by Ada, Sudia Paloma McCaleb (1994) entered into dialogues with Spanish-speaking parents about their lives, including their educational experiences in and out of school, and their aspirations for their children. In some cases, these dialogues provided the seeds for autobiographical narratives that parents then wrote for their children, sharing their own life experiences; in other cases parents and children collaborated on the writing and illustration of stories based on incidents in their lives. These parents wrote in Spanish. In other settings, parents and children have collaborated on family stories created in their second language, English (Nurss & Rawlston, 1991).

To conclude this section: I would maintain that a framework for writing in dual language educational settings needs to acknowledge contexts for writing that already exist in children's homes and communities. Further, parents and other adults need opportunities to contribute to curriculum as they share their expertise and as they write down their cultural stories and personal histories, both bringing these texts into classrooms and expanding the view that parents may have of themselves as writers.

Writing in classroom settings

In addition to the home and community, another powerful context for bilingual children to understand the potential of writing and to develop their abilities as writers is the school and the classrooms in which they find themselves. As I reviewed work on writing that has been done in bilingual and second language classrooms, I found myself considering aspects of this context, such as: the opportunities for writing provided in classrooms; the understandings and beliefs about writing that teachers have and how these influence children; the relative importance attached to writing in two languages, and how this affects children's work. A consideration of these issues follows.

More than 20 years ago Lucy Calkins, Donald Graves, and others began to share the results of in-classroom investigations of children and teachers engaged in writing, with writing defined as the generation/creation of one's own texts. These researchers demonstrated that young children, while still learning spelling, punctuation, capitalization, and other conventions of written language were enthusiastic generators of their own personal stories or narratives. They also demonstrated that young writers were eager to share their work and were able to engage in content revisions based on the comments of others. This writing happened in classrooms where teachers believed that children learn to write by engaging in the craft of writing; that children need authentic reasons to write, audiences to write for, and choice of and control over what they created; and that it is important for children to share their work with adults and other chidren so that what they are creating might benefit from the comments of others (Calkins, 1983; Graves, 1983; Hansen, 1987). Teachers' understandings about writing as a social and collaborative undertaking affected how they organized their classrooms for writing; how they worked with children; and how they helped children work with each other.

The earliest writing-process work was carried out with middle-class, European American, native English-speaking children and their teachers, although it soon expanded to more culturally diverse classrooms (Dyson, 1989, 1993). Many of us working in bilingual and second language settings chose to relate the concept of writing as a process to bilingual classrooms and came to the conclusion that composition was composition regardless of the language. It seemed logical that Spanish-speaking children in bilingual programs would learn to write in Spanish by engaging in the process of writing and by having others respond to their work, rather than by completing worksheets and drills designed to teach sound–letter correspondences and conventional orthography before being asked to create any pieces of their own (Freeman & Freeman, 1998).

As bilingual and second language educators from more traditional backgrounds struggled with a process perspective on writing instruction, they began to engage young children in writing. Evidence began to accumulate that young Spanish speakers could and would engage in writing from the beginning of their school careers if their teachers created classroom enviroments that included opportunities and time for them to write, and if the teachers deliberately encouraged their young pupils to experiment with written communication (Edelsky, 1981, 1986; Edelsky & Jilbert, 1985; Flores & Garcia, 1984; Hudelson, 1981–82). Children in kindergarten and primary grades showed themselves to be capable of using written Spanish to engage in written conversations in interactive journals (Flores & Garcia, 1984; Flores et al., 1986; Garcia, Berry, & Garcia, 1990); to create personal stories, real and imagined; to extend invitations to classroom functions; and to prepare informational work, such as reports (Edelsky, 1986).

The expertise of teachers with regard to writing instruction was also of critical importance with regard to the conduct of writing in classroom settings. In an examination of first through third grade children's writing in Spanish in a bilingual program, Edelsky and her colleagues (Edelsky, 1981, 1986) found teachers who were spending a significant portion of each day having children engage in writing of various kinds: journals, personal narratives, reports, letters, invitations, posters, etc. The teachers created real audiences for the children's writing (for example, the school principal, the bilingual program director, children from other classrooms, pen pals from other schools, parents and other adults).The children enjoyed these activities and produced a lot of writing. However, limitations in the teachers' understandings about writing also influenced the children's processes. The teachers did not view writing as crafting, so they did not engage the children in examining, sharing, and revising their work. They did not view writing as a social process, so the children did not collaborate with each other. They did not publish any work in final, revised and edited form, so the children did not see the real-world need for revisiting one's work, both to examine the content and to attend to conventional written language. Thus the children's writing did not become substantially more sophisticated or conventional in form.

The teachers' views of writing also influenced the children's products. When the teachers believed that the children's efforts had to be spelled conventionally from the beginning, the children's written products resembled worksheets or workbook pages. When the teachers believed that content was more important than the use of conventional forms of writing, the children's writing was much less constrained by concerns for spelling and punctuation. When the teacher believed that longer pieces were preferable to shorter pieces, the children vied to see who could write the longest piece, with no regard for the quality of the text. Thus, Edelsky concluded that teachers' understandings and beliefs made a big difference in what actually went on in classrooms in the name of writing.

Edelsky's work was the first to document in detail what has come to be known as writing process classrooms within the context of bilingual education. She studied classrooms for one year and collected data at four specific times during the year. These data collection times were the only opportunities for observing in classrooms and interacting with teachers and children. More recently, other investigators have spent extended periods of time in classrooms documenting teachers' understandings about how children develop as writers; how teachers set up classrooms to encourage writing; and how teachers and other children interact with child writers as they create texts (for extended vignettes, see Faltis & Hudelson, 1998; Freeman & Freeman, 1994, 1998). A volume that I have found particularly rich with classrooms details is a case study of one bilingual classroom, written collaboratively by university teacher Kathryn Whitmore and third grade bilingual teacher Caryl Crowell (1994). Whitmore and Crowell share details of Crowell's daily writer's workshop, which provides opportunities for children to work on writing of their own choosing in the language that they choose, including ongoing personal narrative writing projects, journal writing, letters, and writing influenced by literature that has been shared in the classroom. Crowell explains how she works with revising and editing, and how she teaches specific skills and conventions. More important, Crowell explicates her understandings of writing as a social, collaborative process. She explains why she works as she does.

The writing process as actualized in classrooms for linguistically and culturally diverse students has not been without its critics. Lisa Delpit (1988a, 1988b) has questioned whether all learners will benefit equally from writing process approaches, which often advocate minimizing or doing away with the teaching of specific writing skills. Delpit argues that children will acquire these skills and conventions through their own writing, through teachers' modeling of conventional forms, and through extensive reading. Delpit has contested this idea, noting that some children, especially non-middle-class minority children, may need explicit instruction in conventions and skills.

With similar issues in mind, Maria de la luz Reyes (1991) examined the literature journals of bilingual fourth graders over the course of several months. The teacher responded to the children's literature log entries with conventionally written entries of her own, but did not directly correct the children's spelling or mechanics. Reyes discovered that the children's spelling did not improve significantly over time, a finding that caused her to question and critique the utilization of writing process pedagogy because of children's needs to be able to use conventional forms in their writing.

My own take on these critiques is the following: First, it has never been my understanding that writing process educators advocated an avoidance of skills instruction. Rather, it has been my understanding that skills were taught, but within the context of children's actual writing, rather than from a workbook and in isolation from children's real texts (Calkins, 1986; Graves, 1983). A description of a second grade bilingual teacher's work as she sought to influence children to revise their writing demonstrates this explicit teaching of skills in context. It also demonstrates the complexity of this kind of contextualized teaching, as the teacher struggles to figure out how much and what kind of direct teaching is appropriate for the developmental levels of her or his students (Zecker, Pappas, & Cohen, 1997). Second, it has been my understanding that writing process teachers advocate teaching specific skills and conventions from selected pieces of text, rather than from every piece of writing children produce. While one could argue that some writing process educators believe that modeling conventional spelling through journal responses should result in learners reading and then using standard forms, it could also be argued that journals and logs have not often been used as texts from which to teach specific skills. Third, in my view it is dangerous to make generalizations about the actions of all writing process teachers on the basis of case studies of a few teachers. Fourth, I readily acknowledge that some writing

process educators, when they first studied writing process philosophy and theory, engaged students in creating their own texts with little or no regard for arriving at conventional forms. The concerns were purely process ones, rather than product. It is my sense that many of these educators have come to understand that conventions and specific skills *are* also important and may need to be taught directly. I also readily acknowledge that some bilingual children may benefit from more explicit instruction than others (Pérez, 1994). However, I would caution against making assumptions about what is occurring in classrooms simply because a label such as "writing process classroom" has been assigned. What needs to happen is a careful look at what actually goes on in bilingual classrooms in the name of writing process (Pérez, 1994, 1995).

One individual who has engaged in such close looking is Kris Gutierrez (1992), who carried out a two-year observational study in five second and third grade bilingual classrooms designated by the school principal as writing process classrooms taught by exemplary teachers. The classroom populations were 90 percent Latino immigrant students. Two classrooms used Spanish as the medium of instruction. In the other three classrooms, because the learners had transitioned into English literacy, English was the medium of instruction. Analysis of videotapes and field notes, child and teacher interviews, and child products revealed that there was

tremendous variation in writing process instruction and in its impact on the children in the classrooms. Some teachers organized writing process instruction as a series of activities to be carried out in a unidirectional fashion, allowing almost no time for talk, generation of ideas, experimentation, or meaning-making. The teachers assumed the role of transmitters of knowledge, managing the writing in ways that provided little opportunity for student interaction or even writing. Gutierrez characterized these classrooms as recitation instruction settings.

In contrast, other writing process instruction was much more open to student talk and interaction, and to students assuming multiple roles as writing contexts tasks varied. Gutierrez characterized this writing as responsive/collaborative. Writing was truly a social process in these collaborative classrooms, and writing time always included time for talking, for working with and helping others, and for receiving appropriate assistance from teachers. When written products were compared, Gutierrez found that the children in the truly responsive/collaborative settings created written pieces that were elaborated, that created and sustained ideas and arguments, and that utilized both children's personal experiences and texts that they had read. In later work with bilingual children's journal writing, Gutierrez (1994) found once again that when children shared journal entries in groups structured by the teacher to be responsive/collaborative, more possibilities existed for children to make revisions to what they had written.

Another example of looking closely at writing instruction comes from the Santa Barbara Classroom Discourse Group and their work in a third grade bilingual classroom where children engaged in story writing as the culmination of a unit of study on space (Tuyay, Jennings, & Dixon, 1995). Children decided to create stories after a class member brought in a book about extraterrestrials. Deciding that the book, which contained elements of both fantasy and reality, was realistic fiction, children chose, in small groups, to create their own realistic fictional stories about planets (Tuyay, 1999). A focus on the child–child and adult–child discourse revealed that collaborative interaction with peers, with the teacher, and with other, more knowledgeable adults was vital to the children's generation and revising of possible texts. Whether working in English, Spanish, or both languages, talk and collaboration were essential to writing. Children needed significant amounts of time to construct text. Not all children accomplished writing within the same time frame. The children's choice of topic and content, along with guidelines from the teacher, were important as children worked to construct meaning both through talk and through writing (1995). An examination of the resulting written products also indicated that the children had successfully combined elements of fantasy and reality in their stories (Tuyay, 1999).

In other bilingual classroom work from Santa Barbara, Ana Floriani (1994) examined collaboration among pairs of sixth graders as the children constructed soical science reports at the conclusion of a two-and-a-half month project in which they worked as social scientists would: observing, collecting data, interpreting evidence, drawing conclusions, and writing up their findings. As the work progressed, the children's writing shifted from a more personal style to a more social-scientific writing style, to writing that was more academic in nature. This work suggests to me that aspects of writing process pedagogy, such as opportunities for talk, collaboration with peers and adults, time for drafting, and opportunities for revision based on adult and peer critiques, need not be limited to the creation of personal stories. More academic writing also benefits from being understood as social in nature. These principles hold in English as a second language as well as in true bilingual settings, although special considerations may need to be made for learners, depending on their English proficiency (Blake, 1992; Hudelson, 1989b; Peyton et al., 1994).

A major issue surrounding writing in dual language settings is the relative importance accorded to writing each language, including questions of whether children should become writers in the Spanish language; how much time is spent in Spanish; what the purposes are for which children write in Spanish and English; when and how English writing should begin; and

whether writing in Spanish should continue once children begin to write in English. In my view, questions like these have to do with the relative status of the two languages, as well as with concerns for children's English language achievement (Edelsky & Hudelson, 1980).

A central premise of many bilingual programs has been that children should develop both reading and writing ability in their native language prior to developing literacy in English. Scholars have pointed out that when children become writers in L1 and use that L1 writing for multiple purposes, they come to understand what writing is and what it can do; they come to appreciate the potential power of written language in people's lives (Hudelson, 1987; Serna & Hudelson, 1993). There *is* evidence that children with better developed Spanish writing abilities write more effectively in English than do children with less developed Spanish abilities (Lanauze & Snow, 1989). There is also evidence that when children develop confidence in themselves as writers in Spanish, they will often choose, of their own accord, to experiment with or to add on English writing (García & Colón, 1995; Hudelson & Serna, 1994), with the result that they begin to use both languages to express themselves in written form.

Over the years I have participated in many discussions about when to transition children to English writing. When are they ready? What kinds of activities/ strategies are appropriate for this period of transition? These are questions I hear frequently. I prefer not to use the term *transition*, for several reasons. The first is that it seems to suggest a unidirectionality, that children are expected to give up writing in Spanish and use only English, as though writing in Spanish had no value in its own right. This strikes me as the wrong message to send children. Spanish is a perfectly valid language for written expression, as millions of Spanish speakers around the world will attest. Even if children are working in English, there may be times when they choose or need to use Spanish, and it is important that they be able to make this choice or use this resource.

Second, in my view, the idea of transitioning does not acknowledge the reality that language-choice norms lead bilingual (and biliterate) individuals to choose the language in which they will communicate with others on the basis of multiple sociocultural factors, including an understanding of others' language abilities (Grosjean, 1982). This means that children who develop as writers in both English and Spanish often choose to use one language or the other for writing on the basis of the L1 of the person to whom they are writing (García & Colón, 1992; Hudelson & Serna, 1994). Topics and purposes for writing may also influence language choice (Hudelson & Serna, 1994). So it is not a matter of discarding writing in Spanish for English; it is a matter of becoming proficient at both.

Third, the question seems to imply that children would not choose to write in English without organized structures and pro-cedures to impel them to do so. Many bilingual educators would question this notion, noting, as I have above, that children often move themselves, or self-transition, into English (García & Colón, 1995), or that they begin to experiment with writing in English because it is functional for them in particular contexts or with particular people (Hudelson & Serna, 1994). The influence of English is very strong—so strong that children in bilingual situations are impelled into English literacy—and teachers must make concerted efforts to retain the Spanish language and Spanish literacy in bilingual classrooms (Shannon, 1995; Turner, 1994).

Thus, instead of concern for moving children out of Spanish writing and into English, dual language programs and classrooms need to be concerned with ways of conceptualizing and organizing the classroom environment and instruction in order to help children become highly proficient writers in both languages and to use their two languages with specific audiences for specific purposes. This article has already noted possibilities for learners to use writing for self-expression in journals and logs, to use writing to share personal stories, to use writing as a way of organizing and presenting information learned in content area study. I wanted to include here mention of two other contexts for writing that bilingual and second language educators have articulated. The first is literary writing, which I am defining as writing in particular genres, such as poetry, fiction, and fantasy. Teacher/researchers have shown that elementary school children are able to create quite sophisticated literary forms in both Spanish and English as a second language. Key to the development of this kind of writing are the reading and discussion of quality pieces of literature, including examination of the writer's craft in producing the text (Espinosa & Moore, in press; Harper, 1997; Samway & Taylor, 1993). The second context is writing that leads young bilingual learners to examine and critique existing social structures and practices and to advocate for social change (Peterson, 1991; Wink, 1997).

Children's Development as Writers

In the previous sections of this article, I have pointed out that Spanish-speaking children's socialization into literacy, and specifically into writing, often begins in homes, families, and neighborhoods. I also have shared some studies done in dual language classroom settings, studies that point to the significant influences of teachers and classroom environments on children's writing. Now I turn to children themselves, to their work of creating or constructing written language and of using that language for multiple purposes. I frame this discussion from both a social interactionist perspective on language acquisition, with its focus on the social nature of language learning, and a constructivist stance, with its emphasis on the child's own intellectual work within multiple social settings. According to the social interactionist view, children learn both spoken and written language as they live their daily lives in the company of others. As social beings, children acquire language because it is useful to them. Growing up in families and communities, children see others use language as one tool to accomplish their purposes. Children work to learn how to use this tool themselves in order to participate in their own worlds (Genishi & Dyson, 1984; Lindfors, 1987).

Within a variety of social contexts, children attend to how those around them use language to get things done. From their observations, they make hypotheses or predictions about how language works, and they try out their hypotheses. Over time, they adjust their hypotheses, or make different predictions. Over time, too, their use of language, whether spoken or written, moves closer to conventional adult use. Thus, within social settings and social interaction, children engage in the creative construction of their language (Lindfors, 1987).

A particular concern of some researchers has been the documentation of how young children's writing emerges and changes over time—that is, of how young children creatively construct the written system of the language or languages with which they are engaged. Scholars interested in emerging writing have examined children's gradual construction of several aspects of written language, including spelling, segmentation (meaning conventional spacing between words), capitalization and punctuation, and the development of particular genre fea-

tures (Weaver, 1994). An especially influential researcher who has documented Spanish-speaking preschool children's construction of the spelling of Spanish is Emilia Ferreiro. Ferreiro has worked independently and in collaboration with Ana Teberosky, in countries such as Mexico, Spain, and Argentina, and with children of varying socioeconomic status. One of the most important contributions of this research has been documentation that, long before children write using the alphabetic principle (that is, using specific letters to represent specific sounds), they are making hypotheses about how written Spanish works (Ferreiro, 1990; Ferreiro & Teberosky, 1979, 1982). This means that children's nonalphabetic writing in Spanish is not merely scribbles; rather, it reflects children's hypotheses about written Spanish at a given point in time.

According to Ferreiro and Teberosky, children's hypotheses change over time. An early hypothesis made by the children they studied was that the length of writing should correspond to the size of the object whose name was being written. (Thus, a child would write a wavy line to represent the word *pato* (duck) and would write a longer line to represent the word *oso* (bear), because a bear is larger than a duck. A different hypothesis that children developed when they began to write using letter forms was that different objects needed to be represented with different forms. For example, the word *gato* (cat) would be represented as *ARTN* and the word *perro* (dog) as *YELC*. As hypotheses

changed, many children decided that any word must be represented by a minimum of four letter forms. Some children also predicted that certain letter forms were significant and should be used in different combinations to create different words. Thus *Aron* was used to write *sapo* (toad); *Aorn* was *pato* (duck), *Iaon* was *casa* (house), and *rAoI* represented the sentence *Mamá sale de casa* (Mom leaves the house). For many children, the letters in their own names were the letters they first chose to use in different combinations.

As the children began to understand that particular letters represent specific sounds, their writing moved into what Ferreiro and Teberosky termed the syllabic phase. Each letter written stood for a syllable, and because of the stability and conventionality of vowels in Spanish, children more often represented syllables with vowels than with consonants. So a word such as *zapato* (shoe) might be written as *AAO*, or a sentence such as *El oso sale* (The bear goes out) might appear as *EOOAE*.

According to Ferreiro and Teberosky, the children began to work from what they called an alphabetic hypothesis when more of the letters of words, including consonants, began to be filled in. Thus *mesa* (table) might be written as *MCA* or *mapa* (map) as *MAP*. Sentences such as *FIMOSAPAKE* could be read easily as *Fuimos al parque* (We went to the park), because of the appearance of most of the sounds even though there was not conventional segmentation between words. This filling in of letters began to occur as children became aware that their writing did not look like the writing they saw around them. The final stage in Ferreiro and Teberosky's description of children's construction of Spanish spelling was figuring out which letter to choose when two letters represented the same sound (as, for example, *c* or *s*, *c* or *k*, *ll* or *y*, *k* or *qu*, *b* or *v*) and utilizing of conventional segmentation between words, again because of examples of written language that surrounded them.

Edelsky and her colleagues (1986) extended Ferreiro's work with preschoolers into the primary grades and into the bilingual context of the United States, as they analyzed first through third graders' writing samples for such features as invented spelling, segmentation, and capitalization and punctuation. In my own work with Edelsky's data (Hudelson, 1981–82), I found that spelling inventions of children who were writing alphabetically were *not* limited to questions of which of two letters to choose for which sound, as Ferreiro suggested. Rather, children created nonconventional spellings for many reasons, among them: (1) spelling a word according to the way it was pronounced in the local speech community or in the individual child's still developing speech, rather than according to its conventional spelling (thus, *fuimos* was spelled *juimos* because that is the way the word was pronounced); (2) Hispanicizing the spelling of the few English words in the piece (thus *Santa Clos* and *Varvi* for the words Santa Claus and Barbie); (3) sounding out words slowly, resulting in elongated pronuncia-

tion and the addition of sounds and letters (such as spelling *maestra* as *mallestra* due to overextended sounding out); (4) substitution of letters that are visually similar, such as *b* and *d*. (5) It also became evident that young Spanish writers were influenced by the phonetic features of some words. Attention to such phonetic features as place of articulation and perceptibility resulted in spellings such as *tabien fuimos al paque* for *también fuimos al parque.*

In addition to extending Ferreiro's work on spelling, Edelsky and her colleagues discovered complexities to children's construction of the rules for spacing or segmenting between words. While Ferreiro demonstrated that, prior to conventional segmentation, children divided sentences according to subjects and predicates, Edelsky (1986) found that children made *multiple* hypotheses about segmentation. These she classified as syntactic hypotheses, which included but were not limited to spaces between subjects and predicates (or NP and VP); phonological/morphological hypotheses based on syllables; anti-syntactic hypotheses and anti-phonological/morphological hypotheses.

More recent work on creative or invented spelling in Spanish has shown that children's predictions based on letters and sounds also change over time. Later hypotheses are more likely to be related to spelling distinctions (for example, *b* or *v*), while early inventions are more influenced by phonetic and dialect or idiolect features. Through their own processes of discovery and

through explicit instruction, children's spelling moves from less to more conventional (Montiel, 1992). So do children's segmentation and punctuation (Ferreiro et al., 1996).

In a previous section of this article, I have noted that children who have become writers in Spanish often begin to add on English writing of their own accord. This frequently occurs without formal instruction when writing in English serves particular communicative purposes. When children choose to add on English writing, they again engage in the creative construction of written language, this time the English language. Their writing reflects multiple hypotheses about how English spelling works. Early on, the central hypothesis appears to be: Spell English as though it were Spanish (Hudelson, 1989a, b; Nathensen-Mejia, 1989). Later ESL spelling reflects children's attention to letter names and sounds in English and to how words appear visually, especially words that appear with frequency in books and in classroom and community environments (Hudelson, 1989a; Hudelson & Serna, 1994).

A central but often unacknowledged reality of children's creative construction of the written language, both in first and second languages, particularly within the context of the school setting, is that it happens at different rates for different children. Using spelling as an example, some children enter the setting of school already sensitive to the alphabetic principle; their writing reflects this understanding. Others enter school still working to distinguish drawing from writing and/or utilizing shapes and forms that are not related to particular sounds and letters. For some, the development and refinement of hypotheses about spelling happens within the first year of classroom experiences with writing; for others this may take significantly more time and may require significantly more explicit assistance from adults and peers (Serna & Hudelson, 1993).

There is also significant variation in children's confidence about and willingness to engage in writing, especially when that engagement means putting down on paper versions of the written language that are not conventional. From the creative construction stance, writing involves risktaking and making mistakes, and not all children are equally comfortable with taking risks. It takes some children significantly longer than others to see themselves as writers. It takes some children longer than others even to begin to generate their own texts, to decide that they can express themselves in writing, especially if that writing is not exactly as adults would create it (Hudelson, 1989a). Studies of children's written language construction have been careful to articulate development over time, rather than to label particular features with a particular age or grade designation. The reality of individual differences and of children's ultimate individual control over their language generation and construction does not mean that teachers should not provide instruction about written language to children. But it does suggest to me that indi-vidual differences in children's developing understandings and utilizations of written language must be acknowledged and respected.

Conclusion

In this article I have set out a framework for planning writing instruction for children in elementary schools' dual language settings. The key features of this framework are:

1. An acknowledgment of and respect for families and communities as literacy teachers

2. An inclusion of family and community experiences, expertise, and stories within the writing curriculum

3. An understanding of and appreciation for writing as a social process that involves talking, sharing, and collaboration as well as individual engagement and struggle

4. A recognition and acceptance of writing as a craft that is time-consuming, messy, and often intensive

5. A vision of writing as a way of learning about and making sense of the world and the individual's place in that world, including the possibility of helping to make the world a more equitable place

6. A balancing of writers' discovery learning about written language with explicit instruction/assistance/scaffolding from teachers and peers

7. A recognition of and respect for the individuality of each writer

8. The provision of multiple opportunities or invitations for children to engage in the craft of writing for multiple purposes, to and with multiple audiences, and in both languages

9. An expectation that bilingual learners are smart and capable and will learn

10. A valuing of and striving for high levels of written proficiency for all learners in both Spanish and English.

My hope is that a consideration of the information presented here will be useful to educators who struggle to offer bilingual children the rich and challenging writing experiences to which they are entitled.

REFERENCES

Ada, A. (1988). The Pajaro Valley experience: Working with Spanish-speaking parents to develop children's reading and writing skills in the home through the use of children's literature. In T. Skutnabb-Kangas & J. Cummins (Eds.), *Minority education: From shame to struggle* (pp. 223–238). Philadelphia: Multi-Lingual Matters.

Blake, B. (1992). Talk in non-native and native English speakers' peer writing conferences. *Language Arts, 69,* 604–610.

Calkins, L. (1983). *Lessons from a child.* Exeter, NH: Heinemann.

Craig, M. (1995). Students as ethnographers. *Practicing Anthropology, 17,* 20–22.

Delgado-Gaitán, C. (1990). *Literacy for empowerment.* New York: Falmer Press.

Delgado-Gaitán, C. (1987). Mexican adult literacy: New directions for immigrants. In S. Goldman and H. Trueba (Eds.), *Becoming literate in English as a second language: Advances in theory and research* (pp. 9–32). Norwood, NJ: Ablex.

Delgado-Gaitán, C., & Trueba, H. (1991). *Crossing cultural borders.* New York: Falmer Press.

Delpit, L. (1988a). When the talking stops: Paradoxes of power in educating other people's children. Paper presented at Ninth Annual Ethnography in Education Research Forum, University of Pennsylvania, Philadelphia.

Delpit, L. (1988b). The silenced dialogue: Power and pedagogy in educating other people's children. *Harvard Educational Review, 58,* 280–298.

Dyson, A. (1989). *Multiple worlds of child writers: Friends learning to write.* New York: Teachers College Press.

Dyson, A. (1993). *The social worlds of children learning to write in an urban primary school.* New York: Teachers College Press.

Edelsky, C. (1986). *Writing in a bilingual program: Habia una vez.* Norwood, NJ: Ablex.

Edelsky, C. (1982). Writing in a bilingual program: The relation of L1 and L2 texts. *TESOL Quarterly, 16,* 211–228.

Edelsky, C. (1981). From "JIMOS-ALSCO" to "7 NARANGAS SE CALLERON Y EL ARBOL-EST-TRISTE EN LAGRYMAS": Writing development in a bilingual program. In B.Cronnell (Ed.), *The writing needs of linguistically different students* (pp. 63–98) Los Alamitos, CA: SWRL.

Edelsky, C., & Hudelson, S. (1980). Second language acquisition of a marked language. *National Association for Bilingual Education Journal, 5,* 1–15.

Edelsky, C., & Jilbert, C. (1985). Bilingual children and writing: Lessons for us all. *Volta Review, 87,* 57–72.

Espinosa, C., & Moore, K. (in press). Understanding and transforming the meaning of our lives through poetry, biographies, and songs. In C. Edelsky (Ed.), *Making justice our project: Teachers working toward critical whole language practice.* Urbana, IL: National Council of Teachers of English.

Faltis, C., & Hudelson, S. (1998). *Bilingual education in elementary and secondary school communities: Toward understanding and caring.* Boston: Allyn & Bacon.

Farr, M. (1994). *En los dos idiomas:* Literacy practices among Chicano Mexicanos. In B. Moss (Ed.), *Literacy across communities* (pp. 9–48) Creskill, NJ: Hampton Press.

Ferreiro, E. (1990). Literacy development: Psychogenesis. In Y. Goodman (Ed.), *How children construct literacy: Piagetian perspectives.* Newark, DE: International Reading Association.

Ferreiro, E., Pontecorvo, C., Moreira, N., & Hidalgo, I. (1996). *Caperucita roja aprende a escribir.* Barcelona: Editorial Gisela.

Ferreiro, E., & Teberosky, A. (1982). *Literacy before schooling.* Exeter, NH: Heinemann.

Ferreiro, E., & Teberosky, A. (1979). *Los sistemas de escritura en el desarrollo del niño.* Mexico City: Siglo XXI.

Flores, B., Cousin, P. T., & Díaz, E. (1991). Transforming deficit myths about learning, language and culture. *Language Arts, 68,* 369–385.

Flores, B., García, E., Gonzalez, S., Hidalgo, G., Kaczmarek, K., & Romero, T. (1985). *Bilingual holistic instructional strategies.* Chandler, AZ: Exito.

Flores, B., & Garcia, E. H. (1984). A collaborative learning and teaching experience using journal writing. *NABE Journal, 8,* 67–73.

Floriani, A. (1994). Negotiating what counts: roles and relationships, texts and contexts, content and meaning. *Linguistics and Education, 5,* 241–274.

Freeman, Y., & Freeman, D. (1998). *La enseñanza de la lectura y la escritura en español en el aula bilingue.* Portsmouth, NH: Heinemann.

Garcia, E., Berry, C., & Garcia, E. (1990). The effects of teacher reaction on students' interactive journals. *Early Child Development and Care, 56,* 35–47.

Garcia, E., & Colon, M. (1995). Interactive journals in bilingual classrooms: An analysis of language "transition." *Discourse Processes, 19,* 39–56.

Genishi, C., & Dyson, A. (1984). *Language assessment in the early years.* Norwood, NJ: Ablex.

González, N. (1995) The funds of knowledge for teaching project. *Practicing Anthropology, 17,* 3–7.

Graves, D. (1983). *Writing: Teachers and children at work.* Exeter, NH: Heinemann.

Grosjean, F. (1982). *Life with two languages.* Cambridge, MA: Harvard University Press.

Guerra, J. (1998). *Close to home: Oral and literate practices in a transnational Mexican community.* New York: Teachers College Press.

Gutierrez, K. (1994). How talk, context and script share contexts for learning: A cross-case comparison of journal sharing. *Linguistics and Education, 5,* 335–365.

Gutierrez, K. (1992). A comparison of instructional contexts in writing process classrooms with Latino children. *Education and Urban Society, 24,* 244–262.

Hansen, J. (1987). *When writers read.* Portsmouth, NH: Heinemann.

Harper, L. (1997) The writer's toolbox: Five tools for active revision instruction. *Language Arts, 74,* 193–199.

Heath, S.B. (1983). *Ways with words.* New York: Cambridge University Press.

Hudelson, S. (1989a). A tale of two children: Individual differences in ESL children's writing. In D. Johnson & D. Roen (Eds.), *Richness in writing: Empowering ESL students* (pp. 84–99). New York: Longman.

Hudelson, S. (1989b). *Write on: Children learning to write in English as a second language.* Englewood Cliffs, NJ: Prentice-Hall.

Hudelson, S. (1987). The role of native language literacy in the education of language minority children. *Language Arts, 65,* 287–302.

Hudelson, S. (1981–82). An introductory examination of children's invented spelling in Spanish. *NABE Journal.*

Hudelson, S., & Serna, I. (1994). Beginning literacy in English in a whole language bilingual program. In A. Flurkey & R. Meyer (Eds.), *Under the whole language umbrella: Many cultures, many voices* (pp. 278–294). Urbana, IL: National Council of Teachers of English.

Lanauze, M., & Snow, C. (1989). The relation between first- and second-language writing skills: Evidence from Puerto Rican elementary school children in bilingual programs. *Linguistics and Education, 1,* 323–339.

Lindfors, J. (1987). *Children's language and learning, 2nd ed.* Englewood Cliffs, NJ: Prentice-Hall.

McCaleb, S. P. (1994). *Building communities of learners.* New York: St. Martin's Press.

Moll, L., Amanti, C., Neff, D., & González, N. (1992). Funds of knowledge for teaching: Using a qualitative approach to connect homes and classrooms. *Theory into Practice, 31,* 132–141.

Montiel, Y. (1992). *Spanish-speaking children's emergent literacy during first and second grades: Three case studies.* Unpublished doctoral dissertation, Arizona State University, Tempe, AZ.

Nathanson-Mejia, S. (1989). Writing in a second language: Negotiating meaning through invented spelling. *Language Arts, 66,* 516–526.

Nurss, J., & Rawlston, S. (1991). Family stories: Intergenerational literacy. *TESOL Journal, 1,* 29–30.

Perez, B. (Ed.). (1998). *Sociocultural contexts of language and literacy.* Mahwah, NJ: Erlbaum.

Perez, B. (1995). The bilingual teacher (Spanish/English) and literacy instruction. *Teacher Education Quarterly,* 1–10.

Perez, B. (1994). Spanish literacy development: A descriptive study of four bilingual whole language classrooms. *JRB: Journal of Literacy Behavior, 26,* 75–93.

Peterson, R. (1991). Teaching how to read the world and change it: Critical pedagogy in the intermediate grades. In C. Walsh (Ed.), *Literacy as praxis: Culture, language and pedagogy* (pp. 156–182). Norwood, NJ: Ablex.

Peyton, J., Jines, C., Vincent, A., & Greenblatt, L. (1994). Implementing writing workshop with ESOL students: Visions and realities. *TESOL Quarterly, 28,* 469–487.

Samway, K., & Taylor, D. (1993). Inviting children to make connections between reading and writing. *TESOL Journal, 3,* 7–11.

Serna, I., & Hudelson, S. (1993). Emergent Spanish literacy in a whole language bilingual program. In R. Donmoyer & R. Kos (Eds.), *At-risk students: Portraits, policies, programs, and practices* (pp. 291–321). Albany: State University of New York Press.

Shannon, S. (1995). The hegemony of English: A case study of one bilingual classroom as a site of resistance. *Linguistics and Education, 7,* 175–200.

Street, B. (1995). *Social literacies: Critical approaches to literacy in development, ethnography and education.* London: Longman.

Taylor, D. (Ed.). (1998). *Many families, many literacies.* Portsmouth, NH: Heinemann.

Taylor, D., & Dorsey-Gaines, C. (1988). *Growing up literate: Learning from inner-city families.* Portsmouth, NH: Heinemann.

Torres-Guzmán, M. Language, culture, and literacy in Puerto Rican communities. In B. Perez (Ed.), *Sociocultural contexts of language and literacy* (pp. 99–122). Mahwah, NJ: Erlbaum.

Turner, E. (1994). *Emerging bilingualism and biliteracy in a primary, multi-age bilingual classroom.* Unpublished honors thesis, Arizona State University, Tempe, AZ.

Tuyay, S. (1999). Exploring the relationship between literate practices and opportunities for learning. *Primary Voices, 7,* 17–24.

Tuyay, S., Jennings, L., & Dixon, C. (1995). Classroom discourse and opportunities to learn: An ethnographic study of knowledge construction in a bilingual third-grade classroom. *Discourse Processes, 19,* 75–110.

Vélez-Ibañez, C., & Greenberg, J. (1992). Formation and transformation of funds of knowledge among U.S. Mexican households. *Anthropology and Education, 23,* 313–335.

Whitmore, K., & Crowell, C. (1994). *Inventing a classroom: Life in a bilingual, whole language learning community.* York, ME: Stenhouse Publishers.

Wink, J. (1997). *Critical pedagogy: Notes from the real world.* New York: Longman.

Zecker, L., Pappas, C., & Cohen, S. (1997). Finding the "right measure" of explanation for Latina/o writers. *Language Arts, 76,* 49–56.

Part II

PRACTICAL APPLICATIONS

NATIVE LANGUAGE & SECOND LANGUAGE INSTRUCTION

Promoting Early Literacy Development Among Spanish-Speaking Children
Lessons From Two Studies

Claude Goldenberg

How do we improve the literacy attainment of children from Spanish-speaking homes? This is surely one of the most urgent questions U.S. educators face. Children from Latino families are more likely to be poor and have a greater chance of failing in school, achieving lower levels of literacy, falling behind in their learning, and dropping out of school altogether than their English-speaking, nonminority peers. Although some educational trends are modestly encouraging (the proportion of Hispanics who completed 4 years of high school, for example, increased from 46% to 51% in the 1980s; U.S. Bureau of the Census, 1991), Hispanic children nevertheless begin school behind their white, non-Hispanic peers, and the variance increases throughout the grades. Language of instruction is not the issue—or at least, it is not the only issue: These children's academic achievement in early elementary school is the same whether they are in a native-language program (i.e., Spanish bilingual education) or in a structured immersion program using only English (Ramirez, Yuen, & Ramey, 1991).

The rapid growth of the Latino population in the United States suggests that the challenge to the educational system will intensify. Currently at least 2.2 million limited-English-proficient (LEP) students are in U.S. schools (U.S. Department of Education, 1991), with some estimates going much higher (Crawford, 1989). Approximately three-fourths of these students have Spanish as their home language. California alone has more than 750,000 Spanish-speaking, LEP students, and the number is expected to continue rising well into the 21st century (California Department of Education, 1992). By the year 2000, at least 35% of California's students will be Hispanic. Now, more than ever, U.S. schools must try to reverse the pattern of persistent underachievement among this population.

Where to begin? We can make plausible arguments for different intervention points—early childhood (e.g., Lazar, Darlington, Murray, Royce, & Snipper, 1982), the beginning of elementary school, or sometime in middle school (e.g., Stevenson, Chen, & Uttal, 1990). One logical place to begin is where children begin their formal schooling, which in most cases is kindergarten. Although earlier intervention is unquestionably desirable, only one-third of the 3- and 4-year-olds most in need and only 22% of Hispanic 3- and 4-year-olds presently attend preschool in this country (Committee for Economic Development, 1991; National Center for Education Statistics, 1991). In contrast, virtually all children in the United States attend kindergarten; in the case of Hispanics, 93% of Hispanic 5- and 6-year-olds in the United States are enrolled in school (National Center for Education Statistics, 1991). Although there is a growing need to make quality prekindergarten experiences available to all children, we should also consider the plausibility of concentrating efforts from the time schooling is virtually universal, that is, when almost all children enter kindergarten at age 5.

Themes and Assumptions

This article describes the results of two related efforts undertaken in a southern California school district to try to improve the early native-language (i.e., Spanish) literacy attainment of Spanish-speaking children. One project was aimed at improving reading instruction in first and second grade. Several themes—perhaps assumptions is more accurate—run through this article.

The first is that children who come to school speaking a language other than English are better served in programs that capitalize on their native language and use it to promote academic and cognitive development for as long as possible during their school careers. The studies reported here involved helping Spanish-speaking students acquire high levels of literacy achievement in Spanish. Children must of course also acquire high levels of linguistic and academic competence in English, but there is no need to accomplish this by quashing the first language. To the contrary: The first language should be seen as a resource to be nurtured and developed rather than squandered (Crawford, 1989).

Many advocates of bilingual education, of course, argue that high levels of literacy in the home language will also help promote high levels of competence in English. The issue is, to say the least, controversial, with numerous ideological and political questions involved. Evaluations of bilingual education programs are complex and

sometimes contradictory; partly as a consequence, discussions become mired in politics and ideology (see, e.g., Crawford, 1989; Porter, 1990). Nevertheless, counter-intuitive though it might be, use of the home language in school does not appear to interfere with the acquisition of English skills. Instead, use of the home language in school might lead to superior achievement in English and academic content areas, as many bilingual education proponents argue (see, e.g., U.S. General Accounting Office, 1987), and its use certainly leads to higher levels of achievement in the home language (see studies cited in Baker & deKanter, 1981). Ideally, therefore, we should be able to produce bilingual and biliterate students, as many countries around the world do, particularly in the case of children who come from homes where another language is spoken. We are still far from accomplishing this important educational goal, however, and the acrimony, vituperation, and politics of the bilingual education debate make it all the more difficult to reach.

Second, despite differences in English and Spanish orthographic systems (particularly the greater orthographic regularity of Spanish) and differences in various structural aspects of the two languages, learning to read in Spanish is probably very similar to learning to read in English. Both are alphabetic languages with predictable spelling patterns. Perhaps more important, in both Spanish and English the key task for the reader is to associate or construct meaning based on written alphabetic symbols. It

is highly likely, therefore, that the same grapho-psycholinguistic processes will be involved in both languages, and what we know about how to help children acquire literacy in English is probably relevant for helping children acquire literacy in Spanish.

Third, and despite these similarities, Spanish-speaking children learning to read in Spanish in the United States face a far different sociolinguistic context—with respect to both written and oral forms of language—than children learning to read English do. Whereas written texts of many types are easily accessible to the English-speaking child, Spanish speakers have fewer such opportunities, despite the existence of Spanish-language periodicals and books. Far fewer Spanish books, magazines, environmental print, activity books, or alphabet books—which all form an important part of the context for successful literacy development (Teale, 1978)—are available in the United States. Educational programs such as *Sesame Street* offer token segments in Spanish, but again, these literacy learning opportunities are scarce in comparison to the relative abundance of English literacy materials and experiences. Parents with whom I have worked have remarked that they find it virtually impossible to find Spanish children's books or other literacy materials in neighborhood markets, even in an area that has a more than 90% Latino population and with many Latino businesses and grocery stores. Some families either have brought books from Mexico or Central America or have them sent by friends or relatives; but they are exceptions.

Finally, the perspective reflected in this article is that creating effective programs to help at-risk children (or to help any group of children) cannot be seen as merely a matter of implementing research findings at particular sites. As important as research is in helping inform decisions, frame questions, and suggest practices, meaningful educational change can take place only through intensive local efforts that are informed not just by research but also by a detailed understanding of the local site and the local issues framing the thinking of teachers and administrators (Goldenberg & Gallimore, 1989, 1991). Although a discussion of the process of educational change and the relationship between rational, scientific knowledge and school improvement is beyond the scope of this article, the studies described here should be seen within this framework: School improvement requires the constructive but complex interplay of local and research-based knowledge.

It follows, then, that to some extent all findings—including the results of program improvement efforts—are local and of limited generalizability. However, this does not preclude transporting successful models from other sites or learning from successful change efforts at those sites. Indeed, many successful and replicable models exist (see, e.g., National Dissemination Study Group, 1989; Slavin, Karweit, & Madden, 1989), as do teaching practices associated with improved student achieve-

ment; but we are likely to learn more about how to help children at educational risk, whatever the language they speak, if we have an understanding of the processes leading to successful change at particular sites.

Promoting Spanish Literacy in Kindergarten

Our project's efforts to promote early Spanish literacy development in kindergarten began in 1986 when I was teaching first grade in a largely Hispanic, low-income school in metropolitan Los Angeles. The majority of families who send their children to this school are Latino and come from Mexico and Central America. Parents of kindergarten children have been in this country for an average of 9 or 10 years; the range is from 1 to more than 30 years. The highly urban district is in one of the poorest areas of the state, and more than 90% of the children receive free or reduced-price meals at the school.

Prior to teaching first grade I had conducted (at the same school) a study of Spanish-speaking first graders who were at risk for poor reading achievement (Goldenberg, 1989). Then, as a first-grade teacher, I became interested in working with other teachers to find ways to improve early Spanish literacy development. In this effort, I drew from my own research and experiences at the school as well as from previous and ongoing early literacy theory and research (e.g., Anderson, Hiebert, Scott, &

Wilkinson, 1985; Chall, 1983), particularly that pertaining to low-achieving minority children (e.g., Kamehameha Schools, 1983).

Simple Spanish Booklets for Kindergarten Children to Read

During the 1985–1986 school year, a kindergarten teacher colleague with whom I was working closely developed some simple booklets in Spanish for her students to learn to read and then take home and share with parents and other family members. The idea generated considerable controversy at the school. Many of the teachers, including the school's instructional specialists, believed that if literacy was to be emphasized in kindergarten— and even this was controversial—teachers should concentrate on children's learning letters, sounds, and phonics rather than reading or pseudo-reading. Other teachers, however, supported language- and meaning-based attempts to help children acquire more knowledge about the forms and functions of literacy, before setting out to teach them to decode.

Despite the local controversy, the idea of providing young children with simple little books even before they could read in a conventional sense was not new and, indeed, is generally accepted. What was new about these booklets was the language in which they were written and the fact that they were easily reproduced and could be sent home for children to keep. Although in English an abundance of materials provides young children with meaning-oriented early literacy opportunities long before they are reading in a conventional sense—e.g., "Instant Readers" (Martin & Brogan, 1971) and "predictable books" (Heald-Taylor, 1987)—in Spanish, there was and continues to be a dearth of readily available, simple books that Spanish-speaking children can hear, learn, and read before mastering the technical aspects of Spanish orthography.

Making such materials available, we thought, might be important because previous research (and our own experiences) suggested that opportunities to deal with age- and development-appropriate texts—e.g., hearing books read and reading or pseudo-reading books—make significant contributions to young children's literacy development. These opportunities are probably the single most important type of prereading experience young children can have, and children who learn to read easily and successfully often come from homes where they have many such experiences (Anderson et al., 1985; Chall, 1983).

Spanish-speaking children in this country rarely have these opportunities. There is a relative scarcity of books in the homes of many U.S. Latino families, and reading to children is relatively infrequent (e.g., Delgado-Gaitan, 1990; Teale, 1986). Ramirez, Yuen, Ramey, and Merino (1986, p. 207, table 146) report that 22% of the parents of Spanish-speaking kindergartners say that they do not read to their children, whereas in a nationally representative sample of parents

from a range of socioeconomic and ethnic groups, only 4% reported either never reading to their children or reading only several times per year (West, Hausken, & Chandler, 1991). Consequently, Spanish-speaking children probably receive comparatively few opportunities with extended, meaningful texts at home. At school, their beginning literacy experiences are likely to be almost exclusively weighted toward what are sometimes called "bottom-up" processes—learning letters, sounds, and phonics, rather than having the opportunity to read (or pseudo-read) themselves. The highly regular Spanish orthography leads most teachers to assume that learning to read in Spanish is a straightforward matter of learning the code. For these reasons, the kindergarten teacher with whom I worked decided to develop simple little booklets for her students and to encourage children's participation, both at home and at school, in meaning-oriented reading—that is, top-down experiences with print. Because we wanted the children to be able to take these books home and keep them, it was essential that they be inexpensive and easily reproduced.

1986–1987 Pilot Study: Unexpected Results

In 1986–1987, we conducted a pilot study to see whether the teacher-created booklets made any contribution to children's early literacy development. Our objective was not to teach reading per se. Durkin (1974-1975) and Hanson, Siegel, & Broach (1987), for example, had already

found that children could be successfully taught to read before first grade. Moreover, Hanson et al. found small but significant effects of learning to read in kindergarten through the end of high school. Our goal was not to attempt to teach reading in kindergarten but to provide Spanish-speaking children with opportunities for interacting with meaningful print and to gauge the effects of these experiences on early literacy growth and knowledge. We predicted that use of the booklets (*Libritos*) at school and at home would lead to increased knowledge of words (sight words), increased ability to derive meaning from familiar print, transfer of knowledge of familiar letters and words to new words, and, in general, greater readiness to learn to read.

To test our hypotheses, two kindergarten teachers in the school used the booklets with the Spanish-speaking children in their classes, and four others served as controls. The latter used the district's reading readiness program (part of the basal series published by Santillana Publishing Co.), supplemented by various other prereading or reading readiness materials. Our measures of literacy development consisted of two group tests in a multiple-choice format, one locally developed for this project and one published commercially, *La Prueba* (Riverside Publishing Co., 1984). Children were tested in the spring of 1987 by instructional aides at the school who had ample experience with young, Spanish-speaking children. Our results were, in a word, disappointing. The experimental and control groups were essentially identical on both measures.

We discovered, however, that our conclusions were premature. When we took a more careful look at the control classrooms, we realized that they did not constitute one group but were instead two distinct pairs of classrooms. Two of the classrooms were indeed standard district kindergartens. Teachers used the district's readiness program, where children learned to trace lines, follow directions, discriminate shapes, sequence events, and so forth. Children heard stories and books read aloud and engaged in a wide range of age-appropriate and developmental activities. However, children's direct opportunities with text were quite limited—they learned a few letters and sounds (mostly the vowels and a few consonants) and, toward the end of the year, some of the more advanced children could read some syllables. There was a decidedly nonacademic focus in the classrooms; certainly there were no systematic attempts to teach reading. To the contrary, teachers tried to promote children's acquisition of readiness concepts, and they explicitly disavowed an academic focus.

The other two control classrooms, however, had a very different program. These teachers—both native Spanish-speaking Latinas—supplemented the district's readiness program with an intensive academic focus actually designed to teach the children to read. After perhaps 2 to 3 months of readiness activities at the beginning of the school year, they systematically taught the children the vowels and their sounds, followed by

the consonants and their sounds, then how vowels and consonants combine to form syllables (e.g., *ma, me, pu, po*) and words (*mamá, ama, papa, puma*). Through a combination of drills, practice, and independent seat work, these teachers stayed in regular contact with parents and sent daily homework beginning in the first week of school with the child's name. Children were expected to complete the homework with the parents' assistance, if necessary, and return it to school the following day.

Instead of a two-group (experimental vs. control) design, by chance we had three groups: the experimental and two distinct controls. We reanalyzed the data, and a different picture emerged. On both the locally developed test and the published readiness test, there were differences among the three groups. This time, there was an experimental effect when the booklets were compared with the standard, general readiness classrooms. However, the classrooms with the strong and direct academic focus scored highest.

Follow-Up Studies: Comparable Results

Because these results were so strikingly unexpected, we conducted a replication in 1988–1989. This time, we knew from the outset that there would be a three-group comparison, and we sampled six children from each of 10 classrooms: four classes at two different schools using the booklets (experimental), four classes at the same two schools with the district readiness program (true controls), and

the two highly structured, academic classrooms, which were located at the same school where the original pilot work had been done.

We also revised the booklets because we suspected that the first set was too simplistic. The new booklets (12 in all, renamed *Libros*) began as little more than caption books and became progressively more challenging. They also contained many elements that made them predictable (Heald-Taylor, 1987), such as rhyme, rhythm, redundant words and pictures, and repeating sentence patterns. In addition, we developed two other sets of materials to accompany the booklets—activity sheets with drawings and words from the booklets and an alphabet book, which also contained many of the characters from the booklets (see Goldenberg, 1990, for a fuller description).

Finally, in contrast to previous years, when we had not concentrated on children's learning the alphabet, teachers in the experimental classrooms were encouraged to teach children the letters and sounds of the alphabet. This added component was a direct result of the impressive results we witnessed in the two academic kindergartens as well as a response to the accumulating evidence that knowledge of letters and sounds makes a positive contribution to early literacy development (Adams, 1990; Chall, 1983).

Instead of using the published readiness test, we also developed a set of individually administered early literacy measures tapping a range of early literacy skills and knowledge, grouped into two clusters: (1) a test of giving the name and sound of each upper- and lowercase letter (presented out of sequence) and (2) a range of early literacy skills and knowledge, comprising *Concepts About Print* (Clay, 1985; translated into Spanish), comprehension of a story read aloud, identification of rhymes and first syllables, reading phonetically regular words, writing or attempting to write self-selected words, and metalinguistic knowledge about literacy. We also administered the group test of word recognition and sentence comprehension that we had used previously.

For the most part, our results were similar to those of the pilot study: The experimental *Libros* classrooms outperformed the readiness classrooms on the early literacy measures, particularly on the group test of word and sentence reading and on individual subtests of letter names and sounds, identification of first syllables, decoding, and word writing. However, the children from the academic classrooms scored highest on the early literacy measures, except for the letter names and sounds, where scores of the experimental and academic classrooms were essentially the same. There were no differences among the three groups on subtests of oral comprehension, *Concepts About Print*, identification of rhymes, or metalinguistic knowledge about print.

There was another noteworthy difference among the groups. The testers (native-English bilinguals with extensive experience working with language-minority children) rated each child on his or her word reading ability, and the three groups produced strikingly different patterns: 42% of the children in the academic classrooms were rated fluent readers, whereas only 25% and 4% of the children in the *Libros* and readiness classrooms, respectively, received this rating. In contrast, 75% of the readiness children were rated nonreaders, and almost none of the children in the other classrooms (8% in the *Libros*; 0% in the academic) received nonreader ratings.

In retrospect, the results of the 2 years seem hardly surprising; but because we were working within a local framework that rejected didactic teaching of reading in kindergarten, they were unexpected at the time. The teachers in the academic classrooms actually set out to teach children to read—something we had not envisioned, much less attempted. They did it systematically, efficiently, and effectively. They insisted on—and got—a high degree of "buy-in" from parents and children. Their classrooms were highly disciplined, smoothly running operations with an unambiguous academic agenda. Although children heard stories and had opportunities to paint and go to "centers," the clear priority was learning to read, write, count, compute, and acquire other pieces of important academic knowledge and skills.

Moreover, these two highly dynamic teachers—both of whom were from Mexican families and had grown up in the Los Angeles area—put an explicitly cultural spin on their classroom practices. For example, in discussing the strict discipline they employed, one of the teachers rejected the criticism that they were being unduly and inappropriately harsh with the children:

We're not being mean, that's the way their parents talk to them. When I say *¿Dónde están tus orejas?* (Where are your ears?) or *¿Qué, no ves?* (What, can't you see?), it's just an expression. People might say it sounds harsh, but that's just the way we talk. My mother talked to me like that. It's not being mean. (fieldnotes, 3/9/89).

Of course, it is impossible to say to what extent these teachers' success is due to their high degree of cultural sensitivity and awareness or their equally high degree of skill and their commitment to Hispanic children's academic achievement. Perhaps both were factors. What is certain, however, were their very impressive results. Additional evidence came from scores on a nationally normed test of Spanish reading achievement given in the fall of first grade (Spanish Assessment of Basic Education, CTB/McGraw-Hill, 1987). These teachers' students had by far the highest scores in the district—at the 70th percentile, according to national norms. The other kindergartens at the school scored around the 60th percentile; the rest of the kindergarten classes throughout the district scored below the 50th percentile.

Our results to date seemed quite clear: Compared with the standard readiness program used in the district, which afforded children little direct exposure to written texts, the booklets and the accompanying materials seemed to provide literacy learning opportunities that could lead to enhanced early Spanish literacy development. The effects were considerable, with effect sizes approximately .7–.8, meaning that the average student in a *Libros* classroom scored .7 to .8 standard deviations higher than the average student in a readiness classroom. These results were concentrated on knowledge of letters, sounds, and word reading and writing. However, the two academically oriented kindergartens produced even better results, with effect sizes ranging, incredibly, from 1 to 3 standard deviation units, for knowledge of letters, sounds, word reading and writing, and simple reading comprehension, but not on oral comprehension, *Concepts About Print*, or metalinguistic knowledge about print.

Final Study: Effects on Language and Affect

In our final study in this series, we were interested in addressing two issues that had previously received scant attention: The first was whether the use of the *Libros* had any effects on children's language. This is an important question, given the importance of language for ongoing cognitive development and communicative competence (Feagans & Farran, 1982) and the concerns about how schools afford children, particularly low-income, minority children, inadequate opportunities for language use and development. When we began our studies, we had originally predicted that using and sending home these meaningful texts would have an effect not only on written literacy development but also on oral language. Our hypothesis was that use of these books at home would pro-

mote more language use between children and parents, and this would then lead to children's greater facility with "book talk." In the course of our home studies, however, we discovered that the *Libros* did not promote more language and meaning-based interactions at home (Goldenberg, Reese, & Gallimore, 1992). We decided, therefore, to see whether a somewhat enhanced intervention with the *Libros* could produce effects on children's language use and production. To test the effect of the enhanced *Libros* intervention, the experimental classrooms (*Libros*-experimental) included two additional components; the readiness classrooms (*Libros*-control) used and sent home the *Libros*, but without these additional components:

1. Teachers in the *Libros*-experimental classroom were encouraged to provide as many opportunities as possible for children to talk about the booklets (and other books or stories) during school time. Teachers were also given copies of the teacher's manual for an oral language and story comprehension program, Story telling and Retelling (StaR), although we never implemented the program in any formal sense. On two to three occasions during the year, I also went into experimental classrooms and demonstrated a model of teaching known as "instructional conversation" (Goldenberg, 1992–1993), which is specifically designed to encourage children to participate orally in discussion

about written texts.

2. We added a last page to each *Libro* in the experimental condition, suggesting to parents that they read and talk about the booklet with their child. The page contained a number of suggested questions to guide possible conversations between parents and children, such as why the child liked the story. (Teachers later reported they used this page during their own classroom lessons.) The experimental teachers also sent home brief notes two to three times per week for parents, reminding them to read and discuss the booklets (or other reading matter) with their children. Parents signed the notes, and children returned them the next day.

The second issue we addressed in our final study was this: Is there any evidence of negative effects of the academic kindergartens on children's attitudes or dispositions? Many recent statements about appropriate learning environments for young children take a strong stand against many of the practices observed in the more academically oriented classrooms (see, e.g., Early Childhood and Literacy Development Committee, 1986; National Association for the Education of Young Children [NAEYC], 1988). The NAEYC specifically warns that "inappropriate instructional techniques are a source of stress for young children." Inappropriate practices include, for example, teacher-directed reading lessons, dividing the curriculum into discrete subjects such as reading and math, and paper and pencil practice exercises or worksheets that children are expected to complete independently (NAEYC, 1988).

Results of Final Year's Study: Something Old, Something New

As happened the previous year, the experimental *Libros* classrooms scored the highest on letter names and sounds, higher, this time, than the academic classrooms. This probably was due to the emphasis we had placed within the project on helping children acquire knowledge of letters and sounds, which served to reinforce further whatever effects the alphabet books had. Again, as before, on the other literacy measures (which we have subsequently found to correlate .73 with standardized reading achievement at the end of first grade), the academic kindergartens outperformed the other classrooms. Except for learning letters and sounds, the academic classrooms were more successful overall in helping children acquire beginning and early literacy knowledge and skills. There were no differences on the early literacy measures (except for letters and sounds) between the experimental classrooms and the control classrooms, both of which were using the *Libros*, although at different levels of implementation. We had two new findings, however.

To permit us to see whether the enhanced version of the *Libros* intervention had any effect on children's productive language, testers showed each child the cover of a book to be read aloud and asked the child to predict what the story would be about. Children's responses were rated from 0 (no response) to 5 (constructs elaborate narrative), then grouped into two response categories—a lower-level response (no response or names only a character or an action, but not both—e.g., *un niño*, "a boy") and a higher-level response (one or more characters and one or more actions in a string or sequence of events— e.g., "*Un niño va a encontrar a su mamá. Va a comprar algo a su mamá. Zapatos y una cadena. Es su compleaños.*" "A boy is going to find his mother. He is going to buy something for his mother. Shoes and a chain [necklace]. It's her birthday.").

Fifty-two percent of the experimental children gave a higher-level response, while only 24% and 27% of the students in the academic and control booklets classrooms, respectively, provided higher-level responses. When we combined the academic and control booklets classrooms, the contrast in higher-level responses—52% for experimentals vs. 25% for others—was statistically significant ($p < .02$). In other words, children in the experimental classrooms, where we had tried to enhance the *Libros* program to promote more language use and language production by children, were more than twice as likely to make more complex predictions than were the children in the other classrooms.

In a second language measure, after reading the story and asking the child several comprehension questions, testers gave children an overall language rating, from 0 (practically nonverbal) to 3 (quite verbal, fluent, and talkative). We again found a significantly ($p = .05$) different pattern among the groups. Children in the experimental group were approximately three times as likely to receive the highest language rating from the testers (44% for the *Libros* vs. 18% and 14% for the academic and readiness classes, respectively). These results, once again, were consistent with our hypothesis that the enhanced *Libros* treatment, where teachers paid increased attention to oral discussion with the booklets and each booklet contained suggested questions at the back, led to higher language performance by the children. When tested in the fall, the groups had been identical in language and prediction ratings and on the Spanish Bilingual Syntax Measure (Burt, Dulay, & Hernández Ch., 1975), an index of syntactic maturity.

Attitudes Toward Reading and Reading Tests

Finally, results of our inquiry into children's affect and attitudes were also quite clear. Children were first asked (prior to beginning tests) two questions: "Do you like to read (or have someone read to you)?" and "Do you know how to read?" More than 90% said unequivocally that they liked to read or be read to, and there were no differences among the three groups. Children gave more varied responses as to whether they knew how to read. In both the experimental and the academic classrooms, 77%

said they could read or could read a little, while in the booklets control classrooms, 52% said they could read or read a little. The differences were not statistically significant (*p* = .07) but, more important, there was clearly no evidence that the academic classrooms had negative effects on liking to read or attitudes toward self as a reader.

A second gauge of children's affective dispositions was obtained by having testers rate children on three measures (apparent self-confidence, motivation, and enjoyment of literacy tasks) after 2 days of individual testing. The three scales were highly intercorrelated, so they were combined into one reliable rating of affective disposition. There were again no differences among the groups, indicating no negative side effects of the more structured academic program.

Kindergarten Spanish Literacy: Some Concluding Comments

In a number of ways, the results of the kindergarten studies yielded unexpected findings and led us in some unexpected directions. First, we had originally anticipated that providing kindergarten children with home and school literacy experiences with meaningful little booklets would help promote their early literacy development. The emphasis, in other words, was on *providing opportunities* rather than *directly teaching*. Our expectation turned out to be only partly confirmed. Compared with the standard readiness classrooms, the booklets did have an effect. In

several respects, however, our experimental *Libros* and accompanying materials were less effective in promoting literacy than were two structured, academic classrooms where children were directly taught letters, sounds, and how they combined to form words, phrases, and sentences. Two things became clear from the various comparisons of the three studies: Kindergarten children learn more about literacy when they are in classrooms that provide additional and direct opportunities for learning about print. They learn even more when directly taught.

Second, as a result of the consistent findings with the academic classrooms, teachers in the experimental classrooms began to include more direct teaching of letters and sounds. We also developed simple alphabet books that teachers used with children at school and sent home for them to keep and use. Once teachers provided a stronger focus on learning the alphabet, we obtained strong and consistent effects on these measures, as might be expected.

Third, our last study suggested that the booklets, accompanied by appropriate verbal interactions with children, could have some important effects, independent of text-based skills such as reading and writing words, knowing letters and sounds, and so forth. We found that a greater emphasis on discussing the stories, encouraging children to talk about them, and including questions at the back that parents and teachers could use in talking about the books had an effect on children's language production.

Finally, this series of studies

suggests there is some basis for rethinking current trends away from academic learning in kindergarten. Although the entire early childhood education establishment appears unanimous in its condemnation of teaching academic skills before first grade, one of the unexpected findings from this series of studies was that children might actually benefit from academic learning and direct nonacademic teaching—if it is skillfully done. Certainly, children's early literacy skills were enhanced in the highly academic classrooms, and there was no evidence whatever of negative socioemotional consequences (Hanson et al., 1987, report similar findings on children they followed to high school). In fact, we have at least anecdotal evidence of positive socioemotional effects on the enhanced academic competence these children experienced. During the 1989 spring testing, one of the testers (who was unaware of the issues and hypothesis in the study) wrote in her notes that the children in these two classrooms "seem quite advanced over [the others tested]—maybe 1 year. Not only did they know much more but their affect was much more positive, i.e., initiated conversation, smiled, appeared higher energy and more confident" (tester fieldnotes, 6/89).

Although I am not necessarily making a case for academic kindergartens, I am suggesting that the current, mainstream revulsion at teaching academic skills to 5-year-olds merits reexamination, particularly when there is evidence that children can benefit from such learning while suffering no adverse side effects. A lot depends on the teaching and the context in which academic learning is expected to take place. The last words go to one of the two teachers in the academic kindergartens, who confounded some of my most cherished assumptions about early literacy development:

Teachers think these kids are so deprived we need to let them play all day here. That really makes me mad because I came from a background like this. [Teachers use assumptions about children's backgrounds] to allow letting kids play all day rather than taking responsibility for teaching them what they need to know so they can be academically successful. These kids can learn, but they have to be taught. If more teachers realized this and did what they were supposed to do, more of these kids would go on to college. (fieldnotes, 8/31/89)

Spanish Literacy Development in First and Second Grades

The next part of the project related to improvement of Spanish reading by first and second graders in the same school where the kindergarten study described previously began—a largely Hispanic elementary school in southern California (see Goldenberg & Gallimore, 1991). As with the kindergarten studies, our project's efforts to improve native-language literacy attainment in grades 1 and 2 also began when I was teaching first grade at the school. This first- and second-grade effort was important because it represented an attempt to extend improved literacy learning opportunities in kindergarten on into early elementary school. Previous studies suggest that preschool literacy gains tend to disappear by mid-elementary school if early elementary programs do not extend and build upon achievement prior to first grade (e.g., Durkin, 1974–1975; however, see also Hanson et al., 1987, which challenges this assertion). We were therefore interested in finding ways to produce high levels of native-language reading development on into the early years of elementary school.

This effort is also significant because it illustrates one of the themes of this article: Successful change did not result from the direct application or implementation of research findings to a particular school site. Instead, it was the result of long-term, cumulative work informed by an understanding of local issues and circumstances, no less than by an awareness of issues and findings generated from research. In many respects, as with the kindergarten studies, the original model envisioned was not the one that eventually emerged. For example, the original emphasis of my efforts to improve early reading achievement assumed that a focus on meaning would essentially displace instruction on letters, sounds, and syllables. This turned out not to be the case, however, and what eventually evolved was a balanced early literacy program where meaning coexisted more or less peacefully with letters, sounds, and syllables.

In fact, a set of fundamental changes evolved in several domains of the early reading program, one of which has already been described for kindergarten. These changes altered considerably the achievement patterns among Spanish-speaking first and second graders at the school. The changes can be grouped into four categories: (1) literacy opportunities in kindergarten; (2) a balanced emphasis on meaning and decoding in first grade; (3) increased home and parent involvement; and (4) improved pacing of instruction.

Changes in School Literacy Program

Increased Attention to Literacy in Kindergarten

The school's kindergarten program went from a readiness orientation prior to 1985 to one that 2 years later placed more emphasis on literacy learning opportunities for children. This was partly the result of the kindergarten studies described previously. Teacher turnover and the arrival of new kindergarten faculty and other personnel also contributed to the shift. The two academically oriented kindergarten teachers transferred from another school and brought with them an explicitly academic focus. On the one hand, this created some tensions with a faculty that was not academically oriented, particularly for kindergarten. On the other hand, it contributed to the emergence of a critical mass of teachers and administrators who shared, at least in this respect, a commitment to changing the early literacy emphasis at the school.

Considerable controversy remained about the early reading curriculum, as reflected by the different orientations of teachers in our kindergarten studies. The controversy mirrored many of the debates in early childhood education; however, the issue was no longer whether kindergarten should include literacy learning opportunities. Instead, the question was what kinds of literacy learning opportunities should kindergartners have? The topic of kindergarten literacy, which previously had been associated with an excessively academic orientation that most of the faculty and administration explicitly rejected, became legitimate, in part, because there were different ways teachers could make literacy opportunities available to children. Although the more explicitly academic classrooms continued to produce the highest levels of achievement, the overall levels and expectations for all kindergarten children at the school shifted considerably. This shift signaled a widespread acceptance at the school that (1) kindergarten children were more capable and ready than most people realized, (2) under the right circumstances they could learn a great deal about print and how it functions, and (3) the school had an important role to play in the children's early literacy development.

Balanced Emphasis on Meaning and the Code in First Grade

Spanish reading instruction tends to be excessively weighted toward a phonics-based, bottom-up approach. The predominant focus is on having children learn two-letter syllables comprising a consonant and a vowel, which constitute the basis for Spanish orthography. As a result, early literacy learning experiences that Spanish-speaking children have in school are often decontextualized and divorced from meaning. Prior to the changes described here, first-grade teachers at the school required children to learn all of the syllables made from the five vowels and the consonants *m, p, t,* and *l* before they could progress in the reading series and begin to read even the briefest meaningful texts.

This focus is potentially of greatest harm to children who have relatively few authentic literacy opportunities outside of school. For some children at the school, especially those who made the slowest progress in learning letters and sounds, reading instruction consisted primarily of games, drills, and various activities focusing on the sounds letters make and how letters combine to form syllables. Throughout first grade, these students had few opportunities to read meaningful texts, phrases, or, in some cases, even words. Even after children got over the hurdle of the syllables, little instruction focused on understanding or deriving meaning from written texts. In a word, the first-grade reading program was unidimensional in the extreme, and the results were very low levels of reading achievement and very slow progress through the reading curriculum.

Gradually, beginning in 1985, meaningful reading began to infiltrate into first-grade reading instruction. For example, short, simple stories—either copied from a book or generated through a language experience approach—were written on charts, and children read and discussed them as whole texts. These activities proved to be valuable, even—perhaps especially—with groups of children that had previously experienced only endless rounds of phonic and syllable drills and exercises. Children learned to read the chart stories through a variety of bottom-up and top-down processes. Individual stories were then copied, and children began to accumulate folders of little stories they could read, take home, illustrate, and so forth. More materials were also introduced, in the form of workbooks and worksheets, that contained more connected text for children to read.

More emphasis on meaning and comprehension also resulted from some informal testing conducted at the school, which revealed that if children were directly taught comprehension skills such as selecting the best title for a simple passage, their performance improved dramatically. Teachers then began to devote more attention to teaching such skills, thereby reinforcing a greater emphasis on the meaning of texts, but also teaching skills that children needed in order to pass end-of-book tests. More attention to meaning might also have resulted from numerous discussions I had with colleagues and several presentations I made about early literacy.

Teachers gradually went from an excessively narrow conception of reading and reading instruction to a broader one, where meaning and reading connected text played more prominent roles. One teacher, in fact, who served on a faculty committee considering reading instruction at the school, successfully argued for a reduced emphasis on phonics as the only means for providing children with literacy learning opportunities. As with the kindergarten program, reading in first grade underwent important changes between 1985 and 1987. Children began reading more connected text, and teachers began to target specific comprehension skills. Phonics and syllables were not banished from the curriculum, but they became part of a more balanced program where children received a wide range of literacy learning opportunities.

Increased Home and Parent Involvement

Prior to 1985, first-grade teachers did not regularly enlist or contact parents to help their children academically. When teachers did contact parents, it was generally for discipline problems. Teachers generally held assumptions that tended to work against promoting the sort of parental involvement that might help children's academic achievement, e.g., parents needed a great deal of training before they could help their children, parents were largely illiterate and deemphasized academic achievement in favor of family or sur-

vival values, families were under such economic stress they could not play a meaningful role in children's academic development, or literacy in the home was not a part of the families' culture.

However, research in the school and community suggested that these assumptions were largely inaccurate. For example, children's homes were not devoid of literacy. Although the overall educational levels of parents were indeed low, they had at least rudimentary reading skills, and many actually read at much higher levels. Similarly, although literacy did not occupy a prominent place in many of the homes, neither was it entirely absent. Virtually all homes sent and received letters to relatives in Mexico or Central America; all received printed flyers or advertisements; most parents reported (and subsequent studies have confirmed) that children consistently asked about signs, other environmental print, or the contents of letters to or from relatives, none of which would be possible if literacy did not exist in the homes at least at some level. Perhaps most important, parents placed great value on educational achievement and its importance for social and economic mobility. One mother, for example, told me this:

> *Uno puede abrirse camino teniendo muchos estudios. En cambio así, uno tiene que andar limpiando, pidiendo de gata porque no puede uno hacer otra cosa.* (If you've studied a lot, you can open up opportunities for yourself. Otherwise, you have to clean houses or ask for handouts because you don't know how to do anything else.) (Goldenberg

& Gallimore, 1991, p. 9)

Other parents explicitly pointed to their own situations as a kind of negative example for their children: *"Nosotros no estudiamos, y mírenos aquí"* ("We didn't study, and look at us here"), one father responded, when asked why he wanted his child to continue with his schooling.

Although doubts continued to persist among teachers about parents' willingness or ability to help their children academically, gradually a new set of practices emerged. Reading books and other literacy materials began to be sent home regularly. In kindergarten, as we have seen, teachers gave children various materials or literacy-related activities to take home and complete, usually with the help or supervision of parents. In other classrooms, teachers sent more conventional homework, such as materials on which children were to practice writing their names or letters of the alphabet.

The textbook policy—which previously did not permit books to be taken home—was changed, and in first grade, reading books and other materials for practice and enrichment began to go home on a regular basis. In all classrooms there was much more emphasis than ever before on having children read at home, which prior research has shown helps improve reading achievement (e.g., Tizard, Schofield, & Hewison, 1982). Teachers also used a number of simple techniques to facilitate practice and reinforcement at home, such as easily reproducible forms where teachers or students wrote down home assignments. Another technique was a cumulative word list, to which key words from reading books were gradually added over a period of weeks.

In this area, too, the successful practices that eventually evolved were not entirely consistent with my original expectations. Previous research suggested that increased opportunities to interact with print at home should promote higher levels of reading achievement (e.g., Anderson et al., 1985; Teale, 1978). Consistent with this and with my previous studies at the school, I hypothesized that providing parents with the appropriate information—suggestions that they read to children, take them to the library, and engage them in various everyday learning activities—would lead to substantial improvements in achievement. Accordingly, at the beginning of each school year, I met with parents to provide them with this information and other information about what children would be learning at school.

Parents were interested and supportive, but there was little evidence that the mere provision of information had a strong effect on home literacy practices or on achievement. We found, instead, that it was important to follow up regularly in the form of homework assignments, of the sort just described, or notes or phone calls home. When we systematically extended children's learning experiences outside school—by sending home books and other materials on a regular basis and consistently monitoring and following through—achievement started to improve.

Improved Pacing of First-Grade Spanish Reading Instruction

In general, and net of other effects, the more material students have an opportunity to learn, the more they are likely to learn (see review in Goldenberg & Gallimore, 1991). The issue of pacing is significant, particularly for lower-achieving students, since these are the students for whom teachers are most likely to slow down the pace of instruction inappropriately, thereby greatly reducing children's opportunities to learn additional and more challenging material (Leinhardt & Bickel, 1989).

At the end of the 1983–1984 school year, no one at the school expected children to proceed through the reading curriculum according to publishers' norms. The staff made a sharp distinction between the publishers' norms and what was reasonable to expect at the school with this population. Children were considered on grade level if they completed and mastered the material in the second of three first-grade preprimers. Exceedingly slow progress through the reading curriculum thus did not alarm anyone. The widespread, not unreasonable, assumption was that, as one teacher said, "You have to take the kids from where they are" and get them as far as possible. Although in theory this made perfect sense, in practice it led to passivity in the face of low achievement levels. This passivity then reinforced very low expectations, which, in turn, further reinforced the absence of any need to do things differently.

Not surprisingly, in 1984, nearly one-half (49%) of the first-grade Spanish readers were still in the first of three first-grade preprimers at year's end, and only 7% were at grade level, that is, reading in a book that was at least minimally appropriate and sufficiently challenging for children who had been in school since kindergarten. However, 3 years later, at the end of the 1986–1987 school year, the situation was exactly the reverse, and more than 45% of the students were in the final preprimer at the end of first grade with only about 10% in the first one. The following year, the situation had improved even more, with nearly 25% of the first graders reading in a second-grade book, and only 1% still in the first preprimer.

One reason for the improved pacing in the reading curriculum was that the principal and one of the instructional specialists had instituted pacing conferences during the 1986–1987 school year. Each teacher met individually with a specialist to discuss the progress that children were making in math, reading, and language. The specialist reported that although at first some teachers expressed some discomfort with this new procedure, the conferences had been beneficial in helping teachers keep in mind the bigger picture, that academic achievement was an ongoing developmental process.

To a significant degree, the improvement in pacing cannot be seen as independent of the other changes already mentioned—the earlier start in literacy learning during kindergarten; the more balanced, substantive approach to reading instruction in first grade; and systematic, regular efforts to involve children's homes and parents in their early literacy achievement. In fact, the dramatically changed picture of student progress in the reading program, as suggested by the data on first-grade book placement at the end of the year, is best understood as the result of the several factors identified here working in concert. Children were learning earlier and learning more about literacy, both in and out of school. Teachers were able to challenge children more, yet appropriately. As a result, there was no longer any need—whether real or perceived—to spend weeks and months in endless rounds of phonic and syllabic drilling. Improved pacing was thus more than a vacuous exercise in turning textbook pages faster, and it was as much an effect of improved achievement as it was a cause.

Effects on Reading Achievement, 1985–1989

What have been the effects of these changes on the early reading achievement of Benson's Spanish readers? To answer this question, we analyzed second- and third-grade test results in Spanish. Achievement tests are administered within the first weeks of school, so student scores presumably reflect previous years' learning. (Demographic changes and grade retentions around the district were also analyzed to rule out the possibility that achievement changes were due to these extraneous factors.)

We found very clear evidence of improvement in reading achievement at the school, both over time and in relation to the other schools in the district. Between 1986 and 1987, CTBS-Español reading scores in the beginning of second grade increased by 20 percentile points, from the 33rd to the 53rd percentile. Scores at the other schools remained essentially unchanged during these years. It is particularly worth noting that whereas in 1985 and 1986 Benson was below the other schools in second-grade Spanish achievement, beginning in 1987, Benson scores became—and remained—higher than those at the other schools in the district.

Third-grade achievement scores demonstrate a similar pattern. Until 1986, third graders at the school, just like the second graders, scored considerably below those in the rest of the district. Again, beginning in 1987, third-grade scores improved both in absolute and in relative terms. The differences in 1987 and 1988 between Benson students' scores and those of the rest of the district are not as large as in second grade. Not until 1989—when they surpassed the 50th percentile on national norms—did they reach statistical significance. The more modest changes in third-grade achievement, in 1987 and 1988, suggest an indirect, or spillover, effect from some of the changes that had occurred in the lower grades. The substantial changes in 1989 scores, however, are probably the results of direct efforts to improve the substance and focus of literacy instruction in second grade. These efforts were an outgrowth of some of the changes described previously, and they represented an explicit attempt to expand the scope of previous work at the school (see Gallimore & Goldenberg, 1989).

Reading achievement improved across the range, but particularly among the lowest-achieving children. The rise in mean scores, in other words, was not simply the result of accelerating the learning of higher-achieving students. At both grades 2 and 3, students' scores at the 10th, 25th, and 50th percentiles were above those of the national sample at those percentile levels. At the 75th and 90th percentiles, second-grade students' scores were virtually indistinguishable from those of the national sample. In third grade, the higher scores dropped off in relation to national norms. At all levels, however, students at the school scored considerably higher than those in the rest of the district (Goldenberg & Gallimore, 1991).

Promoting and Sustaining the Literacy Development of Spanish-Speaking Students

For perhaps understandable reasons, language *use* and language *instruction* have dominated research and policy considerations in the education of Spanish-speaking children. Yet given the patterns of achievement among Hispanic children—whether taught in English or Spanish—there are clearly many more issues involved.

To be sure, language is important: When and how should the native language be used; when and how should English be introduced; should the native language be phased out once children can benefit from English instruction; does learning that took place in the first language then transfer and become accessible in the second language; if so, what transfers and what doesn't? Each of these language-oriented questions is important in its own right, and, to one degree or another, they have received the attention of practitioners and scholars (e.g., California State Department of Education, 1984; Cummins, 1979; Goldman & Trueba, 1987; Wong Fillmore & Valadez, 1986).

A focus on language is not enough, however. Even the most enlightened *language* policy will falter in the context of an ineffective *instructional* program. Yet little attention has focused on the larger issues of school and classroom effectiveness in bilingual education, independent of language matters. I will close by briefly addressing two of these.

Early Reading Instruction in Spanish

One set of issues that must be examined very closely has to do with Spanish-language reading instruction and the literacy learning opportunities we provide Spanish-speaking children. Although attaining high levels of native-language literacy is central to the theory of bilingual education (e.g., Krashen & Biber, 1988; Wong Fillmore & Valadez, 1986), with rare exceptions (e.g., Edelsky, 1986; Goldenberg &

Gallimore, 1991), Spanish language literacy has received very little attention from researchers in this country. Research and descriptions of practice do exist, of course, in Spanish-speaking countries (e.g., Ferreiro & Teberosky, 1982; *Lectura y vida*, a journal published by the International Reading Association), but the different literacy context for the Spanish-speaking child in an English-speaking country might make even this literature problematic for U.S. Spanish-language educators. One clear implication, therefore, is that intensive efforts are needed to develop effective instructional models to help children acquire high levels of literacy knowledge and skills in Spanish.

Results of the studies described here suggest that the provision of increased literacy learning opportunities, both at home and at school, will have a positive effect on Spanish-speaking children's literacy development. Contrary to many professionals' assumptions that these children are generally not ready to learn about literacy when they enter school, we found that they are indeed able and willing learners. As to what kinds of early literacy opportunities are most beneficial, the kindergarten studies described earlier suggest that a strong emphasis on learning letters, sounds, and how they combine to form syllables and meaningful words—that is, a code emphasis—gave kindergarten children an early and valuable start in learning to become literate. This finding is consistent with findings based on research with

English-speaking populations (Adams, 1990; Chall, 1983). A code emphasis might be especially pertinent and useful in Spanish, due to the greater orthographic regularity; or, alternatively, because of the relative transparency of Spanish orthography, a code emphasis might be misplaced. Children might instead benefit more from a well-conceived and implemented-meaning-based approach in which, essentially, they decipher the code for themselves. The results of our studies seem to lend support to the first hypothesis, but clearly these questions warrant investigation and empirical testing. In any event, experiences other than code-based ones are also important for literacy development. We found that reading and discussing stories probably produced effects on children's oral language production, at least as gauged by our simple assessments.

In first grade, a reading program that combines continued learning of letters and sounds, and how they combine to form syllables and words, together with adequate opportunities for reading (and writing) meaningful and extended texts at school and at home, seemed to help children achieve at higher levels than before. However, what this combination should be—in other words, what the optimum balance is between, on the one hand, learning the code and other technical skills and, on the other, reading for meaning and communicative purposes—is another matter. Again, this seems like a fruitful area for continued research and reflective practice.

Through happenstance, I

arrived at a balance in my own teaching that seemed very useful. In my final 2 years at the school, I taught half-time and shared my classroom with a teacher who was code-oriented in contrast to my meaning-based approach. We decided that on the days when she taught, she would emphasize the letters and syllables featured in the lessons or stories that the children were learning. On the days when I taught, I focused on language, meaning, comprehension, and real reading. It was an uneasy alliance at first, but eventually, this 50–50 split seemed to work very effectively. Both of us believed that we had the most successful classes we had ever taught.

Beyond the beginning stages of reading, even less is known about the conditions for promoting sustained reading growth in the native language. Research and theory suggest that the tasks and nature of reading change as children develop as readers (Chall, 1983). Whereas in the early stages of learning to read, a certain emphasis on learning the code supports reading development, the focus of reading experiences beyond this early stage must shift if reading development is to continue. In what Chall calls Stage 2 of reading development (typically, late second and early third grades), children need a great many opportunities to read familiar books and stories in order to confirm and consolidate their knowledge about print and its conventions. In Stage 3 (beginning around fourth grade), there must be more of an emphasis on reading to learn, rather than on learning to read. Expository

prose and the learning of new ideas, facts, and concepts from print become more important, and children require opportunities to read and learn from more complex, challenging, and less familiar materials. It is likely that native-language literacy—even in a non-native-language context—develops in a similar way. Again, it is an area that would benefit from systematic examination by teachers and researchers alike.

Creating Contexts for Change

Finally, we need to consider the larger context within which any instructional or curricular program must exist. Research during the past 20 years has consistently documented the positive effects of certain school contexts on the achievement of at-risk populations, independent of particular teaching methodologies (e.g., Bliss, Firestone, & Richards, 1991; Lucas, Henze, & Donato, 1990). This body of research has identified a number of characteristics that differentiated more and less effective schools, e.g., strong instructional leadership, high expectations for student achievement, a safe and orderly learning environment, an emphasis on basic skills, continuous monitoring of student progress, and clear and well-understood school goals (Davis & Thomas, 1989).

Clearly, this literature represents a potentially useful knowledge base to help practitioners create conditions in schools that will support meaningful and substantive change. Valuable as it is, effective schools' research is limited in its utility since it is large-

ly retrospective. We know, in other words, that a number of factors distinguish more and less successful schools. With few exceptions (e.g., Peterson & Lezotte, 1991), however, we seem to have little knowledge of the transformation process from its inception—that is, how less successful schools came to be more successful.

This dearth of direct evidence is particularly glaring for schools serving language-minority populations. Ronald Gallimore and I reported a case study of a single school serving a largely Spanish-speaking population and how the early native-language literacy program went from being less to more effective (Goldenberg & Gallimore, 1991). Even here the scope of the study was very limited, dealing only with native-language reading achievement in grades 1 and 2. No study has examined how an entire school serving a substantially Latino population has gone from ineffective to effective with respect to student learning and achievement. In the context of the rapidly growing Latino population and the persistent under-achievement among these students, this is a glaring gap.

There are apparently successful models, however, and no doubt other schools are attempting to replicate successful practices elsewhere. Krashen and Biber (1988) report a number of successful bilingual programs. Crawford (1989) also describes a number of bilingual education success stories, the results of a project ("Case Studies in Bilingual Education") initiated by the California State Department of Education. It would seem extremely useful to attempt to implement these or other models, then to document prospectively the processes schools undergo as they attempt to deal more effectively with the educational challenges they face.

We need, in short, intensive local efforts to improve achievement schoolwide and case studies documenting this effort. Shulman (1986, p.11) has argued for the importance of knowledge of specific, well-documented and richly described events as an important component of a professional and theoretical knowledge base. Although context-free research that sets out to test propositions has produced a great deal of useful and important knowledge, the value of cases, according to Shulman, derives from how they can illuminate complex, multifaceted phenomena in particular contexts. Creating school contexts to improve the academic achievement of language-minority children—indeed, to improve academic achievement under any circumstances—is an example of such complex, multifaceted phenomena. We cannot lose sight of this complexity and the serious challenges it poses to practitioners.

This article is a revised version of a paper presented at the symposium *Teaching children to read: The state of early interventions*, American Educational Research Association, San Francisco, CA, April 1992. The research reported here was made possible by a Spencer Fellowship from the National Academy of Education and a subsequent grant from the Spencer Foundation. My thanks to the children, teachers, parents, and colleagues who made this work possible. Special thanks to Ronald Gallimore.

REFERENCES

Adams, M. (1990). *Beginning to read: Thinking and learning about print.* Cambridge, MA: MIT Press.

Anderson, R.C., Hiebert, E.H., Scott, J.A., & Wilkinson, I.A.G. (1985). *Becoming a nation of readers.* Champaign, IL: Center for the Study of Reading, University of Illinois.

Baker, K., & deKanter, A. (1981). *Effectiveness of bilingual education: A review of the literature.* Washington, DC: U.S. Department of Education, Office of Planning, Budget and Evaluation.

Bliss, J., Firestone, W., & Richards, C. (Eds.). (1991). *Rethinking effective schools: Research and practice.* Englewood Cliffs, NJ: Prentice Hall.

Burt, M., Dulay, H., & Hernández Ch., E. (1975). *Bilingual syntax measure.* New York: Harcourt Brace Jovanovich.

California State Department of Education. (1984). *Studies in immersion.* Sacramento, CA: Author.

California State Department of Education. (1992). *BEOutreach, 3* (1), 17.

Chall, J. (1983). *Stages of reading development.* New York: McGraw-Hill.

Clay, M (1985). *The early detection of reading difficulties* (3rd ed.). Portsmouth, NH: Heinemann.

Committee for Economic Development. (1991). *The unfinished agenda: A new vision for child development and education.* New York: Author.

Crawford, J. (1989). *Bilingual education: History, politics, theory, and practice.* Trenton, NJ: Crane.

CTB/McGraw-Hill. (1987). *SABE: Spanish Assessment of Basic Education.* Monterey, CA: Author.

Cummins, J. (1979). Linguistic interdependence and the educational development of bilingual children. *Review of Educational Research, 49*, 222–251.

Davis, G.A., & Thomas, M.A. (1989). *Effective schools and effective teachers*. Boston: Allyn & Bacon.

Delgado-Gaitan, C. (1990). *Literacy for empowerment*. New York: Falmer.

Durkin, D. (1974–1975). A six-year study of children who learned to read in school at the age of four. *Research Quarterly, 10*, 9–61.

Early Childhood and Literacy Development Committee. (1986). IRA position statement on reading and writing in early childhood. *Reading Teacher, 39*, 819–821.

Edelsky, C. (1986). *Writing in a bilingual program: Había una vez*. Norwood, NJ: Ablex.

Feagans, L., & Farran, D. (Eds.). (1982). *The language of children reared in poverty: Implications for evaluation and intervention*. New York: Academic Press.

Ferreiro, E., & Teberosky, A. (1982). *Literacy before schooling*. Portsmouth, NH: Heinemann.

Gallimore, R., & Goldenberg, C. (1989). *Action research to increase Hispanic students' exposure to meaningful text: A focus on reading and content area instruction*. Final report to Presidential Grants for School Improvement Committee, University of California.

Goldenberg, C. (1992–1993). Instructional conversations: Promoting comprehension through discussion. *Reading Teacher, 46*, 316–326.

Goldenberg, C. (1990a). Making success a more common occurrence for children at risk for failure: Lessons from Hispanic first graders learning to read. In J. Allen & J.M. Mason (Eds.), *Risk makers, risk takers, risk breakers: Reducing the risks for young literacy learners* (pp. 48–78). Portsmouth, NH: Heinemann.

Goldenberg, C. (1990b). Beginning literacy instruction for Spanish-speaking children. *Language Arts, 67*, 590–598.

Goldenberg, C., & Gallimore, R. (1991). Local knowledge, research knowledge, and educational change: A case study of first-grade Spanish reading improvement. *Educational Researcher, 20* (8), 2–14.

Goldenberg, C., & Gallimore, R. (1989, Autumn). Teaching California's diverse student population: The common ground between educational and cultural research. *California Public Schools Forum, 3*, 41–56.

Goldenberg, C., Reese, L., & Gallimore, R. (1992). Effects of school literacy materials on Latino children's home experiences and early reading achievement. *American Journal of Education, 100*, 497–536.

Goldman, S., & Trueba, H. (Eds.). (1987). *Becoming literate in English as a second language*. Norwood, NJ: Ablex.

Hanson, R., Siegel, D., & Broach, D. (1987, April). *The effects on high school seniors of learning to read in kindergarten*. Paper presented at the annual meeting of the American Educational Research Association, Washington, DC.

Heald-Taylor, G. (1987). Predictable literature selections and activities for language arts instruction. *Reading Teacher, 41*, 1–12.

Kamehameha Schools. (1983). *Kamehameha Educational Research Institute list of publications*. Honolulu, HI: Author.

Krashen, S., & Biber, D. (1988). *On course: Bilingual education's success in California*. Sacramento, CA: California Association for Bilingual Education.

Lazar, I., Darlington, R., Murray, H., Royce, J., & Snipper, A. (1982). *Lasting effects of early education: A report from the Consortium for Longitudinal Studies. Monographs of the Society for Research in Child Development, 47*, 1–51.

Leinhardt, G., & Bickel, W. (1989). Instruction's the thing: Wherein to catch the mind that falls behind. In R. Slavin (Ed.), *School and classroom organization* (pp. 197–226). Hillsdale, NJ: Erlbaum.

Lucas, T., Henze, R., & Donato, R. (1990). Promoting the success of Latino language-minority students: An exploratory study of six high schools. *Harvard Educational Review, 60*, 315–340.

Martin, B., & Brogan, P. (1971). *Instant Readers teachers' guide, level 1*. New York: Holt, Rinehart and Winston.

National Association for the Education of Young Children. (1988). *Appropriate education in the primary grades*. Washington, DC: National Association for the Education of Young Children.

National Center for Education Statistics. (1991). *Digest of Education Statistics, 1990*. Washington, DC: U.S. Department of Education.

National Dissemination Study Group. (1989). *Educational programs that work* (15th ed.). Longmont, CO: Sopris West.

Peterson, K., & Lezotte, L. (1991). New directions in the effective schools movement. In J. Bliss, W. Firestone, & C. Richards (Eds.), *Rethinking effective schools: Research and practice* (pp. 128–137). Englewood Cliffs, NJ: Prentice Hall.

Porter, R. (1990). *Forked tongue: The politics of bilingual education*. New York: Basic Books.

Ramirez, D., Yuen, S., & Ramey, D. (1991). *Final report: Longitudinal study of structured English immersion strategy, early-exit and late-exit transitional bilingual education programs for language-minority children* (executive summary). San Mateo, CA: Aguirre International.

Ramirez, D., Yuen, S., Ramey, D., & Merino, B. (1986). *First year report: Longitudinal study of immersion programs for language-minority children*. San Mateo, CA: Aguirre International.

Riverside Publishing Co. (1984). *La Prueba Riverside de Realización en Español*. Chicago: Author.

Shulman, L.S. (1986). Those who understand: Knowledge growth in teaching. *Educational Researcher, 15* (2), 4–14.

Slavin, R., Karweit, N., & Madden, N. (Eds.). (1989). *Effective programs for students at risk*. Boston: Allyn & Bacon.

Stevenson, H., Chen, C., & Uttal, D. (1990). Beliefs and achievement: A study of black, white, and Hispanic children. *Child Development, 61*, 508–523.

Teale, W. (1986). Home background and young children's literacy development. In W.H. Teale & E. Sulzby (Eds.), *Emergent literacy: Writing and reading* (pp. 173–206). Norwood, NJ: Ablex.

Teale, W. (1978). Positive environments for learning to read: What studies of early readers tell us. *Language Arts, 55*, 922–932.

Tizard, J., Schofield, W.N., & Hewison, J. (1982). Collaboration between teachers and parents in assisting children's reading. *British Journal of Educational Psychology, 52*, 1–15.

U.S. Bureau of the Census. (1991, October). *The Hispanic population in the United States: March 1991*. Current Population Reports, Series P-20, No. 455. Washington, DC: U.S. Government Printing Office.

U.S. Department of Education. (1991). *The condition of bilingual education: A report to the Congress and the President*. Washington, DC: U.S. Government Printing Office.

U.S. General Accounting Office. (1987, March). *Bilingual education: A new look at the research evidence* (PEMD-87-12BR). Washington, DC: General Accounting Office.

West, J., Hausken, E., & Chandler, K. (1991). *Home activities of 3-to-8-year-olds: Findings from the 1991 National Household Education Survey*. Washington, DC: National Center for Education Statistics.

Wong Fillmore, L., with Valadez, C. (1986). Teaching bilingual learners. In M. Wittrock (Ed.), *Handbook of research on teaching* (3rd ed.), (pp. 648–685). New York: Macmillan.

Spanish Language, Literacy, and Cognition: Keys to Students' Success

Juan R. Lira

Receptive and expressive communication are central to a successful school experience for all students. Successful communication enables students to make sense of instruction and to communicate their thoughts in clear and meaningful ways. These issues seem especially important when considering the needs of English Language Learners (ELLs). Among the most hotly debated issues surrounding this topic is the role of the first language in helping these students eventually to become literate not only in their first language but in the English language as well.

After an exhaustive review of the related literature and following an in-depth analysis of school districts implementing different programmatic alternatives to help ELLs acquire literacy skills in English, Thomas and Collier (1997) concluded that learning experiences provided through the students' native language played a significant role in determining students' future academic success. They found that "students who arrived between the ages of 8 and 11, who had received at least 2–5 years of schooling taught through their primary language (L1) in their home country, were the lucky ones who took only 5–7 years" (p. 33) to acquire sufficient academic English. Krashen (1999a), on the basis of a critical review of related literature, also indicates that content acquired through the use of the first lan-

guage helps to make it comprehensible when it is encountered in English. Krashen further emphasizes the notion that literacy in the first language facilitates literacy development in the second language (L2).

The insights set forth by Krashen and by Thomas and Collier support the notion that the greater the students' cognitive and academic language proficiency in the first language, the faster they tend to progress in their second language. Cummins (1981) explains this phenomenon through the common underlying proficiency hypothesis. In essence, the conceptual and language development achieved through instruction in the students' first language serve as cognitive anchor points for continued learning in English. The interdependent nature of students' bilingual language skills enables them to use their insights into language and communication to understand and express themselves in both their primary language and the second language (e.g., English).

Given the unique importance of language, literacy, and cognitive development in a student's first language, it seems useful to explore how appropriate instructional resources, coupled with developmentally appropriate pedagogical practices, can promote this type of growth among these students. To accomplish this goal, specific attention will be given in this article to the following issues: access to developmentally appropriate books; matching students with appropriate books; provision of adequate time and an appropriate environment to listen to, read, and share ideas concerning books; and different ways to develop students' comprehension.

Not all the research cited in this article deals specifically with Spanish literacy; some of it has been conducted in English literacy settings. Nonetheless, its incorporation was deemed appropriate because of the apparent similarities that English and Spanish literacy share. Goldenberg (1994) has addressed the point specifically by stating:

> Learning to read in Spanish is probably very similar to learning to read in English. Both are alphabetic languages with predictable spelling patterns. Perhaps more important, in both Spanish and English, the key task for the reader is to associate or construct meaning based on written alphabetic symbols. It is highly likely, therefore, that the same grapho-psycholinguistic processes will be involved in both languages, and what we know about how to help children acquire literacy in English is probably relevant for helping children acquire literacy in Spanish. (p. 174)

Importance of Access to Developmentally Appropriate Books

From the beginning of nursery school, books play an integral role in literacy development (Guszak, 1997). Children are often read entertaining books, sometimes more than once. These experiences and subsequent discussions of these stories help children to discover that stories have characters, settings, plots, and resolutions. They also become familiar with the language that is used in books—i.e., "book talk." All of these experiences help children to develop rich backgrounds of knowledge and metalinguistic insights that contribute to the foundation needed for subsequent meaningful interactions with books in formal school settings (Anderson, Hiebert, Scott, & Wilkinson, 1985). These types of experiences help children to "catch" reading (Teale, 1981). However, it is important

for these frequent interactions to continue once youngsters enter kindergarten and move on to the subsequent grades in order to build on that foundation.

Different resources are available for teachers to use in Spanish as part of the literacy instruction provided to children. Pérez and Torres-Guzmán (1996) have provided an extensive annotated bibliography of narrative and expository books for the primary and intermediate grades which teachers may want to review. Also included in this list are some English titles. Graves, Juel, and Graves (1998) (see Appendix A) and Leone and Cisneros (1994) (see Appendix B) have provided sample lists of children's literature which may be useful to teachers working with children developing literacy in Spanish. An additional book, which I have enjoyed, is Joe Hayes' *Tell me a cuento: Cuéntame un Story* (1998, published by Cinco Puntos Press). The four complete stories written in Spanish and English describe different situations in which people may find themselves. For additional information on books written by Joe Hayes, readers may want to consult the Web site http:// www.cincopuntos.com.

Graves et al. also recommend a review of Freeman and Cervantes' (1991) annotated bibliography of over 300 children's books written in Spanish. Graves and his colleagues also suggest that readers visit the Web site of the Center for the Study of Books in Spanish for Children and Adolescents / para el estudio de libros Infantiles y Juveniles en Español at http:// www. csusm.edu/public_html/ yin/intro_eng.html. This site provides monthly updated reviews of over 2,000 books written in Spanish and recommended for children and adolescents.

When teachers are considering reading material for use with their children, it seems important to keep certain factors in mind. For example, books that respect and honor children's home culture may help them find a sense of "connection" and relevance between the home and the school. If appropriate books are not readily available, students can be guided by teachers to "write and publish their own books," or *libritos*, as they have been referred to by Goldenberg (1994). Such pieces of literature may be developed through the use of language experience stories, which eventually get transcribed into small books. The use of technology can help make this task quite manageable. By keeping these stories and others like them in a file or notebook that can be expanded as the number of stories increases, children can practice reading and rereading them multiple times at school and at home. Goldenberg (1994) found that such a practice helped kindergarten students to become comfortable reading at school and at home.

Leone and Cisneros (1994) suggest that first-language printed materials be as abundant as possible. These materials should include books, magazines, newspapers, phone books, posters, signs, labels, student-made books, other reading materials, and an abundant supply of writing resources. Predictable books, picture books, books on tape, books for shared reading (several copies), and read-aloud books may be particularly useful in meeting the diverse reading needs of a variety of students.

Talking to students to determine their reading interests is another means of providing sufficient and appropriate books for students, especially if the topics selected can be tied directly to a theme that will be discussed in class. This way, children's time spent listening, reading, sharing, and writing about texts can also help them to participate meaningfully in other areas of the curriculum.

Matching Students with Appropriate Books

Once books are available, carefully assessing a student's progress in a self-selected book, or in a book the teacher is contemplating for the student, is a key consideration in ensuring that the student's literacy experiences are meaningful and successful. Generally, a student's reading performance is judged to be at the *independent*, *instructional*, or *frustrational* level. Criteria for establishing these levels may vary slightly, but generally involve word recognition and reading comprehension. Some authors (e.g., Guszak, 1997) include *fluency* as an additional criterion to determine the adequacy of fit between a student and a book.

In my work with children over the last 20 years, I have found that all three criteria are quite useful in helping to match students with appropriate books to read. The information in Table 1 (see p.105) was taken from Guszak's (1997) research. I have found it to be very helpful in matching students with appropriate books.

The information suggests that students reading at their *independent* level can do so successfully without support from the teacher. Teacher guidance is essential, however, at the child's *instructional* level, since it is at this point that the student can develop new reading insights and strategies to extend her reading capabilities. Once the student's *frustrational* level is determined, it is important to provide reading experiences below this level so that the student's progress can be enhanced. With frequent, successful, and challenging reading experiences, the student's reading proficiency is expected to grow so that she can eventually enjoy books that were once too difficult.

The following story, at approximately the third grade level, illustrates how the criteria included in the table can be applied to help assess a child's reading behavior.

Ramón, El Corredor
/ Había una vez un niño que quería una bicicleta. Pero como sus padres no tenían bastante dinero para comprársela, él nunca logró tener la bicicleta. Así es que Ramón poco a poco se acostumbró / a caminar. Después de un tiempo, él empezó a correr y le comenzó a gustar.

Ramón corría por todas partes. Corría de la casa a la escuela, a la tienda, y al patio de recreo. Dentro de poco tiempo, Ramón se integró como parte de un equipo de corredores de su escuela. Después de mucha práctica, los niños <u>empezaron</u> a viajar a otros

TABLE 1
CRITERIA FOR READING EASE AND DIFFICULTY

INDEPENDENT LEVEL

Fluency (Rate)		Word Recognition	Comprehension
Book Levels	Minimums		
First	80 wpm	97 percent and better, as based on definite miscues that can alter the meaning of text, such as bad substitutions, words told, and omissions. Indefinite miscues that don't alter the meaning of text are not counted.	80 percent and better
Second reader	90 wpm		
Third reader	100 wpm		
Fourth and up	110 wpm		

INSTRUCTIONAL LEVEL

Fluency (Rate)		Word Recognition	Comprehension
Book Levels	Minimums		
First	60 wpm	92 percent to 96 percent, as based on the definite miscues listed above	60 percent to 79 percent
Second reader	70 wpm		
Third reader	80 wpm		
Fourth and up	90 wpm		

FRUSTRATIONAL LEVEL

Fluency (Rate)	Word Recognition	Comprehension
Rates are below the minimums above. When a pupil drops below the minimum rate, he is considered frustrational despite his word recognition and comprehension scores.	91 percent and less, as based on the previous definite miscues	59 percent and less

Independent reading: To be considered independent in reading materials, the reader must meet or exceed the minimums in rate, word recognition, and comprehension. **Instructional reading:** If the pupil can work within these criteria, it is assumed that he or she can work at this level with some assistance from the teacher, another pupil, or a tape assist. **Frustrational reading** is the usual outcome when pupils read materials that are too difficult. If the pupil falls below any one of the three criteria, that pupil should be placed in easier materials within the instructional criteria.

Source: From *Reading for students with special needs* (2nd ed.) (p. 72), by F. J. Guszak, Dubuque, IA: Kendall Hunt. Copyright 1997 by Kendall / Hunt Publishing Company. Reprinted with permission.

escuelas para competir contra otros equipos. Ramón era uno de los mejores corredores y casi todo el tiempo él y sus compañeros ganaban el primer premio. Los padres de Ramón siempre iban a las competiciones para apollarlo.

/ A Ramón también le gustaba aprender todo lo posible de este deporte para mejorar su capacidad de correr. Así es que siempre leía diferentes libros y revistas relacionadas con temas de correr. Además, / platicaba con entrenadores para aprender como aumentar su capacidad de correr más lejos sin cansarse tanto. Ramón siempre tomaba tiempo para ayudarles a otros estudiantes que también querían aprender a correr y disfrutar de este deporte.

Todo el trabajo le sirvió mucho a Ramón, porque fue invitado a competir contra otros estudiantes en la competición nacional. En este día, Ramón pudo correr los 10 kilómetros más rápido que los demás corredores. Después de la carrera, él le dio las gracias a sus padres, a pesar de nunca haber podido comprarle una bicicleta. Quizás esto le ayudó a Ramón a ser muy buen corredor.

Pregunta de comprensión ¿De qué se trata esta historia?

Respuesta: Nos dice que había un niño llamado Ramón quien al principio quería una bicicleta. Pero como sus padres no tenían bastante dinero para comprársela, él se acostumbró a caminar y luego a correr. Como le gustaba tanto correr, se integró en un equipo de corredores y después de prepararse bien, comenzaron a competir contra otros equipos. Casi siempre ganaban las competiciones. Después de bastante tiempo y mucho trabajo, Ramón fue invitado a competir al nivel nacional contra otros estudiantes. En la carrera de 10 kilómetros, Ramón salió en primer lugar. Después de la carrera, él le dio las gracias a sus padres, a pesar de nunca haberle podido comprar la bicicleta.

The story is about a young boy named Ramón, who wanted a bicycle but never got one because his parents could not afford it. As a result, he got used to walking and then running. Ramón eventually became such an accomplished runner that he joined the school's track team, which frequently defeated opposing schools. After a lot of hard work, extensive reading, and consulting with his coaches, Ramón was invited to compete in a 10 kilometer race at the national level. After winning the race, Ramón thanked his parents for their support and encouragement, even though they were never able to buy him a bicycle.

The two slash marks (at the beginning of the first paragraph and at the beginning of the third paragraph) indicate that the teacher took two rate checks of 15 seconds each during the time the child was reading the story aloud. (It is recommended that the teacher have her own copy of the story to mark while the child is reading, to avoid interrupting the child.) Each rate check began where the first slash mark is indicated and ended where the second slash is placed. The first check indicates that the child read 34 words in 15 seconds. At this rate, the child could be expected to be reading at approximately 136 words per minute. (This figure was obtained by multiplying 34 words times 4, which provides an estimate of the number of words the child could be expected to read in 60 seconds.) The second rate check of 15 seconds was determined to be 33 words (or 132 words per minute). It was taken to check the reliability of the child's performance and also to establish an average reading rate for the student. On the basis of the two rate checks, the child appears to have an average reading rate of 134 words per minute, which suggests that the material is at the student's independent reading level.

To determine if the reading rate was accompanied by appropriate comprehension, the student was asked to explain what the story was about. The response provided, which is consistent with the summary of the story in English, indicates that the student has a clear and accurate understanding of the text. This also indicates that the reading material may be at the student's independent reading level. A teacher may wish to use a ✓+ to indicate a very complete retelling of the story, a ✓ to reflect an adequate retelling, and a ✓– to denote an incomplete rendition of the story. With practice and by comparing students' retellings, teachers can usually become quite accurate in judging the quality of the student's comprehension. A ✓+ can serve as an indicator of independent reading behavior, a ✓ can depict instructional reading performance, and a ✓– may suggest an inappropriate understanding of the story consistent with frustrational level reading behavior. If the teacher is unsure about how to characterize a student's reading comprehension, it is wise to take additional samples by having the child read and retell the meaning of additional stories.

The final consideration focuses on the student's word recognition ability. The three underlined words, or definite miscues, indicate that they were told to the student after she made different attempts to pronounce them. Out of 250 words in the selection, this result indicates a word recognition accuracy rate of 99 percent. Thus, on the basis of the child's reading rate, comprehension, and word recognition accuracy, this material was judged to be at the student's independent reading level.

A rate check can serve as a useful indicator of a student's word recognition and comprehension success. If the reading rate is below the desired minimum levels and tends to remain this way as the student attempts to read on numerous occasions and in different texts, there is probably sufficient reason to ask why this is happening. The answer may lie in the child's inability to decode words quickly, which may also have an adverse effect on his comprehension of the material. According to the automaticity theory (LaBerge & Samuels, 1974), a fluent reader does not have to devote a great deal of attention to the text, since the decoding of the text tends to occur automatically. This ability allows the reader to devote more of his attention to acquiring meaning from the text. However, if the reader needs to devote an extensive amount of energy and attention to decoding the words, then it may be necessary to give the child more suitable reading material.

Providing reading experiences at the child's independent level on a frequent and regular basis is essential to help the student develop a greater sense of confidence as a reader and more fluency. Moreover, since the child can read this material quite easily on his own, reading at this level can free him to explore multiple meanings of the text. For example, perhaps the student could come up with a different ending to the story of La Caperucita Roja (Little Red Riding Hood).

Frequent and regular experiences with reading at his instructional level can help a student to extend his word recognition, comprehension, and fluency skills. With proper guidance based on careful and ongoing assessment of the child's reading progress, a teacher can ensure that the student is placed in and moves through appropriate reading material at a pace commensurate with his rate of progress. In this way, the child can continue to read challenging material that is still within his reach, while also extending his reading rate, word recognition, and comprehension skills.

Among the different issues that teachers need to address once students are properly placed in books is how to ensure that students have enough time to read and share their insights about their books. These issues are essential to the creation of a community of learners capable of functioning in a literate environment.

Allowing Time for Students to Read and Share Books

Besides providing access to meaningful texts, educators need to set aside time at school for students to enjoy and interact with these books and to share their insights with others. Guszak (1997) has underscored the importance of this phenomenon very concisely by indicating that reading is principally caught from books that fit, are read regularly, and are shared. Guszak's observations are well supported. In their list of recommendations, Anderson et al. state that students should spend more time doing independent reading, whether at home or at school. By the time children enter fourth grade, they should be reading independently a minimum of 2 hours per week. Obviously, acquiring this reading habit depends on frequent and successful interactions with texts from an early age, and this practice needs to continue once the child enters school.

In documenting the actions of effective primary grade teachers, Snow, Burns, and Griffin (1998) indicate that these teachers, among other things, create a literate environment which allows children access to a variety of reading and writing materials and time to work with them. Guszak (1997) lists a time schedule, which he has found to be particularly useful in ensuring that students have an opportunity to read and write in class every day. A sample of this schedule is given in Table 2.

Verifying that each child is successfully interacting with a book that is within his or her capability is essential for the reading time to be of maximum benefit. Beginning readers could be asked to look through picture books or to practice reading a predictable book with a partner. Students may also engage in choral, individual, and partner reading. Thus, during both independent-level and instructional-level reading periods, the teacher listens to selected students read on a given day and asks them to retell the story that they are reading. Through this informal monitoring procedure, the teacher can listen to each child in the class read at least once a week and express his or her comprehension of the text. With this information, the teacher is in a better position to determine if the child is making appropriate progress and to adjust the instruction accordingly.

Setting aside time to address reading comprehension and writing activities provides students with opportunities to solidify and extend their comprehension of the material they are reading. Listening time allows the teacher to expose children to new authors or interesting stories that they may want to explore further when they are able and thus extend their appreciation for different types of literature.

In a study of 195 fifth and sixth graders who were asked to keep reading logs from mid-January to mid-May, Taylor, Frye, and Maruyama (1990) found, through the use of a stepwise multiple regression, that the amount of time students spent reading during the reading period contributed significantly to their reading achievement. After an exhaustive review of research on the importance of successful and meaningful reading experiences for children, Krashen (1999b) also concluded that "More reading typically results in better literacy development." (p. 47).

This research clearly indicates that students need access to many books from which they can select to read. Moreover, ample time needs to be provided on a daily basis for these students to read and exchange ideas with others about what they read. Careful monitoring of the pupil–text interaction is essential if teachers are in fact to provide meaningful literacy experiences for all students.

A major factor influencing students' literacy success is their ability to comprehend

---

TABLE 2
SAMPLE SCHEDULE FOR READING AND WRITING IN CLASS

• 8:00–9:00 a.m.	Reading. This time frame may be divided in the following manner:
8:00–8:20	Independent reading
8:20–8:30	Instructional-level reading (Monday – Thursday; content reading occurs at this time on Friday.)
8:40–9:00	Written comprehension (Monday – Thursday; content reading continues at this time on Friday.)
• 9:00–10:00 a.m.	Writing. This time frame may be used in the following manner:
9:00–9:50	Students may draft, revise, edit, or publish their writings.
9:50–10:00	Sharing. Different students are asked by the teacher to share their work with the rest of the class, especially if they are at a point where they are striving to improve upon the quality of their work to date.
	(The timebreak here indicates that other school activities are taking place.)
• 12:25–12:45	Story time: The teacher reads to the students every day immediately after lunch.

what they listen to and read. This issue is directly tied to how teachers can guide students to extend and appreciate not only their own understanding of texts but also others' points of view. The next section of this article deals with issues involving comprehension.

Comprehension and Ways to Facilitate Its Development

The "comprehension hypothesis" has been described by Krashen (1999b) as the acquisition of language and development of literacy through the understanding of messages. This notion clearly indicates the importance of frequent and successful contact by students with meaningful and interesting stories. Reading fluency facilitates the comprehension of text and thus enhances students' chances of "catching the reading bug."

Comprehension and Fluency

In an effort to help students clearly understand and appreciate the meaning of a text, a teacher may seek to enhance their reading fluency by having them reread the material several times. During this time, the teacher would need to attend not only to the students' reading rate but also to their use of prosodic features of language. These include the pitch, stress, juncture, and intonation of language, which are important to understand stories that involve dialogue (Guszak, 1997).

To help a student in need of developing greater fluency, a teacher may ask the child to read two or more times a particular section of a page, or perhaps one or more pages, of a story until a criterion level has been reached—e.g., 85 words per minute (Samuels, 1994). A student may be assisted in this task by listening to a taped version of the story at a particular reading rate. After listening to the taped story several times, the student can then practice reading it until the desired reading rate is achieved. It is recommended that once the reading is done by the student, she be encouraged to explain what she read. This helps ensure

that fluent reading is accompanied by appropriate comprehension.

The effect of repeated readings has been found to extend to other texts, provided that there is a considerable amount of overlap of specific words between the texts (Faulkner & Levy, 1994; Rashotte & Torgesson, 1985). More recently, Shany and Biemiller (1995) found, while working with poor readers from the third and fourth grades, that students' reading rate and comprehension were positively influenced by their reading for 30 minutes four times a week for 16 weeks at their independent reading level from basal reading series that contained words that were repeated across successive selections. Participating students who were helped by the teacher with word recognition read five times more words of text than the control group, while students who listened to audiotaped recordings of the basal series selections read ten times more words of text than the controls.

In 1997, Stahl, Huebach, and Cramond studied 230 second graders who varied from essentially nonreaders to those who could successfully read fourth grade material. The teachers of these youngsters introduced basal stories by reading them aloud to the students, followed by questions posed by both the teachers and the students. Organizational frames, such as story maps and Venn diagrams, were used to help students acquire a deeper understanding of the stories. Children needing extra assistance participated in echo reading by reading a paragraph which had been previously read by the teacher. The child then read the same selection at home to her parents that evening.

For additional practice, the next day at school students took turns reading to each other every page or paragraph of the selection. This activity enabled the teacher to verify that the students were in fact reading, while allowing her to informally assess their performance by moving about the room listening.

Besides reading basal selections several times, students were asked to read books of their choice both during class for 15 to 20 minutes and at home. The different strategies used to promote comprehension and fluency through extensive reading, rereading, and elaborate discussions of the text's meaning resulted in substantial progress. Of 190 students who began second grade in the fall reading at the primer level or higher, only 5 were still incapable of reading at the second grade level by the spring term. Nine out of 20 students who could not even read the primer book when they began the year were able to reach or exceed the second grade level by the spring semester. Finally, all but one of these 20 students could read at least at the primer level.

The practice of repeated readings both at school and at home, coupled with reading comprehension instruction, which includes opportunities for direct teaching and for detailed discussions of stories, seems to hold promise for facilitating students' reading achievement. Comprehension may be particularly enhanced when the reading material contains words that are common across selections and when students have multiple opportunities to listen to taped versions of the passage at desired reading rates with appropriate prosodic features. While students are reading or are listening to a story being read by someone else, it is important for them and their teachers to determine the degree to which the children are, in fact, comprehending what they are reading or listening to.

Process Comprehension

Teachers need to be concerned with the type of thinking they encourage among their students, when reading a story to them and then discussing it as well as when students are doing the reading themselves and are then provided opportunities to share their insights about the text with others. Attention to how students are understanding the text during the actual reading or listening situation indicates that the processes used to comprehend the text are important (Guszak, 1997).

A student who is a successful processor of language can readily retell what a portion of a story or an entire story is about after having listened to it. This student can also generally explain what she is reading about en route to completing a story and after having finished reading the text. Consistent behavior of this type suggests that this student is successfully making sense of the language she is listening to or reading.

A less successful processor is the student who is either unsure about what the story means or simply does not understand the text at all (Guszak, 1997). We often see this reflected in a student's incomplete summaries of the stories. This "dubious processor" may lack relevant background and vocabulary to fully understand the story that he is listening to or attempting to read. The "nonprocessor" is the student who simply has very little or no idea what he is reading or listening to. These difficulties may be the result of limited experiences, limited language, or limited understanding.

Frequent opportunities to listen to and read different types of stories and then share their insights with others can help fill students' apparent conceptual and vocabulary voids, as well as develop their language concepts. Cain's (1996) study of seven- and eight-year-olds whose word recognition was appropriate for their chronological age, but who varied in their reading comprehension, is instructive in this regard. Cain found that successful comprehenders had parents who read to them at home more often than the parents of the children who were not as successful. Cain also found that the skilled comprehenders were more likely to read books with their parents and to talk about books and stories more frequently than their counterparts. Goldenberg (1994) reported similar results while working with kindergarten students learning to read in Spanish. However, in addition to providing parents with information, such as how to read and interact with their children about a story, Goldenberg found that students' achievement began to increase noticeably when a follow-up system was instituted. Parents were asked to sign forms indicating that they had actually sat down to read and interact with the child. On other occasions, they received notes or phone calls reminding them of literacy tasks with which they could help their children. Collectively, this information suggests that we as teachers would do well to read extensively to our students, to encourage them to share their views about stories with us, and to support their efforts to read extensively both at school and at home.

Frequent oral language and writing opportunities can help students acquire deeper meanings of different types of stories (Wubbena, 1983, 1990; Guszak, 1997). Goldenberg (1994) in a longitudinal study involving kindergarten, first, second, and third grade students found that frequent listening, reading, writing, and speaking opportunities were key components of a well-balanced Spanish literacy program. Leone and Cisneros (1994) recommend that language and literacy opportunities revolve around topics that are meaningful to children and that allow them to interact with each other in a comfortable environment. In this environment, use of students' first language (e. g., Spanish) is very important to demonstrate that it is just as viable and respected a means of communication as English.

Children's vocabulary and reading comprehension have been found to increase when they are provided information about the meanings of words and examples of how the words can be used in different contexts (Stahl & Fairbanks, 1986). Opportunities of this type can build students' cognitive and linguistic repertoire, which they will need to handle more cognitively demanding tasks.

In addition to regularly reading from appropriate levels of text, students need to have a purpose for reading. This helps them to focus their attention on key aspects of the story (Guszak, 1997). For example, after listening to the story "Ramón, El Corredor," a student might say, "La historia era de un niño que se llamaba Ramón y ganó una carrera muy grande" (The story is about a boy named Ramón, who won a big race). Although this statement is true, it ignores other important aspects of the story. Thus, in an attempt to focus the student's attention, the teacher could say, "Al escuchar la historia de nuevo, pon atención para determinar como fue que Ramón empezó a correr cuando era niño" (As you listen to the story again, pay attention to the part that tells how it was that Ramón began running as a youngster). Once this part of the story has been read, it is advisable for the teacher to stop and ask the child, "¿Cómo fue que Ramón empezó a correr cuando era niño?" (How was it that Ramon began running as a youngster?). Posing the question at this point helps to ensure that the student is attending to the part of the story indicated. During the ensuing discussion, the child also has an opportunity to confirm or modify his understanding of this part of the story. The nature of a question setting a specific purpose and the amount of text required to respond to it will depend on the teacher's assessment of the child's reading ability.

Additional purpose statements could be developed in accordance with the structure of the story to reflect its most important aspects. For example, after reading the first two paragraphs of "Ramón, El Corredor" and following the student's summary of these passages, the teacher might make the following statement to the children: "¿Qué creen que hacía Ramón para poder seguir mejorándose como corredor?" (What do you think Ramón did to keep improving as a runner?). After students make several predictions, the teacher might say, "Pongan atención en la siguiente parte de la historia para determinar si sus ideas son confirmadas" (Listen to the next part of the story to find out if your ideas can be confirmed). By guiding students to successfully respond to specific purpose statements based on the structure of the stories, the teacher can help them eventually to formulate concise summaries of different types of texts. Such a feat can confirm the students' successful processing of language and text (Guszak, 1997).

The procedure described above is similar to the Directed Reading Thinking Activity, or DRTA (Graves, Juel, & Graves, 1998), since it is designed to help students understand that reading is a thinking process. Although initially demonstrated to students by the teacher, the eventual goal is to guide students into developing their own purposes for reading, then reading to determine if their predictions can be confirmed, and subsequently orally rereading the passage that contains the verifying information. The second phase of the DRTA, the skill training phase, allows students to delve into the meaning of the story more deeply after it has been completed. For example, students could explore the meanings of specific words or phrases, such as *entrenadores* (trainers) or *una carrera de 10 kilómetros* (a 10 kilometer race), and events by drawing semantic webs, summarizing the story, or performing other appropriate tasks. During these activities, it is recommended that there be a gradual release of responsibility from the teacher to the students, since the goal is eventually to have students perform many of these activities on their own. However, this transition of responsibility needs to be monitored very closely during the guided-practice part of the lesson to ensure that students understand the activity and can eventually succeed in using it (Pearson & Gallagher, 1983). Following the reading of the passage, it is important to delve into the ideas that students derived from reading it.

Product Comprehension

Product comprehension refers to the "understanding that remains after the reading act" (Guszak, 1997, p. 116). To explore this issue, it seems important to use a reading comprehension conceptual scheme that encompasses different types of thinking activities that readers can perform to explore various aspects of the text. A tool that I have found to be very useful in this regard is Guszak's (1997, pp. 116–167) concept of PLORE. The term refers to *predicting,*

locating, organizing, remembering, and *evaluating* information.

PLORE is intended to reflect a manner of thinking about what we read. *Predicting* is indicated first, because it drives many of our reading efforts. Reflected in our anticipations as to what a book or story is going to be about, it also extends into our specific purposes for reading and our ability to use context to determine the meaning of words or phrases contained in a selection. Our predictions may be influenced by our background knowledge, which we may have developed, in part, through previous reading and listening experiences. Predictions may be either convergent or divergent. Convergent predictions enable the reader to use the text to verify their accuracy and thus determine if the text is making sense. Divergent predictions, on the other hand, encourage multiple responses designed to promote behaviors such as creativity, humor, and invention.

Locating follows predicting, since it is intended to reflect our efforts to read and locate information that supports or refutes our predictions. Subsequent to the reading of the text, we may want to *organize* it in some fashion to share it with others, perhaps in the form of a summary. *Remembering* plays a key role in this activity, since we need to recall important pieces of information about the text for the summary to be meaningful. *Evaluating,* the last component of PLORE, helps us judge the selection in different ways. For example, we can thoughtfully assess its internal consistency, determining whether the description and sequence of events make sense. We can also judge whether a piece of text is factual or not, and whether it appears to have been written primarily to inform, persuade, or entertain the reader.

An enjoyable story written by Joe Hayes (1998) in English and Spanish entitled "Monday, Tuesday, Wednesday, Oh! Lunes, Martes, Miércoles, ¡Oh!" demonstrates the use of PLORE with actual text. This story describes the plight of a poor woman whose husband dies and leaves her penniless to care for her children. After much deliberation, the poor woman begins working for a rich woman by cleaning her house. After cleaning the house, washing the clothes, and making tortillas from Monday through Saturday, the poor woman finally receives her pay—a stack of dry tortillas that the rich woman had not eaten. Feeling very tired and depressed, the poor woman returns home and feeds her children the dry tortillas. After putting them to bed, she takes a stroll to think about how she can properly feed and care for her children.

While walking, the poor woman hears a song in the distance: "Lunes, martes, miércoles, ¡oh! Lunes, martes, miércoles, ¡oh! " (p. 21). She follows the sound and comes upon a group of little men, whom she approaches, pleasantly greets, and then suggests a way that the song might be improved. The poor woman recommends that the little men sing: "Lunes, martes, miércoles, ¡oh! Jueves, viernes, y sábado, ¡so!" (p. 23). (The new song is "Monday, Tuesday, Wednesday, oh! Thursday, Friday, and Saturday, so!").

The little men try out and like the new song. In appreciation, the leader of the little men tells the poor woman that they will sing this song every Saturday night, and then he gives her a clay pot. The poor woman thanks the little man and then goes home.

Upon arriving home, she uncovers the pot and finds it filled with gold. Feeling very happy and relieved, the poor woman takes one piece of gold to buy food for her children and hides the rest. After being accused by the rich woman of stealing from her while working during the week, the poor woman explains how she obtained the gold. Upon hearing this, the rich woman visits the spot where the little men are singing in an effort to get gold from them to become even wealthier.

After listening to their song, the rich woman embarrasses them for leaving out Sunday. She orders them to add the words "Domingo también" (Sunday too). After several attempts to incorporate these words into their song, the little men eventually become frustrated and conclude that these words do not fit their song. Before departing, the displeased leader of the little men gives the rich woman a clay pot. Without thanking him, she grabs the pot and runs home to open it. Anticipating that it is filled with gold, she is shocked to find it filled with poisonous creatures. She becomes so frightened that she runs out of the house screaming and runs down the road.

The story ends with the poor woman and her children living very happily every day of the week. "Lunes, martes, miércoles, jueves, viernes, sábado,¡y domingo también!" (Monday, Tuesday, Wednesday, Thursday, Friday, Saturday, and Sunday, too!).

The following questions illustrate how different PLORE activities could be structured on the basis of this story. It is recommended that the questions be formulated by the teacher once she has read the story and has closed the book. Such a practice seems to ensure that the questions formulated do indeed reflect key aspects of the story. These questions could be posed to the students once the story has been read to them orally or after they have read it themselves. Students' responses could be obtained orally at first in order to monitor their comprehension. When they are able, students should be supported in their efforts to write each question and then provide a written response in a complete sentence. Students should be encouraged to use words from the question stem to formulate their answers. Guszak (1997) and others, including myself, have found that such written responses help students to clarify and solidify their understanding of the story.

The teacher should adjust the number and types of questions that children are asked to answer so that they are commensurate with the students' capabilities. For example, he may want to ask students to answer predicting and locating questions only, if this is as much as has been covered in reading comprehension instruction. Through a gradual release of responsibility, students can be guided to write various types of comprehension questions, prepare a written response for each, and then check their own work from an answer sheet. Afterward, students would be expected to share and explain their responses to the teacher. This type of interaction can provide a teacher with valuable diagnostic information about the students' reading comprehension and their written communication skills as well. These insights can then be incorporated by the teacher into future lessons, as deemed appropriate. It is anticipated that by second grade, students should be able to respond to the full range of PLORE comprehension questions (Guszak, 1997).

Sample PLORE Questions and Answers in Spanish

The following PLORE questions and sample responses have been arranged in Spanish. Their English translations follow.

Predecir Información

1. ¿Qué le pudiera haber pasado a la señora pobre si no la hubiera ayudado el jefe de los hombrecitos?
   Respuesta:
   Si no la hubiera ayudado el jefe de los hombrecitos, la señora pobre podría haberse enfermado.

2. ¿Qué quiere decir la palabra *tacaña* en la siguiente oración: "Pero la señora rica era *tacaña* y no le gustaba compartir nada con nadie"?
   Respuesta:
   La palabra *tacaña* en esta oración quiere decir que la señora rica no le daba nada a nadie.

Localizar Información

3. ¿Cuál de las siguientes dos oraciones nos da a conocer que la señora pobre quería hacer algo para poder cuidar bién a sus hijo?
   a. La señora pobre regresó a casa y le dió de comer a sus hijos lo mejor que pudo con las tortillas secas. Luego los acostó.
   b. Luego se levantó y salió afuera, esperando que el aire fresco le aclarara la mente para que pudiera hallar como ganarse mejor la vida.
   Respuesta:
   La segunda oración nos a conocer que la señora pobre quería hacer algo para cuidar mejor a sus hijos.

4. ¿Cuál de los siguientes párrafos nos da a conocer lo que hizo la señora pobre para ayudarles a los hombrecitos?
   a. Oigan. Tal vez quieran cantar así: Lunes, martes, miércoles, ¡oh! Jueves, viernes, y sábado, ¡so!
   b. ¡Oh!—dijeron—que buena canción!— Y volvieron a bailar, cantando como la señora les había dicho. Bailaron hasta que el primer gallo cantó en el pueblo.
   Respuesta:
   El primer párrafo nos da a conocer que la señora pobre les ayudó a los hombrecitos por medio de enseñarles una canción nueva.

Organizar Información

5. Prepara una lista de los eventos principales de la historia.
   Respuesta:
   Los eventos principales de la historia son los siguientes:
   • La señora pobre quedó sin dinero después de la muerte de sus esposo, y no sabía como iba a cuidar a sus hijos.
   • La señora pobre comenzó a trabajar por la señora rica, pero no recibió mas que tortillas secas como su pago.
   • La señora pobre se encontró con los hombrecitos y les enseñó una canción nueva.

- El jefe de los hombrecitos le dió una holla de barro llena de oro a la señora pobre porque los ayudó.
- La señora rica trató de obtener oro también de los hombrecitos, pero no lo logró, porque los trató muy mal. En vez de oro, ella recibió una olla de barro llena de bichos venenosos del jefe de los hombrecitos.
- La señora pobre acabó siendo rica, y la señora rica terminó en volviendose loca.

6. Escribe los siguientes eventos de la historia en la orden en que ocurrieron:
- Los hombrecitos están agradecidos a la señora pobre porque les ensenó una canción nueva.
- La señora pobre está preocupada porque se le murió el esposo y no tiene dinero.
- La señora rica comienza a correr gritando y muy asustada.
- La señora rica se encuentra a la señora pobre en la tienda de comida.

Respuesta:
Los eventos de la historia ocurrieron en la siguiente orden:
- La señora pobre esta preocupada porque se le murió el esposo y no tiene dinero.
- La señora pobre les enseña una canción nueva a los hombrecitos.
- Los hombrecitos están agradecidos a la señora pobre por la canción que les enseñó.
- La señora pobre se encuentra a la señora rica en la tienda de comida.

Recordar Información

7. ¿Qué le dió la señora rica a la señora pobre como pago por su trabajo?
Respuesta:
La señora rica le dió tortillas secas a la señora pobre por su trabajo.

8. ¿Qué le dió el jefe de los hombrecitos a la señora pobre?
Respuesta:
El jefe de los hombrecitos le dió una holla de barro llena de oro a la señora pobre.

Evaluar Información

9. ¿A quién crees que los hombrecitos apreciaban más—a la señora pobre o a la señora rica? Explica por que piensas así.
Respuesta:
Los hombrecitos apreciaban más a la señora pobre porque les había enseñado una canción nueva y los había tratado con respeto.

10. ¿Crees que el autor escribió esta historia para divertirnos o para ayudarnos a entender lo importante que es ayudarnos unos a los otros? Por que piensas así?
Respuesta:
Yo creo que el autor escribió esta historia para ayudarnos a aprender lo importante que es ayudarnos unos a los otros. Yo pienso así porque a la señora pobre le fué muy bién después de haberles ayudado a los hombrecitos. Pero, a la señora rica le fué muy mal porque quiso tomar ventaja de los hombrecitos.

Sample PLORE Questions and Answers in English

The following section translates into English the PLORE activities given above in Spanish.

Predicting Information

1. What might have happened to the poor woman if the leader of the little men had not helped her?

Response:

If the leader of the little men had not helped the poor woman, she might have gotten sick.

2. What does the word *stingy* mean in the following sentence: "But the rich woman was very stingy and did not like to share with anyone"?

Response:

The word stingy in this sentence means that the rich woman did not like to give things to other people.

Locating Information

3. Which of the following two sentences tells us that the poor woman wanted to do something to take better care of her children?

   a. The poor woman returned home and fed her children as best she could on the dry tortillas.

   b. Then she got up and walked outside, hoping the cool air would clear her mind, so that she might think of some way to make a better living.

Response:

The second sentence tells us that the woman wanted to do something different to take better care of her children.

4. Which of the following two paragraphs tells us what the poor woman did to help the little men?

   a. Listen! Maybe you would like to sing: Monday, Tuesday, Wednesday, Oh! Thursday, Friday, and Saturday, So!

   b. "Oh!" they said, "That's a good song!" And they started to dance again, singing the way the poor woman suggested. They danced until the first rooster crowed in the village.

Response:

The first paragraph tells us that the poor woman helped the little men by teaching them a new song.

Organizing Information

5. Make a list of the main events of the story.

Response:

The main events of the story are the following:

- The poor woman is left without any money after her husband dies, and she does not how how she is going to take care of her children.
- The poor woman begins to work for the rich woman, but receives nothing but dry tortillas for her pay.
- The poor woman meets the little men and teaches them a new song.
- The leader of the little men gives the poor woman a pot of gold because she helped them.
- The rich woman tries to get gold from the little men too, but she does not get it, because she treats them very badly. Instead, she gets a clay pot filled with poisonous creatures from the leader of the little men.
- The poor woman ends up becoming rich, and the rich woman ends up going crazy.

6. Write the following events in the order in which they occurred in the story:
   - The little men are grateful to the poor woman because she taught them a new song.
   - The poor woman is worried because her husband died and she does not have any money.
   - The rich woman begins to run, shouting and very scared.
   - The poor woman meets the rich woman in the grocery store.

Response:
The events from the story occurred in the following order:

- The poor woman is worried because her husband died and she does not have any money.
- The little men are grateful to the poor woman because she taught them a new song.
- The poor woman meets the rich woman in the grocery store.
- The rich woman begins to run, shouting and very scared.

Remembering Information

7. What did the rich woman give to the poor woman as pay for her work?

Response:
> The rich woman gave dry tortillas to the poor woman as pay for her work.

8. What did the leader of the little men give to the poor woman?

Response:
> The leader of the little men gave the poor woman a pot of gold.

Evaluating Information

9. Whom do you think the little men appreciated more—the poor woman or the rich woman? Explain why you think so.

Response:
> The little men appreciated the poor woman more because she had taught them a new song and treated them with respect.

10. Do you think the author wrote this story to entertain us or to help us learn how important it is to help one another? Why do you think so?

Response:
> I think the author wrote the story to help us learn how important it is to help one another. I think so because the poor woman ended up being happy after helping the little men. But things ended up very badly for the rich woman, because she tried to take advantage of the little men.

By closely monitoring how well students respond to the different types of PLORE questions, teachers will be in a better position to determine when direct teaching of reading comprehension may be needed. For example, the predicting section allows the teacher to determine how well the students can formulate a response based on information included in the story. Such predictions may also involve students' ability to establish cause-and-effect relationships based on textual information. The vocabulary item included also provides the students an opportunity to demonstrate how well they can use graphophonic, syntactic, and semantic cues to figure out the meaning of the word *stingy*. The locating items serve as placeholders of important information which can help the students obtain a deeper understanding of the story. The tasks involved can vary from locating a specific sentence to locating larger sections of text (e.g., paragraphs, pages). It is wise to start with simple tasks and then move into longer passages of text.

If needed, a graphic organizer, such as a story map, may help students acquire a better understanding of the sequence of events in a story (Graves et al., 1998). Encouraging those students who have difficulty remembering important events of a story to stop periodically to recall and rehearse in their minds the main events as they are unfolding can help them use their metacognitive skills to prepare a meaningful summary of the story. Ensuring that students can use text information to formulate reasoned judgments concerning the story helps them develop meaningful insights involving critical thinking.

Additional Product Comprehension Activities

Product comprehension tasks can extend beyond PLORE activities. Activities involving readers' theater, reader response through journal writing, and the use of graphic organizers can enrich students' understanding of the story.

A readers' theater activity can be initiated by asking students to identify different parts of the story they would like to read and then orally rehearsing these parts extensively to help the story come to life. The oral reading of the story may be accompanied by movements, sound effects, and props to help the audience understand the intended meaning of the story. Having children act out the story as it is being read, or having children formulate their version of the story with accompanying dialogue and movements, is an excellent means of helping students develop a more personal meaning of the story. These types of activities were found by Morrow, Tracey, Woo, and Pressley (1999) to be part of the instructional efforts that successful first grade teachers used in working with their children. In my work with children, I have found these types of activities useful for extending children's oral language, reading comprehension, and fluency skills. In addition, they serve as one mechanism through which burgeoning readers can develop self-confidence as successful communicators of meaning.

Teachers may also allow children to reflect upon and then write in their reader response journal the part of the story that they liked the most. Children should be encouraged to explain why they picked a particular section. Subsequently, students may be encouraged to share their journal entry with another student, who may respond in writing to the first child's reaction (Pérez & Torres-Guzmán, 1996). This type of dialogue journal writing can be supported by oral exchanges between students to explain their written comments. Research by Atwell (1987) indicates that this type of interaction can extend students' points of view and appreciation of the texts they read. However, the frequency with which this type of activity occurs should be carefully monitored to ensure that children have sufficient time to read and reflect upon their selections prior to being asked to write their reactions in their journals.

Providing children with additional books and stories that were written by the same author or that deal with same topic can also help them extend their reading comprehension. Reading to the children or encouraging them to read "The Terrible Tragadabas—El Terrible Tragadabas," which was also written by Joe Hayes (1998), could complement the story "Lunes, Martes, Miércoles, ¡Oh! Monday Tuesday Wednesday, Oh!" very nicely. The former story describes how a tiny bee was able to rescue a group of people from a terrible creature by stinging it.

With an extensive and varied supply of books on the same theme or written by the same author, small groups of children (e.g., four to a group) can be formed who are interested in reading the same book. Such "literature circles" or "book clubs" (Daniels, 1994; McMahon, Raphael, Goatley, & Pardo, 1997) provide an excellent opportunity for all students to participate in the discussions related to the meaning of the text, since the groups are small. Guszak (1997) has found that second through eighth graders in such environments tend to produce more elaborate oral than written responses to the text.

Thematic literary instruction can also involve cross-curricular connections. Cunningham and Allington (1999) propose that this type of integrated instruction allows teachers to save time, while also providing students with an opportunity to interact with relevant content in meaningful ways. The authors recommend that integration start with activities planned for one day in which the literacy and content-area instruction for the day revolves around one theme (e. g., helping one another). The two activities described below illustrate how this might be accomplished as an extension to the story "Lunes, Martes, Miércoles, ¡Oh! Monday, Tuesday, Wednesday, Oh!"

Actividades Integradas de Curriculum

La señora que era pobre tiene una olla de oro. Ella quiere comprar comida para prepararles a sus hijos una comida deliciosa y saludable. La señora quiere asegurarse que la comida contenga elementos de las cuatro principales categorías de nutrición, porque ella sabe que sus hijos necesitan comida de cada grupo. Después del nombre de cada categoría de comida, escribe por lo menos dos tipos de comida que la señora podría comprar. Revisa los anuncios en el periódico para ver cuánto puede esperar la señora que va a gastar de su dinero. Puedes discutir tus ideas con un amigo. (La información debajo de cada categoría sirve como un ejemplo de lo que podrían alistar los alumnos.)

Una Muestra de Comestibles que Podría Comprar la Señora

Panes y Cereales

2 barras grandes de pan blanco
($1.00 cada una) $2.00

2 paquetes de tortillas frescas
(Vienen 24 tortillas en cada
paquete; cada paquete se
vende por 85¢.) $1.70

Carnes

1 pedazo de carne de vaca
(Se vende por $1.30 la libra.
La carne pesa 3 libras.) $3.90

1 paquete de 20 rebanadas de pavo . . $4.00

Productos Hechos de Leche

1 galón de leche $4.00

1 galón de nieve $2.60

Frutas y Legumbres

6 libras de plátanos (a 40¢ la libra) . . .$2.40

3 lechugas
(Cada lechuga cuesta $1.00.) $3.00

Costo Total $23.60

The poor woman has a pot of gold. She wants to use some of the gold to buy food so that she can prepare a delicious and healthy meal for her children. The woman wants to make sure that she buys food from the four basic food groups, since she knows that her children need food from each group. After the name of each food group, write the names of at least two foods that the woman could buy. Look over the advertisements in the local newspaper to get an idea of how much the woman is going to have to pay for the food. You can discuss your ideas with a friend. (The information below each category is provided as an example of what students might write.)

A Sample of the Food Items That the Woman Could Buy

Breads and Cereals

2 loaves of white bread
(1.00 for each loaf) $2.00

2 packages of fresh tortillas
(Twenty-four tortillas come in
each package. Each package
sells for 85¢.) $1.70

Meats

1 roast
(The roast sells for $1.30 per
pound. It weighs 3 pounds.) $3.90

1 package of turkey slices
(Twenty slices come in each
package.) $4.00

Milk Products

1 gallon of milk $4.00

1 gallon of ice cream $2.60

Fruits and Vegetables

6 pounds of bananas
(at 40¢ per pound) $2.40

3 heads of lettuce
(Each head sells for $1.00.) $3.00

Total Cost $23.60

ORGANIZADOR GRÁFICO

Categoría de comida	Lo que se de esta categoría	Lo que quiero saber de esta categoría	Lo que he aprendido de esta categoría
Productos de Leche			
Panes y Cereales			
Carnes			
Frutas y Legumbres	Muchos atletas comen plátanos.	¿Por qué son buenos los plátanos para nosotros?	Los plátanos contienen potasio, un elemento que nos ayuda a tener energía.

KWL GRAPHIC ORGANIZER

Food Group	What I Know About This Food Group	What I Want to Know About This Food Group	What I Learned About This Food Group
Milk Products			
Breads and Cereals			
Meats			
Fruits and Vegetables	Many athletes eat bananas.	Why are bananas good for us?	Bananas contain potassium, which is a substance that helps to give us energy.

It is important to know something about the different food groups and how they help us stay healthy. Working in cooperative groups of four students each, prepare a report on this topic by looking for information in different library books or on the Internet. Use the following form to help prepare your report. Each team member is to give an oral report to the class on a particular food group after working on the project for a week.

The following graphic organizer, known as the KWL procedure (Ogle, 1986), is based on what students *know*, what they *want to know*, and what they *learned* about a topic. According to Graves, Juel, and Graves (1998), it is perhaps the best known and most often used method of obtaining information from expository text.

The KWL procedure enables students to activate their relevant background knowledge regarding the topic at hand and then to generate at least one question, which can serve to set a purpose for their subsequent reading. After reading the relevant section(s) of text and reflecting upon them in light of the question, the student is expected to write down in her own words what was learned in response to the question. Once the entire matrix is completed, students can discuss what they have learned on the basis of all the questions generated and then decide how best to present their information in a meaningful fashion to the rest of the class.

While students are reading their content material, if a teacher is unsure as to whether they are understanding the material, she may want to consider using Reciprocal Teaching, a cooperative procedure that begins as a teacher-directed activity (Palincsar & David, 1991; Snow, Burns, & Griffin, 1998) to enhance their comprehension. Reciprocal teaching begins as a teacher-directed activity that involves question generating, clarifying, summarizing, and predicting. The teacher reads a paragraph or two of content material to students and then poses questions about the important ideas contained therein. Students respond to these questions and pose questions about any issues that they do not understand. At this time, discussion should be allowed in an effort to clarify these issues. Subsequently, students should be asked to summarize their understanding of the text up to this point and to predict what is likely to come up next in the material. The process is repeated until the entire piece of text is completed. As the lesson unfolds, the teacher should closely monitor how well the students are dealing with each aspect of this procedure, because as soon as it is deemed appropriate, the students should start gradually assuming more responsibility for leading this activity.

Reciprocal teaching has been found to be quite effective in helping students across different grade levels to understand content material. It is based on the principles that direct instruction, guided practice, comprehension monitoring, and meaningful discussions of relevant and developmentally appropriate content material are valuable means of helping students acquire a deeper understanding of the text. According to Snow, Burns, and Griffin (1998), research on the use of reciprocal teaching with first and second graders has resulted in statistically significant improvements in their listening comprehension and in fewer referrals to special education. In addition, the students' teachers reported having higher expectations for these children as a result of their involvement with the reciprocal teaching dialogues.

Conclusion

Development of bilingual students' receptive and expressive communication abilities in their first language is important in its own right, and it is an endeavor that can be initiated and subsequently maintained by the students' parents. Moreover, it is a viable means of supporting students' efforts to develop into successful second language users. To enhance students' communication capabilities in their first language, it is essential that their exposures to language and print be meaningful, frequent, and challenging. They should also be provided with a supportive and literate environment. In this setting, students need extensive opportunities to listen to, read, and then share the meaning of self-selected books, which they have found to be personally relevant. By ensuring that students are matched with books that they can read at a reasonable rate with appropriate comprehension and word recognition accuracy, teachers can do much to create a literacy environment aimed directly at promoting students' success. Providing students with multiple opportunities to reread text can also help them to develop the automaticity they need to decode words quickly and thus be able to devote more of their attention to discerning the possible meanings of the text.

Allowing students time to share their views concerning the material they are reading or listening to can help solidify their understanding of the text, as well as expand their interpretations of it. This can be facilitated through meaningful and thought-provoking discussions, which allow students to critically examine and appreciate their own viewpoints, as well as those of others. While they are reading, students' use of strategies such as the Directed Reading Thinking Activity (DRTA) can help them focus on important and personally relevant information.

Students' thinking and communication abilities can also be promoted after they have listened to or read a story. Comprehension schemes such as Guszak's (1997) PLORE provide a systematic means through which students can be guided to become actively engaged in thinking about text in different ways and thus obtain a deeper and richer understanding of its significance. By structuring different tasks that allow students to demonstrate their understanding in different ways, teachers can do much to build on and extend students' strengths. Students' success may also be facilitated through direct instruction focusing on the desired objective, followed by a gradual release of responsibility based on the teacher's careful assessment of the students' abilities to perform the task on their own. This notion seems especially important when the focus is on developing students' abilities to monitor their own comprehension and to take appropriate steps to restore it, if it happens to be momentarily lost.

Receptive and expressive communication skills in the students' first language can also be expanded into cross-curricular areas that complement the language arts. Supporting students' efforts to do so can help them find relevance in studying these other aspects of the curriculum. Instructional strategies such as Reciprocal Teaching and KWL underscore the importance of gradual, guided, and closely monitored instruction by the teacher to help ensure that students can eventually complete their assigned and self-selected tasks successfully.

Implications

The evidence to date suggests that there is a great need for Bilingual Education practitioners and researchers to collaborate in carefully examining how research knowledge can be meaningfully applied in specific educational contexts to promote the development of literacy in students' first language (e. g., Spanish). Goldenberg (1994) and Goldenberg and Gallimore (1991) have documented the importance of such a venture by clearly demonstrating how a primarily code-emphasis Spanish Literacy program was transformed into a well-balanced kindergarten to third grade program, which enjoyed strong parental support and participation.

REFERENCES

Anderson, R. C., Hiebert, E. H., Scott, J. A., & Wilkinson, I. A. G. (1985). *Becoming a nation of readers: The report of the Commission on Reading.* Champaign, IL: University of Illinois, Center for the Study of Reading.

Atwell, N. (1987). *In the middle: Writing, reading, and learning with adolescents.* Portsmouth, NH: Heinemann.

Cain, K. (1996). Story knowledge and comprehension skills. In C. Cornoldi & J. Oakhill (Eds.), *Reading comprehension difficulties: Processes and intervention* (pp. 167–192). Mahwah, NJ: Lawrence Erlbaum Associates.

Cummins, J. (1981). The role of primary language development in promoting success for language minority students. In Office of Bilingual Bicultural Education (Eds.), *Schooling and language minority children: A theoretical framework* (pp. 3-49). Los Angeles: Evaluation, Dissemination, and Assessment Center, California State University.

Cunningham, P. M., & Allington, R. L. (1999). *Classrooms that work: They can all read and write* (2nd ed). New York: Longman.

Daniels, H. (1994). *Literature circles: Voice and choice in the student centered classrooms.* New York: Stenhouse Publishers.

Faulkner, H. J., & Levy, B. A. (1994). How text difficulty and reader skill interact to produce differential reliance on word and content overlap in reading transfer. *Journal of Experimental Child Psychology, 58,* 1–24.

Freeman, Y. S., & Cervantes, C. (1991). Literature books en Español for whole language. In K. S. Goodman & Y. M. Goodman (Eds.), *Occasional papers: Program in language and literacy.* Tempe: University of Arizona Press.

Goldenberg, C. (1994). Promoting early literacy development among Spanish-speaking children: Lessons from two studies. In E. H. Hiebert & B. M. Taylor (Eds.), *Getting reading right from the start: Effective early literacy interventions* (pp. 171-199). Boston: Allyn & Bacon.

Goldenberg, C., & Gallimore, R. (1991). Local knowledge, research knowledge, and educational change: A case study of first grade Spanish reading improvement. *Educational Researcher, 20* (8), 2–14.

Graves, M. F., Juel, C., & Graves, B. B. (1998). *Teaching reading in the 21st century.* Boston: Allyn & Bacon.

Guszak, F. J. (1997). *Reading for students with special needs* (2nd ed.). Dubuque, IA: Kendall/Hunt.

Hayes, J. (1998). *Tell me a cuento: Cuéntame un story.* El Paso, TX: Cinco Puntos Press.

Krashen, S. D. (1999a). Condemned without a trial: Bogus arguments against bilingual education. Portsmouth, NH: Heinemann.

___. (1999b). *Three arguments against whole language and why they are wrong.* Portsmouth, NH: Heinemann.

LaBerge, D., & Samuels, S. J. (1974). Toward a theory of automatic information processing in reading. *Cognitive Psychology, 6,* 293–323.

Leone, B., & Cisneros, R. (1994). Whole language in bilingual education: The most meaningful, integrated, and natural environment for fostering biliteracy. In R. Rodriguez, N. J. Ramos, & J. A. Ruiz-Escalante (Eds.), *Compendium of readings in bilingual education: Issues and practices* (pp. 133–149). San Antonio, TX: Texas Association for Bilingual Education.

McMahon, S. I., Raphael, T. E., Goatley, V. J., & Pardo, L. S. (1997). *The book club connection: Literacy learning and classroom talk.* New York: Teachers College of Columbia University Press.

Morrow, L. M., Tracey, D. H., Woo, D. G., & Pressley, M. (1999). Characteristics of exemplary first-grade literacy instruction. *The Reading Teacher, 52* (5), 462–476.

Ogle, D. (1986). K-W-L: A teaching model that develops active reading of expository text. *The Reading Teacher, 39*, 564–570.

Palincsar, A. M., & David, Y. M. (1991). Promoting literacy through classroom dialogue. In E. Hiebert (Ed.), *Literacy for a diverse society: Perspectives, programs, and policies* (pp. 122–140). New York: Teachers College of Columbia University Press.

Pearson, P. D., & Gallagher, M. C. (1983). The instruction of reading comprehension. *Contemporary Educational Psychology, 8*, 317–344.

Pérez, B., & Torres-Guzmán, M. E. (1996). *Learning in two worlds* (2nd ed.). White Plains, NY: Longman.

Rashotte, C. A., & Torgesen, J. K. (1985). Repeated reading and reading fluency in learning-disabled children. *Reading Research Quarterly, 20* (2), 180–188.

Shany, M., & Biemiller, A. (1995). Assisted reading practice: Effects on performance for poor readers in grades 3 and 4. *Reading Research Quarterly, 30*, 382–395.

Stahl, S. A., & Fairbanks, M. M. (1986). The effects of vocabulary instruction: A model-based meta-analysis. *Review of Educational Research, 56* (1), 72–110.

Stahl, S. A., Huebach, K., & Cramond, B. (1997). Fluency oriented reading instruction. *Reading Research Report No. 79.* Athens, GA: National Reading Research Center.

Samuels, S. J. (1994). The method of repeated readings. *The Reading Teacher, 50* (5), 376–381.

Snow, C. E., Burns, M. S., & Griffin, P. (Eds.). (1998). *Preventing reading difficulties in young children.* Washington, DC: National Academy Press.

Taylor, B. M., Frye, B. J., & Maruyama, G. F. (1990). Time spent reading and reading growth. *American Educational Research Journal, 2*, 187–202.

Teale, W. (1981). Emergent literacy: Reading and writing development in early childhood. In J. Readence & R. Baldwin (Eds.), *Research in literacy: Merging perspectives. Thirty-sixth yearbook of the National Reading Conference* (pp. 45–74). Rochester, NY: National Reading Conference.

Thomas, W. P., & Collier, V. (1997). *School effectiveness for language minority students.* Washington, DC: National Clearinghouse for Bilingual Education.

Wubbena, R. (1983). WILSAD: *A reading report.* Weslaco, TX: Weslaco Independent School District.

___. (1990). *Annual report of reading progress.* Weslaco, TX: Weslaco Independent School District.

APPENDIX A

Sample List of Reading Books for Spanish Literacy suggested by Graves et al. (1998)

Ancona. G. *The Piñata Maker/El Piñatero*. Harcourt, 1994. In a colorful manner, this book illustrates the art of piñata making.

Burstein, F. *The Dancer/La Bailarina*. Bradbury, 1993. On the way to a ballet lesson, a little girl and her father have encounters, with a horse, a flower, and others.

Garza, C. L. *Family Pictures/Cuadros de Familia*. Children's Book Press, 1990. Family scenes of fiestas, holidays, and religious ceremonies, among others, are depicted.

Hall, N. A., & Syverson-Stork, J. *Los Pollitos Dicen/The Baby Chicks Sing: Traditional Games, Nursery Rhymes, and Songs from Spanish Speaking Countries*. Little, Brown, 1994. The games and songs are accompanied by colorful illustrations.

Mora. P. *Listen to the Desert/Oye el Desierto*. Clarion, 1994. The sights and sounds of the desert are meaningfully explained.

Reiser, L. *Margaret and Margarita/Margarita y Margaret*. Greenwillow, 1993. The book describes what happens when two little girls meet in a park.

Roe, E. *Con Mi Hermano/With My Brother*. Bradbury Press, 1991. The story describes a young Hispanic boy who admires his brother and wishes to be like him when he becomes older.

APPENDIX B

Children's Literature in Spanish Suggested by Leone and Cisneros (1994)

Ada, A. F., Manzano, Manzano. *Just one more series* (in Spanish). Mariuccia Iaconi Distributors.

Argueta, M. *Los perros mágicos de los volcanes*. Bilingual Multicultural Literature Series. Children's Book Press.

Balzola, A. *Munia y la luna*. Colección Munia. Ediciones Destino. Mariuccia Iaconi Distributors.

Cleary, B. *Ramona y su padre*. Colección Austral Juvenil. Mariuccia Iaconi Distributors.

de Souza, J. *El hermano Anansi y el rancho del ganado*. San Francisco: Children's Book Press.

Lomas, Garza, C. *Cuadros de familia*. San Francisco: Children's Book Press.

Rivera, T. *...y no so lo tragó la tierra*. Houston, TX: Arte Público Press.

Rohmer, H., et al. *El sombrero del tío Nacho*. San Francisco: Children's Book Press.

Turin, A., & Bosnia, N. *Rosa Caramelo. Colección a favor de las niñas*. Mariuccia Iaconi Distributors.

Uribe, G. *El cocuyo y la mora. Colección narraciones indígenas*. Mariuccia Iaconi Distributors.

Teaching Literacy in Spanish

Kathy Escamilla
University of Colorado at Boulder

The least complicated entry into literacy learning is to begin to read and write the language that children already know and speak. What they already know about language can be used to power their literacy learning.

(Clay, 1993)

Introduction

In 1998, the National Research Council, the principal operating arm of the National Academy of Sciences and the National Academy of Engineering, issued a report entitled "Preventing Reading Difficulties." This report's chapter on "Teaching Reading to Language Minority Children" concluded that "initial literacy instruction should be provided in a child's native language whenever possible. Further, literacy instruction should not be introduced in any language before some reasonable level of oral proficiency in that language has been attained" (p. 238). This report supports and further validates the results of numerous research studies conducted over the past thirty years that conclude that initial literacy instruction is most effective when it is provided in the native language of a child (Cummins, 1981; Escamilla, 1987; Krashen & Biber, 1988; Lindholm, 1993; Modiano, 1968; Rodríguez, 1988). For the more than 6 million Spanish-speaking children in U.S. public schools (Brown, 1992), this means initial literacy instruction in Spanish.

Teaching Spanish-speaking children to read and write first in Spanish has long been a cornerstone of the effective implementation of programs of bilingual education in the United States. Further, it has been established that there is a high and positive correlation between learning to read in Spanish and subsequent reading achievement in English (Collier & Thomas, 1995; Greene, 1998; Leasher-Madrid & García, 1985; Ramírez, Yuen, & Ramey, 1991; Thomas & Collier, 1997). The positive relationship between reading well in one language and learning to read well in a second language has come to be called the *transfer effect:* Skills and strategies learned in literacy in one language transfer to reading and writing situations in a second language without having to be relearned.

The knowledge that a child's first language is the best entrance into literacy provides a "best practice" model to schools as they plan and implement bilingual and dual language programs for Spanish-speaking students. However, knowing that you should teach children to read and write in Spanish is only a beginning. Setting up best-practice literacy programs in public schools requires that teachers and school leaders also know *how* to teach reading in Spanish. Further, it is important that teachers know how the teaching of reading in Spanish is similar to, and yet different from, teaching reading in English.

This article will discuss approaches to literacy instruction that may be considered to be universal or applicable to both Spanish and English. It will also give examples of the ways in which literacy instruction in Spanish should be different from English instruction. The article will use examples from a current approach to literacy instruction known as balanced literacy to illustrate why Spanish/English bilingual teachers need specific knowledge about teaching methods related to Spanish reading. The article will also discuss issues in adapting English literacy methods for use with Spanish speakers.

Bilingual Teachers and Spanish Academic Proficiency

It is important to note that only 10 percent of the teachers serving English Language Learners are certified in bilingual education (August & Hakuta, 1997). Further, the majority of Spanish/English bilingual teachers in the United States have had limited opportunities to learn academic language in Spanish (Figueroa & García, 1994; Waggoner & O'Malley, 1984). For the most part, prospective and practicing bilingual teachers have attended U.S. public schools in which the teaching of Spanish academic language either was limited to early elementary grades (via transitional bilingual programs) or was not available at all. After attending K–12 schools in which academic Spanish was not well developed, the majority of Spanish/English bilingual teachers attended U.S. colleges in which classes and teacher preparation programs were also predominantly offered in English (Guerrero, 1997).

Course work in teacher preparation included methods classes in the teaching of reading and language arts. The focus in these classes has been on methods for teaching reading in English. Few universities and colleges offer specific course work in "Methods of Teaching Reading in Spanish." In many of these classes, prospective bilingual teachers are simply told to learn best-practice strategies in English and do them in Spanish. This universalist approach, labeled by some as "one size fits all," has been widely criticized (Ferdman, 1990; Reyes, 1990). However, it remains pervasive in teacher preparation programs.

After becoming certified, teachers continue to learn how to teach reading in Spanish by learning about English literacy methodology through local school district in-service programs. Here, too, bilingual teachers are exposed to best-practice strategies for teaching reading and writing in English and are told simply to utilize them in Spanish. Opportunities for teachers to discuss and learn about approaches to literacy teaching in Spanish are, unfortunately, rare or nonexistent. Equally scarce are opportunities for U.S. bilingual teachers to observe teachers from Spanish-speaking countries and to exchange ideas and strategies with them.

Given all of the above, Guerrero (1997) has concluded that it is unreasonable to expect that bilingual teachers have extensive knowledge of academic Spanish or knowledge about how to best deliver literacy instruction in Spanish. He goes on to say that the solution to this situation is not to blame the teachers for opportunities that they have not had. Rather, it is more important to create opportunities to develop academic Spanish and to learn effective strategies for teaching literacy in Spanish. The remainder of this article will discuss approaches to literacy instruction that bilingual teachers need to consider when planning literacy programs for Spanish-speaking students.

Synthetic, Analytic, and Socio-psycholinguistic Orientations to Reading: Spanish and English

Spanish and English share three similar philosophical orientations to literacy teaching. Methods for applying each orientation, however, vary widely across languages. These include synthetic methods, analytic methods, and the socio-psychological process (Freeman & Freeman, 1997). These orientations have similar meanings in English and Spanish. Each orientation has its proponents and critics.

Synthetic methods are more commonly called part-to-whole methods (Chall, 1967; Braslavsky, 1962). These are methods that start with teaching children parts of words, such as letters and letter sounds. They commonly use letters, syllables, and letter sounds to build up to words. In English, synthetic methods include phonemic awareness, phonological awareness, alphabetic awareness, and phonics-based approaches (Adams, 1990; Foorman, 1995). In Spanish, synthetic methods include *el método alfabético* (the alphabetic method), *el método silábico* (the syllabic method), and *el método onomatopéyico* (the onomatopoeic method). (See Freeman & Freeman, 1997, for a thorough discussion of these synthetic methods for teaching literacy in Spanish.)

Analytic methods are more commonly called whole-to-part methods. These methods start with whole words and break them down for analysis into their various parts. In English, analytic methods are often called sight-word methods (Chall, 1967). In Spanish, analytic methods include *el método global o ideovisual* (the global or visual-concept method), *el método de palabras generadoras* (the generative word method), and *el método léxico* (the lexical method) (Freeman & Freeman, 1997). These orientations focus on word recognition as a goal of reading instruction. Teaching methods to implement these various orientations vary greatly across languages. As will be discussed more thoroughly throughout this article, it is important to note that the more focused a particular approach is on teaching sounds, syllables, and recognition of individual words, the more language-specific the teaching techniques are. Implementing these methods requires a thorough knowledge of the language of instruction. It is not enough simply to know the method in English and apply it in Spanish.

The *socio-psychological process* focuses on the construction of meaning. This orientation to literacy holds that children first develop global understandings about text and gradually come to understand the parts. Reading, in the socio-psychological view, is an enriching experience, not a process of skills mastery. In applying this philosophical orientation, literacy is developed in the context of reading whole stories and texts. The focus is on text interaction, not solely on word recognition. In English, socio-psychological views of reading have been labeled whole-language (Goodman, 1986). In Spanish, this orientation is referred to as *lenguaje integral* (Ferreiro, 1994; Goodman, 1989). The socio-psychological process orientation to literacy instruction is universal, in that the methodology of a focus on the construction of meaning as central to reading instruction will transcend language. Approaches to literacy instruction from this orientation can be applied in either English or Spanish without the need to focus on language-specific constructs or linguistic functions.

Unfortunately, over the past 30 years, these philosophical orientations have often been portrayed in the literature as being dichotomous—incompatible and mutually exclusive. As such, they have been pitted against each other. Teachers, parents, administrators, and policymakers have been asked to take sides and declare themselves to be "whole-language schools" or "phonics schools." Competition among the methods has helped to create a situation known as the reading wars (Chall, 1967, 1999; Fillipo, 1997; Cassidy & Weinrich, 1997). The reading wars have occurred in Latin America around Spanish reading instruction as well (Braslavsky, 1992; Castedo, 1995; Solé I Gallart, 1995).

It is important to note that these orientations are not as dichotomous as they might appear. It has always been a goal for synthetic and analytic approaches to lead to comprehension of text. Similarly, the socio-psychological orientation has never been opposed to skills instruction, as long as such instruction is done in the context of constructing meaning and reading real literature and whole stories. Thus, while the points of departure for beginning literacy instruction may be widely divergent, the goal is the same for all orientations in both languages.

Balanced Literacy Instruction: A Response to End the Reading Wars

Recent attempts to resolve the reading wars have created a different orientation to literacy teaching known as a *balanced approach to teaching reading* (Adams & Bruck, 1995; Cunningham, 1991; Cunningham & Allington, 1994; National Research Council, 1998). Proponents of this approach argue that a balanced approach utilizes synthetic, analytic, and socio-psychological orientations in a way that combines the best of all three.

Proponents of balanced approaches to reading instruction assert that balance does not mean mindless eclecticism or rejection of scientific inquiry. Balance means taking an intelligent approach to reading practice informed by scientific research. Balance involves a program that combines phonological awareness skills and decoding with language- and literature-rich activities. In short, it combines in a thoughtful way synthetic, analytic, and socio-psychological orientations to literacy instruction. An informed approach to reading instruction begins in kindergarten and continues until the child is a fluent reader. Such an approach is thought to be appropriate for children from *all* language, cultural, and social backgrounds (Adams, 1990; Foorman, 1995; Honig, 1996).

The idea of a balanced approach to literacy instruction has great appeal to many educators and policymakers. The appeal has been particularly strong in large urban school districts that are desperate to improve literacy achievement among their students, particularly students from cultural and linguistic minority groups and economically disadvantaged students. The numbers of schools and districts implementing balanced approaches to literacy instruction is growing rapidly. At the forefront of this movement are the California Department of Education, the Dallas Independent School District, the Houston Independent School District, and the Denver Public Schools. Each of these educational settings has adopted some form of balanced literacy program. As a result, each

has also created intensive staff development programs to implement balanced literacy instruction. All the states and districts listed above have large numbers of Spanish-speaking students, and therefore must consider how best to implement a balanced literacy program in Spanish.

As with many educational innovations, balanced literacy approaches in the United States originated in another English-speaking country (New Zealand) and were developed in English (Reutzel, 1998). They are not yet being discussed or widely implemented in Latin American countries. This means that, once again, bilingual educators are learning about an English literacy program that, with little or no guidance, they will have to implement in Spanish.

As stated before, balanced literacy is thought to combine the most powerful elements of the other major approaches to literacy instruction. Components of balanced literacy programs vary slightly from district to district. Reutzel (1998) offers the most comprehensive definition of balanced literacy, and with it, an important caveat. Balanced literacy programs have only recently been implemented in the United States, but they have been implemented for many years in New Zealand (Department of Education, 1985). Balanced literacy programs are more than just inclusions of phonics and whole-language, as they have been developed in the United States. Fully developed balanced approaches consider all of the following:

1. Environmental design
2. Assessment
3. Modeling
4. Guidance
5. Interactivity
6. Independence
7. Practice
8. Oral language acquisition
9. Writing and reading processes
10. Community building
11. Motivation
12. Phonological awareness
13. Print awareness
14. Alphabetic and orthographic awareness
15. Orthographic awareness.

The reader can easily see elements of synthetic, analytic, and socio-psychological orientations to literacy teaching in this list. Given the current trends toward the implementation of balanced reading programs in schools, and the potential of that approach, it is important to ask: How do teachers implement balanced literacy programs in Spanish? Is balanced reading in Spanish the same as in English? Is balanced reading the same for children of all ages and cultural and social backgrounds, as Adams (1990) suggests? What needs to be changed or adapted or both?

I would argue that many important components of balanced literacy programs *cannot* be implemented the same way in Spanish as in English. Research on Spanish reading indicates that a common framework for literacy development in both English and Spanish might be effective because both languages are alphabetic (Jiménez & Haro, 1995; Goldenberg, 1990, 1998; Jiménez, García, & Pearson, 1996). However, the same researchers are quick to caution that there must be accommodations for each language. For example, in Spanish, the basic building block of reading is the syllable, in contrast to the letter or phoneme in English. Further, the two languages differ greatly in their spelling systems, writing conventions, and discourse patterns.

Balanced literacy programs include many synthetic and analytic methods (e.g., phonemic awareness, print awareness, alphabetic awareness), making it critical that consideration be given to how the Spanish language works. Overall, it is important for schools and teachers to discuss the ways in which English-language balanced literacy programs need to be modified if they are to be effective for Spanish speakers.

An additional issue in the United States relates to the interaction in bilingual schools between the Spanish and English languages. It is commonly suggested to teachers that effective balanced literacy programs need to be structured for at least 2 to 3 hours every school day. This is more than half the school day in many cities. For Spanish-speaking children, the issue becomes when and how instruction in English as a Second Language should occur. In the United States, Spanish speakers are expected to learn oral English at the same time they learn to read in Spanish. Thus, bilingual teachers must consider how to integrate oral language acquisition in both Spanish and English into their balanced literacy programs. Conversely, if schools decide that ESL is to be separate from balanced literacy, teachers must consider when it will be taught and how it will fit into the school day.

For balanced literacy to have a positive impact on Spanish-speaking children, schools and teachers must have knowledge about how best to teach alphabetic, orthographic, and phonemic awareness in Spanish, as well as how to integrate the teaching of English into the balanced literacy program and school day for Spanish speakers. Further, they must understand reading and writing processes, how to create print environments that honor and validate Spanish as well as English, and how to motivate students to want to become biliterate. In short, to be effective, schools and teachers must have ongoing, specific conversations about how to implement balanced literacy programs for Spanish-speaking children. An example of the kinds of discussions needed to implement balanced literacy for Spanish speakers is discussed next.

Balanced Literacy—Language-Specific Issues and Modifications from English Methods: *Phonics They Use*

A personal anecdote will serve as an introduction to this section. During the past school year, I was involved in a partner school project with a group of teachers from an inner-city school. The partner school is 87 percent Latino, 44 percent limited English proficient, and 97 percent free and reduced lunch. The school mirrors the school district's demographics. The district is 49 percent Latino, 25 percent limited English proficient, and 70 percent free and reduced lunch. The school was one of several in the district selected to participate in an intensive in-service program designed to teach strategies and methods for implementing a balanced literacy program. As time allowed, I participated in these in-service sessions with teachers from the school.

The in-service program was well organized and informative; however, it was offered entirely in English. Handouts, professional literature, and teaching examples were all presented in English. In contrast, over 75 percent of those attending the in-service program were bilingual teachers who were teaching reading only in Spanish and were also charged with teaching ESL.

At one of the in-service sessions, all the teachers were given copies of Pat Cunningham's book *Phonics They Use* (1995). As a group they read the book and discussed how they could use its many teaching ideas in their own classrooms. Many of the bilingual teachers asked if these ideas were appropriate in Spanish. They were told that the teaching ideas would also work in Spanish. However, not once were bilingual teachers engaged in specific conversations about how to adapt Cunningham's ideas into Spanish literacy instruction.

After the in-service sessions were over, I worked with a group of teachers from the partner school. We generated the ideas presented below about how to modify Cunningham's book for use in Spanish. The reader should note that these ideas represent weeks of work, and that bilingual teachers were expected to individually make these adaptations into Spanish without being given any guidance or extra time. The English literacy teachers had ready-made tools supplied to them, while the Spanish/English bilingual teachers were left to their own devices.

The ideas below are not presented as a criticism of the Cunningham book, which is an excellent resource for teachers. However, it was written for teachers who teach in English. This discussion is meant to illustrate the many important differences between English and Spanish that need to be acknowledged and explained if the ideas for teaching in English are to be successfully transferred to teaching in Spanish. It is also meant to demonstrate the complexities involved in the adaptation of reading approaches across languages. This discussion concerns only one part of the Cunningham book, the section on word walls.

Cunningham suggests that teachers utilize high-utility word walls to help children develop fluency in reading/writing (p. 100). She then provides numerous examples of possible high-utility wall words. To maximize utilization of this strategy, the following need to be considered for Spanish instruction.

1. Separate Word Walls in Spanish and English

Perhaps the most important point is that in many bilingual classrooms, teachers attempt to put Spanish and English side by side or to do two things at once by creating word walls that include both Spanish and English words. This is a questionable practice. For one reason, a two-language word wall could contain words such as *come* (come in English) and *come* (eat in Spanish). While the words are spelled the same, they are read and pronounced differently in different languages, and have vastly different meanings. The attempt to increase reading fluency could create confusion instead.

The vowels in Spanish and English have different sounds. *E* in English (e.g., eat) is not the same as *E* in Spanish, which makes an long *A* sound (e.g., *elefante*, elephant). *I* in English (e.g., ice cream) is not the same as *I* in Spanish, which makes a long *E* sound (e.g., *indio*, Indian).

Teachers who are responsible for teaching literacy in both Spanish and English should make sure that they have *separate* word walls for each language. Attention to separate word walls is an important aspect of balanced literacy related to the environmental design (Reutzel, 1998).

2. Frequently Used Words on Word Walls

Cunningham suggests having frequently used words on word walls. She defines frequently used words as those that make up 50 percent of the words children read and write. Spanish also has words that are frequently used, but they are different from the English words. Frequently used words in English are often words that are phonetically irregular and need to be learned as site words. Frequently used words in Spanish are very often phonetically regular, but learning them as site words helps to increase reading fluency. The following is a widely used Spanish frequent words list (Cornejo, 1972). The list is divided by grade; however, teachers should make their own decisions about which words to use in their own word walls.

3. Word Walls Illustrating Initial Consonant Sounds

Cunningham recommends that word walls in early elementary classrooms contain examples for each initial consonant. The same is true in Spanish, with two exceptions. In Spanish there are some letters that do not occur (or seldom occur) in initial consonant positions even though they are a part of the Spanish alphabet. These letters are *rr* and *ñ*. It would be much more helpful to children if these letters in the medial positions of words were highlighted on word walls as shown below:

Examples: Pe**rr**o or Pe<u>rr</u>o
carro or ca<u>rr</u>o
niña or ni<u>ñ</u>a
piña or pi<u>ñ</u>a

CORNEJO'S SPANISH WORD FREQUENCY LIST

(by grade)

Pre-Primer	Primer	1st	2nd	3rd	4th	5th
a	alto	bonita	ayer	amar	árbol	amistad
azul	flor	arriba	aquí	aquí	bandera	azucar
bajo	blusa	fruta	año	debajo	abeja	contento
mi	ella	globo	cerca	familia	escuela	corazón
mesa	ir	estar	desde	fiesta	fácil	cumpleaños
pan	leche	café	donde	grande	fuego	edad
mamá	más	letra	hacer	hermana	hacia	escribir
lado	niño	luna	hasta	jueves	idea	felicidad
la	padre	luz	hijo	lápiz	jardín	guitarra
papá	por	muy	hoy	miércoles	llegar	estrella
me	si	noche	leer	once	manzana	igual
no	tan	nombre	libro	quince	muñeca	invierno
esa	sobre	nosotros	martes	sábado	naranja	orquesta
el	sin	nunca	mejor	semana	saludar	primavera
en	tras	ojo	mucho	silla	sueño	recordar
cuna	color	pelota	oir	sobrino	señorita	respeto
dos	al	porque	papel	vivir	tierra	tijeras
mi	día	rojo	paz	zapato	traer	último
de	bien	té	quien	tarde	ventana	querer
los	chico	taza	usted	traje	queso	otoño

4. Word Walls with Articles

In Spanish, the use of articles with nouns varies because of gender (feminine and masculine) and because of singular and plural usages. Children need to learn in reading and writing that article/noun agreement is important. For this reason, word walls in Spanish are more powerful if they include articles with nouns (e.g., *el libro*, the book; *la mesa*, the table; *los libros*, the books; *las mesas*, the tables).

Article usage in Spanish has different rules for words that do not end in vowels (e.g., *la navidad*, Christmas; *el reloj*, the watch). Further, there are words that are simply exceptions to the rules (e.g., *el mapa*, the map; *el problema*, the problem). In Spanish, learning rules for noun/article agreement is very important. Word walls with articles and nouns can greatly assist in teaching these concepts.

5. Word Walls That Model Upper- and Lower-Case Letters

Modeling of reading and writing in many contexts and in many ways is an important component of balanced literacy instruction (Reutzel, 1998). Cunningham recommends word walls that illustrate both upper- and lower-case letters (e.g., *A/a; D/d*) as one type of modeling. The same idea could be applied in Spanish, with several caveats. In Spanish, there are several letters that are represented by two letters: *Ch, Ll,* and *rr*. Capitalization of these letters requires that only the first letter be upper case. It is not appropriate to provide the following as a model on a word wall: *LL, CH, RR*. Word walls should model these letters as follows: *Ch/ch; Ll/ll*. The letter *rr* never occurs at the beginning of a word and therefore should never be modeled in the upper case. Further, *ñ* is only rarely capitalized, and in some countries when letters such as *ñ* are capitalized, they lose their tilde (the mark above the *ñ*).

6. Word Walls with Examples for Each Initial Consonant and Vowel

Cunningham suggests that a word wall contain an example word for each initial consonant. Presumably, she does not suggest common words for vowels because of the way vowel sounds change in English. In Spanish, it would be appropriate to provide examples for each initial consonant *and* vowel. Vowel sounds in Spanish are phonetically regular and occur much more frequently in Spanish words than in English words. Including vowels in Spanish is also important because they emerge in writing in Spanish before they do in English (see the letters and words listed below).

It is important to note here that in Spanish, it is often confusing to teach the names of the letters as well as the letter sounds. In learning to read and write, knowing the sound of a letter is much more useful to emergent readers and writers than knowing a letter's name.

Vowels in the order of the frequency of their use in Spanish are as follows:

O/o – el oso (the bear)
I/i – el imán (the magnet)
E/e – el elefante (the elephant)
A/a – el avión (the airplane)
U/u – las uvas (the grapes)

Consonants in the order of the frequency of their use in Spanish are as follows:

M/m – La mariposa (the butterfly)
S/s – El sol (the sun)
D/d – El dedal (the thimble)
F/f – La flor (the flower)
T/t – El tambor (the drum)
C/c (fuerte) – La casa (the house)
C/c (suave) – La ciudad (the city)
N/n – El nido (the nest)
P/p – La papa (the potato)
L/l – El limón (the lemon)
R/r – El ratón (the rat)
G/g (fuerte) – El gato (the cat)
G/g (suave) – El gigante (the giant)
B/b (de burro) – El bebé (the baby)*
V/v (de vaca) – La ventana (the window)*

J/j – La jaula – (the cage)

H/h (muda) – El hilo (the string)†

Ch/ch – El chivo (the goat)

N/ñ – La niña (the girl)

Ll/ll – La lluvia (the rain)

K/k – El kiosko (the kiosk)

Y/y – El yoyo (the yoyo)

Z/z – El zoológico (the zoo)

W/w – *Not* a letter in Spanish; used only when writing foreign words (e.g., *Washington*)

* The letters *B* and *V* make the same sound in Spanish. To help children differentiate the two letters, teachers in Mexico often refer to these letters as *b de burro*, meaning *b*, and *v de vaca*, meaning *v*. Having this language visually displayed on a word wall could also be helpful for children.

† *H* in Spanish does not make a sound. It can easily be represented on a word wall using a picture of a face with eyes, a nose, and no mouth.

7. Word Walls with Examples of High-Utility Words That Are Frequently Misspelled

Cunningham suggests that teachers have word walls that contain common vowel spelling patterns. Again, because of the phonetic regularity of vowels in Spanish, this may not be useful for Spanish-speaking students. However, there are letters and letter combinations that have the same sound and thereby create spelling problems for Spanish speakers. These words are commonly misspelled. In Spanish, frequently confused letters are often called "Monster Letters." They include: *b/v; c/s/z; g/j; h* and *ll/y* (see example below). Having a word wall with commonly misspelled words in Spanish could be very useful.

Examples: Llo boi a la hescuela y despues seno con mis ermanos.

(Yo voy a la escuela y después ceno con mis hermanos).

I go to school and then I eat dinner with my brothers.

8. Word Walls for Contractions

Cunningham suggests having a word wall for common English contractions (e.g., *can't, didn't*). Having a contraction word wall in Spanish makes no sense. There are only two contractions in Spanish (*a + el = al* and *de + el = del*).

9. Word Walls for Common Blends

Having a word wall for common blends in Spanish, as in English, makes good sense. Examples include the following:

Fr – el frío (the cold)

Fl – la flor (the flower)

Br – la brisa (the breeze)

Bl – la blusa (the blouse)

Gr – el grito (the scream)

Gl – el globo (the balloon)

Pl – el plato (the plate)

Pr – el prima (the cousin)

Tr – el tren (the train)

Cl – el clavo (the nail)

Cr – creer (to believe)

Tr – la trucha (the trout)

10. Word Walls with High-Frequency Words That Need Accents/Tildes/Diereses (See Cornejo's list in item 2, above)

There are no accent marks in English, and thus the issue of how to teach students about accents, tildes, and diereses does not arise. However, in written Spanish, various types of accent marks are important. They change word meanings and are important markers of time. For example, *la papa* means potato, but *el papá* means father and *el papa* means the pope. Further, a word like *hablo* means I talk (present tense), but *habló* means he, she, or you talked (past tense). It is critical that teachers teach Spanish speakers rules about when and how to use accents in their writing. At the beginning stages of literacy, teachers may assist students in learning how to use accents by having word walls that show high-frequency words that utilize the markings.

Examples: High-frequency words that need an accent mark
mamá, papá, está, día

High-frequency words that need the tilde
mañana, piña, niña

High-frequency words that need the dieresis
pingüino, bilingüe

11. Word Walls to Demonstrate How to Join Syllables to Make Words

Sample word walls for the most common vowel spelling patterns in English are not appropriate in Spanish. What is helpful to children as they learn to read and write is to learn how syllables are formed and how they combine to make words. A word wall with examples of how to join syllables together to make words would be very useful to Spanish speakers. For a more detailed explanation of how to help children learn to combine syllables to make words and other issues related to teaching word recognition and comprehension, see Ferreiro, Pellicer, Rodríguez, & Vernon (1991).

Examples: pa + to = pato
ga + to = gato
ma + to = mato
ma + lo = malo
pa + lo = palo

12. Word Walls with Words That Children Frequently Use in Their Writing

Word walls with children's favorite or often-used words can be used in both Spanish and English (e.g. *favorito, familia, hermanos, escuela*). However, as stated above, words in the two languages should be placed on separate word walls.

13. Review Rhyme with Word Wall

Cunningham suggests that word walls be used to teach about word families (p. 105) (see the English example below). While a similar technique could be used in teaching Spanish, it is important for teachers to know that word families in Spanish are not the same as word families in English (see

the Spanish example below).

English: at
b + at = bat
c + at = cat
m + at = mat
r + at = rat

Spanish: zapato (shoe)
zapatería (shoe store)
zapatero (cobbler, shoe repairer)

pan (bread)
panadero (baker)
panadería (bakery)

libro (book)
librería (bookstore)
librero (bookseller)

pez (live fish before it has been caught)
pescado (fish after it has been caught)
pescador (fisherman)
pescadería (fish market)

The above examples are all meant for teachers who are teaching in primary grades. Cunningham also provides suggestions for word walls for intermediate grades, which, with teaching ideas and suggested modifications for teaching in Spanish, are summarized below.

1. Word Walls for Commonly Used Homophones

Commonly used homophones make useful word walls in Spanish as well as in English. Again, homophones are different in Spanish and in English. Examples for the highest utility homophones in Spanish are as follows:

Haber / A Ver (dos palabras)
Ola / Hola
Hacer / A Ser (dos palabras)
cayó / calló
haya / halla
coser / cocer
casar / cazar
azar / asar / azhar

2. Word Walls for Commonly Used Compound Words

Commonly used compound words make useful word walls. Compound words, too, are different in Spanish and in English. Examples of compound words in Spanish are as follows:

> cumpleaños
> rascacielos
> tocadiscos
> portavoz
> sacapuntas
> guardarraya
> guardarropa
> guardaespaldas
> sobrecama
> sobremesa
> sobresaliente
> rompecabezas
> paraguas
> parabrisas
> anteojos
> paracaídas
> fotosíntesis

3. Word Walls for Hard-to-Spell Words

Hard-to-spell words make useful word walls. Hard-to-spell words and word patterns are different in Spanish and in English. Useful rules and examples for hard-to-spell words in Spanish are given below. For a more detailed discussion of Spanish spelling rules, see Aguilar (1997) or the Secretaría de Educación Pública (1995).

Rules for H: Se escriben con *h* (you write with an *h*):

Todos los tiempos del verbo *haber*
> he hube habré, había, habría, hay, hubiera, etc.

Todas las palabras que principian con los diptongos *ua, ue, ui, ia, ie*
> huarache, huevo, huir, hiato, hielo

Todos los tiempos del verbo *hacer*
> hago, hice, haré, hacía, hecho

Todos las formas de los verbos *hablar, hallar, habitar*
> hablo, habité, hallé

Las interjecciones
> ¡bah! ¡ah! ¡eh!

Rules for Ll: Se escriben con *ll* (you write with *ll*):

Todas las palabras que comienzan con *fa, fo, fu*
> falleció, fallaste, folletos

Todas las palabras que terminan con *illo* y *illa* (palabras diminutivos)
> costilla, boquilla, panecillo, chiquillo

Los vocablos que comienzan con *lla, lle, llo, llu*
> llamada, llanta, llenar, llorón, lluvia

Rules for B: Se escriben con la letra *B* (you write with a *b*):

Los verbos *haber, saber, caber, deber, beber, trabajar, robar, acabar*

Las terminaciones *aba, abas, ábamos*, de los verbos conjugados en copretérito del modo indicativo
> jugaba, llevabas, caminábamos

Las palabras que llevan *b* antes de otra consonante (*br, bl,* y *bs*)
> brisa, blusa, absolutismo, cobre

Las palabras que tienen las sílabas compuestas *bla, ble, bli, blo, blu*
> bloque, cable, blando, tabla, broma, brusco, bruma, libre

Rules for V: Se escriben con la letra *V* (you write with a *v*):

Todos los verbos que terminan en *servar*
> reservar, observar, conservar

Todos los adjetivos que terminan en *ava, ave, eva, ivo, iva, evo*
> brava, suave, primitiva, agresiva

Los verbos *ir, estar, andar,* y *tener* en sus conjugaciones en pretérito
> con sus compuestos y derivados
> estuve, anduve, tuve, ve, va, van

Las palabras que compiezan con *ven*
> ventaja, veneno, vencedor, vencer, vengar, venir, venta

4. Word Walls for Accent Rules

As stated above, English does not use accent marks. However, they are very important in writing in Spanish (and also very difficult to teach and learn). A useful word wall for intermediate students may be one that illustrates basic accent rules.

Examples:

- Palabras esdrújulas – Todas las palabras que reciben el acento en la antepenúltima sílaba siempre llevan acento. (Words that place the accent (stress) on the third to the last syllable require an accent.)

    Último, exámenes, mayúscula, capítulo, cándido

- En algunas palabras monosilábicas el acento sirve para distinguirlas cuando se hallan en función gramatical diferente. (In some monosyllablic words the accent mark serves to distinguish the word when it is used as a different part of speech.)

    El (artículo) (article), él (pronombre) (pronoun)

    Se (pronombre) (pronoun) sé (verbo) (verb)

    Tu, mi (adjetivos) (adjective), tú, mí (pronombres) (pronouns)

    Si (conjunctivo) (conjunction), sí (adverbio)

- Cuando se usan las palabras *donde, cuando, como, que, por que*, o *cual* en una oración interrogativa. (When you use the words *where, when, how, what, why*, or *which* in a sentence that asks a question, you use a question mark.)

    ¿Por qué no tenemos escuela mañana?
    ¿Cuál es tu libro favorito?
    ¿Cuándo empieza el baile este sábado?

5. Word Walls That Illustrate Contrasts in English and Spanish

A paramount issue for Spanish/English bilingual teachers in the United States is when and how students will begin transition, even if they continue from Spanish literacy to English literacy. In the intermediate grades, a useful word wall might be one that contrasts English and Spanish conventions. This might be helpful as students make transitions from Spanish to English.

Examples:

- Words with capitals in English, but not in Spanish

    days of the week
    months of the year

- Punctuation in English and Spanish: In Spanish, question sentences and exclamation sentences have punctuation marks at the beginning and end of a sentence. In English, they appear only at the end.

    !Qué bonito día!
    What a beautiful day!

    ¿Cuál es tu apellido?
    What is your last name?

- Date notation devices in Spanish and English

    In English, 2/3/96 is February 3, 1996; in Spanish, 3/2/96 is February 3, 1996.

These lists of ideas and examples are by no means exhaustive. However, they are meant to give bilingual teachers ideas for applying appropriate teaching techniques, such as those proposed by Cunningham, in authentic ways in Spanish. If bilingual teachers are to provide the same quality of literacy instruction to Spanish-speaking students as they do to English-speaking students, they must have the same tools, information, and support systems.

To summarize this section, it is important to state once again that methods of teaching reading that have a synthetic or analytic orientation, such as those represented in balanced literacy methods—including phonemic awareness, alphabetic awareness, and phonological awareness—are language-specific. That is, sound methodology and teaching techniques need to be developed by studying the particular language and knowing how it works. For these methods, it is not enough to apply English methods in Spanish. There are, however, a number of approaches in a balanced literacy program that could be considered to be universal. These methods are discussed briefly below.

Balanced Literacy: Universal Approaches Applied in Spanish

As stated previously, many teaching approaches that are recommended for English balanced literacy programs can be applied in Spanish balanced literacy programs without extensive modification. These include modeling, shared reading, guided reading, interactive teaching, independent reading, writing and reading processes, community building, and motivation (Reutzel, 1998). The power of these approaches, in Spanish, is dependent on the ability of the school and teacher to give equal status and time to Spanish literacy instruction. Throughout the history of bilingual education in the United States, providing equal status across languages has been difficult for Spanish/English bilingual teachers (Escamilla, 1992, 1994; Shannon, 1995; Shannon & Escamilla, 1999). Unless both languages have equal status, it is difficult to motivate students to want to learn to read and write in two languages.

Applying equal status to both Spanish and English in bilingual classrooms means that the print environment in these classrooms gives equal attention to both languages. It means that bilingual classrooms and school libraries are well stocked with books in Spanish as well as English. It means that the Spanish book collection includes works that were originally written in Spanish as well as titles that have been translated from English. It means that the English-language collection includes good literature that was originally written in Spanish and has been translated into English. It means that literature collections include works that reflect the cultural, linguistic, and historical heritage of the community. Teachers and schools need to make certain that the same variety of literature that is accessible to English speakers is accessible to Spanish speakers. This includes books written at various levels of difficulty and representing a variety of genres. Bishop (1994) eloquently writes that multicultural book collections in schools are critical in order to serve as mirrors and windows for children of all cultural groups. Mirrors enable children to see themselves in books, and windows enable children to learn about the lives and stories of other cultural groups.

Unfortunately, research on the availability of literature and other books in Spanish in U.S. schools has established that many schools with large numbers of Spanish-speaking students have library collections that are not adequate in Spanish (Pucci, 1994; DeLaurie, 1998). Further, many classrooms and school libraries lack literature that represents the cultural experiences of Spanish-speaking students (Barrera, Linguori, & Salas, 1992; Barrera & Garza de Cortés, 1997; Barrera, 1992). Barrera & Garza de Cortés (1997) found, for example, that between 1992 and 1995, only 67 children's books were published with themes reflecting Mexican-American experiences. Further, twice as many fiction books as nonfiction works were published. Teachers in schools with bilingual programs need to become advocates for themselves and their students by ensuring that the literature collection in classrooms and school libraries is equitable for students from all language groups. They must also ensure that the literature is representative of the cultures and communities of their schools.

Students learning to read and write in Spanish must have daily opportunities to read and write in Spanish in authentic ways and for real purposes. Choral reading, echo reading, readers' theater, literature studies, author studies, and readers' and writers' workshops are all strategies that can be used effectively in Spanish with little need for modification except for the materials. Again, it is important for bilingual teachers to use culturally relevant and engaging materials as they organize their reading programs. For example, many texts can be modified to become readers' theater projects. However, the impact on students is more powerful if teachers choose materials related to student real-life experiences. For example, *Pepita Habla Dos Veces* (*Pepita Talks Twice*, 1995) is a book about a Spanish-speaking girl growing up in the United

States and learning two languages. She becomes tired of using two languages and decides to speak only English in spite of her family, friends, and teacher, who tell her it's wonderful to be bilingual. Pepita sees bilingualism as a burden. Pepita's story is typical of the struggle that many children experience as they learn two languages. The book is easily turned from narrative into a culturally affirming readers' theater piece. Similarly, author studies can be conducted on writers such as Gary Soto, Pat Mora, and Alma Flor Ada, as well as Judy Blume, Shel Silverstein, and Tommy de Paola.

Books representing real-life experiences of Spanish-speaking children should be part of the daily literacy experience in schools. *Los Recuerdos de Chave* (*Chave's Memories*, 1996) is an example of a common experience of Mexican-American children. The book is about a child's memories of yearly family trips to his grandparents' *rancho* (farm) in rural Mexico. Books such as this one make excellent books for literature studies, read-alouds, and independent reading. For suggestions of stories and books written by and about various Latino cultures, see Bishop (1994), Harris (1997), and Escamilla & Nathenson-Mejía (1997).

If equal status is to be given to two languages and if children are to become bilingual and biliterate, they must be assessed in two languages. Achievement in literacy in Spanish must be valued and rewarded by schools in the same way that achievement in English is valued and rewarded. Assessment practices should not be English measures and tools translated and/or adapted into Spanish without careful consideration of how Spanish is different from English. They should be tools that reflect the conventions, the rhetorical and discourse structures, and the cultures of Spanish-speaking students.

Conclusion

To summarize this article, it is important to emphasize once again that teaching children to read in Spanish is *not* the same as teaching children to read in English. While there are a number of similarities, it should not be assumed that a teacher who knows how to teach reading in English is prepared to teach reading in Spanish. Best-practice literacy programs in Spanish need to be grounded in a knowledge base of how the Spanish language works. Spanish literacy programs can and should be further informed by a knowledge base that combines best practice in English literacy with best practice in Spanish literacy.

The number of Spanish-speaking students in the United States continues to grow rapidly. This is one of the fastest-growing school-aged groups. Research and experience have shown that the best entry into literacy for these children is in their native language, in this case Spanish. Many bilingual teachers have not had opportunities to take methods courses that focus on teaching reading in Spanish, nor have they had opportunities to learn formal academic Spanish. Therefore, it is critical that schools create literacy programs that are specifically designed and implemented for Spanish speakers and that engage teachers in learning more about how to teach literacy in Spanish. Teachers need models, examples, and tools that enable them to create exemplary biliterate learning environments for the children they teach. To do this, they must have professional development opportunities, professional books, children's books, and other resources in Spanish that are equivalent in both quantity and quality to these resources in English.

The goal of biliteracy for Spanish-speaking students and others is both worthy and attainable. However, for this goal to become a reality, we must pay careful attention to developing skills and strategies in biliteracy in both our students and our teachers. Moreover, we must build classroom and school environments that honor and validate both languages.

The author wishes to gratefully acknowledge the suggestions and contributions made to this article by the following colleagues: Terry Berkeley, Vivian Cuesta, Diana Geisler, Silivia Latimer, Sally Nathenson-Mejía, and Olivia Ruiz.

REFERENCES

Adams, M. J. (1990). *Beginning to read: Thinking and learning about print*. Cambridge, MA: MIT Press.

Adams, M.J., & Bruck, M. (1995). Resolving the "great debate." *American Educator, 19* (2), 7, 10–20.

Aguilar, Katya S. (1997). *Ejercicios de caligrafía y ortografía*. Mexico, D.F.: Ediciones Aguilar.

August, D., & Hakuta, K. (1997). *Improving schooling for language-minority children: A research agenda*. National Research Council Institute of Medicine. Washington, DC: National Academy Press.

Barrera, R. (1992). The cultural gap in literature-based literacy instruction. *Education and Urban Society, 24* (2), 227–243.

Barrera, R., Liguori, O., & Salas, L. (1993). Ideas a literature can grow on: Key insights for enriching and expanding children's literature about the Mexican American experience. In V. Harris (Ed.), *Teaching multicultural literature in grades K–8*. Norwood, MA: Christopher-Gordon Publishers.

Barrera, R., & Garza de Cortés, O. (1997). Mexican American children's literature in the 1990's: Toward authenticity. In V. Harris (Ed.), *Using multiethnic literature in the K–8 classroom*. Norwood, MA: Christopher-Gordon Publishers.

Bishop, R. (1994). *Kaleidoscope: A multicultural booklist for grades K–8*. Urbana, IL: National Council of Teachers of English.

Braslavsky, B. (1962). *La querella de los métodos en la enseñanza de la lectura*. Buenos Aires: Kapelusz.

Brown, A. (1992). Building community support through local educational funds. *NABE News, 15* (5), 4–5.

Cassidy, J., & Wenrich, J.K. (1997). What's hot, what's not for 1997. *Reading Today*, p. 34.

Castedo, M.L. (1995). Construcción de lectores y escritores. *Lectura y Vida, 16* (3), 5–25.

Chall, J. (1967). *Learning to read: The great debate*. New York: McGraw-Hill.

Chall, J. (1999). Commentary: Some thoughts on reading research: Revisiting the first-grade studies. *Reading Research Quarterly, 34* (1), 8–10.

Clay, M. (1993). Issues in initial reading instruction. Paper presented at the West Coast Literacy Conference, Palm Springs, CA.

Collier, V., & Thomas, W. (1995). *Language minority student achievement and program effectiveness*. Washington, DC: National Clearinghouse for Bilingual Education.

Condemarín, M. (1991). Integración de dos modelos en el desarrollo del lenguaje oral y escrito. *Lectura y Vida, 12* (4), 13–22.

Cornejo, R. (1972). *Spanish high-frequency word list*. Austin, TX: Southwestern Educational Laboratory.

Cummins, J. (1981). The role of primary language development in promoting educational success for language minority students. In *Schooling and language minority students: A theoretical framework*. Los Angeles: Evaluation and Assessment Center, California State University, Los Angeles.

Cunningham, P. (1995). *Phonics they use*. New York: HarperCollins.

Cunningham, P. (1991). Research directions: Multimethod, multilevel instruction in first grade. *Language Arts, 68*, 578–584.

Cunningham, P., & Allington, R. I. (1994). *Classrooms that work: They can all read and write*. New York: HarperCollins.

DeLaurie, A. (1999). Diversity and the library media teacher. *The Multilingual Educator*, 14–16.

Delgado, M. (1996). *Chave's Memories (Los recuerdos de Chave)*. Houston: Arte Público Press.

Department of Education, Wellington District. (1985). Reading in junior classes. Wellington, N.Z., and New York: Richard C. Owens.

Escamilla, K. (1994). The sociolinguistic environment of a bilingual school: A case study introduction. *The Bilingual Research Journal, 18* (1&2), 21–47.

Escamilla, K. (1993). Promoting biliteracy: Issues in promoting English literacy in students acquiring English. In A. Flor Ada & J. Tinajero (Eds.), *The power of two languages: Literacy and biliteracy for America's Spanish-speaking students* (pp. 220–233). New York: Macmillan/McGraw-Hill.

Escamilla, K. (1992). Theory to practice: A look at maintenance bilingual education classrooms. *The Journal of Educational Issues of Language Minority Students, 11*, 1–23.

Escamilla, K. (1987). *The relationship of native-language reading achievement and oral English proficiency to future achievement in reading English as a second language*. Unpublished doctoral dissertation, University of California, Los Angeles.

Escamilla, K., & Nathenson-Mejía, S. (1997). Latino children's literature as a tool for preparing teachers of Mexican and Mexican-American children. Paper presented at the National Association for Multicultural Education (NAME) Conference, Albuquerque, NM.

Ferdman, B. (1990). Literacy and cultural identity. *Harvard Education Review, 60*, 181–204.

Flippo, R. F. (December, 1997). Sensationalism, politics, and literacy: What's going on? *Phi Delta Kappan*, 301–304.

Ferreiro, E. (1994). Diversidad y proceso de alfabetización: De la celebración a la toma de conciencia. *Lectura y Vida*, *15* (3), 5–14.

Ferreiro, E., Pellicer, A., Rodríguez, B., Silva, A., & Vernon, S. (1991). *Haceres, quehaceres y deshaceres con la lengua escrita en la escuela primaria*. Mexico, D.F.: Secretaría de Educación Pública.

Figueroa, R., & García, E. (1994, Fall). Issues in testing students from culturally and linguistically diverse backgrounds. *Multicultural Education*, 10–19.

Foorman, B.R. (1995). Research on "The Great Debate": Code-oriented versus whole-language approaches to reading instruction. *Educational Psychology Review*, *6*, 25–47.

Freeman, Y., & Freeman, D. (1997). *Teaching reading and writing in Spanish in the bilingual classroom*. Portsmouth, NH: Heinemann.

Goldenberg, C. (1998). A balanced approach to early Spanish literacy instruction. In R. Gersten & R. Jiménez (Eds.), *Promoting learning for culturally and linguistically diverse students*. Belmont, CA: Wadsworth.

Goldenberg, C. (1990). Beginning literacy instruction for Spanish-speaking children. *Language Arts*, *67*, 590–598.

Goodman, K. (1989). *Lenguaje integral*. (Trans. Adelina Arellano Osuna). Mérida: Editorial Venezolana.

Goodman, K. (1986). *What's whole in whole language*. Portsmouth, NH: Heinemann.

Greene, J. (1998). *A meta-analysis of the effectiveness of bilingual education*. Unpublished manuscript, University of Texas at Austin.

Guerrero, M. (1997). Spanish academic language proficiency: The case of bilingual education teachers in the U.S. *The Bilingual Research Journal*, *21* (1), 25–43.

Harris, V. (1997). *Using multicultural literature in the K–8 classroom*. Norwood, MA: Christopher Gordon Publishers.

Honig, B. (1996). *Teaching our children to read*. Thousand Oaks, CA: Corwin Press.

Jiménez, R., & Haro, C. (1995). Effects of word linguistic properties on phonological awareness in Spanish children. *Journal of Educational Psychology*, *87*, 193–201.

Jiménez, R., García, E., & Pearson, P. (1996). The reading strategies of bilingual Latina/o students who are successful English readers: Opportunities and obstacles. *Reading Research Quarterly*, *31* (1), 90–112.

Krashen, S., & Biber, D. (1988). *On course: Bilingual education's success in California*. Sacramento: California Association for Bilingual Education.

Lachtman, O. (1995). *Pepita talks twice (Pepita habla dos veces)*. Houston: Arte Público Press.

Lindholm, K. (1993). Un modelo educacional de éxito para estudiantes inmigrantes de origen Latino. *Revista de psicologeia social y personalidad, IX* (2), 85–94.

Leasher-Madrid, D., & García, E. (1985). The effect of language transfer on bilingual proficiency. In E. García & R. Padilla (Eds.), *Advances in bilingual education research*. Tucson: University of Arizona Press.

Modiano, N. (1968). National or mother tongue in beginning reading: A comparative study. *Research in the Teaching of English, II* (I), 32–43.

National Research Council. (1998). *Preventing reading difficulties in young children*. Washington, DC: National Academy Press.

Pucci, S. (1994). Supporting Spanish language literacy: Latino children and free reading resources in schools. *Bilingual Research Journal*, *18* (1 & 2), 67–82.

Ramírez, D., Yuen, S., & Ramey, D. (1991). *Final report: Longitudinal study of structured English immersion, early-exit, and late-exit transitional bilingual education programs for language minority children*. San Mateo, CA: Aguirre International.

Reutzel, D.R. (1998). On balanced reading. *The Reading Teacher, 52* (4), 322–324.

Reyes, M. (1990). Challenging venerable assumptions: Literacy instruction for linguistically different students. *Harvard Education Review, 62* (4), 427–445.

Rodríguez, A. (1988). Research in reading and writing in bilingual education and English as a second language. In A. Ambert (Ed.), *Bilingual education and English as a second language: A research handbook*. New York: Garland.

Secretaría de Educación Pública. (1995). *Ficheros—actividades didácticas en Español, grados 1–6*. Mexico City: Secretaría de Educación Pública.

Shannon, S., & Escamilla, K. (1999). Mexican immigrants in U.S. schools: Targets of symbolic violence. *Education Policy, 13* (4).

Thomas, W., & Collier, V. (1997). *School effectiveness for language minority students*. Washington, DC: National Clearinghouse for Bilingual Education.

Solé I Gallart, I. (1995). El placer de leer. *Lectura y Vida, 16* (3), 25–30.

Waggoner, D., & O'Malley, J. (1984). Teachers of limited English proficient children in the United States. *Journal of the National Association for Bilingual Education, 9* (3), 25–42.

EFFECTIVE TRANSITIONING STRATEGIES: ARE WE ASKING THE RIGHT QUESTIONS?

Lilia I. Bartolomé
Harvard University

Introduction

Much of the current discussion regarding linguistic minority academic achievement in our schools stresses the topic of successful or effective teaching strategies. The term *teaching strategies* refers to an educational plan or a series of activities/lessons designed to obtain a specific goal or result. However, before we can discuss these strategies—transitioning strategies in particular—and their effectiveness or ineffectiveness, it is necessary to discuss their perceived effectiveness within the larger sociocultural context. We must consider why, on the one hand, these strategies are warranted, and on the other hand, why these strategies are deemed effective in a given sociocultural context.

In his letter to North American educators, Paulo Freire (1987) warns against uncritically importing and exporting strategies and methods with no regard for sociocultural contexts. He states that teachers must possess content area knowledge *and* political clarity to be able to effectively create, adopt, and modify teaching strategies that simultaneously respect and challenge the learner. It is critical that educators become so well versed in the theory of their specializations that they own their knowledge. This ownership imbues the educators with confidence while translating theory that enables them simultaneously to consider the population being served and the sociocultural context in which learning is expected to take place. It is equally critical that teachers comprehend that their role as educators is not politically neutral. In negating the political nature of their work, teachers maintain the status quo and their students' subordinate status (status that reflects their group's subordinate political and economic status in the larger society). Conversely, teachers can become conscious of and subsequently challenge the role of educational institutions and their own roles as educators in maintaining a system that often serves to silence students from subordinate groups.

Teachers must remember that schools, similar to other institutions in society, are influenced by perceptions of socioeconomic status (SES), race/ethnicity, language, and gender. They must begin to question how these perceptions influence classroom dynamics. It is especially important for teachers who work with students from subordinate groups to recognize historical (and current) attributions of low status to members of low SES linguistic minority populations and the subsequent mistreatment/underservicing of such populations in the schools.

So, while it is certainly important to identify effective instructional strategies, it is not sufficient to narrow and restrict our focus to instructional issues solely related to teaching methods and activities. This discussion must be broadened to reveal the deeply entrenched deficit orientation toward "difference" (e.g., social class, race/ethnicity, language, gender) in our schools. We must also ask how this view has affected our perceptions of linguistic minority students and shaped our approaches to teaching them.

In this paper I will also argue that by taking this comprehensive approach to analyzing language arts teaching strategies identified as effective within a particular sociocultural reality, we can shift our focus from the strategy itself to more fundamental pedagogical features common *across* strategies. These student-centered features are known by educators to constitute good teaching for any population. More important, in the case of linguistic minority students, they serve to offset potentially unequal relations and discriminatory structures and practices in the classroom. Without underestimating the importance of teachers' knowledge of methodology, such focus is neither sufficient nor a substitute for comprehensive and critical understanding of pedagogy and the teacher's role in its implementation—*especially* as it relates to students from subordinate populations.

For this reason, I will caution readers against the general tendency to reduce complex educational issues (those that reflect greater social, political, and economic realities) to mere "magical" methods and techniques designed to remediate perceived student cognitive and linguistic deficiencies. I will conclude by proposing what Macedo (in press) calls an *antimethods pedagogy* that refuses to be enslaved by the rigidity of models and methodological paradigms. An antimethods pedagogy should be informed by a critical understanding of the sociocultural context that guides our practices so as to free us from the beaten path of methodological certainties and specialisms.

This is a pedagogical process that requires both action and reflection. Using it, instead of importing or exporting effective strategies, teachers are required to re-create and reinvent those effective approaches, taking into consideration the sociocultural limitations *and* possibilities.

Our Legacy: A Deficit Orientation and Unequal Relations in the Classroom

Teaching strategies are neither designed nor implemented in a vacuum. Design, selection, and use of particular teaching approaches and strategies arise from perceptions about learning and learners. It is especially important, when discussing learners from subordinate populations, that we deal candidly with our deeply rooted and traditional deficit orientation toward difference. The most pedagogically advanced strategies prove ineffective in the hands of educators who implicitly or explicitly subscribe to a belief system that renders linguistic minority students, at best, culturally disadvantaged and in need of fixing (if we could only identify the right recipe!) or, at worst, culturally or genetically deficient and beyond fixing. Despite the fact that alternative models are utilized to explain the academic failure of certain linguistic minority groups—academic failure described as historical, pervasive, and disproportionate—the fact remains that our views of difference are deficit-based and deeply imprinted in our individual and collective psyches (Flores, 1982; Menchaca & Valencia, 1990; Valencia, 1986, 1991).

The deficit model has the longest history of any model discussed in the education literature. Valencia (1986) traces its evolution over three centuries.

> Also known in the literature as the "social pathology" model or the "cultural deprivation" model, the deficit approach explains disproportionate academic problems among low status students as largely being due to pathologies or deficits in their sociocultural background (e.g., cognitive and linguistic deficiencies, low self-esteem, poor motivation).... To improve the educability of such students, programs such as compensatory education and parent-child intervention have been proposed. (p. 3)

The deficit model of instruction and learning has been critiqued by numerous researchers as ethnocentric and invalid (Boykin, 1983; Díaz, Moll, & Mehan, 1986; Flores, 1982; Sue & Padilla, 1986; Trueba, 1989; Walker, 1987). Mehan (1992) correctly maintains that new lines of research offer alternative models that "shift the source of school failure away from the characteristics of the failing child, their families, their cultures, and toward more general societal processes, including schooling" (p. 2). Unfortunately, these alternative models often give rise to a kinder and liberal yet more concealed version of the deficit model. Despite the use of less ethnocentric models to explain the academic standing of linguistic minority students, I believe that our deficit orientation toward difference, especially as it relates to low socioeconomic groups, is very deeply ingrained in the ethos of our most prominent institutions, especially schools, and in compensatory programs such as bilingual education. Yet the study of structural factors within the schools has triggered research yielding valuable insights into the asymmetrical and unequal relations and how they are manifested between teachers and students from subordinate groups.

The number of studies that examine unequal power relations in the classroom has increased in recent years. Unequal and discriminatory treatment of students based on their socioeconomic status, race/ethnicity, language use, and gender has been empirically demonstrated. Findings range from teacher preference for Anglo students to bilingual teachers' preference for lighter-skinned Latino students to teachers' negative perceptions of working-class parents compared to middle-class parents, and finally to unequal teaching and assessment practices in schools serving working-class and more affluent populations (Anyon, 1988; Bloom, 1991; Lareau, 1990; U.S. Commission on Civil Rights, 1973). Especially indicative of our inability to deal honestly with our deficit orientation is the fact that the teachers in these studies—teachers from all ethnic groups—were themselves unaware of the active role they played in the differential and unequal treatment of their students.

Furthermore, many research studies that examined culturally congruent and incongruent teaching approaches actually describe the negotiation of power relations in classrooms where teachers unwittingly impose participation structures upon students from subordinate linguistic minority groups (Au & Mason, 1983; Heath, 1983; Mohatt & Erickson, 1981; Philips, 1972). These studies, in essence, capture the successful negotiation of power relations that resulted in higher student academic achievement and teacher effectiveness. Unfortunately, interpretations and practical applications of this research have focused on the *cultural* congruence of the approaches. I emphasize the term *cultural* because in these studies the term is used in a restricted sense devoid of its dynamic, ideological, and political dimensions. According to Giroux (1985), "Culture is the representation of lived experiences, material artifacts, and practices *forged within the unequal and dialectical relations* [emphasis added] that different groups establish in a given society at a particular point in historical time" (p. xxi). I utilize this definition of culture because, without identifying the political dimensions of culture and subsequent unequal status attributed to members of different cultural groups, the reader may conclude that teaching methods simply need to be culturally congruent to be effective—without recognizing that not all cultural groups are viewed and treated as equally legitimate in classrooms.

Given the sociocultural realities in the above studies, the specific teaching strategies may not be what made the difference. It could well be that the teacher's effort to "share the power," treating students as equal participants in their own learning and, in the process, discarding (consciously or unconsciously held) deficit views of the students, made the difference. Utilizing a variety of strategies and techniques, students were allowed to interact with teachers in egalitarian and meaningful ways.

Teachers also learned to recognize, value, utilize, and build upon students' previously acquired knowledge and skills. In essence, these strategies succeeded in creating a comfort zone so students could exhibit their knowledge and skills and ultimately empower themselves to succeed in an academic setting. McDermott's (1977) classic research reminds us that numerous teaching approaches and strategies can be effectively utilized so long as trusting relations between teacher and students are established, and power relations are mutually set and agreed upon.

It is against this backdrop that teachers can begin to interrogate the unspoken yet prevalent deficit orientation used to hide SES, race/ethnicity, linguistic, and gender inequities present in American classrooms. And it is against this backdrop that we turn our discussion to bilingual education and its persistent mirroring of a deficit view of linguistic minority students.

Bilingual Education, the Deficit Model, and the Practice of Transitioning

Despite the fact that current bilingual education models emerged from an enrichment two-way bilingual program designed to serve Cuban refugees in Dade County, Florida, in 1963, government intervention changed the program's focus when it was applied to low SES Mexican-American and Puerto Rican student populations. Crawford (1989) explains that the focus shifted

> from an enrichment model aimed at developing fluency in two languages to a remedial effort designed to help "disadvantaged" children overcome the "handicap" of not speaking English. From its outset, federal aid to bilingual education was regarded as a "poverty program," rather than an innovative approach to (p. 29)

The belief that students from subordinate linguistic minority groups have language problems is very much present in the origins of bilingual education. Flores, Cousin, and Díaz (1991) point out:

> One of the most pervasive and pernicious myths about [language minority] children is that they have a language deficit. This myth is not reserved just for bilingual and non-English-speaking students; it is also commonly held about African-American and other minority students [as well as English dominant linguistic minority students]. (p. 9)

In addition, these students are perceived as lacking valuable life experiences necessary for academic success. The consequent belief is that these deficits, in turn, cause learning problems. Bilingual education is then viewed as a compensatory program designed to remediate students' language problems, referring to their limited English proficiency. Educators often fail to interrogate the deficit model, which may constitute the *real* problem to the extent that it disconfirms rather than confirms linguistic minority native language experiences.

Currently, the Federal government identifies two needs of limited English proficient students: (a) to develop their English proficiency so that they can fully benefit from instruction in English, and (b) to enhance their academic progress in all subject areas (U.S. Department of Education, 1991). The U.S. Department of Education lists three general program types capable of teaching limited English proficient students English language skills necessary for success in school: transitional bilingual education; two-way, or developmental, bilingual education; and special alternative instructional programs. Only the first two programs utilize the student's native language for academic and instructional purposes. Special alternative instructional programs are "designed to provide structured English language instruction and special instructional services that will allow a limited English proficient child to achieve competence in the English language and to meet grade promotion and graduation standards" (p. 17). Of the three programs, transitional bilingual programs represent the largest percentage of programs currently funded by the Federal government (U.S. Department of Education, 1991).

Broadly defined, transitional bilingual education programs allow the use of limited English proficient students' native language in academic settings while they acquire the English language proficiency necessary to transition into English-only settings. Crawford (1989) criticizes the ambiguity of transitional bilingual education as it relates to native language use:

> The definition of transitional bilingual education is broad, requiring only that some amount of native language and culture be used, along with ESL instruction. Programs may stress native-language development, including initial literacy, or they may provide students with nothing more than the translation services of bilingual aides. Contrary to public perceptions, studies have shown that English is the medium of instruction from 72 to 92 percent of the time in transitional bilingual education programs. (p. 175)

Spener (1988) adds that what too often occurs in transitional bilingual education is that "programs provide only a limited period of native-language instruction and do not guarantee English mastery. Thus, these programs often prevent children from attaining fluency in either their native language or in English" (p. 133).

Nevertheless, the common assumption is that students exiting bilingual classrooms and entering "regular" or English-only classrooms necessarily possess native language literacy skills and will therefore transfer or apply these (presumed) skills to their English academic work. The problem is not so much with the assumption that skills transfer from one language to another. A number of recent studies suggest that cross-lingual transfer does occur (Avelar-La Salle, 1991; Clarke, 1988; Faltis, 1983; Hernández, 1991; Reyes, 1987; Zhang, 1990). The difficulty lies in the assumption that students are indeed being taught native language literacy skills.

In addition, we need to question the hidden objective embedded in the transitioning model that requires that limited English proficient students discontinue the use of their native language as they increase their fluency in English. Again, this subtractive view of bilingualism mirrors our deeply rooted deficit and assimilative orientation that often devalues students' native language. In other words, Freire's (1987) requirement that teachers possess political clarity regarding the sociocultural material conditions within which transition takes place will enable them to see the inherent contradiction of the educational language policy. We can accept the native language as long as it is used only minimally and temporarily, that is, until it is replaced with English. Is it not ironic that while we discourage the maintenance of linguistic minority students' native language throughout their education, we require mainstream English-speaking students to study a foreign language as a prerequisite for college— where many continue their foreign language studies for some years.

Even if we accept the underlying deficit notion of transitional bilingual education, we need to question how it is possible to expect students to transfer or apply native language literacy skills to English literacy tasks when, in reality, they have had little opportunity to develop these skills in their native language in school. All too often, students are held accountable and penalized for not possessing the very native language literacy skills that the school has failed to develop in the first place. In situations such as these, we must call into question the assumption that students are allowed to develop native language literacy skills so the transfer of skills really *can* occur. Does shuttling students from so-called bilingual classrooms where English is the medium of instruction from 72 to 92 percent of the time to classrooms where it is the *sole* medium of instruction constitute transitioning, or does it constitute receiving more of the same English-only instruction?

To discuss effective transitioning strategies, it is necessary to contextualize them within the ideal model of bilingual education. That model promotes the development of native language literacy skills beyond basic decoding and encoding skills and teaches English-as-a-second language literacy skills in an additive fashion with native language literacy skills. Building on the assumption that the ideal model is possible, we can then discuss teaching strategies identified as effective for preparing students to learn literacy skills in both the native language and English.

The Politics of Student-Centered Teaching

Numerous teaching strategies and approaches promise to facilitate transfer of native language literacy skills to an English-as-a-second language context. Well-known approaches and strategies such as cooperative learning, language experience, process writing, and whole language activities can be used to create learning environments where students cease to be treated as objects (Pérez & Torres-Guzmán, 1992). In successful applications of these approaches and strategies, students are treated with respect and viewed as active and capable subjects in their own learning.

Student-centered teaching strategies can take many forms. One may well ask, is it not merely common sense to promote approaches and strategies that recognize, utilize, and build on students' existing knowledge bases? Yes, it is. However, it is important to recognize, as part of our effort to increase our political clarity, that these practices have *not* typified classroom instruction to students from subordinate populations. Cummins (1989) reminds us of the need for emancipatory pedagogical practices instead of dehumanizing "banking" notions of learning, where subordinate students are viewed and treated as empty receptacles in need of filling. The practice of learning from and valuing student language and life experiences *often* occurs in classrooms where students speak a language variety and possess cultural capital that more closely matches the mainstream (Anyon, 1988; Lareau, 1990). Unfortunately, this practice is not a given with student popula-

tions traditionally perceived as deficient and lacking. Student-centered teaching strategies in the latter context require teachers consciously to discard deficit notions and genuinely value and utilize students' existing knowledge bases in their teaching. Furthermore, these teachers must remain open to the fact that they will learn from their students. Learning is not a one-way undertaking.

We recognize that no language variety or set of life experiences is inherently superior, yet our social values reflect our preferences for certain language varieties and life experiences over others. Student-centered teaching strategies such as cooperative learning, language experience, process writing, and whole language activities can help to offset or neutralize our deficit-based failure to recognize subordinate student strengths. Our tendency to disconfirm these strengths occurs whenever we forget that learning only occurs when prior knowledge is accessed and linked to new information.

Jones, Palincsar, Ogle, and Carr (1987) explain that learning is linking new information to prior knowledge. Prior knowledge is stored in memory in the form of knowledge frameworks. New information is understood and stored by calling up the appropriate knowledge framework and integrating the new information. Acknowledging and utilizing existing student language and knowledge makes good pedagogical sense. The process also constitutes a humanizing experience for students traditionally *de*humanized and disempowered in the schools. I believe that strategies identified as effective in the literature have the potential to offset that reductive education where "the educator as *the one who knows* transfers existing knowledge to the learner as *the one who does not know*" (Freire, 1985, p. 114).

Creating learning environments that incorporate student language and life experiences in no way negates teachers' responsibility for providing students with particular academic content knowledge and skills. It is important not to confuse academic rigor with rigidity that stifles and silences students. The teacher is the authority, with all the resulting responsibilities that that entails; however, it is not necessary for the teacher to become authoritarian in order to challenge students intellectually. Education can be a process in which teacher and students mutually participate in the intellectually exciting undertaking we call learning. Students *can* become active subjects in their own learning instead of passive objects waiting to be filled with facts and figures by the teacher.

As mentioned earlier, a number of student-centered teaching strategies possess the potential to transform students into active subjects and participants in their own learning. However, for the purposes of illustration, I will briefly discuss one approach currently identified as promising for both English-speaking "mainstream" students and linguistic minority students in upper elementary grades. I will highlight some key features of the strategy and explain its potential to empower teachers and students; in other words, its potential to humanize the educational process. The approach is referred to in the literature as "strategic teaching."

Strategic Teaching and the Potential for Teacher and Student Empowerment

Strategic teaching refers to an instructional model that explicitly teaches students learning strategies that enable them consciously to monitor their own learning; this is accomplished through the development of reflective, cognitive monitoring, and metacognitive skills (Jones et al., 1987). The goal is to prepare independent and metacognitively aware students. Examples of learning strategies include teaching various text structures (i.e., stories and reports) through frames and graphic organizers. *Frames* are sets of questions that help students understand a given topic. Readers monitor their understanding of a text by asking questions, making predictions, and testing their predictions as they read. Before

reading, frames serve as an advance organizer to activate prior knowledge and facilitate understanding. Frames can be used by the reader during reading to monitor self-learning. They can also be used after a reading lesson to summarize and integrate newly acquired information.

Graphic organizers are visual maps that represent text structures and organizational patterns used in texts and in student writing. Ideally, graphic organizers reflect both the content and text structure. Graphic organizers include semantic maps, chains, and concept hierarchies, and assist the student to visualize the rhetorical structure of the text. Jones et al. (1987) explain that frames and graphic organizers can be "powerful tools to help the student locate, select, sequence, integrate, and restructure information—both from the perspective of understanding and from the perspective of producing information in written responses" (p. 38).

Although much of the research on strategic teaching focuses on English monolingual mainstream students, recent efforts to study bilingual and limited-English-proficient linguistic minority students' use of these strategies show similar success. This literature shows that strategic teaching improved students' reading comprehension and conscious use of effective learning strategies in the native language (Avelar-La Salle, 1991; Chamot, 1983; Hernández, 1991; O'Malley & Chamot, 1990; Reyes, 1987). Furthermore, these studies show that students, despite limited English proficiency, are able to transfer or apply their knowledge of specific learning strategies and text structure to English reading texts. For example, Hernández (1990) reports that sixth-grade limited-English-proficient students learned in the native language (Spanish) to generate hypotheses, summarize, and make predictions about readings. He reports:

> Students were able to demonstrate use of comprehension strategies even when they could not decode the English text aloud. When asked in Spanish about English texts, the students were able to

generate questions, summarize stories, and predict future events in Spanish. (p. 101)

Avelar-La Salle's (1991) study of third- and fourth-grade bilingual students shows that strategic teaching in the native language of three expository text structures commonly found in elementary social studies and science texts (topical net, matrix, and hierarchy) improved comprehension of these types of texts in both Spanish and English.

Such explicit and strategic teaching is most important in the upper elementary grades, when bilingual students are expected to focus on English literacy skills development. Beginning at about third grade, students also face literacy demands distinct from those encountered in earlier grades. Chall (1983) describes the change in literacy demands in terms of stages of readings. She explains that at a stage three of reading, students cease to "learn to read" and begin "reading to learn." Students in third and fourth grade are introduced to content area subjects such as social studies, science, and health. In addition, students are introduced to expository texts (reports). This change in texts and text structures and in the functions of reading (reading for information) calls for teaching strategies that will prepare students to comprehend various expository texts (e.g., cause/effect, compare/contrast) utilized across the curriculum.

Strategic teaching holds great promise for preparing linguistic minority students to face the new literacy challenges in the upper grades. As mentioned earlier, the primary goal of strategic instruction is to foster learner independence. This goal in and of itself is laudable. However, the characteristics of strategic instruction that I find most promising grow out of the premise that teachers and students must actively interact and negotiate meaning in order to reach a goal. To assist students in becoming independent, reflective, and empowered learners, Jones, Palincsar, Ogle, and Carr (1987) recommend that teachers follow this instructional sequence:

1. Teachers access and assess current student knowledge about pertinent content and learning strategies via think-aloud and other prereading brainstorming activities. During this phase of instruction, teachers learn about their students' existing knowledge bases as well as students' questions and concerns regarding their own learning.

2. As a result of the above informal assessment, teachers explicitly explain the new content and strategies to students. After considering students' existing knowledge bases and questions, the teacher and students link the new content and strategies with prior knowledge and skills. The teacher and students identify and discuss the target strategy or strategies (declarative knowledge), how they should employ the strategy or strategies (procedural information), and in what context they should employ the strategy (conditional information).

3. Teachers model the new strategy or strategies so that students have the opportunity to witness the thought processes and behaviors involved in the employment of the strategy. For example, in reciprocal teaching, teachers initially model for students the process of formulating questions that will assist students to monitor their own learning during reading.

4. Teachers scaffold the instruction and provide students the time to practice and demonstrate their use of the strategy or strategies. Scaffolding is "a process that enables a child or novice to solve a problem, carry out a task, or achieve a goal which is beyond his unassisted efforts" (Wood, Bruner, & Ross in Jones et al., 1987, p. 55).

5. The teacher apprentices students and provides extensive support of their efforts. This support is temporary; teachers gradually reduce their support so that students assume sole responsibility and become independent learners.

6. Teachers relate strategy instruction to motivation so students recognize the significant role they play in their own learning and academic success. By providing students with experiences in which they see the successful results of strategic learning, it is possible to change students' expectations for success and failure and help them sustain strategy use (modified from Jones et al., 1987).

Throughout the strategic learning process, students are empowered in learning contexts in which teachers allow them to speak from their own vantage points. Before teachers attempt to instruct students in new content or learning strategies, efforts are made to access prior knowledge so as to link it with new information. In allowing students to present and discuss their prior knowledge and experiences, the teacher legitimizes and treats as valuable student language and cultural experiences usually ignored in classrooms. If students are allowed to speak on what they know best, then they are, in a sense, treated as experts—experts who are expected to refine their knowledge bases with the additional new content and strategy information presented by the teacher.

Teachers empower themselves in the process. To carry out this recommended sequence of instruction, teachers must be knowledgeable in both the subject area and the necessary learning strategies for successful learning to occur within that particular subject area or discipline. O'Malley & Chamot (1990) describe teacher empowerment in this type of teaching:

> Teaching becomes an active and decision-making process in which the teacher is constantly assessing what students already know, what they need to know, and how to provide for successful learning. This requires that teachers not only be good managers but also have an extensive knowledge base about their subject and about teaching learning strategies…. Teachers act as models and demonstrate mental processes and learning strategies by thinking aloud to their students. (p. 188)

Teachers are often empowered in the process of implementing strategic instruction because they must become experts in the subject areas they teach as well as in the key learning strategies that will facilitate students' acquisition of the subject matter. In addition, teachers must constantly monitor their students' existing knowledge bases as well as their growing mastery of the new content and learning strategy knowledge.

Furthermore, teachers play a significant role in creating learning contexts in which students are able to empower themselves. Teachers act as cultural brokers of sorts when they introduce students not only to the culture of the classroom but also to particular subjects, and when they prepare students to behave as "insiders" in the particular subject or discipline. Gee (1989) reminds us of the social nature of teaching and learning. He contends that for students to do well in school, they must undergo an apprenticeship into the subject's or discipline's discourse. That apprenticeship includes acquisition of particular content matter, ways of organizing content, and ways of using language (oral and written). Gee adds that these discourses are not mastered solely through teacher-centered and -directed instruction, but also by "enculturation or apprenticeship into social practices through scaffolded and supported interaction with people who have already mastered the discourse" (p. 7).

Models of instruction such as strategic teaching can promote such an apprenticeship. In the process of apprenticing linguistic minority students, teachers must interact in meaningful ways with students. This human interaction often familiarizes individuals from different SES and race/ethnic groups and creates mutual respect instead of the antagonism that so frequently occurs between teachers and their students from subordinate groups. In this learning environment, teachers and students learn from each other. The strategies serve, then, not to fix the student but to humanize the learning environment. Teachers are forced to challenge implicitly or explicitly held deficit attitudes and beliefs about their students and the cultural groups to which they belong.

A Humanizing Pedagogy: Going Beyond Teaching Practices

As discussed earlier, numerous teaching strategies possess the potential to humanize the learning process. It is urgent that teachers break free from lock-step methodologies so they may utilize any number of strategies or features of strategies to serve their students more effectively. When I recall a special education teacher's experience related in a bilingualism-and-literacy course I taught, I am reminded of the humanizing effects of teaching strategies that, similar to strategic teaching, allow teachers to listen to and learn from their students. This teacher, for most of her career, had been required to assess her students through a variety of close-ended instruments and then to remediate their diagnosed "weaknesses" with discrete skills instruction. The assessment instruments provided little information to explain why the student answered a question either correctly or incorrectly, and they often confirmed perceived student academic and cognitive weaknesses. The fragmented discrete skills approach to instruction restricts the teacher's access to existing student knowledge and experiences not specifically elicited by the academic tasks. Needless to say, this teacher knew very little about her students other than her deficit descriptions of them.

As a requirement for my course, she was asked to focus on one limited English proficient special education student over the semester. She observed the student in a number of formal and informal contexts, and she engaged him in a number of open-ended tasks. The tasks included allowing him to write entire texts such as stories and poems (despite diagnosed limited English proficiency) and to engage in "think-alouds" during reading. Through these open-ended activities, the teacher learned about her student's English writing ability, his life experiences and world views, and his reading

meaning-making strategies. Consequently, the teacher constructed an instructional plan much better suited to her student's academic needs and interests; even more important, she underwent a humanizing process that allowed her to recognize the varied and valuable life experiences and knowledge her student brought into the classroom. This teacher was admirably candid when she shared her initial negative and stereotypic views of the student and their radical transformation. Initially, she had formed an erroneous notion of her student's personality, world view, academic ability, motivation, and academic potential on the basis of his Puerto Rican ethnicity, low-SES background, limited English proficiency, and moderately learning-disabled label. Because of the restricted and closed nature of earlier assessment and instruction, the teacher had never received information about her student that challenged her negative perceptions. Listening to her student and reading his poetry and stories, she discovered his loving and sunny personality and learned his personal history. In the process, she discovered and challenged her deficit orientation. The following excerpt exemplifies the power of the student voice for humanizing teachers.

My Father

I love my father very much. I will never forget what my father has done for me and my brothers and sisters. When we first came from Puerto Rico we didn't have food to eat and we were very poor. My father had to work three jobs to put food and milk on the table. Those were hard times, and my father worked so hard that we hardly saw him. But even when I didn't see him, I always knew he loved me very much. I will always be grateful to my father. We are not so poor now and so he works only one job. But I will never forget what my father did for me. I will also work to help my father have a better life when I grow up. I love my father very much.

The process of learning about her student's rich and multifaceted background enabled this teacher to move beyond the rigid methodology that required her to distance herself from the student and confirm the deficit model she unconsciously adhered to. In this case, the meaningful teacher-student interaction humanized instruction by expanding horizons through which the student demonstrated human qualities, dreams, desires, and capacities that close-ended tests and instruction never capture. The specific teaching strategies utilized, in and of themselves, may not be the significant factors. The actual strengths of strategies depend, first and foremost, on the degree to which they embrace a humanizing pedagogy that values the students' background knowledge, culture, and life experiences.

Teaching strategies are means to an end, that is, humanizing education to promote academic success for students historically mistreated and underserviced by the schools. A teaching strategy is a vehicle to a greater goal. A number of vehicles exist that may or may not lead to a humanizing pedagogy, depending on the sociocultural reality in which teachers and students operate. Teachers need to examine critically these promising teaching strategies and appropriate the aspects of those strategies that work best in their particular learning environments. Too often, teachers uncritically adopt "the latest in methodology" and blame students (once again) when the method proves ineffective.

Methods, teaching strategies, and techniques are not panaceas. For this reason, I believe that we cannot reduce transitioning success to a specific strategy or methodological paradigm. More important than strategies are the teacher's political clarity and critical understanding of the need to create pedagogical structures that eliminate the asymmetrical power relations that subordinate linguistic minority students (Freire & Macedo, 1987). As the strategic teaching approach demonstrates, features that lead to a process in which students are treated with dignity and respect make all the difference. In other words, these teaching strategies provide conditions which enable subordi-

nate students to move from their usual object position to subject positions. I am convinced that the transitioning from object to subject position produces more far-reaching effects than transitioning from the native language to English. In fact, if the former transitioning occurs, the latter will present little difficulty.

I believe that educators, particularly bilingual teachers, would be far more effective if they critically understood the complex interrelationship of sociocultural factors shaping the educational context within which they are expected to transition students. The teachers' high level of criticity would empower them to develop the necessary pedagogical structures that cease to view and treat limited English proficient students as lacking, or as having language problems. Teachers could develop pedagogies to enhance those native language skills necessary for application to English language settings. Otherwise, these educators could easily fall into what Macedo (in press) calls an entrapment pedagogy; that is, "a pedagogy that requires of students what it does not give them" (p. 6). An uncritical acceptance of the transitioning model could very well lead to such entrapment. Finally, I would urge educators to understand that, above all, the critical issue is the degree to which we hold the moral conviction that we must humanize transitioning linguistic minority students into the English-only mainstream by eliminating the hostility that often greets these students. This process would require what Macedo (in press) suggests, the "antimethods pedagogy" that

> would reject the mechanization of intellectualism.... The antimethods pedagogy challenges teachers to work toward reappropriation of [the] endangered dignity [of both teacher and student] and toward reclaiming our humanity. The antimethods pedagogy adheres to the eloquence of Antonio Machado's poem, "Caminante, no hay caminos. Se hace el camino al andar." (Traveler, there are no roads. The road is created as we walk it [together].) (p. 8)

REFERENCES

Anyon, J. (1988). Social class and the hidden curriculum of work. In Gress, J. R. (Ed.), *Curriculum: An introduction to the field*, pp. 366–389. Berkeley, CA: McCutchan.

Au, K. H., and Mason, J. M. (1983). Cultural congruence in classroom participation structures: Achieving a balance of rights. *Discourse Processes,* vol. 6, pp. 145–168.

Avelar-La Salle, R. (1991). *The effect of metacognitive instruction on the transfer of expository comprehension skills: The interlingual and cross-lingual cases.* Unpublished doctoral dissertation, Stanford University.

Bloom, G. M. (1991). *The effects of speech style and skin color on bilingual teaching candidates' and bilingual teachers' attitudes toward Mexican American pupils.* Unpublished doctoral dissertation, Stanford University.

Boykin, A. W. (1983) The academic performance of Afro-American children. In Spence, J. T. (Ed.), *Achievement and achievement motives: Psychological and sociological approaches*, pp. 322–369.

Chall, J. (1983). *Stages of reading development.* New York: McGraw-Hill.

Chamot, A. U. (1983). How to plan to transfer curriculum from bilingual to mainstream instruction. *Focus*, vol. 12. Washington, DC: National Clearinghouse for Bilingual Education.

Clarke, M. A. (1988) The short circuit hypothesis of ESL reading—Or, when language competence interferes with reading performance. In Carrell, P. L., Devine, J., and Eskey, D. E. (Eds.), *Interactive approaches to second language reading*, pp. 114–124. New York: Cambridge University Press.

Crawford, J. (1989). *Bilingual education: History, politics, theory and practice.* Trenton, NJ: Crane.

Cummins, J. (1989). *Empowering minority students.* Sacramento: California Association for Bilingual Education.

Díaz, S., Moll, L. C., and Mehan, H. (1986). Sociocultural resources in instruction: A context-specific approach. In *Beyond language: Social and cultural factors in schooling language minority students*, pp. 187–230. Los Angeles: California State University; Evaluation, Dissemination and Assessment Center.

Faltis, C. J. (1983). *Transfer of beginning reading skills from Spanish to English among Spanish-speaking children in second grade bilingual classrooms.* Unpublished doctoral dissertation, University of Arizona at Tucson.

Flores, B. M. (1982). *Language interference or influence: Toward a theory for Hispanic bilingualism.* Unpublished doctoral dissertation, University of Arizona at Tucson.

Flores, B., Cousin, P. T., and Diaz, E. (1991). Critiquing and transforming the deficit myths about learning, language and culture. *Language Arts*, vol. 68, no. 5, pp. 369–379.

Freire, P. (1987). Letter to North-American teachers. In Shor, I. (Ed.), *Freire for the classroom*, pp. 211–214. Portsmouth, NJ: Boynton/Cook.

Freire, P. (1985). *The politics of education: Culture, power and liberation.* South Hadley, MA: Bergin & Garvey.

Freire, P., and Macedo, D. (1987). *Literacy: Reading the word and the world.* South Hadley, MA: Bergin & Garvey.

Gee, J. P. (1989). Literacy, discourse, and linguistics: Introduction. *Journal of Education*, vol. 171, no. 1, pp. 5–17.

Giroux, H. (1985). Introduction. In Freire, P., *The politics of education: Culture, power and liberation*, pp. xi-xxv. South Hadley, MA: Bergin & Garvey.

Heath, S. B. (1983). *Ways with words.* New York: Cambridge University Press.

Hernández, J. S. (1991). Assisted performance in reading comprehension strategies with non-English-proficient students. *The Journal of Educational Issues of Language Minority Students*, vol. 8, pp. 91–112.

Jones, B. F., Palincsar, A. S., Ogle, D. S., and Carr, E. G. (1987) *Strategic teaching and learning: Cognitive instruction in the content areas.* Alexandria, VA: Association for Supervision and Curriculum Development in cooperation with the Central Regional Educational Laboratory.

Lareau, A. (1990). *Home advantage: Social class and parental intervention in elementary education.* New York: Falmer Press.

Macedo, D. (in press). Preface. In McLaren, P., and Lankshear, C. (Eds.), *Conscientization and resistance.* New York: Routledge.

McDermott, R. P. (1977). Social relations as contexts for learning in school. *Harvard Education Review*, vol. 47, no. 2.

Mehan, H. (1992). Understanding inequality in schools: The contribution of interpretive studies. *Sociology of Education*, 65 (1).

Menchaca, M., and Valencia, R. (1990). Anglo-Saxon ideologies in the 1920s–1930s: Their impact on the segregation of Mexican students in California. *Anthropology and Education Quarterly*, vol. 21, pp. 222–245.

Mohatt, G. V., and Erickson, F. (1981). Cultural differences in teaching styles in an Odawa school: A sociolinguistic approach. In Trueba, H., Guthrie, X., and Au, K. H. (Eds.), *Culture and the bilingual classroom: Studies in classroom ethnography*. Rowley, MA: Newbury.

O'Malley, J., and Chamot, A. U. (1990). *Learning strategies in second language acquisition*. New York: Cambridge University Press.

Pérez, B., and Torres-Guzmán, M. E. (1992). *Learning in two worlds: An integrated Spanish/English biliteracy approach*. New York: Longman.

Philips, S. U. (1972). Participant structures and communication competence: Warm Springs children in community and classroom. In Cazden, C., John, V., and Hymes, D. (Eds.), *Functions of language in the classroom*. New York: Teachers College, Columbia University.

Reyes, M. (1987). Comprehension of content area passages: A study of Spanish/English readers in the third and fourth grade. In Goldman, S. R., and Trueba, H. T. (Eds.), *Becoming literate in English as a second language*, pp. 107–126. Norwood, NJ: Ablex.

Spener, D. (1988). Transitional bilingual education and the socialization of immigrants. *Harvard Education Review*, vol. 58, no. 2, pp. 133–153.

Sue, S., and Padilla, A. (1987). Ethnic minority issues in the U.S.: Challenges for the educational system. In *Beyond language: Social and cultural factors in schooling language minority students*. Los Angeles: California State University; Evaluation, Dissemination and Assessment Center.

Trueba, H. T. (1989) Sociocultural integration of minorities and minority school achievement. In *Raising silent voices: Educating the linguistic minorities for the 21st century*. New York: Newbury House.

U.S. Commission on Civil Rights (1973). *Teachers and students: Report V: Mexican-American study: Differences in teacher interaction with Mexican-American and Anglo students*. Washington, DC: U.S. Government Printing Office.

U.S. Department of Education (1991). *The condition of bilingual education in the nation: A report to the Congress and the President*. Washington, DC: U.S. Government Printing Office.

Valencia, R. (1991). *Chicano school failure and success: Research and policy agendas for the 1990s*. New York: Falmer Press.

Valencia, R. (1986, November 25). *Minority academic underachievement: Conceptual and theoretical considerations for understanding the achievement problems of Chicano students*. Paper presented to the Chicano Faculty Seminar, Stanford University.

Walker, C. L. (1987). Hispanic achievement: Old views and new perspectives. In Trueba, H. T. (Ed.), *Success or failure; Learning and the language minority student*. New York: Newbury House.

Zhang, X. (1990). *Language transfer in the writing of Spanish speaking ESL learners: Toward a new concept*. Paper presented at the Fall Conference of the Three Rivers Association of Teachers of English to Speakers of Other Languages. (ERIC Document Reproduction Service No. ED 329 129).

Official Versions: Encouraging Writing in Students' First Language in ESL Classrooms

Paula Wolfe

One common theme in the literature of multicultural education is the call to view cultural diversity in schools and classrooms as a strength rather than a deficit. From this perspective, cultural diversity enables all students to experience and learn from multiple voices. All too often, however, teachers who believe that culturally diverse schools and classrooms are more interesting and richer places perceive cultural diversity as a social rather than an academic strength. In other words, teachers have little difficulty accepting that students from culturally diverse backgrounds bring social and language norms to school, but it seems more difficult to see how these differing norms can actually help these children, and more mainstream children, learn more effectively. Cultural diversity is often seen as a social strength, not an academic strength, and certainly not a language strength. However, this common-sense assumption has been discounted by much of the recent research on becoming literate in a second language

(Ramírez, Yuen, & Ramey, 1991). In contrast to the assumption that literacy in a first language hinders English writing development, much current research argues that the inclusion of first language writing into ESL curriculum is of great benefit to students who are becoming bilingual in an ESL classroom (Lucas & Katz, 1994), regardless of whether or not the teacher is proficient in the language(s) of her students. This article is designed to provide monolingual English-speaking teachers with options for the inclusion of bilingual children's first language in the writing classroom.

Writing in Student's First Language—Why?

According to a recent survey conducted in a large university in the Southwest, even those teachers with an avowed interest in and support for bilingual education did not see the use of Spanish in literacy instruction as "academically useful" for students who are becoming bilingual. These bilingual/ESL

teachers saw the use of Spanish as important mainly for social reasons (Garcia, 1999). Also, as Barrera (1983) points out, when Spanish is included in the classroom, it is often used for oral communication and reading but rarely for writing instruction, yet Lucas and Katz (1994) found that the best ESL programs are those that enable students to converse and write in their native language. Further research seems to point to the folly of ignoring first language writing. For example, Hudelson (1984) has shown that student's first language literacy supports the development of writing in their second language and furthermore that children discover the process of connecting letters to sounds through their own writing and then apply this knowledge to reading. Similarly, I argue that the inclusion of students' first language literacy in ESL classrooms is an effective tool not only for creating increased ties between the school and the student's community but also for facilitating all students' control over the conventions of written English.

Writing in Student's First Language—How?

While there is much debate regarding how best to incorporate first language literacy into ESL classrooms, what seems to be emerging as most effective is an approach based on several fairly clear ideas regarding language and literacy learning in general (Davies Samway & McKeon, 1999). One of these ideas is that first language literacy is best incorporated into ESL classrooms for real purposes; in other words, students use their first language when it is necessary to use it (e.g., for communication with someone from their home community). Another idea, one that is explored in this article, is that the separation of language purposes between students' first and second languages provides for the successful development of literacy in ESL students.

The concept of the separation of language purposes in authentic writing activities is fairly straightforward. As literate adults, we understand that we write differently for different purposes: we write a shopping list differently from a memo, and we write an academic essay differently from a letter to the editor. Different kinds of literacy conventions are appropriate for different purposes. This simple rule applies equally as a guide to including children's' first language in the writing classroom. It is more appropriate to write in Korean if your audience is the Korean community, and it is appropriate to write in English if your goal is to communicate with your monolingual English classmates. The teacher's job is to find authentic purposes and audiences for the children's writing in their first language. In this way, there is a separation of language purposes between the two languages; the languages are used for different purposes. Often teachers of bilingual students see first language writing as a preliminary to the translation of the piece of writing into English. In this way, the "official" version of the piece of writing is always in English. This paper, however, argues that it is necessary for teachers to think of first language and second language writing as serving different language purposes and, by extension, different audiences. The questions are: What is the goal of the writing, who is the audience, and which language best serves the purpose and audience? For example, the production of a newsletter for the student's home community would probably be written in the child's first language, while a newsletter for the school would be written in English.

The following case studies [1] explore how three different transactional classrooms, based on three different approaches to writing instruction, (specifically, writer's workshop, theme cycles, and Frierian problem posing) included literacy in the students' first language. What is clear from each of the three case studies is that because of the separation of language purposes between the students' first language and second language, these students—and in one case the monolingual English students, also—developed a greater facility in the written conventions of English.

In addition, the inclusion of ESL students' first language literacy in all cases led to a greater connection between the classroom and the ESL students' home community. These case studies are offered not as ideals to which teachers are expected to aspire, but as examples of what can happen when students' first language writing is welcomed in the classroom. As the following three case studies indicate, the separation of language purposes for first language and second language has two main benefits: first, children gain a sense of the value of their native language along with a better control over the written conventions of English; and second, there is a greater involvement between the school and the child's home community.

Case 1: Jamie and the Writer's Workshop Approach

Jamie, a sixth grade student in an ESL classroom, was a quiet, isolated boy who almost never spoke in class. A recent immigrant from Mexico, Jamie usually sat apart from the other students, brushed his red hair over his eyes, and spent his day writing in silence. If you did not read Jamie's work, you might think that his capacity with English was minimal. However, by looking at his writing, you can see that his ability with language far outreaches his level of oral communication.

Near the beginning of the semester, Jamie's teacher announced a writing contest in honor of Martin Luther King, Jr.

Day. Students were asked to produce an essay regarding who they saw as a peacemaker in their community and why. Jamie raised his hand when the teacher asked who wanted information on the contest, and for the rest of the writer's workshop period he sat looking at the contest information. Over the next week Jamie sat quietly writing and covered his paper with his arm whenever his teacher passed by his desk. Finally the teacher, Mr. Sennet, pulled up a chair next to Jamie.

"Jamie, really, it's killing me! I want to know what you are working on. The curiosity is driving me crazy."

Jamie smiled but looked concerned. Finally, he said in his quiet voice to Mr. Sennet, "I'm not really writing yet, I'm just making notes." As Jamie said this, Mr. Sennet glanced down at the paper and discovered the reason for Jamie's secrecy: He had been writing in Spanish.

"You know, I don't care if you write in Spanish. It's fine with me," Mr. Sennet said.

"I didn't know if you would care, Mister," Jamie answered. "I know I just can't write in Spanish, not for the contest."

"Listen, we'll worry about getting this ready for the contest later. Don't worry about that right now. I just really want to know what you are writing. I haven't talked to you for five days."

"Uh, the contest, the peacemaker?"

"Uh-huh, who did you pick? Who are you writing about?" Mr. Sennet asked.

"Me, I'm the peacemaker," Jamie answered.

"You are? I don't get it. It's an interesting take on this, though. Why don't you tell me what you are writing?"

"OK. Well, you know, I am writing in Spanish, you know, 'cause I'm trying to say how the lowriders and La Raza (a Mexican American cultural movement) have made me not want to get into fights. All the Cholos in my neighborhood? They all want me to, but I read the lowrider magazines, on Sunday I read them when I have time. And they make me think I should have pride in my background and not fight."

"Wow, that's a great idea. I bet no one else in the contest is going to write about how they themselves can be peacemakers. I didn't get it when you first said it, but now I do. What have you got so far?"

Jamie went on to explain his first draft to Mr. Sennet. The first draft in Spanish was a collection of stories about lowrider cars and Jamie's experiences in his neighborhood. The two then discussed the fact that an essay has to have one main idea that all the other ideas support. They finally came up with the thesis of the paper, that peace is not made through grand gestures but through small, everyday decisions. Mr. Sennet flipped Jamie's paper over and wrote the thesis statement in English on the back. Mr. Sennet then encouraged Jamie to continue to write his experiences and ideas but to try to begin to relate everything back to the main idea of the essay.

"Mister, can I still do it in Spanish?" Jamie finally asked.

"Of course you can. Just out of curiosity, though, why do you want to?"

"It's just easier, you know, it's hard to write about La Raza in English. I don't know how to explain some things that don't make sense in English and then I get stuck."

Jamie continued to draft his essay in Spanish until he felt that he had all the ideas he wanted set out and organized around the main idea. Mr. Sennet then had Jamie write his first draft in English on the computer. However, Mr. Sennet encouraged Jamie to leave in Spanish anything that did not make sense in English; the main thing was to get an initial draft typed out. Over a long period of time Jamie and Mr. Sennet continued to work on the essay in English. Jamie seemed to have an inexhaustible interest in continuing to redraft the piece. While working with Jamie, Mr. Sennet kept a list of conventions of written English that Jamie learned in the production of the essay. These conventions included the generation of a thesis statement, relating specific examples to the main idea, moving from the general to the specific in writing, the structure of a personal essay, and writing good leads. As an example of Jamie's greater facility in English writing, one only has to look at the beginning sentences of his essay. In the first several drafts Jamie's opening sentence had been, "Who is a peacemaker?" While it is not a bad strategy to repeat the question one is trying to answer in the first line of an essay, clearly this sentence does not mark Jamie's essay as especially interesting. In contrast, Jamie's opening sentence of his final draft (after a short conference with his teacher on writing good leads) was: "Sunday is a fine day. Sunday is the day that I have time to be filled with the beauty of my culture."

The point of this case study is that Jamie used Spanish and English for very different purposes. He used Spanish to communicate personal and cultural knowledge. In an attempt to explain how important La Raza had been to him, he had written in the language that understood and could explain what La Raza was. In other words, in order to communicate his experiences, he had to write in the language of those experiences. However, for the writing contest, Jamie was equally capable of producing successive drafts of his essay in English. One more point here is necessary: in the final draft of his essay, Jamie included several Spanish words and phrases, which added immense richness and interest to his writing.

While Jamie's writing in Spanish allowed for his growing control over the conventions of written English, it also had an effect on the rest of the class. Although Jamie was too shy to share his writing with the class, Mr. Sennet often spoke of his essay to the other students, who were also writing for the peacemaker contest. Based on Mr. Sennet's conversations, one student who had been writing about Cesar Chavez as a peacemaker changed the structure of his essay and instead interviewed his mother, who had been active in the United Farm Workers movement and had marched with Chavez. Roberto's essay changed from a fairly typical "I think

Cesar Chavez is a peacemaker because…" into a deeply personal exploration of his mother's commitment to the cause of equality. Roberto was able to generate a highly complex thesis that argued that it is only through justice and equity that we can achieve peace. This interest in their own cultural history led to a classwide exploration of the representation of minority cultures in the mass media.

Jamie's communication of his personal and cultural knowledge in Spanish, then led not only to his greater control over the conventions of written English but also to a greater awareness of the connection between the classroom and the students' home community and cultural history.

Case 2: Tyson and the Theme Cycles Approach

Tyson was a bright, talkative boy with a ready smile and shining black eyes. Along with several other students in his first grade classroom, Tyson was bused to the school from the Native American reservation where he lived. Although fluent in English and Cree, Tyson had yet to "break code" and could not write in English. One day his student teacher, Megan, read the class a story about bears. Tyson threw up his hand excitedly and said, "My grandfather killed a bear." His student teacher had no idea how to deal with something like this. Wouldn't the idea of bears dying be traumatic to the children in the classroom?

"It wasn't a bear like the one in the story, though, was it, Tyson?" she asked.

"No," Tyson answered. "It was

a real bear."

"So what's the difference, do you think?" his teacher asked.

"I know," Alicia answered. "Real bears don't talk to people."

"Uh-huh, they do," Tyson answered loudly.

"They do?" Mrs. Jackson asked, "Are you sure, Tyson, real bears talk to people?"

"YES!" Tyson said, "My grandpa, he says that, he says that he thanked the bear when it died, and he tells stories of bears who talk."

"You know, I don't know anything about those stories," Tyson's teacher, Mrs. Jackson, said. "Would your grandpa be willing to tell you those stories so you can write them down and share them with us?"

"But grandpa doesn't speak, he only speaks Cree mostly."

"OK, how about you tape record your grandpa telling you the story and then you can take notes about it and share it with the class, explain to us what he is saying?"

"OK, we have a tape deck."

Tyson eventually interviewed his grandfather, recorded the story, and made notes about the story in Cree. He later shared his grandfather's story with the class and taught them Cree words. Finally, Tyson produced a bilingual book with a Cree version and an English version (written by the teacher) based on his grandfather's story.

Beyond Tyson producing his first bilingual story, his comment led to a classwide theme cycle based on the study of real versus imaginary bears. This cycle involved: studies of conservation efforts in the Canadian Rockies; mathematical graphing of declining bear populations in comparison with human populations; discussions about how one signals in writing that the characters are real or imaginary; musical productions of *The Teddy Bear's Picnic*; and a series of student-produced reports, drawings, poems, and letters about bears.

At the end of the theme cycle, the student teacher, Megan, sat at a large round table in the corner of the classroom. Alicia, dragging a fuzzy gray teddy bear and holding tight to a piece of paper, ran over to her. "Miss Megan, I brought Oscar and I finished my bear story!"

Megan smiled. "That's great, Alicia. Will you read it to me?" Alicia read her story slowly, and at the end Megan asked, "I notice you changed the beginning of the story. Why did you decide to do that?"

"I didn't like the way 'Once upon a time' sounded. It wasn't that kind of a not-fiction story."

"Well, I think it sounds wonderful as a nonfiction story. Is this your published copy?"

"Yep, I'm going to read it to Mom when she comes for the picnic this afternoon." Alicia ran back to her desk.

Not only had the inclusion of Tyson's Cree interview and subsequent story allowed him to produce a much longer narrative than he had previously, it had also lead to a greater control over the conventions of English writing for the monolingual English speakers in the class. Alicia's example shows that she learned that the opening "Once upon a time" is an indicator that the story and the characters are fictional. This heightened awareness of genre allowed the

students to produce a much wider variety of writing as they moved away from strictly personal narratives. In addition, the awareness of differing story conventions in Cree and in English allowed the students to produce stories that were actually more conventionally like typical English stories. In other words, because students became aware that English stories involve a beginning, middle, and end, while Cree stories typically do not (Tyson's grandfather's story had a four-part structure), students were able to produce English narratives that had a more conventional structure.

It is important to note, however, that not only did Tyson and the other students gain a greater control over conventions of written English through the inclusion of Tyson's writing in Cree, but the theme cycle also allowed for greater contact between the classroom and the reservation community. The day of the student's presentation of *The Teddy Bear's Picnic*, Tyson's family came to the classroom to share a traditional dance. Tyson's grandfather told his story in Cree while the monolingual English students followed in the bilingual book that Tyson had created. Once again, the inclusion of students' first language writing served both academic and social purposes. In fact, it is clearly difficult to separate one set of purposes from the other.

Case 3: Chen and the Problem-Posing Approach

Chen was a small, thin girl with bobbed hair and round, gold glasses. Chen's pull-out ESL class-

room teacher was participating in a large project whereby middle school teachers were attempting to institute Freirian problem posing in their classrooms. Problem posing is widely referred to in education literature as critical literacy (for a fuller explanation of problem posing as pedagogy, see Wolfe, 1996). Critical literacy helps students to explore their own communities and through their exploration reveal values imbedded in community structures and institutions. Freire's approach to critical literacy is defined by Lankshear and Lawler (1987) as consisting of a three-step process:

> In the first step, something from daily life is observed in detail . . . in the second step it is investigated . . . and in the third it is resolved . . . This is to problematize social reality, to take something that is everyday and present it as one aspect or facet of an overall structured social practice that serves human interest unequally, and that needs to be transformed if the interests of people at large are to be met more justly. (p. 168)

In this project Chen's teacher was attempting to combine transactional, student-centered pedagogy with critical literacy, or problem posing.

The first project of the year in Chen's class involved the teacher asking Chen and the other students to do observations and note taking in their neighborhoods to try to find out what some of the problems were. Chen went home that day with her notebook but without many answers about what she was supposed to observe. As she walked in the door of her house, however, she realized that there was a perfect opportunity right in her own living room. Her grand-mother was meeting with a group of friends from her church. Chen asked if she could listen in and found that once tea was served the talk shifted from issues of the church to issues of the women's everyday lives.

Chen listened to the discussion as the Korean grandmothers excitedly discussed the high prices of food in the local super-market. Ever since the big super-market opened, they argued, food prices had skyrocketed.

Trying to keep up, Chen wrote notes for herself quickly in Korean. "I'll translate them later," she thought.

The next day at school Ms. Venda, Chen's teacher, had one-on-one meetings with several of the students. When it was Chen's turn, Ms. Venda pulled up a chair alongside her and asked, "So, what was your research about?"

Chen told her of observing her grandmother's meeting and about the claims of the women regarding the food prices. Ms. Venda listened intently and said, "I think this sounds really good, like really good research. What other investigating are you going to do?"

Chen thought for a moment. "Well, I thought that when my mother goes shopping, I will go and keep track of the prices of what she buys at the supermar-ket." "OK," said Ms. Venda. "So what will that tell you?" Chen looked puzzled. "What I mean is, didn't your grandmother say that prices had gotten higher, gone up?" Ms. Venda said, point-ing skyward, "So the question is, WHY have they gone up? And are they just as high in other places? And if not, why not?"

"I don't, I don't know," Chen answered, "how would I, what do I do?"

"Well, I think your first idea of keeping track of prices is a good one. Is there any way you could compare those prices to another store in the city?"

Chen said, "Yes, the church van picks up food donations from other stores. I could go with them."

"Great! So that's the next step in your research."

Over the next two weeks, Chen rode with her pastor to pick up food donations, and he helped her develop a list of foods and their prices at several stores around the city. Chen kept detailed notes in Korean about the stores' locations and her impressions of the neighbor-hoods. After collecting her data, she met again with Ms. Venda to show her all her findings.

After Ms. Venda looked at the food prices and listened to Chen's description of the stores, she said, "This looks great, it's so much work!" Chen smiled proudly. "So, what does all this mean? I mean, what's your gen-eral impression of why the prices are higher in some areas than others?"

Chen looked confused. "Why? I don't really know why."

"But you have a lot of infor-mation in your notes, just reread them once more and see if you have an impression." After rereading for several minutes, Chen answered, "Well, where there are many stores together, they are close to each other, the prices are better." "Aha, so one reason is competition, right? Close stores compete with each other to attract customers?"

"Uh-huh," Chen replied. "But in our neighborhood, there used to be little stores, like Korean stores, but then the big store came and they closed."

"You know what that's called? It's a monopoly. The big store that has lots of money came and I bet started with lower prices so the neighborhood stores lost money and then after the little stores had left, I bet the prices went higher."

"Well, grandmother said, the ladies said the prices had gotten higher after the Korean store closed."

"So you know the interview, the talk with your grandmother could be part of your data for your report about how big stores move into neighborhoods and charge higher prices."

"And the ladies, you know, they don't have much money and the prices are higher." Chen looked up, her voice rising above her normally quiet whisper. "You're right, it doesn't seem fair that the people who have the least money have to pay the highest prices."

"You know what?" Ms. Venda pulled the data toward her. "Why don't you write something for the people in your neighborhood about the better prices in other stores? Is there a newspaper or anything?"

"Uh-uh, no," Chen answered, "but the church has a newsletter that has, like, community things in it."

"Perfect," Ms. Venda remarked. "Why don't you write a short sum-mary of your findings for the newsletter?"

"But, uh, the newsletter is in Korean and the ladies don't really understand English," Chen answered shyly.

"Fine, write it in Korean. You can do a different kind of report for class."

Chen's report for the class turned out to be a photo essay on her research, showing prices on similar foods and plotting prices by neighborhood. The accompanying script was written in English and was used, in a slightly expanded form, for Chen's final assignments. The Korean version of the report was published in the church newsletter, and after reading it, the pastor arranged for the elderly women in the neighborhood to accompany him in the church van to the lower-priced stores once a week to do their shopping.

Ms. Venda had followed the problem-posing methodology, and the result had been that Chen was able to institute some kind of social action that helped her community. However, it is important to note that this social action would not have happened had Ms. Venda not allowed, indeed encouraged, Chen to write in her first language. What is not immediately evident is the increased mastery on Chen's part over the conventions of written English. What Chen became able to do through this assignment was: conduct research, formulate a research question, and provide data to support an argument. Also, she developed genre knowledge in that she was able to produce both a verbal script and a written report based on the same data. Once again, the student's first language writing led both to a greater control over the conventions and processes of writing in English and to greater connections between what happened in the classroom and what hap-

pened in the student's home community.

Implications

These case studies contradict several prevailing myths about the use of student's first language for literacy development. This section explores how the points made by the case studies can be understood as answers to three of these prevailing myths, identified by Davies Samway and McKeon (1999).

1. *First language writing is useful for social reasons but not for academic ones.* In each of the cases discussed, the inclusion of writing in the student's first language served both social and academic goals. Social goals were served in that students got increased opportunities to explore and explain their home communities. In each case, the student's writing led to the inclusion of knowledge from the community and made that knowledge the subject of instruction and learning. Even for those ESL students who are not literate in their first language, the inclusion of community knowledge is important in the development of English literacy (Pérez & Torres-Guzman, 1992).

By making community knowledge the subject of academic exploration, writing in the first language also served academic goals. Each of the students in the case studies, and, indeed, other students in the case study classrooms, gained a much greater facility

with the conventions of written English because of the inclusion of literacy activities in their first language. In at least one case, the inclusion of first language writing allowed even monolingual English students access to academic concepts such as genre norms in writing and comparison in mathematics. The classrooms in these case studies contradict the prevailing belief, as shown by the survey mentioned in the introduction, that first language inclusion is primarily oral and serves primarily social goals.

2. *The use of first language writing interferes with second language development.* The second myth is that students' writing in their first language will somehow interfere with their development of written English. However, what each of these case studies has shown is that when there is a separation of language purposes, the inclusion of first language writing actually leads to a greater control over the conventions of written English while still valuing the first language. When English is not simply used for translation—in other words, when a student does not just write a story in Korean and then translate it into English to give to the teacher—but the two languages are used for distinctly different purposes (e.g., writing a newsletter versus writing a script for a classroom report), then the student's first language is especially powerful in the process of learning to write in

English. Even for the case study student who did translate his story (with the help of the teacher) from Cree to English, the purpose was clearly separated. He wrote the story in Cree to tell the story as his grandfather had told it but wrote it in English so that his classmates could follow along with the telling.

What is important to note is that the separation of language purposes involved the provision of audiences for the student's writing that moved beyond the teacher. Whether it was classmates, grandfathers, writing contests, or churches, the writing was produced for someone besides the teacher to read. This understanding leads to the third myth about first language writing that these case studies seem to challenge.

3. *If the teacher is not a speaker of the student's first language, she can't encourage first language writing.* One of the most prevalent myths in the area of ESL teaching is that monolingual English-speaking teachers cannot encourage the use of students' first languages in the classroom. However, as mentioned earlier, Lucas and Katz (1994) have shown that the best ESL programs do exactly that. For each of the cases discussed in this paper, the teacher's lack of fluency in Spanish or Cree or Korean had very little effect on the written pieces produced in the student's first language or in English. What was key, however, was the teacher's belief that writing in

any language is valid and that not all writing has to have an "official" version that is understood and graded by the teacher.

More than expertise in any particular language or community, it was these teachers' efforts to validate students' literacy attempts in either language, as well as the creation of a classroom in which students are encouraged to write for real purposes and for diverse audiences that made possible for the students' successful efforts at the development of biliteracy.

Conclusion

It is perhaps not surprising that so many teachers do not see the inclusion of first language as academically useful. Because most teachers were trained as top-down information providers, seeing what students bring to the classroom as topics for academic exploration is difficult. What sets the teachers in the case studies apart is that although each has a different writing program with different expectations and goals, each is committed to organizing a student-centered, transactional classroom. Perhaps it is only through reinterpreting how we as educators see children in our classrooms (as empty vessels or as active contributors) that we can begin to see the academic power of including students' first languages writing in the ESL curriculum.

NOTES
1. These case studies, although representing actual students and teachers I have observed, have been

constructed out of an amalgam of observations in several different classrooms.

REFERENCES

Barrera, R. (1983). Bilingual reading in the primary grades: Some questionable views and practices. In T. Escobedo (Ed.), *Early childhood bilingual education: A Hispanic perspective* (pp. 164–184). New York: Columbia University Press.

Davies Samway, K., & McKeon, D. (1999). *Myths and realities: Best practices for language minority students.* Portsmouth, NH: Heinemann.

Garcia, A. (1999). Attitudes of bilingual education students regarding the use of Spanish in classrooms. Poster session presented at Arizona State University, Tempe, AZ.

Hudelson, S. (1984). Kan yu ret an rayt en ingles: Children become literate in English as a second language. *TESOL Quarterly, 18,* 221–237.

Lankshear, C., & Lawler, M. (1987). *Literacy, schooling, and revolution.* New York: Falmer Press.

Lucas, T., & Katz, A. (1994). Reframing the debate: The roles of native languages in English-only programs for language minority students. *TESOL Quarterly, 28,* 537–561.

Pérez, B., & Torres-Guzmán, M. E. (1992). *Learning in two worlds: An integrated Spanish/English biliteracy approach.* White Plains, NY: Longman.

Ramírez, J.D., Yuen, S.D., & Ramey, D.R., (1991). *Executive summary of final report: Longitudinal study of structured English immersion strategy, early-exit and late-exit transitional bilingual education programs for language minority students.* San Mateo, CA: Aguirre International.

Wolfe, P. (1996). Literacy bargains: Toward critical literacy in a multilingual classroom. *TESOL Journal, 5,* 22–26.

Two-Way Bilingual Education: The Power of Two Languages in Promoting Educational Success

Kathryn J. Lindholm, *San José State University*

Rosa Molina, *San José Unified School District*

We are at an important crossroads in educating our nation's children. We can join the ever increasing movement to promote English at the cost of other languages—OR—empower all children with two or more languages! Two-way bilingual education is an educational model that is gaining in popularity, even as the English-only enthusiasts surge with well-financed efforts to dilute bilingual education, including two-way bilingual education. As we forge ahead with implementing and refining two-way bilingual education, it is critical that we take considerable care in establishing programs that promote educational success in all our students, including those who are ethnically, linguistically, and economically diverse. Programs that do not serve the educational needs of language minority students will come under increasing scrutiny. This scrutiny must further motivate us to design our programs attentively so that they are optimal for promoting academic success. Unfortunately, many language education programs—both traditional and two-way bilingual—exist in schools that do not well serve the needs of linguistically diverse students. In addition to underserving these students, such programs reinforce the negative opinion that the media perpetuates—that bilingual education does not work. Our objective in this article is to present the definition, theoretical framework, some implementation guidelines, and evaluation outcomes to serve as a catalyst for promoting high-quality two-way bilingual education programs—to empower our nation's children with the power of two languages.

What Is Two-Way Bilingual Education?

Two-way bilingual education combines features of full bilingual education for language minority students and early total immersion education for English-speaking students. Language minority and language majority students are integrated for academic instruction that is presented separately through two languages. For both groups of students, one of the languages is their native language and one is a second language. The definition of two-way bilingual education (TWB) encompasses *four critical features*: (1) The program essentially involves some form of two-way bilingual instruction, where the target language is used for a significant portion of the students' instructional day [target language is used here to distinguish the second, or non-English, language of the program]; (2) the program involves periods of instruction during which only one language is used; (3)

both native English speakers and native speakers of the target language are participants; and (4) the students are integrated for most content instruction. The major goals of the program are that: (1) students will develop high levels of proficiency in their *first* language and in a *second* language, (2) academic performance will be at or above grade level as measured in both languages, and (3) students will have high levels of psychosocial competence and positive cross-cultural attitudes. (For further information about TWB programs, see Christian, Montone, Lindholm, & Carranza, 1997; Lindholm, 1997, in progress; Lindholm & Molina, 1998).

More than 225 public schools in 23 states have developed TWB programs at the elementary level. Most of these programs are Spanish/English, but there are other languages that combine with English, such as Korean, French, Cantonese, Navajo, Arabic, Portuguese, Japanese and Russian (McCargo & Christian, 1998).

Rationale and Theoretical Underpinnings

Two-way bilingual education has been constructed on three major theoretical and conceptual building blocks so that it can meet the language and academic needs of both native and non-native speakers of English: (1) social context of language education; (2) effective schools, and (3) language development (see Lindholm, 1992, in progress).

The *social context of language education* refers to the attitudes and policies that are held regarding the language education program and its participants. There are several features from this body of literature that have influenced the development of the TWB model. (1) The model is additive for both English-speaking and target-language-speaking students. This additive aspect is important in two regards. First, all students are provided the opportunity to acquire a second language at no cost to their home language and culture. Second, target-language-speaking students are given the chance to further develop high levels of proficiency in their native language rather than to advance through the usual process of primary language loss. (2) Encouragement of positive and equitable interactions between teachers and students and between target-language-speaking and English-speaking students fosters equity in the classroom. (3) Balancing the proportion of target-language-speaking and English-speaking students in each classroom facilitates an environment of educational and linguistic equity and promotes interactions among both groups of students.

Two-way bilingual education, like immersion education, is grounded in *language acquisition* research in several respects. (1) Language input to the students is adjusted to their conceptual and linguistic level, using many features of sheltered instruction, including "motherese," to facilitate language comprehension and acquisition on the part of the students. (2) Balanced with the need to make language comprehensible for second language learners is the necessity to make language input challenging for students operating in their first language (Swain, 1991). (3) Concentrated exposure to language is important to promote language development. Several studies have shown that it takes somewhere between four and seven years to develop full proficiency in a second language (Collier, 1987; 1984). Part of the importance for developing full proficiency relates to the Threshold Hypothesis discussed by Cummins (1979) and Toukomaa and Skutnabb-Kangas (1977). They speculate that there may be threshold levels of linguistic proficiency a child must attain to avoid cognitive disadvantages and to allow the potentially beneficial aspects of becoming bilingual to influence cognitive growth. This hypothesis assumes that a child must attain a certain minimum or threshold level of proficiency in both languages to enable bilingualism to exert a significant long-term effect and to positively influence cognitive growth. (4) The two languages are kept distinct and never mixed during instruction.

Several reasons for keeping the languages separate include: a) it improves the quantity and quality of teacher delivery, particularly the teacher's preparation (e.g., vocabulary, materials) for lesson delivery in the target language; b) students need sustained exposure to the minority language in a variety of contexts to obtain native speaker levels; c) the target language needs sociocultural and political protection to assure that English does not encroach in the domains of language use because of its dominant status; d) avoidance of language mixing and switching allows for more reliance on comprehensible input, negotiation of meaning, and comprehension checks in both languages.

Over the past several years, a large body of literature has been amassed on effective schools. There are several critical characteristics of effective schools that have implications for the success in implementing the two-way bilingual education model. (1) The bilingual program is integrated within the total school program, strong support for the program is given from the school district administrators and local Board of Education, and the principal is very supportive of and knowledgeable about the program. (2) Parental involvement and collaboration with the school is highly valued. (3) Students receive their instruction from certified teachers who have native or native-like ability in either or both of the language(s) in which they are instructing.

Program Features

A few salient program features will be discussed in this section, including (1) language distribution and use, (2) curriculum and instructional approaches, (3) instructional strategies, (4) student population, (5) staff, and (6) cross-cultural and self-concept components.

Language Distribution and Use

There are two common instructional designs in TWB programs. In California, most programs follow the 90:10 model whereas outside of California, the majority of programs use the 50:50 model. We will focus our discussion on the 90:10 model because the 50:50 design is similar to the 90:10 model in grades 4–6.

The distribution of languages for instruction varies across the grade levels in the 90:10, but not 50:50, design. In the 90:10 model, at kindergarten and first grade, 90% of the instructional day is devoted to content instruction in the target language and 10% to English. Thus, all content instruction occurs in the target language and English time is used to develop oral language proficiency. Reading instruction begins in the target language for both target-language-speaking and English-speaking students. At the second and third grade levels, students receive 80% of their day in the target language and 20% in English. As in the previous grade levels, all content is taught in the target language, with the exception of music, art, or physical education which may be taught during English time at some school sites. In second grade, English time is still largely spent in developing preliteracy skills and academic language proficiency. Students begin formal English reading in third grade. By fourth and fifth grades (and sixth grade, if it is included at the elementary school site), the students' instructional time is balanced between English and the target language.

In the *50:50/partial TWB* model, instructional time is evenly divided between the two languages across all grade levels, as in grades 4–5 for the 90:10 model. However, reading instruction begins in both languages or in the student's native language initially.

For both the 90:10 and 50:50 models, the content areas taught in each language depend on the available curriculum materials and supporting resource materials and on particular needs at each school site. However, an attempt is made to assure that students are given opportunities to develop academic language in each of the major curricular areas.

As indicated previously, teachers never mix the languages during instruction. In most school sites at the early grade levels, teachers may team together so that they are models of only one language. The most common strategy for both the 90:10 and the 50:50 designs is to separate the languages by time of day, so that students study in one language in the morning and another language in the afternoon.

Curriculum and Instructional Approaches

The instructional curriculum is based on state and local school district guidelines. Thus, the curriculum that the TWB students receive is equivalent to that for students at the same grades not enrolled in the two-way bilingual education program. Schedules are carefully structured for teaching all required academic subjects using methods appropriate not only for specific grade levels, but suitable also for enabling both English-speaking and the target-language-speaking students to acquire language skills in both English and the target language.

Instructional Strategies

Instructional strategies vary by language and grade level. In the early grades in the 90:10 model, the target language is used to teach content, and it is usually not taught as a subject area. There is little variation across school sites in the use of the target language for almost exclusive teaching of content. In addition, students are typically grouped heterogeneously, rather than by ability, when they are grouped at all. School sites, and even teachers within a grade level at a particular site differ in whether they teach grammar at the upper elementary levels. Some teachers believe that the target language grammar will be learned as the target language is used and thus they do not think that it is necessary to teach the students the target language grammar. Consistent with reports in the French immersion programs (e.g., Lapkin & Swain with Shapson, 1990; Lyster, 1990), more TWB teachers are realizing that it is impor-

tant to incorporate grammar into their content instruction.

During English time there is considerable variation in how English instruction is carried out and whether it is used as the language for content instruction in the early grade levels. In some school sites at the early grade levels, students are separated for English time, with the target-language speakers receiving English as a Second Language (ESL) strategies and the English speakers working on further English language development. In other school sites at the early grade levels, the students are kept together for English time, and all students are given oral input through content such as music, stories, drama. Unfortunately, not enough attention has been paid to English time in many school sites where English time has been used for assemblies, P.E., or other activities that do not provide a good basis for the development of academic English.

Student Population

As indicated earlier, classroom composition is a balance of native English speakers and native target-language speakers. In many school sites, segregated communities surrounding the school make it virtually impossible to include equal numbers of target language speakers and English speakers. Typically in the first or second year of model implementation, schools may have more difficulty recruiting a balanced population. After two or three years, though, most schools are able to balance their populations without much difficulty. The populations represented in the two-way bilingual education model are heterogeneous by school site. Many times the target-language and English-speaking populations are not comparable in important ways that we will briefly describe below.

Target Language Speakers

As a group, target language speakers can be characterized as largely immigrant, from families in which the parents are a part of the working class and have typically 5–6 years of formal education. It is important to note that there is variation within this group, though. While some target language-speaking students are U.S. born or have parents who are highly educated and middle class, most target-language-speaking students live in run-down inner cities or in rural areas in broken down trailer homes without electricity or indoor plumbing. Some of these students' parents are very involved in their children's education and understand how to promote achievement in their children, and other parents are not involved for various reasons or have no formal education to enable them to help their children with their schoolwork. In programs in which the language combinations include Korean, Chinese, Japanese, or Portuguese, there is also diversity with respect to immigration status and socioeconomic status. However, language minority students in these language groups are more likely to be middle class and to come from homes with educated parents.

English Speakers

The English-speaking population is also diverse in social class and parental education as well as in ethnic composition. In some schools, most of the English speakers are middle class and European American. In other schools, the majority of English speakers are African American students living in the poor and run-down sections of the city. In still other schools, the English-speaking population is diverse, including middle-and working-class European Americans, African Americans, Hispanics, and Asian Americans.

Special Needs Students

Students with special education needs or learning disabilities are accepted at most, but not every, TWB site. The only exception to this policy of admitting all students is where students have a speech delay in their native language, in which case a decision for admittance is carefully conducted on an individual case-by-case basis. Further, students are typically not moved from the TWB program because of special education or learning disability needs.

Staff

Teachers in two-way bilingual education programs tend to have appropriate teaching certificates or credentials, have good content knowledge and classroom management skills, have native or native-like proficiency in one or both languages in which they are instructing, and are trained with respect to the two-way bilingual education model and appropriate instructional strategies. In reality, however, the quality of teachers does vary considerably by school site and even by grade level within the same school, in large measure because of the tremendous shortage of bilingual teachers in the United States.

At some school sites, teachers do not work together as a team but rather plan and teach in isolation. In other school sites, teachers at the same grade level plan together and team for instruction. The amount of coordination and planning within and across grade levels varies by school site, but a higher level of coordination across grades is almost always associated with more successful programs.

Many classrooms have an instructional assistant for some amount of time, though the amount of time, and whether there is any assistance, varies by school site and even grade level. In some classrooms, there is an instructional assistant all day and in other classrooms, there may be a four- or six-hour a day assistant that is shared among two or three classrooms. In addition, some classrooms have parent volunteers for a few hours a week.

Cross-Cultural and Self-Concept Components

Psychosocial and cross-cultural competence are carefully integrated into the two-way bilingual education model in various ways. These features are built into the model through the social context components of additive bilingualism and positive and equitable interactions between teachers and students and between target-language-speaking and English-speaking students as indicated above. In the ideal—and successful—models, teachers are trained to treat all students equally, regardless of their background. Each student is expected to perform, to participate in different roles in the classroom or group, to serve in leadership roles, and so on. Further, students are expected to treat each other equally and with respect.

Developing the Strongest Two-Way Bilingual Education Program: Some Important Hints

The implementation of two-way bilingual education programs is not without its challenges. As school staff works to market and attract participants into the program, teachers and administrators must be engaged in the careful planning and development of their instructional practices and methods to produce a program that is additive and equitable for both the language minority and English-speaking students.

Some of the most successful two-way programs in the U.S. first began in schools that had an impressive track record in bilingual education for language minority students. The teaching staff had developed their expertise in using appropriate strategies and methodologies to plan a program in the first language (L1) for language minority children. Teachers knew how to plan for literacy in the L1 and ESL/ELD for the students in their L2, and they could use this experience to serve as the knowledge base in which to incorporate English speakers into the language learning mix without compromising the program for the native speakers.

This shift from a bilingual program serving language minority students to one encompassing both language majority and language minority students, however, requires extensive planning time and professional inservice in the areas of immersion education, cooperative grouping, second language acquisition strategies, and educational equity. Such training assists the teacher in developing techniques to make the curriculum comprehensible for all students. Even the most experienced teacher must draw the best practices from the research on bilingual education, immersion education, linguistics, and foreign language education to inform their program planning and consciously determine the linguistic and academic objectives for both language groups in their classrooms. Program practitioners must work to consistently raise the status of the target language for both groups of students to motivate all students to become second language learners. Increasing the prestige of the language and motivating English speakers to learn it also raises the status of the minority language students who are the target language models!

One of the greatest challenges facing two-way teachers is determining the correct level of difficulty in the target language for each student in the classroom. The most successful teachers focus their instruction on the needs of the minority language students, to ensure academic and linguistic success for both language groups. Research of achievement and language proficiency results in two-way bilingual education demonstrate that English speakers are meeting the appropriate expectations for language development and academic progress but language minority students continue to lag behind the English speakers. This finding has been a wake-up call for two-way practitioners. These research findings compel classroom teachers and program developers to carefully analyze their practices and review their decisions on language use, scheduling, introduction of English, and the development of the curriculum at each grade level, because these decisions have a direct impact on the L1 and L2 development of the language minority students. If teachers unnecessarily attenuate the target language so that English speakers can keep up, the target language speakers are adversely affected by the reduction of academic and linguistic rigor in their L1. Classroom practices and language must be rigorous enough for the native speakers of the language to grow academically and linguistically, and comprehensible enough for the second language students. A variety of instructional strategies, other than oral use of the language, must be employed! This requires extensive professional development, and coaching and planning time for the teachers implementing this program.

If the underlying goal of two-way programs is to narrow the gap between language minority and language majority students, then the program implementers must make a conscious decision to keep the focus on the needs of the target language students–those whose language continues to be "at risk" even in the best programs. No language group is expendable! The administration, teaching staff, and parents must share a commitment to the vision of equity and academic success for all children in their two-way classrooms. Without a watchful approach to the quality of the program and the instructional practices of the classroom teachers, program administrators might find themselves tragically exploiting the target language speakers they had hoped to help for the benefit of the English-dominant students in the program.

Evaluation Outcomes at the Elementary Level

Evaluation efforts have sought to determine the levels of first and second language proficiency, the levels of reading and content area achievement in both languages, and the levels of psychosocial competence and cross-cultural attitudes.

To provide information about the students' progress in TWB programs, data will be presented and briefly discussed from four school sites in California. These school sites were selected because they have implemented a 90:10 model for at least four years and there is consistent data for the students. Each school began implementation of a two-way bilingual education program at the kindergarten and first-grade levels because the TWB model was considered the most promising model to promote high levels of bilingualism, biliteracy, and academic achievement. Each school also received funding from the U.S. Department of Education to develop its program.

Data Collection

A variety of data was collected from 555 third- through seventh-grade students representing four schools implementing a 90:10 TWB program in Spanish and English. About 56% of the students were Spanish Bilinguals (students who began the program as Spanish speakers) while 44% were English Bilinguals (students who began the program as English speakers). While all of the Spanish Bilingual (SB) students were Hispanic, the English Bilingual (EB) students comprised different ethnic backgrounds: European American (57% of EB students), Hispanic (31% of EB students), and African American (13% of EB students). Only 19% of the EB students were low income (based upon participation in the Free School Lunch program defined according to home income by the U.S. government) as compared to 75% of the SB students. Thus, it is important to understand that the two groups of students (SB and EB) at these schools were not comparable and differed with respect to the educational background and economic resources of the parents.

Data collection instruments included: (1) norm-referenced, objectives-based achievement tests in reading and mathematics for both Spanish and English, which were designed to measure achievement in the basic skills normally found in curricula at the state and local levels; and (2) the Student Oral Language Observation Matrix (SOLOM), a rating scale in which the teacher assesses the student's oral language proficiency in five domains: comprehension, fluency, vocabulary, pronunciation, and grammar. This instrument, which can be used in any language, produces a rating for each domain and provides an indication of whether the student is fluent/proficient in each language. The top score in each domain requires native speaker proficiency. In addition, students, teachers, and parents completed questionnaires regarding their attitudes toward various aspects of the program (teachers and parents) or achievement-, language- and cross-cultural attitudes (students).

Language Proficiency Outcomes

Examining the results from the perspective of the students' language proficiency in their L1, all SB and EB students maintained high levels of proficiency in their first language. With respect to proficiency in L2, both the SB and EB students made great gains in L2 oral language proficiency across the grade levels. By fifth grade, most students were rated by their teacher as communicatively proficient in the second language, though some teachers may have overinflated the Spanish proficiency ratings of the English speakers. Classroom observations showed that while most SB students were clearly fluent in English, many EB students lacked the fluency, vocabulary, and grammar to converse entirely in Spanish about a variety of topics, as Swain and her colleagues have reported with regard to EB students in French immersion programs (e.g., Lapkin & Swain with Shapson, 1990).

Reading Achievement Outcomes

Students completed tests in both languages that measured their vocabulary and reading comprehension. According to this assessment of academic language skills, there was significant variation in students' scores depending on which school they attended, their grade level, and the socio-economic status of the student. In Spanish reading, SB and EB students scored at grade level, though their scores dropped during grades 4–5, as they focused more on English literacy. Performance in Spanish rebounded to grade level by grades 6–7.

English reading achievement varied substantially by school sites, social class (participation versus non-participation in free lunch program), and language background. Beginning at third grade, the year they started formal reading instruction in English, the EB students scored average to very high. Spanish speakers did not attain grade level performance at any school site (with the exception of a couple classes of students), though they made good gains at most school sites.

Content Area Achievement Outcomes

Overall, students scored at grade level in mathematics achievement measured in Spanish, though there was significant variation across school sites in students' achievement. At most schools, EB students scored average to very high, while SB students performed in the average range. English mathematics achievement also varied significantly across the different school sites. English speakers at most sites scored average to very high. At some sites, SB students scored average, while at other sites their scores were below grade level. There was a highly significant correlation between mathematics achievement in English and Spanish $R = .75$, $p < .0001$).

In science and social studies, performance was average to very high for both EB and SB students.

It is important to realize that all of these programs are located in California, which has the sad distinction of its students receiving among the lowest test scores in all the 50 states of the U.S. (Bazeley, 1997). Thus, to report that TWB EB and SB students were scoring at or above grade level in reading and mathematics means that these students were scoring better than most students in California.

Self-Esteem and Cross-Cultural Attitudes

Students demonstrated average to high levels of self-esteem, rated their academic competence as high, and held very positive attitudes toward other languages, speakers of other languages, and people they perceived as different from themselves. Almost every student reported that s/he enjoyed studying in English and Spanish and wanted to continue in the TWB program. Most students also believed that being bilingual had made them smarter, able to perform better in school, able to think better, and would someday help them get a better job.

How Do Students Compare to Their Peers Not in TWB Programs?

In comparisons of the SB TWB students with SB students in bilingual education programs, the SB TWB students scored significantly higher in every area that could be compared: Spanish and English reading and mathematics achievement. Similarly, when the EB TWB students were compared to English monolingual students educated only in English, the TWB students scored higher in English reading and English mathematics than their monolingual English peers (Lindholm, 1992, 1997).

Follow-Up Study of TWB Students at the Secondary Level

A total of 101 tenth-grade through twelfth-grade students participated in the study; they had been enrolled in a two-way immersion program since kindergarten or first grade at one of three schools in California. Approximately equal numbers of boys and girls were represented among the students.

Of the 101 students, 57% were Hispanic Spanish bilinguals (SB); 24% were Hispanic English bilinguals (EB); and 19% were Euro American English bilinguals (EB). Students in these three groups differed significantly in mother's educational background, with higher levels of education among the Euro American students, followed by Hispanic EB students, and lowest levels of education among Hispanic SB students.

Results from this study have indicated that:

- Over half of all students say they like reading, mathematics, and school.

- Most students agree that learning two languages helped them do better in school, helped them to think better, made them smarter; challenged them to do better and gave them a sense of accomplishment; gave them the confidence to do better in school; and the program will help them get a better job. (When there are significant group differences, Hispanics score higher than Euro students)

- Most students indicated that they were not going to drop out of school. Thus, they did not feel that the two-way program kept them from dropping out of school, though more Hispanic than Euro students felt that the program kept them from dropping out.

- Majority of students of all backgrounds plan to attend a four-year college (63%); most students (80–94%) agree that they want to go to college, that getting a good education is important, and that good grades are important; and most students agree that their parents want and expect them to do well in school and to go to college (85–100%).

- Many students report average grades (Bs and Cs) in language arts, social studies, math, and science. (Grades in these areas vary by ethnic/language group.)

- Many students felt that the program gave them a sense of identity, but many students do not report being bicultural. (Group differences.)

- Most students agree that they enjoyed being in the two-way program, would like to continue being educated in two languages, and would recommend it to other students.

- Most students are proud that they are bilingual; their parents are proud that the students are bilingual.

- When asked what was the most important benefit to studying Spanish, students selected job benefits first, though strong identity and having gotten a good education were also among the most important benefits.

Study of Teacher Attitudes

In examining teacher attitudes in TWB programs, results with 126 teachers (45% Hispanic; 55% European American) indicated that:

- Teachers had fairly high levels of satisfaction (M=3.9) and teaching efficacy (M=3.9) [on a scale of 1=low to 5=high].

- Teachers perceived medium support from the local school district and school board (M=3.2), good support from the principal and non-TWB staff (M=3.8), and high support from parents (M=4.2). [These attitudes varied by school site.]

- There were significant school SES and ethnic density effects: teachers in schools with more English speakers on free lunch and with greater ethnic density (more ethnic minority students) had higher mean scores in satisfaction, self-efficacy, perceived support from principal/staff, agreement that there is program planning, agreement that the needs of all students are met, and mastery-oriented beliefs and practices. The only deviation from this pattern was that perceived support from the district and board of education was higher in schools with fewer English speakers on the free lunch program and schools with a lower ethnic density.

- Teaching efficacy and satisfaction were much higher when TWB teachers perceived support from the principal, non-TWB staff and parents, and when the school site was engaged in effective program planning and meeting the needs of the diverse TWB student population (Lindholm, in progress; Lindholm & Gavlek, 1997).

Study of Parent Attitudes

A total of 201 parents, representing one elementary school, participated in the study. Parents were categorized as: Euro American (EURO) parents–32%; Hispanic-English speakers (Hisp-ENG)–15%; Hispanic-Bilinguals (Hisp-BIL)–34%; and Hispanic-Spanish speakers (Hisp-SP)–19%. Parents varied considerably across these ethnic/language groups in terms of their educational background: EURO and Hisp-BIL parents had the most education, followed by Hisp-EO, and lastly by Hisp-SP parents.

Children's grade levels were categorized as kindergarten only (first year of program), grades K/1/2 (parents with a first or second grader and possibly a kindergartner as well, prior to English reading instruction), grades 3–5 only (after beginning English reading instruction but prior to mastery of English reading), and older (parents with students in grades 6-8 who may also have students in earlier grade levels—full experience of elementary program and skills it developed in students).

Results indicated that:

- Parents were satisfied that their child was receiving access to the subject matter (M = 4.4 – 4.9), though this varied by ethnic/language group. While EURO parents were satisfied (M = 4.4), their level of satisfaction was lower than that of Hispanic (M = 4.6 – 4.9) parents.

- Parents were highly consistent that they would recommend the program to other parents (M= 4.8 – 5.0), regardless of their ethnic/language background.

- Parents perceived that the staff were successful in promoting diversity and that they balanced the needs of Spanish- and English-speaking parents, though Hispanic Bilinguals (M = 4.7) and Spanish speakers (M = 4.8) were more confident that the staff balanced the needs of the students than were the English-speaking EURO and Hispanic (M = 4.2) parents.

- Most parents also saw the value in their child studying Spanish: to be comfortable with other Spanish speakers (M = 4.3 – 4.6), to meet and converse with varied people (M = 4.5 – 4.8), to understand Hispanic culture (M = 4.3 – 4.8), and to participate in activities with people of other cultures (M = 4.5 – 4.8).

- Parents also believed that studying Spanish was important for their children because: they will need it for their career (M = 3.8 – 4.8), it will make them more knowledgeable (M = 4.5 – 5.0), and it will make them smarter (M = 3.5 – 3.9).

- Parents' attitudes toward the program and toward bilingualism did not vary significantly according to ethnic/language background, with the following exception: Hispanic English/Bilingual parents scored significantly higher than English-speaking European and African American parents in the importance of Spanish for career advantages.

- Another analysis was conducted to determine whether parent satisfaction differed according to their children's grade level. There were large differences according to grade level. Parents of kindergartners were all completely satisfied (M = 5.0), followed by parents who had older children in grades 6–8 (M = 4.8). Parents of children in grades 3–5 were least satisfied, though their scores still registered as "agree" that they were satisfied (M = 4.3).

- Somewhat similar findings were obtained in examining whether parents were satisfied with their child's progress in English reading. Parents who only had a kindergartner or who had children in upper grades (6–8) were most satisfied with their children's progress in English reading (M = 4.7–4.8). Those parents who had first and second graders were least satisfied (M = 3.9), and those with third through fifth graders in between (M = 4.2). We might expect that parents who enroll their kindergartner are optimistic about the program, especially toward the end of the year when both groups of children are beginning to use the second language and demonstrate preliteracy skills in Spanish. By second grade, we typically see the lowest levels of satisfaction. Since children do not begin formal English reading until third grade, parents see their children reading in Spanish but not in English, and become concerned that their children will fall behind. This is a typical outcome observed in 90:10 programs among parents, particularly English-speaking parents. When children begin English reading instruction in third grade and become competent readers in English by fifth grade, there is less concern. By grades 6–8, parents are not at all concerned; they know their children can do all of their academic work in English.

These results clearly show that parents are very happy with the program, that parents are involved, and they have very positive attitudes toward bilingualism both for social and academic purposes for their child.

Conclusions

Since the TWB program is a combination of a bilingual education program for language minority students and an immersion program for language majority students, model development has been based on program features of both these language education programs. In addition, various features have been incorporated into the model on the basis of the theoretical and empirically based literatures on the social context of language education, effective schools, and language development to more adequately address the cultural, ethnic, and linguistic diversity represented in TWB classrooms. However, it is important to note that not all TWB program coordinators and staff are even aware of all these program features. Thus, the quality and effectiveness of the TWB model implementation varies tremendously from school to school. Results demonstrate that the TWB model can be successful: students demonstrated bilingual proficiency—fluency in their first and a second language; students were developing biliteracy—achievement at or above grade level in reading as measured in both languages; and students achieved grade level or above in mathematics, social studies, and science. Also, parents and teachers were satisfied with the program and student outcomes. However, variations in outcomes among schools demonstrate the importance of carefully designing the program to meet the educational needs of both groups of students. Only then will we ultimately demonstrate the power of two languages in promoting educational success.

REFERENCES

Bazeley, M. (1997, February 28). The sad state of math skills. *San Jose Mercury News*, pp. A1, A26.

Christian, D., Montone, C., Lindholm, K., and Carranza, I. (1997). *Profiles in two-way bilingual education*. Washington, D.C.: ERIC Clearinghouse book series.

Christian, D. and Whitcher, A. (1995). *Directory of two-way bilingual programs in the United States*. Washington DC: Center for Applied Linguistics/The National Center for Research on Cultural Diversity and Second Language Learning.

Collier, V. (1989). How long? A synthesis of research on academic achievement in a second language. *TESOL Quarterly, 23*, 509–531.

Cummins, J. (1987). Bilingualism, language proficiency, and metalinguistic development. In P. Homel, M. Palij, and D. Aaronson (Eds.), *Childhood bilingualism: Aspects of linguistic, cognitive and social development* (p. 57–73). Hillsdale, NJ: Lawrence Erlbaum Associates, Publishers.

Lapkin, S., and Swain, M. with Shapson, S. (1990). French immersion research agenda for the 90s. *The Canadian Modern Language Review, 46*, 638–74.

Lindholm, K. J. (1992). Two-way bilingual/immersion education: Theory, conceptual issues, and pedagogical implications. In R. V. Padilla and A. Benavides (Eds.), *Critical perspectives on bilingual education research*. Tucson, AZ: Bilingual Review/Press.

Lindholm, K. J. (1994). Promoting positive cross-cultural attitudes and perceived competence in culturally and linguistically diverse classrooms. In R. A. DeVillar, C. J. Faltis, and J. P. Cummins (Eds.), *Cultural diversity in schools: From rhetoric to practice*. Albany, NY: State University of New York Press.

Lindholm, K. J. (1997). Two-way bilingual education programs in the United States: In J. Cummins and D. Corson (Eds.), *Encyclopedia of language and education, volume 5: bilingual education*. (pp. 271–280). Boston: Kluwer Academic Publishers.

Lindholm, K. J., and Molina, R. (1998). Learning in dual language education classrooms in the US: Implementation and evaluation outcomes. In J. Arnau and J. M. Artigal (Eds.), *Immersion programmes: A European perspective* (pp. 707–717). Barcelona: Universitat de Barcelona.

Lindholm, K. J. (in progress). Dual language education. Avon England: Multilingual Matters.

Lyster, R. (1990). The role of analytic language teaching in French immersion programs. *The Canadian Modern Language Review, 47*, 159–175.

Swain, M. (1984). A review of immersion education in Canada: Research and evaluation studies. *Studies on immersion education: A collection for United States educators* (pp. 87–112). Sacramento, CA: California State Department of Education.

Swain, M. (1991). Manipulating and complementing content teaching to maximize second language learning. In R. Phillipson et al. (Eds.), *Foreign/second language pedagogy research* (pp. 234–250). Avon, England: Multilingual Matters.

Toukomaa, P., and Skutnabb-Kangas, T. (1977). The intensive teaching of the mother tongue to migrant children of pre-school age and children in the lower level of comprehensive school. Helsinki: The Finnish National Commission for UNESCO.

Turning Transformative Principles into Practice: Strategies for English-dominant Teachers in a Multilingual Context

Joan Wink, *California State University, Stanislaus*
LeAnn G. Putney, *University of Nevada, Las Vegas*

Introduction

When we first encountered the Faltis Framework in 1993, we felt that we had found a golden nugget, a book that brought together a way for English-dominant teachers to work with multilingual students in their classrooms. We struggled with the paradox of trying to make visible the need for primary language instruction for non-English-dominant students, within the reality of schools with few teachers capable of providing bilingual instruction. Faltis (1993) also recognizes the superiority of primary language teaching while recognizing the reality of many English-dominant teachers. We knew then that this work was important and that we would use it in our own educational spaces, but little did we realize that we would find it even more important six years later. Even though much has changed during those ensuing years, much has also stayed the same.

Across the nation we have encountered a shortage of qualified teachers. At a time when policymakers are attempting to find ways of increasing test scores and elevating standards of teaching, more teachers than ever are entering classrooms with emergency credentials, finding themselves in a situation they could not have anticipated. They are English-dominant teachers in a multilingual context, and they want to know what they should do.

In the context of meeting the needs of these teachers and the students who are in the process of acquiring English and simultaneously struggling with core curriculum, we will examine what it means to put into practice a set of transformative principles to foster communication while promoting social integration in diverse classroom settings. The construct of *joinfostering* is built from four principles, which we refer to as the Faltis Framework: the need for (1) two-way communication, (2) social integration, (3) knowledge of second language acquisition, and (4) parental participation in all classrooms. In this article, we present vignettes to examine what these principles might look like from the point of view of teachers and students who practice them as part of their daily routines.

This article will take us down two main paths: First, we will demonstrate examples of classroom practice, which reflects four principles, found in the Faltis Framework (Faltis, 1993; Faltis, 1997; Faltis & Hudelson, 1998). This section illustrates the individual parts of the framework with vignettes from various classrooms. We will draw from various types of classroom settings in different types of schools to help make visible that these principles work under different conditions. Second, after showing how each principle can be established in a classroom setting, we will demonstrate how one project can incorporate and integrate all four principles simultaneously.

The Four Principles of the Faltis Framework

In this section, we will look at each of the four principles of the Faltis Framework and show how each of them can be turned into meaningful classroom practice. These principles become a foundation for the ways in which teachers and students construct their learning. From this perspective, the relationship between teaching and learning is dynamic and socially constructed through the interactions of teachers and students in their daily work and over time (Tuyay et al., 1995). The principles that we will illustrate throughout this section are not prescriptive. Rather, they become guidelines for teachers to use in their everyday practice.

Principle 1: Two-way Communication

The first principle of the Faltis Framework is promoting two-way communication between teacher and students. When teachers apply this principle, they first recognize the knowledge that students bring with them to the classroom. Teachers promoting two-way communication also encourage interactive exchanges for all students, regardless of their level of English proficiency. These teachers find a way to incorporate the students' experiences into classroom topics and discussions.

One way of incorporating two-way communication in the classroom is to establish working relationships in small groups so that students who share a common linguistic background can work together to solve problems in their primary language to facilitate their understanding of the content before they display their answers in English. Discussion in small groups engages students in a more natural form of communication than the question-and-answer routine of the conventional classroom, and allows time for students whose first language is not English to generate knowledge and make meaning of the curriculum. To the degree that it is possible, teachers create small groups that include native speakers of English, and at least two students representing other language groups. By doing this, the speakers of other languages are able to negotiate meaning both through their emerging English and through their primary language.

...Into Practice: Math Quips with Mrs. Burke

"Mrs. Burke, can we do Math Quips today?" asked Lucinda. Mrs. Burke immediately thought back to yesterday, when they had done Math Quips. The students enjoyed the challenge of trying these math problems in their table groups. They could discuss the problems, but they could not use paper and pencil to work them. They had to listen to the teacher's oral clues about place value and placement of the numbers in sequence, then figure out the six-digit number combination that she had in mind. She used their guesses as clues and reminders as she listed them on the overhead projector for all to see.

Ordinarily, Mrs. Burke would be delighted to have her fifth grade students pleading to do Math Quips, but yesterday's experience has made her think twice. Two of her students, Javier and Elena, were unable to participate in this activity because they knew very little English. How was she going to capture their interest and help them participate when she spoke no Spanish? Mrs. Burke was about to tell the students that they would not have time for Math Quips today when Lucinda spoke up again.

"Mrs. Burke, could I sit with Javier and Elena this time?" Lucinda asked. "I can translate the clues for them into Spanish. They know how to do the math. I saw them do the work yesterday from our problem of the day. But they just don't know what you are saying when you give the clues in English."

"Lucinda, I think that will work just fine, but let's find out what the rest of the class thinks about that. Class, what do you think of Lucinda's suggestion?" asked Mrs. Burke.

The rest of the class responded with encouragement. They enjoyed playing Math Quips, and they wanted Javier and Elena to participate, too. Lucinda worked with them as the groups played the game. Javier and Elena were delighted when they solved the second round before anyone else in the class.

In this example, the non-English-dominant students were not prepared to participate in two-way communication, since English was the only language spoken in the classroom. However, that does not mean that they did not want to participate. Lucinda was able to recognize that the community was not complete without Elena's and Javier's contribution, and her offer to facilitate the communication was also supported by the teacher and the other students. Only when they entered into true two-way communication were all the students offered access to the content of the lesson.

How did Mrs. Burke convey the principle of two-way communication into practice? She encouraged Lucinda to speak with Javier and Elena in their dominant language when discussing content that was presented in English.

Principle 2: Social Integration

Faltis (1993) refers to social integration of minority language students in classrooms where English is the dominant language. We have come across another type of social integration that we want to address here. *Inclusion* is a term often used in schools to refer to a process in which all students are in the mainstream for at least part of the day. Students who might have previously been in Special Education for the major segment of the day are now also included in mainstream activities. While there are many valid reasons for doing so, it means that teachers without experiences and training with Special Education students feel insecure about their own ability to work with this diversity in the mainstream classroom.

...Into Practice: "Now All of You Are Teachers"

Palmer spoke a language different from that of the other children in the first grade class when he entered Mrs. Casey's classroom the first day of school. Palmer spoke *echolalia*, meaning that he repeated the same sentences and phrases over and over while using his hand as a puppet. The resource teacher informed Mrs. Casey that this was Palmer's way of communicating because he was autistic and that this was his first experience in a mainstream classroom. This was Mrs. Casey's first experience with mainstreaming an autistic child.

So how would she establish an integrative experience that would be beneficial for Palmer as well as the other students? Mrs. Casey's initial reaction was that perhaps there was little that she could do for this student. The resource teacher said that for Palmer to be successful, she would have to change her integrative teaching style, give up doing the activity centers, and add more structure. Mrs. Casey was not at all certain that she could accomplish this, nor did she want to believe that it would be necessary.

The Friday before classes started was the first time Mrs. Casey came to understand the severity of Palmer's autism as she observed him during her quick orientation session. While she was reviewing her teaching philosophy, homework policy, and supplies list, she noticed that Palmer was walking around the room, touching everything, talking in a loud, shrill voice, and making stroking gestures in the air as he babbled. His mother followed him and calmly redirected his actions so that he would not cause harm to himself or to anything or anyone in the room. In conferring with Palmer's mother after the orientation, Mrs. Casey realized clearly that she had hopes for him in this classroom setting, mostly in terms of social integration.

Throughout the first week of school with Palmer, Mrs. Casey continued to monitor his actions while trying not to take too much attention away from the other students. The resource teacher offered to come to class and talk with the students about autism so that they could better understand why Palmer acted the way he did. The students and the resource teacher sat in a circle discussing the realities of autism, with the students offering some of their own observations and questions about Palmer's actions. As if in response to their talk, Palmer started wiggling and squirming and throwing himself around. Attempts to get him to sit down and cross his legs seemed futile until the students began to offer themselves as examples for him. After the resource teacher had gone, the students and Mrs. Casey continued to talk. Then as they moved back to their desks, Melissa suddenly exclaimed, "Mrs. Casey, look at Palmer!" Palmer was still sitting in the circle space, this time with his legs crossed. The students congratulated him, and they started clapping and exclaiming, "Good job, Palmer!" Their acceptance of him and their enthusiasm were echoed in Palmer's face, lit up with a huge smile.

Mrs. Casey explained that they were lucky to have Palmer in their classroom because he would teach them about being patient, and they could teach him about being a first grader.

"What do you call someone who shows another person how to do something and then they are able to do it?" asked Mrs. Casey. The students sat for a minute and really gave careful consideration to what she was asking.

"A teacher?" Miguel spoke up first.

"That's right," Mrs. Casey responded, "And now all of you are teachers because Palmer doesn't know very much about being a first grader and how to act in school, but you are here to teach him. You are all teachers now."

In this vignette, Mrs. Casey and her students demonstrate the potential power of social integration. We are not suggesting that it is an easy task. Nor do we intend to imply that all went smoothly after this first week. There were struggles ahead for all, but there were successes for all as well. Those successes often were measured in tiny, yet highly significant, increments.

When a new student came to class in January, Palmer began to pay close attention to the particular dialect this student spoke because it was different from that of the other students. One day, Palmer perfectly imitated Leon's request to go to the bathroom, the first question Palmer had ever asked in class. When he received permission to do so, he now had to process the notion that asking a question could lead to permission to proceed with his request. Soon he was imitating all the questions initiated by other students. Mrs. Casey answered them so that Palmer could make the connection

between wants and needs and the spoken request to fulfill them. Her other students soon chimed in and helped answer Palmer's questions. Before long, Palmer was generating his own questions, not only in class but also to other teachers he saw in the hallway.

So in this example the verbalizations of the other students, and their work together in small groups throughout the day, served as the jumping-off point for Palmer to make his own connections. Mrs. Casey did not have to change her teaching strategies or her learning centers, nor did she have to change her integrative approach to a more structured, skills-based approach for Palmer's benefit. Rather, she maintained a classroom community that prompted the students to demonstrate for Palmer what it meant to be a successful first grader. Through their explicit modeling and encouragement, the students and teacher together supported Palmer's social and academic learning.

How did Mrs. Casey convey the principle of social integration into practice? She encouraged students to reflect, to discuss, to demonstrate their learning, to question, to summarize, and to generate ideas through social interaction.

Principle 3: Knowledge of Second Language Acquisition

In endorsing this principle, Faltis (1993) defines *language acquisition* as a socially interactive process in which students must have access to what is going on in a particular context and must also be able to participate fully in

ongoing classroom discourse. He further establishes that what is needed for students to succeed in acquiring language is comprehensible invite (Faltis, 1997)—that is, inviting oral and written language from teachers and fellow students that encourages them to respond in a genuine way that promotes social construction of knowledge.

...Into Practice: Silence or Engagement?

"Speak English, you know we only speak English in this classroom," exclaimed the ninth grade ESL teacher. Mrs. Rogers was conducting an oral review for a social studies exam, and the students were chattering in their primary language while they debated the answer to her question.

Silence immediately reigned among the previously engaged students.

"But, Mrs. Rogers, these questions are hard," explained Berta, one of the more outspoken students in this linguistically diverse classroom.

"I know they are hard, but you need to be able to answer them in English. I hoped that we could make this review more fun and interesting by making a game of it. That is why, when I ask a question, someone in your row is supposed to give me the answer. If your row can't get it, the next row gets a chance to answer, in English."

By invoking one of "the rules," Mrs. Rogers did not seem to understand how she was setting up these non-English-dominant students for failure to participate in this classroom situation. While they may have been comfortable using English in conversational settings, the students knew that it would take much longer to develop the academic language necessary to succeed in school. In this classroom setting, they did not want to take a chance that they had misunderstood the question, resulting in a wrong answer for their team. Only the most outspoken and proficient English-speaking students bothered to take a stab at the answer to the next question. Without being able to clarify possible answers in advance with their classmates, those who were not as comfortable in speaking English simply remained silent rather than give a wrong answer to their teacher. This was not a safe environment in which to try out this relatively new and scary language.

What could this teacher have done to put the principle of understanding second language acquisition into practice with these students? She could have provided students with an opportunity to talk first in their primary language so that they felt prepared to answer before the entire class in English, which would have afforded access to the academic content.

Principle 4: Parental Involvement

An approach to involving parents in the education of their children means that teachers and school officials need to open the lines of communication and invite the families to participate. This is a first step. However, we have found in our own practice that inviting families to participate is an insufficient, though necessary, aspect of involvement.

For example, in many school districts, families may find that they do not speak the language *in* or *of* the school (Lin, 1993). By this we mean that if the school is one in which "English spoken here" is the norm, families whose primary language is other than English may not feel ready to speak to school officials. That is language *in* the school. At the same time, even families who readily speak English may be intimidated by the language *of* the school. We educators are so immersed in the words we use to describe education that we forget others may not be in tune with what we are trying to convey about their children's education. Furthermore, we may be so ready to *tell* families what it is that they need to hear that we forget first to *listen* to their needs and respond accordingly (Putney & Wink, 1998).

...Into Practice: How to Do It with Them
One of the most successful elementary school teachers we know in respect to parent involvement begins each year by sending a letter home to the parents, after reading it aloud in class with her students. This letter gives some of her own background so that the parents can feel that they know her better. She also outlines what she hopes the class will accomplish together, and she invites the parents to write back, with their child participating as a homework assignment, a letter stating what they hope their child will accomplish. This letter writing continues after the parent-student-teacher conferences, in which the children share the work from their

portfolios with their parents. The teacher writes what she feels their strengths have been as classroom members, and the parents write to their children about what they have witnessed throughout the year in terms of their learning process.

In her elementary school, a year-round school in a Southern California metropolitan area with 87 percent of the children identified as non-English-proficient, the school officials have taken the responsibility of initiating family literacy activities. To ensure that the families have various opportunities to read with their children and have access to books and print materials in both English and their native language, the school officials invite family members to come read with the children for the first 30 minutes of the school day. The number of family members participating in their family reading activities is astounding. Each day over 200 family members enter classrooms to read with their children. In addition, their family nights have over 200 attendees each week, and their story time usually attracts 50 preschool siblings along with their moms and grandmas. This is a school that believes the family is a valuable resource in developing and supporting their child's literacy.

What can school faculty and staff do to put the principle of family involvement into practice? Recognize the importance of involving families in classroom and school activities, while making the activities available and accessible to family members.

Integrating the Faltis Framework Into One Holistic Pedagogical Process

In the preceding section, we demonstrated how each of the four principles can be changed into dynamic classroom practice. In this section, our goal is to demonstrate how one holistic pedagogical practice can simultaneously integrate all four principles into transformative classroom practice.

Creating Classroom Big Books

Big Books can be created in multiple ways with students and families. In this section, we will look at various processes of authoring and publishing books in the classroom and community. The principles of the Faltis Framework are inherent within the various ways of generating authentic literacy.

We have chosen to use the words *Big Books* because in our experience the books that teachers, students, and families create together often are written and illustrated on large pieces of paper for small-group and whole-group reading activities. We have observed many teachers who, first, capture the language of the children on the chalkboard. Second, they transfer this story to a large piece of paper so that all students in the room can see the book. Third, teachers ask students to copy the story from the chalkboard to their own paper so they can read it at home with their families.

Initial questions about making Big Books:
- Do they have to be big?
- In what language do we write them?
- Why do we do what we do?

Do the books have to be big? No, if you and the students prefer to generate smaller books, we encourage you to follow your own professional judgment concerning the needs of the students. What matters is that teachers, families, and students join together to generate their own authentic literacy based on the students' lived experiences.

In what language do we write the books? It depends on the specific objective of your lesson. If your objective is to generate literacy and knowledge, we suggest that you create the books in the dominant language of the students. However, if your objective is to teach English to non-native speakers, it is effective to create the books in English. In this section, we will see that Dawn and Verónica often created their books in Spanish; Sharon and Fernando often created their books in English. The students in Joan's classes created their books in English, Spanish, Hmong, Cambodian, Lao, and Vietnamese.

Why do we do what we do? Never an easy question. We build Big Books in class to create processes that enhance the four theoretical principles of two-way communication, social integration, knowledge of language acquisition, and parental involvement. We want classrooms that bring in the voices of students and families. Our goal is to ground our human and pedagogical interactions around curriculum that not only generates literacy but also reflects the families' knowledges, literacies, and cultures.

In the remainder of this section, we will share two separate portraits that integrate these principles into holistic literacy practices. It is our hope that other teachers will take these activities and adopt and adapt them to fit their own classrooms.

One Way of Doing Big Books: Sharon

Sharon is English-dominant and teaches a combination class of kindergarten and first grade to students who are Spanish-dominant and Russian-dominant; the students entered school speaking no English, and are mandated, by California Proposition 227, to speak and learn in English. The district mandates a specific parts-to-whole basal approach to literacy development. However, in this district, teachers are also encouraged to make time for more holistic and creative ways to enhance literacy development. When Sharon began this process of generating authentic literacy with students, she was nervous, insecure, and somewhat confused about how she "should" do it. Finally, she decided to begin by working with the students' knowledge about the community.

Sharon's First Big Book Project: A Book About Places in the Community

Sharon wrote a short letter to the families explaining (1) what they were doing in class and (2) why they were doing it. She explained that in class they would make a large book based on what the students knew about places in the community. The letter was written in English, Spanish, and Russian, the languages of the families. Sharon explained that she had taken pictures of specific places around the community that she thought her students might recognize: fast-food restaurants, a drugstore, a playground, and a discount store. She had photocopies made of her pictures and sent a set of them home with each letter. Each family was asked to write on one page about one of the places for the class. Eighty percent of the students' families returned their written stories to be included in the class book. The students who did not return a story from home wrote their stories in the classroom.

After the families returned the stories to class, Sharon realized that these stories allowed her to learn a great deal about the language and literacy of each family. After recognizing this, she realized that a new question had emerged which she needed to answer: Should she edit the language the families had used before making the book for the class? Every teacher who begins generating authentic literacy with students and families will eventually face this question. Sharon knew from her years in teaching that many have very strong feelings on both sides of the question. Some say: Yes, edit. Some say: No, maintain the authentic voice. Sharon understood both perspectives, but needed to find the right answer for the context of her classroom and community. Sharon wanted to retain the authentic voice of each child and each family, but

she didn't want to expose any grammatical or spelling errors to the scrutiny of all who might read the book. After reflecting on the multiple perspectives of the question, she found her answer while visiting with the students. She told the students about other authors who write books. Their language is edited before the final book is published. The students decided that if this is the way other authors do it, so would they. Sharon edited the language, compiled the stories onto the pages, and took the book to a copy store for binding. The book is now in the classroom. The students love it and read it again and again. When families come to pick up their children, they look with pride at their languages, their cultures, and their histories.

The truth is that this book cost Sharon a lot of money, which raises other questions. Our perspective is that many, many teachers give to their classrooms in multiple ways all year, every year. If you are a teacher and have never done this, keep a running list of everything you buy with your own money to use in class for just one year. We guarantee that you will be shocked at how much you spend to support the teaching and learning in your own classroom. Our sense is that the public is largely unaware of this private subsidy program which supports public education nationwide.

Sharon's Second Big Book: Five Pictures from Home

The second Big Book project also involved photos, as Sharon had discovered that this was a good way to initiate the process. First, she bought five disposable cameras to take to school. She wrote another letter to the families explaining that the class would be making its second Big Book.

On day one, Sharon sent the five cameras home with five students and asked the families to take five pictures of people or things that were important to the child. In her letter, Sharon asked these five families to return the camera on day two. All five cameras were returned successfully and safely.

On day two, Sharon sent these same five cameras home with five other students. This process continued for four days, as she has 20 students in her class. Within this four day period, 100 percent of the students returned the cameras as instructed, on the following day. Many of Sharon's colleagues told her that the cameras would never be returned. However, Sharon believed in her students and their families; she had faith in the learners (Freeman & Freeman, 1998).

Sharon got the pictures developed and pasted them in composite collages on large pieces of paper. Below and around the collages, Sharon wrote the students' sentences about their family. In this second book, each student did not have a separate page; rather, each student's family was represented as a part of the larger community. After the creation of the second Big Book, Sharon noticed more families walking their children to her class in the morning and afternoon. Soon families began to linger in the class before and after school to talk about the books and the pictures. Her goal now is to have the families read the Big Books with the students at the beginning and end of the school day.

This is an explicit example of how schools can, and must, go beyond inviting parents to participate. Give the families an authentic reason to come to school with their kids and they will come. It must have been evident to those parents that Sharon valued what they valued, since the literacy activities came from the families' pictures and ideas.

Sharon's Third Big Book Project: The Daily News

Whereas the first two Big Book projects were very carefully planned, organized, and implemented with Sharon's direct guidance, the third project happened spontaneously. Sharon had the pedagogical knowledge and wisdom to recognize the significance of the moment, and the pedagogical courage to follow the students' interest. Thus, the Big Book project moved from teacher-centered to student-centered.

"I saw a dead cat on the way to school," Miguel said. With this one sentence, Sharon decided to make her third Big Book a creation that the students eventually named *The Daily News*. "Teacher, look at my pretty haircut," Rosa said as she came flying into the classroom. Her beautiful waist-length hair was now beautiful shoulder-length hair. Sharon commented on how

nice it looked and realized that she had yet another opportunity for literacy development based on the lived-experience of students. Rosa was thrilled with her haircut and even more thrilled that Sharon quickly wrote *Rosa has a pretty new haircut* on paper and prepared the second page of *The Daily News*.

Since the spontaneous beginning of *The Daily News*, the students arrive eager to share with their teacher. Sharon writes their language in the book—one page per child per day. At the end of the day, she simply staples or tapes the pages together for the published book. Suddenly the students are authors. The students love telling the teacher their news and illustrating their individual page each day. *The Daily News* is available for them during free, voluntary reading time.

In summary, this is how Sharon creates Big Books:

1. Students talk in their emerging English, and Sharon writes what they say on a large piece of paper.

2. Students write (copy) the language from this page to an 8 1/2"x11" paper to make their own copy of *The Daily News*. In this smaller, individual book, the students copy not only their individual story (or sentence) but also all of the stories of the day.

3. Students each illustrate their own page in the Big Book.

4. Sharon binds the Big Book and the individual smaller books with staples during the day, so that *The Daily News* is written and published daily.

5. Students take their own books home to read with families.

6. Sharon and students together read *The Daily News* from the Big Book each day while the students look at the Big Book or follow along in their smaller books.

7. Students come to school and have access to yesterday's *Daily News* during free, voluntary reading time.

What Is Different in Sharon's Class Now?

"Language. Language. Language." This is a quotation taken directly from Sharon's journal after she had been doing Big Books with her class for five months. Sharon learned experientially what we have learned from our studies of Vygotsky's description of the relationship between thinking and speaking (Putney et al., in press; Vygotsky, 1978; Vygotsky, 1986; Wink, 1997; Wink, Putney, & Bravo-Lawrence, 1994, 1995). We have learned that thinking and speaking are in a reciprocal and dynamic relationship with each other and with our experiences. Each language experience in which we engage builds more thinking, and more thinking builds more language, especially when the school concepts we are learning are related directly to our own home learning. By bringing the students' own experience directly into the classroom, Sharon was first valuing what the students in her classroom already knew. Beyond that, she was valuing what they wanted to come to know and share as a class, and she built upon that every chance she had.

The culture of the classroom has changed. Sharon's journal also indicates that the students enter the classroom with a perspective that assumes: "In this room we are authors; we read, we write, we publish." So we can see that as the students learned more from Sharon's teaching, so Sharon was learning from her teaching, and from the students' learning (Floriani, 1997; Putney & Floriani, in press).

How was this learning from teaching a transformative act in Sharon's classroom?

- Previously, the reading program was teacher-centered; now the literacy development is student-centered.
- Previously, Sharon had to "teach" the isolated sounds; now, the students author their own books.
- Previously, the students approached reading time with a sense of apprehension (remember, they were being asked to read in a language they did not yet know); now, the students have a pride in and ownership of their literacy.
- Previously, the students lost interest in the mandated drill of individual sounds; now, the students love their stories.

Importance of Illustrating as Communication

One of the unexpected consequences of this project for Sharon was that it reminded her of the importance of art. When books are made, students always do an illustration. As the students in the classroom are five or six years old and do not yet speak English, Sharon is always alert to other forms of communi-cation: art, in this case. She has relearned that the illustrations in the Big Book project provide insights into the world of the children.

She learned from Miguel's illustration that his mom had to go to Mexico because her mother was sick. Miguel was very sad and expressed this through his art. Sharon also learned that Miguel and his family had moved to a new house. Miguel was happy about this and drew a picture of where his bed was in the new house. Sharon learned that when Hector fell from the play bars and broke his arm, he made a new friend.

Changes in the Perspectives of Some Families

As Sharon reflected on the beginning of the school year, she also saw changes in the ways some of the families acted toward her and toward others in the classroom. As the following vignette shows, much can happen in a relatively short time when you demonstrate the value of all students in your classroom.

"I don't want my girls in class with 'those Mexicans,'" the Russian-dominant father said to Sharon on the first day of school. Much has changed since then for Sharon, the students, and their families. It has only been five months since beginning this process of developing literacy based on the students' lives, but Sharon worked diligently to build bridges to the community by building books with her students. Fast-forward from a concerned father's remarks on the first day of school to his child's progress five months later.

"I want a pencil," Anna, a Russian-dominant six-year-old, said to Sharon.

"What?" Sharon responded with surprise.

"I want a pencil," Anna said again in a complete sentence.

"Of course, Anna," Sharon replied with absolute joy.

This was the first sponta-neous, complete sentence that Anna had uttered in English. Sharon and Anna both knew what a significant moment this was. Sharon started to pat Anna on the shoulder. In an instant, Anna fell against Sharon, and they hugged. They smiled and celebrated the moment.

When Anna's dad came, Sharon told him about Anna's emerging English language.

"Yes, and Anna and her sister are going to Russian language school at our church on Friday nights," he told Sharon.

"Wonderful," Sharon replied. "Their continued study of Russian will make their acquisi-tion of English easier and faster," she continued. "And, while they are learning English, they can continue to learn in Russian," Sharon told the dad.

"See you *mañana*," the dad said with a twinkle in his eye.

"Soon, you and Anna will be speaking three languages," Sharon called to the dad as he and Anna left school. All three of them smiled. "And this is the man who did not want his girls with *those Mexican kids*," Sharon thought. However, that was before they all came to know each other better through the Big Book project.

A Second Way of Making Big Books: Fernando

Another way of beginning the process of making Big Books is to start with a piece of literature. Begin with any good story that captures the hearts and minds of the listeners. Fernando chose to begin the process with the book *Crow Boy* by Taro Yashima, which was a winner of the prestigious Caldecott Honor Award. He chose this story because he has discovered that many students, teachers, and families will have a similar experience somewhere in their past: a story of rejection and, finally, victory over difficult conditions. *Crow Boy* is a story that triggers more stories. Also, this is a story that will capture 5-year-olds, 15-year-olds, and 55-year-olds. Fernando was working with a large group of K–12 teachers. The majority of these teachers were English-dominant and were working with multilingual students. The teachers in this specific example are exactly the target audience for turning the theory of the Faltis Framework into classroom practice.

First, Fernando read the story aloud with the students. He asked that the teachers simply sit back and enjoy the story for its intrinsic value. He explained that there would be no comprehension test; no questions at the end of the story; no vocabulary or spelling test based on the story. Fernando only wanted them to listen and enjoy the story.

Second, Fernando asked the large group of teachers to share with those sitting near them. His only question was: What do you think about this story? Initially, the room was quiet as many were still just musing and enjoying the story. Within five minutes, the roomful of teachers was filled with meaningful conversation.

Third, Fernando asked the group to share any similar experiences they might have had. While the group was talking, Fernando quickly taped to the wall a large piece of paper divided into four sections. On this paper, it was easy to see that Fernando had written a short story and had drawn pictures to accompany his own story.

In the quickly drawn sketches, the teachers were easily able to see a young boy on his bike with his helmet and football equipment strapped to the handlebars and the back of the bike. The boy was biking up hill on a dirt road; the back tire of the bike kicked up dust, indicating the movement of the bike. The second picture showed a station wagon with wooden panels on its sides, passing the boy as dust and rocks flew in the boy's face. The third frame of the story showed a small boy standing on the football field watching practice; he was wearing his football gear and just waiting to get to practice with the other boys. The fourth picture showed the return trip home. The boy was riding downhill on his bike, which was again laden with heavy football equipment, and the wood-paneled station wagons were driving by him and kicking up dirt in his face. Fernando shared the story of what he remembered from his high school days when he had tried out for the football team. For the entire season, he rode his bike to practice but was never included in the group.

Fourth, Fernando provided each participant with a small piece of paper that had a story board and asked the teachers to write and illustrate any "crow boy" experience they ever had. Many just sat and reflected for awhile; some were even resistant to writing. Fernando kept walking around the room and did not engage in conversation. Without words, his classroom practice was saying:

It is okay to think, to remember, to feel. And, then you will write and illustrate your own story. This is not a time to talk and visit.

Within 20 minutes, everyone's head was down, and the only sound was that of pencils moving across paper. This fourth step would be easy for a teacher to omit within the context of the class. However, students will share and write only if the teacher models these behaviors first, just as Fernando did. His classroom practice demonstrated that he was not asking anyone to do something that he had not already done.

Teachers often say they want the students to write. We ask: Do you write? Teachers often say they want the students to read. We ask: Do you read? Many powerful classroom practices are effective only to the degree that the teachers also do what is asked of the students.

Fifth, Fernando asked the teachers to share. It began slowly; we are often hesitant to be so vulnerable with our colleagues, just as students are with their classmates. Before long, many had shared in the large group. The remainder of the teachers preferred to share in the smaller groups. When the sharing session ended, there were very few dry eyes in the room.

Conclusion

In this chapter, we have provided glimpses into various classrooms of teachers who are working to create a transformative curriculum for themselves and the students who learn with them. While there are many more examples we could have used, we are optimistic that these particular examples will be useful for teachers who are willing to work toward constructing a transformative classroom. Our purpose was to make visible the practices of teachers who are engaged in the principles that have been presented in the Faltis article in this book.

To promote transformative classroom practice, we advocate the engagement of teachers and students in meaningful interactive discourse while promoting social integration of all students in the classroom. Further, when second language acquisition principles are combined with content instruction in an interactive setting, the language skills of second language learners are able to evolve while their knowledge base in the content areas develops. We saw Javier and Elena participating more in Mrs. Burke's classroom when Lucinda offered to work with them in their primary language to understand the math problems. Let us not forget how Palmer was able to begin to interact in meaningful ways beyond his autistic world because of the examples and the caring provided by his first grade classmates.

We also encourage teachers to recognize the resources of their bilingual students and to draw on their cultural experiences to facilitate learning. One way to bring those cultural experiences into the classroom is to welcome and facilitate family involvement through the making of Big Books. Verónica made this visible in her Big Book adventure. Turning the transformative principles into classroom practice also involves a change from a teacher-directed recitation classroom to one that is more student-centered. We saw this kind of transformation in Sharon's class as she discovered the success of her students in producing *The Daily News*. By working with their topics for the news publication, she ensured their interest and genuine purpose, which also encouraged communication within the classroom, at home, and between families and the school.

This process of turning principles into practice is not an easy one, nor is it ever complete. The process is dynamic, reflexive, and reconstructive. Once you begin to transform your teaching, you will find your own ways to incorporate these principles and others into your practice. And the more you discuss it with colleagues who care, the more energized you will become about trying to do even more. We hope that these vignettes of classroom life have stirred you to begin your own involvement with transformative principles, to grapple with them, to make them your own, and to turn them into transformative practice in your own educational spaces.

NOTE

The authors would like to thank Fernando Peña, the Coordinator of California Mini-Corps at California State University, Stanislaus, who has been instrumental in implementing this project with many students and families in the Central Valley of California. Templates for use in making Big Books are available from Fernando at 7433 Heathrow Way, Hughson, CA 95326; **minicorp@toto.csustan.edu.** We also thank Sharon Whitehead, who has taught us the importance of using cameras to bring the students' lives into literacy development. We are indebted to Verónica Manzo for her collection and publication of oral histories, which was fundamental in focusing our interest again on literacy development based on the lived experiences of students. We also thank Deborah Swaffer for her assistance in critical reading and editing.

One Way to Bind Big Books

After pages are written and illustrated, it is time to bind the book. It is preferable that each author be sitting at a table because the binding process for Big Books requires a little room. If you are making smaller books, an individual desk will suffice.

Tape is needed for the binding. For very small books, cellophane tape will function. For larger books (8 1/2" x 11"), masking tape will work better. For large books, which can be used with a small or whole group, you will need masking tape, if not something stronger. Strapping tape is often used if the participants want to laminate each page prior to the binding process. Remember, laminate first.

Before beginning with tape, it is helpful to practice the following 10 steps with Post-its. Begin with a five-page book only.

1. Place the last page, face up, on the desk in front of you.

2. Tape the left (vertical) side of the page; half of the long strip of tape will be on the edge of the page and the other half will be taped to the desk. Remember, half on/half off.

3. Place the second-to-last page on top of the last page, which is now taped to the desk. Place the tape exactly as directed in step 2.

4. Repeat step 2 with all pages, including title page and cover. All pages of your book are taped to each other and to the desk. You will be looking at the cover of your book.

5. Detach all pages of the book from the desk and turn over, face down, on the desk, with the sticky side of the tape facing up.

6. Place half of another long piece of tape on top of the sticky part of the tape (which is facing you) and the other half of the tape on the desk. The front of the book is now facing down and is still taped to the desk.

7. Detach the book from the desk. Fold the only remaining sticky part over to the back of the book's spine.

8. Take another long piece of tape and tape half of it vertically to the front of the book and the other half vertically to the back of the book.

9. Cut excess tape from top and bottom.

10. Share your book.

REFERENCES

Faltis, C. (1993). *Joinfostering: Adapting teaching strategies for the multilingual classroom.* New York: Macmillan.

Faltis, C. (1997). *Joinfostering: Adapting teaching in the multilingual classroom* (Vol. 2). New York: Merrill.

Faltis, C. J., & Hudelson, S. J. (1998). *Bilingual education in elementary and secondary school communities.* Needham Heights, MA: Allyn & Bacon.

Floriani, A. (1997). Creating a community of learners: Opportunities for learning and negotiating meaning in a bilingual classroom. Unpublished Ph. D. dissertation, University of California, Santa Barbara.

Freeman, D., & Freeman, Y. (1998). ESL/EFL teaching: *Principles of success.* Portsmouth, NH: Heinemann.

Lin, L. (1993). Language of and in the classroom: Constructing the patterns of social life. *Linguistics and Education, 5,* 367–409.

Putney, L. G., & Floriani, A. (in press). Examining transformative classroom processes and practices: A cross-case analysis of life in two bilingual classrooms. *Journal of Classroom Interaction.*

Putney, L. G., Green, J. L., Dixon, C. N., Duran, R., & Yeager, B. (in press). Consequential progressions: Exploring collective-individual development in a bilingual classroom. In C. D. Lee & P. Smagorinsky (Eds.), *Constructing meaning through collaborative inquiry: Vygotskian perspectives on literacy research.* New York: Cambridge University Press.

Putney, L. G., & Wink, J. (1998). Breaking rules: Constructing avenues of access in multilingual classrooms. *TESOL Journal.*

Tuyay, S., Floriani, A., Yeager, B., Dixon, C., & Green, J. (1995). Constructing an integrated, inquiry-oriented approach in classrooms: A cross-case analysis of social, literate, and academic practice. *Journal of Classroom Interaction, 30* (2), 1–15.

Vygotsky, L. S. (1978). *Mind in society: The development of higher psychological processes.* Cambridge, MA: Harvard University Press.

Vygotsky, L. S. (1986). *Thought and language.* Cambridge, MA: MIT Press.

Wink, J. (1997). *Critical pedagogy: Notes from the real world.* White Plains, NY: Addison-Wesley-Longman.

Wink, J., Putney, L., & Bravo-Lawrence, I. (1994, September/October). Introduction: La voz de Vygotsky. *CABE Newsletter, 17,* 10–11, 13–14.

Wink, J., Putney, L., & Bravo-Lawrence, I. (1995, March/April). Vygotsky's zone of proximal development: What in the world is it? *CABE Newsletter, 17,* 12–13, 24.

L1 Teachers and L2 Students: What Mainstream Classroom Teachers Know and Need to Know About English Language Learners*

Luisa Garro and Olga Romero[†]
Bank Street Graduate School of Education

The Changing Demographics of American Public Schools

I want to know what stifles [English language learners], what encourages them in their learning. I want to know about the research. I want to know about everything that can help me with these children.

—First grade mainstream classroom teacher, New York

In the three decades since the Bilingual Education Act of 1968, there has been a wide range of efforts to provide children who lack a solid foundation of English language skills with the special assistance needed to ensure their future academic success. While the programs and approaches designed to help English language learners (ELLs)** have been almost as diverse as the over 300 languages spoken by these students, most of the programs have shared one key feature: they provided services to students outside the context of mainstream classroom instruction. Sometimes the services constituted an entire academic program that ran parallel to the regular school program, and sometimes they were special pullout sessions that complemented in-class work; but in either case, instruction was provided by educators specially trained to work with ELLs (bilingual teachers, ESL instructors, language development specialists, etc.).

More recently, the trend has been to keep immigrant students and other ELLs in the mainstream classroom. This move away from discrete bilingual programs has been underscored by a number of political initiatives, including the revocation of Michigan's bilingual education law in 1995, the 1998 Unz Initiative in California, and Rep. Frank Riggs' (R-CA) introduction of the English Fluency Bill in 1998. To a certain extent, mainstreaming has been necessitated by the changing demographics of American schoolchildren. In many cities, the large numbers of children coming from homes in which English is not the first language vastly exceed the spaces available in existing bilingual programs. Similarly, there are insufficient numbers of trained bilingual teachers to serve the growing ELL populations across the nation. As a result, many school districts have had little choice but to place ELLs with their English-speaking peers in mainstream classes. As one local example of the policy implications of this trend, New York City places ELLs who score above just the 40th percentile on the Language Assessment Battery in monolingual English classrooms—a score that would otherwise be indicative of a serious need for remedial services.

The Result of an Unprepared Teaching Force: Academic Failure for ELLs

While some say linguistic mainstreaming supports the practice of inclusion, the effective impact has been that many ELLs find themselves thrust into a sink-or-swim situation. As Christina (1992:19) reports, "A majority of mainstream teachers are in need of strategies to work effectively with English language learners." Although the TESOL (1995:11) statement recommends "training on the nature of second language acquisition...and language-sensitive content teaching methodologies" for all K–12 teachers, Crawford's 1997 study, "Best Evidence: Research on Language-Minority Education," maintains that fewer than a third of the teachers whose classrooms include ELLs have had "some" training in supporting the educational development of children who are not native English speakers.

Unfortunately, because most teachers lack the training to meet the linguistic needs of ELLs, an untenably large number of these young learners are viewed as being culturally deficient and incapable of succeeding in a rigorous, inquiry-driven program of instruction (Cavazos, 1990; Ruby & Law, 1987; Stoddart & Neiderhauser, 1993). The results of this situation are as predictable as they are undesirable: academic failure, a dropout rate as much as four times higher than the national average, and a significant number of "young adults [who] do not have the basic level of education that is thought to be essential in today's economy" (National Center for Economic Statistics, 1997); see Table 1.

Table 1

Group	Dropout Rate
Total (16 – 24-Year-Olds)	11.1 percent
All Immigrants	25.3 percent
All Hispanic	29.5 percent
Hispanic Immigrants	44.1 percent

From NCES's Dropout Rate in the United States, 1996

The larger significance of these dire results is made all too clear in Crawford's 1997 report, in which he documents the sheer magnitude of the ELL population. Using 1990 Census data, Crawford establishes that one in seven American households speak a language other than English, with nearly 2.4 million children between the ages of 5 and 17 having at least some difficulty with English. According to state education agencies, these students account for at least 7 percent of the nation's school population, with annual increases averaging nearly 10 percent. Crawford (1997:2) maintains that "this total is surely an under-count." For those states with a continued influx of immigrants, such as California, Texas, Florida, and New York, estimates are that by the year 2000 close to 30 percent of all students attending public schools will come from homes where the primary language is not English.

New Directions Needed in Research: How to Improve Education for ELLs

Recognizing a direct connection between a lack of teacher preparation and the subsequent underachievement of mainstreamed ELLs, researchers have begun to call for an exploration of how to improve teacher training and preparation. In their report "Improving Schooling for Language-Minority Children," August & Hakuta (1997:267) highlight the need for more empirical research on how "to develop effective methods for use in preparing teachers of English language learners." Similarly, the 1997 OBEMLA symposium report, "High Stakes Assessment: A Research Agenda for English Language Learners," identified several areas for future research with close links to teacher preparation. Among those areas, two have shaped and informed the study described in this article:

1. The importance of assessing "the access of English language learners to necessary resources and conditions, such as adequate and appropriate instruction" (p. 12)

2. The need to find ways "to assess language proficiency appropriately, both discrete language skills (e.g. vocabulary, grammar, etc.) as well as more authentic and holistic uses of language" (p. 11).

By investigating these interrelated issues of instruction and assessment, this study seeks to provide crucial information on how to help English language learners attain educational success within the mainstream classroom. The specific objectives of the study are:

■ To identify the baseline of information (or misinformation) that mainstream teachers currently have about ELLs, along with the existing teaching methodologies employed in their work with ELLs; and

■ To identify a common knowledge base that mainstream teachers need to acquire in order to implement strategies that have been effective in supporting the educational development of ELLs.

Gathering the Data: The Focus Groups

To identify what mainstream classroom teachers currently know about working with ELLs, we hosted a series of two-hour focus group meetings. To participate, teachers had to meet the following criteria:

1. To be teachers in regular education classrooms (K-3);

2. To have in their classrooms students who were English language learners; and

3. To self-identify as English monolingual—i.e., as not knowing a second language or as having very limited skills in a second language.

Four focus groups were held with teachers from the New York metropolitan area. The groups ranged in size from five to eleven. We found that the ideal group size was between six and eight participants. This allowed all teachers to engage fully in the discussion.

The first focus group meeting was held at Bank Street College of Education. The participants were all Bank Street graduates. Some of them were teachers at the Bank Street School for Children and some were public school teachers. With this group we tested whether our questions and the structure for the focus group were appropriate. We also tried our own abilities as facilitators.

After minor revisions, we held the next three focus group meetings. We held one at Bank Street with participants representing the city public and private schools and the last two in the suburbs, attempting to represent a broader geographical and institutional spectrum of the New York metropolitan area.

The teachers responded to two scenarios and a more formal questionnaire (see Tables 2 and 3 below, respectively). The questionnaire was modeled after the one used by Christina (1992) and Faltis (1997).

By answering first in writing to the scenarios and the questionnaire, the teachers had time to reflect about their experiences with ELLs. Also, having jotted down some ideas lessened the pressure of responding on the spur of the moment when the conversation began. The focus group discussions were audiotaped and transcribed.

Table 2 SCENARIOS

In preparation for the discussion, think about the following:

1.   A child arrives in your classroom and does not produce any or much oral language for several weeks. Think about what you would do. We'd like you to share some of your ideas with the group.

---

2.   Think of a specific situation where you were frustrated in your effort to teach something to a child in your class who was an English language learner. We'd like you to share this experience with the group.

Table 3
FOCUS GROUP QUESTIONNAIRE

Please answer the following questions. Your answers will give us a better idea of what teachers might need.

1. How many students do you have in your classroom? _____

2. How many English language learners are there in your classroom now? _____

3. Have you had any English language learners in your classroom before?

	Yes	No
4. How do you determine who are English language learners?		
School records	____	____
Information from parents	____	____
A language test in the first language	____	____
A language test in English	____	____
Other (specify):	____	____
5. How did you learn the strategies for teaching English language learners? Check as many as apply.		
Workshops (How many?)	____	____
A college course or seminar	____	____
Concentration in degree	____	____
On your own	____	____
Other (specify):	____	____
6. What supports would you need to improve your teaching techniques with English language learners? Check as many as apply.		
Workshops (How many?)	____	____
Ongoing staff development in English as a second language	____	____
Access to English as a Second Language and Bilingual teachers in your school as resources and experts in the field	____	____
A written set of guidelines on stages in second language learning	____	____
A written list of exemplary teaching practices to reach all the students in your classroom	____	____
A teacher group in school where issues of English language learners are discussed on a regular basis	____	____
Other (specify):	____	____

Your name: _____ Years of teaching experience _____

Grade you currently teach: _____ What grades have you taught? _____

School where you teach: _____

Years of teaching experience: _____

What follows is a preliminary summary and analysis of our findings.

What Mainstream Classroom Teachers Know

In general, it was both enlightening and encouraging to find that mainstream teachers as a group have not only many insights into the needs of ELLs but also many questions and a genuine desire to find answers to those questions. The information these teachers shared with us is not based on research or scholarship; it's mostly based on intuition and gut feeling as they make decisions about how to teach ELLs. They have learned through trial and error, from other teachers and from using their own common sense. What we have attempted to do in creating the eight charts that follow is to weave together the threads of individual teachers' knowledge into a tapestry that reflects the wealth of information that mainstream teachers have as a group.

The eight categories represented in the charts emerged as we examined the data from the four focus group discussions. They reflect different aspects of the daily academic interaction between teachers and ELLs, and they present ideas, suggestions, and tried practices as well as questions and specific needs.

To validate the soundness of the ideas and strategies articulated by the teachers, we include in the charts citations of some of the existing literature and research that support their practices.

Our attempt to summarize and present our initial findings in chart form could be misleading, however. Teachers shared information with us in bits and pieces. No one individual teacher, not even one focus group, had all the information. The charts are intended to show not only what mainstream teachers know but also how much more they want and need to know.

Chart 1

INFORMATION GATHERING: GETTING TO KNOW ELLS

- Parent questionnaire: Language survey and other information on child's linguistic, academic, and family history (Echevarria & Graves, 1998; Gonzalez, 1997; Pease-Alvarez & Vasquez, 1994)

- Prior teachers and current school specialists (Gonzalez, Brusca-Vega & Yawkey, 1997; Peregoy & Boyle, 1997)

- School records (Peregoy & Boyle, 1997)

- Direct observation of the child (Hamayan, 1994; Peregoy & Boyle, 1997)

- Hard to assess what ELLs know because teacher does not know their native language

Chart 2
HOW TEACHERS SUPPORT ELLS IN THEIR CLASSROOM

- Have a buddy system; best buddy is not always the most verbal child but the most compassionate (Peregoy & Boyle, 1997)
- Have classroom translators (Faltis, 1997)
- Give ELLs time; do not force the use of L2 (De Avila, 1997; Krashen, 1994; McKeon, 1994)
- Acknowledge that ELLs can be silent (Krashen, 1994)
- Emphasize socialization at the beginning (Faltis, 1997; Freeman & Freeman, 1998; Tabor, 1997; Toohey, 1998)
- Connect with ELLs at an emotional level (Faltis, 1997; McKeon, 1994)
- Make ELLs feel safe, accepted, and comfortable, e.g., by creating a play environment (Krashen, 1994; Peregoy & Boyle, 1997)
- Be ELLs' advocate (Cazden, 1986); sometimes ELLs are used as scapegoats by other kids
- ELLs may express themselves physically because they do not have the language to express what they feel
- Use signs, gestures, and visual aids for communication (Cummins, 1996; Faltis, 1997; Garro, 1998; Peregoy & Boyle, 1997)
- Teach sign language to the class
- Applaud ELLs' efforts; help ELLs feel successful in their learning (Faltis, 1997; Peregoy & Boyle, 1997)
- Be attentive and sensitive to ELLs' feelings and cues (e.g., resistance to speaking or reading in the native language) (Peregoy & Boyle, 1997; Willett, 1995)
- Support the native language of ELLs: make it part of the classroom routines; have books in the native language of ELLs (Cummins, 1986; Freeman & Freeman, 1994)
- Bring members of the ELL's family into the classroom to tell stories, to cook, etc. (Flood et al., 1997; Pease-Alvarez & Vasquez, 1994)
- Give importance to classroom routines (Faltis, 1997; Tabors, 1997)
- Have pets in the classroom; ELLs can be the pet caretakers
- Learn the native language and about the culture of ELLs (Freeman & Freeman, 1998; Peregoy & Boyle, 1997)
- Think of their own experiences learning a second language that allow them to connect with ELLs' experience (Freeman & Freeman, 1998)
- Teach other kids in the class acceptance of diversity through songs and poems in the foreign languages represented. For whole-group meetings use literature about the cultures represented by children in the class (Faltis, 1997; Freeman & Freeman, 1998)
- Tell children in the class to think about an activity in which ELLs can participate that does not require language
- Educate English-speaking parents about what ELLs are experiencing (Miramontes, Nadeau, & Commins, 1997) through their children's play dates
- Use ELLs' talents (e.g., ELL who liked computers taught other students) (Freeman & Freeman, 1998)
- Feel frustrated because they do not know how ELLs feel about themselves, the classroom, the school because they cannot express it
- If you are a good teacher you follow your instincts in trying out new ideas and discarding them if they do not work (Clair, 1995). You should not be bound by a lesson plan.

Chart 3
WHAT TEACHERS KNOW ABOUT SECOND LANGUAGE LEARNING

- ELLs learn in concrete ways through immersion in functional environment, cooking, block building, field trips, movement, art (e.g., ELL made flags and other kids added words to his art or sculpture describing what he had made). (Thomas & Collier, 1997)

- ELLs learn through modeling, repetition, and imitation from teacher and other kids. (Bayron-Resnick, 1997; Echevarria & Graves, 1998; Garro, 1998; Peregoy & Boyle, 1997)

- ELLs understand more than they produce (Krashen, 1994): first receptive, then expressive. Silent period: ELL is physically on periphery or turns his back; eventually ELL says all the words for communication (e.g., "Do you want to play checkers?"). Other children celebrate the breakthrough.

- Older kids use curse words to be like the other kids. (Krashen, 1994)

- Learn set phrases (e.g., from the computer "Way to Go"). (Willett, 1995)

- ELLs do more talking at play than at meetings. (Faltis, 1997)

- ELLs go from simple to more complex language: first words, then phrases and conversations. (De Avila, 1997; Gonzalez, Brusca-Vega & Yawkey, 1997)

- Personality and style influence rate of L2 acquisition. (Echevarria & Graves 1998; Krashen, 1994; McLaughlin, 1992; Willett, 1995)

- ELLs passive at first; then they communicate their frustrations in physical ways. Could be socially frustrated.

- ELLs get tired listening to English all day (e.g., teachers give ELLs a break to run an errand in the school). (Flood et al., 1997)

- It's better to learn a second language early.

- Correct what ELLs said incorrectly; correct English must be used.

- Support the native language of ELLs; knowledge of L1 is important in learning L2. (Cummins, 1986; Freeman & Freeman, 1994)

Chart 4
WHAT TEACHERS KNOW ABOUT ELLS' ACQUISITION OF LITERACY

- Teachers need patience and willingness to wait. (De Avila, 1997; Krashen, 1994)
- Encourage ELLs to speak first.
- Label things in L1 and L2 in the classroom (Hudelson, 1994); not clear if a rich print environment will lead to academic success.
- Use poems and songs, dramatization. (Faltis, 1997; Flood et al., 1997; Freeman & Freeman, 1998)
- Use Living Books, CD-roms, and books on tape. (Echevarria & Graves, 1998)
- Send home with the book an audiotape of the class reading the story. (Freeman & Freeman, 1998; Peregoy & Boyle, 1997)
- Create a book of words in which parent writes words and child draws the pictures (Freeman & Freeman, 1998)
- It's important to have a rich language experience at home. (Tabors, 1997; Peregoy & Boyle, 1997)
- Encourage parents to read at home in native language. (Miramontes, Nadeau, & Commins, 1997)
- Upper grade teachers think that primary language takes care of literacy skills. Literacy in first language is important in learning a second language. (Cummins, 1986; Freeman & Freeman, 1994) Teachers did not know when to start pushing ELLs in second language or how to set limits in the use of L1, especially in writing.
- Have ELLs write in any language (Hudelson, 1994); but then what do teachers do if they cannot read what ELLs wrote?
- Some ELLs are great decoders but have no comprehension.
- Support concept development in any language. (Cummins, 1986; Met, 1994)
- Use nonfiction for older ELLs. They love to see pictures of real things (e.g., Eyewitness books). Favorite book *I Hate English*. (Hudelson, 1994)
- Teach ELLs how to use dictionaries.
- Uncertain about copying as a strategy (Hudelson, 1994)
- With basic math ELLs can be successful without knowing the second language well, but have more difficulty with word problems (e.g., "How much more…"). (Short, 1993)
- See a philosophical conflict between outside consultants and school reading teachers

Chart 5
LEARNING DISABILITY VERSUS SECOND LANGUAGE LEARNING

- Hard to decide if it is a language or a learning issue.
- ELLs are more at risk for misidentification. (Cummins, 1984; Fueyo, 1997; Gonzalez, Brusca-Vega & Yawkey, 1997)
- Vicious cycle in determining whether it is LD or language learning because there is low self-esteem in both situations due to sense of failure.
- To decide whether to refer or not, ESL teacher is consulted; a teacher turned an ESL evaluation into a preliminary evaluation for special education.
- Follow their gut feelings with respect to LD issues.
- Emotional issues are getting in the way of learning and might contribute to the perception of a learning disability.
- Teacher complained about revolving-door classroom—too many pullout programs.
- For ELLs who have been in the United States since kindergarten, it is easier to say they have a language problem.
- Teachers feel the responsibility to report possible learning problems by third grade.
- A school does not check native language knowledge to diagnose LD issues.
- Some schools have teachers present cases to a school team, forcing teachers to be alert for developmental milestones.
- People who test children are not available to teachers for follow-up conferencing.
- Parents can identify language problems in some cases; other parents are in denial.

Chart 6
SCHOOL SUPPORT OF NEW TEACHERS

■ No support from the school for new teachers. (Faltis, 1997)

■ Teachers want a language policy from the administration regarding ELLs and their parents (liaisons, translators, etc.). (CEEE, 1996)

■ ESL teacher helps out the mainstream teacher. (Faltis, 1997; Short, 1993)

■ ESL, special education, and classroom teachers should have some way of communicating about ELLs. (CEEE, 1996; Cummins, 1996)

■ Initiative to create teacher forums or support groups should come from the teachers and the administration. (CEEE, 1996; Clair, 1995)

■ Some teachers visited other schools with bilingual programs as part of a second language initiative in the district. One school experimented with Spanish as a second language, but there was no support for implementation.

■ Administration pushes for tests; teachers have to deliver. You have to move kids along, but what about the goals for every kid?

Chart 7
HOW TEACHERS RELATE TO THE PARENTS OF ELLS

- Some teachers do not know how to communicate with parents. (Miramontes, Nadeau & Commins, 1997)
- Some teachers may find it frustrating when their values clash with those of the parents.
- Some teachers do not know how to be parent advocates. (Miramontes, Nadeau, & Commins, 1997)
- Expect support for parents from the school or district; parenting and literacy workshops exist. (Miramontes, Nadeau, & Commins, 1997)
- Understand the emotional exhaustion families go through.
- Teachers want parental involvement in the education of ELLs. (August & Hakuta, 1997; Miramontes, Nadeau, & Commins, 1997)
- Bring parents in to read a story in their native language (Flood et al., 1997; Freeman & Freeman, 1998), and give English-speaking kids clues to decipher the code.
- Some teachers believe that differences in home environment are determined by social class and poverty.
- Even middle-class and rich kids can be in a nonverbal L1 environment.
- Parents who also speak English can help teachers understand how the children feel at the beginning and at the end of the day.
- Parents do not know how to access school resources. (Miramontes, Nadeau, & Commins, 1997)
- Parents want their children's teachers to teach in English.
- Parents have limited availability because of jobs; school meetings are usually scheduled during the school day in the suburbs.
- Parents are overwhelmed (Miramontes, Nadeau, & Commins, 1997) by amount of information at the beginning of the school year, specially for kindergarten.
- Some parents do not have high expectations. They just want ELLs to get through. Others care about boys succeeding but not girls.
- Parents have negative attitudes toward their own native language and toward bilingual education.
- Parents do not receive information in a language that they can understand; school should have staff who speak the language and can translate. (Miramontes, Nadeau, & Commins, 1997)
- Some Anglo parents get upset when Hispanic parents come to read in Spanish.

Chart 8
WHAT MAINSTREAM TEACHERS WANT

- ESL methodology courses (August & Hakuta , 1997; Clair, 1995)
- Information on stages of second language acquisition (Peregoy & Boyle, 1997; Reagan, 1997)
- Linguistic knowledge: how languages are different or similar (Hamayan, 1994; Peregoy & Boyle, 1997; Reagan, 1997)
- Having a professional library, bibliography, journals, resources, and videos on ESL (August & Hakuta, 1997; McLaughlin & McLeod, 1997)
- District to provide teachers with knowledge they need (CEEE, 1996)
- Attending an ESL conference instead of a reading conference
- Visit ESL exemplary classrooms; create a list of sites (Clair, 1995)
- Read what other teachers have written on ESL (CEEE, 1996)
- Find out about specific ESL techniques (Clair, 1995; Reagan, 1997)
- Have a chance to talk about ESL with people outside the system, to connect with people with expertise
- More conversations with other teachers (Clair, 1995)
- Know how to pick up signs of trouble to seek another opinion
- Know about culturally determined behavior (e.g., tying a boy's shoelaces)
- Have bilingual materials, books in the native language of ELLs (Freeman & Freeman, 1994)
- A compilation of frequently used phrases in Spanish (Freeman & Freeman, 1994)
- Have someone in the building who can speak to parents of ELLs in their native language; more translators (Faltis, 1997; Miramontes, Nadeau, & Commins, 1997)
- Instruction in the native language of ELLs in the classroom (Cummins, 1986; Freeman & Freeman, 1994, 1998)
- A computer program that translates
- PTA meetings translated and held when parents can attend (Miramontes, Nadeau, & Commins, 1997)

What Mainstream Classroom Teachers Want and Need to Know

Notwithstanding the areas of strength exhibited by the teachers, our preliminary analysis of the data revealed some glaring gaps and misinformation in their knowledge base: areas where it is evident that teachers need to sharpen their skills if their work with ELLs is to be effective. Having audiotaped and transcribed our conversations with the teachers, we can use their own words as springboards into the specific areas in which they want and need to increase and solidify their knowledge about ELLs.

"I don't know, but [the children] seem to understand more before they produce."

"I don't know, but [the children] seem to understand more before they produce."

It became obvious to us, and it came as no surprise to the teachers, that they had no formal knowledge of how children learn a second language. Without exception, the mainstream teachers we interviewed blamed their lack of information on their college preparation. It was clear to them that their teacher education courses had not equipped them to deal with immigrant children. For most of them, their knowledge in this area was based on commonplace assumptions such as "The younger you learn a language, the easier it is," or even on pseudo-facts concerning the role of the left or right areas of the brain in the acquisition of languages. Beyond statements such as "Children learn a second language through imitation" or "...by going from simple to more complex language," their understanding of stages of second language learning was a veritable *tabula rasa*.

The implications of this gap in teachers' knowledge can be far-reaching. It explains many of the problems that the teachers encounter in all their day-to-day dealings with ELLs, from initial efforts at integrating a new ELL into the classroom to the use of techniques that can enhance the student's learning of English.

"It takes seven years for a child to learn English fluently, but when do they use the language? I still don't know."

"It takes seven years for a child to learn English fluently, but when do they use the language? I still don't know."

Mainstream classroom teachers had conflicting information regarding the length of time that it takes a student to master the various aspects of the English language. Teachers who expect the process of language learning to be very lengthy and laborious may expect very little of their students, while those who believe that children should learn a second language in no time at all may decide that the ELLs in their classrooms are slow or have learning disabilities.

Even though several teachers articulated the importance of first language competence in the acquisition of English, their efforts to support the development of the first language were understandably insufficient in a mainstream environment. Interestingly, even those who mentioned children in their classroom whose mastery of the first language might have been an asset in their learning of English were really not aware of the level of competence that the children had in their first language. In general, schools do not consider it a priority to establish a child's ability in his or her first language unless there is a problem with the acquisition of English. Similarly, teachers had no access to assessment instruments that could give them a clue about the level of competence that the ELLs in their classrooms had achieved.

One teacher put it quite bluntly: "Each child is different, each culture is different. What I found is that it's trial and error that works."

Many of the teachers expressed a desire to learn more about languages and linguistics. They wanted to know how the native language of ELLs can help or hinder their learning of English and how the written expression of their native language, alphabetic or ideographic, contributes to literacy development. They also wanted to know how the age at which ELLs are first exposed to the second language can affect their progression in the acquisition of English.

"My Korean children are excellent decoders but don't really understand. The comprehension is not there."

Another area in which teachers' knowledge was lacking is, in essence, an extension of the one discussed above: Teachers were pretty much baffled in their efforts to introduce and develop literacy in the second language. Again, unaware of the literacy level of ELLs in their first language, the teachers found it difficult to make decisions about methodology and content level. They also mentioned that they had never received instruction in how to teach literacy skills to ELLs. This is another element missing from their teacher preparation courses.

Even though they had notions about using poems, songs, and dramatization as a way to engage ELLs in the classroom, going specifically into reading and writing was a struggle for the teachers. Labeling objects in the classroom was a good beginning for many of them, but they had difficulty moving beyond this strategy.

We were surprised to learn, for instance, that many teachers were thoroughly confounded by the fact that many of their ELLs had very good decoding skills but very low comprehension levels. The idea that ELLs needed more time to learn oral vocabulary and syntax totally eluded these teachers. Those teachers who allowed ELLs to write in their first language did not know when or how to begin to encourage the child to take chances with English.

Some of the teachers were of the opinion that ELLs' literacy skills in the primary language would take care of their literacy skills in English. This attitude of "benign neglect" could be extremely dangerous in that it could lead to academic failure for the older child.

Although several of the teachers told us that they encouraged parents to read to their children at home in the native language, it was not clear whether they even knew about the parents' literacy level, and it was painfully obvious that they were unable to suggest appropriate literature to the parents.

The teachers' inability to discern ELLs' skills in their first language was often a source of great frustration to them. If a child was not learning English at a rate that seemed appropriate to the teacher, the teacher was bound to question whether the child had a learning or language disability.

"It might be an ESL issue or something else, or language processing, or a reading thing...it is frustrating."

Most of the teachers we interviewed mentioned this as one of the most intractable problems they faced within the school system. Fearful of "labeling" a child unnecessarily, some teachers waited until the child's problems reached an untenable level. Others rushed prematurely to refer the child for a special education evaluation, thus putting in motion a process that would result in ELLs being labeled incorrectly as learning, language, or emotionally disturbed.

To our surprise, there are still schools in which ELLs are not evaluated in their first language when a problem is suspected, and there are schools in which unqualified interpreters are used during evaluations. Barring these unfortunate

"My Korean children are excellent decoders but don't really understand. The comprehension is not there."

"It might be an ESL issue or something else, or language processing, or a reading thing...it is frustrating."

circumstances, teachers were stymied when it came to differentiating between the normal process of second language learning and a bona fide disability. Some spoke of following "your gut feeling," and trusting "your intuition"; others had made the decision that if ELLs are not learning according to the school's standards, they must be referred for an evaluation by third grade.

In cases in which ELLs were receiving additional services in school, such as ESL, speech and language therapy, occupational therapy, and counseling, teachers described their classrooms as having a "revolving door" system in which the children who need it most are never consistently present in the classroom and thus are always behind their peers and not quite integrated into the group.

Teachers reported that with "ESL students," their label for children who have recently migrated into the United States, it is easier to decide whether they have a learning problem than in the case of "bilingual" children, those who have received most of their education in the United States. What teachers labeled as "cognitive issues" involving the latter group of children revealed the teachers' lack of knowledge about the effects of language attrition in children. Teachers need to know that language attrition, the consequence of subtractive bilingualism, can have deleterious effects on a child's ability to learn a second language and that the problems that ELLs may present, while real, are often pedagogical in origin.

Teachers still speak of many of the ELLs as coming to school with "no language." Such comments, perhaps not malicious in their intent, reflect the types of myths that spread and take root among the population at large and that end up creating or confirming already existing negative stereotypes.

Our sense was, and some teachers confirmed it, that academic expectations for ELLs, in both their native and second languages, are lower than those for native English speakers.

"I would like to have the parents more involved; those parents who are intimidated because they don't speak English [I wish would] come in more."

In general, we found that teachers lack knowledge about the cultural characteristics of the parents of ELLs. This lack of knowledge leads to many misunderstandings and misinterpretations of behavior and to an understandable discomfort in having to deal with these families.

A teacher described her relationship with a Japanese mother in the following terms: "When he [an eight-year-old Japanese boy] arrived, he was very hostile, aggressive. . . . they had to drag him upstairs to third grade. The cultural differences too. The mother would come into the room entirely bent over. She would not look at me. I thought she had a back problem." Eventually, this teacher understood that the mother's demeanor would have been entirely appropriate in the relationship between parent and teacher in Japan.

The teachers spoke often about the difficulty they have in bringing the parents of ELLs into the school. Their own discomfort about having the parents in the school, finding appropriate ways to communicate with them, and planning to use the parents' language and talents in the classroom arose only peripherally, but it was clearly there.

There was an honest effort on the part of the teachers to understand the plight of many of the parents: "They work long hours"; "It's all too confusing for them"; "They're exhausted." Yet there was an undercurrent of resentment when they talked about the parents speaking about "going back to my country," as if

"I would like to have the parents more involved; those parents who are intimidated because they don't speak English [I wish would] come in more."

the United States were not their country, "so they're not going to try to assimilate because they're going to go back," or the fact that "the children go back and forth to their native countries," so they fall behind in school.

There also seems to be a feeling among the teachers that the parents cannot or will not help with homework and that the children "go home to no language."

Issues of social class and racial discrimination also surfaced, especially in suburban schools where immigrant populations are relatively new. Teachers are very conscious about the situation but feel helpless in the face of institutionalized racism: "It's no accident that there are no Spanish people in my school, let alone blacks," commented one of the teachers, or that white parents do not want their children placed in a "dark classroom," code words for a classroom with many non-English-speaking children. This points to a larger problem to which teachers alluded very clearly: The lack of support on the part of many schools when it comes to helping both teachers and parents.

"I would like to have someone in the building who can translate and speaks the native language of the parents."

"I would like to have someone in the building who can translate and speaks the native language of the parents."

The needs of teachers are as basic as those expressed by this teacher. There are indeed schools with large immigrant populations where arrangements have never been made to have an interpreter so that teachers and parents can communicate.

Even when a classroom aide is available, some teachers voiced their concern about the fact that ELLs did not want to use their native language with the aide. An easy explanation might be that ELLs do not want to be singled out as different and that the effort to have a student communicate with a special adult would create discomfort in the child. The situation could also be examined from a political point of view: What is the status of aides within a classroom or in the school as a whole? Do ELLs perceive the status of the person who speaks their native language and reject the person based on "low status by association"? How many of the head teachers that ELLS encounter belong to their own ethnic or linguistic group? Would a child be more inclined to use the native language with the highest status person in the classroom, namely the head teacher?

The mainstream teachers we interviewed understood the needs of the parents but felt enormously frustrated by the lack of response from the administration. In one district, the directive is that every communication that goes out to parents must be in English. The fact that a large percentage of parents cannot read English seems to be of no consequence to the administration. A teacher reported that in her district, policy dictates that teacher–parent meetings be held during school hours: "[The school] would not consider that there are people who cannot take off from work.... It's not that they do not want to be here, but economically they cannot be here."

The teachers are articulating quite explicitly the task at hand at the level of policymaking and district leadership: The administration has to make a commitment to the education of immigrant children, and certain practical arrangements have to be implemented to welcome parents and to prepare teachers.

Summing Up

English language learners are the fastest-growing group in schools today, and our findings show that mainstream classroom teachers are not prepared to educate these students. However, the teachers have an intuitive knowledge of the children's needs. They use their instinct, gut feeling, and common sense to meet some of these needs, and they are quite aware of what they lack as teachers to serve ELLs in an effective way.

When asked to give us a wish list, teachers spoke about professional development in the form of workshops and conferences. They want to learn about linguistics and second language learning; they want to know more about literacy development in the second language; they want the schools to supply them with books in the native languages of the children; they want special ESL materials to use in the classroom; they want more communication with ESL teachers, learning specialists, and other colleagues; they want the school to organize study groups so that teachers can bring up and discuss their concerns about specific children.

In this article, our intention was to reflect on our findings and to offer some suggestions that schools and districts can start implementing now to support mainstream classroom teachers. Our preliminary review of the literature clearly shows that there is a great deal of research and information that both teachers and administrators could use (see the next section for references by topic). Why is it that this information has not reached mainstream teachers? How can we share with them the knowledge that they expressly want and need? The next phase of our project is to find ways to make our research findings available to them. Our ultimate goal is to be true conduits of information from the proverbial "ivory tower" into the ranks of mainstream classroom teachers.

As we revisit the teacher's quote that opens this article, the mandate could not be more explicit: "I want to know what stifles [English language learners], what encourages them in their learning. I want to know about the research. I want to know about everything that can help me with these children."

English language learners will continue to fill mainstream classrooms in the United States. How can we prepare and support the teaching force to be ready for them?

How to Learn More About ELLs

Our preliminary review of the literature has revealed some sources to which mainstream teachers, administrators, and anyone else working with English language learners can refer to learn more about what they need to know. Listed below are specific areas of interest, followed by the numbers of relevant articles and books that are cited in the references that appear at the end of this article.

Second language acquisition and development (oral expressive, receptive, and written language)
a. Theories: 2, 11, 18, 22, 23, 24, 32, 42, 47
b. Stages: 2, 17, 18, 23, 24, 27, 32, 34, 42, 45, 56, 57
c. Literacy: 1, 7, 11, 18, 19, 20, 22, 23, 24, 26, 27, 28, 29, 31, 35, 40, 47, 54

Misconceptions about ELLs: 14, 16, 18, 23, 24, 27, 34, 56

Recognition of differences
a. Cultural sensitivity: 2, 3, 6, 16, 18, 19, 24, 27, 34, 42, 45, 52, 56
b. Language differences (use, acquisition, and development): 10, 12, 14, 16, 18, 19, 24, 27, 34, 37, 40, 45, 49, 55, 57

Assessment
a. Placement: 1, 10, 17, 18, 23, 24, 26, 27, 40, 45, 49
b. Ongoing: 1, 18, 19, 21, 23, 34, 36, 40, 42, 45, 49
c. Learning differences: 10, 14, 19, 27, 42

Classroom applications
a. Teaching methods and philosophies: 3, 6, 7, 9, 12, 16, 17, 18, 21, 22, 23, 24, 26, 27, 28, 35, 37, 40, 42, 44, 45, 47, 49, 53, 55, 56
b. Strategies for integrating ELLs: 2, 7, 12, 17, 18, 19, 20, 21, 23, 24, 27, 35, 37, 40, 44, 47, 49, 53, 55
c. Specific tips and activities: 2, 3, 9, 18, 19, 20, 21, 24, 25, 27, 28, 35, 40, 42, 44, 47, 49

Home and school connection: 6, 16, 18, 20, 22, 24, 27, 35, 37, 40, 41, 44, 50, 53, 56

Professional development: 1, 6, 9, 18, 20, 22, 23, 27, 34, 37, 40, 41, 42, 43, 53

Suggestions for additional resources: 1, 6, 18, 32, 35, 37, 42, 43, 49, 52, 53

To learn more about ELLs on the Web:
Center for Applied Linguistics: http://www.cal.org
National Clearinghouse for Bilingual Education: http://www.ncbe.gwu.edu
Teachers of English as a Second Language: http://www.tesol.edu

This study has been made possible through a 1998 field-initiated research grant from the Office of Bilingual Education and Minority Language Affairs, U.S. Department of Education.

REFERENCES

1. August, D., and Hakuta, K. (1997). *Improving schooling for language-minority children: A research agenda.* Washington, DC: National Academy Press.

2. Baker, C. (1996). *Foundations of bilingual education and bilingualism (2nd ed.).* Philadelphia: Multilingual Matters Ltd.

3. Bayron-Resnick, N. (1997). *Strategies for helping limited English proficient children communicate in the classroom.* Unpublished manuscript. New York: Bank Street College of Education.

4. Cavazos, L. (1990). *Strategies for educating gifted, disadvantaged youth.* UMI Evaluative Report. Ann Arbor, MI.

5. Cazden, C. (1986). ESL teachers as language advocates for children. In P. Rigg and S. Enright (Eds.), *Children and ESL: Integrating perspectives* (pp. 9–21). Washington, DC: TESOL Press.

6. Center for Equity and Excellence in Education (CEEE) (1996). *Promoting excellence: Ensuring academic success for limited English-proficient students.* Arlington, VA: George Washington University. http://r3cc.ceee.gwu.edu

7. Chamot, A.U., & O'Malley, M. (1996). The cognitive academic language learning approach: A model for linguistically diverse classrooms. *The Elementary School Journal, 96* (3), 259-273.

8. Christina, B. (1992). *An in-service training course designed to increase teachers' strategies for working effectively with second language learners in the elementary school mainstream classroom.* New York: BETAC.

9. Clair, N. (1995). Mainstream classroom teachers and ESL students. *TESOL Quarterly, 29,* 189-196.

10. Cloud, N. (1994). Special education needs of second language students. In F. Genesee (Ed.), *Educating second language children: The whole child, the whole curriculum, the whole community* (pp. 243–277). New York: Cambridge University Press.

11. Collier, V. (1995). *Acquiring a second language for school.* Washington, DC: National Clearinghouse for Bilingual Education.

12. Cox, C., and Boyd-Batstone, P. (1997). *Crossroads: Literature and language in culturally and linguistically diverse classrooms.* Upper Saddle River, NJ: Prentice Hall.

13. Crawford, J. (1997). *Best evidence: Research foundations of the Bilingual Education Act.* Washington, DC: National Clearinghouse for Bilingual Education.

14. Cummins, J. (1984). *Bilingualism and special education: Issues in assessment and pedagogy.* Clevedon, England: Multilingual Matters.

15. Cummins, J. (1986). The role of primary language development in promoting educational success for language minority students. In California State Department of Education (Ed.), *Schooling and language minority students: A theoretical framework* (pp. 3–50). Los Angeles: Evaluation, Dissemination, and Assessment Center.

16. Cummins, J. (1996). *Negotiating identities: Education for empowerment in a diverse society.* Ontario, CA: California Association of Bilingual Education.

17. De Avila, E. (1997). *Setting expected gains for non- and limited English proficient students.* NCBE Resource Collection Series, 8.

18. Echevarria, J., & Graves, A. (1998). *Sheltered content instruction: Teaching English language learners with diverse disabilities.* Boston: Allyn & Bacon.

19. Faltis, C. (1997). *Joinfostering: Adapting teaching for the multilingual classroom.* Upper Saddle River, NJ: Prentice Hall.

20. Flood, J., Lapp, D., Tinajero, J.V., & Hurley, S. (1997). Literacy instruction for students acquiring English: Moving beyond the immersion debate. *The Reading Teacher, 50* (4), 356–358.

21. Freeman, D., & Freeman, Y.S. (1991). Doing social studies: Whole-language lessons to promote social action. *Social Education*, 29–32.

22. Freeman, D., & Freeman, Y. (1994). *Between worlds: Access to second language acquisition.* Portsmouth, NH: Heinemann.

23. Freeman, Y., & Freeman, D. (1998). *ESL/EFL teaching: Principles for success.* Portsmouth, NH: Heinemann.

24. Fueyo, V. (1997). Below the tip of the iceberg: Teaching language-minority students. *The Council for Exceptional Children*, 61–65.

25. Garro, L. (1998). *English language learners.* Unpublished manuscript. New York: Bank Street College of Education.

26. Genesee, F. (Ed.) (1994). Educating second language children: *The whole child, the whole curriculum, the whole community.* New York: Cambridge University Press.

27. Gonzalez, V., Brusca-Vega, R., & Yawkey, T. (1997). *Assessment and instruction of culturally and linguistically diverse students with or at risk of learning problems: From research to practice.* Boston: Allyn & Bacon.

28. Hamayan, E.V. (1989). *Teaching writing to potentially English proficient students using whole language approaches.* National Clearinghouse for Bilingual Education, *11*, 1–17.

29. Hamayan, E.V. (1994). Language development of low-literacy students. In F. Genesee (Ed.), *Educating second language children: The whole child, the whole curriculum, the whole community* (pp. 278–300). New York: Cambridge University Press.

30. Hernandez, H. (1997). *Teaching in multilingual classrooms: A teachers' guide to context, process, and content.* Upper Saddle River, NJ: Prentice Hall.

31. Hudelson, S. (1994). Literacy development of second language children. In F. Genesee (Ed.), *Educating second language children: The whole child, the whole curriculum, the whole community* (pp. 129–158). New York: Cambridge University Press.

32. Krashen, S. (1994). Bilingual education and second language acquisition theory. *In Schooling and language-minority children: A theoretical framework* (2nd ed.). Los Angeles: California State University, National Evaluation, Dissemination and Assessment Center.

33. McKeon, D. (1994). Language, culture, and schooling. In F. Genesee (Ed.), *Educating second language children: The whole child, the whole curriculum, the whole community* (pp. 15–32). New York: Cambridge University Press.

34. McLaughlin, B. (1992). *Myths and misconceptions about second language learning: What every teacher needs to unlearn.* National Center for Research on Cultural Diversity and Second Language Learning, *5*, 1–9.

35. McLaughlin, B., & McLeod, B. (1997). *The impact statement on practice and knowledge: Educating all of our students. Improving education for children from culturally and linguistically different backgrounds.* Washington, DC: National Clearinghouse of Bilingual Education.

36. Met, M. (1994). Teaching content through a second language. In F. Genesee (Ed.), *Educating second language children: The whole child, the whole curriculum, the whole community* (pp. 159–182). New York: Cambridge University Press.

37. Miramontes, O., Nadeau, A., & Commins, N. (1997). *Restructuring schools for linguistic diversity: Linking decision making to effective programs.* New York: Teachers College Press of Columbia University.

38. National Center for Educational Statistics. 1997. Email: nces@ed.gov

39. OBEMLA. (1997). *High-stakes assessment: A research agenda for English language learners.* Washington, DC: National Clearinghouse for Bilingual Education.

40. O'Malley, M., & Valdez-Pierce, L. (1996). *Authentic assessment for English language learners: Practical approaches for teachers.* New York: Addison-Wesley.

41. Pease-Alvarez, C., & Vasquez, O. (1994). Language socialization in ethnic minority communities. In F. Genesee (Ed.), *Educating second language children: The whole child, the whole curriculum, the whole community* (pp. 82–102). New York: Cambridge University Press.

42. Peregoy, S.F., & Boyle, O.F. (1997). *Reading, writing, and learning in ESL: A resource book for K–12 teachers* (2nd ed.). White Plains, NY: Longman.

43. Reagan, T. (1997). The case for applied linguistics in teacher education. *Journal of Teacher Education, 48* (3), 185–196.

44. Rennie, J. (1993). *ESL and bilingual program model.* Washington, DC: ERIC Clearinghouse on Languages and Linguistics. (ERIC Document Reproduction Service No. ED36 20 72).

45. Richard-Amato, P.A., & Snow, M.A. (Eds.). (1992). *The multicultural classroom: Readings for content-area teachers.* White Plains, NY: Longman.

46. Ruby & Law, R. (1987). *School dropouts: Why does the problem prevail?* Paper presented at the Annual Meeting of the National Association of School Psychologists, New Orleans.

47. Schirmer, B., Casbon, J., & Twiss, L. L. (1996). Diverse learners in the classroom: Innovative literacy practices for ESL learners. *The Reading Teacher, 49* (5), 412–414.

48. Stoddart, T., & Neiderhauser, D. (1993). Technology and educational change. *Computers in Schools, 9,* 5–22.

49. Short, D.J. (1993). Assessing integrated and language instruction. *TESOL Quarterly, 27* (4), 627-656.

50. Tabors, P. (1997). *One child, two languages: A guide for preschool educators of children learning English as a second language.* Baltimore: Paul Brookes.

51. TESOL. (1995). *"Is your school helping its language minority students meet the national educational goals?"* ERIC ED389160.

52. TESOL standards: Ensuring access to quality educational experiences for language-minority students. (1993). *NABE News,* pp. 7, 20.

53. Thomas, W., & Collier, V. (1997). *School effectiveness for language-minority students.* Washington, DC: National Clearinghouse for Bilingual Education.

54. Tinajero, J.V., & Ada, A.F. (1993). *The power of two languages: Literacy and biliteracy for Spanish-speaking students.* New York: Macmillan/McGraw-Hill.

55. Toohey, K. (1998). Breaking them up, taking them away: ESL students in grade 1. *TESOL Quarterly, 32* (1), 61–84.

56. Willett, J. (1995). Becoming first graders in an L2: An ethnographic study of L2 socialization. *TESOL Quarterly, 29* (3), 473–503.

57. Wong-Fillmore, L. (1985). Second language learning in children: A proposed model. In *Issues in English language development.* Washington, DC: National Clearing House for Bilingual Education.

NOTE

* We are using the term *mainstream* as defined by Faltis (1997:2) "grade-level...English-speaking teachers who have been prepared for elementary classroom teaching in an all-English education program.

† We want to thank the members of our Research Advisory Board for their suggestions.

** We have chosen the term *English Language Learners* to emplhasize the fact that these students are learning an additional language. We have tried to avoid the phrases *limited English proficient* and *minority language*, sometimes used to describe this group of learners, because the terms *limited* and *minority* carry a controversial or negative connotation.

Sheltered Strategies: An Integrated Approach to Reading Instruction for Second Language English Speakers

Julie Jacobson, *San Diego Unified School District*
Diane Lapp, *San Diego State University*
James Flood, *San Diego State University*

Teacher: What do you think about the reading activities we did this year?
Juan: The reading activities make us speak in English.
Gloria: All the activities are good because we have to think using ideas, the plot of the story, the moral, and everything. We learned by putting the words together, especially when we described a message in the story.
Maria: I think we learned a lot from retelling the story in our words.

This conversation occurred in a Sheltered English classroom in which grade-level subject matter was presented in English for students who possessed basic literacy skills in their first language, which was not English. The goal of the sheltered approach was to combine the best of communicative language teaching with the best of challenging content instruction. While focusing less on formal language drills and grammar rules than does traditional language teaching, sheltered English was designed:

1. to be task-based and thematic in orientation
2. to encourage scaffolded instruction in such a way that students could safely take risks and reach higher levels of proficiency with the help of their teachers or their more capable peers
3. to employ a variety of cooperative structures, including dialogues and skits that allowed all students to use and work with the language concepts as each shared diverse perspectives
4. to incorporate and use informational or narrative texts, which provided additional contexts within which students could experience English.

Finally, curricula were based on the cyclical reintroduction of concepts at increasingly higher levels of complexity and interrelatedness, as opposed to a linear progression of items. This instruction was designed to ensure that learners approached the content-area issues in many different ways over a significant period of time as they assimilated the language.

What Is New About Sheltered Strategies?

Sheltered strategies are already widely recognized as excellent teaching methods. However, in regular content-area classes, in which students who are acquiring English are placed, as well as within Sheltered English Instructional programs, there is a need to use them more extensively and continuously, building scaffolds as the need arises. For this reason, lessons involving limited English-proficient speakers must be tailored to meet students' individual needs.

While a native speaker may understand and practice a concept after two tasks, the second language learner may need four or five different tasks to acquire a firm grasp of new material. In Sheltered English Instruction the most basic concepts need to be amplified as students assimilate the new language (Sizer, 1991). In this way, students can glean as much academic knowledge from the mainstream subject matter as their native-speaker counterparts can.

Approaching second language acquisition through avenues where language is contextualized and supported by reading experiences affords the second language learner opportunities to synthesize information while learning a new language. As with listening, speaking, and writing processes, the reader's lexical and syntactical knowledge of the first language assists comprehension of the second. Moreover, reading promotes analytical and cognitive skill development when readers strive to ascertain the meaning of printed texts. Flood and Lapp (1997) assert that meaningful contexts that enhance literacy skills for first language learners can also be employed to responsibly and creatively meet the challenge of addressing the needs of second language learners.

An important concept of both first and second language literacy is that universal reading skills and learning strategies that are applicable to reading move from language to language (Cummins, 1988). The "common" underlying proficiency, according to Cummins, makes possible the transfer of cognitive/academic or literacy-related skills across languages. Students are able to build on what they already know in their native language to learn new skills in the second language. Moreover, strategic assistance that occurs before, during, and after the processing of text in the target language can compensate for inadequate linguistic as well as textual knowledge.

Instruction that focuses on comprehension should be based on principles that acknowledge the student's role as the meaning-maker in the reading act. The teacher's role in the scaffolding process is to provide necessary and meaningful support toward each learning objective. According to Applebee (1984), the scaffolding process requires the student to take ownership for learning and the teacher to provide appropriate direction and support in teaching. It requires a form of collaboration between teachers and students in which both work together to ensure that students internalize rules and strategies for meaning-making. The following components of sheltered language instruction are methods that support the needs of second language learners and provide for optimal language arts learning:
1. Reciprocal teaching
2. Cooperative grouping
3. Cross-age tutoring.

How Is Reciprocal Teaching Implemented in the Sheltered Classroom?

Sheltered instructional classes foster learner autonomy through the explicit teaching of strategies. Strategies enable learners to successfully complete academic tasks (Palincsar & Brown, 1985). Reciprocal Teaching is an example of one such strategy, because the activity provides the student with immediate feedback and is a means for both the learner and the teacher to engage in a process of scaffolding. As with other kinds of interactions in the classroom, reciprocal teaching should be modeled and practiced as a whole class first, then in pairs. Palincsar and Brown (1985) explain that reciprocal teaching methods provide the teacher or more capable peers with an opportunity to guide learners to an optimal level of understanding. It is a process whereby the teacher structures an interaction, assesses a student's comprehension from the response, and restructures the interaction to clarify or correct student responses. Duffy and Roehler (1987) explain that discussion is a critical part of this type of teaching and learning. After several sessions of guided practice, control can be released to students. When proficient readers engage in deriving meaning from the text with less competent readers through reciprocal teaching, pairs of students can read the text together, questioning each other, developing their own "good" or strategically designed questions, and trying to solve problems related to their understanding of the text. The procedure outlined in Figure 1 may support using a reciprocal teaching strategy.

Figure 1 - PROCEDURE

1. Student A reads one paragraph aloud. A stops and asks B one or two "good" questions.
2. B answers the questions or explains why she or he cannot answer. A and B discuss questions and answers.
3. Text changes hands. B reads next paragraph aloud and asks A one or two "good" questions.
4. A answers the questions or explains why she or he cannot answer. A and B discuss questions and answers.
5. Finally, A and B summarize the paragraphs and predict the main idea of the next section they will read.

As students engage in this reciprocal teaching activity, the questioning process shown in Figure 2 will help them with comprehension.

Figure 2 - TYPES OF QUESTION–ANSWER RELATIONSHIPS
(Raphael, 1982, 1986)

1. Right There: The reader can immediately identify the answer because it is explicitly stated in the text.
2. Think and Search: The answer is implicit in the text. The student has to "think and search" for relevant information throughout the text. The reader must analyze, infer, draw logical conclusions, etc.
3. On My Own or Knowledge-Based: The reader has questions related to the topic that are not included in the text.
4. Writer and Me: If the reader were right in front of the author, what questions would he or she ask?

How Does Reciprocal Teaching Promote Second Language Learning?

Reciprocal teaching is a very collaborative interaction that promotes oral language and reading comprehension The following benefits occur when a collaborative approach is implemented in a second language classroom:

1. Collaborative learning activities generate varied paths of access to language and academic knowledge.
2. Collaborative learning lends itself to purposeful engagement and individualized instruction.
3. Teachers can show students not only what to learn but how to learn.
4. Group interaction lends itself to varied learning styles.
5. Acquisition of knowledge through cultural and cognitive variations in approaches to learning is addressed.
6. Collaborative learning yields greater motivation, particularly for students at risk.
7. The interactive learning philosophy lends itself to provide opportunities to assimilate patterns of language through strategic problem solving, yielding the development of higher-level cognitive skills.
8. Students accept new responsibilities through cooperative approaches.
9. Students' self-esteem is enhanced through shared responsibilities.
10. Complexity and variety of input produce higher-level cognitive development.

How Does Cooperative Grouping Promote Second Language Learning?

Students must be given support and encouragement in order to realize that reliance upon teacher input is not the only means by which tasks can be completed. Through cooperative grouping, which is also very collaborative, students gradually assume responsibility for their learning. Successful collaborative outcomes require: (1) a student's willingness and confidence that his or her own contributions are valuable, (2) an understanding that teamwork is effective, and (3) an awareness that attempts toward comprehension and mastery of material are worthwhile and of value.

The important goal of a student's ability to generate his or her own literary products will enhance self-esteem. As students become aware of the importance of their work and the impact it can have on their teachers and classmates, they will not only come to appreciate their accomplishments more fully, but also gain the self-confidence necessary to encourage others. Group activities provide the teacher with opportunities to become familiar with each student's abilities and to effectively identify and address individual needs. Cooperative learning best provides the non-native speaker with opportunities that are similar to the social experiences within which the native speakers have acquired the language.

Successful techniques of collaborative instruction include the utilization of a task structure that requires students to work cooperatively in four- to six-member groups of heterogeneous ability (Stevens, 1983). Cooperative learning methods are most effective when there is individual accountability. Cooperative lessons also include an initial structured introduction of material.

Jigsaw Teaching

The cooperative learning method that is most appropriate for situations in which students must extract information from text is called jigsaw teaching (Aronson et al., 1978; see Figure 3). The basic idea of jigsaw teaching is that each member of a mixed-ability learning group becomes an expert on one aspect of a topic the class is studying. The experts read information on their topics and then meet with others who were assigned to the same topic. Then the experts return to their teams to take their turns teaching their teammates about their topics. An appealing feature of Jigsaw is that it gives each team member a unique area of expertise, so students feel that they are making a valuable contribution to their oral language teams, which is a way to provide a format for enhanced communicative practice.

Figure 3 - PROCEDURE FOR JIGSAW TEACHING

1. The teacher presents a lesson on a topic. (e.g., the history of the Olmec civilization.)
2. Each member of a mixed-ability learning group becomes an expert on one aspect of a topic the class is studying (e.g., geographic location, archaeological structures, religion, crafts, Olmec traders, the rain forests of Central America.)
3. The experts meet with others assigned to the same topic (a group studying archaeological structures, for example). Students work in four-member learning teams to master material, discussing concepts, completing projects together, and drilling one another on worksheet items, or working problems separately, comparing answers, and discussing discrepancies.
4. The experts then return to their teams to take their turns teaching their teammates about their topics.
5. Students take individual quizzes. Teams may earn certificates based on the average of all team members' scores.

The principal advantage of Jigsaw II, outlined in Figure 4, is that the strategy uses existing textbooks and requires creation of four topics and a brief quiz for each unit. The approach provides extended means for second language learners to hear language modeled, to communicatively express their ideas, and to access information within a supportive environment.

Figure 4
PROCEDURE FOR
JIGSAW II

1. Students work in heterogeneous teams.
2. Students are assigned chapters or other units to read, and are given expert sheets, which contain different topics for each team member to focus on when reading.
3. Students from different teams with the same topic meet in an expert group to discuss their topic.
4. The experts then return to their teams and take turns teaching their teammates about their topics.
5. Students take quizzes that cover all the topics, and the quiz scores become team scores.

Jigsaw II can be used whenever the material to be studied is in written narrative form. It is most appropriate in such subjects as social studies, literature, some parts of science, and related areas in which concepts rather than skills are the learning goals. The instructional material for Jigsaw II should usually be a chapter, story, biography, or similar narrative or descriptive material.

In Jigsaw II, students work in heterogeneous teams. For the second language student, cooperative structures provide a context for extended practice and opportunity to assimilate the new language and concepts pertinent to the lesson. The students are assigned chapters or other units to read, and are given *expert sheets*, which contain different topics for each team

member to focus on when reading. When everyone has finished reading, students from different teams with the same topic meet in an *expert group* to discuss their topic. The experts then return to their teams and take turns teaching their teammates about their topics. Finally, students take quizzes that cover all the topics, and the quiz scores become team scores.

In a class of 32, for example, the teacher divides students into eight heterogeneous teams of four. Each home team then decides who will act as member A, B, C, or D. The teacher then directs all A group members to one area of the room, B members to another area, and so on. The four groups constitute expert teams that are responsible for discussing and mastering the information indicated to them through an *expert sheet* designed by the teacher. The expert sheet is a series of questions upon which students should focus their attention in preparation for teaching their team members and for taking a quiz on the material. The A members from each team meet to discuss question number 1, while B members discuss question number 2, and so on. Once all group members have grasped the material, each returns to his or her home team to teach the other group members. During the sharing session with home team members, all students impart the information they learned during discussions with the expert groups.

Figure 5 shows an expert sheet for a U. S. history lesson as well as one that can be used to review the literary elements in a story. Through *extension questions*, the literature review sheet provides students with an extended opportunity for communicative engagement. After students have taught one another in their home teams, extension questions can be included as a means to encourage conversation among group members and to provide opportunities for second language learners to express themselves using new information, vocabulary, and concepts.

Figure 5
SAMPLE EXPERT SHEETS

Social Studies
The United States Becomes an Urban Nation

Expert Group Discussion Questions
1. Why did immigrants come to the United States? What type of life did they face when they arrived?
2. How did immigrants contribute, along with other factors, to the rapid growth of the cities?
3. Discuss a typical labor strike and why it started.
4. What were the strike's consequences, and how was it settled?

Literature Review

Expert Group Discussion Questions
1. What is the theme?
2. What is the main conflict in this chapter? Which characters are involved?
3. What are the steps that led to the conflict?
4. Has the conflict been solved? Provide examples.

Extension Questions
1. How would you react in the same situation?
2. Write a short letter to _____. Explain your point of view and the reasons for your opinion. What question would you ask this character?

After students have answered the questions, the teacher reviews the material with the class and gives students an opportunity to ask further questions. During this session, the teacher can focus students' attention on main concepts. In addition, students may be called upon to summarize areas presented throughout the reading material. At the end of the review session, the teacher administers a test to the entire class. Each home team member's score is recorded on a *Team Summary Sheet*. Each home team can decide on a name for their team. The total team score, as well as the team average, is calculated. The team with the highest average may be given special recognition or a special privilege as a reward for their high scores. Figure 6 shows a sample team summary sheet after the first test.

Figure 6 - SAMPLE TEAM SUMMARY SHEET

TEAM NAME: Sensational Six			
CARLOS	92		
LIN	83		
IRENE	92		
ALFONSO	100		
JENNIFER	81		
JOSE	94		
TOTAL TEAM SCORE	542		
TEAM AVERAGE	90		
TEAM AWARD	SUPER TEAM		

Informational Texts and Storybook Activities

Collaborative experiences that are promoted through reciprocal teaching and cooperative grouping can be developed through the use of multiple sources. These include narrative and informational trade books, newspapers, magazines, pamphlets, reference resources, and any other type of print medium that has purpose and relevance. For the second language student, the trade text provides an opportunity to experience both languages as well as novel concepts in an often familiar context where interaction with people, places, and ideas can occur. In addition, other materials such as stories can help form bridges to the information presented in the text.

Trade Texts

According to Young (1991) and Swaffar (1991), authentic texts provide the most effective means by which second language students derive meaning from reading experiences. When students are familiar with stories, they can readily use concept-driven processing strategies as they read. These include skimming, looking at pictures, anticipating content, integrating information, and recognizing text structure. From a communicative perspective of language instruction, the reading of trade texts can serve to supplement textbook material and can help students to clarify concepts.

Teachers may also use the materials to provide students with opportunities to summarize, question, discuss, evaluate, or learn to persuade in order to solve a problem. Trade texts provide the stimulus for sharing and processing information. Both are valued goals of second language instruction, according to Long and Harlow (1988). Through reading, writing, listening, and speaking, second language learners participate in comprehensive engagement of the language through contextualized, meaningful experiences.

How Does Cross-Age Tutoring Enhance Second Language Learning?

Cross-age tutoring is a third collaborative learning strategy that engages students in focused conversation that will support their second language development. The cross-age tutoring format provides an opportunity for students to study and learn together. Through purposeful engagement, cross-age tutoring gives learners a legitimate reason for practicing in order to improve reading performance (Johnson, Maruyama, Johnson, Nelson, & Skon, 1981; Slavin, 1983). In addition, cross-age or peer tutoring has also been found to promote positive reading attitudes and habits (Boland-Willms, 1991).

According to Gaustad (1993), the strategy is beneficial because the process allows tutors expanded opportunity to review material, to contemplate the purpose as well as the intended outcome of a task, and to improve communication skills. Peer tutoring has resulted in students' enhanced enjoyment of working with partners, increased requests for help, expanded friendships extending outside the treatment setting, and improved attitudes toward writing (Utay & Utay, 1997). Cohen (1986) explains that organizing material to teach "facilitates long-term retention, as well as aiding in the formation of a more comprehensive and integrated understanding." Furthermore, tutors can be instructed to scaffold information, adapting instruction to the learner's pace, learning style, and level of understanding. Tutees can receive immediate feedback, answers to questions, and correction within a tutoring format.

If the goal of language instruction is that of performing authentic communicative tasks, according to De Costa (1987), not only must learners be given opportunities to function in the language, but classroom instruction must be examined for the extent to which (1) students are allowed to perceive the language as functional, and (2) communication takes place within a relevant context. The benefit of varied grouping formats, she continues, is that members of the group become genuinely interested in each other's opinions, feelings, and interests, and feel comfortable expressing themselves on the topic or in the presentation.

Figure 7
PROCEDURE FOR INTEGRATING RECIPROCAL TEACHING, COOPERATIVE LEARNING, AND CROSS-AGE TUTORING

1. The teacher engages students in a conversation regarding their prior knowledge of the story or story theme.

2. The teacher narrates the story in Spanish, from a pictorial story board depicting the major events in the story.

3. Students act out the scenes as the teacher narrates the story. The class watches the actions of the student actors as well as the gesturing from the teacher as vocabulary and action words are represented on the story board.

4. The teacher assists students as they create story boards, illustrating the sequence of the story. Sentences are developed in the target language, describing each picture.

5. Students read their illustrated narratives to the class in the target language.

6. In small groups, students read stories aloud, each taking turns reading a paragraph. Teacher should provide groups with a tape recorder so that students may listen to themselves read.

7. Students can create individual pictorial representations of their favorite scenes from the stories, using the story books as a reference for their descriptions. Depictions can be presented orally to the class.

8. Classmates work together to answer both textually explicit and implicit questions developed by the teacher. Questions should require students' comprehension of the material as well as an application of the story's theme or characters to their lives.

9. A cross-age peer group reading program can be established between different grade levels, using trade texts as a means to provide students with additional reading experiences.

10. The class may work as a collaborative group in order to develop a skit based on the story.

11. Students write summaries of the story in the target language after performing skits.

12. The instructor associates the themes or concepts from trade text information to the textbook.

Figure 8
A PEDAGOGICAL OVERVIEW OF STRATEGIC SHELTERED INSTRUCTION

Scaffold (Domain)	Appropriate Tasks	Benefit to the Reader
1. Modeling	Teacher models task and provides examples. Individual/Group oral reading, repetitions. Direct experience through practice.	Clarifies concepts Provides understanding of objective
2. Connecting content	Questions in: Think-Pair-Share Three-step Interview Quick-writes Anticipatory charts Brainstorming	Addresses students' prior knowledge Provides a personal connection between learner and theme of the class
3. Creating a context	Visualizations Focus questions and: Use of manipulatives Self-involvement Instructor provides an experiential environment. Students demonstrate knowledge for authentic audiences.	Enhances context and concept familiarity
4. Bridging concepts	Compare/Contrast matrix used as advanced organizer Story graph used to skim through a text Cooperative Jigsaw activities	Students gain heightened insight into the varied uses of language. Students develop connections between concepts.
5. Perceptual understanding	Reciprocal teaching Self-monitoring Self-assessment Students discuss and model reading strategies.	Self-autonomy is fostered. Students' knowledge of strategies is enhanced through a conscious focus on the processes.
6. Extensions	Drama Journal writing Story boards Collaborative posters with text Eyewitness accounts Postcards/Letters	Students extend their understandings and personal relevance as they apply information to novel formats.

Summary

Reciprocal teaching, cooperative grouping, and cross-age tutoring are approaches within the pedagogical framework of sheltered English instruction. They can provide enhanced opportunity for interactive learning among students who are acquiring English as their second language (see Figure 7 on page 216). The implementation of an integrative program of study skills can have mutual and enriching benefits for both first and second languages. In addition, integrated language activity constitutes a strong foundation from which acquired study skills can be applied throughout the various content areas. Specifically, the six domains listed in Figure 8 on page 217, encompassing the principles of learning through a sheltered approach and intrinsic to language learning, should be addressed in all content area classrooms with limited-English-proficient students. Additionally, Figure 8 details various strategies that can enhance both reading comprehension and the oral language proficiency of second language learners.

As Figure 8 shows, communicative proficiency in a second language is rooted in content-based instruction that includes proficiency in reading, writing, listening, and speaking (Mohan, 1986). Good readers are strategic readers who actively construct meaning as they read; they are self-motivated and self-directed (Paris, Lipson, & Wixson, 1983); they monitor their own comprehension by questioning, reviewing, revising, and rereading to enhance their overall comprehension (Baker & Brown, 1984). Furthermore, proficient readers who have experiences with integrated literacy instruction create meaning by associating a personal significance to the information they read. These same strategies will be the foundation of writing and oral language development.

REFERENCES

Aronson, E., Stephan, C., Sikes, J., Blaney, N., & Snapp, M. (1978). *The jigsaw classroom.* Beverly Hills, CA: Sage.

Applebee, A. N. (1984). Writing and reasoning. *Review of Educational Research, 54,* 577–596.

Baker, L., & Brown, A. L. (1984). Metacognition skills and reading. In P. D. Pearson (Ed.), *Handbook of reading research.* New York: Longman.

Cummins, J. (1988). The role and use of educational theory in formulating language policy. *TESL Canada Journal, 5* (2), 11–19.

Duffy, G. G., & Roehler, L. R. (1987). *Characteristics of responsive elaboration which promote the mental processing associated with strategy use.* Paper presented at annual meeting of the National Reading Conference, St. Petersburg Beach, FL.

Flood, J., & Lapp, D. (1997). Literacy instruction for students acquiring English: Moving beyond the immersion debate. *The Reading Teacher, 50* (4).

Long & Harlow (1988). *The newspaper and the five skills.* (ERIC Document Reproduction Service No. ED 336 939).

Mohan, B. (1986). *Language and content.* Reading, MA: Addison-Wesley.

Palincsar, A. M., & Brown A. L. (1985). Reciprocal teaching activities to promote reading with your mind. In E. J. Cooper (Ed.), *Reading, thinking, and concept development: Interactive strategies for the class.* New York: The College Board.

Paris, S. G., Lipson, M. Y., & Wixon, K. K. (1983). Becoming a strategic reader. *Contemporary Educational Psychology, 8,* 293–316.

Sizer, T. (1991). No pain, no gain. *Educational Leadership,* May, pp. 32–34.

Swaffar, J. (1991). *Reading for meaning: An integrated approach to language learning.* Englewood Cliffs, NJ: Prentice Hall.

Young (1991). Activating student background knowledge in a take-charge approach to foreign language reading. *Hispania, 74,* 202–208.

Developing Biliteracy in a Two-Way Immersion Program

Jennifer Martínez and Julie A. Moore-O'Brien, with assistance from Ginger Dale and María Juárez-Cruz
Windsor School District, California

Walking down the corridor toward my classroom one spring morning, something on the playground caught my attention. The March breeze carried the faint sounds of children singing and chanting in Spanish. I stopped and stood mesmerized as I watched 12 or 15 of my first-grade students actively engaged in a game of jump rope. I listened intently to the rhythmic chants of rhymes and poems we had been reciting and reading in class for the past several weeks. I gazed down the line of children awaiting their turns and saw a jumble of blond, brown, and black hair blowing wildly in the breeze. I listened to them encourage each other, criticize each other, and argue over turns, as all six-year-olds do. What made this particular scene so unique was the fact that the conversations were entirely in Spanish; yet only about a third of the children were native speakers of Spanish.

It's not to say that their utterances were error free. I heard shouts of "¡Yo quieres más turnos!" (¡Yo quiero más turnos!—I want more turns!), "¡Yo no brincas mucho!" (¡Yo no brinco mucho!—I don't jump much!), or "¡Ayúdenme! ¡Yo no sabo jump!" (¡Ayúdenme! ¡Yo no sé brincar!—Help me! I don't know how to jump!). However, none of these typical second language learner errors interfered with the negotiation of meaning. In fact no one even acknowledged their miscues. The conversations, the chanting, and the arguing flowed as freely as in any children's game. It wasn't long before several second graders from the English-only class next door abandoned their own game of jump rope and filed into line with the younger children. When the turn came for the first second grader to jump, one of my students ordered, "Say it in English. She's not in the Spanish class." The children changed gears without a thought and began chanting "Cinderella." When the second child prepared to jump she requested, "Say something in Spanish for me. It sounds neat."

Although I had a list of chores awaiting me in the classroom, I stood on the corner and watched for nearly 20 minutes. When I greeted my students in line at the start of class a particularly observant little boy asked, "Maestra, ¿por qué estás llorando?" (Teacher, why are you crying?) How could I begin to explain the feelings of hope and pride that overwhelmed me as I witnessed some of the early effects of our Two-Way Immersion Program?

Introduction

We became bilingual teachers because we wanted to offer equal educational opportunities to Hispanic students who were failing in English-only classrooms. We knew that bilingual classrooms certainly improved the educational experiences of our Spanish-speaking students. Still we recognized certain program limitations or inherent contradictions that limited the effectiveness of the *transitional bilingual model*. For example, Spanish-speaking students rarely received enough instruction in Spanish to fully develop their primary language. This not only led to low levels of Spanish language proficiency, but also resulted in low levels of English language proficiency. English speakers enrolled in these same programs never had the opportunity to learn to speak, read, or write Spanish fluently.

As dedicated bilingual teachers who have actively participated in the evolution of bilingual education, we are convinced that Two-Way Immersion Education is the bilingual education model of the future. It eliminates the contradictions in bilingual programs by guaranteeing that both language majority and language minority students value and have equal access to both Spanish and English. The Two-Way Immersion Program at Windsor Union School District is in its sixth year. In the upcoming school year we will have 17 Immersion classes, K–6, with three classes at most grade levels. It has not been an easy journey to the point where we are today, but we are ensuring a future that will bring dramatic and lasting changes in the quality of education we offer our students.

We have divided this article into two main sections: "What Is Two-Way Immersion?" and "Developing Biliteracy." Although it is impossible to write about everything that we do in the Two-Way setting, we have included all the main instructional strategies we employ and given concrete, practical examples of how we develop bilingualism and biliteracy in the classroom.

What Is Two-Way Immersion?

In Two-Way Immersion classrooms, Spanish is the primary language of instruction for both Spanish-speaking and English-speaking students in the early grades. Our classrooms are made up of approximately 50 percent Spanish-speaking students and 50 percent English-speaking students. This ratio is necessary to maintain an environment of educational and linguistic equity and to promote optimum interactions among speakers of both languages. All students learn to read and write in Spanish first and are later introduced to these skills in English.

It is important to remember that in the social context of the United States, Spanish is the language at risk for both Spanish- and English-speaking students. Spanish-speaking students are almost certain to choose English as their preferred (and often only) mode of communication within the first few years after entering school. English-speaking students will have no chance to develop full bilingualism unless Spanish is used as the primary language of instruction. Two-Way Immersion Programs elevate the status of the Spanish language and thus offer both groups of students an unmatched opportunity to maintain both languages. Such programs also greatly enhance students' understanding and appreciation of other ethnolinguistic groups while maintaining positive attitudes toward their own cultural group.

In order to understand the differences between the Traditional Bilingual Model and the Two-Way Immersion Model, it is useful to see a side-by-side comparison.

Traditional Bilingual	**Two-Way Immersion**
English and Spanish used on alternate days as language instruction for class rituals, P.E., art, science, social studies.	Spanish is primary language of instruction. Amount of English instruction increases at each grade level.
Children develop literacy in their dominant language.	All children develop literacy in Spanish initially.
Spanish speakers are transitioned into English.	Both Spanish and English speakers develop and maintain literacy in both languages.
Children are separated into homogeneous language and ability groups for literacy instruction.	Children are grouped heterogeneously for all instruction.
Teachers model both English and Spanish.	Teachers are monolingual role models in either language.

Goals

The goals of the Two-Way Immersion Program reflect the unique educational, linguistic, and social needs of both minority and majority students. The following are the goals of our Two-Way Immersion Program:

1. fluency in communication and literacy in two languages;
2. academic achievement in all subject areas following state frameworks;
3. appreciation and understanding of other cultures while developing positive attitudes among students, their families, and their communities; and
4. opportunities for students to develop the positive values of self-reliance, initiative, kindness, cooperation, resourcefulness, creativity, responsibility, and love of learning.

Program Design

The number of minutes of instructional time to be conducted in each language at each grade level was determined by research results from the fields of bilingual and immersion education. Windsor's Two-Way Immersion model uses Spanish for about 75 percent of the *total program* instructional time by beginning with 90 percent of the kindergarten instruction in Spanish and slowly increasing the percentage of time in English until a 50/50 balance is reached in the sixth grade.

Due to the importance of teachers serving as monolingual role models, students receive Spanish instruction from one teacher and English instruction from another. We accomplish this through a team approach in which program teachers at the same grade level exchange classes for the English portion of the day. For example, from 12:45 P.M. to 1:10 P.M. the three first-grade teachers take over each other's classes for whole-group English language development. The three teachers involved in this team are bilingual, since in the early stages of the program students are encouraged to interact in either language and they must be confident that their teacher will understand them. The teachers adhere to their monolingual role very seriously and step outside the classroom if they need to respond to an English-speaking parent. Even in the upper grades we feel it is important that the teacher maintain a monolingual role with students. This ensures that Spanish remains the language of prestige in the classroom and is not slowly undermined by the ever-present influence of English.

The following graph illustrates the percentage of instructional time allocated to each language in Windsor's Two-Way Immersion Program.

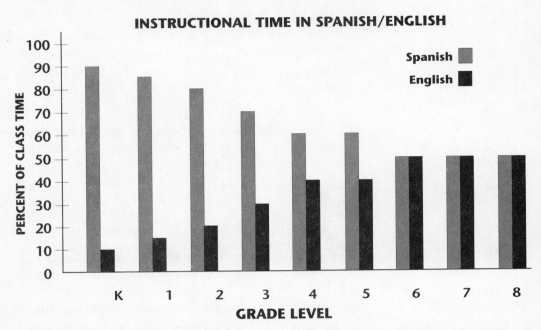

INSTRUCTIONAL TIME IN SPANISH/ENGLISH

- In grades K, 1, and 2 all subject matter is taught in Spanish without translation. The students receive oral English language development for 20–40 minutes daily.

- In grade 3 all subject matter is still taught in Spanish. English instruction is increased to 60–90 minutes daily. English literacy is formally introduced while maintaining Spanish literacy.

- In grades 4 and 5 Spanish is used for most subject matter. English instruction is increased to 90 minutes daily.

- In grade 6, 7, and 8 Spanish is used for half of the instructional time and English the other half. Subjects taught in Spanish one year may be taught in English the following year.

How Does an Immersion Classroom Function?

Our classrooms are set up in centers revolving around reading, process writing, interactive journal writing, math, language enrichment, art, and science activities. The activities are set up each morning in the centers that correlate to the current thematic unit of study, and children rotate to the centers in small groups. Each classroom is also equipped with a special area filled with books, stuffed animals, and a comfortable place to read. We are fortunate to have classroom aides, as well as extra help from parent volunteers.

Our interdisciplinary curriculum design provides students a situation similar to the world outside the classroom by not isolating learning into subject areas. This prepares students for independent learning and problem solving in their daily lives. The curriculum is planned around a theme integrating all the traditional subject matter primarily through literature and learning center projects. We systematically integrate language use, development, and complexity of structure into all curricular content. Special effort goes into ensuring that units of study represent a variety of cultures and cultural perspectives. An emphasis is placed on the Hispanic heritage, since over 50 percent of our students share that culture. The curriculum is designed to develop children's knowledge and skills in all developmental areas. Integration of physical, emotional, social, and cognitive developmental domains forms a base from which teachers prepare the learning environment and plan appropriate curricular activities.

In our classrooms, students are active participants in the learning process. The teacher's primary role is that of facilitator, guiding children through interactive, experiential learning activities in a meaningful context. We subscribe to Cummins's (1985) contention that students must be viewed as "explorers of meaning, as critical and creative thinkers who have contributions to make both in the classroom and in the world beyond" (p. 2). We employ a critical pedagogical model that incorporates instructional factors that promote high levels of first and second language competence, biliteracy, academic achievement in two languages, high self-esteem, and positive cross-cultural attitudes. Each child is recognized as a unique person with an individual pattern and timing of growth, as well as individual personality and family background. Attention is given to the different needs, interests, experiences, and developmental level of all students. Both the curriculum and the teacher's interactions with children are responsive to individual and cultural differences.

We take great care in planning and organizing contacts between minority and majority students so that the achievement of both groups can be maximized. Our classrooms are structured so that students work together in small cooperative teams, with each team member contributing to the task at hand.

Both majority and minority students benefit tremendously from cooperative learning. Cooperative learning is an excellent setting for conceptual learning and critical problem solving. It teaches prosocial behavior and takes advantage of academic differences by teaching children to teach each other.

We heterogeneously group our students to ensure that they are never segregated or grouped based on perceived ability or level of language proficiency. The importance of heterogeneous grouping is magnified in the Two-Way Immersion setting, where language acquisition is a primary goal. Language development in both languages is accelerated when interactions between native and non-native speakers are increased. The self-esteem of all students is enhanced because they have the opportunity to be the language model for either English or Spanish.

The language skills of children in our classrooms are developed through sheltered language techniques that make the social and instructional features of classroom language more clear. We accomplish this by simplifying the input through slower speech rate, clear enunciation, repetitive vocabulary, and simplified sentence structure. Another technique we employ is the use of contextual clues such as gestures, facial expressions, dramatization, props, realia, and visuals. Our teachers extend students' speech by putting incomplete verbalizations into complete sentences or thoughts. We engage students in the process of negotiating for meaning by elaborating, checking for comprehension, requesting clarification, rephrasing, and contextualizing.

At the same time, our teachers meld these sheltered language techniques with complex language appropriate for fluent native speakers. One example of how this can be accomplished is by reading traditional language-rich literature to all students, while using gestures, facial expressions, and dramatization to make it comprehensible for non-native speakers. Native speakers are encouraged to assist their teacher by paraphrasing the story and describing the illustrations. The teacher also uses various levels of vocabulary and questioning strategies with different students based on their linguistic background.

Developing Biliteracy

Our approach to biliteracy is based on Cummins's theory of a common underlying proficiency (Cummins, 1989), which posits that knowledge learned in one language transfers to the second language once students have acquired the linguistic skill to express that knowledge. For this reason, in kindergarten through second grade we focus on Spanish literacy. Beginning in third grade we formally introduce English literacy to all students. Predictably, many children learn to read simultaneously in both Spanish and English, but this is not a program expectation. It is important to note that we continue Spanish literacy instruction through all the grades.

This section of our article emphasizes the development of Spanish literacy, although most of the same strategies are eventually employed in the development of English literacy. At the end of this section we will give a more detailed description of our English literacy component.

Holistic Language and Literacy Acquisition

In Two-Way Immersion students are provided with authentic language and literacy events in which language acquisition (both oral and written) is a natural process developed through social interaction and need. For language minority students, immersion in their native language provides the necessary linguistic and academic foundation for the later acquisition of English and the further development of proficiency in both languages (Lindholm, 1989). When schools develop and reinforce the native language while introducing the second language, students experience additive bilingualism (Lambert, 1987). Additive bilingualism is an enrichment process through which students acquire a second language with no fear of native language loss or abandonment of their own cultural identity and values. This is associated with high levels of proficiency in both languages and higher levels of scholastic performance.

For the native English-speaking students a second language is best developed through immersion in that language (Genesee, 1985). Children learn a second language similar to the way in which they acquired their first language. In promoting second language acquisition we re-create the conditions that are present in the home, where the children learn their first language. This process necessarily involves trust, language models, interaction, feedback, and a genuine purpose for language use. In a literate, print-rich environment, literacy development occurs naturally for most children. Written language will develop when children have real purposes for reading and writing.

Our literacy program is built around children's literature integrated into the content curriculum through thematic units. Thematic units provide a focal point for inquiry, cultural content, use of language, and cognitive development. Students encounter the same vocabulary in a variety of contexts.

Language-rich Environment

In our Two-Way Immersion Program, language is never the focus of learning but rather a tool for learning. Input provided by the teacher is carefully adjusted to guarantee that it is comprehensible to all learners, but at the same time stimulating and enriching for native speakers. A language-rich environment makes use of stories, poetry, songs, games, chants, finger plays, etc., to reinforce and motivate language use. Many of these have been borrowed from folklore, passed down through generations, and are culturally and linguistically rich and engaging for students.

Print-rich Environment

The first thing we accomplish is to surround children with print. One of our first activities at the beginning of the year is to label everything. We often include a statement from a child about a particular object as well as a name label. For instance, the teacher's chair might have two labels: *silla* ("chair") and *La maestra se sienta en esta silla* ("The teacher sits in this chair"). It is a wonderful way to reinforce vocabulary that children are already familiar with, and it also serves as an introduction to new language. New labels are added and old ones are changed throughout the year as we refer to them often in our daily activities. It is not uncommon to see a child using a label to help spell a word or remember the name of a classroom object.

We also start the first day of school with a wall dictionary waiting to be filled with children's favorite words. The first words to be placed on the wall dictionary are the children's and teacher's names. Each day students are asked to choose words from books we are reading or topics we are studying to add to the dictionary. In kindergarten, these wall dictionary cards also have a picture of the object on them so that children can identify the words. Student name cards are adorned with a photograph of the student. It is amazing how quickly and painlessly children develop an awareness of the relationship between letters of the alphabet and their sounds. A frequent comment is something like, "Esa palabra comienza como *Maribel*. Comienza con la *m*." (This word starts like *Maribel*. It starts with an *m*.) Soon children begin to keep dictionaries of their own, entering words that are interesting and important to them. Name cards are not restricted to the wall dictionary but are used in many ways, especially during the first weeks of school. They are worn around children's necks, used to make lists and to label places to sit and work.

As new songs and poems are introduced, the words are put on colorful charts and displayed throughout the room. Once students are familiar with the words, we use the charts to read as we recite or sing. Children are frequently observed using the charts to generate ideas for a journal entry or a new book or to check for the correct spelling of a word. They also enjoy standing in front of the charts and reading the words when they have finished a task early.

In the older grades, the wall dictionary becomes a wall thesaurus. Students are very enthused about finding synonyms in their literature books and in their units of study that they can add to the thesaurus. Poetry and song charts reflecting the current theme fill the room. Other good sources of authentic print include recipes, graphs, lists, jokes, student-authored materials, comic books, magazines, maps, ads, signs, newspapers, etc.

In all the Immersion classrooms a variety of students' work is displayed. Units of study can be easily identified from the process writing books, book reports, projects, etc., that adorn the rooms. The print-rich environment helps children to internalize language structure and new vocabulary. This is equally important for both language minority and language majority students, particularly for those children who have had limited exposure to literacy in the home environment.

Reading

Reading to Students

Reading aloud to students is a daily activity; it exposes them to good literature they cannot yet read for themselves. It teaches them structures of language and areas of knowledge they cannot yet acquire through reading independently. Additionally, it familiarizes learners with a variety of moods and styles. This activity continues throughout the grades.

Spanish Literacy in the Early Years

A wide variety of materials are used at the reading center. In kindergarten and first grade, most of our activities center around Big Books and predictable books. Big Books allow children to see the text and join in a choral reading with the teacher until they are gradually able to read the text without the assistance of the teacher. We use smaller copies of the same story for more independent reading. Big Books are read again and again. Detailed teacher-student dialogues take place when children are familiar with a particular story. We also incorporate the Creative Reading Method as proposed by Alma Flor Ada (1986).

As children are able to read the book independently, we talk about the strategies they used to figure out what was coming next or what the text said. We utilize many extension activities such as an oral cloze activity. The next step may be a written cloze task where several words are deleted from the text and must be filled in by children. At first we do this together on the chalkboard, but later children work with individual copies of the text. As they become familiar with the activity, it is fun to try to change the story by adding new words that make sense in the spaces.

Many of the Big Books are predictable in nature, as are the majority of the other books we use at the kindergarten and first-grade levels. Predictable books are characterized by rhyme, repetition of vocabulary, familiar content and story structure, and cyclical sequencing. We discuss what "helped" them read the book, and children readily discover that the repetitive language pattern and picture clues assisted them in reading. They soon begin to match up printed words with their voices and notice letter/sound correspondences.

As we choose words from these books to place in the wall dictionary, students begin to pay more and more attention to the alphabet and its relationship to the reading process. By putting the text on sentence strips to manipulate in the pocket chart, we are able to help children discover the phonetic relationships needed to read that particular text. Although we do not teach phonics in an isolated fashion, children are quick to discover sound/symbol relationships in the context of a motivating story.

Predictable books also provide the setting to study such elements of literature as cause and effect, problem and solution, and lists and sequences. These kinds of discussions are usually not introduced until children are very familiar with a number of different predictable stories. Children never seem to tire of these books because the vocabulary is not controlled for readability as it is in most basal readers, nor is the language stilted. Predictable books encourage a reader's meaning-based interaction with a text from the very first reading experience, while the reader begins to generalize about the phonetic similarities between words in a natural and meaningful manner.

After learning to read a predictable story, students often create their own variations of the book based on similar language structures. They also use the books as resources for their own writing—locating words and phrases they need for a particular piece. We make many class books in which each child contributes a page based on the pattern of a familiar book. These books are bound and placed in the classroom library where they are read time and time again.

A very important component of our program is the process of having students make their own books. In the early grades they usually make a copy of most of the books we read at the reading table so that they will have a collection of books in Spanish to be read and enjoyed at home. Both students and their families have enjoyed this aspect of the program. One parent of a kindergarten student reported that every night at bedtime her child insisted on reading a book that she had made in class. Reading her own version of a classroom book to her mother became a nightly ritual that they both looked forward to and enjoyed.

We also create a lot of our own books to be used with children in the early grades when trade books are not available or appropriate for our needs. This is especially true at the kindergarten level. For example, the first kindergarten books focus on skills such as tracing, cutting, pasting, and coloring, and on developing students' vocabulary of common nouns, adjectives, and color concepts. The basic sentence structure of the beginning series of books is simple and repetitive so that students become familiar with it quickly and can predict the text easily—*La manzana es roja* ("The apple is red"). Each page of the book involves a number of carefully designed activities that ground the vocabulary and concepts in hands-on, sensory experiences for students. *Manzana* ("apple") becomes part of the child's daily vocabulary when she/he has had the opportunity to taste, touch, and smell it and to use the word in a variety of contexts. At the art table the child has made apple prints in paint. At the math center she/he has made patterns with combinations of green and red apples. At another station she/he has planted an apple seed and learned how apple trees grow. At whole group time she/he has participated with the class in making apple graphs comparing size differences. She/he has been reading stories about apples and apple trees. In this way the curriculum is designed in layers, with each new layer reinforcing and building on previously taught concepts, vocabulary, and skills. For children to experience success in reading, they must be able to predict text and be familiar with the vocabulary on the page.

We have designed many books using the words of songs and rhymes that utilize particular skills (such as memory, number sequencing, color, and number words) or that complement a curricular unit of study. We are also careful to build specific language structures into our books and curriculum so that children can practice them in a natural manner. The possibilities are endless, and children are always elated to take their treasured books home after the class has had ample opportunity to enjoy them.

Literature Studies

Beginning in kindergarten, we also choose several titles of quality literature with genuine plots and rich, aesthetic language to complement each unit of study. In the early grades, these books may be too difficult for some children to read independently, but the primary goal of our literature studies is to develop a love of reading and also a love of books. In literature studies we involve students in comparing and contrasting literature to their own experiences. Students live in the author's world by choosing a piece of literature to read independently and later study in small groups. Students analyze and critique components of literature such as style, character, setting, theme, symbolism, and plot. The teacher is a participant, empowering children by valuing their knowledge and opinions. The emphasis is on enjoying literature and examining the author's craft, not on developing isolated reading skills.

At the kindergarten and first-grade levels we find that children love to listen to the stories on headphones and read along in individual copies of the book. They enjoy listening to the same story many times. Children respond to the literature in many ways. They make story maps, rewrite the endings, describe their favorite characters, describe and illustrate their favorite parts, convert the stories into plays or puppet shows, write letters to the author, and relate the stories to events in their own lives.

As children progress through the grade, they choose pieces of literature to read independently and later study in small groups. The selection of titles usually reflects the themes of study in the classroom (i.e., fairy tales, Native American legends, immigration, etc.).

A favorite activity among the older children is to cooperatively decide how they will present their piece to the rest of the class or other classes. Their ideas are endless: plays, puppet shows, television shows, mobiles, dioramas, versions of Big Books, etc. Students create their own scripts and any props needed for the presentation. They cooperatively decide who will take what role and are responsible for putting the presentation together from beginning to end.

For the past several years we have been developing an extensive Spanish core literature list. Our literature selections represent a wide range of reading levels, genres, cultural values, and human values. At each level we may include books written in repetitive, rhythmic language, as well as books with rich, complex language structures. As children get older we include as many works as possible that were originally written in the Spanish language in a wide range of Spanish-speaking countries in addition to the translated classics of children's literature.

Writing

Interactive Journal Writing

Children need to be immersed in writing just as they are immersed in reading. Children desire to and think they can write from a very young age. We expect children to write from the very first day of kindergarten. Children are encouraged to spell creatively. The development of the writing process may progress from linear scribbles to combinations of letters, symbols, and numbers, to letters in random order, to experiments with creative spelling, followed by the first standard spellings, and then to standard spellings not represented by speech sounds. Each child progresses at a different pace and may skip some of these stages entirely.

Beginning in kindergarten, each child keeps a journal to which the teacher responds on a daily basis. Students record their thoughts, ideas, experiences, and messages, and the teacher responds to the content rather than to the structure or form. The journal is a daily interaction between child and teacher, and ultimately very personal thoughts are shared. In the primary grades the entries may begin with one-word entries copied off the walls, such as *caballo* accompanied by a picture of a horse. They progress to things like *un cabayo café* (un caballo café—a brown horse). Naturally, as they begin to invent their own spellings rather than copy print from the room environment, we see more words misspelled, as this entry by a native Spanish speaker illustrates: "oY FuiAl m A r iNAbE so Lo Nos AviA co mNAdAr." (Yo fui al mar y nadé solo. No sabía como nadar.—I went to the ocean. I swam alone. I didn't know how to swim.) It is not uncommon in these early entries to find entire journals filled with familiar sentence structure such as "A mí me gusta el gato" (I like the cat), "A mí me gusta la naranja" (I like the orange), "A mí me gusta la pelota" (I like the ball), etc.

It pays to be patient because many children rapidly acquire the skills and the confidence to share very meaningful messages. Many children begin to record daily events such as "Hoy fimos a la bibbotka." (Hoy fuimos a la biblioteca.—Today we went to the library.) One disappointed child wrote, "Hoy era el dia de paletas pero yo no gare una paleta porque la mayestra no nos dío la nota." (Hoy era el día de paletas pero yo no agarré una paleta porque la maestra no nos dio la nota.—Today was the Popsicle day but I didn't get a Popsicle because the teacher did not give us the notes.)

Even non-native speakers soon begin to use their journals as a place to share their innermost feelings, as evidenced by this first-grade entry: "Mi mama esta en el hospytal. Le dwele la espalda. Yo voy a la casa de Lauren prque mi mama esta en el hospytal. Yo no ciero ir. Ciero ir con mi mama. Yo y mi papa y mi ermana van a visitar mi mama. No puetho espar." (Mi mamá está en el hospital. Le duele la espalda. Yo voy a la casa de Lauren porque mi mamá está en el hospital. Yo no quiero ir. Quiero ir con mi mamá. Yo y mi papá y mi hermana vamos a visitar a mi mamá. No puedo esperar.—My mother is in the hospital. Her back hurts. I am going to Lauren's house because my mother is in the hospital. I don't want to go. I want to go with my mother. My father and I and my sister are going to visit my mother. I can't wait.)

We find it very helpful to keep class journals to record what we have studied or done in class. This helps children at early stages of writing to grasp the idea of recording thoughts and events. As approximately half of our students are learning to read and write in their second language, it is even more important to keep the focus on meaning, enabling young readers to make sense of the world around them.

Journal Entries

un dia yo fui al zoo. Yo vi un coneJos y un león. yo vi un caballo yo vi un toro. yo vi unamariposa yo vi una aralla. Yo vi un hago. Me gusta mucho el zoo.

(Un día yo fui al zoo. Yo vi un conejo y un león. Yo vi un caballo. Yo vi un toro. Yo vi una mariposa. Yo vi una araña. Yo vi un chango. Mue gusta mucho el zoo.)

(One day I went to the zoo. I saw a rabbit and a lion. I saw a horse. I saw a bull. I saw a butterfly. I saw a spider. I saw a monkey. I like the zoo.)

Native Spanish Speaker—First Grade

oY FuiAl m   A r iNAbE so   Lo Nos AviA   co mNAdA r

(Yo fui al mar y nadé solo. No sabía como nadar.)
(I went to the ocean. I swam alone. I didn't know how to swim.)

Native Spanish Speaker—Kindergarten

Yo tiengo una prima y. Ella NO ES MUY BUENA ELlA TIRO
MIS JUGETES Y
ROMPIO MI CAMA

(Yo tengo una prima y ella no es muy buena. Ella tiró mis juguetes y rompió mi cama.)

(I have a cousin and she is not very good. She threw my toys and ripped my bed.)

Native English Speaker—First Grade

Hoy en mi grupo yo vas a ser una corazon y tienes mi nombre en la corazon y tienes que trazar mi nombre con pegadura y luego vaz a poner gliter en mi nombre y luego yo vaz aponer decoraziones.

(Hoy en mi grupo yo voy a ser un corazón y voy a tener mi nombre en el corazón. Tengo que trazar mi nombre con pegadura y luego voy a poner gliter en mi nombre y luego yo voy a poner decoraciones.)

(Today in my group I am going to be a heart and I will have my name in a heart. I have to trace my name with glue and later I will put glitter on my name and later I will put decorations on it.)

Native English Speaker—First Grade

I like Oregon. Everything is so green and beautiful. The air smells so clean. If you go walking on a trail you will see and hear birds and lots of other animals. If you go to the ocean you will see alot of clear blue water. You will smell salt in the air. That is why I like Oregon.

Native English Speaker—Fourth Grade

Process Writing

Beginning in first grade, we utilize the Process Writing approach advocated by Donald Graves (1983), which allows children to acquire writing skills by engaging in activities that utilize writing as a communicative tool. Our teachers assume the role of facilitator, guiding students through a process where they generate ideas, receive a response to their work, revise and edit successive drafts, and participate in postwriting activities that enable them to share their work with an authentic audience (i.e., publishing a book or report, mailing a letter, etc.). Of course, at the first-grade level the revision and editing process is greatly simplified and the teacher serves as the final editor.

Most of the direct teaching of skills occurs during the revisions of student writing and the editing of final drafts. Children are encouraged to write for content without focusing too much on mechanics in their first drafts. They have learned that things like grammar, spelling, and punctuation will be addressed during the editing stage. Errors are viewed as valuable tools that give teachers insights into where the children are in their development as writers. We look for the logic behind the errors and patterns in the errors that serve as the basis for individual, small group, and/or whole group minilessons. As children progress through the grades, daily minilessons focus on more complex literary elements such as order, detail, voice, point of view, etc. The teachers often use samples of student drafts or journal entries as a starting point for group revision.

The importance of minilessons at the editing stage is intensified in the Immersion classroom. The teacher continually needs to provide guidance and instruction in language forms as well as spelling and punctuation. Classroom peers are wonderful resources when it comes to helping students recognize and correct second language learner errors. As children begin formal literacy in English, they have many questions about the structural differences between Spanish and English that can be addressed during the editing of their own pieces.

We have found that it is important for young writers to publish often. At first we publish every piece a child writes to help develop a sense of the audience, as well as of accomplishment. Soon children are able to select their favorite pieces for publication.

Each child's work is kept organized in a writing folder, which has proven to be a valuable tool for the teacher and child alike. It provides the child with a visible collection of his or her best ideas and fosters a strong sense of accomplishment. The writing folder also serves as a valuable record of the child's progress to share with parents. Additionally, it provides the teacher with a record of a year's development from which to discover problems and assess needs.

We are always absolutely astounded by the energy, joy, and determination we witness in our students as they work each day at the writer's workshop. All children are able to participate, sharing a small part of what was important and meaningful to them with each word. Even those at the very beginning stage of invented spelling approach the craft of composing with confidence. English-speaking students often seek help with vocabulary from their Spanish-speaking peers, yet the same children are often able to help others with spelling. In the first-grade Immersion classrooms we see many first drafts full of non-native speaker errors like "Mi tío pescaste tres peces." (Mi tío pescó tres peces.—My uncle caught three fish.) However, they provide the perfect focal point for a mini-lesson during conferencing. It is truly amazing how often children help each other correct such errors without any teacher intervention. Children take their role as writers very seriously and create a nurturing atmosphere for others.

Process Writing Samples

Había una vez dos pandas muy enamerados. Uno se llama Janet y el otro se llama Rudy. Un día fueron a la feria y Rudy le pregunta a Janet si se queria casar y Janet te contesto - ¡sí! ¡claro que sí! El siguiente día se casaron y para su luna de miel fueron a Hawie y en Hawie fueron a nadar. Janet traia un biquini muy bonito y Rudy tenia un short muy bonito.

(Once upon a time there were two pandas who were very much in love. One was named Janet and the other was named Rudy. One day they went to the fair and Rudy asked Janet if she wanted to get married and Janet answered him, "Yes, definitely I do!" The next day they got married and for their honeymoon they went to Hawaii and in Hawaii they went swimming. Janet brought a very pretty bikini and Rudy had on very nice shorts.)

Native Spanish Speaker—Fourth Grade

Despues que compro un crete que tenia pistola se fue a un planeta que se llama Micka. Se fue cuando luego vio que los dinosaurios eran muy grande muy muy pero muy grande. El fue porque dijeron que pudia agarar dinero rapido. El choco en el el suerlo y los pedasos de sacate eran gigante. "¿Donde estan los dinosaurios?" Bume "¡un temblor"! grito pero solo via un pie. El supio en ella asi pudria ire mas rapido y quesas ver a donde va a ire. Qisase va a vere donde esta y como ira a otro planeta. Otra ves su crete se fue muchuca de los pies del grande gigantesca muy muy pero muy grande asi fue.

(Later he bought a rocket that had a pistol in it and he went to the planet called Micka. He left when later he saw that the dinosaurs were very big very, very but very big. He went because he was told that he could get money quickly.

He crashed into the ground and the even the pieces of grass were huge. "Where were the dinosaurs?" Bume yelled "an earthquake!" but it was only a footstep. He climbed back in so that he could go more quickly and perhaps see where it was going to go. Perhaps he would see where he was and how to go to another planet. Again, his rocket went into the feet of a great giant very, very, but very big—that's how it was.)

Native English Speaker—Fifth Grade

Developing English Literacy

In kindergarten through second grades, we focus on oral language development in English. We do not separate language minority and language majority students for instruction. We have discovered that children acquire a tremendous amount of language through interaction with their peers and are more likely to develop positive cross-cultural relations when they work and learn together.

As with our Spanish instruction, we meld sheltered language techniques with the use of complex language appropriate for native speakers. We choose language goals for our language minority students and then use many interesting mediums to immerse students in comprehensible oral language. We include many books off the district's English core literature list so that children begin to develop story schemata and acquire story language in English. This contributes to an easier transition into English literacy.

In third grade we introduce children to interactive journal writing in English. Sometimes we encounter resistance from a few third-grade students when they are first given a blank journal designated for writing in English.

We do daily editing exercises by lifting excerpts from students' journal entries to revise and edit as a class. This enables us to focus on errors that are universal, as well as individual needs. It provides the perfect setting for minilessons on English spelling, grammar, punctuation rules, and opportunities to work on voice and style. The following journal entry by a native English speaker is a perfect piece to use for a minilesson on capitalization: "This Saterday my friends Bernadette, Alexandria and I are going to 'great America' for my Birhday party. They are going to spend the night friday and in the morning were going to go. My sister is bringing a friend to come too. I have bin to 'great America' before but Alexandria has'nt." This next journal entry by a native Spanish speaker was publicly recognized as a good beginning example of descriptive writing and served to motivate many children to experiment with descriptive writing: "My worst vacation was when we went to México. The time that I spent ther was on my 6th birthday. We went to México D.F.. The air was pouluted. I could smell the smok. The sky looked dark. I cuold fell the hard wind on my face. The sound of cars racing and beping at each other hurt my ears. I could almost tast the dust the cars left behind."

The third graders also participate in literature studies in English. We do not use "watered-down" or simplified texts but rather choose quality pieces of literature that might be found on any third-grade core literature list. Strategies such as choral reading, cooperative learning, and peer partners build confidence and encourage risk taking.

In fourth and fifth grades, children are able to participate in all of the same literacy activities in English that they do in Spanish. Spelling and punctuation are still areas of weakness for children and are emphasized through process writing and other authentic literacy experiences. We have found that it is important not to replicate activities in each language. For example, while students are writing historical biographies in Spanish, we might focus on poetry in English. Children also receive some subject matter instruction in the intermediate grades.

Promoting Literacy in the Home

Dr. Alma Flor Ada has worked with our district in training our teachers in how to implement the "Padres, Niños, y Libros" (Parents, Children, and Books) program. Many of our parents and children have become authors through the influence of this program. Parents are led through the process of reading and discussing a piece of children's literature to help them in working with their children. Parents who cannot read are able to listen to the story and retell it to their children using the illustrations.

Next, parents write a book together around a variety of topics such as "Consejos para nuestros hijos" (Advice for our children), "Nuestros sueños para nuestros hijos y como podemos ayudarles para que se lleven a cabo" (Our dreams for our children and how we help them to realize them), and "Nuestros recuerdos" (Our memories). By putting parents' statements and ideas on chart paper in front of the group and later transcribing them on the computer and publishing them in book form, these parental thoughts are validated and recognized for the golden pieces of wisdom and poetry that they are. Here are the words of one father describing his dreams for his children:

"Yo deseo que mis hijas prosperen en sus estudios para que ayuden a toda la comunidad. Voy a apoyarlas—tener más atención y escucharlas. También tener cuidado con ellas para que hagan su trabajo en la casa." (I want my girls to prosper in their studies so that they can help the whole community. I am gong to support them by giving them more attention and listening to them. Also, I will care for them so that they can do schoolwork at home.)

To encourage parents to continue the process of writing books with their children, we have developed a home learning kit called "La caja de aprendizaje." The home learning kit contains a tape recorder, book/tape sets of children's literature, blank tapes, crayons, scissors, construction paper, writing paper, glue, pencil, eraser, blank books for writing stories, etc. Parents check out the kit and receive training on how to use it with their children. They also receive guidance on a variety of activities that they have the materials to experiment with. We publish, bind, and distribute all of the books that parents and their children write to all of the families who are participating and to each kindergarten through third-grade Immersion classroom. Teachers read the books in the class and put them in their libraries. Children and their families are authors who are recognized and encouraged by their peers.

Padres, Niños, y Libros and the home learning kit component are a vital part of supporting parents in their quest to develop their own and their children's literacy skills. We continually work with families to challenge them to creatively undertake the task of writing books with their children. We motivate parents to record and share their childhood and experiences with their children in this way. Many families ask for multiple copies of their books so that they can send them to their families in Mexico. The history, tradition, and "oro" of the family is preserved and is utilized as a tool to promote literacy in the home and to enrich the classroom.

Parents who have participated in the Parent Education Program have asked us to provide parent literacy training. We hold biweekly ESL classes on the school site and provide child care and transportation so that parents can attend. The child's school becomes the parent's school also. Parents are models for their children of how education is an important part of their lives, and the children tell all of their friends that their parents come to school here, too!

Conclusion

Never doubt that a small group of thoughtful committed citizens can change the world. Indeed it's the only thing that ever has.

—*Margaret Mead*

These words have been an inspiration for the parents and teachers who have worked together in a partnership to develop and implement the Two-Way Immersion Program. Our vision is global:

Un mundo sano donde hay armonía y cada persona se siente que puede alcanzar sus metas y sueños en una sociedad que valore la diversidad cultural y la igualdad.

A healthy, harmonious world where all people are empowered to pursue their dreams and goals in a society that values cultural diversity and equality. Our mission is challenging:

Asegurarnos de que existan oportunidades sin límites en el futuro de nuestros hijos uniendo a los padres y maestros, como socios, para crear un sistema educacional que:

- promueva excelencia académica, igualdad y responsabilidad en la comunidad;
- abra las puertas a la diversidad lingüística y cultural;
- valore el desarrollo personal, la felicidad y la autoestimación;
- inspire a todos a luchar por sus ideales.

To ensure that boundless opportunities exist in our children's future by empowering parents and teachers, as partners, to create an educational system that:

- promotes academic excellence, equality, and community responsibility;
- welcomes cultural and linguistic diversity;
- values personal development, happiness, and self-esteem;
- inspires all individuals to strive for their ideals.

As teachers, we dedicate ourselves to adopting a clear vision of the kind of society and individuals we want to develop. We challenge each of you to empower yourselves and your students by critically examining your curriculum, your interactions with students and their families, and especially the types of interactions your school encourages among students. By committing ourselves to effecting change, we can create an educational system that promotes optimum achievement, the ability to think critically and generate new ideas, and an understanding and appreciation for the diverse peoples of our society in all our students.

We are no longer naïve about the commitment or struggle that is involved in fostering this type of program, philosophy, and environment. There are many elements of the system that oppress our children, our teachers, and especially the minority members of our community. We have seen the flag of racism raised high and propelled on the chilling winds of fear and anger. There have been many times when we have had to make tough personal decisions about whether or not it was worth it to keep going. In those moments, we have reaffirmed our vision and taken strength from the words of Albert Einstein, "Great spirits have always encountered violent opposition from mediocre minds." For if our program has nothing else, it has great spirit!

As for our thoughts about the wonders of creating bilingual, biliterate students in our educational system, we would like to share this story related by one of our teachers, Ginger Dale. Like most of our Immersion teachers she has her own children enrolled in the program. She was listening one day while her son and two of his Immersion friends were playing a game of superheroes, and each had to decide what power he would possess. One said he would be the strongest in the universe and the rest agreed. One said that he would be able to become invisible and the rest agreed. The last child said that he would be able to speak all the languages of the world. The two others chimed in, "No, **that's not fair. That's too powerful!**"

REFERENCES

Ada, A. F. (1986, November). Creative education for bilingual teachers. *Harvard Educational Review*, vol. 56, no. 4.

Cummins, J. (1989). *Empowering minority students*. Sacramento: California Association for Bilingual Education.

Cummins, J. (1985). *Special needs in French immersion*. Paper presented at Canadian Parents for French Annual Conference, Whitehorse, Canada.

Dale, G., Moore, J., and Reynolds, J. (1989). *How to plan and implement a two-way Spanish immersion program*. Title II Federal Grant administered by the California Post Secondary Education Commission and the California State Department of Education.

Genesee, F. (1985, Winter). Second language learning through immersion: A review of U.S. programs. *Review of Education Research*, vol. 55, no. 4, pp. 541–561.

Graves, D. (1983). *Writing: Teachers and children at work*. Portsmouth, NH: Heinemann Educational Books.

Lambert, W. E. (1987). The effects of bilingual and bicultural experiences on children's attitudes and social perspectives. In Homel, P., Paliz, M., and Aaronson, D. (Eds.), *Childhood bilingualism: Aspects of linguistic, cognitive and social development*. Hillsdale, NJ: Lawrence Erlbaum Associates, Publishers.

Lindholm, K. J. (1989) *Student progress after two years in a Bilingual Immersion program*. Paper presented at the 1989 14th annual CABE Conference, Anaheim, California.

A Word Study on Word Study: Teacher-Researchers Use Computers to Accelerate Word Study in a Multicultural School with a Two-Way Bilingual Immersion Program

Dennis Sayers

*The Ann Leavenworth Center for Accelerated Learning–
Fresno Pacific University Teacher-Researcher Partnership*

This article explores some new developments in the ways teacher-researchers are using computers to address the demand for student mastery of the complexities of standard written English usage in "mainstream" and bilingual education classrooms.

Balancing reader-based and writer-based literacy learning strategies

Schema-based, or—to use a common designation among researchers—top-down, reading theories, which are drawn from cognitive psychology, and ultimately from the Piagetian psychological notions of assimilation and accommodation, present a dynamic picture of the process of emergent literacy. Young readers attempt to predict meaning by bringing to their encounter with a particular text a wealth of background knowledge of previously experienced situations as well as their current, emerging world view. Of course, their experiences are, by definition, limited, and their world view has gaps in terms of conceptual and practical knowledge. Learning to read becomes a process of anticipating meaning based on prior schema while encountering new realities and concepts, which need to be accommodated to previous schema as these conceptual webs become more sophisticated.

Early reading instruction in the primary grades, whether in English or in the language learners' primary language, has traditionally exploited the power of fictional narrative—children's stories—to create a productive encounter between young readers and the written word. Intriguing make-believe characters, their clever resolution of difficulties as they overcome obstacles, and surprising twists in storybook plots are the staples of formal initial reading instruction. Indeed, it would be hard to imagine a more compellingly pleasurable and therefore fertile ground for marshaling young readers' existing schema in order to better anticipate a text's meaning, all the while experiencing, in a fictive realm, new concepts and situations that can enrich children's understanding of the world.

But what happens when young readers confront the very different demands of making sense of expository writing? Jeanne Chall's distinction (1983) between learning to read in the primary grades and *reading to learn* in the upper elementary grades—and beyond—is still useful: the goal of primary literacy instruction, though initially focused on predictable texts and sound–letter correspondences, is to forge a tool for efficiently acquiring an expanding body of subject matter knowledge. And this reality is very much a felt reality: Around third grade, young backs begin to ache under the strain of lugging home heavier content-area textbooks, books with a very different organizational scheme than fictional storybooks.

Fascinating characters are replaced by subject-matter topics, and exciting story lines by dense paragraphs chock full of information, broken only occasionally by a descriptive diagram or a summarizing list. While children's storybooks are reflected and reinforced in the popular media—in movies, children's television shows, and so on—as well as in children's dramatic fantasy play, very little in the wider society prepares the learner for the radically different demands that expository prose places on its readers. The rush of new information to be accommodated often overwhelms young readers' ability to rapidly adapt their existing schema. One outcome is that many measures of reading achievement show a dramatic dip at the third and fourth grade levels, precisely when nonfiction reading of expository prose gains ascendancy in school settings (Chall, 1983).

In the last ten years, approaches to reading instruction have been developed that respond to this challenge in various ways. The amount and availability of nonfiction material for primary grades have increased, often in attractive "big book" formats which lend themselves to large-group shared reading activities. An impressive effort has been made in many school districts to expose young readers to expository prose from the earliest moments of schooling, recognizing that a balance must be established between fictional and nonfictional texts if students are to be readied for the increased demands of the informational reading they are sure to face in the upper grades. Another important initiative has been to develop *reader-based strategies* for encouraging the use of prediction in nonfiction reading. Readers are encouraged to search for graphic organizers to help "pre-read" an expository text, looking for clues to its overall meaning in titles, headings, and subheadings, lists, diagrams, topic and summary sentences, and so on. Jim

Cummins has described a multimedia computer-based program that uses any electronic text as input and creates a supportive context for reading, with bilingual dictionaries with translations and cognates as well as target language dictionaries available by clicking on any word (1998).

The advent of the Internet and the possibility of engaging in joint curriculum projects with distant "classmates" has renewed an opportunity to introduce more *writer-based strategies* into reading instruction. I say "renewed" because the first educators to systematically explore the potential of distance exchanges to foster literacy development actually predated the computer era by several decades.

As Jim Cummins and I described in more detail in *Brave New Schools: Challenging Cultural Illiteracy Through Global Learning Networks* (1997), the French pedagogue Celestin Freinet established in the 1920s what was to become a vast multilingual network of collaborating educators, spanning countries and continents. Today we have the Internet; then, the teachers who composed the Ecole Moderne relied on national postal services to create an elaborate yet effective network for exchanges between *learning clusters* of twinned "partner classes." Students in distant classes engaged in joint learning projects on identical topics—for example, local geography comparisons, dual opinion surveys on controversial topics, and parallel science investigations—and then shared and compared their results via the postal system on a weekly basis with their partner class, and once a month with the other classes in their learning cluster.

Freinet and his colleague teachers in the Ecole Moderne wrote numerous monographs on the various teaching techniques with which they were experimenting, including several books that outlined a new approach to literacy instruction. The learning of reading skills within Freinet's global learning network was, and remains today, a result of the complex interplay between children's greater familiarity with highly contextualized, locally produced texts and their desire to understand the more decontextualized texts—though centered on a common topic—which they receive from distant partner classes.

> To our way of thinking, our students know how to read when they can easily read all the works they and their classmates have written for their partner classes, and when they can read with acceptable ease and fluency the texts sent to them from their partner classes. (Balesse & Freinet, 1961/1973, p. 68)

Written exchanges between classes engaged in parallel projects in the context of global learning networks exert a powerful motivation for students to summon the discipline they need in order to master language mechanics.

An opening is created for students willingly to confront the demands of accepted discourse standards. Students immediately understand that faulty spelling and grammar in messages destined for their partner class will reflect poorly on them. Thus, they are receptive to—indeed, they often demand—their teachers' assistance on what are no longer the "details" of grammar and spelling, much more so than when writing for themselves or for just a local audience. This motivation to "get it right" only increases when they wish to fully comprehend the communications they receive from their distant colleagues.

> If on the one hand the child ... creates new texts to satisfy his need for self-expression, utilizing words and expressions without worrying about the technicalities of syllables and letters, then on the other hand the practice of sharing learning projects between classes places literacy in an entirely different light....
>
> This is the moment at which the child really moves into decoding and becomes aware of it as a process. Familiar words are immediately discovered and ones that have never been seen are analyzed perspicaciously.... Our intervention, even an exercise sheet, is wanted to aid in easily decod-

ing those words that might clarify for us what we want to know. The teacher's observations and help with syllabification and spelling are not an imposed system, but rather a necessity integrated with something that is lived, and are therefore received with the same enthusiasm as everything that extends the child's life. (Balesse & Freinet, 1961/1973, pp. 64–65)

And so students in Freinet's Ecole Moderne—as in our latter-day Internet-based global learning exchanges—have an opportunity to balance and contrast *reader-based* interpretation of abstract, published expository writing with *writer-based* strategies that they must employ in their efforts at describing their own communities, lives, and world view for a distant audience of peers. Students write the descriptive prose which before they had merely attempted to read in published books; and they write not only for their teacher but also for an *unknown but knowable* audience of distant colleagues, partners in a common learning enterprise. To enhance their descriptions, students make lists, provide annotations, design diagrams, and anticipate possible questions from their distant readers with topic and summary statements. And they are motivated to use these expository devices, not merely to recognize them. Their efforts at self-expression are juxtaposed with a simultaneous attempt to make sense of the parallel, distinct world view of their distant colleagues. Moreover—and this is key—local and distant students *can ask questions* about what they have read and *can be asked questions* about what they have written.

As Freinet pointed out, participation in global learning networks increases students' motivation to master language mechanics such as grammar and especially spelling, both to produce well-formed communications and to interpret accurately messages received from distant colleagues. Any teacher would welcome any such "teachable moments." Yet the blessing is a mixed one. Are we educators, as a profession, in a position to respond adequately, with appropriate materials and techniques, to these often unpredictable teachable moments arising from a "lived" literacy encounter? Students seek (1) focused, specific practice aimed at perfecting a problem area in their developing reading or writing skills, in order to get on with the learning exchange at hand; and (2) broad, "big picture" approaches to language mechanics that give students the tools necessary to confront, on their own, new and unpredictable reading challenges and to become more independent in their fluency with standard written language—again, so as to pursue with fewer interruptions their learning partnerships.

Many contemporary language arts curricula, materials, and methods ill equip the teacher to respond with immediacy to these learning needs. Practice materials that are focused on a specific skill area are frequently difficult to locate and, if available, are too often piecemeal and rarely related to a larger, coordinating framework that could guide more independent mastery of language mechanics.

Teacher-research in a multicultural setting

As we begin to discuss more recent developments in the use of technology to enhance literacy learning in primary and second languages, it is critical that we understand that the "language mechanics learning dilemma" confronting educators who wish to involve their students in global learning networks, while seemingly context-specific, is identical to the one faced by the majority of teachers under a wide variety of circumstances. Certainly, primary language literacy educators everywhere are confronted with the challenge of ensuring students' productive exposure to high-quality children's literature and nonfiction writing, while addressing students' need to master the complexities of language mechanics—spelling, grammar, and standard usage—that are required of all literate citizens in a technological age, no matter what their cultural and linguistic background.

And all this in the highly conflictive context of a time when back-to-the-basics literacy curricula, in the form of phonics-first—or even phonics-only!—approaches to initial literacy, are being trumpeted in the popular media and by politicians as the antidote against what are simplistically viewed as the failures of whole-language, literature-based teaching. Indeed, a time when the primary and second language learning needs of the children of recent immigrants—often the majority of students in many urban, suburban, and rural schools—are actively disregarded, as in the case of post-Proposition 227 California in the wake of voter approval of an ill-conceived ballot initiative that effectively eliminated primary language instruction for millions of students in that state.

The remainder of this article chronicles the efforts of a group of teacher-researchers in a multicultural school in California's Fresno Unified School District (FUSD), a school in which bilingual education is far from dead or dying. Indeed, it is flourishing, experimenting, and innovating. The Ann Leavenworth Center for Accelerated Learning is a K–6 elementary school in Fresno that opened its doors for year-round schooling in August of 1994. Its founding principal, Glenna Encinas, and the talented faculty she has brought to the school serve slightly under 1,000 students, 95 percent of whom are from "minority" backgrounds. At Ann Leavenworth Center, minority is an anachronistic designation, since most schools in both rural and densely populated communities throughout the state of California, like so many urban districts in other parts of the nation, have student enrollments whose minorities are the majority. "Asians" are the 41 percent of students from Hmong and, to a lesser extent, Laotian and Khmer-speaking backgrounds. "Hispanics," in this case referring to students of Mexican descent, form 48 percent of the the student tally. "English Language Learners" are 64 percent of all students. At Ann Leavenworth, poverty is the rule rather than the exception, with 93 percent of the student body from families on AFDC (Aid to Families with Dependent Children).

The Ann Leavenworth Center has based its curriculum on the research of Henry Levin (1987), stressing a "teaching up" philosophy of high academic and social expectations that replaces compensatory, remedial approaches with curricular activities usually associated with programs for gifted and talented students. One example, among many, of a school culture that encourages problem-posing, reflective teaching is the Teacher-as-Researcher Partnership with Fresno Pacific University, coordinated by the author with the close involvement of two distinguished bilingual education and second language acquisition researchers, Yvonne and David Freeman. The Teacher-as-Researcher Partnership has two distinct but interrelated components:

■ A "partner teachers as researchers" study of biliterate and prosocial development within the two-way bilingual immersion program; and

■ A schoolwide "teachers as action researchers" inquiry into best classroom practices for computer-mediated literacy learning—research in progress that is discussed in this article.

Teachers as Action Researchers

Kurt Lewin (1946) introduced the term *action research* to describe field-based research undertaken by reflective practitioners with the goal of improving their practice, exploring an innovation, or testing a theory's application. Since teachers involved in action research projects are first and foremost teachers, care must be taken to ensure that the methodology for data collection of the project is not so time-consuming as to interfere with instructional delivery; yet teachers must have confidence that the data they collect will be sufficiently reliable to allow them to develop and modify hypotheses that hold promise for informing improved classroom instruction (Hopkins, 1985).

The classroom practice selected by teachers at Ann Leavenworth School for our teacher-as-action-researcher inquiry is *accelerated word study of English*, a phrase we usually shorten to "the spelling research." Teacher concern with students' lack of spelling mastery and its impact on overall reading skills arose during their weekly grade-level meetings. Indeed, third and fourth grade teachers undertook independent efforts to gather data on student spelling performance, although they eventually linked their inquiries. (This was a natural development because these two grade levels are paired for "looping," a system whereby students remain with each teacher for two consecutive grades—the general practice at Ann Leavenworth.) Fifteen teachers are involved in the inquiry: third grade teachers Debbie Friesen, Carol Jones, Sheri Martin, Susan Schmale, and bilingual teachers Julia Amavisca and Jessie Torrez, led by Kim Kirste, grade-level chair, and fourth grade teachers Karen Perkins, Julia Richardson, Jane Quiring, Elaine Schneider, and bilingual teacher Virginia Chavez, chaired by Marta McConnell.

Teachers voiced dissatisfaction with the current approaches to teaching English spelling, including the spelling program in the adopted reading series utilized throughout the district. Both informal spelling inventories and standardized achievement measures indicated low scores on word analysis and spelling. The district-mandated language arts assessments, our school's own extensive literacy assessments, and our anecdotal experience all pointed in the same direction: our students were far from accelerated in their spelling achievement. The SAT-9 results provided corroboration when we compared our classrooms, looking for patterns in our students' scores on the Word Study Skills and Spelling subtests. Third grade results from eight classrooms illustrated a pattern that was repeated in our five fourth grade classrooms. In seven of the eight classrooms the scores of more than 50 percent of the children fell in the "below average" category on either the Word Study Skills or the Spelling subtest, and on both subtests in three of the seven classes. On the Word Study Skills subtest, six classes indicated that vowel analysis was harder than consonant analysis. On the Spelling subtest three classes performed more poorly on vowel spellings than on consonant spellings, and three more classes showed equally "below average" performance on vowel and consonant spelling; just two classes showed slightly better consonant spelling performance. These test scores pointed to a general picture of low spelling achievement, with greater difficulty in vowel analysis as compared with consonant analysis; further, the Word Study Skills subtest showed equally poor performance on short- and long-vowel analysis, with no clear area of strength.

Previous staff development efforts by the district's language arts coordinators had stimulated interest among teachers in recent curriculum research on what has come to be called *word study*, a "discovery-oriented" approach to teaching spelling and vocabulary development relying on various inductive-learning activities, chief among them *extensive word card sorting*. Many of the teachers at Ann Leavenworth had read *Words Their Way* (Bear et al., 1996) and had found compelling its solid grounding in current findings from research into developmental spelling. Yet in unison teachers voiced their concerns with both the *classroom logistics* and the *appropriate corpus* for word study with their grade level's students.

Managing word study activities posed logistical challenges for teachers. While some commercial word sorting materials are available, most classroom materials for word study are teacher-made and place daunting organizational demands on teachers to create, file, and store large numbers of word cards for ready use by students, the teacher, and, ideally, parents. And teachers need to design these materials for use in a variety of teaching situations, including whole-class instruction, with small groups facilitated by the teacher, and for independent, student-monitored learning.

Deciding the appropriate corpus for word study activities was also a concern of teachers. Which words should be studied, and in what sequence, and through which discriminatory lenses should these words be viewed as candidates for word sorting activities? There are four potential sources of word lists for sorting:

- Design and collect locally a sample of typical texts encountered or produced by learners, and then analyze the collected corpus using several of the word frequency analysis programs that are now available for personal computers (Higgins, 1991).

- Collect teachers' own limited recollections of exemplary words for specific pronunciations and spellings. Such recollections are usually drawn from fading memories of how they themselves were taught, and most teachers lack ready knowledge of *enough* exemplary words to illustrate and practice a particular pronunciation or spelling.

- Search for the numerous published word lists for educators, an eclectic hodge-podge of listings, usually either (a) idiosyncratic lists of high-frequency words illustrating a particular pronunciation/spelling point or (b) short lists of rime words drawn from similarly spelled "phonograms," such as *long, strong, wrong, along, belong*.

- Generate customized word lists, in electronic and print formats, from specially designed databases of high-frequency words like Visual Spelling (Sayers, 1981, 1998) with the capability of grouping word lists by their common vowel and consonant sounds, spellings, and syllabification, by their rhymes and rimes, and by the rank order frequency of each word, specific to every grade level from first through twelfth, and based on values derived from recent computerized word frequency analyses of a huge sampling of typical grade-level-appropriate reading materials (Zeno et al., 1995).

The first three sources posed problems for teachers in terms of, first, collecting word lists and, second, producing word cards for word study activities. We elected to build our own word sorting lists using Visual Spelling.

Obviously, questions of classroom logistics are interrelated with the selection of an appropriate corpus for word study. Let us first consider the issues that arose as we generated a suitable corpus of words for grade-level-specific word study. Visual Spelling is capable of producing an enormous number of grade-level-specific word lists across 22 stressed vowel sounds and 44 possible vowel spellings, and in a variety of consonant settings, including final consonants, and both final and onset consonant blends. This kind of discriminatory power is an embarrassment of riches; no teacher could monitor such an astronomical number of sorting possibilities. Teacher-researchers instead chose

Figure 1
THE -/ t / EXTENDED WORD FAMILY

short a	short e		short i	short o	short u	short oo
that	**get**	-**better**	**it**	**not**	**but**	put
at	**let**	-getting	**bit**	**got**	**cut**	*pushed*
sat	**set**	-**letter**	**sit**	**lot**	**shut**	
cat	**yet**	--except	**hit**	**hot**	*just*	foot
flat	**met**	--forget	*picked*	**spot**	*must*	*looked*
hat	**wet**	-letters	*list*	**pot**	*jumped*	
fat	**pet**	-metal	-little	*stopped*	*hunt*	
asked	**went**	--**present**	-city	*lost**	--result	
last	*left*	--effect	-sitting	*soft**		
can't	*next*	--western	-cities	*cost**	what	
fast	*felt*	--**percent**	-written	--cannot	*want**	
past	*best*		-kitten	-bottom	-wanted*	
plant	*kept*	--against	--political	--**forgot**		
act	*rest*				*front*	
fact	*sent*	*meant*	*built*	*want*		
-matter	*helped*			*walked*		
-faster	*west*		-pretty	*watched*		
	spent			-water		
laughed	*test*			-wanted*		
aunt						
				caught		
				taught		
				thought		
				brought		

*Alternate pronunciation (see diphthong /aw/)

to use Visual Spelling as a tool for studying English spelling patterns in order to design a simplified and accelerated word study and spelling curriculum. In other words, we used Visual Spelling to engage in our own word study.

Visual Spelling offers many possibilities for informed curricular decision making in this regard. The database generates and displays 19 "Extended Word Families," a unique array of high-frequency short and long vowel rhyming words ending in the consonant sounds -/b/, -/ch/, -/d/, -/f/, -/g/, -/j/, -/k/, -/l/, -/m/, -/n/, -/ng/, -/p/, -/s/, -/sh/, -/t/, voiced and unvoiced -/th/, -/v/, and -/z/, in addition to one Extended Word Family, devoted to words with stressed syllables for 22 different vowel sounds. Figure 1 presents the largest of these 20 word families, the - /t/ Extended Word Family.

The Extended Word Family array displays far more information than traditional

Figure 1
THE -/ t / EXTENDED WORD FAMILY (continued)

long a	long e	long i	long o	long u	/aw/
late	**eat**	**right**	*don't*	*used*	*want*
state	**heat**	**night**	*most*	--*produced**	*walked*
ate	**seat**	**might**	*won't*		-*water*
rate	**meat**	**light**	-*noticed*	**long oo**	-*wanted*
placed	*reached*	**bright**		--*produced*	
-*later*	*least*	**sight**	**boat**		*lost*
	east	**fight**	**coat**		*soft*
wait	-*eating*	--**tonight**	coast		*cost*
paint					
-*waiting*	**feet**	**white**	**wrote**		**caught**
-*waited*	**street**	**quite**	**note**		**taught**
straight	**meet**	**write**			
		kite			**thought**
great	--**complete**	*liked*			**brought**
-*greater*		--*united*			
					*aunt**
eight		--*writing*			
weight					/ow/
					out
					--**about**
					--**without**
					-*shouted*
					--*amount*
					--**through-out**
					/oy/
					point
					-*pointed*

*Alternate pronunciation (see <u>long oo</u>. Note that newscasters and the British favor this style of pronunciation)

word lists of isolated "phonograms" or "word families," which are usually listings of rimes (rhyming words whose endings are spelled exactly alike), such as *bring, sing, string*. In Visual Spelling's Extended Word Families, all high-frequency words with stressed short and long vowels that end in a particular consonant are displayed together, forming a cluster of rhyming or "near-rhyming" words. Under each stressed vowel heading, different spellings for that vowel sound are grouped together. For each spelling,

- monosyllabic words are presented together, with the highest-frequency word first and others following in descending rank order;
- monosyllabic words with final blends are provided second, again in descending rank order, and are underlined, to distinguish them clearly from VC and CVC word patterns; and
- multisyllabic words are provided last, with dashes indicating the syllable where the vowel stress, and hence the word's rhyme, falls.

Finally, all rimes are **boldfaced**.

The usefulness of Extended Word Families as a presentation scheme is that it allows teachers of word study and spelling to create word sorts over a large array of stressed vowel distinctions, and offers students opportunities to develop a "big picture," comprehensive working knowledge of all stressed vowel sounds and their spellings. Equally important, Visual Spelling permits comparisons between Extended Word Families, making clear that some are much larger than others. Figure 2 shows the number of words, drawn from the first 1,000 most frequent rhyming words, as they appear in each of 20 Extended Word Families. It is clear that just six Extended Word Families (-/t/, -/d/, -/n/, -/z/, -/s/, and the Extended Family of rhymes ending in vowels) account for the preponderance of high-frequency words, with the remaining sixteen families accounting for only a third of the first 1,000 most frequent rhymes. We

had uncovered our first principle for focusing and accelerating our word study curriculum: *Use the largest Extended Word Families as a focal point for word sorting activities.*

As an aid in our effort to sequence and streamline our word study curriculum, we used Visual Spelling to generate further reports on the sortable characteristics of the first 1,000 most frequent words for our grade levels. Again, although the combinatorial possibilities are huge, patterns emerged that helped justify curriculum sequencing decisions. For example, Figure 3 illustrates the complexity of the task confronting students as they attempt to match graphemes with stressed vowel phonemes; yet it makes clear that students' efforts at word study of certain troublesome spelling areas could provide a basis for understanding the patterning of a great number of words.

The outline emerged of a second principle to guide our effort toward designing an accelerated sequence for a word study curriculum: *When sorting for phoneme/grapheme correspondence, focus on those graphemes which provide the greatest "explanatory power" for the broadest number of phonemes.* The "silent e" challenge was preeminent in this regard, with 21 vowel sounds represented across nearly 225 words from the first 1,000 most frequent for our grade levels. The single-letter graphemes -a- and -o- were also clear contenders for accelerated word study, as were the often confusing -ea- and -ee- vowel digraphs and the contrast between -oo-, -ou-, and -ow- graphemes.

We utilized Visual Spelling to help us generate a third principle for curriculum sequencing, but only later, after we began to pilot test our word study curriculum at Ann Leavenworth. The first implementation, in January 1999, was as a "Spelling" module, taught by the author, for an after-school program called Academic Excellence, offering a range of one-hour enrichment activities three days a week. All teacher-researchers could nominate two children for this five-week module, and fifteen students participated. It was in this module that we began to confront the logistical challenges of our deci-

Figure 2
EXTENDED WORD FAMILIES

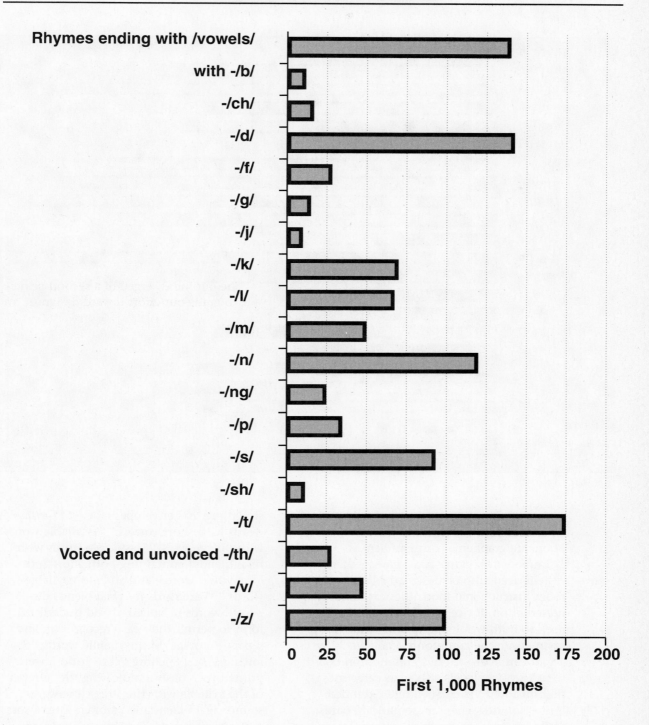

Figure 3
STRESSED VOWEL SPELLINGS

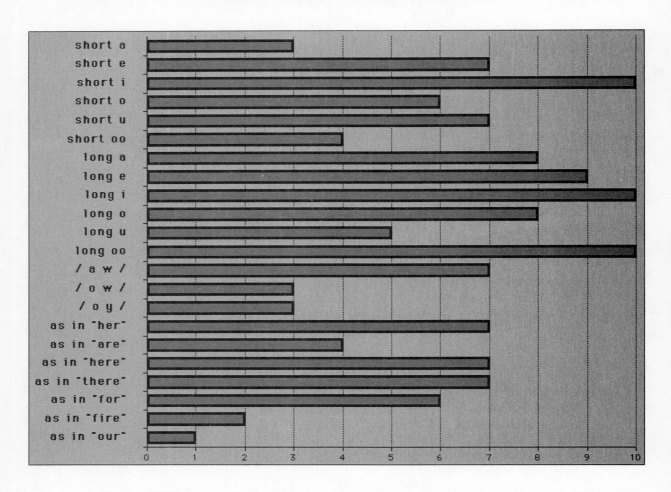

sion to focus on the corpus for the six major Extended Word Families and the thorniest phoneme/grapheme correspondences.

Immediately, a materials management system needed to be designed and classroom instructional modalities explored. A presentation device was developed that lent itself to both whole-group and small-group instruction: the commonly available 3- by 4-foot cardboard tri-fold presentation board with 15 vowel labels affixed as categories that mirrored Visual Spelling's Extended Word Families. These presentation boards could be stood up for display purposes or opened on a table for small-group work. Word cards for each Extended Family were

stored in vinyl envelopes labeled "1-syllable words with short vowels," "1-syllable words with long vowels," "1-syllable words with final blends" containing both short and long vowel words, and all "multisyllable words." Word cards for final blends displayed words in italicized and underlined form to permit their easy recognition and separate storage. Multisyllablic words, following Visual Spelling's convention, were printed with dashes indicating the number of the syllable with the stressed vowel sound, again facilitating storage after a sort was completed, while focusing student attention on vowel stress during the word sort activity.

The decision to use no more than four envelopes to store word cards for each Extended Word Family was a compromise. At this point, we were not sure into how many vowel categories students could productively sort word cards. Most word study curricula use a limited number of sorting categories, often just two or three. But with 15 vowels to account for, we wanted to avoid having a separate envelope for each vowel sound. With a four-envelope system, teachers who wanted to contrast only two or three vowel sounds could empty an envelope and quickly select the words they wanted. Those who wanted to explore sorting across more categories could simply use an envelope's contents in their entirety; or, to extend the number of categories even further, they could mix the contents of the short and long vowel envelopes. Yet the system was simple enough that teachers and students could quickly store word cards after completing a word sort, an important feature for the use of our materials in independent student-monitored learning situations.

A typical week's sessions began with a whole-group presentation, with word cards distributed and students asked to affix their word on the Extended Word Family display board. These were followed by word study using table boards in small groups of three to five students at learning stations. A typical week's culminating activity was to randomly create teams, who attempted to achieve the highest scores for accurate word sorting for one or several Extended Word Families.

It immediately became clear that we teachers had underestimated our students' capabilities for sorting across multiple categories. Initially, most could easily handle the six short vowels together, and after a week's practice, most could sort across all 15 short and long vowels at once. This meant that all monosyllabic words from the six Extended Word Families could be sorted extensively during our first five-week module. Results seemed impressive: By the end of five weeks, random groups of five could sort large numbers of words across 15 different vowel sounds (spending 10 minutes with each of three different word families, including more than 100 words each, and moving on to the next). Two out of three of the small groups had an impressively low three errors in sorting 350 words, and the third group had only 15 errors. This Academic Excellence "Spelling" module continues; indeed, it has been extended to two five-week modules. Pairs of students from our third and fourth grade classes continue to participate, and the modules are facilitated by a parent volunteer, Martha Moreno.

A major finding from the first after-school module was insight into the most troublesome vowel sound contrasts faced by students. Learners from both native English and other language backgrounds had difficulties "tuning their ears" to the following contrasts:

short e Visual Spelling; **short i** (157 and 132 words, respectively)

short o, Visual Spelling; the **diphthongs /aw/** and **/ow/** (83, 54, and 37 words, respectively)

short u and **short oo** Visual Spelling; **long u** and **long oo** (94, 29, 22, and 46 words, respectively)

the **"-/ r / colored" vowels** (170 words), including words that rhyme with *her, are, there, here, fire, for,* and *our.*

We therefore developed word sorting units that focused on these contrasts. Our third principle to guide corpus selection for an accelerated word study curriculum had emerged: *Provide study opportunities with those words which contain troublesome vowel sound contrasts.*

We returned to Visual Spelling seeking a basis for further insights into other ways our curriculum could be accelerated. Finally, we developed a fourth principle related to selection of our corpus of words: *Apply parsimony to word sorting activities.* We sought to winnow our learning units to a core suite of sequenced activities, trying to eliminate any redundant, repetitive word study and retaining units in which a particular phoneme or grapheme had been productively sorted in the broadest sorting context. The result has been the development of teacher kits of word cards for word sorting, organized into 15 study units.

A second phase of implementation has begun as we have introduced these word study materials into our classrooms. As part of this effort, the author has facilitated a learning station for two weeks in each third and fourth grade class, working out the logistics for leading small-group instruction and establishing independent learning stations. A general presentation pattern has developed; for example, word study of an Extended Vowel Family follows this sequence:

- Display presentation board (or a set of vowel sorting cards) on a table.

- Teacher reviews all vowel sounds.

- Empty contents of Word Family envelope(s) on table and ask students to divide up word cards.

- Students take turns reading one or two words aloud, then place them under vowel headings.

- Students read all the sorted words aloud. Teacher then asks students about each vowel sound: "How many ways do we spell this vowel sound?" as students "sub-sort" by spellings. Students reread all the words.

- Students replace word cards in appropriate Word Family envelopes.

Our independent learning groups build on this model, with students working in pairs or in groups as they sort, check, and record their sorting accuracy levels.

Conclusions

What have been our observations on the impact that our word study curriculum has had on student achievement in word analysis skills and spelling? One important finding has been the immediacy of its favorable influence on reading skills in some children who are performing below grade level. Four teachers have pointed out surprising growth in the reading performance of these students. Participating students have been assessed using miscue analysis and have shown gains associated with the growth of fluency in reading. Others have jumped five levels on our schoolwide literacy assessment, approximately a third of a year's growth, after only two weeks of organized word study. We hypothesize that our word study curriculum is encouraging the development of a wider array of word analysis strategies, as students listen for and self-correct errors when reading stressed vowels. Further, we anticipate our research will suggest that as increased skill with self-correction enhances a reader's fluency with written text, that student will meaningfully encounter a greater number of words, an experience that will assist in developing improved spelling skills.

While third and fourth grade teachers have provided the leadership in this teacher-as-action-researcher study designed to benefit all students at the Ann Leavenworth Center, it is important to understand that this effort is closely related to the concerns of our two-way bilingual immersion teacher-researcher colleagues at the center.

The initial language of literacy in every 90/10 model two-way program is the "minority" language, in this case Spanish. Formal English language literacy instruction is postponed until third grade, or late in the second grade at the earliest, after students have firmly established reading and writing in their initial language of literacy. If this initial language is one of the many languages with a high degree of correspondence between phonemes and graphemes, such as Spanish or Korean, then students inevitably face a daunting challenge when they confront their second language of literacy, English. In our situation, students have achieved fluent mastery of the five vowel sounds of Spanish which, depending on the consonant sound they appear with, are represented by usually one and sometimes two graphemes. Suddenly, they are confronted by the 22 vowel sounds of English, each one of which has as many as ten and rarely fewer than three different graphemes. While many of the consonant spellings of Spanish and English are identical, the discrepancy and multiplicity of vowel sound spellings are considerable.

Most students in two-way bilingual immersion programs—and there are thousands of students in several hundred programs within the United States alone—are faced with the challenge of becoming literate in a second language, but this time around in a much more complicated language to read and spell, English. Yet it is important to understand that this challenge is dissimilar to the one they initially faced when learning to read and write their first language of literacy. Students in two-way programs—like students in regular bilingual education classrooms—do not need to learn to read a second time; indeed, an axiom among bilingual educators is, "You only learn to read once." Most of the conceptual groundwork that makes fluent reading possible has already been laid through several years of Spanish language literacy instruction; it will easily transfer to English and, for that matter, to all future languages a learner will acquire during her or his lifetime. English orthography, however, must be learned on its own terms, and we believe that our word study curriculum should prove useful in stimulating English language learning in both our traditional bilingual and two-way bilingual immersion classes.

REFERENCES

Baleese, L., & Freinet, C. (1973). *La lectura en la escuela por medio de la imprenta*. F. Beltran, trans. Barcelona: Editorial Laia. (Original work published in 1961 as *La lecture par l'imprimerie á l'école*. [Reading through printing in schools.]

Bear, D.R., Invernizzi, M., Templeton, S., & Johnston, F. (1996). *Words their way: Word study for phonics, vocabulary, and spelling instruction*. Columbus, Ohio: Merrill.

Cazden, C. (1988). *Classroom discourse: The language of teaching and learning*. Portsmouth, NH: Heinemann.

Chall, J. (1983). *Learning to read: The great debate*. New York: McGraw-Hill.

Cummins, J. (1998). Using text as input for computer-supported language learning. *Computer-Assisted English Language Learning Journal, 9* (1), 3–10.

Cummins, J., & Sayers, D. (1997). *Brave new schools: Challenging cultural illiteracy through global learning networks*. New York: St. Martin's Press.

Higgins, J. (1991). Looking for patterns. In T. Johns & P. King (Eds.), *Classroom Concordancing. Birmingham University: English Language Research Journal, 4*, 63–70.

Levin, H. M. (1987). Accelerated schools for disadvantaged students. *Educational Leadership, 44* (6), 19–21.

Zeno, S.M., Ivens, S.M., Millard, R.T., & Duvvuri, R. (1995). *The educator's word frequency guide*. Brewster, NY: Touchstone Applied Science Associates, Inc.

Part III

LANGUAGE AND LITERACY DEVELOPMENT
ACROSS CONTENT AREAS

Content Area Instruction for Students Acquiring English: Focus on Social Studies

Carrol Moran
Educational Consultant

Abstract

Content area instruction for students acquiring English must be sensitive to the cultural and linguistic background of the student. Basic program models are discussed that should be chosen based on the characteristics of the student population and staff capabilities. The program model will determine to a great extent the amount of primary language developed during content area instruction. Regardless of the program model chosen, the following elements will create a more effective approach to content area instruction in primary or second language:

(1) Curriculum is grounded in the knowledge and experience the student brings to the classroom. (2) Organizational strategies are provided—tools that fit a concept into the bigger picture as well as organize bits of information within the context or the topic. (3) Acquisition of academic language is facilitated through focusing on new vocabulary and concepts and providing interaction with the language and con-cepts in relaxed, informal ways. (4) Synthesis of new information occurs immediately after process-ing, and reporting or sharing is encouraged through a variety of modes of expression. (5) Students reflect on the process of how they learned as well as on what they learned. This will increase the probability of transfer of the learning to new situations.

Throughout the discussion of these important elements I have woven in practical teaching strategies that incorporate the above elements in social studies, science, and math, drawn from authentic teaching situations.

Introduction

If you've ever entered a movie late, rendering you unable to make sense of the scenes before you, the importance of back-ground knowledge is clear. If you've been caught in a conver-sation between two computer hackers comparing megabytes, you know the "dumb" feeling a lack of vocabulary or language proficiency can create.

This is the experience of many students acquiring English in content area classes. Even with basic English communication skills, students are often at a loss to make sense of the informa-tion. They often lack both the academic language (Cummins, 1981) and the schemata, or maps, to make sense of the mate-rial. Many times they don't know what the bigger picture is that a concept fits into, nor do they see how it relates to their lives.

There are a variety of approaches developed by teach-ers and researchers to help stu-dents acquiring English achieve success in content curriculum. The basic program models out-lined here provide the frame in which content curriculum is taught to students acquiring English. Local demographics and policies determine which model is used, which in turn deter-mines the extent to which pri-mary language is utilized. I will discuss some strengths and weak-nesses of the basic models. Then I'll lay out the basic elements of instruction that benefit all stu-dents regardless of the program. These elements are the ones that connect new learning to the known and give road maps and guideposts to students to help them understand where the curriculum "is going." I will intersperse specific activities that incorporate the effective elements discussed. Finally I'll offer a brief checklist for teachers to utilize in self-assessing content area lessons.

Program Models

In the context of bilingual programs there are a variety of program models for making use of the primary language while developing English. The determining factors in the teaching situation that should determine the type of program used (local politics and policies notwithstanding) include student and staff characteristics such as: ethnicity, language proficiency, degree of literacy in each language, number of students of any one language background, etc. The program model chosen will in turn determine the extent to which the primary language is developed.

In programs with sufficient bilingual staff, an alternate day or alternate week program may be instituted. With this approach, literacy is generally taught in homogeneous groups according to the strengths of students, and the content area instruction is in heterogeneous groups that switch language on a daily/weekly basis between the first and the second language.

The advantage to such an approach is that children continue to develop cognitive academic language in the primary language at the same time that they begin to build vocabulary in English. Sometimes, however, students don't see the connection between the academic language and concepts in their primary language and the vocabulary in English. This is a bridge that is often missed for students. In a study of the advantages of a primary language on a student's learning of a third language (Swain & Lapkin, 1991), where both the primary language (Italian or Spanish) and the third language (French) were Romance languages, students generally did not make use of cognates between the languages to acquire meaning. Swain suggests that perhaps this needs to be taught. Discussions that explicitly focus attention on the similarity of the languages could help students to more readily transfer meaning from one language to another (Moran & Calfee, in press).

Immersion programs, such as those in Montreal, Canada, place students of the language of prestige (in this model, English) into a classroom where all teaching is done in French. All students in the class are beginning the language together. Content areas are taught in French. Literacy in English is introduced in the third or fourth grade. This model has proven itself effective in producing balanced bilinguals who outperform their monolingual peers on some tests of cognition (Peale & Lambert, 1962). Unfortunately, the Immersion Model is sometimes misinterpreted, and programs are set up that place minority language children in English-only programs competing with native English speakers, and the title "Immersion Program" is misused on "submersion," also known as "sink-or-swim," models (Cummins, 1981).

Dual-language programs are an adaptation of the French Immersion Model from Canada. In dual-language programs, English-speaking students are immersed in the minority language (Spanish) alongside native speakers. Instruction in literacy as well as content areas is in the minority language for the first three years. English is gradually introduced (Lindholm, 1990). This approach has proven successful at grounding minority language students in content area concepts in their own language as well as preparing them to move into English in the intermediate grades. Majority language students appear to do as well as or better than their peers in English-only programs in both literacy and content area work (Lindholm, 1990).

A team-teaching model is often used in bilingual programs where monolingual English-speaking teachers are incorporated into the program, providing a majority-language as well as a minority-language model for students. In these models, content area subjects may be taught in the students' dominant language or may vary according to the topic. Team teaching may also be used to allow teachers to build their strength in one or two subject areas rather than teach all subjects in the elementary schools. One teacher might teach all the science, another all the social studies. Or, a modified teaming approach may be used that allows flexibility for teachers to move between homogeneous and mixed language grouping. For example, three teachers might teach a unit on geology. One teacher might focus on plate tectonics, and a short lecture or movie may require homogeneous language grouping. Students may then be heterogeneously grouped to build volcanoes or make plaster-of-paris fossils and process the learning from the direct teaching experience.

A concurrent approach is still utilized in some bilingual classrooms. This is basically translating back and forth between the two languages. The purpose of this kind of instruction is to keep all students involved. The drawback to this model is that students tend to listen only to their dominant language and so are not encouraged to build their second language. In addition, it can be tedious to bilingual students to hear everything twice.

A preview-review approach may also be used in content area instruction. A lesson is previewed in one language. The introduction—an explanation of what is going to be taught—is given in language "A." Then the lesson itself is conducted in language "B." Then the lesson is discussed and comprehension checks are done in language "A" to be sure that all students understand what is being taught. This pattern may be consistent with language "B" always being the language of instruction, or it may switch back and forth as in the alternate day/week model.

When bilingual staff is not available in the language of the child, there are a number of models used by schools. Whatever the model, some form of a "Sheltered English" approach is generally followed. Sheltered English is a form of instruction all in English that relies on the following strategies to create comprehensible input for students acquiring English: (a) Speech is modified by using shorter, less complex sentences, slowing the pace, and using nonverbal cues such as gestures and facial expressions or repetition and paraphrasing to convey meaning. (b) Visuals including props, pictures, projected images, etc., are used with specific pointing to provide a clear reference. The drawback to Sheltered English is that often the name is used where the principles are not applied. When the principles are applied, it is sometimes a watered-down approach to the content, so that students acquiring English are not gaining the academic skills and knowledge to succeed.

Essential Elements of Content Area Instruction

Whatever the configuration of students or the program models used for teaching students acquiring English, there are a number of elements of content area instruction that will provide effective instruction for students acquiring English. Integrated throughout all of these principles must be a linguistic and cultural sensitivity toward the student, subtle focus on language strategies when appropriate, and alternative means of expression. Incorporating the following elements into instruction will make content area classes more effective for students acquiring English.

(1) Curriculum is grounded in the knowledge and experience the student brings to the classroom (Díaz, Moll, & Mehan, 1986; Heath, 1983; Maria, 1989). It is important to find out what the student knows about the topic and find some bridge to connect the curriculum to his/her life. (2) Organizational strategies are provided, tools that fit a concept into the bigger picture as well as organize bits of information within the context of the topic (Calfee, 1981; Hernández, 1989). (3) Acquisition of academic language is facilitated by focusing on new vocabulary and concepts and providing interaction with the language and concepts in relaxed, informal ways. Let students learn from each other (Reyes, 1991; Hudelson, 1989). (4) Synthesis of new information occurs right after processing, and reporting or sharing is encouraged through a variety of modes of expression. It doesn't have to be a written report. (5) Students reflect on the process of how they learned as well as on what they learned. This will increase the probability of transfer of the learning to new situations.

All pieces are interwoven in effective instruction. Interaction, for example, can be involved in all phases of instruction. Organizational tools are utilized at every level of the process but are given a separate section in this text to emphasize the variety of tools available. Suggestions for supporting language development and alternative modes of expression are woven throughout the text. The following matrix exemplifies how the interweaving of the elements occurs throughout the instructional process.

FIGURE 1

Sources of Information	Language Support	Tools of Organization	Expression, Presentation
Connections Where do students get the information they bring to school? Parents, community	Visuals, props, gestures	Diagram of a chain of events in the learning process	Quick-write Pair share
Interaction Break up information: Cooperative groups Paired work Collaborative work	Shorter text, labeled props, mixed language groups	Assigned student roles	Checklist of group interaction Sharing group procedures
Synthesis Explain charts Analysis of information Report back within group	Word lists: transitions comparatives	Hierarchy, student-made pictures	Posters, skits, explain pictures Write-up of work
Reflection Rethinking the process of how we learned what we know	Sentence frames: We used to think…but now we know… Transition terms: *first, then, finally*	Venn diagram	Groups share thinking processes and process of accomplishing tasks with the class

Making Connections— Building Background

On my first day of chemistry in high school I sat memorizing the chart of chemical elements. As soon as I learned five, I would forget three of them. I remember thinking, "What does this have to do with my life?" If anyone had informed me that chemistry can explain how bread rises, or meat tenderizes, or how plastic is made, I would have been fascinated. As it was, I dropped chemistry. This is what happens to many students acquiring English, with school in general,

and particularly with science, social studies, and math. They have no sense of how these topics fit into their lives. Combined with the challenging language, the motivation is often not strong enough to succeed.

In introducing a topic we need to bring out what students know about that topic. "If there is a gap, teachers should avoid the temptation to fill it by simply supplying the information; background knowledge cannot simply be presented to children who lack it, although this may seem efficient" (Maria, 1989, p. 299). There are a variety of ways to bridge the gap. Some people start with a large sheet of butcher paper on which they write, "What do you know? What do

you want to know?" Others create a semantic map with the topic in the middle, having students brainstorm about the topic (Pearson & Johnson, 1978). A five-minute "quick-write" is a way to have students think about what they know. Students acquiring English may write in their own language or pair with another student to write in English. A "think-pair-share" encourages students to think quietly for a short time, then pair with a peer and talk, and paraphrase and share what their peer said (Kagan, 1989). Sometimes this knowledge check will demonstrate that more background building is necessary before students can get involved in a topic.

In social studies some concepts are rather vague for students. For example, "discrimination" or "majority rule" may need to be experienced before a discussion can take place to draw out a student's prior knowledge or experience. A simulation, where students actually experience the concept briefly (Hernández, 1989), can provide such experience. Giving real experiences through field trips or hands-on activities is another way to connect children's experience with new concepts. Narrative text— stories, biographies, historical fiction, etc.— can also bridge the distance between personal experience and historical events or even scientific concepts (Wong & Calfee, 1988).

If the selection of topics to be studied is negotiated with students, they can choose topics that have inherent interest for them. When students are involved in choosing topics that relate to their lives, they will be able to engage in their own forms of social science or ethnographic research on the topic.

In *Ways with Words*, Heath (1983) describes a science class of fifth graders (mainly African American boys reading below the second-grade level) who became ethnographers researching local folk theories and methods of agriculture. Students were told to find at least two sources of information, one oral and one written, to validate their work. They interviewed community people, read newspapers, and so on, to gain information about agriculture in their community.

Learners in this science classroom had become ethnographers of a sort; in so doing, they had improved their knowledge of science. In addition, they had learned to talk about ways of obtaining and verifying information; terms such as *sources, check out* (the sense of *verify*), *summarize*, and *translate* had become part of their vocabulary. They had come to recognize, use, and produce knowledge about the skills of inquiring, compiling, sorting, and refining information. They had not only made use of inquiry and discovery method skills discussed in science and social studies methods texts; they had acquired the language to talk about these skills. (Heath, p. 320)

A group of Latino students in Arizona were introduced to social science inquiry techniques (Díaz, Moll, & Mehan, 1986) when they created their own surveys to inquire about the language attitudes and practices of people in their community. They used the information they found as a basis for writing expository text. Their ownership of the writing project was evident from their choice of topic, creation of interviews, and feedback from the community. Writing became a meaningful activity.

When students become ethnographers within their own community, they bridge the gap between home and school. Their learning validates and integrates both home life and academic life. Academic skills are learned incidentally amidst involvement in the project. Ethnographic work can begin as simply as making homework assignments relate a topic to the home. In math, for instance, when children are first learning multiplication or division, they can interview family and community members to find out when these skills are used in their home or community. This information can be used to create word problems that come out of their own lives—using names of people they know, involving happenings in their own community. In social studies, when a particular aspect of history is studied, students can find out where their parents, relatives, or ancestors were and what they might have been doing during the time the event took place. Particularly when studying broad concepts such as liberty, injustice, and freedom, students will ground their knowledge by discovering what these terms mean to their own families. This kind of ethnographic work can be done on a daily basis and enrich class discussions to the benefit and sometimes enlightenment of all students as well as teachers; at the same time the content becomes grounded in the students' life. In addition, students learn to formulate questions, validate sources, organize information, and express that information through writing or explaining what they learned.

Creating these connections between what students bring to the learning and the new learning allows students to begin to construct conceptual understandings, which then become the basis for the inquiry work. According to the Conceptual Change Perspective of Science, which grew out of cognitive science studies of learning and knowing in knowledge-rich domains:

This web of knowledge, or the individual's conceptual ecology (Posner et al., 1982), only becomes useful and meaningful to students when it is integrated with the learner's own personal knowledge and experiences with natural phenomena. Students come to science classes with many ideas and explanations about natural phenomena. Their ideas are experience-based and often stand in stark contrast to the scientific explanations studied in school. A central goal of science teaching is to help students change their intuitive, everyday ways of explaining the world around them—to incorporate scientific concepts and ways of thinking into their personal frameworks. (Roth, 1989, p. 19)

Organizational Structures and Tools

To avoid the feeling of having entered in the middle of a movie when a new topic is introduced, it is important to put topics in a larger context so they can be seen as part of the whole. If it is a historical event, it needs to be placed in its chronological or social context. If it's a scientific experiment, its evolution or application needs to be under-

stood. In addition, some way of breaking down the topic or organizing the information for comparison or understanding will improve comprehension. Schema building is a powerful verbal learning tactic (Derry, 1988). Schema building is done by showing organizational structures through diagrams known as "graphic organizers" to organize thinking as well as reading and writing. The following graphic organizers can be used successfully from kindergarten onward. They can be introduced as whole-class activities, incorporated into small group work, and later used by pairs and individuals for organizing information.

A *semantic map* (Pearson & Johnson, 1978), as described earlier, is a simple way for students to brainstorm ideas in a group or on their own. Brainstorming can begin as a whole-class project, with small groups or partners adding to the semantic map as new ideas occur. Other organizational tools can then be introduced to work from the semantic map or to organize information from texts.

A *matrix* is a powerful organizing tool to make comparisons. A matrix is often the format of tables in social studies books. Students acquiring English may need help as to how to read the tables. Practice creating prose out of the tables by reading across as a group. Writing down the words needed to make sense of the tables will help students acquiring English. It allows students to see relationships between aspects of a topic. It also is an excellent way to build vocabulary around a topic. As the matrix is used to compare or contrast, finer distinctions are made in word meanings, and the topic gives the student a "mental file folder" in which to store this new vocabulary. Any matrix of different peoples, for example, might list elements of culture across the top for comparison (see Figure 2) and list the different cultures being studied down the side.

In science this same matrix can be used to compare attributes of different plants or animal species. Students can bring in fruits, vegetables, leaves, or other plants. As a group the class can brainstorm the most salient

FIGURE 2 - *Matrix*

Regional Group	Housing & Shelter	Food Source	Clothing	Tools
Plains Indians	Tepees	Buffalo	Deerskin Buffalo robes	Bows and arrows Travois and stone knives
Coastal Indians	Tule Huts	Seafood, acorns, berries	As needed, deerskin, rush skirts, and rabbit capes	Baskets, grinding stones
Southwestern Indians	Pueblos Adobe	Fry bread Corn and other vegetables	As needed, skins, blankets, and other adornments	Baskets, pots, dig sticks, grinding stones

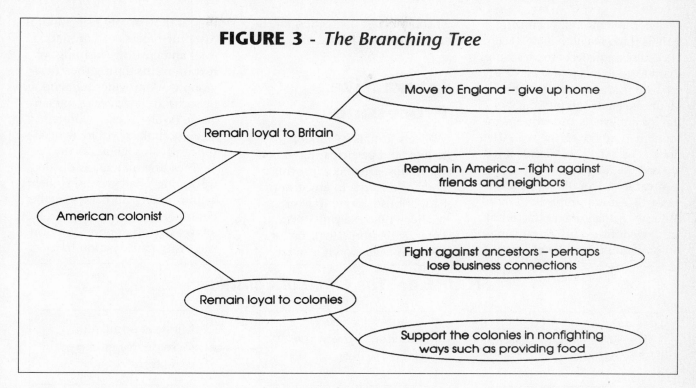

FIGURE 3 - *The Branching Tree*

- American colonist
  - Remain loyal to Britain
    - Move to England – give up home
    - Remain in America – fight against friends and neighbors
  - Remain loyal to colonies
    - Fight against ancestors – perhaps lose business connections
    - Support the colonies in nonfighting ways such as providing food

attributes (e.g., have seeds, grow above ground). The possible attributes can be listed across the top, and the names of the fruits (or other objects) can be placed down the side. Students can then decide which categories fit each of the fruits and place an *x* for the ones that work. As they work together they are not only building labels for the objects but the aspects of each object as well. In math the matrix is very powerful in solving logic problems. This is a simple tool for problem solving that is often not taught until a student is studying for college placement exams. It can easily be used with third or fourth graders in cooperative groups.

Venn diagrams are very useful in comparing any two things, groups, different points of view, different books, or different objects. The two overlapping circles allow a student to see readily what is different about each group, and where the overlap occurs is what is the same about them.

A *branching tree* (Figure 3) is another important structure for helping students problem-solve as well as for understanding how certain kinds of text are organized (Calfee, 1981). A branching tree begins where "two roads diverge in a yellow wood" or at any point of two possible choices. It then branches out into the consequences of either of those choices. In studying the American Revolution, for example, you could discuss what the dilemma might have been for a colonist—stay with England or become independent. Then look at what might have been the consequences of each of those decisions and which might bring up a new dilemma. For example, loyalists might want to return to England or fight against their neighbors.

The branching tree is a tool that students can use in thinking through decisions in their own lives, such as involvement in drugs, staying in school, etc. In addition to being a powerful problem-solving tool, it can be a useful linguistic tool for helping students utilize and understand complex grammar related to their lives. If a student draws a branching tree of a decision from his/her own life, even using simple pictures rather than words to convey the dilemma, a discussion can ensue and the student will have the opportunity to learn to express such experiences in sophisticated grammar, e.g., "If I had gone with that gang, I would have been arrested." Moving from prose to a diagram such as the branching tree and back to prose again is useful in organizing and thinking through ideas as well as building language skills.

Another powerful organizing tool is the *chain of causality* (Figure 4). Cause and effect are sometimes hard for students to discuss or to pick up in their reading. If students are guided to pick out important events and write them in sequenced boxes, they can then look at each box and decide if it caused the following event. Did "A" cause "B," or did it just precede "B"? It is a simple but powerful way to analyze both historical and scientific events. Organizing information from a text helps to

of content area instruction for students acquiring English.

Interactive Processing

We learn to talk by talking, listening, and participating in conversations. There is a growing body of research to attest to the benefit of small-group work (Cohen, 1986; Kagan, 1989; Lotan & Benton, 1990; Taylor, 1982). If a classroom is quiet,

than if they simply read about it. Also, the process of negotiating roles and creating meanings of text or events during theatrical group work provides tremendous opportunity for developing language (Wolfe, 1992). Content area vocabulary will increase significantly in such a process.

If reading material is divided up among small groups, students acquiring English have a smaller chunk of text to read. This allows a greater opportunity for successful participation in the

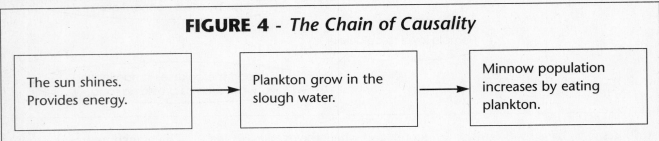

FIGURE 4 - *The Chain of Causality*

organize our thinking. Organized thinking leads to organized writing. This chain of causality can become a lifelong skill for student growth.

In addition to helping in the background-building, connection-making stage of a lesson and the processing of information, organizing structures can help keep groups on task and provide an easy means for a group to divide up a chore. If a group decides a matrix will best organize the information, each student may be responsible for one of the rows or one of the columns on the matrix. When it is time to report back information, the organizing structure can be used to help organize the report or provide the notes to talk from. Working in groups is facilitated by the use of organizational tools, and such interactive processing is an important aspect

students are not developing language. On the other hand, noise alone does not mean that students are acquiring language and concepts as effectively as possible. Creating experiences for students to interact in constructive ways is essential for content area classrooms where students are acquiring language (Reyes, 1991; Hudelson, 1989). Interaction may be with the whole group, small heterogeneous groups (homogeneous groups may be beneficial for limited purposes), pairing of students, or mixing with other classes or community members. The interaction must be planned and facilitated with students' language abilities and growth in mind.

Students working in small groups to produce skits or plays to portray a historical event will remember more of the content

group and greater potential for learning the content, for example, if a chapter on the American colonies is divided up assigning one colony to each group to create a skit or mural or poster for the class. All students spend less time plowing through text and more time negotiating, analyzing, and synthesizing information to share with the class. The productions by each group give the whole class access to the content. Nothing is lost, and a great deal of participation, language, and concept development is gained. In a study done on nine bilingual classrooms, grades two through four, looking at cooperative groups using a math/science program, Cohen found:

> Talking and working together clearly has favorable effects on learning, especially conceptual

learning. In this study, children who were seen as highly problematic by their teachers showed excellent learning gains. The sharpest learning gains were made by fully bilingual children and by developmentally precocious children whose pretest scores were below the state norms on CTBS. (Cohen, 1984, p. 186)

Cohen also cautioned against the negative effects of heterogeneous grouping without teacher intervention. Status characteristics present in the class at large come into play in any group: "Higher status students will have higher rates of participation and influence" (1984, p. 186). Cohen suggests that status characteristics in the class will be played out in the group. Status may be attributed to attractiveness, reading ability, athletic ability, race, gender, etc. She notes that teachers can mitigate these effects or actually change the status of members of the class through a variety of strategies.

Strategies for mitigating status might include choosing the lower-status students to be trained on certain aspects of a task or to be given certain responsibilities that carry status. It might also mean choosing topics or tasks for which lower-status students would have greater knowledge or expertise. For example, if Southeast Asian students seem to have lower status in the class, then studying Southeast Asia or some aspect of that culture will give these students the opportunity to be the experts. If Hispanic girls seem to have lower status in math activities, then train them on the use of a new manipulative and have them train their groups. (For

more suggestions on creating successful groups, see *Designing Groupwork*, Cohen, 1986.)

Interaction doesn't have to mean groups. Heterogeneous pairs of students can work effectively together on a project learning to negotiate plans and meanings. My fourth and fifth graders planned trips across the country. They were given a budget and the task of planning a two-week trip. Their job was to decide where they were going each day, and how much they would spend on food, transportation, lodging, and activities. They plotted the trip on maps, calculated gas mileage, researched points of interest, and drew pictures of what they would see. At one point two boys came running back from the office where they had gone to call a travel agent: "Guess what! There's a special to Arizona; we can go round-trip for under $200." These boys were so engaged in their project that it had become real to them. One of these boys researched in English, the other in Spanish. They pooled their information and created a report that they gave in both Spanish and English.

Whether group work is done in a large group, small groups, or pairs, it is important that students analyze their findings and pull them together to report information back to the larger group. The analysis and synthesis of an activity is what makes the difference between "fun activities" and "fun learning experiences."

Synthesize the Content: What Did We Learn?

I once taught a unit on African folktales. We had done extensive background building on Africa and its peoples. After reading eight different folktales, in the midst of producing plays or stick puppet theater on four of the tales, I asked the class one day in a quick-write to tell me what a folktale was. I realized from their responses that they didn't have a clue beyond its being a story. I was expecting them to distill the essence of folktales from reading and participating in them. They clearly weren't capable of doing this without some tools.

The purpose of synthesis is to think through the content that has been digested and make some sense out of it, see the patterns, find what it adds to our understanding of the world, and how it changes our conceptual understandings (Roth, 1989). This may be done by a group, in pairs, or individually. However it is done, students will need specific tools and guidance to get started. In a study of four classrooms teaching a six-to-eight-week unit on photosynthesis, which consisted mainly of interactive activities, "eighty-nine percent of the students in the study failed to grasp the central concept of the unit: that plants get their energy-containing food only by making it internally out of carbon dioxide and water" (Roth, Smith, & Anderson, 1983, in Roth, 1989, p. 19).

To remedy this dilemma in our folktales unit we brainstormed what these stories seemed to have in common. After some discussion (and extensive thinking and rereading) we came up with a list of elements we thought they had in common: (a) They came from oral traditions in different parts of Africa; (b) They had characters who acted like people; (c) They had a moral or message; (d) They gave us some information about the people who created the story (we decided to call this world view); (e) They were entertaining.

We created a matrix with these elements across the top and the stories we had read down the side. We started with the stories being performed, and each of the four groups analyzed the story they were performing. Working in pairs within the groups, students drew a picture and wrote a paragraph explaining how a particular characteristic was true for their play. For example, one student wrote: "We learn from the folktale of 'Anansi and the Spiders' that stories are very important to the people of Africa and that stories are for everyone not just one person." The pictures and paragraphs were pasted onto a large wall matrix. We then could compare both across stories and across elements to validate our explanation of African folktales. In addition, the students shared the characteristics of their story orally when they introduced the performance of the play or puppet show.

We analyzed more stories for our matrix. The students then wrote their first essay on what folktales were. They were encouraged to use their fellow students' work on the matrix as sources.

We practiced how to turn the elements listed at the top into topic sentences and how to provide support for the topic sentence by choosing examples from several different folktales. I posted lists of transition phrases such as "for example," "in addition," and "finally" on the wall, and we practiced how to use them in an essay. All students acquiring English (after six months in English reading) were able to write excellent three-to-four-page essays on "Why you should read folktales" or "What folktales are." This is the kind of scaffolded expository writing that builds success in second language writers.

Another way to scaffold writing for purposes of synthesis is to help students use available formats to synthesize their information. There are a number of repetitive formats in "patterned stories" that allow students to pick up the pattern and imitate it in their own writing. Using well-written trade books as models of writing can get a reluctant writer started. An example of a simple format that can help students conceptualize their ideas is the English folktale, "The House That Jack Built." There are many popular versions of this story. The simplest one I have heard is as follows:

> This is the house that Jack built. This is the cheese that stayed in the house that Jack built. This is the rat that ate the cheese that stayed in the house that Jack built. [The story continues until the last line sums up the entire story.] This is the priest that married the boy and the girl, the boy that kissed the girl that milked the cow that tossed the dog that chased the cat that caught the rat that ate the cheese that stayed in the house that Jack built.

This story format has been used by many teachers over the years in both social studies and science. The following is an example of how a fourth-grade class used the format to recount their scientific knowledge and observations on a field trip to a nearby slough area. I will share just the last line which sums up the pattern story, "The Sun That Shines on Elkhorn Slough":

> This is the sun that shines on the great hawk that grasped the little rabbit that nibbled the grass that grew in the dirt that formed with the help of micro-organisms, the micro-organisms that decomposed the dead seal that floated past the leopard shark that swallowed the minnows that ate the plankton that get energy from the sun that shines on Elkhorn Slough. (Alianza Bilingual School, Ms. Petritz)

This kind of synthesis of content provides a product that all students can take home with them and share with their families. Another way to synthesize content that also provides a great language learning opportunity is to create a "museum" or "fair" to show off the learning that students have done. Students can work in pairs or groups to gather artifacts of an era or to create science experiments or solve complex applied math problems. Once everything has been gathered and studied, students can create a short talk to share with students from other classes as they wander through the museum or fair to see the display. This allows students to practice their short speech for a purpose and repeat it over several times for different classes. The elevated adrenaline of performance and repetition ingrain the speech in the long-term memory.

Over the years I have observed many teachers doing exciting and interesting group activities. Unfortunately, the synthesis needed to move from an exciting activity to a learning experience is often lacking. Students need the tools to organize the information gained from their activities and to synthesize this information. Graphic organizers and adaptable formats help students to bring together the information they are learning and to process it in such a way that they can make sense out of it.

Reflecting on the Process

Reflection on the process, on how we learned what we learned, can be done in journals, diaries, or five-minute quick-writes (students write everything they can think of in a five-minute period without worrying about punctuation and spelling). It can also be done by students sharing their products with another class and explaining to the class the process by which the product came about. The importance of this step is that it provides the metacognitive understanding of the process. Metacognition, or knowing what we know and how we know it, helps us to transfer knowledge to new situations.

To continue the example of the essays on African folktales, when the essays were written

students were so proud of them (and so were we) that we decided they should share them in other classes. They were practice-reading the essays when someone stopped by and asked how they had done such wonderful work. To my chagrin none of them could explain the process. I realized that if they didn't remember how they had done it, they would not be able to do it again. We discussed this problem and decided that rather than just read their essays, they would take the matrix to other classes and explain, step by step, how they had written the essays. (Now we had a purpose for going back over the process.)

We spent several class periods going back over the steps and practicing how to share these steps with another class. They then went off as teachers to explain expository essay writing using a matrix as an organizing tool to the other fourth and fifth grades. This served not only as reflection and metacognition on their part, but also as staff development for other teachers and the introduction of a process to other students. It was well worth the extra few days spent to finish off the unit.

The reflective process can take a variety of forms. Quick-writes about a problem-solving process provide fast feedback as to what students remember about the process. Student math journals provide an excellent opportunity for individuals to write about how their cooperative group solved a particular math problem. A math journal is kept by students after their problem solving to reflect on the process and

experience of what they have done. They are encouraged to draw pictures of the problem and write step by step how it was solved. A class journal or log of an ongoing science project can be kept to see what each "scientist" has observed or what procedures were performed on the project. Having one group share its process with another group or having pairs form into groups of four to share how a problem was solved or which procedures were used on a science experiment are alternatives for providing reflection on the process.

There is always the lament, "There's not enough time to do all this," but time can be divided in many ways. Language arts can be combined with content areas to allow more time to spend on synthesis and reflection (which are language arts). Time for students acquiring English can be wasted trying to cover too many topics, read too much material, and move on too quickly. Limiting the number of topics covered and dividing material to be shared in highly engaging interactive activities that culminate with synthesis of the content learned and reflection on the process will be much more cost-effective in terms of time spent.

In Summary

There are many ways to approach the teaching of content to students acquiring English. It is preferable to provide instruction in the primary language as well as in English, and there are a variety of models to be adapted for that purpose that should be determined by the characteristics of students as well as the availability of staff. Whatever program model is chosen, there are basic elements of effective content area instruction that are summarized in the following checklist to help teachers and administrators think through content area lesson planning.

■ **Connections**
How have students been involved in the selection of topics? Will the number of topics allow in-depth study? Have students contributed as sources of knowledge on the topic? Are context and necessary background developed?

■ **Organizational Tools**
Do students have the big picture, where the topic fits in the whole? Have we broken the topic into sizable chunks to study? Are students able to utilize a graphic organizer to make sense of information from a variety of sources? Can students move from the text to the graphic organizer and from the graphic organizer to prose?

■ **Interactive Processing**
Are students talking and interacting with peers most of the time? Do we utilize a variety of effective grouping strategies? Does status within the group vary and do all students participate in the groups?

■ **Synthesis of Content**
Have students discussed and expressed what they learned? Have there been alternative ways to express the learning?

■ **Reflection on the Strategies and the Processing**
Have students reflected on how they accomplished their goals? Can they apply their learning process in a new situation?

REFERENCES

Calfee, R. (1981). *The book.* Unpublished Project READ training manual. Stanford University.

Cohen, E. G. (1986). *Designing group-work: Strategies for the heterogeneous classroom.* New York: Teachers College Press, Columbia University.

Cohen, E. G. (1984). Talking and working together: Status, interaction and learning. In Peterson, P., Wilkinson, L. C., and Hallinan, M. (Eds.), *The social context of instruction.* New York: Academic Press.

Cummins, J. (1981). The role of primary language development in promoting educational success for language minority students. In *Schooling and language minority students: A theoretical framework.* Los Angeles: California State University; Evaluation, Dissemination and Assessment Center.

Derry, S. (1988, January). Putting learning strategies to work. *Educational Leadership.*

Díaz, S., Moll, L., and Mehan, H. (1986). Sociocultural resources in instruction: A context-specific approach. In *Beyond language: social and cultural factors in schooling language minority students*, developed by Bilingual Education Office, California State Department of Education. Los Angeles: California State University; Evaluation, Dissemination and Assessment Center.

Heath, S. (1983). *Ways with words.* Cambridge University Press.

Hernández, H. (1989) Development of a multicultural curriculum. In *Multicultural education: A teacher's guide to content and process.* Columbus, OH: Merrill Publishing Company.

Hudelson, S. (1989). Teaching English through content-area activities. In Riggs, P., and Allen, V. G. (Eds.), *When they don't all speak English.* National Council of Teachers of English.

Kagan, S. (1989). *Cooperative learning resources for teachers.* San Juan Capistrano, CA: Resources for Teachers.

Lindholm, K. (1990, December). *Promoting bilingualism and academic achievement among English and Spanish speaking children.* Unpublished paper presented at Stanford University.

Lotan, R., and Benton, J. (1990). Finding out about complex instruction: Teaching math and science in heterogeneous classrooms. In Davidson, N. (Ed.), *Cooperative learning in mathematics: A handbook for teachers.* Menlo Park, CA: Addison-Wesley.

Maria, K. (1989, January). Developing disadvantaged children's background knowledge interactively. *The Reading Teacher.*

Moran, C., and Calfee, R. C. (in press). Comprehending orthography: Social construction of letter-sound systems in monolingual and bilingual programs. *Reading and Writing: An Interdisciplinary Journal.*

Peal, E., and Lambert, W. E. (1962). The relation to bilingualism and intelligence. *Psychological Monographs: General and Applied,* vol. 76 (Nov. 27), no. 564.

Pearson, P. D., and Johnson, D. (1978). *Teaching reading comprehension.* New York: Holt, Rinehart and Winston.

Posner, G. J., Strike, K. A., Hewson, P. W., and Gertzog, W. A. (1982). Accommodation of a scientific conception: Toward a theory of conceptual change. In *Science Education, 66* (2), pp. 211–227.

Reyes, M. (1991). Instructional strategies for second-language learners in the content areas. *Journal of Reading,* vol. 35, no. 2.

Roth, K. (1989, Winter). Science education: It's not enough to "do" or "relate." *American Educator.*

Swain, M., and Lapkin, S. (1991). Additive bilingualism and French immersion education: The roles of language proficiency and literacy. In Reynolds, A. G. (Ed.), *Bilingualism, multiculturalism, and second language learning.* The McGill Conference in Honor of Wallace E. Lambert. Hillsdale, NJ: Lawrence Erlbaum.

Taylor, B. P. (1982). In search of real reality. *TESOL Quarterly,* vol. 16, no. 1.

Wolfe, S. (1992). *Learning to act/acting to learn: Language and learning in the theatre or the classroom.* Unpublished doctoral dissertation, Stanford University.

Wong, I., and Calfee, R. (1988). *Trade books: A viable supplement to textbooks in earth science.* Paper presented at AERA, New Orleans.

Literacy and Science: Connections for English Language Learners

Sally Blake, Sandra Rollins Hurley, and Josefina V. Tinajero
The University of Texas at El Paso

The United States has drastically changed as technology has become ingrained in all aspects of life. There are fewer unskilled, high-paying jobs available to those without technical preparation. Projections indicate that after the year 2000 one-third of new entrants to the work force will be citizens and immigrants from minority groups, many of whom are second language learners (Clark, 1996). We know that in order for individuals to enter careers in science, they must have opportunities to learn science, they must achieve in science, and they must make the decision to enter science-related careers (Oaks, 1990). However, science education in the United States finds itself in a state of crisis concerning the underrepresentation and underachievement of minority group members, particularly those who are also second language learners. Schools face the challenging responsibility of reversing these trends. Part of the answer lies in the preparation of teachers skilled in providing all students with a rich intellectual diet based on best practices and high academic standards.

This article begins with a demographic overview of the United States and a discussion of how those demographics are reflected in science. Contextualized within these demographic realities is a discussion of the movement toward standards-based teaching and learning in science and literacy and some implications for teachers of English language learners (ELLs). Subsequently we demonstrate ways to make connections and support student learning through integrated inquiry by considering cognitive learning research. The article concludes with a sample multilevel integrated inquiry project that supports both content and concept development and language acquisition.

English Language Learners and Science Education

Students from designated minority groups (e.g., Hispanic American, African American, Native American) are seriously underrepresented at every level of science, from the elementary school science student to the professional scientist. Hundreds of reports on science and mathematics education have been issued, almost all of which reveal a serious underrepresentation of minority group students in the fields of mathematics and science (American Council on Education, 1988; Ayers et al., 1992; National Science Foundation, 1997, 1996a, 1996b, 1996c, 1994). According to the National Science Foundation (1994), racial and ethnic minorities constitute 20 percent of the total population but only 8 percent of the science and engineering labor force. In 1990 Latinos constituted only 3.1 percent of the science and engineering work force. Currently, Latinos make up 11 percent of the college-age population but earn less than 5 percent of science and engineering degrees. Underrepresentation in science is also evident in the number of professionals who are minority group members and serve as science faculty members.

Elementary teachers provide the first socialized experiences in science for all students in the United States. They may be the key that unlocks the science barrier in American schools. At least 50 percent of U. S. teachers will have one or more English language learners in their classes at some point in their careers; however, most receive little or no preparation in working with students whose first language is not English (McKeon, 1994). This occurs despite the fact that most students acquiring English as a second language spend the majority of their time in mainstream classrooms; thus, the responsibility for their education is largely up to mainstream teachers (Anstrom, 1998). The underrepresentation and underachievement of minority group students in science can be traced in part to these early school experiences. Lack of preparation in science among linguistic and cultural minority students in the elementary grades determines, in large part, their enrollment and success in secondary-level school programs and, ultimately, in college and career choices later in life (Clark, 1996). It is no surprise, therefore, that low numbers of students from linguistic and cultural minority groups experience the level of success in science and mathematics in school that would encourage them to seek higher education and careers in science or technology.

Science and Literacy: Making the Connections for English Language Learners

Language is more than the means by which thoughts are shared between human beings. Vygotsky (1984) suggested that the primary function of language is social, to communicate meaning from one person to another. Language is also a learning tool because it helps us construct meaning for ourselves through social interaction. Current research supports the acknowledgment of prior experiences of all students, including second language learners within their subject matter settings: "Children want to be a part of their new cultural and linguistic setting without having to cast aside the cultural heritage that gives structure and meaning to their lives" (Tinajero, 1997a, p. T21). Because thought and language are so closely connected, building on children's cultural heritage gives structure and meaning to science and literacy learning. We use language to help us remember; to find and construct knowledge; to organize our ideas; to make what we know more precise by reorganizing, transforming, and interpreting facts; and to apply what we know to new situations (Fisher & Terry, 1990). Language is what makes it possible to associate facts with concepts and ideas. For example, a child may be able to "decode" a word like *caterpillar*, but if the child has no concept of what a caterpillar is, the word is without meaning. The youngster who sees the word *caterpillar* has difficulty talking about it without knowledge of a fuzzy, multilegged insect.

The use of the integrated inquiry approach is one way for teachers to help children associate facts with concepts and ideas. Integrated inquiry can give children an opportunity to explore languages while exploring the world and can help them build on their existing knowledge. Looking at pictures and videotapes and handling caterpillars, cocoons, moths, and butterflies during an integrated inquiry project centered on life cycles, for example, will enable children to learn concepts and vocabulary within a meaningful context (Hurley & Blake, 1997).

Literacy processes are the root system for growth in science: they are the symbolic means by which science content is conveyed by students and teachers. There is a solid research base indicating that people learn language when they are in real situations where communication is valued (De la Cruz, 1998). Integrated inquiry in science encourages students to use language to learn and to communicate. The scientific paradigm provides an opportunity for a variety of oral and written language uses crucial for optimal language and literacy development. It also provides opportunities for asking questions, gathering and interpreting data, and explaining findings. Through science activities, students investigate, gather, organize, analyze, and evaluate information—skills vital to literacy development. These activities are congruent with national standards and are based on best instructional practices derived from brain research and learning psychology.

Standards-Based Teaching and Learning for All Students

Over the past decade, educators have moved toward standards-based curricula. This movement to establish what children should know and should be able to do at particular benchmark grade levels is designed to raise expectations and achievement. However, educators must simultaneously develop pedagogical methods to enable all children, including those learning English as a second language, to reach the standards. Science education standards have been articulated by the National Research Council (1996) and the American Association for the Advancement of Science (1993). Literacy standards have been articulated by the National Center for Education and the Economy (1999), and the Standards for the English Language Arts (1996) have been developed by the International Reading Association and the National Council of Teachers of English.

The National Science Education Standards (NRC, 1996) are based on seven principles, the first three of which directly address equity issues for linguistic and cultural minority students in science education:

- All students, regardless of gender, cultural or ethnic background, physical or learning disabilities, aspirations, or interest and motivation in science, should have the opportunity to attain higher levels of scientific literacy than they do currently.

- All students will learn science in the content standards.

- All students will develop science knowledge as defined in the content standards and an understanding of science that enables them to use their knowledge as it relates to scientific, personal, social, and historical perspectives.

Science and technology today demand higher levels of literacy than were needed by previous generations. Prior to World War I, persons were deemed literate by the U. S. Census Bureau if they could read a simple sentence and write their own name. However, the National Literacy Act of 1991 defines *literacy* as the "ability to read, write, and speak in English and compute and solve problems at levels of proficiency necessary to function on the job and in society, to achieve one's goals, and to develop one's knowledge and potential." The implications of changing literacy demands are clear, and the implications for educators of second language learners are profound. Issues of access to science, technology, literacy education, and equity for all learners are serious and cannot be ignored if all children are to have opportunities to succeed.

The national literacy standards focus explicitly on the needs of second language learners.

- Standard 9. Students develop an understanding of and respect for diversity in language use, patterns, and dialects across cultures, ethnic groups, geographic regions, and social roles.

- Standard 10. Students whose first language is not English make use of their first language to develop competency in the English language arts and to develop understanding of content across the curriculum.

Another focus of the standards is to give students the tools to comprehend, interpret, evaluate, and appreciate a wide range of texts. When science, literacy, and second language learning are taught through integrated inquiry, it is much easier for educators to help *all* students achieve at the high levels established by national standards. The three language arts standards listed below are natural to integrate with the science standards.

- Standard 4. Students adjust their use of spoken, written, and visual language (e.g. conventions, style, vocabulary) to communicate effectively with a variety of audiences and for different purposes.

- Standard 7. Students conduct research on issues and interests by generating ideas and questions and by posing problems. They gather, evaluate, and synthesize data from a variety of sources (e.g., print and nonprint text, artifacts, people) to communicate their discoveries in ways that suit their purpose and audience.

- Standard 8. Students use a variety of technological and informational resources (e.g., libraries, databases, computer networks, video) to gather and synthesize information and to create and communicate knowledge.

Standards and the Opportunity for ELLs to Achieve Them

According to August (1994), language minority students can greatly benefit from the movement toward higher standards for all. Setting high expectations for all children could further the cause of educational equity. August maintains that

> all too often, the goal is frustrated by a myopic focus on English acquisition, to the virtual exclusion of other subjects. To break the self-perpetuating cycle of low expectations and academic failure, [ELL] children must be provided access to challenging content while they are acquiring English. For children who face language barriers to achieve high standards, schooling must be tailored to their strengths and needs. (p. 6)

Salient among the recommendations by August on how content can be most effectively taught to ELLs are the following: (1) incorporate the cultural background and life experiences of students; (2) provide high-quality instruction; and (3) establish a multifaceted approach to enhancing opportunities to learn with provisions to ensure that the unique educational needs of ELLs are met. The use of integrated inquiry projects meets these recommendations.

Use of Integrated Inquiry Projects to Support Science and Literacy Learning for English Language Learners

To help English language learners meet the goals established in the science and literacy standards, teachers must adopt instructional approaches and teach specific strategies that make text more comprehensible to students. Integrated inquiry projects are especially appropriate because they are multilevel, thus allowing for personalized instruction and assessment of each student. Further, such projects use elements of the language experience approach, which has been used successfully in ESL and bilingual education classrooms for decades (Tinajero & Calderon, 1988; Van Allen, 1973).

While a variety of teaching methods are used daily in most classrooms, the national standards seem clear in their support of inquiry teaching. Inquiry teaching allows students who traditionally were not encouraged or given the opportunity to learn science (females, students of color, and students with limited English proficiency) to approach learning from a variety of cognitive levels. Full inquiry involves:

1. Asking a question

2. Completing an investigation

3. Answering the question

4. Presenting the results to others.

Teaching Standard A from National Science Standards (National Research Council, 1996) provides suggestions for planning an inquiry approach to teaching science: "Teachers of science plan an inquiry-based program for their students" (p. 30). Inquiry-based planning involves five main elements.

1. Develop a framework of year-long and short-term goals for students. Planning is critical to inquiry teaching. A vision of what students will be able to do provides the framework used to build science literacy. Once the framework of goals is determined, teachers need to remain flexible. Teaching for understanding requires listening and responding to students, so strategies and plans are constantly revisited and adapted to fit the learning situation.

2. Select content and adapt and design curricula to meet the interests, knowledge, understanding, abilities, and experiences of students. Teachers need to become familiar with the history and culture of the diverse groups of students in the classroom to be successful in integrating multicultural content into the curriculum (Clark, 1996). It is vital to take into consideration the local population during the planning process. Language-minority classrooms need to present science as a sense-making practice (Warren & Rosebery, 1992). A major component of inquiry learning is using questions from students to guide discussions and planning. Teachers are also advised to consider their own strengths and weaknesses and available resources.

3. Select teaching and assessment strategies that support the development of student understanding and nurture a community of science learning. Inquiry into authentic questions generated from student experiences is the central strategy for science teaching. Teachers can guide students as they acquire and interpret information from sources such as the library and computerized databases or as they gather information from experts.

4. Teachers must decide when and how often to use small-group and large-group instruction. Cooperative learning activities provide students with opportunities to associate with their peers and to learn from and gain respect for each other (Clark, 1996).

5. Individual and collective planning is the cornerstone of science teaching. This collaborative effort provides modeling for heterogeneity and builds respect for other cultures and ideas.

Inquiry therefore lends itself to integration across the curriculum. As teachers develop integrated inquiry projects, it is helpful to use the following three steps.

1. Identify a Theme. First a theme and related subtopics are identified. Questions to consider include:

■ What do I expect students to learn as a result of participating in this unit?

■ Is this something children are naturally curious about?

■ Do the children have experience with or background knowledge about this theme? If not, how can I best develop their experiential background?

2. Create Specific Activities. Next, brainstorm (perhaps with another teacher) ideas for specific teaching and learning activities. Consider such questions as:

■ What types of activities naturally lend themselves to this project?

■ Is each activity developmentally and culturally appropriate for my students?

■ Is every activity meaningful, worthwhile, and related to the content and performance standards?

3. Implement the Project. As implementation begins, teachers ask themselves questions such as the following:

■ What is an intriguing way to begin the project that will capture students' interest?

■ Does the classroom need to be rearranged?

■ What resources (e.g., books, mathematics and science manipulatives and instruments, guest speakers) will be needed?

■ How can the project be ended effectively? What are good closure activities?

■ How will student learning be assessed?

Reflection, including the use of journals, during and after the project as well as while planning will help identify refinements and improvements (Hurley & Blake, 1997).

The following section describes a sample integrated inquiry project.

A Sample Integrated Inquiry Project: "Asking Questions"

Objectives. Students will develop a question related to science concepts taught in the core book, complete an investigation into possible answers, answer their question, and present the results to others.

Background. This sample integrated inquiry project, "Asking Questions," is centered on Pamela Allen's (1980) picture book, *Mr. Archimedes' Bath*. The book is a loose retelling of the legend of how Archimedes, a Greek mathematician, discovered a way to find the volume (the amount of space occupied) of an object that has a nongeometrical shape. The legend is that while Archimedes was turning the problem over in his head, he chanced to come to the bathing place, and there, as he was sitting down in the tub, he realized that the amount of water that flowed over the edge of the tub was equal to his own volume. In his joy he leaped out of the tub and rushed naked toward his home, crying out with a loud voice that he had found what he sought. As he ran, he shouted in Greek, "Heuréka, heuréka" ("I have found it!") (Clagett, 1968, p. 480).

Learning Activities

■ *Water Levels.* Fill a clear bowl three-quarters full of water. Mark the water level on the outside with masking tape. Provide different-size objects and have children predict how the water level will change when they place each object in the water. As children place objects in the water, mark the new level with tape. Somewhat older students could make a chart showing how the water rises and falls in relation to the size of the object placed in it. Guide discussions to help children infer that mass influences the water level in the container. As second language learners participate in the discussion, keep in mind that their receptive skills may be stronger than their expressive skills. Thus, they may understand concepts but have difficulty expressing them. When students offer responses, their developing pronunciation may be nonstandard and their grammatical constructions may include elements from their first language. When this happens, accept the response, model the correct form in a tactful and unexaggerated way, and praise students for their contributions. Help them express their ideas by using semantic expansion techniques; that is, start with something the student said and elaborate to clarify or add to the meaning of something he or she said. Sensitively use structural expansions, in which you rephrase a grammatically incorrect utterance correctly. Ask confirmation-check questions to confirm what you think the student has said or to recall a definition or related information. Make clarification requests, in which you ask students to clarify, elaborate on, or restate what has just been said by another student or you. Clarify the meaning of difficult and abstract concepts by pointing to pictures and objects. The use of these strategies will help students express their thoughts and ideas even if they are not yet fully fluent in the language (Tinajero, 1997).

■ *Equivalency Measures.* Use nonstandard capacity containers (e.g., plastic bowls, cups, hairspray tops) and have children estimate which one contains the same amount of water as the water that was displaced. The use of manipulatives and hands-on activities help students understand complex and abstract concepts presented in this lesson as they are learning English as a second language. The use of concrete objects helps students represent scientific ideas and helps them move from understanding simple, concrete concepts to understanding more difficult and abstract ones. Activities that get students actively involved in solving problems through experimentation, measuring, charting, and weighing—such as the ones in this example—are particularly good.

■ *Make Boats.* Place students in cooperative work groups (Johnson & Johnson, 1991; Slavin, 1990). Provide each group with the same amount of clay. Instruct them to work together in their group to make a boat that will float and hold marbles (more marbles than any other group's boat). Set a time limit of perhaps 10 minutes. Encourage children to talk and to listen to others in the group as they design and build the boats. Have each group think of a name for their boat. List the names on the board or a chart tablet. Have the groups, one at a time, launch their boats in a small tub of water. If the boat floats, they begin adding marbles one at a time until it sinks. The number of marbles each boat held successfully is written on the chart next to the name of the boat.

Name of Boat	Number of Marbles
Charlie the Champion	8
Rapid Racer	7
El Rápido	10
Unsinkable Sally	11

Such cooperative group work is excellent for second language learners. It maximizes interaction with peers and creates contexts for purposeful communication. When it comes to language acquisition, students often learn more from their peers than they do through formal instruction. Cooperative group work increases the frequency and variety of interactions among students and provides opportunities for them to act as resources for each other. Second language learners also experience less anxiety in cooperative settings and become valued participants in the classroom.

Follow-up activities center on discussing why some boat designs were successful and others were not. Guide students to infer a relationship between the amount of water a boat can displace and the boat's ability to float and carry a load. Allow students to redesign and test float their boats as many times as they wish throughout the course of the project. During this process they can draw or write their observations, collect data on which designs hold the most marbles, and ask why. The use of multilevel strategies can help teachers tailor the level of participation and responses required of students. For example, students at the pre- or early-production level of English proficiency can be asked questions that require short phrase responses or short explanations; students at the intermediate or advanced fluency level can be asked questions that require the use of higher-order language and that require them to produce language with varied grammatical structures and vocabulary.

■ *Boat-Related Activities.* The numbers collected may be charted and graphed to illustrate the data in various ways; for example, all the first attempts might be compared, or multiple attempts by one group might be compared. Numbers can be ordered from smallest to largest, or vice versa. Children can calculate the average number of marbles held. Students can write persuasive papers or advertisements extolling the benefits of a particular boat or design. They can write directions for "how to build a successful boat." Language experience principles (Tinajero & Calderon, 1988; Van Allen, 1973) can be applied. Children can read about and look at pictures of boats built for various purposes by people in different cultures or geographic areas.

■ *Eureka! and Other Words.* Engage children in word play by asking them to share words they use to express excitement, joy, or pleasure. Draw examples from students' cultural backgrounds and experiences—for example, *¡Bravo!* from Spanish speakers. Use analogies to relate the teaching of new vocabulary words to experiences in the students' backgrounds, homes, and neighborhoods. Compile an experience chart of their words. Ask them to have parents and others in their family help them collect more words to add to the chart.

■ *More Books.* Provide more books related to the main theme of "Asking Questions" and related subthemes, such as water, bathing, and animals. One example might be *No More Water in the Tub* by Tedd Arnold. *The Gullywasher/El Chaparron Torrencial* by Joyce Rossi is filled with Leticia's questions to her *abuelo* (grandfather). The book also explores some effects of staying in water too long, like wrinkled skin. It lends itself wonderfully to beginning an inquiry on storms. Both informational books about goats, wombats, and kangaroos (animals featured in *Mr. Archimedes' Bath*) and fiction like Mem Fox's *I Love You, Koala Lou,* which pictures wombats, kangaroos, and other animals from New Zealand, are appropriate.

■ *History and Geography Questions.* Consider with children the reasons why a Greek mathematician was in Rome working and taking Roman baths. Where are Greece and Rome? How did people in Archimedes' time travel from one place to the other? Use a variety of visuals, including maps, to help students understand distances and the location of the two countries. The use of visuals and other multisensory input provides students acquiring English with important support in building comprehension and establishing the context-rich environment that fosters language acquisition and understanding of abstract concepts.

■ *Fact or Fiction—More Questions.* Help children look for and find the answers to questions they wonder about. Schools can encourage students to use encyclopedias on CD-ROM and Net searches to look for information to answer their questions. Were there really kangaroos, wombats, and goats in Italy during Archimedes' time? Why can boats made of heavy materials like steel float? What is the formula for the displacement of water, and why is it important? What do mathematicians do when they go to work? What else did Archimedes do? Rather than isolate students acquiring English, have them work in heterogeneous groups or in pairs with more proficient English speakers so that they can help one another (DeVillar, 1990). Grouping together students of varying proficiencies provides them all with the opportunity to use newly acquired language, to act as resources for each other, and to assume a more active role in learning English and science concepts.

■ *Art.* Provide wet chalk or water colors and encourage children to respond to the story by creating an original picture. Try bubble art by adding food coloring to bubble mixture. As children blow colored bubbles, have them try to catch them on paper. When the bubbles pop, they leave a colored ring. Have children put drops of tempera or water paint on paper and blow on the paint with a straw to create images of lightning or raindrops. Such visuals help second language learners to understand and verbalize abstract ideas.

■ *Sink or Float.* Provide an assortment of objects that will sink or float. Allow children to put objects in a container of water and then mark on a chart whether each one sinks or floats (Hurley & Blake, 1997). Have students work coorperatively in groups or pairs.

Assessment

Students will maintain a portfolio of project activities/products which they will self-assess using the rubric in Figure 1 (page 276). They will also conference individually with the teacher, using both the project portfolio and the completed self-assessment rubric. Together the teacher and student will assess the integrated inquiry project holistically, using the summary checklist in Figure 2 (page 277). The teacher will also assess the student's progress in the acquisition of English (see Figures 3 and 4, pages 277–278).

The Teacher's Role in Inquiry

1. Focus and Support Inquiries While Interacting with Students. The teacher naturally serves as the filter of science learning. Teachers will constantly try to balance taking the time to allow students to pursue an interest in greater depth and the need to move on to new areas to be studied. Second language learners need a variety of teaching styles and strategies to support both language and concept development. Teachers must use meaning-centered strategies to provide students with access to grade-level content in science together with strategies that facilitate language acquisition. The English teaching process becomes an orchestrated visual and verbal performance in which teachers use the environment, physical activities, and visuals to teach important new words for concept development in science. That is, teachers use as many extra-linguistic clues, gestures, and other representations of vocabulary and reality as possible. Teachers make content comprehensible by paraphrasing, by emphasizing, and by explaining key concepts prior to a science lesson. Teachers also involve all students in the interaction process as well as at different levels of science conceptualization. Teachers must also keep in mind that individual English language learners are at different levels of English proficiency. Thus, teachers must be aware of the levels of receptive and productive language that students bring to the task as well as their levels of science knowledge and background. There may be some students who are not ready to begin producing oral English. They may be experiencing the "silent period" of language learning, during which they listen rather than produce language. Since children's receptive language skills develop earlier than their productive ones, it is important to keep in mind that language learning is taking place during this time. Children don't always need to respond in order to learn new language skills. Similarly, the lack of verbal participation does not necessarily reflect their thinking. They can benefit greatly from the opportunity to absorb the conversations of others (Krashen, 1988; Rice, 1989).

Student inquiry in the science classroom encompasses a range of activities. Some activities provide a basis for observation, data collection, reflection, and analysis of firsthand events and phenomena. Effective teachers continually create opportunities that challenge students and promote inquiry by asking questions.

2. Orchestrate Discourse Among Students About Scientific Ideas, and Accept Use of the Home Language. One stage vital to inquiry is the oral and written discourse that focuses the attention of students on how they know what they know. Teachers require students to record their work, teaching necessary skills as appropriate, and promote many different forms of communication. The teacher's role is to listen, encourage broad participation, and judge how to guide discussion and writing so that students will reflect on their learning. Meaning-centered strategies involve the use of the home language to facilitate the learning of subject matter. There is pedagogical evidence that academic content acquired in the first language will transfer positively to English. Data from a number of studies (Cummins, 1989; Ramirez, Yuen, & Ramey, 1991) suggest that providing content-area instruction in the native language may be the most educationally sound method of helping ELLs learn the academic uses of school English.

Figure 1
RUBRIC FOR SELF-ASSESSMENT OF PROJECTS

■ Directions: Look carefully at your project portfolio. On the list below, put a number 1 on the line before each statement that is true. Add up your points. That represents the number of points you think your project deserves. Bring the completed list with you for our end-of-the-project conference.

> 9–11 points: Outstanding, I really did a good job on this.
> 6–8 points: Nice job. Could do with a little fine tuning.
> 3–5 points: Pretty good, but... (But I'll do even better next time.)
> 1–2 points: I need to improve.
> 0 points: Uh, oh—give me a chance to rewrite and resubmit.

1. _____ The project is complete; every assignment is included.

2. _____ My work shows that I have learned more about language arts and science.

3. _____ I used questions to guide my inquiry project.

4. _____ I used reading, writing, and thinking about science in this project.

5. _____ I used speaking and listening about science in this project.

6. _____ I used language to view and to make my own visual representations (pictures, drawings, charts, graphs, etc.) about science in this project.

7. _____ I used a variety of resources in learning (books, computer, talking to parents or other adults, etc.).

8. _____ I did an experiment and/or collected data.

9. _____ I looked at, thought about, and redid parts of my work to make it better (written drafts, conferences with teacher or other students, etc.).

10. _____ I found an answer to my question, or if I didn't find an answer now I have more and better questions about my topic.

11. _____ I presented the results to others (class presentation, letter to editor of local paper, shared with another class, wrote a report, etc.).

_____ **TOTAL POINTS**

On the back of this sheet, write a paragraph stating what you liked best and what you liked least about this project. Also, tell three important things you learned from doing this project.

Figure 2
INTEGRATED INQUIRY PROJECT SUMMARY CHECKLIST

4 Excellent, exceeds expectations for age and developmental level

3 Very good, meets expectations in all areas and exceeds them in some areas

2 Good, meets expectations

1 Needs to improve in one or more areas

	1	2	3	4
Evidence of development in language and science				
Evidence student asked questions				
Evidence student did an investigation				
Student found answers				
Student presented findings				

Figure 3
UNSINKABLE BOATS

Use the following rubrics to assess students' English proficiency.

Critical Thinking: **Relate Cause and Effect**

During the sharing of observations from the boat activity, the student talks about cause and effect.

___ Yes ___ Not Yet

1 nonverbally (pointing to illustrations or concrete object)

2 nonverbally or with one- or two-word labels ("Boat sink," etc.)

3 with longer phrases and greater detail ("More marbles," "Boat sinked)

4 with connected discourse that includes the language of cause and effect and few errors ("The marbles maked the boat sink.")

5 by using the language of cause and effect comparably to native-speaker peers

Figure 4
PROJECT ON BOATS

Language Functions: Ask for and give information.

As project groups talk to each other, the student asks for and gives information:

1 nonverbally (by pointing or gesturing)

2 with several words ("What this do?" "This for boat")

3 with short phrases and some details ("He putted marbles on boat big")

4 with longer, more detailed phrases with few errors ("This marbles are too many on the boat.")

5 comparably to native-speaking peers

3. Challenge Students to Take Responsibility for Their Own Learning. The teacher of an inquiry-based classroom creates opportunities for students to take responsibility for their own learning, individually and as a group. Teachers support the students' ideas and questions and encourage independent thinking and assessment by students of their own work and learning.

4. Recognize and Respond to Student Diversity and Encourage All Students to Participate Fully in Science Learning. Skilled teachers recognize the diversity in their classes and organize the classroom so that all students have the opportunity to participate fully. Teachers monitor the participation of all students carefully to determine if all members of a collaborative group are working with materials. English language learners are encouraged to use their own language as well as English and to use forms of presenting data, such as pictures and graphs, that require less language proficiency (National Research Council, 1996). Activities should be designed to foster success on the part of the student (Clark, 1996). In providing activities, teachers need to be sensitive in selecting materials, speakers, and role models. Students need to see that women and men of all cultures and ethnic groups have made significant achievements in scientific and technological fields and that a career in science is a realistic option for all people.

5. Encourage and Model the Skills of Scientific Inquiry, as Well as the Curiosity, Openness to New Ideas, and Skepticism That Characterize Science. Teachers who are enthusiastic and interested, and who speak of the power and beauty of scientific understanding, will instill in their students some of those same attitudes (National Research Council, 1996). Teachers are models for the students they teach. How a teacher approaches teaching science may directly influence the student's attitudes and future success in the field of science. Teachers whose actions demonstrate respect for differing ideas, attitudes, cultural backgrounds, and values support a disposition fundamental to science classrooms.

Integrated inquiry can include all of the following instructional practices recommended by the National Science Foundation for fostering a high level of learning in science:

- ■ "Minds-on" student involvement
- ■ Hands-on interaction
- ■ Problem-solving experiences
- ■ Prolonged, in-depth contact with a central or unifying concept
- ■ A community of scholars in which both teacher and students learn and where respect is shown for student opinions and prior knowledge
- ■ Communication, demonstrated by presentations of ideas and group interactions
- ■ Assessment that emphasizes the process of arriving at the answer and application of knowledge to new situations. (NSF, 1996a, p. 35)

Summary: Creating an Equitable Environment for All Science Students

Equity research recommends particular practices to ensure that all learners acquire science and literacy concepts, processes, and skills. These ideas have proven useful in developing curriculum, methods, and environments conducive to the development of learner-centered classrooms, particularly for English language learners. The following recommended practices from equity research are inherent in the integrated inquiry approach described above.

1. Set High Standards.

Set clear, high goals or standards for what all students should know and be able to do. Schools that work respond to poor and minority students by accelerating learning. These schools are demonstrating every day of the school year that poor and minority students achieve at the highest levels if they are taught at the highest levels (Education Trust, 1996).

2. Provide a Challenging Curriculum for All Students.

Remove watered-down course work, give all students the opportunity to learn from a standards-based curriculum. Education Watch (Education Trust, 1996) states that many poor and second language students are aware of the low-level curriculum they receive. Others only realize it when they go to college and find that the A's they received in high school weren't like the A's their peers in the suburbs received. A recent study (McLeod, 1996) of exemplary schooling for ELLs highlights schools that have successfully met the challenge of providing equal educational opportunities to all students regardless of differences in English proficiency. The exemplary schools (1) provided ELLs with a rich intellectual diet in all areas of the curriculum; (2) expected ELLs to achieve to high standards in English literacy; (3) used curriculum approaches and instruction that were congruent with recent educational reform trends, emphasizing depth, critical thinking, hands-on learning, exploration process, and connections across disciplines; and (4) had ELLs engaged in intellectually enriching activities in both English and their native language in all areas of the curriculum.

3. Give All Students Expert Teachers.

Invest in professional development and demand high standards from teacher education preparation programs. All students deserve teachers who are highly skilled in teaching strategies and secure in content knowledge.

4. Use a Variety of Teaching Strategies.

Suggested teaching strategies include simulations, debates, plays, outdoor activities, research projects, cooperative learning, and creative writing. All teaching styles and strategies should be sensitive to cultures and appropriate for all students.

- Cooperative learning—small groups of students who help each other master material will develop interpersonal relationships and tolerance for diversity (Slavin, 1991).

- Peer tutoring—effective for cultures valuing cooperation and mentoring (Eddington & Hunt, 1996).

- Mastery learning—assumes that most students will master the curriculum if given enough time. Involves teaching and reteaching to enhance understanding.

- Curriculum integration—connect subjects through a literature-based curriculum.

5. Provide a Risk-Free Environment.

Allow opportunities for conversation and cultural exchange. Encourage students to experiment and let them know that it is all right to fail as long as they try again. Provide experiences that allow more than one correct answer and more than one way to solve problems.

In such classrooms, students take an active part in their own learning, engage in activities they view as meaningful, build on their own understanding and efforts, and participate in collaborative and socially constructed contexts for learning to read, to write, and to share while learning the science content. Teachers surround children with literature that connects to the science curriculum; they make science and literacy a family affair; they integrate and unify the curriculum; and they give all children ample opportunities to engage in science learning while they acquire higher and higher levels of proficiency in English.

CHILDREN'S LITERATURE CITED

Allen, P. (1980). *Mr. Archimedes' bath*. New York: Angus & Robertson, an imprint of HarperCollins Publishers.

Arnold, T. (1995). *No more water in the tub!* New York: Puffin Books.

Fox, M. (1989). *Koala Lou, I love you*.

Rossi, J. (1998). *The gullywasher/El chaparron torrencial*. Flagstaff, AZ: Northland Publishing.

REFERENCES

Advisory Board, National Science Foundation (1997). *Shaping the future*. Arlington, VA: National Science Foundation.

American Council on Education (1988). *One-third of a nation*. Report by the Commission on Minority Participation in Education and American Life. Washington, DC.

American Association for the Advancement of Science (1993). *Benchmarks for Science Literacy*. Washington, DC: Author.

Anstrom, K. (1998). *Preparing secondary education teachers to work with English language learners*. NCBE Resource Collection Series No. 10. Available online at http://www.ncbe.gwu.edu/ncbepubs/resource/ells/language/index.htm.

August, D. (1994, Fall). For all students: Limited-English-proficient students and goals 2000. *Occasional Papers in Bilingual Education*, No. 10.

Ayers, D., et al. (1992). *A study of the participation and achievement of black, Hispanic, and female students in mathematics, science and advanced technologies in Virginia secondary schools*. Richmond: Virginia State Department of Education.

Clagett, M. (1968). Archimedes. In W.D. Halsey (Ed. Dir.), *Collier's Encyclopedia* (p. 480). New York: Crowell-Collier Educational Corporation.

Clark, J. V. (1996). *Redirecting science education: Reform for a culturally diverse population*. Thousand Oaks, CA: Corwin Press.

Cummins, J. (1989). *Empowering minority students*. Sacramento: California Association for Bilingual Education.

De la Cruz, Y. (1998). Issues in the teaching of math and science to Latinos. In M. L. Gonzalez, A. Huerta-Macias, & J.V. Tinajero (Eds.), *Educating Latino students: A guide to successful practice* (pp. 143–160). Lancaster, PA: Technomic Publishing Co.

DeVillar, R. A. (1990). Second language use within the non-traditional classroom: computers, cooperative learning and bilingualism. In R. Jacobson & C. Faltis (Eds.), *Language distribution issues in bilingual schooling* (pp. 133–159). Clevedon, England: Multilingual Matters.

Eddington, S., & Hunt, C. (1996). *Teaching consultation process sourcebook*. Stillwater, OK: New Forums Press.

Education Trust (1996). *The education watch*. Washington, DC: Education Trust.

Fisher, C.J., & Terry, C.A. (1990). *Children's language and the language arts*. Boston: Allyn & Bacon.

Hurley, S. R., & Blake, S. (1997). Animals and occupations. Why theme-based curricula work. *Early Childhood News*, 20–25.

International Reading Association and National Council of Teachers of English (1996). *Standards for the English language arts*. Newark, DE, and Urbana, IL: Authors.

Johnson, D. W., & Johnson, F. (1991). *Joining together: Group theory and group skills* (4th ed.). Englewood Cliffs, NJ: Prentice Hall.

Krashen, S., & Biber, D. (1988). *On course: Bilingual education's success in California*. Sacramento: California Association for Bilingual Education.

McKeon, D. (1994). When meeting common standards is uncommonly difficult. *Educational Leadership, 51* (8).

McLeod, B. (1996, February). *School reform and student diversity: Exemplary schooling for language minority students.* Internet: NCBE Resource Collection series No. 4.

National Center on Education and the Economy (1999). *New standards: Primary literacy standards in reading and writing.* Learning and Research and Development Center at the University of Pittsburgh and National Center on Education and the Economy.

National Research Council (1996). *National science education standards.* National Academy Press. Washington, DC.

National Science Foundation (1996a). *Indicators of science and mathematics education.* Arlington, VA: Author.

National Science Foundation (1996b). *The learning curve: What we are discovering about U.S. science and mathematics education.* Arlington, VA: Author.

National Science Foundation (1996c). *Shaping the future: New expectations for undergraduate education in science, mathematics, engineering, and technology* (draft). Arlington, VA: Author.

National Science Foundation (1994). *Women, minorities, and persons with disabilities in science and engineering.* Washington, DC: Author.

Oakes, J. (1990). *Lost talent: The underparticipation of women, minorities, and disabled persons in science.* Santa Monica, CA: Rand Corporation.

Ramirez, J. D., Yuen, S.D., & Ramey, E. (1991). *Final report: Longitudinal study of structured English immersion, early-exit transitional bilingual education programs for language-minority children.* U. S. Department of Education, Contract No. 300-87-0156. San Mateo, CA: Aguirre International.

Rice, M. (1989, February). Children's language acquisition. *American Psychologist, 4* (February), 149–156.

Slavin, R. E. (1990). *Cooperative learning: Theory, research, and practice.* Englewood Cliffs, NJ: Prentice Hall.

Tinajero, J.V. (1997). Becoming bilingual: A personal experience. In J.V. Tinajero & A. Schifini, *Into English, Teacher's Guide* (p. T21). Carmel, CA: Hampton-Brown Books.

Tinajero, J. V., & Calderon, M. E. (1988). Language experience approach plus. *Journal of Educational Issues of Language Minority Students, 2,* 31–45.

Van Allen, R. (1973). The language experience approach. In Robert Karlen (Ed.), *Perspectives on elementary reading: Principles and strategies of teaching.* New York: Harcourt Brace Jovanovich.

Vygotsky, L.S. (1984) *Mind in society: The development of higher psychological processes.* In M. Cole, V. John-Steiner, S. Scribner, & E. Souberman (Eds. and trans.). Cambridge, MA: Harvard University Press.

Making Inequality: Issues of Language and Meanings in Mathematics Teaching with Hispanic Students

Lena Licón Khisty

How should we explain the disproportionately and consistently poor achievement of Hispanic students in mathematics in the United States? Recent data indicate that the general population of Hispanic students performs well below the average national level in this subject (Matthews, Carpenter, Lindquist, & Silver, 1984; Moore & Smith, 1987). In comparing recent National Assessment results with previous assessments, Matthews and her colleagues (1984) indicate that Hispanics showed only small gains in the lower cognitive areas of knowledge and computational skill and no gains in understanding or application. As we examine these data, it is important to bear in mind other demographic factors that relate to this population. First, the National Center for Education Statistics (1981) has projected that the school population of limited-English-proficient (LEP) students will reach 3.4 million in the year 2000; Spanish-speaking students will constitute 77% of this population in the year 2000. Second, although this population is growing very rapidly, educational institutions remain virtually static in their response to the issue. One in four teachers has LEP students in his/her classroom, but only 3.2% of the nation's teachers have had the academic preparation to teach them (U.S. Department of Education, 1982). Through an analysis of these data, we begin to see a framework of inequities that suggests factors to account for the underachievement of Hispanic students.

Traditional perspectives on the generally poor performance of minority students have focused attention first on factors related to individual characteristics and then on factors related to the cultural background of the student. Since the 1960s, the predominant paradigms that have guided investigations into this phenomenon have assumed that the problem resides, if not necessarily in genetic deficits, then in cultural deficits. Such models concentrate on pinpointing and describing what students do not know, what experiences they presumably do not have, or what language and behavior differences they possess that result in a mismatch with the norms of the school. Actions and policies consistent with these pathology models are based, therefore, on changing the student and/or the family—on remedying the assumed imperfections.

However, we can look at the problem in a fundamentally different way. At the heart of this paradigm shift is the premise that there is a process of school failure that involves inadequate or inappropriate instructional decisions that de facto handicap poor and ethnic-minority students. Moll and Diaz (1987) describe it this way:

> Although student characteristics certainly matter, when the same children are shown to succeed under modified instructional arrangements it becomes clear that the problems these working-class children face in school must be viewed primarily as a consequence of institutional arrangements that constrain children and

teachers by not capitalizing fully on their talents, resources, and skills. . . . This conclusion is pedagogically optimistic because it suggests that just as academic failure is socially organized, academic success can be socially arranged. (p. 302)

The research presented here reflects this later paradigm. In essence, it is based on the argument that the teaching and learning process consists of an interaction between persons for the purpose of developing and sharing meanings. It logically follows that language is crucial if the development and negotiation of meaning are to occur. Consequently, if we are to fully understand instructional dynamics—and obstacles that arise in the process that constrain minority children—we must examine not only curriculum and classroom activities, but also classroom discourse—that is, what is said and how it is said. In the case of students for whom Spanish is a home and/or dominant language, language use in classrooms is naturally critical (e.g., Cazden, 1986).[1]

Furthermore, consistent with the contention that no pathology resides within the student, the focus of attention is on the discourse characteristics of the teacher. However, this is not to suggest blaming the teacher. Rather, it is the teacher who makes instructional decisions and determines instructional contexts; it is the teacher who explains new concepts and poses questions to stretch students' thinking and understandings; and it is the teacher who represents the element that completes our understanding of classroom processes and, more important, becomes the agent of change (e.g., National Council of Teachers of Mathematics, 1989).

In what follows, I first present the general results of observations of mathematics teaching in five classrooms with sizable populations of non-English-proficient (NEP) and limited-English-proficient (LEP) students of Mexican descent. The teachers in the classrooms are fluently bilingual and are able to instruct using the primary language of the student. Next, I offer a closer look at the dynamics of teacher discourse in mathematics with two contrasting case studies. Just as the zoom lens of a camera provides more detail of the subject, the microethnography of just two classrooms provides detail that reveals how a simple concept such as talk becomes a political tool that either empowers students or disenfranchises them.

Background

This research has been informed by three major areas of inquiry. The first relates to the work by sociohistorical psychologists (e.g., Moll, 1990; Scribner & Cole, 1981; Vygotsky, 1978; Wertsch, 1985) on the critical role of social interaction in learning. Vygotsky (1978) in particular has offered a framework of socially constituted development of higher mental processes. Within his framework, there are many interrelated factors that must be present, one of which is an "enabling other." This is a more experienced person who embodies and, consequently, models the intended outcome for the learner. In this case, modeling corresponds to a traditional pattern of direct instruction and imitation, rather than to what exists in an apprenticeship, where the mentor exposes the novice to, and enculturates her/him with, new behaviors in a spontaneous and informal manner. In this mode of instruction, there is no artificiality of conversation and, therefore, little loss of contact with the purpose of dialogue. For all of this to be accomplished, the enabling other must provide a scaffold for the learner via dialogue that includes probing questions and cues that extend talk as well as the intellectual range of the learner. Let me illustrate this modeling-and-scaffolding process with an example taken from the work of Tharp and Gallimore (1988):

A 6-year-old child has lost a toy and asks her father for help. The father asks where she last saw the toy; the child says, "I can't remember." He asks a series of questions: "Did you have it in your room? Outside? Next door?" To each question, the child answers no. When he says, "In the car?" she says, "I think so," and goes to retrieve the toy. . . . Through this small domestic collaboration, the father is rousing to life significant cognitive functions. Such teaching—understood as assisted performance of apprentices in joint activity with experts—becomes the vehicle through which the interactions of society are internalized and become mind. (pp. 7–8)

Research on the role of modeling or assisted performance in the teaching of language arts supports the need on the part of students to have teachers model new concepts (e.g., Au & Jordan, 1981; Langer, 1987; Tharp &

Gallimore, 1988). It also is clear that for the modeling to be effective, language use must be carefully considered, as in the situation just described, in which the father chooses to ask a series of questions instead of making a declarative statement that might have quickly informed the child.

The second area of inquiry consists of the work that has been done concerning effective instruction for bilingual or language-minority students. One of the most significant findings relates to the academic benefits that result from use of the student's primary language—in this case Spanish—in instruction, particularly when it is used in the teaching of concepts (e.g., Cummins, 1981; Garcia, 1988).[2] It is only reasonable that when new meanings are being developed, the language that the child comprehends best should be the one used. However, use of the primary language in instruction also provides the support needed while the student continues to develop proficiency in the second language, specifically as it is used academically in classrooms and textbooks. This proficiency in the cognitive academic language is not easily acquired and can take as long as seven years to achieve (Cummins, 1981). This suggests that English language development be integrated with academic skill development and that during instruction, attention be paid to students' acquisition of new terms for concepts, or simply new vocabulary and syntax modes (e.g., Tikunoff, 1985). Consequently, both the native language (L1), Spanish, and the second language (L2), English, are used in instruction;

however, the languages are kept separate and are not mixed.

In regard to mathematics, the use of the primary language may be very necessary in order to clarify confusions that result because of the differences between Spanish and English mathematical terms (e.g., Casteneda, 1983; Cuevas, 1984). This may be particularly important when Spanish is used at home by parents and other adults, and children may develop certain understandings that are not necessarily the same as those in school, where instruction is usually in another language. Without attention to making bridges between meanings and terminologies developed in the two contexts, that is, home and school, mathematical discussions could be less than effective and may even be incomprehensible.

The third area of inquiry concerns the nature of the language we use to communicate mathematical ideas, or the mathematics register. This is not to be confused with the special terminology used in mathematics. Rather, the mathematics register extends to the use of the natural language in a way that is particular to a role or function (Halliday, 1978). In other words, it is a set of unique meanings and structures expressed through everyday language. The development of a mathematics register is accomplished in many ways, including reinterpreting existing words such as *carry, set, face, point,* and *reduce* (Halliday, 1978). Thus, the register can present many instances in which words have meanings different from what children expect, and this can be especially hazardous for

LEP students. For example, it is easy to imagine limited-English-proficient students being confused by the mathematical meaning of the word *left* (as in, How many are *left*?), when commonly it is the directional meaning of the word that is stressed in the learning of English. It also would not be unusual for LEP students to be confused by words such as *sum* and *whole*, which have nonmathematical homonyms. Such words would not necessarily present the same kind of difficulty for native English speakers, since they do not have to deal with comprehension of the language in the first place, which makes it easier to identify the subtleties between the different meanings.

Comprehending mathematical talk is made more difficult because symbolically we can have one statement (e.g., $10 - 4 = 6$), but verbally, we can express it several ways ("Ten take away four is six," or "Four from ten leaves six"). Moreover, these expressions are often unthinkingly and freely interchanged by teachers as they instruct (e.g., Pimm, 1987).

The issue surrounding the mathematics register does not lie in the register itself nor in whether students should learn it for its own sake. Instead, the issue is one of identifying mathematics with its language. If Hispanic students do not know the language for, or do not have the means of expressing, mathematical ideas, they cannot, in essence, do the mathematical work; they are curtailed from participating in those activities that develop and enhance mathematical meanings and comprehension. The issue is compounded for students for whom English is a second language because they must contend with multiple language variables all at the same time. Therefore, the existence of the register needs to be brought to students' attention and its structure needs to be taught, along with the rest of mathematics, in order for students to develop sufficient control in its use as a way of communicating mathematically.

The importance of these points is that learning mathematics involves language in a way that appears to be much more crucial than previous studies of mathematics education with language-minority students might suggest. If we accept Vygotsky's premise that the more able other (i.e., the teacher) has to model the desired cognitive behavior, and if we accept that learning is most effective in the child's primary language and that mathematics entails unique language use, then we have to explore further those verbalizations and development strategies the mathematics teacher uses.

Methods

As part of a larger project, school administrators, as well as bilingual and mathematics curriculum directors, were asked to identify teachers whom they considered effective in the teaching of mathematics with Hispanic students. Classrooms were selected from elementary schools with a significant population of Hispanic LEP and NEP students. Data gathered in five of these classrooms form the basis of the present discussion. Three classrooms are at the second-grade and two are at the fifth-grade level. Consistent with ethnographic methods, field observations were carried out at

various times over a year, and each classroom was videotaped intermittently for 7 to 10 hours when the teacher indicated that new concepts would be introduced and explained. In addition, an entire week of each teacher's mathematics lessons (e.g., introduction of new concepts, review, etc.) was videotaped to get a sense of consistency across the lessons, and one whole day was videotaped to get a sense of how mathematics related to the rest of each teacher's curriculum. Each teacher was asked a prepared set of questions regarding personal and teaching background, academic and language backgrounds of his or her students, and perceptions of teaching mathematics. Informal interviews were conducted with each teacher after a videotaped lesson, in order to identify and clarify instructional decisions that were made. Informal interviews were also used with randomly selected students to assess their grasp of the mathematical meanings presented in the lesson and to enhance the observations.

The analysis of the videotapes, the primary source of data, focused on the following constructs: (a) the nature and use of a mathematics register; (b) the nature and use of L1 (Spanish) and L2 (English); (c) instances of language use for the negotiation of meaning, or for emphasizing rote learning; and (d) the clarity or ambiguity of language used in concept development. Triangulation among three independent observers was used to provide validation of the items deemed to be linguistically troublesome.

It is important to note that

although all of the teachers for this particular discussion were bilingual, there were important differences among them. One had had all of her schooling (including higher education) in Mexico. Two other teachers were not native speakers of Spanish, but did have extensive academic training in the language and had lived in Spanish-speaking countries. The last two were Hispanic, had had most of their schooling in the United States, and had varying degrees of fluency in Spanish.

General results

As we look inside these five classrooms, two patterns of teacher discourse emerge that are particularly relevant to our discussion. The first relates to the differences among teachers in their efforts to attend to the language of mathematics.

Effective techniques used by some of the teachers included emphasizing meanings by variations in voice tone and volume, and by pausing either before or after a word is spoken in order to draw students' attention to it. Also, at times as a word was spoken, it was written or pointed to among a previously prepared list of words.

Another effective technique was the frequent "recasting" of mathematical ideas and terms. As Spanos and his colleagues (1988) have pointed out, mathematics has many linguistic features that present problems to students, including a semantic structure composed of synonymous words and phrases that can be used to signal a single mathematical operation. The recasting observed in this study attempted to provide students not only with some of the synonyms relevant to the particular problem, but also with other ways of looking at the problem within the immediate context of discussing it. The following excerpt demonstrates this recasting technique.

In this episode, the teacher is giving directions to a second-grade class on how to make a paper cat that each student will use to illustrate his or her own story. The teacher is weaving the development of various geometric concepts into her directions that students will eventually follow on their own. She has just introduced the word *perimeter* as the concept of an outline of a figure.

Please note that dialogues in Spanish have been translated into English and the translations are in italics. However, it should be recognized that there are many instances in which the subject code switches between Spanish and English and uses the two languages within the same sentence or paragraph.

T: ¿Qué es un contorno? A ver tú.
    (What is an outline? Let's see, you.)
S1: Ahm, un, una figura.
    (Ahm, a figure.)
S2: Un rededor de figura.
    (A line around a figure.)
T: *Very good! Good job, you are a good listener, I like you.* Un contorno, el contorno es el rededoro, el perímetro, la línea que encierra la figura. El contorno es el rededor de la figura. La figura puede ser una persona, un animal, una cosa, un pedazo de papel, un...
    (An outline, the outline is the surrounding, the perimeter around the shape, the line that encloses the figure. The outline is the line surrounding a figure. The figure can be an animal, a thing, a piece of paper...)
S1: Un juguete. *(A toy.)*

As can be seen, recasting during instruction provides students with a repertoire of mathematical talk and perspectives for comprehending the talk. In this case, the teacher provides not only synonyms but also examples of how the word is used in sentences. Moreover, this example suggests that it is not enough simply to provide a formal definition of a term or even to translate the item into English.

Clearly, if a student knows only one way of expressing a mathematical concept, it will be very easy for the student to get lost in a discussion when synonymous terms are freely interchanged. For example, in the following excerpt from a discussion in an upper-grade classroom, we can see almost the reverse of what occurred in the example just given. In this case, a student gets lost in the teacher's explanation because no attention is given to making sure students recognize the interchangeability of *three-fourths* and *three-quarters*.

T: Now we can take three-fourths of this. OK, what's three-quarters of this number [pointing to a number]? Can someone tell me?
    [Chorus of correct and incorrect student responses]
S: Teacher, I don't understand. How did you get three-quarters?
T: Here [pointing to 3/4 and proceeding to work out the problem].

In the interview with this student, it was found that he had understood *three quarters* to mean coins. He did not know that *three-fourths* and *three-quarters* are register terms for the same concept and are interchangeable. On the other hand, the teacher's response suggests that an assumption was made that the student had these terms in his cognitive repertoire and simply needed to be reminded. Consequently, the response, which was intended to clarify, was meaningless.

Less effective techniques were characterized by missed opportunities to establish and clarify the mathematics register. In an earlier paper related to this research (Khisty, McLeod, & Bertilson, 1990), my colleagues and I described a teacher's use of the Spanish word *decena* (meaning a group of 10) during an explanation of place-value and regrouping. This is a specialized word that would not be familiar to most young students; it is also very similar to the word *docena*, which means dozen. The two spoken words can easily be confused (as often occurs with *eights* and *eighths*), particularly if the teacher's accent is difficult to understand. During the lesson, no steps were taken to draw attention to the word *decena* and its meaning, nor to contrast it with the other word. As a result, students found the discussion incomprehensible since they were not able to make a connection between what they thought they heard as directions to form groups of twelve and what they saw in the teacher's demonstration of regrouping by ten.

In the following dialogue, we can see how another teacher gives care and attention to developing students' understanding of the mathematics register. The teacher is using the context of constructing paper houses to develop concepts of rational numbers with her students. She has just explained how each student will get half of a piece of paper to use in their projects, and now introduces the concept of a fourth and its relationship to a half. Notice that the teacher draws the students' attention to the fact that *cuarto* in Spanish can mean both "fourth" and "room," and she specifically clarifies which meaning is being used.

T: Y cada partecita se va a lla-mar…
    (And each little piece will be called…)
S1: Fourth.
T: Fourth. Este es un cuarto y este es un cuarto [holding two pieces of paper]. No un cuarto de la cocina ni un cuarto de la casa. Es un cuarto del entero. ¿Si este lo doblamos … en otro, en una …en una mitad, este… medio, cuantos cuartos va haber en este medio?
    (This is a fourth and this is a fourth. It is not the room as in kitchen nor as in a room in a house. It is a fourth of a whole. If we fold this… into a half, this…half, how many fourths will there be in the half?)

This example also points out that the mathematics register is not language-specific. Each language has its own unique way of expressing mathematical concepts. Mathematical meanings, which can be confused in one language (e.g., *cuarto* for both "room" and "fourth" in Spanish, and *sum* and *some* in English), may not present confusion in another language. Consequently, we cannot assume that if you know the mathematics register in one language, you know it in another. For LEP students, this means that attention must be given to clarifying confusions caused by both the Spanish and English mathematics register, and to making connections between ways of expressing concepts in both languages.

Thus far, we have looked at the various effective and ineffective techniques teachers used to clarify the mathematics register. We have seen how teachers may specifically draw students' attention to key words and phrases and make sure that students distinguish the specialized meanings of the mathematics register from alternative everyday meanings of the same words. I have also noted that teachers, on the other hand, tend to miss opportunities to develop the register; either they forget to do so, or they seemingly do not recognize its importance to student understanding. However, there were also several instances in teachers' explanations when they actually made errors in using mathematical terms and phrases. For example, let us examine the following dialogue from a lesson with upper-grade students. The errors in this episode are of two types: First, the teacher presents a dot completely out of context and asks for its mathematical meaning; second, the Spanish word for "one-tenth" is used to refer to all decimal numbers.

The teacher's objective in this lesson is to introduce addition with decimals to the students. The teacher has just completed leading the class in solving an ordinary whole-number addition problem and now puts a dot on a blank overhead screen:

T: ¿Quién sabe que es esto? Who knows what that is [pointing to the solitary dot]? ¿Quién sabe? Who knows? ¿Quién sabe? ¿Quién sabe? [The teacher is translating as he goes along.] [Students raise their hands and one is called on.]
S1: Un décimo. *(A tenth.)*
T: Right, décimo. *(tenth).* How do you say it in English? Decimal [with a very specific Spanish pronunciation]. ¿En español? Décimo. *(In Spanish? Tenth.)* [Teacher and students are saying the key words, *décimo* and *decimal*, pronounced as in Spanish, in unison.]

Throughout the rest of the lesson, the solitary dot is referred to as the "decimal," and there is no further explanation of how it is used in the context of rational numbers. The significance of this lies in its potential to mislead because, mathematically, a dot is also used to mean a "point" in the line. In many countries, including those in Latin America, the dot is used in place of a comma to set off particular whole-number place values. Lastly, in this episode, the stage has been set for confusion by the free interchange of *decimal*, pronounced as it would be in Spanish, and *décimo* (one-tenth), which is not the translation for *decimal*. By the end of the lesson, students could be heard using the words interchangeably among themselves just as the teacher had.

The second pattern of teacher discourse to emerge from the data concerns the very little Spanish that was actually used in the mathematics context. This was true at both grade levels for all of the teachers except one, in spite of the fact that in all of the classrooms, there were students who spoke no English or for whom English was clearly a weaker language. The Spanish that was used fell into two categories, which I have chosen to refer to as "instrumental use" and "markers of solidarity." In the first case, teachers tended to use Spanish in a perfunctory manner as an "instrument" to impose discipline, to call students' attention to the subject of the lesson, or to punctuate a statement. In the second case, Spanish was used to give encouragement and to motivate the class. However, in these situations, Spanish was most often used as a shared but private mode of expression when a teacher worked individually with a student. In general, these uses of Spanish can represent appropriate applications of the language in teaching. In fact, a "marker of solidarity" can be particularly useful because it serves to draw students into classroom processes. The issue surrounding the use of Spanish in the ways I have described is that the language is not used in the context of making meaning in mathematics.

Overall, very few whole thoughts during mathematical explanations were conveyed in Spanish. Individual Spanish words or phrases were sprinkled in the teachers' talk, or sentences were not completed. In light of

this, it is natural to ask whether Spanish was used more extensively at any other time or for any other subject. In other words, was Spanish particularly excluded from the mathematics context, or was this the general state of affairs for all instruction with these students? Observations of instruction at different times of the day revealed that Spanish was used more frequently to develop concepts related to reading and/or language arts instruction. This is consistent with the findings of others, which suggest that mathematics does not require as much consideration of language use or discourse as other subjects (e.g., Cazden, 1986). As I argue later in this discussion, however, this is not true. It also points to the tendency of bilingual teachers to see themselves as language and culture brokers. The implication is that there is an accompanying tendency to make Spanish relevant only in the areas of language development and cultural ties. Given additional curriculum and policy constraints, districts can be less concerned about developing concepts equally across all academic areas (Khisty, 1991). Therefore, it becomes easy to overlook the need to use extended talk and students' primary language in teaching mathematics. This is no small matter, since these techniques constitute critical links to success in the subject for Hispanic students.

However, interviews with the teachers suggest other contributing factors besides the inclination to give priority to language development issues above other areas. The teachers who used Spanish the least in a mathemat-

ics context had learned Spanish either in an academic setting or informally within their families. The teachers for whom Spanish was a second language did not have any training in the technical aspects of the language; this is to be expected, since few foreign-language programs address this area. In essence, they had not had access to the Spanish mathematics register. In many of our observations of these teachers, it was noted that some English mathematical terms and phrases were directly translated into Spanish and, as a result, were not always correct. All of the teachers in interviews expressed a sense of helplessness about speaking mathematically; they recognized that there were times when they really did not have a command of the Spanish vocabulary needed to explain concepts thoroughly. On the other hand, for them, mathematics was also simply a difficult subject to explain (Khisty, 1991).

It should be noted that the only teacher to spend a considerable amount of time developing mathematics by way of explanations, questions, and cues to extend student talk was the teacher who used the most Spanish in instruction. Also, while some of the other teachers tended to use a concurrent translation method (switching frequently between Spanish and English), which often resulted in incomplete sentences, this teacher tended not to mix languages. She spoke in one language for longer periods of time and her talk stands out because of its pattern of complete thoughts, as contrasted with the other teachers' broken discourse. Furthermore, while she used a considerable amount of Spanish, this was balanced with the active development of English skills in highly contextualized situations. This is the same teacher who had had all of her schooling in Mexico. Moreover, from observations of her teaching, it is clear that her primary instructional goal was to teach concepts and not to develop language skills only.

The Politics of Talk

The foregoing discussion is intended to provide a general overview of teacher discourse characteristics found in the classrooms used for this study. As can be seen, in these environments there are clearly language strategies in instructional practices that are questionable because of their effect in constraining Hispanic students' learning of mathematics. If students are unable to understand instructors' presentations fully because words are used in such a way as to distort what is being said, or because instruction is simply in a language students do not understand, or have to struggle to comprehend, then it is small wonder that Hispanic students have trouble developing proficiency in mathematics.

However, there is another aspect to learning in addition to simply comprehending words and phrases used in explanations and problems. It has to do with communication processes that encourage a sense of what it means to do mathematics, that foster the internalization of the subject, and that enculturate the learner into the world of mathematical activity. In essence, it has

to do with minimizing feelings of alienation from mathematics.

The enculturation process is multidimensional and complex, and many factors contribute to it. But one crucial means by which students become enculturated is by having ample opportunities to talk about mathematics, to ask questions that test their understandings, to engage in debates about various mathematical processes, and, in general, to participate in the higher cognitive levels of the subject that accompany active dialogue.

Clearly, this is the process by which shared meanings are developed and advanced. It is also the means by which meanings become personalized. Without participatory dialogue, learning remains outside the person; it is something that is removed from personal experiences and mental connections, and it is elusive and difficult to hold onto (e.g., Bishop, 1991). Freire (1970) also suggests that the acquisition of the "word which names the world" is what gives an individual power to participate in the world. Talk, therefore, is the critical vehicle by which an individual internalizes meanings, becomes enculturated, and develops a sense of personal power in mathematics.

The following section is intended to illustrate how talk or the absence of talk results in either drawing students closer to mathematics or alienating them from it. The two subjects discussed here are experienced second-grade teachers who are very concerned about mathematics; they spend a lot of time teaching it and thinking about how to improve their instruction. Both

are competent bilingual instructors, although one uses English considerably more than the other.

Teacher 1

This teacher generally presents information and develops ideas in English and then provides a more basic and less detailed translation in Spanish. The mathematics lessons seldom have a conceptual introduction to the day's activities that connects them to any previous or future activities. The classroom is arranged so that each table has a group of four to six students seated around it. However, students spend their time working quietly and independently on completing worksheets. The problems students work on are part of a currently popular manipulative-based mathematics curriculum. With this instructional arrangement, the teacher spends her time walking around the room answering individual questions, and students often spend a good deal of time waiting for the teacher's attention.

During the lesson described here, a group of Spanish-speaking students have been separated from the rest of the class to receive special attention. The teacher and four students sit around a table. The lesson is on chip trading and place value, and very closely follows the teacher's guide for this curriculum. The teacher and each student have square boards in front of them, and there is a basket of red and black plastic objects on the table. The teacher pulls out one red and four black objects, puts them in the middle of the table, and says something too low for anyone to hear clearly.

Then, she begins again and as she points to each black object, she says: "Uno, dos, tres, cuatro" *(one, two, three, four)* and as she puts her finger on the red object, she says "manzanas" *(apples)*, as a name for the collection. She then signals with her hand for all the students to join in and repeat the chant that she has just demonstrated. In unison, the chant is completed twice and then each individual child is signaled to take a turn. The third time through the group chant, one of the young girls makes a mistake and says *cinco (five),* instead of *manzanas,* She is told to do the chant again. Once the teacher is satisfied that the routine has been mastered by everyone, she then directs each student to move the black objects as they are counted to one side of the board, and when they come to *manzanas,* the red object is exchanged for the others. This routine of regrouping in base 5 proceeds for several turns, and then the process is reversed in the same strict order. The only talk that takes place is the counting described. There is no discussion of why *manzanas* is used in place of *five,* nor of the cognitive relevance of this activity to the nature of regrouping in general and to base 10 in particular.

Teacher 2

Just as English is the primary language used in Teacher 1's classroom, Spanish is what is most often heard in Teacher 2's room. Also, just as students spend most of their time working individually in the other classroom, in this room, they spend their time working in groups on various projects that integrate mathematical skills related not only to adding and subtracting with multidigit whole numbers, but also to basic understandings of rational numbers. They also spend considerable time sitting in a group on a carpet in front of the teacher, who sits on a small chair. In this arrangement, teacher and students engage in lively discussions focused on mathematics. By traditional standards, this class is very noisy. The following is an example of Teacher 2's lessons. Each student uses a slate for writing the problem.

T: Okay…write…one hundred and three, one hundred and three, ciento tres, ciento tres,…¿Si digo ciento tres, cuantos lugares voy a tener ocupados?
(… one hundred three, one hundred three…. If I say one hundred three, how many places are going to be occupied?)

Sch: Ciento tres, ciento tres! [Sch. indicates that many students are talking at the same time.]

S1: Tres. *(Three.)*

S2: Tres. *(Three.)*

T: Voy a tener tres lugarcitos…. ¿Van a estar los tres lugares ocupados?
(I'm going to have three places…. Will the three places be occupied?)

Sch: Sí. *(Yes.)*

S1: No.

S2: No.

S3: Yes.

S4: No, porque está un soldado. *(No, because there's a soldier.)* [Students use "soldier" to describe the zero place holder.]

The discussion continues with various students offering opinions, asking questions, and sometimes freely changing the subject. The teacher brings the students back to the original topic.

T: Okay, ciento tres, we have how many hundreds?

Sch: One.

T: Yes, one hundred. What do we mean when we say we have one hundred, what do we mean by that? [The teacher translates her statements.] ¿Qué quiere decir…qué queremos decir cuando decimos que tenemos una centena?

S1: Una…una vez cien. *(One…one times a hundred.)*

Sch: Diez!

S2: Yo dije…cero veces diez. *(I said…zero times ten.)*

A debate among the students ensues and a correct interpretation is arrived at with the help of the teacher, who both questions and explains. Then another multidigit number is offered and the discussions begin again.

On a subsequent day, the students are about to start a project of baking a cake. The project is intended to reinforce skills in reading and following directions, as well as basic concepts of measuring and rational numbers. The students are to work in small groups, with each group having its own box of cake mix. Before starting the project, the students gather together on the floor in front of the teacher for overall directions on how to proceed. Shortly after the teacher begins, one of the students interrupts with a question about the picture of a slice of cake that is on the box. The student has recognized that the slice must be a fraction of the cake; the question has to do with what fraction is represented. The following dialogue is another example of how this teacher seizes opportunities to engage her students in mathematical talk and thinking.

S1: What is this? [The student is indicating the picture of a slice of cake on the box.]

S2: Son de chocolate.
(They are chocolate.)

T: What?

S1: Mira, le quitaron uno.
(Look, one has been taken.)

S3: De chocolate.
(Of the chocolate.)

T: Oh, I see, you guys, le quitaron un pedazo a la fracción, ¿verdad?
(Oh, I see, you guys, a piece was taken that's a fraction, right?)

Sch: ¿Qué fracción es ésta? [indicating the cake slice]
(What fraction is this?)

S1: Era un tercio.
(It was a third.)

T: ¿Creen ustedes que este es un tercio?
(Do you think this is a third?)
[The students all say yes.]
Pero está muy chiquita para ser un tercio. Miren el tercio grande que está allí [pointing to a picture on the wall of a pie-shaped third the students had made].
(But this is too small to be a third. Look how big the third is over there.)

S2: Un cuarto.
(A fourth.)

S3: Miren que tan chiquito [pointing to another picture on the wall of a pie-shaped fourth].
(Look, it's too small.)

S4: Teacher, teacher, si le quitan...un poquito del tercio.
(Teacher, teacher, if you take...a little from the third.)

The students continue offering guesses, making comparisons with what they already know abut fractions, and justifying their own analysis. After a short while, one of the students finally asks: "How will we figure it out?" The teacher responds with a question that invites the class to offer ways to figure out what fraction is represented by the slice. The students accept the challenge and spend part of the afternoon trying to measure the cake slice instead of doing the baking project.

From these examples, we can infer each teacher's assumptions about the role and purpose of talk in mathematics. In Teacher 1's classroom, students' talk is controlled through the use of repetition and choral speaking. There is no room for personalization by a student, since deviations in responses are met with corrections and implicit herding back into the group.

Teacher 2, on the other hand, carries on active discussions, with many instances of positive challenges to students to explain what they mean and to use what they know to solve a problem not encountered before. There are many variations in the student responses and clear indications that everyone can and has a right to offer his or her own idea or to ask a question.

In essence, what we can see here are two very different messages being given to Hispanic students via communication processes. In the first class, students are being told implicitly that they cannot really participate in mathematics, that mathematical knowledge is beyond them, and that this knowledge is something that someone else has to give them. In the second class, the implied message is just the opposite: Mathematics is participatory, it resides within each one of us because of universal experiences with quantities, and it is socially constructed, meaning that all students have equal chances in mathematics.

Summary and Concluding Remarks

Throughout this discussion, I have argued that there is nothing inherent about Hispanic students or their culture and family life that should handicap them to the extent indicated in recent national studies (Matthews et al., 1984; Moore & Smith, 1987). Instead, I have offered alternative hypotheses that focus on the nature of teachers' language use in the instruction of mathematics. I have pointed to issues concerning teachers' clarity of wording and choice of language—that is, English or Spanish. I also have offered a perspective that connects the relatively simple concept of speaking with a more crucial and formidable aspect of mathematics teaching and learning related to the alienation or empowerment of minority students in mathematics.

I wish to conclude with a reminder of my opening remarks

to the effect that consideration of a shift in paradigms away from students and toward school processes, including teaching, is not to suggest fault finding or cynicism about teachers. My position is that teachers are genuinely goodhearted and concerned about providing the best instruction possible. In fact, as I noted earlier, the teachers in this study recognized their shortcomings with respect to explaining mathematics and being able to change their instructional practices. They also felt a sense of powerlessness when it came to acting on their intuitions about effective instruction.

What I am suggesting is that variables related to teacher discourse, learning environments that promote student talk, and educational policies that encourage and support instructional change in light of these variables have not gotten sufficient attention as we discuss Hispanic students' performance in mathematics. We have operated too long with the myth that mathematics teaching and learning transcends linguistic considerations. As I hope I have demonstrated, such a mythology is particularly detrimental to the educational advancement of high-risk students.

Nor are the issues I have put forth easily reduced to improving bilingual teachers' clarity of speech or engaging students in classroom discourse. We must begin to ask questions about the content of teachers' conceptual explanations and about teachers' abilities to use questions and cues to extend student talk and thinking, all in two languages. We must ask questions about how to carry out principles of teacher and student dialogues in those cases when the participants speak different cultural languages. We must ask questions about the use and quality of contextualized situations so that they genuinely engage minority students in higher-level critical thinking in mathematics rather than in superficial, and ultimately lower-level, thinking. Most important, we should ask questions about our teacher-training policies and activities and how they affect and interact with the foregoing issues. Are all teachers provided with sufficient and specific opportunities to acquire appropriate knowledge and skills with which to implement effective instruction in mathematics in multilingual and multicultural contexts?

Last, what sets these issues and questions apart from a more generalized discussion of improved instruction for all students? Why is it not enough to assume that "good teaching is simply good teaching"? The answers lie in the implied assumption that we can ignore socially contextualized instruction, which considers the unique sociolinguistic and cognitive needs of language-minority students. Improved instruction for Hispanic students in mathematics is grounded in the process of redefining teaching as creating learning environments that capitalize on students' home language and experiences rather than ignoring or devaluing them.

ACKNOWLEDGMENTS

The research reported in this paper was supported in part by National Science Foundation grant number MDR-8850535. Any opinions, conclusions, or recommendations are those of the author and do not necessarily reflect the views of the National Science Foundation.

I wish to express my debt and gratitude to colleagues who assisted me along the way. I would like to thank the very dedicated teachers and students who allowed me into their classrooms and shared their time and insights with me; I promised them anonymity and so I must thank them collectively. I would also like to thank members of the research team: José Prado, who started work on the project as a high school apprentice and is now a confirmed college student; Kathryn Bert and Jennifer Cowgill, research assistants, who spent many hours videotaping and transcribing; Gilberto Cuevas, Hugh Mehan, and Alba Gonzalez Thompson, who served as consultants throughout the project; and Verna Adams and David Pimm for their thoughtful comments on earlier drafts of this work. Finally, but not least, I am grateful to Douglas B. McLeod, a special colleague and collaborator from the beginning.

NOTES

1 The focus of the research and discussion in this chapter is on Spanish-speaking children of Mexican descent, to whom I refer with the generic term *Hispanic*. However, many of the issues and concepts discussed herein pertain equally well to any group of students who are non-English-proficient or limited-English-proficient.

2 For additional discussion and a comprehensive review of research in bilingual education, the reader is referred to L. Wong Fillmore

and C. Valadez (1986), Teaching Bilingual Learners, in M. Wittrock (Ed.), *Third Handbook of Research on Teaching* (pp. 648–685), New York: Macmillan. Also, a good review of successful programs and their characteristics can be found in S. Krashen and D. Biber (1988), *On Course: Bilingual education Success in California,* Sacramento: California Association for Bilingual Education.

REFERENCES

Au, K., & Jordan, C. (1981). Teaching reading to Hawaiian children: Finding a culturally appropriate solution. In H. Trueba, G. P. Guthrie, & K. Au (Eds.), *Culture in the bilingual classroom: Studies in classroom ethnography* (pp. 139–152). Rowley, MA: Newberry House.

Bishop, A. (1991). *Mathematical enculturation.* Norwell, MA: Kluwer.

Casteneda, A. (1983). Mathematics and young bilingual children. In T. H. Escobedo (Ed.), *Early childhood bilingual education: A Hispanic perspective* (pp. 139–147). New York: Teachers College Press.

Cazden, C. (1986). Classroom discourse. In M. C. Wittrock (Ed.), *Third handbook of research on teaching* (pp. 432–463). New York: Macmillan.

Cuevas, G. (1984). Mathematics learning in English as a second language. *Journal for Research in Mathematics Education, 15,* 134–144.

Cummins, J. (1981). The role of primary language development in promoting educational success for language minority students. In *Schooling and language minority students: A theoretical framework* (pp. 3–50). Evaluation, Dissemination and Assessment Center, California State University, Los Angeles.

Freire, P. (1970). *Pedagogy of the oppressed.* New York: Continuum.

Garcia, E. (1988). Attributes of effective schools for language minority students. *Education and Urban Society, 2,* 387–398.

Halliday, M. A. K. (1978). *Language as social semiotic.* Baltimore, MD: Edward Arnold.

Khisty, L. L. (1991). *Program and policy issues in the mathematics education of Hispanic bilingual students.* Unpublished manuscript. University of Illinois at Chicago, College of Education.

Khisty, L. L., McLeod, D., & Bertilson, K. (1990). Speaking mathematically in bilingual classrooms: An exploratory study of teacher discourse. In G. Booker, P. Cobb, & T. Mendicutti (Eds.), *Proceedings of the Fourteenth International Conference for the Psychology of Mathematics Education* (Vol. 3, pp. 105–112). Mexico City: CONACYT.

Krashen, S., & Biber, D. (1988). *On course: Bilingual education success in California.* Sacramento: California Association for Bilingual Education.

Langer, J. (1987). A sociocognitive perspective on literacy. In J. Langer (Ed.), *Language, literacy and culture: Issues of society and schooling* (pp. 1–20). Norwood, NJ: Ablex.

Matthews, W., Carpenter, T., Lindquist, M., & Silver, E. (1984) The third national assessment: Minorities and mathematics. *Journal for Research in Mathematics Education, 15,* 165–171.

Moll, L. (Ed.). (1990). *Vygotsky and education: Instructional implications and applications of sociohistorical psychology.* New York: Cambridge University Press.

Moll, L., & Diaz, S. (1987). Change as the goal of educational research. *Anthropology and Education Quarterly, 18,* 300–311.

Moore, E., & Smith, A. (1987). Sex and ethnic group differences in mathematical achievement: Results from the national longitudinal study. *Journal for Research in Mathematics Education, 18,* 25–36.

National Center for Education Statistics. (1981). Projections of non-English background and limited-English-proficient persons in the U.S. to the year 2000. *Forum: Bimonthly Newsletter of the National Clearinghouse for Bilingual Education, 4,* 2.

National Council of Teachers of Mathematics. (1989). *Curriculum and evaluation for school mathematics.* Reston, VA: Author.

Pimm, D. (1987). *Speaking mathematically.* New York: Routledge & Kegan Paul.

Scribner, S., & Cole, M. (1981). *Psychology of literacy.* Cambridge, MA: Harvard University Press.

Spanos, G., Rhodes, N. C., Dale, T. C., & Crandall, J. (1988). Linguistic features of mathematical problem solving: Insights and applications. In R. Cocking & J. Mestre (Eds.), *Linguistic and cultural influences on learning mathematics* (pp. 221–240). Hillsdale, NJ: Erlbaum.

Tharp, R., & Gallimore, R. (1988). *Rousing minds to life.* New York: Cambridge University Press.

Tikunoff, W. (1985). *Applying significant bilingual instruction in the classroom.* Rosslyn, VA: National Clearinghouse for Bilingual Education, United States Department of Education (1992). ERIC: Instructional features in the classroom, Part 3.

U.S. Department of Education. (1982). *The condition of bilingual education in the nation, 1982.* A Report from the Secretary of Education to the President and the Congress. Rosslyn, VA: National Clearinghouse for Bilingual Education. (ERIC Document Reproduction Service No. ED 262 555).

Vygotsky, L. S. (1978). *Mind in society: The development of higher psychological processes.* Cambridge, MA: Harvard University Press.

Wertsch, J. V. (1985). *Vygotsky and the social formation of mind.* Cambridge, MA: Harvard University Press.

Wong Fillmore, L. & Valadez, C. (1986). Teaching bilingual learners. In M. C. Wittrock (Ed.), *Third handbook of research on teaching* (pp. 432–463). New York: Macmillan.

LANGUAGE AND LITERACY AS A BRIDGE TO MATHEMATICS: INTEGRATING THEORY WITH PRACTICE

Eva Midobuche
Arizona State University West

Abstract

*T*he focal point of this article is the use of literacy, language, and mathematics in working with linguistically and culturally diverse students. This article specifically addresses the use of two languages in presenting mathematics in a multi-age and multi-grade bilingual classroom in the Southwest. The material presented emphasizes bringing theory into practice through the use of language. The article also introduces a new technology-based software program that promotes the teaching of select NCTM Curriculum and Evaluation Standards as well as the NCTM Professional Standards for Teaching Mathematics through the use of literacy and language for language-minority students.

Upon entering the classroom, you are struck by the voices of young children in animated discussion. The scene is a multi-age third, fourth, and fifth grade classroom in an ethnically and linguistically diverse southwestern city. The school had recently had a "bee alarm" drill. In order to make this drill seem more realistic, the teacher had brought in a newspaper article about a swarm of Africanized "killer bees" found recently in the community. In the middle of this discussion, one realizes that the focus of the teacher's lesson is not only literacy development, but also mathematics. Incorporated into her animated use of this everyday source of literature are elements of the National Curriculum and Evaluation Standards and Professional Teaching Standards for Teaching of Mathematics as well as strategies for first and second language development.

A saying in education has it that mathematics, as the Jaime Escalante character says in the movie *Stand and Deliver* (1988), is "the great equalizer". Secretary of Education Riley (1998) notes that "Mathematics equals opportunity." In a general sense, these statements are true. People who know mathematics usually inspire awe in others. Therefore, if people know enough mathematics, they are considered successful. Riley also states that if high school students take gateway courses like Algebra I and Geometry, they go on to college at higher rates than those who do not—83 percent, compared to 36 percent. For low-income students, the rate is almost three times higher—71 percent versus 27 percent. However, what happens when the student is not yet proficient in English? Escalante's students as portrayed in the movie are Latino, but are not limited English proficient. It has become quite evident that the ability to speak English has a direct effect on the learning of mathematics in an English-speaking classroom (Mather and Chiodo, 1994; Aiken, 1972; Cuevas, 1984; Dawe, 1983; Kessler et al., 1985).

Furthermore, Secada (1983), Lass (1988), as well as Mather and Chiodo (1994) help to dispel the myth that mathematics is a universal language. All languages are tied to culture, and therefore many cultures interpret mathematics differently. The National Council of Teachers of Mathematics (NCTM, 1991), acknowledges that more proficiency in the language of instruction leads to a greater understanding and learning of mathematics. The NCTM further states: "Teachers' knowledge of their students' cultural backgrounds and [of] the implications of this knowledge for their teaching is crucial in recognizing the impact of language on learning" (p.146).

Buchanan and Helman (1997, p. 3) report that in 1994, the NCTM position statement on language-minority students further clarified this issue by stating: "Cultural background and language must not be a barrier to full participation in mathematics programs preparing students for a full range of careers. All students, regardless of their language and cultural background, must study a core curriculum in mathematics based on the NCTM standards." According to Garrison (1997, p. 132), "Mathematics instruction should become much more language dependent, [with students] now expected to read, write, listen, and speak about their mathematical understanding.... Now more than ever, mathematics has language as one of its central foci."

To add to the literacy dimension, Balas (1997) states that to communicate in the world, you need letters, symbols, and numbers: Letters form words that symbolize objects or actions in reading; numbers symbolize amounts, patterns or relationships in mathematics. Balas (p. 2) also states, "Success in reading and mathematics is based on process skills that incorporate the integration of contextual information with prior knowledge to produce meaning." She concludes that there is a natural connection for the integration of reading and mathematics.

The Curriculum and Evaluation Standards for School Mathematics (1989, pp. 5–6) published new goals for students that include (1) learning to value mathematics; (2) becoming confident in one's own ability; (3) becoming a mathematical problem solver; (4) learning to communicate mathematically; and (5) learning to reason mathematically. Whitin (1992, p. 24) states, "There is no more powerful vehicle for meeting new goals in mathematics than the use of children's literature in the classroom." Whitin (1992) concurs with NCTM that students will do more writing, reading, and discussing of mathematical ideas and stresses that this is the ideal place for children's literature. He states that:

> 1) children's literature can help learners value mathematics; 2) children's literature helps learners build their confidence in their own mathematical abilities; 3) children's literature encourages learners to be mathematical problem solvers; 4) children's literature provides a meaningful context for children to communicate mathematically; and, 5) children's literature supports learners in reasoning mathematically. (pp. 24–25)

In addition, Whitin, Mills, and O'Keefe (1990) maintain that children become mathematically literate in the same way they became literate in reading. Mathematics is more than just numbers, as language is more than just letters. Mathematical concepts may be presented in a nonthreatening manner through children's literature.

Hudelson (1984) points to the relations among reading, writing, listening, and speaking in the development of proficiency in speaking and reading English. Allen (1993) discusses the integration of mathematics and its great potential for second language development. The most effective content-area instructional programs for second language learners are the ones that incorporate instruction for math literacy along with language-building activities, thus minimizing the gap between language and content-area instruction (Chamot, 1985; Kessler, 1987; Dale and Cuevas, 1987; Garcia, 1991; Short, 1991; Kang and Pham, 1995; Carrasquillo and Rodriguez, 1995). Thus, the opportunities for the understanding of subject matter and English proficiency by language-minority students are increased (Tinajero, 1994; Peregoy and Boyle, 1993; Reyes and Molner, 1991; Secada, 1993).

Bickmore-Brand (1993, cited in Balas, 1997, p. 5) contends that language learning strategies that can be applied to enhance the learning of mathematics include the following:

- Creating a meaningful and relevant context for knowledge, skills, and values of mathematics
- Realizing that the starting point of interest in mathematics is the knowledge base of the student
- Providing opportunities for the learner to see the skills, processes, and values of mathematics by the teacher's modeling
- Continuing to build on the knowledge base and challenging the students' scaffolding
- Facilitating the metacognition of the student by helping the student identify the learning processes and how he or she learns
- Assisting the learner to accept the responsibility for the construction of knowledge
- Building a community of learners in a risk-free learning environment.

In improving mathematics instruction for bilingual students, Lass (1988, p. 481) provides an excellent if not comprehensive list of instructional procedures. She suggests the following:

1. Develop bilingual students' first language (L1) competence, especially to improve later mathematical ability in English
2. Develop bilingual students' second language (L2) proficiency
3. Teach mathematics to bilingual children bilingually
4. Recognize the role of language in mathematical problem solving
5. Recognize that mathematics is not necessarily a "universal language" for bilinguals
6. Teach mathematics vocabulary directly and systematically
7. Consider pairing L2-dominant students with L1-dominant students as one grouping method for English mathematics instruction
8. Teach problem-solving skills directly
9. Understand that social interaction patterns can affect mathematical achievement
10. Use culturally relevant situations and illustrations
11. Use individualized instruction and a diagnostic-prescriptive approach
12. Provide extensive staff development, including opportunities for bilingual mathematics teachers to develop their own materials
13. Develop a planned parent-participation model
14. Recognize the positive effects of bilingualism on mathematics learning.

The use of both languages with linguistically and culturally diverse students should be an important consideration in the instructional approach used. Today, evidence suggests that the use of two languages with linguistically and culturally diverse students increases their achievement in learning mathematics. (Cardelle-Elawar, 1990; Santos, 1992; Christian, 1995; Garrison, 1997; Wilde, 1991; Secada, 1993).

The NCTM and the National Standards

The National Council of Teachers of Mathematics (NCTM) is a nonprofit professional association dedicated to the improvement of mathematics education for all students in the United States and Canada. NCTM recognized that a change was needed in the manner in which mathematics was taught after *A Nation at Risk* 1983, was published. The development of the NCTM standards occurred over time, with mathematics education teachers, researchers, mathematicians, parent groups, and business and political leaders providing input (Price, 1997). Setting high standards for each student, NCTM developed the Curriculum and Evaluation Standards for School Mathematics in 1989. These standards outline the processes and the content that should be taught in the elementary, middle, and high school grades to ensure a high-quality mathematical background for children who will constitute the primary workforce for the early twenty-first century.

In 1991, NCTM published the Professional Standards for Teaching Mathematics. These standards develop the pedagogical methods, standards for classroom climate, and the role of the teacher and student considered necessary to meet the vision of the Curriculum and Evaluation Standards (math.ed.ology, 1997).

In 1995, the Assessment Standards for School Mathematics were published. Along with the Curriculum and Evaluation and Professional Standards, they represent guidelines that can be used to shape a mathematics curriculum in accordance with the philosophy that all students can—and must—learn mathematics in every school, in every state (Price, 1997).

According to Balas (1997), the 1989 NCTM Curriculum and Evaluation Standards of School Mathematics acknowledged the integration of mathematics and reading in its Standard 2, "Mathematics as Communication," in the following grades:

In grades K–4:
- Mathematics can be thought of as a language.
- Reading children's literature about mathematics, and eventually text material, needs more emphasis in the K–4 curriculum.
- Children can meaningfully learn mathematics; teachers can help the process by providing opportunities for them to communicate and to "talk math" with their friends.
- Use connections to construct knowledge, learn alternative ways to think about ideas, clarify thinking, and communicate about problems. (p. 9)

In grades 5–8:

- Use the skills of reading, listening, and viewing to interpret and evaluate mathematical ideas. (p. 10)

In grades 9–10:
- Use of skills provides opportunities for interpretation of data and statistics regarding social issues in this manner: mathematics helps students develop an understanding of the events in society (p. 11)

Garrison (1997) states that these standards are in alignment with current teaching strategies in bilingual education and do not place the emergent English speaker at risk. Also, when properly implemented, the NCTM standards can provide all students with a meaningful and powerful mathematics curriculum. Secada (1993) concurs, adding that some of the techniques developed by the reform movement in mathematics are effective with linguistically and culturally diverse students, whether the instruction is provided in the students' native language or in English. Furthermore, Secada (1993) points out that instruction in mathematics can promote students' fluency in English when used with other bilingual instructional methodologies.

To incorporate literacy, first and second language strategies, and NCTM standards into a mathematics lesson may be difficult for teachers of language-minority students. The Mathematics as Communication Standard will be particularly difficult for these students to attain if they do not understand the language of instruction. The students may even find it problematic to explain their mathematical reasoning in their native language. It becomes very difficult for the teacher to determine if the students' problems are mathematical or linguistic (Garrison, 1997). This point is also made by Khisty (1995), who observed classrooms with Mexican American students in which the teacher spoke primarily English or Spanish. The teaching of mathematics to language-minority students was examined through actual classroom observations. She concluded that the process of mathematics instruction can be hindered for minority and language-minority students because classroom discourse may exclude them.

Seago (1996, p. 4) states that the Professional Teaching Standards (1991) describe discourse as:

> an active discussion of mathematics; where students defend solutions and strategies to each other as well as the teacher; where conjectures are made, argued and verified; where multiple ways of thinking are encouraged, valued and listened to; where students are at the center of the discussion and their making sense of the mathematics is the reason for orchestrating discourse.

A student whose proficiency in English is limited may find these standards difficult to meet, as Khisty (1995) notes. Seago (1996) states that students are more likely to take risks if they are not afraid of making mistakes or being ridiculed. McLaughlin (1992) also indicates that children can be extremely anxious if they are singled out to perform in a language they are in the process of acquiring. Therefore, linguistically and culturally diverse students should be allowed to use their native language in answering a question. Students who are taught in their native language will transfer that knowledge to English as their language skills improve (Secada, 1993). Secada and De La Cruz (1996) also point out that sometimes the precise use of mathematical language can be learned through the use of the children's own language. Writing in both their native language and the target language for students becoming literate in a second language helps to develop concepts in both languages. Sometimes students writing first in their native language paves the way for writing in the target language (Wilde, 1991). This allows students to concentrate on one skill at a time—first on their mathematical thinking, then on their English (Garrison, 1997).

An Innovative Approach

In classrooms attended by linguistically and culturally diverse students, mathematics is not the only concern. Bilingual education teachers are expected to be knowledgeable in mathematics content and to be able to teach it fluently in the students' native language while transitioning both math and language skills to English. This is not an easy task when there are few qualified mathematics teachers and even fewer who also have preparation as bilingual education or ESL teachers (Midobuche, 1998). Fern (1998) reports that 27 percent of mathematics teachers do not have a background in mathematics and the proportions are much higher in high-poverty schools. Despite this shortage, teachers must deal with the increasingly growing population of limited-English-proficient students in our schools. According to Macías (1998), the national student enrollment of limited-English-proficient students for 1996–1997 was 3,452,073.

The shortage of qualified bilingual education and ESL mathematics teachers is alarming. The math.ed.ology program, an innovative, technology-based teacher preparation program with a mathematical focus and a special emphasis on Hispanic students, was created at Arizona State University to address this shortage. The math.ed.ology program can be accessed through CD-ROM or the Internet. Math.ed.ology (1997) is a set of multimedia professional development resources intended to help teachers increase the mathematics achievement of elementary students. In math.ed.ology, teachers are observed through video vignettes, teaching mathematics lessons in their classrooms and modeling many of the NCTM standards. (Midobuche, 1998; math.ed.ology, 1997). This program aims to promote a better understanding of those standards especially those pertaining to discourse and curriculum. In some of these classroom videos, the teacher preparation standards for bilingual education teachers (NABE, 1992) are clearly evident. Commentaries by experts in mathematics and math methods, language specialists, and the teachers themselves are presented in each segment of the lessons. The program is very realistic in examining and bringing forth the "real" student and teacher composition found in many of our schools today. Some featured classes consist entirely of students whose first language is Spanish. Others may contain Hispanic students with wide-ranging English proficiencies, along with non-Hispanic, monolingual English speakers. The amount of Spanish used varies with the language proficiency of the students in each classroom (Midobuche, 1998).

The Actual Lesson

The opening paragraph of this article's introduction is an observation from one of the lessons shown in math.ed.ology. The classroom is multi-age, multicultural, and bilingual. The students are at various stages of acquiring the English language. The teacher uses both English and Spanish to teach. The students are allowed to choose which language they feel more proficient in for use during classroom participation. This validation of the students' language and culture is important and obvious throughout the lesson.

Students in this class are studying bees. The mathematics lesson is designed to accompany that study and to provide an opportunity for estimation of the size of very large numbers, as well as a review of geometrical concepts such as congruent shapes and the definition of *square*. A brief description of the lesson includes the teacher reading a newspaper article on Africanized killer bees. She informs the students that they will be hearing numbers and that they need to make sense of them. As the article is read, the measurements of an 11-by-13-foot beehive are mentioned. Some students spontaneously react to the size of the beehive, which indicates that they consider it unusually large, while other students need to be encouraged to construct

number meanings. The teacher probes for more information. In order to have a sense of the size of the hive, the students are asked to visualize it and make comparisons to other objects that are familiar to them, including the height of their classroom and the lengths of a Siberian tiger and a white shark. The teacher engages the students in a real-world situation in order for these numbers to have meaning. She connects them to experiences outside the classroom.

Newspaper articles are an excellent source of stories that contain information based on numbers. This particular one not only establishes a context for exploring large numbers in terms of relative magnitude but also provides a great stimulus for a discussion of large objects and numbers.

Next the teacher reviews data displayed on the classroom walls about the number of flowers (60,000–90,000) that bees must visit in order to make a thimbleful of honey. An actual thimble is shown as a referent. The students react to the fact that so many flowers are needed for so little honey. The students are asked to estimate how long it would take them to make 10,000 flowers out of paper. The students' reaction to quantities of 10,000 and 90,000 show that they appreciate that these are large numbers. The teacher stresses the importance of understanding numbers this large.

As an added connection to literature and an introduction to a variety of flowers, the students are read a book about flowers in a garden. After the book is read, viewed, and discussed, to further develop the meaning of large numbers, the teacher asks the students to predict how many flowers they think the class can make in 30 minutes. The students make and justify their predictions. These predictions are recorded on the chalkboard. The students are reminded to listen critically to the estimates and see if they make sense. The students are given square pieces of paper and asked to use them to make the flowers. Specific directions are given to make origami flowers. The estimates are thus connected to reality. The students are also challenged to prove that the piece of paper given them is actually a square. Students discuss the properties of a square and prove that all sides of a square are congruent. Students then work individually in making the flowers. After 30 minutes, each group counts the flowers made by each member and writes the total on the chalkboard. The students then calculate the totals for the entire class. The students are asked to share their mental math strategies (math.ed.ology, 1997).

The teacher provides an environment in which students readily express their thinking and intuitions about numbers. The lesson is also presented in both languages. The teacher uses Spanish to instruct and communicate. She clarifies new technical vocabulary, paraphrases, and translates salient points when she feels it is appropriate. She tries to ensure that the language-minority students comprehend the meaning of the information presented in the lesson. She uses several techniques—the native language, simplified English terms, visuals such as posters, actual items such as the thimble, the hands-on activity of making flowers, and literature—to motivate and stimulate interest and to activate the students' prior knowledge. The story about the flowers in the garden provides the students not only with information on different flowers but also with visuals that clarify new words. The teacher builds her instructional activities on the students' real-life experiences with the newspaper article and their own bee alarm drills in school. Bringing the students' prior experiences into mathematics creates situations in which interaction of teacher and students can occur. These activities not only stimulate the learning of mathematics and literacy but also promote language acquisition. The classroom is a stress-free environment in which students' affective filter is lowered and comprehensible input is promoted (Krashen, 1994). Even bilingual students who are confident and proficient speakers of English often have difficulty grasping specialized vocabulary of academic content. If support in their first language is withdrawn too early, they are placed at a disadvantage. In this lesson, the students' language and culture are validated in every gesture, word, and action of the teacher. This is a very important aspect of teaching linguistically and culturally diverse students.

Student Learning of Content

This mathematics lesson was very rich and comprehensive. Through the incorporation of literacy and the students' first and second languages, mathematical concepts were brought to the fore and became a real part of the students' lives. Through the use of both languages, students were empowered to construct meaning from the mathematical concepts and standards listed here. The following is a list of the mathematical concepts addressed and presented in this lesson:

Understanding large numbers, place-value concepts, counting strategies, grouping strategies, different uses of numbers in the real world, cardinal/ordinal numbers, benchmarks for measurement, operations (addition, subtraction, multiplication, division), relationship among the operations, facts and algorithms, mental math, estimation, choosing the best strategy for solving a problem, describing shapes, classifying shapes, attributes of shapes, and geometry in the real world (math.ed.ology, 1997).

NCTM Curriculum and Evaluation Standards Taught

Using the newspaper as a stimulus, this particular lesson focused on developing understanding of number sense, numeration, and geometry. The NCTM Curriculum and Evaluation Standards identified in this lesson include the following:

Standard 6: Number Sense and Numeration

C6.1 Posing questions and tasks that elicit, engage, and challenge each student's thinking

C6.3 Develop number sense

C6.4 Interpret the multiple uses of numbers encountered in the real world

Standard 9: Geometry and Spatial Sense

C9.1 Describe, model, draw, and classify shapes

C9.2 Investigate and predict the results of combining, subdividing, and changing shapes

C9.3 Develop spatial sense

C9.4 Relate geometric ideas to number and measurement ideas (math.ed.ology, 1997)

The Role of Discourse

The environment created by the teacher in this lesson promoted appropriate mathematical discourse by both teacher and student. The use of real literature, visuals, and the native language plays a prominent role in allowing mathematical discourse to take place and have meaning. The discourse standards from the NCTM Professional Development Standards identified in this lesson include the following:

Standard 2: The Teacher's Role in Discourse

D2.1 Posing questions and tasks that elicit, engage, and challenge each student's thinking

D2.2 Listening carefully to students' ideas

D2.3 Asking students to clarify and justify their ideas orally and in writing

D2.4 Deciding what to pursue in depth from among the ideas that students bring up during a discussion

D2.5 Deciding when and how to attach mathematical notation and language to students' ideas

D2.6 Deciding when to provide information, when to clarify an issue, when to model, when to lead, and when to let a student struggle with a difficulty

D2.7 Monitoring students' participation in discussion and deciding when and how to encourage each student to participate

Standard 3: Students' Role in Discourse

D3.1 Listen to, respond to, and question the teacher and one another

D3.2 Use a variety of tools to reason, make connections, solve problems, and communicate

D3.3 Initiate problems and questions

D3.4 Make conjectures and present solutions

D3.5 Explore examples and counterexamples to investigate a conjecture

D3.6 Try to convince themselves and one another of the validity of particular representations, solutions, conjectures, and answers

D3.7 Rely on mathematical evidence and argument to determine validity

Standard 4: Tools for Enhancing Discourse

D4.2 Concrete materials used as models

D4.3 Pictures, diagrams, tables, and graphs

D4.5 Metaphors, analogies, and stories (math.ed.ology, 1997)

Summary and Conclusions

Given that bilingual education teachers are in very short supply, schools need to make every effort to attract these types of teachers. The shortage of qualified bilingual/mathematics teachers only makes this situation more critical. Therefore, it is very important that schools begin their own staff development programs in order to help themselves. Universities also need to encourage mathematically inclined bilingual students to pursue degrees in teaching.

Since it was possible for this article to present only a small portion of what was observed in this lesson, one must surmise that providing sufficient time for this type of learning activity is very critical. Time is also needed to plan literacy and native language development, as well as second language strategies, and to integrate them into the lessons. This is in addition to incorporating the appropriate NCTM standards.

The intent here, however, is to give the reader a realistic sense of the learning possibilities for linguistically and culturally diverse students presented by this mathematics lesson. It is easy to see that this lesson was much more than mathematics. It was also much more than the teaching of mathematics through the use of literature. This particular lesson was about mathematics being taught to linguistically and culturally diverse children through the use of literacy in order to bring the reality of current events into the classroom.

What one can actually say about this type of mathematical discourse is that it operationalizes the notion of comprehensible input (Krashen, 1994). The importance of this type of meaningful discourse for these students cannot be overstated. This meaning is further enhanced by teachers who promote the native language and culture of the students. For the linguistically and culturally diverse student, this has the effect of expanding the world of mathematics beyond the classroom.

REFERENCES

Aiken, L.S., Jr. (1972). Language factors in learning mathematics. *Review of Educational Research, 42,* 359–385.

Allen, B. (1993). Integrating English as a second language and mathematics instruction in the elementary grades. ERIC Document Reproduction Service No. ED 368 188.

Balas, A. (1997, June). The mathematics and reading connection. ERIC Digest Clearinghouse for Science, Mathematics, and Environmental Education. URL: http//www.ericse.org/digests/dse97-2.html

Bickmore-Brand, J. (1993). Applying language-learning principles to mathematics teaching. In M. Stephens, A. Waywood, D. Clarke, & J. Izard (Eds.), *Communicating mathematics: Perspectives from classroom practice and current research* (pp. 79–90). Hawthorn, Australia: Australian Council for Educational Research, Ltd.

Buchanan, K., & Helman, M. (1997). *Reforming mathematics instruction for ESL literacy students.* ERIC Document Reproduction Service No. ED 414 769.

Carrasquillo, A.L., & Rodriguez, V. (1995). *Language-minority students in the mainstream classroom.* Philadelphia: Multilingual Matters, Ltd.

Cardelle-Elawar, M. (1990). Effects of feedback tailored to bilingual students' mathematics needs on verbal problem solving. *Elementary School Journal, 91* (2), 165–176.

Chamot, A.U. (1985). English language development through a content based approach. In *Issues in English language development* (pp. 49–55). Rosslyn, VA: National Clearinghouse for Bilingual Education (NCBE).

Christian, D. (1995). Two-way bilingual education: Students learning through two languages. Santa Cruz, CA: National Center for Research on Cultural Diversity and Second Language Learning.

Cuevas, G. J. (1984). Mathematics learning in English as a second language. *Journal of Research in Mathematics Education, 15,* 35–144.

Dale, T. C., & Cuevas, G.J. (1987). Integrating language and mathematics learning. In J. Crandall (Ed.), *ESL through content-area instruction: Mathematics, science, social studies* (pp. 9–54). Englewood Cliffs, NJ: Prentice Hall Regents.

Dawe, L. (1983). Bilingualism and mathematical reasoning in English as a second language. *Educational Studies in Mathematics, 14,* 325–353.

Fern, V. (1998, July). What are the characteristics of the bilingual teacher shortage? How do we best prepare teachers for linguistically culturally diverse settings? National Clearinghouse for Bilingual Education. AskNCBE. Vol. 14 [On-line] URL: http: askncbe@ncbe.gwu.edu.

Garcia, E.E. (1991). *Education of linguistically and culturally diverse students: Effective instructional practices.* Santa Cruz, CA: National Center for Research on Cultural Diversity and Second Language Learning.

Garrison, L. (1997). Making the NCTM's standards work for emergent English speakers. *Teaching Children Mathematics, 4* (3/4), pp. 132–138.

Hudelson, S. (1984). Kan yu ret an rayt en Ingles: Children become literate in English as a second language. *TESOL Quarterly, 18,* 221–238.

Kang, H., & Phan, K. T. (1995). From 1 to Z: Integrating math and learning. Paper presented at the 29th Annual Convention of the Teachers of English to Speakers of Other Languages, Long Beach, CA. Eric Document Reproduction Service No. ED. 381 031.

Kessler, C. (1987). Linking mathematics and second language teaching. ERIC Document Reproduction Service N. ED 289 357.

Kessler, C., Quinn, M.E., & Hayes, C.W. (1985, October). *Processing mathematics in a second language: Problems for LEP children*, Newark, DE: Paper presented at the Delaware Symposium VII on Language Studies. ERIC Document Reproduction Service No. ED 268 821.

Khisty, L.L. (1995). Making inequality: Issues of language and meanings in mathematics teaching with Hispanic students. In W.G. Secada, E. Fennema, & L. B. Adajian (Eds.), *New directions for equity in mathematics education* (pp. 279–297). New York: Cambridge University Press.

Krashen, S.D. (1994). Bilingual education and second language acquisition theory. In C.F. Leyba (Ed.), *Schooling and language-minority students: a theoretical framework,* 2nd ed. (pp. 47–75). Los Angeles: Evaluation, Dissemination and Assessment Center, School of Education, California State University, Los Angeles.

Lass, M. J. (1988). Suggestions from research for improving mathematics instruction for bilinguals. *School Science and Mathematics, 88* (6), 480–487.

Macias, R. F. (1998). *Summary report of the survey of the states' limited-English-proficient students and available educational programs and services, 1996–97.* National Clearinghouse on Bilingual Education, Contract No. T295005001, U.S. Department of Education.

McLaughlin, B. (1992). *Myths and misconceptions about second language learning: What every teacher needs to unlearn* (Educational Practice Report: 5). University of California. Santa Cruz, CA: The National Center for Research on Cultural Diversity and Second Language Learning.

math•ed•ology (CD-ROM software program). (1997). Tempe; Arizona Board of Regents, Arizona State University, Technology-Based Learning and Research.

Mather, J.R.C., & Chiodo, J.J. (1994). A mathematical problem: How do we teach mathematics to LEP students? *Journal of Educational Issues of Language Minority Students, 13,* 1–12.

Midobuche, E. (1998, November 1). Preparing bilingual/ESL mathematics teachers through innovative technology. *NABE News, 22* (3).

National Association for Bilingual Education. (1992). *Professional Standards for the Preparation of Bilingual/Multicultural Teachers.* Washington, DC: National Association for Bilingual Education.

National Commission on Excellence in Education. (1983). *A nation at risk: The imperative for educational reform.* Washington, DC: U.S. Department of Education.

National Council of Teachers of Mathematics. (1989). *Curriculum and evaluation standards for school mathematics.* Reston, VA: NCTM.

National Council of Teachers of Mathematics. (1991). *Professional standards for teaching mathematics.* Reston, VA: NCTM.

National Council of Teachers of Mathematics. (1994). *News Bulletin.* Reston, VA: NCTM.

Peregoy, S. F., & Boyle, O.F. (1993). *Reading, writing, and learning in ESL: A resource book for K–8 teachers.* New York: Longman.

Price, J. (1997, April). The NCTM standards: Helping shape a mathematically literate society. *Notices of the American Mathematical Society.* [On-line] URL: http://www.ams.org/notices/199704/forum-price.html.

Reyes. M., & Molner. L. (1991). Instructional strategies for second language learners in the content areas. *Journal of Reading, 35,* 96–103.

Riley, R. W. (1998, January). *The state of mathematics education: Building a strong foundation for the 21st century.* Address given at the Joint Mathematics Meeting, Baltimore. URL: http://www.ms.org/notices/199804/riley.pdf.

Santos, S.L. (1992). Mathematics instruction in bilingual education. In R.V. Padilla & A.H. Benavides (Eds.), *Critical perspectives on bilingual education research* (pp. 242–256). Tempe, AZ: Bilingual Press/Editorial Bilingüe.

Seago, N. (1996, December). Mathematical discourse—What does that mean? *CMC ComMuniCator 21* (2), 4–5.

Secada, W. G. (1983). The educational background of limited-English-proficient students: Implications for the arithmetic classroom. Washington, DC: Office of Bilingual Education and Minority Languages Affairs. ERIC Document Reproduction Service No. ED 237 318.

Secada, W. G. (1993). Teaching limited-English-proficient students to understand and use mathematics. ERIC Clearinghouse on Urban Education Digest No. 70. URL: http//eric.web.tc.columbia.edu/digests/dig70.html.

Secada, W., & De La Cruz, Y. (1996). Teaching mathematics for understanding to bilingual students. In J. L. Flores (Ed.), *Children of la frontera: Binational efforts to serve Mexican migrant students* (pp. 285-305). Charleston, WV: ERIC Clearinghouse on Rural and Small Schools.

Short, D. (1991). Integrating language and content instruction: Strategies and Techniques. National Clearinghouse for Bilingual Education Program Information Guide Series 7.

Stand and Deliver (1988) [Film]. (Musca, T. (producer), & Menendez, R. (director). Available from Warner Brothers, Inc.)

Tinajero, J.V. (1994). Are we communicating? Effective instruction for students who are acquiring English as a second language. *The Reading Teacher, 48,* 260–264.

Whitin, D. J. (1992). Explore mathematics through children's literature. *School Library Journal, 38* (8), 24–28.

Whitin, D. J., & Gary, C. (1994). Promoting mathematical explorations through children's literature. *Arithmetic Teacher, 49* (2). 4–11.

Whitin, D. J., Mills, H., & O'Keefe, T. (1990). *Living and learning mathematics: Stories and strategies for supporting mathematical literacy.* Portsmouth, NH: Heinemann.

Wilde, S. (1991, February). Learning to write about mathematics. *Arithmetic Teacher,* 39–43.

Part IV

TECHNOLOGY

GLOBAL LEARNING NETWORKS: HEARTBEATS ON THE INTERNET[1]

Kristin Brown
Center for Language-Minority Educational Research

Las telecomunicaciones en la sociedad deben servir, como los electrocardiogramas, para transmitir los latidos de amor del corazón humano. (Instead of viewing the Internet as an information superhighway, we should see telecommunications in our society as an electrocardiogram whose purpose is to transmit our heartbeats, to make it possible for the love beating in our human hearts to be felt by others.)

Daniel Reyes (1949 –1997), Founder, "Red Telar" (Todos en la Red), Argentina

Linking Students Across Distances

As educators of culturally and linguistically diverse students, we cannot afford to underuse the Internet. Rather than viewing it as a super-encyclopedia, intimidating and expensive to page through, we should see it as an opportunity for our children to make real connections in the real world. Rather than just looking for information, we should be looking for people.

When students can move beyond passive "surfing" and individualized learning to develop investigative and cross-cultural communication skills, they are allowed to look at realities of their own and other cultures. Their learning takes on a personal feeling and a powerful relevance as students discover how sharing information through collaborative, project-based learning changes their lives—and the lives of others.

The concept behind global learning networks—that classrooms in different parts of the world should link up to work on common projects—is relatively simple. Yet if teachers are to tap into the immense potential of educational networking, they must go beyond linking individual students as "pen pals" or "key pals," and actively link classes to promote dynamic and relevant investigation. This article describes how educators working with bilingual and diverse student populations have integrated global learning networks into the curriculum at their schools within a framework of collaborative and critical inquiry and purposeful social action.[2]

Teachers who want to create lively, equitable, and more effective educational experiences for their students must concern themselves with issues beyond the classroom walls. Inside the classroom, students are isolated from many experiences that would help them understand the past in meaningful ways and thus develop skills for democratic participation in the future. Many culturally diverse students enter schools where they see little from their backgrounds reflected in the curriculum or on the walls of the classroom. Schools tend to be cut off from students' families, communities, and languages, and from knowledge of the world in which the students live. When schools fail to build on the skills and experiences that students bring to school, students are more likely to absorb the message that cultural diversity is a problem to be solved rather than an asset to society, and they become less likely to attend, either intellectually or physically. Even if they are not absent, they literally are "not present." Global networking projects can act as a strong and positive antidote to such intellectually and emotionally stifling classroom situations.

Fortunately, with the Internet, it has never been easier for teachers to extend the walls of their classrooms and to maintain a close, ongoing dialogue with other communities and other cultures. We need to see students' lives as works in progress that neither begin nor end at the schoolhouse door. Schools can be places to develop and nurture relationships and form communities in which learning takes on its own momentum as students build knowledge with others and critically examine their place in the world. Schools can be places that expand the mind by nourishing the heart and motivating deeper learning.

Deepening the Curriculum

The idea that intercultural learning networks can be organized around community learning, group dialogues, and critical inquiry as an integral part of the curriculum has a long and rich history, even predating the introduction of computers into schools. In 1924, French educators Celestin and Elise Freinet developed three highly successful teaching techniques: daily "learning walks" through town to connect learning with the students' direct experience; the composition of "group texts" (using moveable-type printing presses) centered on the students' impressions of community life; and interscholastic exchanges, in which students exchanged these writings globally along with "culture packages," small packages sent through the mail containing photos, tapes, maps, schoolwork, and local memorabilia. To this day, French teachers enjoy free franking privileges, paying nothing to use the national postal service for educational projects. At the time of Celestin Freinet's death in 1966, the interscholastic network that he and Elise founded, the Modern School Movement, involved 10,000 schools in 33 countries.

We can use new technologies to build on the success of the Freinets' techniques. The Internet offers several kinds of communication tools for classes engaging in global networking projects. With electronic mail, messages are exchanged between two or more e-mail accounts, speeding information across a continent or an ocean in just a few seconds. E-mail reduces the turnaround time and greatly facilitates communication between two partner classes. Another useful tool is computer-based conferencing, or newsgroups (also called electronic bulletin boards), which foster communication among a number of classes participating in a group project built around a topic of common interest. On electronic bulletin boards, messages are stored and displayed online—a more permanent record in a public place—so that newly joining classes can easily become up-to-date on project activity. These "asynchronous" forms of communication are especially useful tools in project-based learning across distances, because they allow students time to discuss and reflect on their partner class's comments before responding. "Synchronous" communication tools, such as live chats or audio- or videoconferences, can be scheduled at key points in the project for students to meet informally, exchange project updates, or make quick decisions in "real time."

Although the technologies employed by classes participating in global networks have changed, we must remember that the pedagogical underpinnings remain the same. Students in distant classes engage in a collaborative project that builds on the curriculum in the participating classes and provides opportunities for interdependent, cooperative activity in small groups at each site. Examples of successful long-distance team-teaching projects include comparative investigations (e.g., dual community surveys, joint science investigations, or contrastive geography projects), shared student journalism and publishing (e.g., newsletters or literary journals), and oral histories and folklore compendia (e.g., community narratives or intergenerational collections of proverbs or folk tales). As Cummins and Sayers (1995) have noted, "The common element of all networking projects that focus on social and cultural inquiry is the emergence of a community of learning that thrives on incorporating alternative perspectives in its search for understanding. These alternative perspectives derive from both the partner classes and the use of a much wider range of sources for research inquiry than just the traditional textbook." These sources may include the Internet. Yet the motivation for searching out new forms of information is quite different from the kind of passive surfing for information mentioned at the beginning of this article. The information sought will be interpreted, analyzed, extended, and critiqued in light of the specific project at hand.

A Few Examples

As bilingual teachers and their students gain practice in jointly designing collaborative projects, they become highly skilled at planning activities that extend the curriculum in both classes, finding areas of common relevance and motivation, and addressing issues of equity at their school sites. The following examples help illustrate how technology can add a layer of sophistication and richness to project-based learning.

In one exchange, a middle school geography teacher responsible for teaching mapping skills engaged in an e-mail exchange with a teacher interested in oral and family histories. The geography teacher in San Diego, working mainly with immigrants from Latin America, Asia, and the Pacific Islands, designed an exchange with Cape Verdean students in Boston in which students in both classes interviewed parents and grandparents to learn about migration and to identify the birthplaces of several generations of family members. Instead of sending the partner class the names of the cities in which students, their parents, and grandparents were born, students sent the latitude and longitude of the birthplaces; instead of revealing the dates of birth of these family members, they noted a famous or important event that had taken place in their culture during the year of birth. These data were sent to the partner class in the form of a geographical guessing game. Because the classes needed to type in only a small amount of text, they needed only minimal access to technology—only one computer per class. Even so, as students shared the history of each class's families, plotting the birthplaces on a world map and noting the dates and cultural events on a timeline, they were able to trace patterns of immigration on the east and west coasts of the United States.

Other teachers learned of this project and took advantage of computer conferencing to organize a larger group exchange involving classes from a dozen countries to investigate what motivates migration and how people from different cultural, racial, and linguistic backgrounds are received by their new communities. This project examined an even wider range of transitions, including moves from rural China to Beijing, African American migration from the south to the north within the United States, immigration from Mexico, Puerto Rico, Southeast Asia, and the Pacific Islands to the United States, and moves from one part of Latin America to another. In this project, dubbed "New Places" by the participating classes, students who had moved described their experiences; students who hadn't moved interviewed peers at their school about how they were received in their new schools and communities. One of the outcomes of this project was that together the students analyzed the linguistic, cultural, and institutional barriers at their schools and drew up guidelines for teachers and students about how to make their schools better places for newcomers. The idea that collaborative problem solving might make the world a better place motivates much online learning.

The Internet not only provides a forum for student discussions but also makes it easier for educators to share teaching strategies, exchange lesson plans, and discuss such challenges as implementing new curriculum standards. Teachers in Puerto Rico and the United States held an online discussion about the teaching of math and the new math standards, which call for connecting math, problem-solving, and communication skills. Curiously, as they discussed these matters, a mutual concern became clear: the underrepresentation of girls and minorities in high school and university math courses. What had begun as a discussion about curriculum led to an interest in exploring how online projects might be used to address issues of equity. For example, curricular divisions in schools usually link math with science in isolation from the social studies curriculum. In the networking project these teachers designed, mathematics was instead taught "across the curriculum" and used to uncover stereotypes, understand history, and examine issues of inequality.

In an environmental project, students studying pollution levels locally are getting together with others around the world to look at environmental decision making. Their goal is to document wise and sustainable decisions. Students everywhere are concerned with the health of the planet and environmental pollution and often form eco-clubs at their schools. Water pollution is an immediate and tangible form of environmental destruction and a global problem. Frequently it directly affects the children's lives, homes, and families. Studying pollution provides a window to see how people and institutions make decisions about environmental and societal resources. In this project students begin by gathering descriptive and quantitative data in order to describe a local environment or ecosystem through their own eyes. Younger students visit local water habitats regularly and take photos and keep journals of their observations. Older students monitor pollution levels of nearby rivers and lakes in their science classes. The students conduct interviews in the community to learn how decisions have been made concerning the water resources in their town or region. They examine how wise and unwise decisions may have been made and publish a report on the Internet and in print so that all participating classes will have a document to share with others in their community. This is an example of technology aiding a truly collective research project, in which even young students can make a substantial contribution.

Cross-cultural learning constantly occurs in global learning networks and challenges teachers and students to discover new techniques and approaches in planning classroom activities to meet their academic and social goals. Teachers in a federally mandated desegregated San Francisco school organized a project around an exchange of cultural packages. Two teachers, a Spanish-speaking bilingual teacher and her African American colleague, sought innovative ways to confront the growing tensions in the school between newly arrived Latino children of Mexican heritage and the African American students. To do so, they established a distance team-teaching partnership with a bilingual teacher in New York City who worked with Spanish-speaking students from the Caribbean. By linking their group with Spanish-speaking Latino students of African descent, they hoped to address intergroup prejudice at their school.

> Since the partner class in New York would include Spanish-speaking Latino students of African descent, we would be linking San Francisco's Latino students with faraway colleagues who in many ways were like them—students who spoke the same mother tongue and shared the experience of learning English as a second language—but whose physical attributes and pride in their African heritage more closely resembled their African-American schoolmates. In this way we hoped to provide a bridge between the African Americans and the Latinos who saw one another everyday at school but whose interaction was distorted by fears and deep-seated prejudice. (Cuellar and Brown, 1995)

The two San Francisco classes and their New York partners shared cultural packages and videos for a year, including an exchange of folk games from Mexican, Caribbean, and African American cultures. The exchange successfully engaged students from different cultures at the school in small-group activities. By the end of the year, Latino students participated actively in after-school programs in the African American neighborhood, and parents of three African American students had requested that their children be allowed to study Spanish in the bilingual program. While teachers found that the complex issues involved required much more exploration and discussion, this project had helped open a dialogue.

In addition to engaging in a curriculum project between two or more classes, teachers usually find it helpful to exchange what have come to be known as "discovery packages," "group self-portraits," or "culture packages" sent through the mail. Discovery packages may be envelopes or small boxes filled with student autobiographies, maps, photographs, audio- and videotapes, and other carefully selected articles from the school and the community, such as postcards, school newspapers, and student artwork. Many teachers find this activity so valuable that packages are exchanged throughout the year, each time exploring more fully with students the provocative question, "What is culture?" and then, "How might we communicate to another group the cultures represented in our class and community?" Teachers can encourage students to identify metaphors and symbols to include that represent the values, ways of knowing, and social relationships that have helped members of their culture survive and thrive. The least interesting packages are random collections of artifacts; the most interesting are carefully composed collections of symbolic items that reveal values and relationships within the community.

Technology plays two important roles in "amplifying the volume" in a long-distance exchange. Telecommunications facilitates a rapid turnaround time for messages, so that a sense of immediacy and dialogue is created and sustained between the two classes. Photographs, audiotapes, and videotapes help students get to know one another and help ensure that the distant class has a strong presence in your classroom between exchanges. In the words of the children who engage in these partnerships, technology helps make the distant partners more "real" and more "human."

Perspective with Distance

How do long-distance curriculum projects differ from the kinds of project-based partnerships that might take place between two classes within the same school or with a neighboring school in the community? Greater distances bring greater differences. These differences not only bring additional perspectives, which enhance a curricular project, but also provide opportunities for students to learn about one another while learning about the topic at hand.

Students face new challenges when they write to others from a distinct geographic, cultural, or linguistic reality. They can't necessarily assume that the other students share the same assumptions and background information. When people are forced to explain their lives, culture, and country to someone from another country or culture, they are forced to take a step back and rethink the world in which they live—a process that we have termed "distancing" (Brown, Cummins, Figueroa, & Sayers, 1998). These exchanges not only have the ability to promote cross-cultural understanding by introducing students to people from a different culture or background, but also have the potential to force students to re-analyze their own worlds, thereby enhancing their understanding of their own lives.

Decades ago, Elise and Celestin Freinet recognized that partnerships between faraway classes served as precursors to a more profound and active engagement with social realities much closer to home. These long-distance learning partnerships create a context for students to collaborate more intensively with people in their own classroom and community.

> When we live very close to our surroundings and to people, we eventually come not to see them. ...But thanks to the questions sent from our distant colleagues, our eyes are opened. We question, we investigate, we explore more deeply in order to respond with precise verifications to the inexhaustible curiosity of our distant collaborators, based on a natural motivation. This gradually leads to an awareness of our entire geographic, historic, and human environment. (Gervilliers et al., 1968/1977, pp. 29–30)

Through this activity, students could come to replace an unquestioning view of their world with a more objective, more conscious, and more critical perspective.

> The student, because she needs to describe them, develops an awareness of the conditions of her life, of the life of her town or her neighborhood, even of her province.
> ... She had been living too close to these conditions and through inter-school exchanges she has distanced herself from them in order to better comprehend the conditions of her life. (Gervilliers et al., 1968/1977, p. 31)

Yet "distancing" is not the only outcome. Students also discover multiple opportunities for purposeful engagement with their day-to-day reality. According to Freinet, reflective distancing leads to social action: "Inter-school networks. . . are conducive to a true cultural formation, offering to each individual several possibilities of action over his surroundings, and causing a profound engagement with human beings and with things past, present and future" (p. 15). In the next section we explore further how to take advantage of a pedagogy of distancing in our own work.

Creating Contexts for Collaborative and Critical Inquiry

Teachers concerned with equity issues and with ensuring that all students learn to high standards must pay attention to what happens beyond the walls of their classrooms as they restructure what happens inside. It is not enough to provide students with access to new resources; teachers must also consider the relations and structures of power in the society that influence their students in school. Teachers can create educational spaces in which linguistic diversity is an asset rather than a problem to be solved, in which parents are regarded as resources rather than obstacles, and in which students' own communities, no matter how poor, hold the keys to understanding the world.

How can teachers create these spaces? Once we have established a methodology, technology can help. One framework that we have found particularly useful in designing global networking projects to promote critical inquiry is the "Creative Reading Methodology" of Alma Flor Ada, whose work draws on the philosophy of Brazilian educator Paulo Freire. Ada's framework integrates in a straightforward way several key principles of learning for culturally and linguistically diverse students:

1. Ensuring relevance of the instruction, with links to family and community knowledge

2. The development of critical literacy and critical thinking skills

3. The importance of students acting on what they are learning and, more generally, taking an activist, constructivist approach to learning.

By applying Ada's four phases of creative reading, diagrammed in Figure 1, to global networking projects as I will demonstrate below, we can help ensure that students go beyond being passive recipients of knowledge to being investigators, knowledge constructors, detectives, social activists, and teachers.

Figure 1

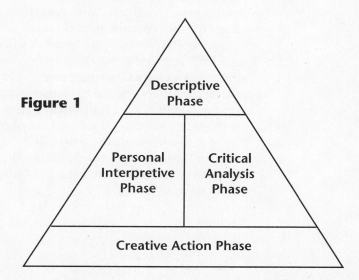

315

Students as Investigators

Traditionally, in the *descriptive phase* of a lesson, the focus of interaction between students and teachers in schools has been information found in a text. Teachers assessed students' comprehension by asking them such questions as "What did the text say?" and "What happened next?" Technology, including Web browsers, word processors, and databases, can bring access to a much wider range of information than was previously found in textbooks and school libraries. Students also have access to a greater variety of sources of information through the proliferation of media. Students need skills in gathering information from both print and electronic sources, but unless they are also able to act upon or process the information they find, knowledge will remain inert rather than becoming a catalyst for further inquiry.

Students as Constructors of Knowledge

In the *personal interpretive phase*, students are encouraged to relate the topic to their own experiences and feelings. Teachers might ask, "What do you know about the topic or issue? Have you ever seen or experienced something like this? How did it make you feel?" Teachers show students that their experiences and feelings are valued. This phase also strengthens students' comprehension of the topic or issues by grounding the curriculum in the students' lives and histories. Global networking exchanges encourage the sharing of personal and local histories. As students prepare their culture packages or write their introductory messages to their partner class, they become aware that only by revealing their own world can they expect others to show them theirs. When students later respond to the questions they receive from afar, they take on the role of local experts, with new opportunities to learn about and understand their own community.

Students also have the opportunity to see their peers through new eyes. Class-to-class partnerships promote new kinds of interactions at the local level. To respond to the probing questions that are raised by their distant colleagues, students often discover that they need to draw on the unsuspected talents of their classmates. A class may find that students who were once reluctant to speak up in class have specialized language skills or knowledge of their community that make their active participation valuable.

Teachers interested in bringing all students in their class into participation can use global learning networks to help reverse patterns of discrimination at their school. For example, in a partnership between schools in Connecticut and Puerto Rico, the teachers designed a newspaper publishing project that valued Spanish language skills in the Connecticut school. The prestige of the Spanish-dominant Puerto Rican immigrants was enhanced in the eyes of their English-speaking Puerto Rican schoolmates, who eagerly sought out their linguistic and translation skills for the exchange. Other teachers have created databases of oral histories or community research exchanges, validating the knowledge of parents and other family members.

Students as Detectives and Critical Thinkers

In the *critical analysis phase* of a project, students engage in a more abstract process of critically analyzing the issues or problems that have been raised. This involves drawing inferences and making generalizations. Teachers can guide students through this process by asking such questions as: "Who is affected? Does it benefit everyone alike? Are there alternatives to this situation? How have people of different cultures, classes, and genders reacted differently to the situation?" Distant partnerships add valuable information to a student's understanding of complex social issues.

In a global networking project, teachers can help students raise questions by encouraging them to notice similarities as well as differences and discontinuities between their local realities and the distant realities of their partners. In a cultural package exchange, for example, asking students to reflect on what they learned, what they found most interesting or surprising, and what questions they still have is a strategy that students of any age can respond to. The kinds of questions that emerge don't necessarily lead to answers that they or their partners can provide, but they do lead to an awareness of the complexity of many social and equity issues and then become the basis for further exchanges and investigations.

In these networks, students often take on the role of detectives. Investigating and making comparisons help them see patterns and think in terms of broader social issues. For example, when a class in Argentina expressed surprise to their partner class in Pennsylvania after the Argentine teacher found a penguin on their beach much farther north than expected, the students found a clue in the oil on the penguin's wings. Students and teachers discovered that the penguins were driven north because the beaches in the south had been polluted with oil. Because tankers are not allowed to dump bilges near the United States, they had done so in the southern hemisphere, where currents carried the oil to the tip of South America. When students are encouraged to make these kinds of connections, complex issues become accessible to even quite young students.

Teachers can also encourage students to reflect on the gaps in their own thinking and to explain the difference between what they found and what they expected to find in their exchanges. When students receive a text or self-portrait from a distant class, teachers may ask: "What was surprising about this? How did our expectations differ from reality? What do we know so far? What might we expect to hear? What do we predict their response will be to the questions we posed?" This, in turn, can lead to evaluating how opinions are formed. For example, in an international telecommunications exchange entitled "The Eradication of Poverty," second graders in California's Central Valley whose parents worked long days in the fields designed and shared a survey that investigated the assumption that if one just tried harder, one wouldn't be poor. By interviewing people of lower-, middle-, and upper-class occupations in their town, students came to question this assumption. They began to see the links between poverty, race, and educational opportunities.

As students learn about the variations in social and environmental policies, about the history of decisions that have been made in their own communities, and about how public opinions are formed in different parts of the world, they begin to envision alternatives to the way things are. They also come to understand that structures and institutions are created by people and can be changed.

Students as Social Activists and Teachers

The *creative action phase* translates the results of the previous phases into concrete action—and here again technology can help. Examples of such action might be desktop-publishing the results of an investigation in a community newsletter and faxing letters to government officials. The water project described earlier offered multiple opportunities for action both locally and globally. Primary grade students exchanged observations of their fresh-water pond via e-mail with their distant classmates for three years, visiting their local pond regularly. As they reported, they became disturbed by changes in the habitat. Equipped with photos and journals, they approached the city council and were able to persuade them to change city planning policies. Other students involved in the water project were concerned by reports from children in Nicaragua that they and their families walked miles each morning to carry drinking water back to the home in buckets. They organized a multi-school effort, raising money to build wells for clean water. For $250 a village could build a well with a water pump made entirely from the parts of old bicycles, which meant that the community could easily repair the pumps in the future.

Conclusion: Schools of Heart and Learning

Students need opportunities to question social realities and to "talk back to the world." Through global networks, they learn that their work and opinion have value as they see the impact of their efforts. Students who have edited newspapers and conducted opinion polls on issues of concern to communities around the world are now well-equipped with research and analytical tools to effect change and mobilize support in their own communities. These students have also gained a deeper understanding of the need for change. Through exposure to new and more diverse perspectives of social problems, their thinking reflects a more complete understanding of sociopolitical and environmental issues. Instead of seeing events in isolation, young people come to see in a more sophisticated way how local incidents may be manifestations of broader patterns of oppression. Through global learning networks, learning can be transformed into action as students gain a working knowledge of what it means to "think globally and act locally." Technology is an important tool for teachers who wish to create schools of heart and learning—schools of thoughtful transformation—in which differences are seen as resources and in which students are empowered to apply their skills to better their own and others' lives.

NOTES

1. This article has been expanded from a chapter entitled "Global Learning Networks" (also authored by Kristin Brown) that appeared in *Virtual Power* (1998), edited by Gerda de Klerk, published by the Pacific Southwest Regional Technology in Education Consortium, Long Beach, CA, and reprinted and adapted by permission of the PSRTEC.

2. Many of the projects and approaches in global networking described in this article were developed collaboratively by Kristin Brown, Enid Figueroa, and Dennis Sayers, co-directors of the teacher partnership network, De Orilla a Orilla. For a detailed discussion of collaborative critical inquiry, see *Brave New Schools* (Cummins and Sayers, 1995).

REFERENCES

Brown, K., & Cuellar, J. C. (1995). Global learning networks as a catalyst for change: Confronting prejudice between "minority groups." *NABE News*, *18* (6).

Brown, K., Cummins, J., Figueroa, E., & Sayers, D. (1998). Global learning networks: Gaining perspective on our lives with distance. In Enid Lee, Deborah Menkart, & Margo Okazawa-Rey (Eds.), *Beyond Heroes and Holidays: A Practical Guide to K–12 Anti-Racist, Multicultural Education and Staff Development*. Network of Educators on the Americas.

Cummins, J., & Sayers, D. (1995). *Brave new schools: Challenging cultural illiteracy through global learning networks*. New York: St. Martin's Press.

Literacy and the Role of Technology: Toward a Framework for Equitable Schooling

Robert A. DeVillar
University of Texas at El Paso

Introduction: Literacy—Its Nature, Forms, and Disparities

Defining Language and Literacy

Language and literacy are sociocultural, symbol-related acts of constructing, conveying, and interpreting meaning for oneself and others through the five senses in interaction with cognition ("the faculties of the mind," as stated by Chomsky, 1975, p. 12). Thus, the senses of hearing, sight, touch, smell, and taste—in interplay with cognitive faculties—can singly or in combination form a system of language or literacy. The symbolic forms that result, and the phenomena they represent, are socioculturally determined; they are not universal. Jespersen (1964), writing in 1921, described and interrelated the individual, social, interpretive, and community-specific elements associated with language:

> The act is individual, but the interpretation presupposes that the individual forms part of a community with analogous habits, and a language thus is seen to be one particular set of human customs of a well-defined social character. (p. 8)

Bell (1999), addressing the language of dance and its instructional relationship to first and second language development, quotes from Kazantzakis's (1953) novel, *Zorba the Greek*, to characterize the nature of language as a social act and, simultaneously, the limitations of spoken language as the sole device for communication:

> Zorba remarks, "Ah, if you could only dance all that you've just said, then I would understand"... But dance is more than a nonverbal language; it is a conversation. (p. 28)

Bell's passage holds the continuum of the elements to which I refer: from the world that we experience to the media that we use to re-present it, and from our individual expression of that re-presentation to its social (shared, and therefore reconstructed) meaning. Put another way, Bell's passage highlights the distinction and interrelationship that can be made among the following:

1. *Language* as a culturally specific code (all cultures, of course, generate language)
2. *Speech* as an individual phenomenon that accesses and constructs from the code based on one's need or desire to re-present and share experience, or to understand and respond to another's re-presentation of experience.

3. *Communication* ("conversation") as the attainment of mutual intelligibility, that is, of meaning, about the re-presented experience through the process of social interaction and its fundamental characteristic, negotiation.

Literacy as a Socially Constructed Act

Meaning, as characterized in the above examples, is variable; it is socially, not individually, constructed. Eisner (1991) points out:

> The process of re-presentation is a process of construal, a reconstruction, and as such it reconstitutes the experience from which it originates. We have no mirror for nature. (pp. 40-41; emphasis added)

Thus, we engage in a social process to arrive at a common understanding of what we have experienced. Furthermore, we attempt to re-present experience through expressive-communicative media (e.g., utterances, dance, music) that must be socially negotiated and constructed to be accepted as meaningful. It is this negotiated re-presentation of our world through symbols that makes the language act for Ortega y Gasset (1957) "irrational."[1] Since the era of the Sophists in Greece, approximately 400 B.C., the conundrum between that which is natural *(phúsei)* and what is convention *(thései)* in society and language has persisted (Jespersen, 1964; see also Durant, 1966).

School Notions of Language and Literacy

In their more conventional applications, the respective acts of language and literacy—although not distinct from one another in an absolute sense—may be operationally differentiated by alluding to their perceived traditional channels of expression: sound through the human voice in the case of language; visual or tactile (i.e., Braille) in the case of literacy (see, for example, discussions on definitions in Ducrot & Todorov,

1994; Richards, Platt, & Platt, 1992). More specific to our purpose here, in schools and society in the United States, *language* is that term applied to a student's command of a particular communicative system (e.g., English) through its spoken expression, while *literacy* translates traditionally and fundamentally into the integrated skills of reading and writing in that particular language.

What Determines Literacy?

Literacy attainment requires that the individual make two fundamental connections of convention. First, the learner must realize that particular symbols in written form correspond to the sounds of one's own language. Second, he or she must realize that those same symbols can combine in such a way as to produce written equivalents of spoken language. Symbol combinations, moreover, can range from a single letter to a word to an infinite string of utterances (e.g., sentences). The type of symbol combination varies according to the genre in which a person engages as a producer or recipient, and ranges from the conventionally accepted (e.g., newspapers) to the literati-challenging (e.g., James Joyce's *Ulysses*) (see, for example, Chaika, 1982, *Language, the Social Mirror*, and Joos, 1967, *The Five Clocks*, regarding numerous styles of English usage).

Learning to be literate is not solely an individual process. It requires that each individual engage in a complex and interdependent cognitive process. This process involves the presence and successful interrelationship of diverse elements from distinct contexts, including psychological, social, institutional, cultural, and technological. Thus, to be regarded as literate, one must be able to act upon the symbol-correspondence and symbol-combination connections made to meaningfully produce and decode written symbols in one's own language at expected levels of increasing performance. As noted at the outset, these levels are socioculturally determined and prescribed during one's elementary through post-secondary school experience (see, for example, Cook-Gumperz, 1986, *The Social Construction of Literacy*).

Who Determines That One Is Literate?

A student's degree of literacy is evaluated throughout his or her schooling experience according to prescribed (that is, conventional) standards of literacy development. The International Reading Association (IRA) describes the role and expectations of schooling in this literacy development process:

> Literacy requires an understanding of reading and writing in many forms, including print and electronic images, intertwined with the ability to interpret critically and apply new information to existing knowledge. Thus, school literacy programs must involve students in learning to read and write in situations that foster critical thinking and in the use of literacy for independent learning in all subject areas. (Professional Standards and Ethics Committee, IRA, 1998, p. iv)

Literacy Tools

Students of literacy and those who are already literate engage in the literacy process by using various tools, either singly or in combination. Literacy tools in schools have commonly included pencils and paper, chalk and boards, and books. Since 1984, microcomputers and various other types of electronic equipment and media have been important additions to the literacy toolbox.

Literacy and Equity

While most children learn to read and write, there are obvious and critical differences in equity—that is, in access to, and participation in, developmental reading experiences, and in the associated benefits that accrue to students. These differences are especially apparent in reading attainment by students belonging to particular ethnic, racial, and socioeconomic groups in the United States. Hence, the reading process and its outcomes, aside from being an individual learning issue, are an issue of equity for students belonging to various groups.

Equity, as used here, consists of three elements: access, participation, and benefit (see DeVillar, 1998, 1986; DeVillar & Faltis, 1994, 1991, 1987). The term differs from its near-cognate *equality* in that equality is associated with rules of law. Equity, in contrast, is associated with principles of natural justice which, ultimately, can guide, challenge, or change—in a word, supersede—law-governed equality (see, for example, Scruton, 1982, *A Dictionary of Political Thought*). Aristotle's (384–322 B.C.) characterization of the term in his *Nicomachean Ethics* stated this notion succinctly:

> Our next subject is equity and the equitable...and their respective relations to justice and the just.... [The] equitable is just, but not the legally just but a correction of legal justice.... And this is the nature of the equitable, a correction of law where it is defective. . . . (Aristotle, quoted in Commins & Linscott, 1966, pp. 110–111)

Equity and Academic Achievement

Traditionally, the degree of equity that particular groups of students have experienced at school has had implications for their reading, and other academic, processes and outcomes. In the United States, students from European American households of middle-class income and above have traditionally fared better than their low-income and minority group counterparts with respect to literacy and general academic outcomes. Since the widespread introduction of computers in schools beginning in 1984, disparities have also persisted in technological access and usage based on household income. Selected data on comparative reading scores, dropout rates, and technology access and use in the United States illustrate the type and degree of disparities in each of the above categories:

- Comparative average reading proficiency rates in 1996, for example, among 17-year-old African American, European American, and Hispanic American students were, respectively: 265, 294, and 265 (NCES, February 8, 1999). The interpretation of scores approaching the 300 mark is that students can "understand complicated information"; students scoring closer to the next lower level (250) can "interrelate ideas and make generalizations" (NCES, June 1, 1998).

- Dropout rates across students from African American, European American, and Hispanic American backgrounds differ significantly. Census Bureau figures from October 1996 cite the dropout rates, among 22- to 24-year-olds, for each of the groups mentioned above as 14.9 percent, 12.6 percent, and 35.3 percent, respectively (U.S. Census Bureau, April 5, 1999). Mexican-origin students from this same age group exhibit even a greater lack of school completion: 41.9 percent (U.S. Census Bureau, April 5, 1999). Hispanic immigrants, who constitute 56 percent of all immigrants, account for almost 90 percent of all immigrant school dropouts (Secada et al., 1998).

- In a similar manner to income, race, and ethnicity, the introduction of computer-supported technology in schools and homes over the past 15 years has exacerbated the equity issue in light of the differential distribution of computer-supported literacy opportunities, development, and outcomes across these same groups (NCES, Indicators 3 & 4, June 1,

1998). This particular difference will be elaborated upon in the following sections.

Equity, Literacy, and Computer-supported Settings

In 1998, the National Research Council's (NRC) Committee on the Prevention of Reading Difficulties in Young Children addressed, in part, this persistent phenomenon of differential reading achievement. It surveyed and analyzed the research literature on reading and made recommendations about future research, policy, and practice. The committee's findings and recommendations touch upon the distinct contexts (e.g., from psychological to technological) identified earlier as being associated with successful reading development. Thus, selected NRC Committee's findings and recommendations will serve as a platform to launch a critical discussion concerning the theoretically and research-informed uses of computer-based technology to promote successful reading development among students.

Generally, the profile of students to which I refer reflects those who are Spanish-language-dominant, or ethnically identified as Hispanic American,[2] from low-income households, who participate in some form of dual language learning context. I use the term *dual language* here in a conceptual sense to embrace a broad array of instructional settings. These settings range from linguistically heterogeneous classroom settings in which English is the sole medium of instruction to those in which the alternation of English and, say, Spanish is used pedagogically and linguistically for bilingual and subject matter development over the course of a student's elementary school years. Students, to differing degrees, complement or supplement their formal and traditional classroom experiences with other kinds of learning activities. Thus, I review nontraditional instructional settings—specifically, those which are characterized as computer-supported and which transpire within the regular school day—and informal ones, including after-school learning contexts and the home. Finally, I address the degree to which these different settings are comparable from a perspective of educational equity.

Technology, Language Policy, and Reading

The NRC Committee reported that "critical attention to the instructional quality of… educational software…is both distressingly absent and urgently needed" (Snow, Burns, & Griffin, 1998, p. 334). It recommended that local education agencies establish "specific standards of evidence of efficacy for reading-related materials" (Snow et al., 1998, p. 334). Although providing reading opportunities in a first or second language through software was not directly mentioned in its recommendation, the committee acknowledged the relationship between reading development and language development:

> Non-English speakers have much less basis for knowing whether their [English] reading is correct because the crucial meaning-making process is short circuited by lack of [second] language knowledge. Giving a child initial reading instruction in a language that he or she does not yet speak thus can undermine the child's chance to see literacy as a powerful form of communication, by knocking the support of meaning out from underneath the process of learning…. [Thus, we] urge initial literacy instruction in a child's native language [and] suggest that literacy instruction should not be introduced in any language before some reasonable level of oral proficiency in that language has been attained. (Snow et al., 1998, pp. 237-238)

In our K–12 schools, there are more than 2 million students who speak a primary language other than English and do not speak or comprehend English well enough to receive instruction through it (National Council of La Raza, 1998). Nearly three of every four of these English language learners (73 percent) have Spanish as their native language (August & Hakuta, 1998). The Hispanic-origin population, moreover, is growing, and at a faster rate than most other U.S. groups, whether designated along cultural, linguistic, or ethnic dimensions. For example, in 1980, the Hispanic American child population accounted for 9 percent of the total U.S. child population; in 1996, it accounted for 14 percent; and in 2020, it is predicted to account for more than 20 percent (Sable & Stennett, 1998).

The committee assessed the research literature on initial reading instruction and learning in non-native-English-speaking classroom contexts. It recommended—with particular reservations, and in some cases contradictory language—that English language learners "be taught how to read in their native language while acquiring oral proficiency in English and subsequently taught to extend their skills to reading in English" (Snow et al., 1998, p. 325). [3] Thus, one may infer from the consistency of the committee's interpretation of the research literature and the recommendations which ensued, that the committee understands and generally promotes the value of providing quality software in a language other than English for initial reading development by early English language learners.

Technology, Income, Ethnicity, and Reading

Issues of Equity: The Past and Present

In 1986, I drew several conclusions upon reviewing the literature on access and use of microcomputers in education in the United States (DeVillar, 1986). The inequitable conditions and trends associated with computer-supported learning across income, racial, ethnic, and language categories which warranted the conclusions drawn in 1986, prevail today, and these of course influence literacy development opportunities and outcomes.

Reading disparities are not merely a function of children being dominant orally in a language other than English. The NRC Committee presents data from various research studies (e.g., Coleman et al., 1966; Herman & Stringfield, 1997; NAEP, 1996; Puma et al., 1997; Stringfield, 1997) which report that African American and Hispanic American children, and children from high poverty or rural areas, tend to have lower initial reading scores than their middle-class and above European American counterparts. Lamentably, this phenomenon increases as these student groups continue through school. As an example, NAEP data reflecting reading outcomes in 1996 indicate that Hispanic students at age 17 were reading at levels comparable to that of European American 13-year-olds (Sable & Stennett, 1998). [4] Hispanic American students from high poverty households, moreover, increased from 33 percent in 1985 to 40 percent in 1996, while that of European American children decreased from 12 percent in 1990 to 10 percent in 1996 (Sable & Stennett, 1998).

Income exerts effects on technology-supported reading opportunities at school and at home. Disparities by income group relative to computer use in these two contexts were evident and persisted from 1984 through 1993. [5] Students from high- and middle-income households have been more likely to use a computer at school or at home than students from lower-income households, as indicates.

Table 1

PERCENT OF STUDENTS, GRADES 7–12, USING COMPUTERS IN SCHOOL OR AT HOME

(by family income)

YEAR	1984		1989		1993	
INCOME LEVEL	SCHOOL	HOME	SCHOOL	HOME	SCHOOL	HOME
LOW	20	2	37	5	41	4
MIDDLE	30	8	39	18	56	22
HIGH	38	30	43	42	60	57

Source: U.S. Department of Commerce, Bureau of the Census, October 1998, *Current Population Survey.*

Note: Percentages are approximate, as data were presented in decimal-scale form.

Access to opportunities for reading through technology is constrained in a parallel form along racial and ethnic categories (Table 2). From 1984 to 1993, *access* to computers at home by African American or Hispanic American students maintained approximately a 1-to-3 ratio when compared to European American students. There also was a reported differential use at home by Hispanic American students who had computers at home. In 1993, for example, 68 percent of Hispanic American students *having* computers at home reported *using* their computers there versus 75 percent of their European American counterparts. The percentage differential increases for both Hispanic American and African American students vis-à-vis their European American counterparts when the combined use of computers (that is, whether at home or at school) is also notable. Sixty-one percent of European American students were reported as using computers *any place* versus a 46 percent combined use by either African American or Hispanic American students. The growth rate in combined use, nevertheless, has been greater for Hispanic American (171 percent) and African American (188 percent) students than for their European American counterparts (85 percent) over the 1984–1993 period.

This same income-to-opportunities-for-use relationship holds for Internet access. Public schools with high minority-student enrollment (50 percent or higher) or that serve low-income students have less access to the Internet than do schools serving higher-income or non-minority students. In fall 1997, for example, 88 percent of schools (virtually 9 of 10) who had fewer than 11 percent of their student body eligible for free or reduced-cost lunches had access to the Internet (National Center for Educational Statistics [NCES], 1998). During

Table 2

PERCENT OF STUDENTS, AGES 3–17, HAVING ACCESS AND USING COMPUTERS AT SCHOOL OR AT HOME

(by ethnic or racial designation)

YEAR	1984			1989			1993		
ETHNIC OR RACIAL DESIGNATION	SCHOOL	HOME ACCESS	HOME USE	SCHOOL	HOME ACCESS	HOME USE	SCHOOL	HOME ACCESS	HOME USE
AFRICAN AMERICAN	16	6	76	35	11	65	51	13	67
EUROPEAN AMERICAN	30	17	74	48	27	72	63	36	75
HISPANIC AMERICAN	18	5	67	38	10	64	53	12	68

Source: U.S. Census Bureau, Population Division, Education and Social Stratification Branch, maintained by Laura K. Yax (Population Division). Last revised March 30, 1999.

this same period, 63 percent of schools (6 of 10) who had 71 percent or more of their student body eligible for free or reduced-cost lunches had access to the Internet. Thus, there was a 40 percent differential in Internet access between schools serving predominantly middle- to high-income student bodies and those serving predominantly low-income student bodies.

The differences across income, racial, and ethnic groups persist. These differences occur in the formal learning context of school and the informal learning contexts of home, camps, community centers, and the like. Moreover, these differences reflect a 15-year persistence in the inequitable distribution and use of computers across particular groups and in the relative degree of literacy benefits, and other social and academically related (*ergo*, socioacademic) benefits, derived from their use.

Literacy, Equity, and Democracy

This section presents theoretical orientations and practices that confront the schooling and informal learning conditions and outcomes described above. In so doing, the section's contents challenge, yet again, our societal status quo, as Dewey and other educator-activists have done in the United States since the end of the nineteenth century. Equitable and critical schooling, as Dewey (in Westbrook, 1996, p. 137) bravely and eloquently pointed out in 1898, moves us toward realizing the democratic vision:

> Men will long dispute about material socialism, about socialism considered as a matter of distribution of the material resources of a community, ...but there is a socialism regarding which there can be no such dispute—socialism of the intelligence and of the spirit. To extend the range and the fullness of sharing in the intellectual and spiritual resources of the community is the very meaning of community.

The degree to which these orientations and practices ultimately lead to change in the form of general educational equity—and distinct schooling configurations with respect to materials, curricula, methods, and outcomes—within U.S. schools remains to be determined. As Cuban (1986) points out after his analysis of U.S. schools over the 1890–1980 period, schools are highly resistant to change. He might have added that so, too, are societies. Nevertheless, these alternative orientations and practices construct computer-supported instructional environments within formal and informal contexts that foster equitable learning experiences—in literacy and beyond—for students from Hispanic American and other underrepresented groups. Ultimately, the school context—particularly the classroom—is where each student must experience meaningful and positive learning. Putting these theoretical orientations into practice significantly enhances students' access to and participation in meaningful learning experiences and serves to enhance, through computer-supported technology, their academic, language, and literacy development.

Enhanced literacy and other learning-related outcomes are important for students' identity formation (Cummins, 1994, 1995) and for the continual development and refinement of our negotiated national democratic culture, as noted by Tarcov (1996):

> Education ought not simply to promote democracy or democratic qualities, but must remember that ours is a liberal constitutional democracy, and that democracy is not simply the liberation of the people from the power of oppression of the few, but a responsibility, even a burden for the people. Thoughtful students ultimately want to know that the qualities they are acquiring are needed not merely to preserve their form of government but to improve their own souls. Education for wisdom and virtue does not simply serve democracy, but can be an end in itself. (pp. 33–34)

As students' degree of risk decreases, the probability of their completing the K–12 schooling cycle and university studies increases. Success in their schooling experience enables enhanced interaction—

through literacy-related and political activities—within the larger society. Enhanced, organized interaction—through multiple means, including technological ones—by significant numbers of individuals from underrepresented groups, in turn, raises the probability of effecting equitable change and fostering negotiated culturally pluralistic development at the national level. Negotiation in this instance is the transformative agent and process that converts *individual meaning* (whether the unit of analysis is a sole individual or a particular culture) to *shared meaning*. Shared meaning by its very nature embodies change, for both parties have transformed their previously individual meanings to a common meaning.

Literacy is an important element in the equation of communicative power for, as Freire (1973) notes, it enables *engagement* (as opposed to passivity or silence) by the individual or group:

> As [groups] amplify their power to perceive and respond to suggestions and questions arising in their context, and increase their capacity to enter into dialogue not only with [others] but with their world, they become "transitive." …Without dialogue, self-government cannot exist. (pp. 17, 24)

Moreover, groups must develop for themselves and their national context a "critical transitivity" that "is characteristic of authentically democratic regimes and corresponds to highly permeable, interrogative, restless and dialogical forms of life—in contrast to silence and inaction (Freire, 1973, pp. 18–19).

A corollary skill that is lacking in the general populace and that schools must develop in their students-cum-community participants through active physical and dialogic engagement is *civic literacy*:

> We suffer, as Benjamin Barber has said, from a dearth of "civic literacy," which he characterizes as "the competence to participate in democratic communities, the ability to think critically and act with deliberation in a pluralistic world, and the empathy to identify sufficiently with others to live with them despite

conflicts of interest and differences in character" (Westbrook, 1996, p. 125)

Thus, literacy is a process that enables a person to think about and interact within his or her context in order to construct, negotiate, and share meaning through the use of symbolic forms to re-present experience, whether real or imagined. In the United States, literacy is intimately associated with power—of the individual, of a particular group, and of the nation. Hence, the greater the degree of disparity in literacy opportunities—especially reading and writing—among particular individuals or groups, the greater the gap in power between them. The equity-based principles and practices described in the following section illustrate the type of change-agent strategies that—to the degree that they were generalized—could narrow the power gap at the intergroup level in terms of educational experiences and outcomes and, in the larger sense, could enable underrepresented groups "to participate and intervene in the historical process" (Freire, 1973, referring to K. Mannheim's *Freedom, Power, and Democratic Planning*, 1950).

Critical Literacy, Technology, and Equity

To acquire literacy is more than to psychologically and mechanically dominate reading and writing techniques. It is to dominate these techniques in terms of consciousness; to understand what one reads and to write what one understands; it is to communicate graphically. Acquiring literacy does not involve memorizing sentences, words, or syllables—lifeless objects unconnected to an existential universe—but rather an attitude of creation and re-creation, a self-transformation producing a stance of intervention in one's context.

—*Paolo Freire*

The socioacademic achievement framework introduced by DeVillar and Faltis in *Computers and Cultural Diversity* (1991) identified three elements critical to equitable schooling experiences and outcomes in the United States: *integration, communication,* and *cooperation.* The three elements relate, respectively, to aspects of Allport's (1954, 1959) social contact theory, Vygotsky's (1962, 1978) social learning theory, and various research-based perspectives of cooperative learning theorists, particularly those espoused by D. and R. Johnson (1981, 1986, 1988, 1994).

DeVillar and Faltis applied the principles of their framework to analyze and critique the works of early theorists and researchers of computers in education and computer-supported instructional programs that were then current. They found that computer-supported instruction, and the philosophy upon which it is based, did not support social integration, meaningful communication at the teacher–student or student–student level, or a structured cooperative learning context. Research-based findings and principles associated with integration, communication, and cooperation led DeVillar and Faltis to the premise that successful academic and general school experiences by underrepresented groups of students (as opposed to individual students) can occur only if the interdependent principles of integration, communication, and cooperation functionally describe the learning context.[6]

Cummins (1994, p. 365) refined the socioacademic achievement framework by incorporating the following elements with those of integration, communication, and cooperation to determine the degree of success of underrepresented students at the group level: (1) societal power relations, (2) negotiation of identity between educators and students, and (3) curriculum content and critical inquiry. Cummins, in earlier writings (e.g., Cummins, 1988; Cummins & Sayers, 1990), posited the value of engaging students in collaborative and critical inquiry—including within computer-supported learning contexts—if educational change in the form of successful social and academic achievement, particularly by students from underrepresented groups, was to

occur. By 1988, Cummins had integrated his "interactive/experiential approach to pedagogy" (see Cummins, 1984), and its fundamental elements, to computer-supported settings, including communicating electronically across distances:

> Our global future will depend more on our children's ability to critically analyze situations and collaborate with others (both locally and in distant locations) in creatively solving problems. These critical thinking skills require discussion, interaction, and negotiation between teachers and students rather than solitary work at a computer. (Cummins, 1988, p. 3)

Additionally, Cummins described how the interactive/experiential approach within computer-supported settings would influence positively the development of language and literacy among students. He presented examples involving students from the continental United States, Britain, and Canada interacting across distances via computer networks with schools in Mexico, Hawaii, Alaska, Japan, and Puerto Rico, and concluded:

> If [the] computer is used within an interactive approach to pedagogy, it can dramatically enhance the learning experiences of all the children in the classroom by acting as a catalyst for cooperative learning, process writing, critical literacy and discovery approaches to science. (Cummins, 1988, p. 12)

The interactive/experiential elements upon which Cummins (1988, pp. 3–4) based his model of learning (and challenge to the transmission model of learning) were articulated from research conducted in England, beginning in the mid-1960s, and which became recommended policy there in 1975. [7] The cognitive and language works of Vygotsky (1962)—including their relationship and extension to reading and writing—were integrated profoundly within the British research paradigm. Vygotsky's work on language and thought was evident in U.S. research and thought (e.g., Bruner,

1966), although not to a comparable degree during the same period (see Macdonald & Leeper, 1966, for an example of U.S. research and paradigm orientation). These interactionist principles were soon assimilated, and they continue to drive language research inquiry in U.S. classrooms, including within computer-supported learning settings (see, for example, Gallego, 1998; Pearson & Iran-Nejad, 1998).

The interactionist principles do not differ from the principles of educational observation, philosophy, and practice experienced, articulated, and espoused by Dewey, Vygotsky, or Freinet during the first 30 years of the twentieth century (see, for example, DeVillar, 1999, and, more recently, Freire, 1973, 1978). Statements by Freire (1978) and Dewey (1916) demonstrate the significant relationship between authentic language and group-specific action:

> The fact is that language is inevitably one of the major preoccupations of a society which, liberating itself from colonialism and refusing to be drawn into neocolonialism, searches for its own re-creation. In the struggle to re-create a society, the reconquest by the people of their own world becomes a fundamental factor. (Freire, 1978, p. 176)

> Knowledge which is mainly second-hand, other men's knowledge, tends to become merely verbal.... In the degree in which what is communicated cannot be organized into the existing experience of the learner, it becomes mere words: that is, pure sense-stimuli, lacking in meaning. To be informed... is to have at command the subject matter needed for an effective dealing with a problem, and for giving added significance to the search for solution and to the solution itself. (Dewey, 1916, p. 367)

The development of language and literacy is at the heart of this common paradigm of principles, for it is ultimately and generally through these skills that humans communicate inwardly and externally. Anticipating Freire's construct of *praxis* (the harmonious relationship between thought and action), Ortega y Gasset (1957), delivering a lecture in 1939, used the term *ensimismarse* ("to go within oneself") to describe the application of the intellect (thought) to distance oneself from one's setting for the sake of thought itself: "As if thought could awaken and function of its own motion, as if it began and ended in itself, and was not—as is the true state of the case—engendered by action, with its roots and its end in action!" (p. 30). For Ortega y Gasset, the danger to society of one-way distancing—that is, of intellectualism, or thought neither based on action nor, as a consequence, leading to it—was that its "deification" by the official structure of the state demanded that "Human life was to put itself at the service of culture because only thus would it become filled with worthy substance. From which it would follow that human life, our pure existence, would itself be a mean and worthless thing" (p. 31).

The construct and role of one-way distancing recently has been defined differently and operationalized in a two-way sense (i.e., thought and action in a reciprocal, transformative relationship) within computer-supported learning settings (Brown, Cummins, Figueroa, & Sayers, 1998), although the construct of praxis remains intact in the way that Dewey, Vygotsky, Ortega y Gasset, and others had posited—specifically, that thought and language are intimately and fundamentally connected. Brown et al. (1998) summarize the logic and expectations associated with their revised notion of *distancing:*

> It is not until people are forced to take a step back and rethink the world in which they live—a distancing process— that they can re-analyze their own worlds, enhance their understanding of their own lives and day-to-day realities, and finally reflect on that world and take decisive action to improve it.... We feel that a pedagogy of distancing, greatly facilitated through global learning networks, is one that changes attitudes and fosters learning and critical questioning through dialogue within classes and between classes—across cultures, distances and differences. (p. 335)

This description also reflects the thought of Dewey, both in terms of a student's individual development and, as indicated below by Dewey's speeches in Asia during 1919 and 1921, social action (see, for example, Archambault, 1964; Westbrook, 1991):[8]

> [Social conflict is fundamentally] conflict between classes, occupational groups, or groups constructed along ideational, or perhaps even ethnic lines.... Social conflict occurs not because interests of the individual are incompatible with those of his society, but because the interests of some groups are gained at a disadvantage of, or even by the oppression, of the interests of other groups.... We must devise means for bringing the interests of all the groups of a society into adjustment, providing all of them with the opportunity to develop, so that each can help the other instead of being in conflict with them. We must teach ourselves one inescapable fact: any real advantage to one group is shared by all groups; and when one group suffers disadvantage, all are hurt. (Dewey, quoted in Westbrook, 1991, pp. 245–246)

In summary, the interactionist [9] principles address and guide the nature of teaching and learning as a social process, where equity must prevail, in all settings, computer-supported or otherwise, for all—a noun that should, by definition, need no qualification. Thus, literacy development is for power: the power to learn and achieve in school; the power to develop one's identity in a healthy and dignified manner; the power to realize one's personal and professional aims; the power to "challenge structures of injustice in schools and other institutions of society" (Brown et al., 1998, p. 335); the power to live and participate actively and significantly in the historical process of one's democratic context.

Recent social constructivist perspectives (see Blanton, Moorman, & Trathen, 1998; Wells, 1998) on learning within computer-supported settings echo the need and basis for a learning context operating within the set of principles mentioned earlier. In terms of need, the lack of equity, the persistent differential processes and outcomes of schooling at the intergroup level, and the mandate for developing higher-order thinking skills and technological competency among students, are cited (Blanton, Moorman, & Trathen, 1998, pp. 236–237). The basis for applying the social constructivist perspective rests on the notion that learning is a socially mediated and constructed phenomenon, in which tools play a fundamental role in the construction and transporting of group meaning over time, and a system in which the group, as well as the individual, experiences learning outcomes in relation to the quality and appropriateness of its structures (Blanton, Moorman, & Trathen, 1998, p. 239). Vygotsky, Leont'ev, and Luria were the founding theorists of this particular social constructivist perspective. To what extent are these principles visible in computer-supported programs, particularly teacher education programs? A study by Blanton, Moorman, & Trathen (1998) reviews and analyzes 52 articles from a pool of nearly 800 relative to the use of telecommunications within teacher education programs. (The almost 750 articles excluded reflect an assessed lack of rigor according to the reviewers' criteria.) Blanton, Moorman, and Trathen (1998, p. 259) conclude that the research they review is "philosophically and theoretically barren."

In an earlier study, Blanton and his colleagues (Blanton, Moorman, Hayes, & Warner, 1997) compared the reading scores of 26 students, grades 3 through 6, involved in the Fifth Dimension, a computer- and tutor-supported after-school program founded on social constructivist principles, to those of 26 students who had not been involved. The posttest reading achievement scores of the students who attended the after-school program were significantly higher than those of the control group. Positive outcomes in reading and math posttest scores led the investigators to conclude that the results "demonstrate that children who participate in the Fifth

Dimension master knowledge and skills and acquire practices that transfer to measures of academic achievement" (Blanton et al., 1997, p. 379). The investigators acknowledge that the students who participated in the Fifth Dimension program had access to enhanced literacy and math development experiences through the use of computers and tutors and made connections between their after-school activities and classroom activities. Also, the after-school program was fun, organized, and socially interactive. Thus, all or some of these factors may have influenced the outcomes. [10] This particular after-school, computer-supported context was designed along social constructivist principles (also called Cultural-Historical Activity Theory, or CHAT). Subsequent similar investigations could contribute to our knowledge base relative to how "artifacts and cultural practices" constructed socially within one context (e.g., an after-school, informal learning setting) "are transported to mediate activity" in another context (e.g., a formal classroom setting).

Conclusion

I conclude with a summary of the elements comprising the effective learning principles discussed in this article, particularly as they pertain to literacy development within computer-supported contexts:

1. Learning settings must be places where students can, with the teacher and among themselves, through jointly constructed, tool-based activities, (a) engage in authentic experiences, (b) reflect, and (c) communicate—through speaking, reading, writing, and comprehending.

2. The language and experiences within the learning setting must be associated closely with the students' prior experiences and development. Continued subjection of English language learners to content classes with teachers who do not speak their language, a phenomenon generally compounded by segregation from native or fluent English-speaking students, will not likely lead to changes in language, lit-

eracy, or general academic achievement.

3. Learning must be an active, social discovery process, guided by the teacher, rather than a transmission process controlled by the teacher. Knowledge is a co-constructed phenomenon.

4. Language and literacy must *permeate* subject matter across the curriculum rather than be studied independent of other subject matter. [11]

5. A learner is a critical thinker *and* an engaged participant; each role informs and transforms the other. The use of the qualifier *critical* is necessary because schools can, and do, produce students whose assessed performance in this area is not satisfactory: "It is clear that the public schools need to do a better job teaching students to think, not just in order to (supposedly) rescue an ailing economy but to serve broad civic purposes as well" (Tyack & Cuban, 1995, p. 38). [12]

Computers and related technology, regardless of attributes such as speed, capacity, programs, entertainment value, and language, will not by themselves lead to the language and literacy development that millions of our students need. As tools, technologies must be designed along pedagogical lines that will complement the teaching-learning experience. The problem is compounded in that we have to change the general orientation of instruction from transmission to social learning. I have offered some indications of viable pedagogical orientations and outcomes here. However, current and historical data at the national level reflect that schools and informal learning programs generally do not use technology or instruction in ways that foster enhanced literacy development or academic achievement for significant numbers of students from underrepresented groups. This outcome is not a new phenomenon; rather, it reflects a persistent difference in educational experiences, expectations, opportunities, and outcomes for students from underrepresented groups that predates the introduction of computers and related technologies. This historical reality will persist until schools and universities integrate the types of social learning principles suggested here in a general and equitable manner.

Notes

[1] All human language—however distinct one may be from another—is a codified, yet dynamic, construction of sounds, potentially coherent to members within a particular speech community. Language is the sound code pool from which a person draws to construct and convey meaning through speech. The person, of course, wishes to use language in such a way as to accurately construct and convey past, present, or future phenomena. Hence, language is not what is, but the selective representation of what is sensed as being. Thus, language is an imperfect tool for individual meaning-making, meaning-conveying, negotiation of meaning between two or more individuals, and, ultimately, attaining shared meaning. The Spanish philosopher Ortega y Gassett (1957) addresses this imprecise and social characteristic of language:

> Language is a social usage that interposes itself between [two individuals], between their two inwardnesses, and whose exercise or use by indiviuals is predominantly irrational. The most scandalous and almost comic proof of this is that we apply the words "rational" and "logical" to our most intelligent behavior—when these words come from *ratio* and *logos*, which in Latin and Greek originally meant "speech," a performance that is irrational. (p. 224)

[2] Labeling groups is a necessarily awkward process. The category *Hispanic American*, for example, is a group designation that includes Basque Americans (of Spanish origin), Cuban Americans, Mexican Americans, Puerto Ricans/Puerto Rican Americans, Spanish Americans, and other groups from Central or South America (with the exception of Brazil). Acknowledging this and other limitations, in this article I use the following terms to *generally* identify a particular category of collectively labeled groups and trust the text to disassociate the terms from any offensive connotations: African American, Anglo American, Asian American, European American, Hispanic American, and Native American. I also use a more *specific* group category (e.g., Mexican American) when alluding only to a particular group, also acknowledging that the descriptive value of any ethnic label is susceptible to challenge.

[3] The NRC Committee's statement is untenably narrow in its designation of who should receive initial literacy development: "If language-minority children arrive at school with *no* proficiency in English. . .these children should be taught how to read in their native language" (Snow et al., 1998, p. 325; emphasis added). This recommendation reflects the *doublethink* process—advanced by Orwell (1949) in his novel *1984* and extended to contemporary academic and public discourse regarding dual language instruction by Cummins (in press)—in which scholars and other academicians can hold simultaneously contradictory views that, on the one hand, acknowledge the reseach-informed needs and benefits to English language learners of native language (i.e., non-English) instruction and, on the other, recommend all English-language instruction except under conditions such as "no proficiency in English."

[4] Sable and Stennett (1998) point our that the NAEP analyses do not control for recent immigration or English language proficiency, and that students whose English is judged to be too low are excluded from taking the tests. Although the criteria employed to determine this particular level of English language proficiency are not described, it does raise the question whether children whose English is "judged not to be appropriate" represent students designated as recent immigrants or with "language difficulties."

[5] In March 1994, the Bureau of the Census redesigned its data collection methods and introduced 1990 census controls and population undercount adjustments. The figures cited here are the most recent available.

[6] In an earlier work, *Language Minority Students and Computers* (Faltis & DeVillar, 1990), the authors provided, in the words of one reviewer,

> both theoretical and practical information to a burgeoning audience of educators concerned with language minority students [in the form of] serious and substantive essays, research and project reports. . .written by highly respected research writers, along with computer technologists and classroom practitioners. The authors bring together a range of subjects from ideology to methodology, and from theory to application. (Roland, 1992)

[7] Cummins (1988) notes that the interactive/experiential approach elements he cites stem from the Bullock Report (HMSO,1975). These elements reflect substantive and innovative research initiated in England in the mid-1960s to investigate ways students and teachers

spoke, wrote, and read language in the classroom (cf. "A Language Policy Across the Curriculum," in Barnes et a., 1971). Moreover, this body of research set the tone, and, arguably, the standard, for classroom language research in the United States—a standard that continues to the present. This research into language and literacy behaviors of teachers and their students, and among the students themselves, extended and refined U.S. classroom language research. Prior to the mid-1960s, classroom language researchers were concerned primarily with categories and distribution of talk, rather than the "details of the ebb and flow" of talk itself (Barnes et al., 1971, p. 12; cf. Amidon & Hough, 1967.

[8] See Pacheco (1999) for a discussion of the dilemma within U.S. society between *education* and *schooling*—the former characterized as the process which leads to the development of a self-identity with social contexts; the latter characterized as the process that leads to the development of the *civic* self.

[9] I use this term only for purposes of convenience. The term serves as a composite of the schools of thought, past and present, and the common set of principles which they espouse, presented throughout this article.

[10] See DeVillar & Jiang (1999) for a report on student attitudes toward the Fifth Dimension program.

[11] Educators from Dewey (writing in 1899 and published in Archambault, 1964, p. 310) to Freire (1971, p.17) have used this specific term in making connections between meaningful learning at the individual and social level and meaningful participation in the democratic process.

[12] This educational outcome and need to rectify it is not too surprising, given the factory model for the organization and operation of schools (Caine & Caine, 1991):

> In traditional factories, products are manufactured on an assembly line, and the final product is the combination of readily identifiable parts that are made using precisely measurable materials. Work is done according to specific schedules, with precise times for beginning, taking breaks, and ending. Speed, accuracy, and the amount of output are rewarded. (p. 13)

REFERENCES

Allport, G. (1959). Normative compatibility in the light of social science. In A. H. Maslow (Ed.), *New knowledge in human values* (1970 edition, pp. 137-150). Chicago: Henry Regnery.

Allport, G. (1954). *The nature of prejudice* (1958 edition). Garden City, NY: Doubleday/Anchor.

Archambault, R. D., (Ed). (1964). *John Dewey on education, selected writings.* Chicago: University of Chicago Press.

August, D., & Hakuta, K. (Eds.). (1998). *Educating language-minority children.* Washington, DC: National Academy Press.

Barnes, D. (1971). Language in the secondary classroom: A study of language interaction in twelve lessons in the first term of secondary education. In D. Barnes, J. Britton, H. Rosen, & the London Association of Teachers of English, (Eds.), *Language, the learner and the school* (rev. ed., pp. 11–77). Middlesex, England: Penguin Books.

Barnes, D., Britton, J., Rosen, H., & the London Association of Teachers of English, (Eds.). (1971). *Language, the learner and the school* (rev. ed.). Middlesex, England: Penguin Books.

Barnes, D., Britton, J., Rosen, H., & the London Association of Teachers of English (1971). A language policy across the curriculum. In D. Barnes, J. Britton, H. Rosen, & the London Association of Teachers of English, (Eds.), *Language, the learner and the school* (rev. ed., pp. 160–168). Middlesex, England: Penguin Books.

Bell, D. (1999). Rise, Sally, rise: Communicating through dance. *TESOL Journal, 8* (1), 27–31.

Blanton, W. E., Moorman, G., & Trathen, W. (1998). Telecommunications and teacher education: A social constructivist review. In P. D. Pearson & A. Iran-Nejad (Eds.), *Review of research in education* (pp. 235–275). Washington, DC: American Educational Research Association.

Blanton, W. E., Moorman, G., Hayes, B. A., & Warner, M. L. (1997). Effects of participation in the Fifth Dimension on far transfer. *Journal of Educational Computing Research, 16* (4), 371–396.

Britton, J. (1970). *Language and learning.* Middlesex, England: Penguin Books.

Brown, K., Cummins, J., Figueroa, E., & Sayers, D. (1998). Global learning networks: Gaining perspective on our lives with distance. In E. Lee, D. Menkart, & M. Okazawa-Rey (Eds.), *Beyond heroes and holidays: A practical guide to K–12 anti-racist, multicultural education and staff development.* Network of Educators on the Americas.

Bruner, J. S. (1966). *Toward a theory of instruction.* Cambridge, MA: Belknap/Harvard University Press.

Caine, R. N., & Caine, G. (1991). *Making connections, Teaching and the human brain.* Alexandria, VA: Association for Supervision and Curriculum Development.

Chaika, E. (1982). *Language, the social mirror.* Rowley, MA: Newbury House.

Chomsky, N. (1975). *Reflections on language.* New York: Pantheon Books.

Commins, S., & Linscott, R. N. (1966). *Man and man: The social philosophers.* New York: Washington Square Press.

Cook-Gumperz, J. (Ed.). (1986). *The social construction of literacy.* Cambridge, England: Cambridge University Press.

Cuban, L. (1984). *How teachers taught: Constancy and change in American classrooms, 1890–1980.* New York: Longmans.

Cummins, J. (in press). The ethics of double-think: Language rights and the bilingual education debate. In R. A. DeVillar & T. Sugino (Eds.), *TESOL Journal (Special Issue: One world, many tongues: Language policies and the rights of learners).* Alexandria, VA: TESOL Journal.

Cummins, J. (1995). *Negotiating identities: Education for empowerment in a diverse society.* Ontario, CA: California Association for Bilingual Education.

Cummins, J. (1994). The socioacademic achievement model in the context of coercive and collaborative relations of power. In R. A. DeVillar, C. J. Faltis, & J. P. Cummins, Eds., *Cultural diversity in schools: From rhetoric to practice* (pp. 363–390). Albany: State University of New York Press.

Cummins, J. (1988). From the inner city to the global village: The microcomputer as a catalyst for collaborative learning and cultural interchange. *Language, Culture and Curriculum, 1* (1), 1–13.

Cummins, J. (1984). *Bilingualism and special education: Issues in assessment and pedagogy.* Clevedon, England: Multilingual Matters.

Cummins, J., & Sayers, D. (1990). Education 2001: Learning networks and educational reform. In C. J. Faltis & R. A. DeVillar (Eds.), *Language minority students and computers* (pp. 1–29). Binghamton, NY: Haworth Press.

DeVillar, R. A. (1999, January). *Del interludio cotidiano al potencial cultural: Comunidades de aprendizaje como construcción social.* Keynote address presented at the IV Binational Conference: In Search of a Border Pedagogy, El Paso, Texas/Juárez, México.

DeVillar, R. A. (1998). Indigenous images and identity in pluricultural Mexico: Media as official apologist and catalyst for democratic action. In Y. Zou & E. T. Trueba (Eds.), *Cultural diversity in schools: From rhetoric to practice* (pp. 187–219). Albany: State University of New York Press.

DeVillar, R. A. (1986, March). Computers and educational equity within the United States: An overview and examination of computer uses in education. Stanford-UNESCO Symposium on Computers and Education, Stanford University, 1–28.

DeVillar, R. A., & Jiang, B. (1999). The Fifth Dimension extended day program: An affective context for effective learning—A descriptive survey of student perceptions. *Selected Proceedings 1998 Research Symposium.* Fresno: University of California, Davis/ California State University, Fresno, 10–19.

DeVillar, R. A., & Faltis, C. J. (1994). Reconciling cultural diversity and quality schooling: Paradigmatic elements of a socioacademic framework. In R. A. DeVillar, C. J. Faltis, & J. P. Cummins (Eds.), *Cultural diversity in schools: From rhetoric to practice* (pp. 1–22). Albany: State University of New York Press.

DeVillar, R. A., & Faltis, C. J. (1991). *Computers and cultural diversity: Restructuring for school success.* Albany: State University of New York Press.

DeVillar, R. A., & Faltis, C. J. (1992). Editors' response to G. Roland's review. *Journal of Computing in Teacher Education, 9* (1), 29–31.

DeVillar, R. A., & Faltis, C. J. (1987). Computers and educational equity in American public schools. In *Capstone Journal of Education, 8* (4), 1–8.

Ducrot, O., & Todorov, T. (1994). *Encyclopedic dictionary of the sciences of language* (originally published in 1972, in French). Baltimore: Johns Hopkins University Press.

Durant, W. (1967). *The story of philosophy.* New York: Washington Square Press.

Eisner, E. (1991). *The enlightened eye, Qualitative inquiry and the enhancement of educational practice.* New York: Macmillan.

Faltis, C. J., & DeVillar, R. A., (Eds.). (1990). Language minority students and computers, *Computers in the Schools* (Special Issue), *7* (1/2).

Fisher, M., Perez, S. M., Gonzalez, B., Njus, J., & Kamasaki, C. (1998). *Latino education: Status and prospects. State of Hispanic America 1998.* Washington, DC: National Council of La Raza.

Freire, P. (1978). *Pedagogy in process: The letters to Guinea-Bissau.* New York: Seabury Press.

Freire, P. (1973). *Education for critical consciousness.* New York: Seabury Press. (Original work written in 1965 and published in 1969.)

Gallego, M., (Ed.). (1998, Spring Quarter). *Activity theory preconference readings.* AERA Preconference Seminar, San Diego, CA.

Jespersen, O. (1964). *Language: Its nature, development and origin.* New York: W. W. Norton.

Johnson, D. W., & Johnson, R. T. (1994). Cooperative learning in the culturally diverse classroom. In R. A. DeVillar, C. J. Faltis, & J. P. Cummins (Eds.), *Cultural diversity in schools: From rhetoric to practice* (pp. 57–73). Albany: State University of New York Press.

Johnson, D. W., & Johnson, R. T. (1981). Effects of cooperative and individualistic learning experiences on interethnic interaction. *Journal of Educational Psychology, 73* (3), 444–449.

Johnson, D. W., Johnson, R. T., Holubec, Johnson, E., & Roy, P. (1988). *Circles of learning: Cooperation in the classroom.* Alexandria, VA: Association for Supervision and Curriculum Development. (Original work published in 1984.)

Johnson, R. T., Johnson, D. W., & Stanne, M. B. (1986). Comparison of computer-assisted cooperative, competitive, and individualistic learning. *American Educational Research Journal, 23* (3), 382–392.

Joos, M. (1967). *The five clocks.* New York: Harcourt Brace Jovanovich.

Macdonald, J. B., & Leeper, R. R., (Eds.). (1966). *Language and meaning.* Washington, DC: Association for Supervision and Curriculum Development.

Ortega y Gasset, J. (1963). *Man and people.* New York: W. W. Norton. (Original copyright, 1957; essays date from 1939.)

Pacheco, A. (1999). Moving toward democracy: Lessons learned. In K. A. Sirotnik & R. Soder (Eds.), *The beat of a different drummer: Essays on educational renewal in honor of John I. Goodlad* (pp. 231-243). New York: Peter Lang.

Pearson, P. D., & Iran-Nejad, A., (Eds.). (1998). *Review of research in education.* Washington, DC: American Educational Research Association.

Professional Standards and Ethics Committee. (1998). *Standards for reading professionals, revised.* Newark, DE: International Reading Association.

Richards, J. C., Platt, J., & Platt, H. (1992). *Dictionary of language teaching and applied linguistics* (2nd ed.). Essex, England: Longman.

Roland, G. (1992). Book reviews. *Journal of Computing in Teacher Education, 9* (1), 25–29.

Rosen, C., & Rosen, H. (1973). *The language of primary school children.* Middlesex, England: Penguin Education.

Sable, J., & Stennett, J. (1998). The educational progress of Hispanic students. *The condition of education 1998.* Washington, DC: National Center for Education Statistics. October 2.

Secada, W. G., Chávez-Chávez, R., García, E., Muñoz, C., Oakes, J., Santiago-Santiago, I., & Slavin, R., (Eds.). (1998). *No more excuses: The final report of the Hispanic Dropout Project.* Washington, DC: Office of the Under Secretary, U.S. Department of Education. February.

Snow, C. E., Burns, M. S., & Griffin, P., (Eds.). (1998). *Preventing reading difficulties in young children.* Washington, DC: National Academy Press.

Tarcov, N. (1995). The meaning of democracy. In R. Soder (Ed.), *Democracy, education, and the schools* (pp. 1–36). San Francisco: Jossey-Bass.

Tyack, D., & Cuban, L. (1995). *Tinkering toward Utopia: A century of public school reform.* Cambridge, MA: Harvard University Press.

U.S. Census Bureau, Population Division, Education and Social Stratification Branch (October 1996). *Report: School enrollment— Social and economic characteristics of students: October 1996 (Update).* April 5, 1999.

U.S. Department of Education, National Center for Education Statistics (1998). *The condition of education 1998.* Washington, DC: U.S. Department of Education (Indicators 3, 4, 16).

Vygotsky, L. S. (1978). *Mind in society: The development of higher psychological processes.* Cambridge, MA: Cambridge University Press.

Vygotsky, L. S. (1962). *Thought and language.* Cambridge, MA: MIT Press. (Originally published in 1934, in Russian.)

Wells, G. (1998). Dialogic inquiry in education: Building on the legacy of Vygotsky. In M. Gallego, (Ed.). (1998, Spring Quarter), *Activity theory pre-conference readings* (pp. 110–145). AERA Pre-Conference Seminar, San Diego, CA.

Westbrook, R. B. (1996). Public schooling and American democracy. In R. Soder, (Ed.), *Democracy, education, and the schools* (pp. 125–150). San Francisco, CA: Jossey-Bass.

Westbrook, R. B. (1991). *John Dewey and American democracy.* Ithaca, NY: Cornell University Press.

Part V

HOME AND COMMUNITY

Mother-Tongue Literacy as a Bridge Between Home and School Cultures

Alma Flor Ada
University of San Francisco, California

In this essay, I will address the importance of the mother tongue and its maintenance. After a brief overview of the many perspectives from which additive bilingualism (maintaining one's home language while acquiring a second one) can be defended, I will then focus on one in particular—the importance of strengthening the relationship between parents and children and children's ties to their cultural communities of origin.

Schools can never be neutral in this regard, especially in the case of language/ethnic minority and/or working-class/poor children. The conscious or unconscious practices of the school, including its approach to literacy, serve either to validate or to invalidate the home culture, thus helping or hindering family relationships.

Yet once our commitment is clear, we can find simple yet powerful means to develop our students' literacy in a way that honors and strengthens their connection to their community, home culture, and language.

I will begin by reflecting on something that we often take for granted—the significance that the development of language has had on our evolution as humans. Through the creation of the symbolic system of language, we have developed our abilities to communicate our ideas, to express our feelings, to build relationships, to transmit knowledge gathered through generations, to record our past, and to plan our future.

Though communication is at the heart of language, we do not always need to have another person present in order to speak. Sometimes we speak with ourselves. As the great Spanish poet Antonio Machado said:

> *Quien habla solo*
> *espera hablar a Dios un día . . .*
>
> He who talks to himself
> hopes to talk to God someday . . .

And in our solitude, language often becomes a means to express the richness of the human soul, a way to turn one's feelings and emotions, one's anguishes and concerns, one's doubts and reflections into a song, a poem, a story, a novel, or a play, and thus contribute to the sum total of human culture.

Language is one of the very first elements of communication between the newborn child and the world. Even before birth, the child begins listening to the mother's voice in the womb as the sound is carried by the amniotic fluid. As a result, the newborn child has been shown already to recognize his or her own mother's voice.

We soothe babies with our words, we encourage them, we praise them, we rock them to sleep, we show our love and caring for them through our words as well as our gestures, thus creating a deep connection between the mother tongue and the young child, the young person.

Research has shown that the babbling of all human infants is identical during the first few months of life, but shortly afterwards, and long before the child is capable of pronouncing any distinguishable words, the sounds of the babbling change in response to the phonological features more common to the language or languages spoken around the infant. This occurs to the extent that a phonetician can determine the languages of the caretakers from the inflections of the infant's babbling.

Many years ago I received a valuable lesson from a very young child, a lesson that I have never forgotten. I would like to share that experience in memory of that child and of all children whose maintenance of their mother tongue is being threatened.

Back in the days when I was a young college student, one of my teachers, a Chicano nun, led a group of us who volunteered to work on Saturdays at an orphanage in a "barrio" of Denver, Colorado. Our major task was to give the children their weekly bath, but we also took time to interact and play with the children.

I developed a great love for the children, and in particular for one little three-year-old girl. As I have always loved to tell stories, I would often gather the children around me for storytelling time. While the children were all Mexican, most of them had lost their Spanish, and so I usually told the stories in English.

One Saturday afternoon, as I was telling stories with the little girl on my lap, she whispered in my ear: "Speak the other way, please, speak the other way." I realized that she was asking me to speak in Spanish, and I was surprised by her request. "Why do you want me to speak Spanish if you don't understand it?" I asked. And then, with a feeling in her voice that moves me to this day, she said: "I don't understand it, but that's the way my mother used to sound."

"That's the way my mother used to sound" has resonated in my ears ever since. Those few words taught me the lesson that no child should ever be deprived of the opportunity of knowing, developing, or enjoying the language in which her or his mother "used to sound."

It is a human, inalienable right to develop the legacy that was created through thousands of speakers:

> cuántos millones de bocas
> tienen pasadas
> viene el ayer hasta el hoy
> va hacia el mañana . . .

> how many millions of mouths
> have these words traveled through
> in them yesterday reaches today
> and journeys toward tomorrow . . .

says the poet Pedro Salinas in his eloquent poem "Verbo," written in honor of his language, our Spanish.

Unfortunately, we live in a society where frequently languages other than English are perceived as a threat instead of a richness. There is no valid rationale for this hurtful and damaging attitude. No one denies the value of a common language, nor the fact that English has historically been the common language and will continue to fill that role. What we disagree with are the false assumptions that language is an either/or choice, that in order for the nation to have a common language, individuals have to give up their own mother tongue. That is what cannot be explained nor justified, because it should be obvious that being fully bilingual is not detrimental in any way; on the contrary, it can be useful and rather fun.

No one questions the importance of the full development of English skills in every child, in every young person, and in every adult in this country. Everyone needs to be able to use our common instrument of communication effectively and efficiently. Yet at the same time, there is no basis for promoting the acquisition of English at the expense of losing one's mother tongue. Instead, much research strongly concludes that the most effective route to "good" English as a second language is a strong foundation in one's first language.

The soundness of promoting additive bilingualism, or the acquisition of a second language while maintaining one's first language, can be supported from various perspectives:

- **Psycholinguistic Factors** The strong affective identification with the mother tongue is exemplified by the little child from Denver who longed to hear the language that represented "how my mother used to sound."

- **Pedagogical Reasons** A language is best learned at a young age, both because children have an innate ability for learning languages and because acquiring a language is a long process. It has been shown to take up to six or seven years to reach near-native fluency in a second language. The European curricula have traditionally included foreign languages for children, on the pedagogical premise that one should learn a skill or a content area at the age at which one is most suited to learn it.

- **Social Reasons** Languages are natural resources. Speakers of multiple languages can be an asset for international relations, trade, cultural exchange, and enrichment of the cultural heritage of the nation.

- **Reasons of Justice** As long as some of the best universities in the country maintain foreign language requirements for admission and give credits for learning a foreign language, it should be argued that schools that allow children to lose their mother tongue are passively encouraging the loss of what would otherwise be a future academic advantage for those children.

There are, then, several aspects from which one could defend the principle of additive bilingualism. I have chosen to focus my current efforts on one aspect that I consider to be the most significant—the right of every parent to be able to communicate fully with her or his children and the need for every child to engage in meaningful communication at home.

A fundamental part of the present-day crisis in our society is the diminishment of parent-child interaction. When there is no communication between parents and children, there is no passing on of family history, no sharing of experiences that can become models for our young people, and no exchange of ideas or negotiation of meaning in a search for alternatives, for conflict resolution, or for planning and creating the future.

The greater the risks and difficulties our students face—drug abuse, early pregnancies, gang violence, as well as increasing racism, practically nonexistent social services, and severe lack of economic opportunities—the stronger the need to have meaningful parent-child interaction.

I do not believe, and I am not proposing, that schools should take over the responsibility of the family. I am saying that we cannot afford to disown the fostering of parent-child interaction, since the more that we can strengthen it, the more manageable our own roles as teachers become.

Parents of language minority students usually send their children to school with great expectations. Many times these parents are convinced that their own social conditions may never change, but they hope that, by means of education, their children will be able to have a better future.

Speaking of the parents I know best, I can attest that while most Hispanic parents wish for a professional career and economic betterment for their children, their hopes do not stop there. Their dreams also include the hope that their children will "bring honor to their community," "know how to respect others, so that they in turn will be respected," "be good human beings," "be kind and generous," "be honest," "help make the world a better place," "assist other people in their communities," "contribute to society, to the world." These are all direct quotes from different parents. These same thoughts are repeated over and over again, in countless different wordings, by the Hispanic parents I encounter in my work.

The parents believe that the schools will know how to make those dreams come true. They have full trust in the schools, which many consider as a "second home" for their children. Often, children are told that they should consider the teacher their "second mother" or their "second father."

The children who come to school from these homes often encounter the contradiction that, while their parents tell them to value the school and what the school teaches, the curriculum and the school practices do not in turn honor and respect children's parents and home environment.

Schools emphasize literacy, and rightly so. Books are presented as repositories of knowledge, as doors to all that there is to know. Most classroom activities revolve around books. Yet in the books children find in the classroom, there is often little or no recognition of themselves, their families, and their communities. And when children go home, often there are no books. Their parents do not own books, do not go to the library to borrow books, most certainly have never authored a book. How must children feel about the discrepancy between the emphasis on the value and importance of literacy they often encounter at school and the lack of literacy they encounter at home?

For many children, the explicit parental message to respect the school environment and the school's lack of respect for the home environment result in a conviction that the school culture is the "right" culture. Disconcerted about their parents, who don't seem to fit the "accepted" images proposed by school and society, students internalize the attitude that in order to belong, they must distance themselves from their families. Most often in an unconscious manner, they begin by feeling ashamed of their parents and their origin, rejecting their home language, anglicizing their names, and accepting the mores and attitudes that they perceive as superior.

They are often at grave risk of internalizing negative self-images of inferiority and defeat. It is these same students who, having become effectively alienated from their families and cultural communities, are most in danger of fulfilling their need to belong by succumbing to peer pressure, with unfortunate gang affiliations often substituting for missing family ties. Other children may react differently. Perhaps because their family and community affiliation is strong, they may never feel quite comfortable in schools, an environment that they perceive to be alien. And so they respond in a passive manner, simply awaiting the first opportunity to leave the system.

Undoubtedly, there are some children who manage to reconcile the two worlds. They maintain their admiration and appreciation for their parents, their community, and their culture, as they learn and integrate the best of the school culture, perhaps with an inner commitment to someday restore the omissions found in the school culture. Nevertheless, I am afraid that this is an enormous demand to place on children; only a few succeed at it.

What can schools do to address this issue? How can they counter the damage that they often create through unconsciously devaluing homes where literacy is not a common practice or whose culture is markedly different from that of the school?

Experience has shown me that this is not a hopeless situation. There are simple yet effective ways that teachers can affirm and include children's families and cultural backgrounds, thus strengthening the parent-child interaction of which we spoke earlier. They can do this even in situations where they do not speak the children's home language and in situations where there are many different languages spoken in the classroom.

I travel frequently. A standard question one encounters on planes is "What do you do?" If I am tired or want solitude, I answer, "a college professor," but if I want to engage in conversation, I answer instead, "an author."

The following anecdote is an example of how this prestige bestowed by print can be used to empower parents. In Windsor, California, in a parent program supported by Even Start, a first-grade boy wrote a book about a camping trip that his family had taken. There were a few pages depicting how the mother had announced that the family was going camping, how they had packed the car, and where they had gone. A couple of lines of text on each page accompanied the boy's delightful drawings. As with all books written by the children in this program, the book was "published." The story was typed, the child's drawing's were pasted onto the pages, the book was photocopied, and each parent in the program received a copy.

A few months later, on one of my visits to the program, a strong young man approached me to introduce himself. As we shook hands, he told me proudly, "I'm Mr. Lara, from 'The Lara Family Goes on Vacation.'" Every time that I share this anecdote after having shown the book in question, the audience laughs, because it is touching that a parent would choose to introduce himself as a character in his six-year-old son's story. But if we reflect on it, the anecdote points to the significance of being recognized, in print, as a protagonist.

For the last several years, I have been encouraging teachers to create in their classrooms books written by the children about themselves and their parents, family, and community.

Depending upon the age of the children, they may take questionnaires home, tape-record interviews, or simply ask their parents to discuss with them different themes related to the family experience. Subjects that teachers have successfully experimented with include:

- **The Family Immigration Experience** How long has the family lived at its current location? Where did they live before? How were these places different? Who made the decision to move? What were the major difficulties encountered? The saddest moments? The happiest? In what way could things have been different?

- **The Family's Present Life Experiences** What are the things that they miss most from their previous life? What things do they like most about the United States? Which do they like least? What things would they like to change?

- **The Parents' or Relatives' Childhood Memories** How was life different then? What are some things that existed in their parents' childhood that are not present now? What is present now that was not present then? What were their favorite activities? Who were their friends?

- **Important Moments in the Parents' Lives** How did they meet? How did they decide to get married? What do they like about each other?

- **Names in the Family** How were the parents named? Who chose their names? What do their names mean? Who chose the child's name? Is there anyone else in the family with the same name? What does the name mean?

These are only some examples. The possibilities are endless. They can relate to any aspect of the curriculum being taught. What is significant is that they transmit the message to children and to parents that their experiences are important and valued by the school.

One way to ensure the success of these activities is to have the teacher model them first. Teachers who have sent home copies of books made by themselves, sharing their own life stories and family stories, have experienced greater ease in connecting with students and their parents. The teacher's book sends the message that the teacher is also a human being, that parents, teachers, and children all share the same human condition—having a mother and a father, being part of a family.

Fear of the parents' possible illiteracy or their lack of knowledge of the English language should not be deterrents to carrying out the proposed activities. Children can interview their parents orally, copy down the parents' responses, or even tape-record them. And if the home language is not English, then it is even more important that the school validate the interaction between students and their parents in the home language.

In a bilingual classroom, books can be produced in both languages. This is, of course, optimal, as students will be developing their literacy skills in both languages. But this approach is by no means limited to bilingual classrooms. In classrooms where the teacher does not speak the students' home language or languages, students can create books in English, even though the original research may be carried out in the home language. In addition to fostering immediate parent-child interaction, the process will be promoting the acceptance and maintenance of the home language—and thus the possibility for future family integrity—while also developing valuable translating and interpreting skills on the part of the students.

Teachers doing this kind of work have made valuable discoveries. To begin with, they have discovered themselves as authors. Their students are excited to read and discuss books written by their teacher, and a closer student-teacher relationship develops as a result of shared personal experiences.

The process of sharing life stories with parents helps break down communication barriers, and parent-teacher relationships also improve and deepen. Parents are often more willing to participate in classroom activities as a result.

By incorporating knowledge of the students' home and community life, the curriculum gains greater relevance. Student interest, attention, and even attendance have improved as a result.

Some teachers' success stories have surpassed all our expectations. A Houston teacher had all of the Spanish-speaking parents contribute a story. The stories were compiled to create a class book entitled "Continuando nuestra cultura" ("Continuing Our Culture"); copies were distributed to all of the parents.

When the teacher was proudly sharing the book at a teachers' conference, it caught the eye of a representative of a major publishing house. Four of the parents received contracts to have their stories incorporated into a new major reading series.

But it is not the spectacular success stories that I want to emphasize here, inspiring as they may be. Rather, it is the cumulative effect of the continuously reiterated message to the students about the value of their parents, their language, and their culture that I believe holds the potential for bridging the gap between home and school.

Inspired by the words of one of the parents of Windsor, who, when asked for advice that he would give his children, said, "We are here to make the world a better place," other teachers are encouraging their students to ask their parents for words of advice. Parents' words, then, are featured and studied with the same kind of attention and reverence that the sayings of famous people have traditionally received.

For some time now, we have been aware of the importance of having cultural diversity in textbooks and in children's books. The negative effects of the current imbalance are recognized in the following words of a migrant parent:

> Why can't I find books for my children that portray me and my family, that show our values and our way of life? Why do they discriminate against us? We farm workers do not discriminate against anyone. The work of our hands feeds all. Do they discriminate against us because our skin is burnt by the sun? Don't they know that the sun is the source of warmth, of light, of life?

As educators, we want publishers to be aware of the need to publish books that indeed tell all the stories, portray all of the people. But it is not enough to make known our demands that such books be available on the market. We also need to facilitate the creation of those books in our classrooms, where indeed every one of our students and their parents or caretakers can be protagonists and authors.

In the process, we hope that students and their parents will reclaim the strength of their voices and the power of the human gift of language. We want to help them reclaim the role of protagonists of their own life story and authors of their own reality. Together we can redefine "success" as being not an individual achievement that separates and alienates us from our communities, but rather a measure of the strength of the connections we have with each other and our ability to facilitate the empowerment of our communities.

SOCIOCULTURAL CHANGE THROUGH LITERACY: TOWARD THE EMPOWERMENT OF FAMILIES

Concha Delgado-Gaitán

In arguing for a theory of literacy as a social practice, Street (1984) challenges the concept of an autonomous model that represents literacy as neutral technology, acquired through formal schooling and detached from other specific social contexts. The autonomous model isolates literacy as an independent variable, a collection of discrete cognitive skills. In contrast, Street takes the position that literacy practices are always accompanied by specific forms of social organization. Literacy, then, becomes the concrete social form and the institution that gives meaning to the discrete practices of reading and writing (95–125).

This perspective provides a context in which literacy practices take different forms depending on the organizational nature of the family. It takes into account the ecocultural niche that explains the family's socio-economic level, social and political relations, religious beliefs, regional ecological location, as well as the family's relationship to other institutions including neighborhood, media, health institutions and schools (Delgado-Gaitán, 1990; Moll & Díaz, 1987; Trueba, 1984). These activities are culturally variable in that there is wide diversity among families as they interact in different settings. Literacy in particular enters as a socioculturally constructed activity (Leichter, 1984; Schieffelin & Cochran-Smith, 1984). At the same time, families' linguistic interaction, especially through

questioning, plays a significant part. Research on questioning in family and school settings (Green, Wade & Graham, 1988; Heath, 1982) affirms that asking questions is a sociocultural activity and that there is diversity in formulating and responding to questions, especially among those children who are not reared in middle class White families. Further, it is clear from my work that as families interact in new settings and acquire new literacy skills, they become empowered through the process of social interaction and community organization (Delgado-Gaitán, 1990).

Empowerment principles state that people who have been historically underrepresented can organize and through a process of critical reflection recognize their potential and state their goals for access to resources, thus power. Empowerment process principles have been advanced by Freire (1970), Freire and Macedo (1987), Delgado-Gaitán (1990), Delgado-Gaitán and Trueba (1991), and the Cornell Empowerment Group (Allen, Barr, Cochran, Dean & Green, 1989). Theoretically, in order to understand families as contexts for human development, we need to consider not only how family members interact with each other in their daily activities but also the social and structural systems that surround the family, including institutional systems such as workplaces and schools. For example, how families exercise their power relative to schools speaks to the level of involvement parents have with the schools and their knowledge about their role as educators in the home.

The Family Matter Program designed by Bronfenbrenner and Cochran in 1976 has successfully exemplified how empowerment occurs on a continuum that varies for everyone involved. Cochran (1988) suggests that empowerment occurs in varying stages for families in the study because families start at different points in the process. Five stages are outlined, depicting sociocultural change leading to empowerment in the community:

1. Positive changes in self-perception

2. Alteration of relations with members of the household or immediate family

3. Establishment and maintenance of new relations with more distant relatives and friends

4. Information-gathering related to broader community involvement

5. Change-oriented community action

The interrelationships among individuals, the social context, and acquisition of social knowledge establish the conditions for social change—the fifth stage—to occur as noted. This framework for empowerment has significant implications for the family literacy study reported here.

The families' perception of social reality and need to enhance communication within their family gave rise to the study reported here. In this case, the research team departed from the current trend of defining family literacy as benefiting children's academic achievement in school, as others have done (Clark, 1984; Goldenberg, 1987; Seppanen, 1988). Beyond the need to improve children's academic performance is the parents' desire to understand how they, together with their children, read to learn, a concept raised as a theoretical construct for literacy in practice by Auerbach (1989). Reading to learn focuses on literacy as a means for deriving meaning from text in relation to the reader's sociocultural experience as it occurs in the natural setting (Auerbach, 1989; Cook-Gumperz, 1986;

Taylor, 1983). In this theoretical framework, the emphasis is on the readers' literacy practices for the purpose of enhancing their self and group identity and/or for instrumental means to accomplish a specific goal. It underscores the five stages of change outlined in Cochran's empowerment process.

This article presents the results of the Carpinteria family-literacy study (Delgado-Gaitán, 1990) pursued from a sociocultural perspective with regards to empowerment for Spanish-speaking children and their families. In particular, the Carpinteria community case is used to illustrate the potential of collective work in parents' learning to read with their children for the purpose of understanding texts in relation to their experience.

Family literacy has power as its basis because it creates access to participation and breaks patterns of social isolation. When change occurs by choice, as a result of self-reflection, it is accepted and internalized by those affected. This allows the person or group to determine its own direction and change. Implicit here is knowledge and responsibility for one's behavior and willingness to take action to help shape it as desired.

Outcomes of the empowerment process manifest themselves through access to resources. Power is the capacity to influence foreseen and unforeseen effects for oneself and others, and the increased ability to create desired change as the individual, parents, family, teacher, and school deem appropriate. At an individual level, empowerment takes place by building self-esteem and self-confidence. At the family level empowerment occurs when barriers are removed or incentives provided in local settings.

Research has found that parents teach more than the mechanics and strategies of reading during this activity with children; they impart sociocultural knowledge based on their own experience (Heath, 1983; Leichter, 1984; Wells, 1986). They convey values, a world view about their position in society, and they imbue their children with a sense of confidence that they are important enough to receive their parents' attention.

Ada (1988) attempted to examine the intersection between children's literature, parent-child interaction with each other and the text, questioning strategies for reading comprehension, and the notion of self-concept through Freire's notion of liberation. Following Freire's (1970) concept of liberation and his work on literacy with Brazilian peasants, Ada attempted to have parents learn how to motivate their children to read by utilizing four questioning strategies. These strategies were intended to teach the children to reflect on their own experience and liberation. She reasoned that if parents were to apply knowledge of their status and experience in society by teaching their children to do the same thing, they would require primary experience in examining text for their own purposes. They would become better teachers if they read texts that interested them and that were relevant to their own experiences. Parents who reflected on their own experience relative to the material they read would be better able to teach their own children how to relate storybooks to the children's experience.

Ada proposed four categories of questions that framed the interaction between adults and children: descriptive, personal interpretive, critical, and creative. Descriptive questions solicited factual recall; for example, "What did the female elephants wear?" Personal interpretive questions asked readers to think about their personal experience in relation to what they read; for example, "Have you ever felt that you were prevented from doing things that others had permission to do? How did you feel?" Critical questions revealed the child's ability to analyze the text in terms of sociopolitical perspective; for example, "Could the male and female monkeys have divided the work and responsibilities better?" Creative questions made readers think about ways they would resolve similar questions to those in the story; for example, "If you had been one of the female monkeys, what could you have done to improve the situation?"

Essentially, Ada found that Spanish-speaking children and their parents become empowered when they learn to interpret literature in relation to their own experience and reality. She showed that parents of Spanish-speaking children learned to read to their children by reading selected children's literature books and using a hierarchy of questions designed to generate discussion between children and parents.

The Intervention Study

Studying Family Literacy

Four years prior to the beginning of the study reported here, I conducted an ethnographic study on home and school literacy and parent involvement in Carpinteria, California (Delgado-Gaitán, 1990). The results indicated that by the time Spanish-speaking children reached the third or fourth grade, parents were intimidated by the language barrier presented in homework, which was almost totally in English. This intimidation was a distancing factor in the parent–child relationship that was crucial to maintaining a supportive system for children.

Another issue emerged in that study: because homework consumed most of the children's time at home, parents found little time to do leisure reading with their children. The findings of this study were shared with a parent group, COPLA (Comité de Padres Latinos), which had been organized to deal with issues pertaining to their children's education. As parents became aware of their literacy practices in the home they expressed an interest in increasing their reading at home with their children; parents who had children who did not excel in reading were especially interested. When I was funded to conduct an intervention study, the focus of the research was decided jointly by the researchers, their assistants, the COPLA committee, and school administrators. Family literacy received strong support as a potential project for children. Students in the third and fourth grades who needed support in their reading skills seemed likely participants, according to earlier findings by Delgado-Gaitán (1990). The students were evaluated by their teachers as Spanish-speaking readers who could benefit from additional support in their reading. Three major research questions guided this study:

1. How does parental use of literature with their children influence the parents' perception of self efficacy regarding literacy tasks?

2. How are household relations affected as a result of parent–child literacy activity?

3. How did the literacy project create new social networks for parents?

Over a five-year period, ethnographic data were collected in Carpinteria, California, on home–school communication in second, third and fourth grades, especially pertaining to literacy activities in home and school. In addition, ethnographic data on parents' involvement with the school district, from preschool to high school, were collected. Data from the latter included policies and practices. Data on the community parent organization showed the development of the power base for Spanish-speaking parents.

Using the background data on children's literacy performance in school, families, and the home–school relationships, the research team consulted with the parents and Morgan Elementary School for their input on a literacy project that would best suit their needs and goals. We created a family literacy program where parents could engage in reading with their children at home.

The eight books for the project were screened intentionally for topics that would generate discussion in families in this community. Nonsexist, nonracist, and nonclassist stories received major consideration. We departed somewhat from the recommendation of Ada (1988) in her curriculum simply because we considered some of the books used in the Pajaro Valley project inappropriate, potentially offensive, or uninteresting. We did overlap with Ada's recommended

list when our criteria fit. The books selected were: *Rosa Caramelo, ¿A dónde vas osito polar?, Historia de los bonobos con gafas, El primer pájaro de Piko-Niko, Tío Elefante, El perro del cerro y la rana de la sábana, Monty,* and *Mira como salen las estrellas.* The project began with the shorter books and progressed to the longer ones.

The parents of the selected children learned how to discuss book content with their children. At eight monthly sessions, held in the school setting, parents were given a children's literature book and taught the four types of questioning strategies that would improve their child's involvement in reading. Parent-participants were then observed reading to their children in the natural home setting on five different occasions. A recording was made during each of these periods. These occasions provided the researchers with observation and interview data on parent–child interaction regarding literature content.

At each monthly meeting parents discussed the new books. Working in small groups, they asked each other questions to model possible ways of interacting with their children. Mrs. Reyes, a parent from the community who had a great deal of experience in reading with children and in working with the COPLA parent group, assisted in the literacy classes, and another parent, Mrs. Mata, organized childcare during the parent meetings. By involving active parents in the project in a variety of capacities, the family literacy project was strengthened because parent leaders served as role models to those learning new practices regarding their children's schooling.

Three major areas in family literacy are delineated in the sections that follow, including background of families, parent–child interaction around literature texts, and parent–parent interaction.

Findings: Family Literacy

Parents' Backgrounds

Families shared a number of characteristics. They were immigrants from Mexico, working class, and predominantly Spanish-speaking. Reading skills of the parents varied along two continua. One was that of Spanish reading and writing: only two parents who had attended school in Mexico had gone beyond the sixth grade. Table 1 describes the families who participated in the intervention project.

All parents valued literacy skills for their children and had definite opinions about what a good or poor reader was. Most of the parents provided a detailed profile of their child as a reader and of their reading competencies. In giving a definition of what makes a good or poor reader, the parents usually described a good reader as a person who read all types of materials, read avidly, and read well, in contrast to a poor reader as a person who did not like to read and had difficulty reading text. Most of the parents read with their children at home prior to the intervention, although many said that they did not read regularly due to time constraints. Once children moved into higher grades in school, parents waited for their children to initiate a reading activity that usually involved school texts.

Table 1
BACKGROUND DATA ON FAMILY

Family Name	Number of Siblings in Household	Parents' Schooling		Parents' Employment	
		Mother	Father	Mother	Father
Romo	2	12th	12th	housekeeping	clerk
Alvarez	3	6th	6th (Mexico) 2 yrs. HS (US)	factory	gardener
Samora	3	1st	2nd	factory	unemployed
Gómez	3	5th	2nd	factory	gardener
Lara	4	6th	4th	housekeeping	tree cutter/ gardener
Méndez	2	1st/US	5th/City College	housewife	gardener
Quinta	2	6th	6th	housewife	gardener
Ríos	7	none	none	housewife	gardener
Macías	2	7th/US	10th/US	self-employed caterer	divorced
Soto	3	did not finish primary	attended secondary school	Supv. of maids hotel	driver, delivery

Parent–Child Interaction

Ada (1988) stated that the four questioning strategy categories (descriptive, personal, critical, and creative) comprise a hierarchy from simple to more complex, which suggests that the more complex questions, in the creative mode, are more likely to evoke the kind of reflection that enables the child to be analytical about sociocultural conditions. Ada's (1988) literature curriculum designated types of questions for teachers to use with the students. Her initial intent was to train teachers to use her literature books and then rely on the children's enthusiasm to motivate the parents to come to the school to learn about the books. She intended that parents, in her study, use similar questioning strategies as those of the teacher.

In the Carpinteria family-literacy study, a principal criterion of analysis was the question–response interaction in the literacy activity in the home. Our project in Carpinteria varied somewhat from Ada's project in that we began training the parents rather than the teachers. However, we maintained the concept of the questioning strategy as a way of organizing the presentation of children's storybooks to the parents. The different themes of each book lent themselves to discussion. Another variation in our project was to have the parents design their own questions for each book. We as the researchers had a preconceived notion based on the concept of empowerment; given the opportunity to create their own questions about the storybooks, parents could build on their personal experience and knowledge. In the parent-training meetings, adults were allowed to spontaneously create the questions they would ask their children when reading the project's books. In order to ascertain how parents actually used these questions with their children in a reading activity, the intervention included an opportunity to discuss the content of the books with them. They practiced constructing questions with each other. By devising these questions, they learned how to think about the story and its relationship to their experience, making it possible to pose appropriate questions for their children.

The five phases of videotaped observations yielded rich data about the way that parents posed questions to children about the text. The first videotaped session was collected prior to the intervention. Four subsequent sessions were scheduled on alternate months during the project.

Although parents read to their children in most of the families, the first preintervention video revealed that all but one set of parents listened to their children read without verbal interaction. The one exception was the Alvarez parents, who asked several questions as they read the book to their child. Table 2 shows a general pattern of parent–child interaction regarding text through descriptive and experiential (personal, opinion, creative) questions. The numbers in and of themselves are not meaningful unless the development of the interaction among the families can be seen along a time continuum. Each family has its own particular story about its experience with literacy before and during the project. For the purpose of this chapter, however, I will discuss briefly three individual family cases to illustrate empowerment within the family as well as with the community.

Ríos Family

The Ríos family was particularly significant to the project with respect to the development of their effort to participate in their daughter Rosa's reading. Nahuatl is the family's first language, Spanish is the second, and English is the third one for the children. The ten family members live in a small dirt-floor shack high up on the mountainside in the outskirts of town. They tend the ranch on the land where they live. In the first project session, both parents attended and brought one of their oldest sons with them; all their other children went to the childcare room. When the parents introduced themselves to the group they revealed that they had to bring all of the younger children because the owner of the ranch did not allow the children to stay in the shack unsupervised, and that they were interested in supporting their children's literacy because they had not had the opportunity to study in either Nahuatl or Spanish in Mexico.

Neither Mr. nor Mrs. Ríos could read Spanish. Their son, Rogelio, sat next to them and read aloud. During the first class all their children joined the parents in the classroom to listen to a story. I asked the children questions about the text. Rosa, a fourth grader, was the only child who raised her hand and responded to the questions enthusiastically. It was apparent to the research team that this family's literacy

Table 2

BOOKS, THEMES, AND QUESTIONING CATEGORIES

	Pre-intervention		Rosa Caramelo Theme: Gender Socialization		A dónde vas osito polar Theme: Separating and Reuniting		Historia de los bonobos Con gafas Theme: Gender Equality and Status		El primer pájaro de Piko-Niko Theme: Self-Discovery and Identity		Tío Elefante Theme: Separation and Familial Support		El perro del cerro y la rana de la sábana Theme: Rhyming		Monty Theme: Problem Solving		Mira como salen las estrellas Theme: Immigration	
	D	E	D	E	D	E	D	E	D	E	D	E	D	E	D	E	D	E
Romo (David)	0	0							15	6							0	2
Romo (Mona)	0	0							8	4							0	2
Alvarez	10	0					45	19	11	8							19	6
Samora	1	2					10	0	19	1							9	3
Gómez	3	0					10	12	7	2								
Lara	0	0					45	14									29	10
Méndez					10	2	17	1	52	6							15	0
Quinta	0	1									14	12	12	4			5	30
Ríos	0	0							5	0	18	0					26	0
Macías	1	2			13	9											4	9
Soto	0	0					1	4	7	0							7	5

D = descriptive   E = experimental

development held great promise and they deserved close observation over the course of the project. In point of fact, we found ourselves involved with the Ríos family sooner and more deeply than we had anticipated. The family had transportation problems that prevented them from continuing the literacy classes. Round-trip transportation was arranged, thanks to other families in the project, and the Ríos family was able to continue participating.

A new challenge was raised, however, when the older son called, a short time later in the project, to state that Mr. Ríos had to work late every Friday night (when class was scheduled) and that Mrs. Ríos was getting along in her pregnancy to the point where the trip to class was too tiring. He concluded his telephone call with the reluctant conclusion that they would have to "drop out" of the project. But the research staff would not permit this; they had quickly become enamored of the family for personal as well as scholarly reasons, and arranged to have Rogelio assume the responsibility of working with his enthusiastic little sister, Rosa. Following the first class, we learned that generally the parents did not listen to the children read, rather that the older brothers helped the younger ones with their schoolwork. Therefore, Rogelio's participation was appropriate.

Before starting the literacy classes in this project, Mr. Ríos listened to Rosa read but did not interact with her verbally in any way. He did express an interest in her reading to him.

The second video session showed Rogelio and Rosa in their home reading the book *El primer pájaro de Piko-Niko*. This book is about a bird who was born in a part of the forest that did not have other birds and who therefore did not know how to fly. He sought his identity with other animals but they could not help him. Just as he was falling from a cliff he passed a group of birds who called out to him "¡Vuela, pájaro, en el viento!" (Fly, bird, in the air!) The bird did so and discovered his identity as a bird.

This session showed Rogelio asking a few questions referring to particular facts of the story. The questions were of a descriptive nature: for example: "A dónde fue?" (Where did the bird go?), to which Rosa answered, "A una cueva" (To a cave).

The third reading was *Tío Elefante*. This story was considerably longer than the previous one, with five short chapters of a few pages each. The story concerned a baby elephant that had been separated from its parents. An uncle tried very hard to help the baby elephant to deal with his sorrow and the pain of not knowing his parents' whereabouts. He took him on a train trip to his own house and helped him to pass the time by playing a variety of games such as counting houses, telephone poles, and peanut shells.

During this third video interaction, Rogelio posed numerous questions to Rosa. Although the questions to Rosa appeared to be mostly of a descriptive nature, they differed qualitatively in their complexity. Earlier questions required brief direct responses, while Rogelio's questions in this third video showed growth, as responses required Rosa to consider purpose on the part of the character as opposed to simply name or location. For example, this set of questions called for Rosa to complete the question with actual text. Pointing to the text, Rogelio asked, "¿Qué intentó?" (What did he intend?); Rosa answered, "Intentó contar las casas" (He intended to count the houses). Recalling the character's intentions meant that Rosa had to understand his role.

Immigration was the theme in the eighth book read by the families in the project. *Mira como salen las estrellas* was the title and it was read on the fourth videotaping of the family in the home. The story was about a young boy and girl who took a long trip to America on a ship with their aunt to join their father and mother. The story was told from the children's point of view, relating their experiences on a ship with other people who were immigrating to America. Various trials and tribulations, such as watching others become sick and die, were reported by the children. Their arrival and reunion with their parents made it all worthwhile.

Rogelio and Rosa's interaction concerning this book was somewhat different from the three previous ones. He asked Rosa over twenty predominantly descriptive questions involving causal links, such as "¿Por qué se iban temprano a la cama?" (Why did they go to bed early?), to which she answered, "Para ver como salían las estrellas" (To see the stars come out). Development was evident in this video as Rogelio posed so many questions that they engaged Rosa into formulating a sequence of events almost at a level of summarizing the story with precise detail. Increased interaction between Rosa and Rogelio during their reading sessions over the course of the project reflected Rogelio's growth in checking on Rosa's comprehension for sequencing events and in developing a format that allowed her to demonstrate her recall on the "what, why, where, when, and how" questions. Rosa became more focused on the text, which built a strong foundation for other types of questions involving her opinion or relating the text to her experience. Revealed in the videotapes also was Rosa's marked enthusiasm for answering the questions, which indicated the importance of being challenged as Rogelio's questions encouraged her to think about what she had read.

Quinta Family

Luis Quinta, a third grader, was having a particular problem with reading, as well as in his overall social adjustment in school, in spite of the fact that his parents read at home. His parents believed that Luis was discouraged because the teacher scolded him when he made mistakes. Luis's overall attitude toward reading and school suffered as a result and the parents were concerned. They had met with the teacher and tried to find out how to help him at home. Although the parents encouraged him to do his homework and rewarded him by taking

him for a ride, he defied them and the problems persisted. On some nights, Luis's parents read to him from the Bible, but usually they read only the school texts, since his academic work was in jeopardy.

The first session we videotaped with the Quinta family showed the father reading Luis's favorite story about a pirate and a treasure at sea. About midway through the book Mr. Quinta stopped reading and asked Luis if he wanted to read part of the book. Luis declined by not responding to the invitation.

The second video, however, showed over twenty question and answer responses between Luis and his father as they read the book *Tío Elefante* (Uncle Elephant). The father, for example, asked "¿Por qué lo invitó el tío elefante?" (Why did his uncle elephant invite him?), to which Luis responded, "Porque el niño estaba solo" (Because the little boy was alone). Mrs. Quinta also posed questions to Luis as she listened to him read. She asked a variety of questions that required Luis to call on his experience. "¿Alguna vez te has sentido solo, triste?" (Have you ever felt alone, sad?) "No." "¿Alguna vez te pasó algo parecido?" (Have you ever had something like this happen to you?) Luis was reluctant to answer his parents' questions, but they were quick to elicit the information with a variety of questions.

In the third session, a number of question-answer interactions were recorded as the parents and Luis read the book *El perro del cerro y la rana de la sábana*. This was a very small book of a nonsensical nature written in rhyme verse, and it provided material for some comparison questions that the parents asked Luis. "¿Quién crees tú que sea el más valiente, el perro o la rana?" (Who do you think is braver, the dog or the toad?) "El perro" (The dog). "¿Por qué?" (Why?) "Porque el perro es más grande" (Because the dog is bigger). Even though the book was brief and of a comical nature, the parent–child interaction advanced in the question-answer formulation.

Parents continued to elaborate on their interaction with their son and the storybooks. Both Mr. and Mrs. Quinta joined Luis in reading the book in the fourth recorded session, *Mira como salen Las estrellas*. An increased number of interactions showed a focus on Luis's opinions and personal experience. For example, "¿Tú qué piensas, por qué estaban contentos?" (What do you think, why were they happy?) "Porque miraban la Estatua de la Libertad" (Because they saw the Statue of Liberty). "¿Y eso qué quería decir?" (And what did that mean?) "Que estaban en América" (That they were in America). "Si a tí te hubiera pasado una cosa así, ¿tu qué hubieras sentido?" (If something like that had happened to you, what would you have felt?) "Alegría." (Happiness). Luis was also asked to imagine what the children in the book might have liked to read: "¿Cuáles historias crees que le gustan?" (What stories do you think he likes?) "De cuando estaba chiquito" (Stories from when he was little). "¿Por qué te gusta que te cuenten historias?" (Why do you like stories told to you?) "Porque hacen que me duerma" (Because they help me go to sleep).

Both parents read together with Luis during the sessions dealing with the project, although they indicated that at other times it was either the father or mother who read with him. Each asked different questions within the same categories to get Luis to think about his reading and simultaneously create meaning with him.

Alvarez Family

The Alvarez family read a great deal at home. Mr. Alvarez had learned to read in Spanish in Mexico and spent two years in a high school in the United States, where he learned to read in English. Both parents in the Alvarez family had a history of reading with Mona, but Mrs. Alvarez admitted that she read less with the children than her husband. Mr. Alvarez had been very involved in the parent group, COPLA. He attended meetings regularly and was very vocal about parents assuming responsibility for their children's success in schooling. The reading sessions reflect the systematic work

that the Alvarezes did with their children.

In the first reading session prior to the intervention, Mr. Alvarez did not pose any questions to Mona when she read, except to ask if she liked what she read. She answered, "Sí." When Mrs. Alvarez read with Mona, a few parent–child interactions were noted; most of them were descriptive questions to which Mona gave factual answers about the story. A couple of times Mrs. Alvarez told Mona to talk to her about what she had read and Mona recounted the story.

Mrs. Alvarez read to Mona and asked her a few questions; then Mona read to her mother and asked her questions. The book they read was *El primer pájaro de Piko Niko*. As her mother read, Mona asked questions such as, "¿Qué es floresta?" (What is a grove?), to which her mother replied, "Como un tipo de selva florestal" (Like a type of dense jungle). "¿Qué apareció en el cielo?" (What appeared in the sky?) "Un pajarito" (A bird).

The two reversed roles and Mona read the book while her mother asked questions, "¿Por qué no le salía la voz, mi hija?" (Why didn't he have a voice, dear?) "Porque estaba muy espantado" (Because he was very shocked). "¿Como tú por ejemplo, si te encontraras en un lugar oscuro te iba a salir la voz, si te dijeran, entra ahí?" (Like you for example, if you found yourself in a dark place wouldn't you lose your voice, if someone told you, enter there?)

In the third session, Mr. Alvarez allowed Mona to read the entire book, *Historia de los bonobos,* and he posed the questions after she finished reading the story. He asked a variety of questions within the framework of questions we suggested—some descriptive, others more personal.

"¿Y los bonobos, qué era lo que hacían?" "Ellos nomás comían y parloteaban." "¿Si alguien hiciera mucho ruido en tu casa, te enfadarías también?" "Sí." (And what did the monkeys do?) (They just ate and talked without stopping.) (If someone made too much noise in your home where you lived would you become fed-up too?) (Yes.)

Mr. Alvarez tried to engage Mona to talk about her feelings about someone invading her territory. Framed as a yes-no question, Mona found it easy to respond with one word. Mrs. Alvarez succeeded in inviting more reflection in subsequent questions, as in the illustration that follows. Mona read the book *Mira como salen las estrellas* to her mother, and Mrs. Alvarez interacted with her daughter to induce her to recall her personal experience.

"Como cuando nosotros fuimos a México. ¿Te acuerdas cuando tú estabas más chiquita, que fuimos para allá y tu papá no fué? Estabas feliz con tus tías y tus primos, ¿verdad? ¿Pero lo extrañabas a él?" "Sí." "¿Y cuando volvimos qué sentiste?" "Contenta." "¿Y le diste un abrazo?" "Ya no me acuerdo." (Like when we went to Mexico, do you remember? When you were younger, we went over there and your father didn't go? You were happy with your aunts and cousins, right? But, you missed him?) (Yes.) (And how did you feel?) (Happy.) (And did you give him a hug?) (I don't remember.)

The Alvarezes exemplified a family who read regularly together and demonstrated the importance of relating text to personal opinions and experiences in their lives. The mother encouraged Mona to think about her feelings about her father's absence, prompting her experience of being distant from her father.

The three families discussed here varied in their development in the sense that they entered the project at various points on the continuum of empowerment from changes in self-perception to community action. Regarding the questioning strategies, for example, the families generally stayed within the descriptive phase of questioning when reading, but they gradually ventured into framing a more elaborate discussion about the text. As parents read more with their children and became more experienced, they developed a more expanded repertoire of questions. Further, we observed a strong bond developing within the families as they shared a special time and space.

Parents also increased their confidence in dealing with the schools because they had become more experienced in academic tasks, as was revealed in the follow-up interview with the families a year after the family literacy classes ended. They also developed networks with other parents in the family literacy classes and were encouraged to become more involved in the COPLA organization to continue their learning about their children's schoolwork. Parents who were active in COPLA made it a point to contact families who were enrolled in literacy classes.

Parent Classes

The format of the literacy classes was designed purposely not only to encourage parents to practice cognitive skills but also to provide them with a setting that invited discussion about their perceptions, emotions, fears, and concerns, and with a place where they could link with others who shared their experience in learning literacy in a new culture. The literacy classes began with an introduction about the beauty of stories. The trainer/researchers and the community member/trainer talked to the families about the importance of reading in the home and the parents' role in that activity. Conditions for participation in the Family Literacy Project were discussed with particular emphasis on the following:

1. The parents should meet regularly with researchers and other parents, including a community leader, to share and discuss storybooks they would read to their children at home

2. Both parents (where possible) should attend the monthly classes and read to their children nightly

3. A quiet time should be allotted daily to read with the child and discuss the story by asking the child appropriate questions

4. Television time should be minimized and substituted with reading activity

5. Monthly reports should be submitted by the families on the books read by the children during the month

6. Families should be available for an interview and videorecording on alternate months during the course of the project

Agreements between the parents and researchers were necessary to establish continuity for the Family Literacy Project. In addition to the parents' role, the researchers were required to provide specific things to the families during the course of the project:

1. Each family would receive one storybook per month

2. Childcare would be provided at every class meeting

3. Home visits would be made on alternate months of the scheduled project at the parents' convenience

4. A nominal monetary compensation would be allocated to each family for their participation in the project

Structure and content were particularly significant in the literacy classes. The format was designed to involve parents. It was intended to facilitate the presentation of text content, which, for the most part, was in the form of a discussion using a variety of questioning strategies.

Parents welcomed the opportunity to participate in the literacy classes although some were rather reticent at first because of their own limited literacy skills. The class format accommodated the variation of literacy skills among the adults. Those parents who opted not to read because they felt embarrassed or because they lacked the skills were allowed to refrain from reading in the small groups. As the classes progressed, however, those parents who initially would not read at all were encouraged to read along with other parents in choral reading. In one case, the couple's older son sat in the classes and read the book to the parents so that they were able to follow along with the group. By the last class, parents who initially did not want to read aloud in the small group sessions were observed reading aloud, even though some read very slowly. They also were encouraged to participate more in the group discussions about the themes of the stories and to share their personal experiences to illustrate. Parents left their children at childcare in a nearby room while they attended class in the library.

At the beginning of the class, I welcomed the parents and we talked informally about general issues of urgency to them such as the possible difficulty in dealing with their children's schoolwork or meeting with the teacher. This was usually an opportunity for the parents who were active in the COPLA parent organization to invite others to participate and to learn about getting involved in the schools and helping their children in this manner.

Following the opening discussion, Mrs. Reyes, the experienced parent, read the new story to the group as they listened and responded to her questions. When Mrs. Reyes completed the story the parents separated into three small groups led by herself and two researchers.

In the groups, parents took turns reading the story that had been read to them and asked questions of each other. At least four of the parents had approached this entire task rather reluctantly because they considered themselves nonreaders. During earlier classes they were allowed to skip their turn to read, but gradually they were encouraged to read aloud with the entire group. In this way they could follow the text as they read aloud with the group. These parents were also encouraged to listen to others read and pose questions about the content; this led to group discussions about the theme of the book. Thus, by the third meeting at least two of the parents who initially claimed to be nonreaders were actually participating in the discussion with the other parents.

As presented to the parents, the questioning strategies—descriptive, personal, critical, and creative—lent a framework to generate discussion. Initially, the questioning strategies were described to the parents as four types of questions to ask children during a reading activity. We soon realized the mistake of describing the strategies as labeled categories. Parents were quite capable of generating questions about the story on their own, and in fact, their questions fit well into the four categories we presented. Yet, when they saw the white sheets of paper with the four types, upon which they were to write their own questions, they became confused as to this competence. The error was in imposing an artificial structure on the process of organizing their thoughts about the texts so that they lost confidence and spontaneity in the discussion.

For the duration of the project, the seven months that followed, some time in class was spent undoing that mistake. When parents asked questions in their small groups, they usually prefaced it by commenting, for instance, "No sé que tipo de pregunta es ésta, pero, ¿Qué hacían los bonobos en los árboles?" (I don't know what type of question this is but, what did the monkeys do in the trees?) Eventually, the confusion of what the abstract categories meant dissipated, or so we thought. On the last interview with families in their homes, two parents, one of them Mrs. Alvarez, mentioned to me that they were so grateful for what they had learned in their classes, but one thing concerned her: "Yo nunca pude aprender los cuatro tipos de preguntas. Eso siempre me confundía." ("I never could learn the four types of questions. That always confused me.) Of course, I assured them that the labels were not important since they had actually accomplished a great deal in the way they interacted with their children about the stories.

How did parents learn ways to discuss the book with their children? Parents learned through modeling, group discussion, and actual practice, which allowed them to define what ideas they had about the story and through open discussion.

Parents approached each book from their experience, which shaped the discussion. At the beginning of each class, Mrs. Reyes modeled the reading activity and she posed questions to them as a group, just as they would read with their children at home. The research team reinforced the practice in the small-group sessions.

By the sixth session, the parents who had become integrated into the reading process had begun to read text in the small groups. Mr. Samora claimed not to be able to read and when we visited their home, he always let Mrs. Samora read with their son. In class, he learned to quietly ask a question or two during group discussion. By the sixth class, Mr. Samora actually read a page from the text with his wife's assistance, as she read along with him. In the small-group sessions of the last class, Mr. Samora read a page by himself without his wife's assistance, and in the last video session recorded in their home, he read with his son and asked him questions. His wife, overburdened by her solitary role as Augusto's tutor, was grateful for Mr. Samora's assistance. In the project, she learned that her husband, too, had developed new skills. Before the project, Mr. Samora expressed discomfort about reading because he had only completed the first grade in Mexico. In the process of learning cognitive skills in reading, parents also learned to express feelings about their relationship to literacy and to redefine it.

Parent–Community Interaction

Mrs. Reyes played a key role not only as a project trainer but also as a cultural broker between the COPLA parent group and this group of parents who had been less involved in the schools. After the first phase of the classes terminated, the School District Migrant Programs sponsored a one-day conference for Spanish-speaking families. The organizers asked the COPLA organization to participate, and Mrs. Reyes volunteered to work with Mrs. Mata, the childcare provider for the Family Literacy Project, to present a workshop on literacy for other Spanish-speaking parents in the larger community. The conference sessions were videotaped and the two parents used them to evaluate their performance. The teacher, Mrs. Reyes, and Mrs. Mata held two two-hour workshops. They had about twenty participants (both men and women) in each session and they used the same format of reading and discussing as was done in the Family Literacy Project. Mrs. Reyes read the story *Rosa Caramelo:*

A herd of elephants discriminated against the female elephants by making them dress in pink frilly collars and pink booties. The only different one in the bunch was a grey elephant that was quite unhappy because she could not do a lot of things that the male elephants did until one day she broke out of the fenced area where the female elephants were restricted. The other female elephants liked what they saw and joined the grey elephant. (Translated from Spanish).

This gender theme was of particular interest to the parents. Mrs. Reyes read the story and posed questions to the group in the familiar way she had done in the literacy class. The parents separated into two smaller groups, where they engaged in a discussion about the unfair treatment of the female elephants. In one group, for example, this position was countered with arguments that girls should be protected and if given too much freedom they might get into trouble. This seemed to sway the conversation to the need to protect all children because of drugs and other evils "allá en el mundo" (out there in the world). Following their half-hour discussion, parents returned to the large group and Mrs. Mata and Mrs. Reyes guided the discussion, inviting both groups of parents to share ideas that emerged about the book.

Another level of extended community awareness that resulted from the Family Literacy Project was the increased networking of parents with the COPLA organization. When the literacy classes began, only Mr. Alvarez, Mrs. Mata, and Mrs. Reyes were active. The classes became a focal area for recruitment for COPLA because the parents saw the importance of linking what they were learning with the rest of the Spanish-speaking community. They believed that by working together to transmit this type of knowledge to others, they could all better assist their children, and COPLA was the vehicle by which they could unite and share this knowledge. Mr. Alvarez usually announced forthcoming activities for the local COPLA meetings. The increase in participation in monthly meetings became evident about five months after the literacy project began. The attendance was more consistent than it had ever been once parents from the literacy class began attending. This meant the end of organizational difficulties in the school, but it also indicated the need for the school to reach out to parents in a way that is meaningful to them. Furthermore, it showed the influence of forming parent networks for the purpose of sharing knowledge and skills to find ways to help their children both at home and at school.

A year after the literacy classes ended, one of the parents gave testimony to the importance of using parental classes as linkages to other parent organizations. Mr. Quinta attended a district-wide meeting of the COPLA organization where he spoke to the issue:

Yo he visto que es muy necesario que uno como padre de familia tome interés en la escuela de sus hijos. Nosotros (yo y mi esposa) participamos en el proyecto de lectura para la familia y hemos visto que nuestro hijo se ha desarrollado mucho y yo creo que es porque nosotros tenemos más interés en su lectura y él sabe que nos importa. También hemos aprendido mucho en las juntas de COPLA sobre los derechos que tienen los padres en las escuelas. Y, pues, yo estoy muy agradecido del apoyo que nos han dado todos.

(I have learned that it is very necessary that parents take an interest in their children's schooling. We (me and my wife) participated in the Main School Family School Project and we have seen our son develop so much and it's because we have taken more of an interest in his reading and he knows that it is important to us. We have also learned a great deal from the COPLA meetings about the rights that parents have in the schools. I, for one, am very appreciative of everyone's support.)

Much was learned about empowerment in this study by observing how parents and children drew meanings from reading together and how they shared and related their experiences to the texts. As we learned more about empowerment by the families vis-à-vis the schools and the community, the families in the study increased awareness of their identity as community members who shared a common cultural base. Sharing this cultural heritage, as they read the books with their children, provided parents with support and confidence. On another level, the empowerment families obtained in this process encouraged them to teach other parents. In a real sense, then, the project had a networking effect and strengthened the empowerment of the group as well as individuals.

Conclusion

Literacy in the Carpinteria project was much more than interpreting text from a book and relating it to the individual's experience. Embedded in a social process, literacy transforms people's organization in the home as a result of the new ideas and practices acquired. Parents and children may have been engaged in a direct question-and-answer interaction about the storybook text, but what they shared was more; they shared values and opinions about the importance of family, identity with a group, emotional support, and freedom. This sociocultural knowledge was transmitted and reconstructed in their literacy classes.

Increased awareness among parents was evidenced by a positive change in their self-perception and efficacy in being able to participate directly in their children's literacy learning. In the cases where reading with their children was not a common activity, parents accepted changes in their family organization to accommodate the new behavior. Through classes they established new relationships with other members of their cultural group and shared common concerns, fears, and successes as they learned from one another. Part of the families' overall development was evident as they reached out to other members of the community by teaching what they learned in the literacy project and by becoming involved in COPLA activities. Although the project was designed to deal only with family literacy within the home, the ramifications extended beyond the household. Families became empowered on numerous levels beyond the home reading activity as parents became knowledgeable about the importance of encouraging literacy in the home, learning collectively with other community members, and becoming more involved in their children's education through an established parent group.

I am grateful for the research assistance of Martha Allexsaht-Snider and Hector Mendez. Funding for parts of this study were provided by John Hopkins Center for the Study of Disadvantaged Students and the University of California, Santa Barbara, Center for Chicano Studies.

REFERENCES

Ada, A.F. (1988). The Pajaro Valley experience: Working with Spanish-speaking parents to develop children's reading and writing skills in the home through the use of children's literature. In T. Skutnabb-Kangas & J. Cummins (Eds.), *Minority education: From shame to struggle* (pp. 224–238). Philadelphia: Multilingual Matters.

Allen, J., Barr, D., Cochran, M., Dean, C., & Green, J. (1989). Empowerment process. Empowerment Project, College of Human Ecology, Cornell University. Unpublished manuscript.

Auerbach, E. (1989). Toward a social-contextual approach to family literacy. *Harvard Educational Review, 59,* 165–181.

Clark, M. (1984). Literacy at home and at school: Insights from a study of young fluent readers. In H. Goelman, A. Oberg & F. Smith (Eds.), *Awakening to literacy* (pp. 38–50). Portsmouth, NH: Heinemann.

Cochran, M. (1988). Between cause and effect: The ecology of program impacts. In A.R. Pence (Ed.), *Ecological research with children and families* (pp. 143–169). New York: Teachers College Press.

Cook-Gumperz, J. (Ed.). (1986). *The social construction of literacy.* Cambridge: Cambridge University Press.

Delgado-Gaitán, C. (1990). *Literacy for empowerment: The role of parents in children's education.* London: Fálmer Press.

Delgado-Gaitán, C., & Trueba, H. (1991). *Crossing cultural borders: Education for immigrant families in America.* London: Falmer Press.

Freire, P. (1970). *Pedagogy of the oppressed.* New York: Seabury Press.

Freire, P., & Macedo, D. (1987). *Literacy: Reading the word and the world.* South Hadley, MA: Bergin and Garvey.

Goldenberg, C.N. (1987). Low-income Hispanic parents' contributions to their first-grade children's word recognition skills. *Anthropology and Education Quarterly, 18,* 149–179.

Green, J.L., Wade, R., & Graham, K. (1988). Lesson construction and student participation: A sociolinguistic analysis. In J.L. Green & J.O. Harker (Eds.), *Multiple perspective analyses of classroom discourse* (pp. 11–48). Norwood, NJ: Ablex.

Heath, S.B. (1982). Questioning at home and at school: A comparative study. In G. Spindler (Ed.), *Doing the ethnography of schooling: Educational anthropology in action* (pp. 102–131). New York: Holt, Rinehart & Winston.

————. (1983). *Ways with words.* New York: Cambridge University Press.

Leichter, H.J. (1984). Families as environments for literacy. In H. Goelman, A. Oberg & F. Smith (Eds.), *Awakening to literacy* (pp. 38–50). Portsmouth, NH: Heinemann.

Moll, L., & Diaz, S. (1987). Change as the goal of educational research. *Anthropology and Education Quarterly, 18,* 300–311.

Schieffelin, B., & Cochran-Smith, M. (1984). Learning to read culturally: Literacy before schooling. In H. Goelman, A. Oberg & F. Smith (Eds.), *Awakening to literacy* (pp. 3–23). Portsmouth, NH: Heinemann.

Seppanen, P.S. (1988). Community education as a home for family support and education programs. Research Report, Harvard Family Research Project. Harvard University.

Street, B. (1984). *Literacy in theory and practice.* Cambridge: Cambridge University Press.

Taylor, D. (1983). *Family literacy: Young children learning to read and write.* Exeter, NH: Heinemann.

Trueba, H.T. (1984). The forms, functions and values of literacy: Reading for survival in a barrio as a student. *NABE Journal, 9,* 21–40.

Wells, G. (1986). The language experience of five-year-old children at home and at school. In J. Cook-Gumperz (Ed.), *The social construction of literacy* (pp. 69–93). New York: Cambridge University Press.

Part VI

ASSESSMENT

ALTERNATIVE ASSESSMENT FOR LATINO STUDENTS

Ann Del Vecchio, Cyndee Gustke, and Judith Wilde
New Mexico Highlands University

Introduction

In determining how best to assess Latino students, several issues must be kept in mind. First, as described by the Joint Committee of the American Educational Research Association, American Psychological Association, and American Council on Measurement (referred to hereafter as Joint Committee), there are at least thirteen standards for testing bilingual persons. As a basic premise, these standards state that a test that relies solely on the English language is confounded (Joint Committee, 1985); it is impossible to know whether the score reflects content area knowledge or English language knowledge. In addition, the Joint Committee standards specifically:

- prohibit the translation of a test from one language to another

- encourage testing in the primary language[1] as well as English

- suggest that "several dimensions" of language proficiency must be assessed

- point out that when testing bilingual students, testing time, home culture and language background, and training for those administering the test must be considered

Obviously, these standards speak about the bilingual or Spanish-speaking Latino student. However, even for English-speaking Latino students the importance of culture and language background must be remembered. Clearly, then, all of these factors emphasize the need for assessment that is more culturally and linguistically fair to Latino students.

Gardner (1993) contends that currently used testing formats (specifically, NRTs) are decontextualized. This seemingly objective format does not benefit students because it is so unlike real-life situations. He adds that testing in the past involved an apprentice-like situation, in which students were expected to demonstrate the skills necessary to become a master in the field. Gardner suggests a return to more performance-based approaches that are apprentice-like in order to provide students with greater opportunities to demonstrate their strengths (Gardner, 1993).

This article will suggest ways to assess Latino students in a manner that will benefit them and their school system. In such a format, students will show their abilities and skills in the best possible light. Different types of alternative assessments and possible scoring mechanisms will be described. In addition, collecting and managing alternative assessments within a portfolio system will be suggested.

Alternative assessments and portfolios are unique because when designed appropriately they can be used with preliterate, biliterate, and monoliterate (English or Spanish) Latino students. These measures actively involve and empower students and educators. They can be modified easily to meet the needs of students with different linguistic abilities and cultural backgrounds. Furthermore, many alternative assessments can be used as part of the curriculum, without the necessity for a specific testing period.

Alternative Assessment

Gardner (1993) describes assessment as the obtaining of information about the skills and potentials of individuals, with the dual goals of providing useful feedback to the individuals and useful data to the surrounding community. The competency of students can be determined by a variety of strategies. All of these are characterized as "nontraditional" measures (Baker et al., 1993), as opposed to "traditional" paper-and-pencil tests. Many educators who work with Latino students and communities find that they can assess students more effectively with alternative measures that allow them to document growth within the context of meaningful instruction. Alternative assessment tasks are designed to resemble real-life or real learning activities. They focus on what students actually can do, as opposed to focusing on students' deficits. Other benefits of alternative assessments include:

- information gathered over time from a range of classroom experiences

- assessments that indicate a student's broad progress in basic skills, conceptual understanding, problem solving, and reflective thinking, as well as motivation toward learning and attitudes toward school

- a focus on the process involved in learning or mastery, not on drill and practice

- measurements based on an understanding of diversity in backgrounds, learning styles, and developmental learning

- active student, teacher, and family reflection, ownership, and involvement in assessments of growth and needs

- a climate of trust with strong partnerships between teachers and students and families

The need for alternative assessments generally is agreed upon by some theoreticians (for example, Gardner, 1993) and practitioners [such as, Teachers of English to Speakers of Other Languages (TESOL) Standards, in Appendix]. The nontraditional nature of alternative assessments is agreed upon (Baker et al., 1993), as are the various benefits of alternative assessments (Navarrete et al., 1990). What remains is to understand exactly what these assessment strategies are and how they are to be used.

Types of Alternative Assessments

There is a great deal of variety in both the design and purposes of alternative assessments. The content (reading, writing, math, art, social studies, etc.) and the purpose (diagnostic, evaluation, grading, self-reflection, etc.) will of course determine the form an alternative assessment takes. The forms of alternative assessment range from simple checklists to week-long performance-based assessments. More complex alternative assessments may require students to show evidence of specific skills and to produce written, graphic, dramatic, or other kinds of products.

Figure 1
EXAMPLE ALTERNATIVE ASSESSMENTS

Student: Observer:		Grade:	
Area	Date	Language	Comment/ Observation
Reading			
Writing			
Math			
Oral			
Coop Learning Groups			
Play			

Anecdotal Records

A common informal method used to capture evidence of cognitive processes and behaviors is an *anecdotal record*. Teachers, parents, educational assistants, and/or others who work with a group of students simply record their observations of students. These observations may document student growth or student needs. This process can become more formal when observations are recorded on a given time schedule, for individual students, for a specific behavior or purpose. An example anecdotal record is provided in Figure 1.

Checklists

A more formal method for observation involves the construction and use of checklists. Checklists can be developed with as few or as many items as necessary to capture progress in a specific area. The checklist consists of a series of expected behaviors that can be scored to indicate whether or not the behavior is present. It can also be scored with a more elaborate rating scale that allows the observer to indicate the degree to which a task is completed or a behavior is evident. A sample checklist is located in Figure 2.

Figure 2
SAMPLE CHECKLIST

Check the box for "yes" or "no" whether the student uses each of these strategies as s/he reads through a familiar passage.

Name _____ Date _____

Language _____

Teacher _____

Book Title _____

	Yes	No
Uses picture clues	☐	☐
Comments:		
Uses context to get meaning	☐	☐
Comments:		
Substitutes another meaningful word	☐	☐
Comments:		
Uses phonics	☐	☐
Comments:		
Backtracks to get meaning	☐	☐
Comments:		

Classroom Products

Classroom products may be used to measure student achievement, attitudes, and proficiency levels. These may include journal entries, writing samples, video productions, collaborative and/or individual work reports, essays, debates, reading lists, problem solution descriptions, artistic media, storytelling, and read-alouds. A sample writing process rating scale for use by teachers is presented in Figure 3. Other instruments that may be used to assess students include question naires, Cloze reading tests, miscue analysis reading assessments, criterion referenced tests, self-assessments (see Figure 4), peer reviews, and parent questionnaires (see the sample parent questionnaire in Figure 5). These methods are described more fully in Bratcher (1994), Del Vecchio et al. (1994), Goodman et al. (1992), Holt (1994), Navarrete et al. (1990), and various materials developed by Stiggins (1990) at the Northwest Regional Educational Laboratory.

Although many of these assessments emphasize student achievement, they can also be used to assess language proficiency in any language. The Council of Chief State School Officers (1992) suggests that all four modalities (reading, writing, speaking, and listening) should be assessed to determine language proficiency. With alternative assessment, a single well-designed instructional activity can generate measures of language proficiency across all four modalities (Del Vecchio et al., 1994).

Figure 3 - SAMPLE WRITING PROCESS RATING SCALE

Name and grade of student _____

Teacher _____ **Language(s)** _____

Circle the number that most closely indicates the student's use of skills. Use the following rating scale:

1 Always or almost always   2 Sometimes   3 Rarely or Never

Does the student

write during designated time?	1	2	3
use constructive strategies for getting drafts started?	1	2	3
show growth in understanding the differences between revising and editing?	1	2	3
use the support systems in the classroom, (manuals, spelling aids, resourse books?)	1	2	3
participate in peer conferences seriously?	1	2	3

Modified from Goodman, Goodman, & Bird, 1992.

Figure 4 - SAMPLE STUDENT SELF-ASSESSMENT

Name

Date

Complete the sentences below.

• Today in science I

• I learned more about

• I still have the following questions

Overall, I would rate my performance in science as

_____ Excellent

_____ Satisfactory

_____ Poor

Figure 5 - SAMPLE EARLY CHILDHOOD PARENT QUESTIONAIRE

Nombre del estudiante

Pecha   Grado

Nombre del adulto en la familia

Mi hijo/hija	siempre	a veces	poco
le gusta hablar	❑	❑	❑
hace preguntas	❑	❑	❑
le gusta contar cuentos favoritos	❑	❑	❑
le gusta hablar en inglés	❑	❑	❑
le gusta hablar en español	❑	❑	❑
le gusta escribir de mentiritas	❑	❑	❑
hace preguntas tocante a lo escrito que ve en el ambiente	❑	❑	❑
le gusta que alguien le lea cuentos	❑	❑	❑
le gusta jugar a leer	❑	❑	❑
tiene cuentos favoritos	❑	❑	❑

Methods for Scoring Alternative Assessments

There are many types of alternative assessments. In addition, there are many ways to assign scores to alternative assessments and products. The type of scoring method used is dependent upon the purpose of the assessment. Some of the more common methods are described briefly below; examples are provided in the accompanying figures.

Holistic rating scales are used to judge the whole product or performance. Specific criteria are identified with holistic "rubrics," or rating scales. Generally, these are scored with symbols (e.g., +, ✓ or –), letters (e.g., A to F), or numbers (ranging from a minimum of 1 to 3 to a maximum of 1 to 10). An example holistic rubric for math is included in Figure 6.

If it is desirable to examine particular parts of a performance or product, *primary trait scoring* can be used. For a written product, a primary trait rubric might be applied to the organization, mechanics, voice, and creativity of the piece. Each part or trait of the piece (e.g., organization) has specific criteria upon which to base the score. The ratings for each part then can be either summed to provide a total score for the piece or left as separate parts. As with holistic scoring, the range of scores generally is between 1–3 and 1–10. A sample primary trait scoring rubric for writing is presented in Figure 7.

Figure 6 - SAMPLE HOLISTIC SCORING FOR MATH

An individual paper or portfolios are likely to be characterized by some, but not all, of the descriptors for a particular level. The overall score should be the level at which the appropriate descriptors are clustered.

Novice
- ❑ Indicates a basic understanding of problems & uses strategies
- ❑ Implements strategies with minor mathematical errors but without observations or extensions
- ❑ Uses mathematical reasoning & appropriate mathematical language some of the time
- ❑ Uses few mathematical representations
- ❑ Indicates a basic understanding of core concepts; uses few tools

Apprentice
- ❑ Indicates an understanding of problems & selects appropriate strategies
- ❑ Accurately implements strategies with solutions, with limited observations or extensions
- ❑ Uses appropriate mathematical reasoning & language
- ❑ Uses a variety of mathematical representations accurately & appropriately
- ❑ Indicates an understanding of core concepts with limited connections; uses tools appropriately

Proficient
- ❑ Indicates a broad understanding of problems with alternate strategies
- ❑ Accurately & efficiently implements & analyzes strategies with correct solutions, with extensions
- ❑ Uses perceptive mathematical reasoning & precise & appropriate math language most of the time
- ❑ Uses a wide variety of mathematical representations accurately & appropriately
- ❑ Indicates a broad understanding of some core concepts with connections; uses a wide variety of tools appropriately

Distinguished
- ❑ Indicates a comprehensive understanding of problems with efficient, sophisticated strategies
- ❑ Accurately & efficiently implements & evaluates sophisticated strategies with correct solutions; includes analysis, justifications, & extensions
- ❑ Uses perceptive, creative, & complex mathematical reasoning; sophisticated, precise, & appropriate mathematical language throughout
- ❑ Uses a wide variety of mathematical representations accurately & appropriately
- ❑ Indicates a comprehensive understanding of core concepts with connections throughout; uses a wide variety of tools appropriately & insightfully

Modified from the Kentucky Instructional Results Information System, Kentucky Department of Education, 1993.

Figure 7 - SAMPLE PRIMARY TRAIT AND ANALYTIC SCORING RUBRIC FOR WRITING

Trait *Weight*	Score	Criteria
Content *x4*	1	Topic & purpose unclear; limited reflection of own thinking
	2	Topic basically understood; some supporting detail & reflection of own thinking
	3	Topic & purpose clearly understood; includes a variety of supporting detail & strongly reflects own thinking
Organization *x3*	1	Limited use of process, sequence illogical, purpose unclear
	2	Completed most steps of writing process; final lacks either introduction, body, or conclusion
	3	Writing process completed; well organized; includes introduction, body, & conclusion; is well developed, coherent
Sentence Structure *x1*	1	Limited use of logical sentences, several problems with sentence structure
	2	Sentences contain few errors, are logical, & vary somewhat in length
	3	Sentences are complete, with few or no errors, vary in length, are logical, concise, & energetic
Voice *x1*	1	Sense of awareness of audience or voice is not evident
	2	Sense of awareness of audience & author is somewhat evident; language is natural
	3	Strong sense of audience & author's presence; strong flavor & tone of task completed

Note: weights are used only with analytic scoring and may be adjusted as appropriate.

Analytic Scoring

The most complex type of score procedure is the *analytic*. In this variation of primary trait scoring, particular traits are considered more important than others and are weighted accordingly. For instance, the organization of a written piece might be three times as important as mechanics, and twice as important as voice. These weightings might be based on recent topics within the curriculum, the weaker areas in a student's products, or other factors. An example of changing a primary trait rubric to an analytic scoring method is indicated in Figure 7 by italicized print.

Although these methods for scoring alternative assessments do not include all possible techniques, they reflect the practices used commonly today. These methods can be extremely useful for working with culturally and linguistically diverse students. They are flexible and can be used with instruments developed in any language. The most important points to remember in using any of these methods are:

■ to set well-defined standards for what is to be assessed

■ to describe these standards clearly and completely

■ to provide instructional opportunities that match the assessments

It is important to keep in mind that alternative forms of assessment should reflect actual teaching practices, with students, families, and teachers understanding how the assessments will be used. Students should be informed of the criteria used to determine grades, and may be involved in the actual development of the criteria.

Creating and Modifying Assessments

Few NRTs and alternative assessments have been developed to assess Latino students' knowledge in content areas. Therefore, it is important to understand the process involved in creating and adapting instruments. Ramírez (in press) has outlined a set of guidelines for developing assessment procedures for Potentially English Proficient (PEP) students. These guidelines involve an eleven-step process, strongly encourage a planning team, and are appropriate for developing materials for all Latino students. They can be summarized into four general areas: (1) deciding about the curriculum framework; (2) determining the frequency of assessment; (3) creating methods and procedures for assessment; and (4) planning professional development about the curriculum framework and the assessment process.

Although all the steps in these guidelines are not essential to developing a specific assessment measure for Latino students, Ramírez's (in press) guidelines provide a broader framework within which to consider any assessment development. They also ensure the generalizability of the assessment to contexts outside the school setting by providing a standardized process for development.

The essential elements necessary to develop or modify alternative assessments are to: (1) identify the purpose for the assessment; (2) generate or find ideas for the assessment that fit with the curriculum; (3) design a prototype instrument and field-test it; and (4) modify the instrument based on the results of the field test. This process is not as linear as it may appear and is iterative; that is, some steps may need to be repeated several times before a good instrument is developed. The procedure is described in more detail in the next section, with Figure 8 providing a brief example of the development of an instrument.

Identify the Purpose for the Assessment

Assessment purposes fall into several broad categories and usually are linked closely to the audience(s) that will use the results of the assessment. Stiggins (1993) suggests that users, as well as uses, of assessment results can be categorized into three levels:

- instructional—including teachers, students, and parents
- leadership/support—including principals, counselors, program directors, support teachers, and curriculum directors
- policy-making—including superintendents, schools, state departments of education, federal and state education agencies and funding sources, community members, and legislators

The purpose of assessment is different for the individuals within each of these levels. As an example, teachers need information about student progress in a particular content area. They can also evaluate their own instructional methods and content coverage, assign grades, and/or identify the need for special programs or instructional methods. On the other hand, students and parents use the results of assessments to inform themselves about the student's academic progress. Superintendents and state departments of education use assessment results to identify schools or districts in need of additional resources.

Defining the purpose of the new assessment (or the revised assessment) is a critical step that must be completed early in the development process. In addition, identifying purposes and designing assessments can help educators, communities, and students raise their awareness of what they see as important goals and priorities for education.

Find the Idea for the New Assessment

The idea for an assessment can come from a variety of sources, including state competencies, instructional activities, textbooks, newspaper articles, the evening news on TV, another teacher, conversations with friends and family, student interests, or life in general. Some of the best ideas are generated by the students themselves; these are more likely to be meaningful for them and to include aspects of their own language and culture. There generally are three steps to this phase of development: (1) talking about the idea with colleagues, (2) thinking about the language of assessment, and (3) considering whether or not this idea can be transposed into a measurable assessment that matches instruction and has meaning and merit

Figure 8 - EXAMPLE INSTRUMENT DEVELOPMENT

Basic Steps	Detailed Process
Identify the Purpose for the Assessment	1. Who is the audience? Who will use the assessment? 2. Will the assessment be used to inform instruction? for diagnostic purposes? to evaluate a program? other purposes?
Find the idea	1. Consult the students first for ideas. 2. Ask colleagues. 3. Consider the curriculum content and identify real-life community problems and issues related to the curriculum. The newspaper, local news, and community groups sometimes have problems that can be used as the basic idea for an assessment. 4. Make sure the idea is culturally relevant—asking the students allows them to include aspects of their culture and language in the assessment.
Design the Assessment	1. Define your objectives (refer to your curriculum). 2. Draft a plan including the objectives, the type of task, instructions to the students, a timeline, and possible problems to be addressed. 3. Consider response formats such as written exercises or reports, presentations, group discussions, experiments, etc. 4. Keep notes on the development process so that others could use your ideas. 5. Determine who will judge the assessment (teacher, students, parents, a committee). 6. Develop a method to score the assessment. This could be a rubric, a checklist, or some other method for identifying the quality of the students' efforts. It should be related closely to the curriculum objectives, and the standards or evaluation criteria the students are expected to reach should be clearly defined. 7. Furnish the students with information about the evaluation criteria. 8. Consider attitudes and attributes you hope to see (motivation, group cooperation, interest). 9. Identify a method to establish reliability for the task. Can it be used or scored by other teachers with the same results?
Modify the Assessment	1. Try the task out. Do not attach stakes (grades) to it during the pilot test. 2. Use feedback from the students and other teachers to modify the assessment. 3. Revise the task and/or the system for scoring it as necessary. 4. Document revisions in your notes. 5. Try it out again.

in the community. For Latino students, English- or Spanish-language assessments might be appropriate. If Spanish is used, a determination of the "type" of Spanish (vernacular from a geographic area or "standard") in which to write items and directions, as well as in which to accept responses, must be made.

Design and Field-Test the Assessment

There are four steps to this phase of instrument development: (1) refining objectives to include how and when the instrument will fit into the curriculum; (2) drafting a plan that includes a description of the task, the purpose (objectives) for it, directions for the students, possible formats, scoring guidelines, and nondirective questions to encourage students to find solution strategies; (3) creating a rough draft of the instrument, including scoring, and sharing the draft with colleagues; and (4) revising the draft and using the instrument in a field test. The field test should include students' feedback about the assessment; there should be no stakes (grades) attached to performance at this time. Notes taken throughout the process will allow replication in the future.

Modify the Instrument

If the instrument already exists, but is not fully appropriate for current students, this phase will be used to revise the instrument. The instrument can be shared with colleagues, including the purpose(s) for which it was designed originally, and then a revised version can be drafted. This draft should be field-tested with students, still asking for their feedback and not grading it.

After the field test, the instrument should be modified based on the feedback from students and colleagues and from student performance. The final step in the development process is to evaluate the assessment based on notes and a personal judgment about how it worked. Things to consider at this time are the cost-benefit ratio—perhaps the assessment provided valuable information but it took too long to administer and/or to score. All available information should be considered at this point and the instrument revised as necessary. It may be necessary to repeat these two steps, field-testing and modifying the instrument, several times before the instrument meets the program's needs.

Portfolio Assessment

Once alternative assessments are selected as the means for assessing student performance, how they can be combined and utilized in the best possible fashion must be considered. One of the more popular and powerful methods is through the portfolio. The most common definition of *portfolio* comes from the Northwest Evaluation Association: "A portfolio is a purposeful collection of student work that exhibits the student's efforts, progress, and achievements in one or more areas" (Northwest Evaluation Association, cited in Arter, 1992, p. 2). The portfolio is an organizational structure that allows the systematic accumulation of various types of assessments. The portfolio may include any of the alternative assessments defined in the previous section, NRTs, CRTs, audio/video tapes, and more. How the portfolio is framed is based on its purpose.

Purposes for a Portfolio

Gottlieb (1992) has proposed six specific purposes for portfolios: to collect, reflect, assess, document, link, and/or to evaluate. Using the first letter of each word, this becomes the CRADLE approach to portfolios. (See Figure 9 for a fuller definition of each term.) If the full approach is used, a teacher (or a program, school, or school district) might begin at stage one, collecting, and gradually move toward stage six, evaluating. Another person might identify where she/he wants to be on the CRADLE continuum and begin directly at that point.

Another approach to portfolio assessment is to view the portfolio as monitoring either a product or a process. In looking at products, a series of "best" works is selected by students and teachers to include in the portfolio. These best works, across a school year, show the progress and achievement of the student. In looking at a process, a series of draft materials and notes leading to one final product would be collected in the portfolio. These materials show the student's growth as she/he researched, studied, drafted, and refined a particular project or assignment. The portfolio also might contain

Figure 9 - Gottlieb's (1992) CRADLE Approach to Portfolios

Portfolios can be used to...

Collect	Encourage an open-ended selection of entries
	Provide a working repository for individual students
	Allow for experimentation
Reflect	Emphasize metacognitive and affective learning
	Focus on the process of acquiring knowledge
	Represent student-centered activities
Assess	Include primary and secondary evidence
	Specify criteria for authentic tasks and projects
	Rely on systematic data collection
Document	Evidence from multiple sources (including NRTs) over time
	Maintain a record of student achievement
	Comply with designated regulations
Link	Bridge communication among home, school, community
	Facilitate connections among teachers
	Show relative language and cognitive development of students
Evaluate	Assign a value to tasks and projects
	Summarize and make meaningful assessment findings
	Serve as a system of accountability at many levels

both works-in-progress and best efforts.

Whatever the purpose of the portfolio, a procedure for planning and organizing it is essential. According to EAC-West (1993), a portfolio of student work should contain, at a minimum:

- the criteria or guidelines for selecting and judging students' work
- the student's own selection of work
- evidence of the student's self-reflection

For large-scale or group assessment, this collection also should articulate clearly (1) the schedule and management plan for collecting students' work; (2) measurable and specified criteria that can be used fairly and without bias for all students; and (3) reasonable procedures for summarizing students' portfolios for grading and/or reporting purposes. Other components that frequently are included in a portfolio are input from teachers, parents, and peers, as well as district information such as local or national test information.

Planning and Organizing a Portfolio

Portfolio assessment systems allow the user to track the progress of an individual student over the course of an entire school year or more. Valencia (1990) suggests that assessment must be a continuous, ongoing process in order to chronicle development. Portfolio assessment allows us to observe and collect information continuously. In this way a student's progress is documented, rather than just the outcome of learning (the product). Valencia feels that this sends a very different message to students and parents: learning is never completed; instead, it is always evolving and changing. As an example, a project in New York collects three documents from students each year from the first grade to the seventh grade. The portfolio follows the student from one grade to the next. At the end of seventh grade, the student's portfolio has a total of twenty-one documents showing growth (Keene, 1994).

Scoring the portfolio has become a major issue. Four choices generally are available: (1) using the portfolio as a collection point without grading either papers or portfolio; (2) grading papers within the portfolio (either all or some papers); (3) grading the portfolio as a whole (without grading specific papers); or (4) grading the portfolio as a whole based on the scores of some specific papers. The type of scoring and the extent to which papers/portfolios are scored are based on the purpose of the portfolio. Thus, clearly defining the objectives for portfolio assessment is imperative.

Portfolios can be used within one content area (e.g., math, English language arts) or can be used to link two or more content areas (e.g., combining language arts with science and history in a paper on the use of water along the Rio Grande). Because portfolios can include such a variety of assessments, a table of contents that lists the items to be included and the timeline for collecting the information is essential for any portfolio. Figure 10 provides tables of contents for two

Figure 10 - EXAMPLE TABLES OF CONTENTS FROM TWO PORTFOLIOS

KIRIS Writing Portfolio Assessment
Grade 4

1. Table of Contents
   Include the title of each portfolio entry, the study area for which the piece was written, and the page number in the portfolio
2. One personal narrative
3. One poem, play/script, or piece of fiction
4. One piece of writing, the purpose of which is to
   a. present/support a position, idea, or opinion, or
   b. tell about a problem and its solution, or
   c. inform
5. One piece of writing from a study area other than English/Language Arts. Any of the other portfolio entries may ALSO come from other study areas.
6. A "Best Piece"
7. A Letter to the Reviewer: a letter written by you discussing your "Best Piece" and reflecting upon your growth as a writer

From the Kentucky Instructional Results Information System, Kentucky Department of Education, 1993.

KIRIS Math Portfolio Contents
Grade 4

1. Table of Contents
   A listing of the titles of the pieces in your portfolio, with page numbers
2. Letter to the Reviewer
   A letter you write to the person who will read your portfolio. In it you might write about what you've learned from keeping a mathematics portfolio, explain which entry is your best and why, tell about your favorite piece and why it's your favorite, and/or tell from which entry you learned the most and why.
3. 5–7 Best Pieces
   Pieces that show many ways of doing mathematics; involve lots of topics such as estimation, geometry, patterns, and graphs; include the many ways you represent numbers; use mathematics to solve real world problems; and use different mathematical tools.

From the Kentucky Instructional Results Information System, Kentucky Department of Education, 1993.

portfolios currently in use for school, district, and state-wide assessment. As can be seen from these examples, the purpose, depth of description, type of materials, and number of materials within portfolios are quite diverse. For example, the purpose of the Kentucky (KIRIS) writing and math portfolio is state-wide accountability (see Figure 10).

Not only are portfolios across programs diverse, but portfolios within a program need not be the same. The grading system, amount of work, and types of work can be adapted (Krest, 1990), as well as the language of the work. Students can be encouraged to take risks and experiment with their language skills as well as with their content skills. As such, portfolios are an ideal method of assessing various linguistically/ethnically diverse groups. In particular, they are ideal for assessing groups such as Latinos who speak the same general language (Spanish and/or English), but with different cultural backgrounds and vernaculars.

Use of Alternative Assessment/ Portfolios in Evaluation

Assessment and evaluation clearly are related. Assessing student achievement across a period of time allows teachers to evaluate their work as a whole and to assign grades. Aggregating students' scores and grades allows the evaluation of a program, school, or district. Because alter-

native assessment procedures are relatively new, there tends to be confusion over their role within the school assessment process. Given that alternative assessments provide teachers, parents, students, and other key stakeholders with important information about student achievement, methods for including the results of these measures in a grading system and in program evaluation must be considered.

Technical Standards

When thinking of "standards," most people think of standardized tests. But, in order to have confidence in a measuring tool, be it an NRT or an alternative assessment, the procedure must be standardized. What is meant by a standardized procedure? Basically, the instrument must be presented and scored in the same manner for each administration. More specifically, a standardized testing procedure is one in which:

- written and oral instruction
- specific items
- length of testing and time of testing
- method of scoring
- purpose for the assessment

are the *same* each time the instrument is used. Only with a standardized procedure can the results of the instrument be compared from one administration to the next, from one group of students to the next.

There is no guarantee that an instrument will be "good." In fact, there is no specific definition of what constitutes a "good" instrument. To be sure, everyone agrees that an instrument must

(1) be trusted and (2) provide information that describes how well a student really is doing. As the stakes become higher, the quality of the instrument becomes more important. For instance, a teacher may want immediate feedback about whether students have conquered particular content. The assessment needs to provide only broad-based information; its quality may not be of great concern. Another teacher might want to assign grades based on the alternative assessment. The stakes for the students are higher in this example. A "better" set of alternative assessments is needed. Finally, the stakes are higher still in program evaluation. If an administrator wants to know how well students in a specially funded program are doing, the instruments must be the best possible. Some authors recommend that validity, reliability, and inter-rater criteria are essential to ensuring that an instrument is valuable. These characteristics can be applied to NRTs, alternative assessments, and portfolios.

Linn et al. (1991) suggest that the *validity* of an assessment is tied closely to its use. Validity should include the context in which the assessment is used and whether or not that use has unintended consequences; teaching to the test is an example of an unintended consequence. Validity is described as the degree to which an assessment actually measures what it claims to measure and whether appropriate inferences can be drawn from the student's performance (Messick, 1989; Navarrete et al., 1993). To increase validity, results from an alternative assessment should:

- provide an accurate picture of how well that student knows the targets of achievement proficiency
- be based on at least five different tasks measuring similar skills
- be generalizable to other tasks to infer "real" mastery

Reliability refers to the likelihood that a score would be the same if the assessment were taken again at another time or if it were rescored by someone else. It is a measure of the consistency or stability of an assessment. Reliability also refers to the extent that overall performance can be generalized from a single or small number of performances. To increase reliability in alternative assessments:

- Design multiple tasks that lead to the same outcome.
- Use trained judges, working with clear criteria, from specific anchor papers or performance behaviors.
- Monitor periodically to ensure that raters use criteria and standards in a consistent manner.

Establishing inter-rater reliability for alternative assessments is an essential and straightforward task. The following steps are involved: (1) agree on the criteria that will be used to assess the student's work or behavior; (2) select student work as sample scoring materials; (3) practice scoring the samples of work using the same criteria and the same rating or scoring form; (4) compare the scores to determine the extent of agreement on the scoring criteria; and (5) score independently with frequent reliability checks to avoid inconsistencies in the rating process.

Two people working together will allow a review of reliability by comparing the ratings. Then, any misunderstandings or uncertainties about the criteria can be clarified. Disagreements about the criteria and ambiguities in the criteria can be resolved by implementing the procedures of inter-rater reliability. Well-established inter-rater reliability should ensure accuracy in the rating of students' performances.

Grading with Alternative Assessments

Methods for scoring individual alternative assessments were described earlier. Scores, in a given content area, are combined to create a grade. Thus, grades are summary measures of aggregated scores. As such, they provide a measure of student progress or achievement in a specific content area. How, though, can a grade be created when there are many different ways to score alternative assessments?

First, the instructor must consider the purpose of the grade. As defined by Bratcher (1994), grading is "communication between teacher and student that is designed to enhance the student's [skills]" (p. 9). The teacher must consider how the grading procedures can be used best to work with students, as well as provide information to other teachers, decision-makers, and parents.

The traditional method for grading involves the simple *averaging* of scores—numbers of checks, holistic scores (changing symbols such as +, ✓, – to numbers such as 3, 2, 1), and others—to create a grade. Typically, 90% of the total points possible or above is an A, 80–89% a B, and so on. According to Bratcher (1994), this method of grading often is referred to as the "common value system" (p. 81). Such converting of scores to letter grades is a method used by a majority of teachers, up to 82% of classrooms at some grade levels (Robinson and Craver, 1989).

Another method for grading is to utilize a *checklist of traits* and characteristics to record student progress. Rather than maintaining the scores on individual assignments, the teacher creates a list of skills that s/he expects students to achieve during the grading period. When a student successfully demonstrates a skill (by achieving a set score on an assessment, through the use of other checklists, or on materials in the portfolio), that skill can be checked off the list. At the end of the grading period, the grade is based on the number of skills actually demonstrated by the student. This type of grading can be considered a criterion-reference method, since the skills the students are to demonstrate, and the degree of accuracy or proficiency, are determined in advance. Robinson and Craver (1989) refer to this as a method of "nonscale alternatives" that provides "more detail of strengths and weaknesses than other methods of grading" (p. 16). The checklist is used across all grade levels, but is seen most in kindergarten and lower elementary classrooms (Robinson and Craver, 1989, p. 29).

A third option is to create a *contract* for each student. Within the contract, students indicate what work they intend to do, and the grade that the successful completion of that work merits. Such an approach can be especially useful (1) in a class of culturally diverse students, such as Latinos, in which different types and amounts of work might be appropriate for different students, or (2) when using portfolios, for which different tables of contents could be developed, each one representing the contract for that student.

Finally, Stiggins (1990) suggests combining these three methods to form a bandwidth methodology. The instructor can develop grades based on percentages. However, since all grading is somewhat subjective, and since students might do poorly on any individual assignment for a variety of reasons, a bandwidth or "gray area" can be established. For instance, if 90% is the breaking point between an A and a B, the gray area might be between 88% and 92%. Students whose average score falls within this gray area are either given a grade such as A/B, or further questions can be asked to determine which grade should be assigned, such as: How many ungraded homework assignments were completed? Did the student start the semester poorly, but then show greatly increased skills as the semester progressed? Did the student attempt extra work to practice skills? These and other

sources of data can help determine whether the bandwidth grade should be raised to A or lowered to B.

Grading *"on the curve"* is not a recommended practice. This procedure is based on grading students relative to one another. The best students receive As and the weakest students receive Fs, regardless of their actual performance. When grading on the curve, it would be possible for a student with an average of 75% to receive an F. Grading on the curve is appropriate only with a large number of students (some authors suggest at least 150), when relative grading is acceptable.

Another method *not* recommended is the *descriptive grade*. Rather than giving specific grades, descriptive grades include anecdotal records, written letters, and/or other comments by teachers. While some proponents argue that information pertaining to student achievement is more fully and individually communicated in this manner, others argue that descriptive grading increases the influence of teacher biases and provides no systematic and cumulative record of student progress toward school goals (Robinson and Craver, 1989).

Also, assessments of attitude, interest, and motivation should not be included in grading procedures. These assessments do not measure skills or proficiencies. Although they may be helpful in planning curricula, the information is not of a type to be important in grading.

Some school districts are using other methods for reporting stu-

dent progress to families, the district, and the community. These methods are based on alternative assessments of student achievement; they are not traditional grade report cards. Such changes in the traditional grading system require re-education, careful planning, and "buy-in" from teachers, families, administrators, and others in the educational community. While they may be a promising practice for the future, it is difficult to define guidelines for them at this point.

Program Evaluation with Alternative Assessments

The use of alternative assessment and portfolio assessment to document student progress for the purpose of accountability to funding sources has a number of advantages. It allows the student, teacher, and program to provide a clear picture of progress when the assessments are well designed to clearly specified and meaningful standards. This kind of assessment allows students to show what they know and how they know it, because the assessment can be designed in the students' native language to include facets of their cultural background, values, and beliefs. For Latino students who are not familiar with the mainstream concepts and values that form the foundation of many of the current NRTs, this may be the only opportunity they have to show what they know.

Traditionally, evaluation has been defined as formative or summative. *Formative* evaluation is utilized early in a program and leads toward modifications and refinements to improve the program. *Summative* evaluation generally is the final, year-end report that summarizes information for the program and determines whether the program's objectives have been met. A newer methodology is the *dynamic evaluation*, which is a more ongoing process (Figueroa, 1990). Dynamic evaluation allows the program to "keep tabs" on students to determine their progress and make modifications in the program as the need is identified.

Funding agencies generally require an annual evaluation of programs that they fund. Evaluation requirements often include documentation of technical standards for all measures of student achievement/progress. When using alternative assessment to meet funding agency evaluation requirements, it is important to report:

■ the process used to develop the assessment

■ methods and kind(s) of reliability established for the measure

■ the context and validation process for the assessment

This article has outlined the manner in which alternative assessment procedures can be standardized while developing alternative assessments. Although it may seem like a costly and time-consuming enterprise, the return on this investment is usually substantial in terms of the rich information it can provide about student progress.

SUMMARY

Psychometricians and educators are beginning to recognize that a single assessment cannot provide an adequate measure of students' capabilities; multiple measures are needed. Concomitantly, there is increased knowledge and awareness of the problems and limitations inherent in standardized tests. This has led to the growth in popularity of alternative assessments, sometimes referred to as authentic assessments, performance-based assessments, or curriculum-based assessments. Educators are discovering that alternatives are empowering to them and to their students. These alternative forms of assessment are ongoing, reflect instruction, are sensitive to individual differences and developmental considerations, and, most important, actively involve students. Alternative assessments also can inform instruction by providing valuable information as to the effectiveness of the instructional activities being implemented in a classroom. Culturally and linguistically diverse Latino students can benefit greatly from the opportunities available with alternative assessments to demonstrate growth and competency within the context of meaningful learning.

The way alternative forms of assessment are designed, used, and graded depends greatly on the specific purpose for their use. As with standardized tests, issues of validity, reliability, and interrater reliability are important to consider when designing or using alternative forms of assessment. Although establishing technical standards for alternative assessments can be a time-consuming and labor-intensive process, the benefits to be derived from alternative measurements are substantial. They can be developed in the native languages of the students to include elements of the students' culture and background. This makes for assessment that is meaningful and more fair for Latino students who may have values and background experiences different from those of the traditional mainstream population that are embedded in many of the current NRTs.

Just as alternative assessments allow a broader and more in-depth view of the student, so do the evaluations that are based on alternative assessments. A formative, dynamic, or summative evaluation should include both NRTs and standardized alternative assessments. In this way, the view of the program will provide the greatest information.

The greater needs of Latino students cannot be met solely through the use of alternative assessments; they must be met within the context of the whole school. A whole-school program that incorporates effective practices for Latino students must be more than an "add-on" to the school's core curriculum. Assessment that looks at what students actually can do (as opposed to what they cannot do) and creates an environment where students are comfortable taking risks is an essential component of meeting the needs of diverse students in whole-school programs. In such schools will we find successful Latino students.

APPENDIX: TESOL STANDARDS[2]

Access to a Positive Learning Environment

(1) Are the language minority (LM) students' schools safe, attractive, and free of prejudice?

(2) Is there a positive whole-school environment? This is defined as one in which the administrative and instructional policies and practices create a positive climate, there are high expectations for all students, and learning experiences are linguistically and culturally appropriate for LM students.

(3) Do teachers, administrators, and other staff receive professional development related to the needs of LM students?

(4) Does the school environment welcome parents of LM students? This includes recognizing parents as at-home primary teachers of their children and as important participants in the life of the school.

Access to Appropriate Curriculum

(5) Do LM students have access to appropriate instructional programs? These programs must support second language development and match the full range of instructional services offered to majority students.

(6) Does the core curriculum designed for all students promote (a) sharing, valuing, and developing both first and second languages and cultures and (b) higher-order thinking skills?

(7) Do LM students have access to the instructional programs and related services that identify, conduct, and support programs for special populations in a district?

Access to Full Delivery of Services

(8) Are the teaching strategies and instructional practices used with LM students developmentally appropriate, attuned to students' language proficiencies and cognitive levels, and culturally supportive and relevant?

(9) Do students have opportunities to develop and use their first language to promote academic and social development?

(10) Are support services (such as counseling, career guidance, and transportation) available to LM students?

(11) Do LM students have equal access to computers, computer classes, and other technologically advanced instructional assistance?

(12) Does the school have institutional policies and procedures that are linguistically and culturally sensitive?

(13) Does the school offer regular, nonstereotypical opportunities for native English-speaking students and LM students to share and value one another's languages and cultures?

Access to Equitable Assessment

(14) Are LM students assessed for language proficiency and academic achievement in the content areas using measures that are appropriate to students' developmental level, age, and level of oral and written language proficiency in the first and second languages? Are these measures reliable, valid, and appropriate? Are the results of such assessments explained to students and their families in their home language?

(15) Are LM students' special needs assessed appropriately? Again, access is further defined by using measures that are nonbiased and relevant, the results of which are explained to the family in their own language.

REFERENCES

Arter, J. A. (1992). "Portfolios in practice: What is a portfolio?" Paper presented at the Annual Meeting of the American Educational Research Association, April 1992, San Francisco, CA.

Baker, E. L., H. F. O'Neil, and R. L. Linn. (1993). "Policy and validity prospects for performance-based assessment." *American Psychologist, 48* (12): 1210–1218.

Bratcher, S. (1994). *Evaluating Children's Writing: A Handbook of Communication Choices for Classroom Teachers.* New York: St. Martin's Press.

Council of Chief of State School Officers. (1992). *Recommendations for Improving the Assessment and Monitoring of Students with Limited English Proficiency.* Alexandria, VA: Council of Chief State School Officers.

Del Vecchio, A., M. Guerrero, C. Gustke, P. Martínez, C. Navarrete, C. Nelson, and J. Wilde. (1994). *Whole School Bilingual Education Programs: Implications for Sound Assessment.* Program Information Guide #18. Washington, DC: National Clearinghouse for Bilingual Education.

Evaluation Assistance Center-West (EAC-West). (1993). *A Brief Guide to Using Student Portfolios in Title VII.* Albuquerque, NM: Evaluation Assistance Center-West (EAC-West).

Figueroa, R. A. (1990). "Best practices in the assessment of bilingual children," in *Best Practices in School Psychology—II* (pp. 93–106). A. Thomas and J. Grimes, eds. Washington, DC: National Association of School Psychologists.

Gardner, H. (1993). *Multiple Intelligences: The Theory in Practice.* New York: Basic Books.

Goodman, K. S., L. B. Goodman, and L. B. Bird. (1992). *The Whole Language Catalog Supplement on Authentic Assessment.* Santa Rosa, CA: American School.

Gottlieb, M. (1992). "Portfolios." Paper presented at the Meeting of Title VII Developmental Bilingual Education Grantees. December, 1992, Los Angeles, CA.

Holt, D., ed. (1994). *Assessing Success in Family Literacy Projects: Alternative Approaches to Assessment and Evaluation.* Washington, DC, and McHenry, IL: Center for Applied Linguistics and Delta Systems.

Joint Committee of the American Educational Research Association, American Psychological Association, and American Council on Measurement. (1985). *Standards for Educational and Psychological Testing.* Washington, DC: APA.

Keene, D. (1994). "Performance-based assessment and evaluation in developmental bilingual education," a panel presentation at the Developmental Bilingual Education Pre-Institute Conference, National Professional Development Institute. October, 1994. Washington, DC.

Kentucky Instructional Results Information System. (1993). *KIRIS Math Assessment Portfolio, Grade 4, 1993–1994.* Frankfort, KY: Kentucky Department of Education.

Krest, M. (1990). "Adapting Portfolios to meet the needs of students." *English Journal, 79* (2): 29–34.

Linn, R., E. Baker, and S. Dunbar. (1991). "Complex Performance-Based Assessments: Expectations and Validation Criteria." *Educational Researcher, 20* (8): 15–21.

Messick, S. (1989). "The Once and Future Issues of Validity: Assessing the Meaning and Consequences of Measurement," in *Test Validity* (pp. 33–46). H. Wainer and H. I. Braun, eds. Hillsdale, NJ: Lawrence Erlbaum.

Navarrete, C., J. Wilde, A. Del Vecchio, R. Benjamin, M. Guerrero, P. Martinez, and C. Nelson. (In press). A New Framework for Assessing Students in Bilingual Education.

Navarrete, C., J. Wilde, C. Nelson, P. Martínez, and G. Hargett. (1990). *Information Assessment in Educational Evaluation: Implications for Bilingual Education Programs.* Program Information Guide #3. Washington, DC: National Clearinghouse for Bilingual Education.

Ramírez, D. (In press). *Assessment of Limited English Proficient Students: Program Guidelines for Teachers and Administrators.* Sacramento, CA: Bilingual Education Office.

Robinson, G. E., and J. M. Craver. (1989). *Assessing and Grading Student Achievement.* Arlington, VA: Educational Research Service.

Stiggins, R. (1993). "Users and uses of assessment results." Paper presented at the Large Scale Assessment Conference of the Council of Chief State School Officers. June 1993. Albuquerque, NM.

Stiggins, R. (1990). *Classroom Assessment Training Program: Trainer's Instructional Package.* Portland, OR: Northwest Regional Educational Laboratory.

TESOL. (1994). The *TESOL Standards: Ensuring Access to Quality Educational Experiences for Language Minority Students.* Alexandria, VA: Teachers of English to Speakers of Other Languages.

Valencia, S. (1990). "A Portfolio Approach to Classroom Reading Assessment: The Whys, Whats, and Hows." *The Reading Teacher, 43* (4): 338–340.